Advance Praise for *Debunking 9/11 Debunking*

"David Ray Griffin's *Debunking 9/11 Debunk~* ~ompendium of the strong body of evidence showi~ ~overnment story of what happened on Septe~ ~ertainly a monstrous series of lies. Tr~ ~eign and domestic policies since that ~ ~nost certain falsehoods. This single book ~ ~vide the basis for the United Nations, Internati~ ~uce, or some specially constituted global body (indep~ ~ne U.S.) to investigate with highest priority, and publicly rep~ ~its findings about, the charge that unknown elements within the U.S. Government, and possibly some individuals elsewhere closely allied to the U.S., caused or contributed to causing the events of September 11 to happen."

—Bill Christison, former senior official of the CIA

"In this astonishing and fearsome book, David Ray Griffin rigorously and brilliantly first dissects and then demolishes the recent published accounts that purport to debunk the critics of the Bush Administration's official explanations of the events of 9/11. Dr. Griffin reveals how the purported 'debunkings' ignore the blatant inconsistencies and obvious cover-ups in the official accounts. No amount of spin can honestly account for the pulverization and nearly free-fall collapse of the World Trade Center buildings by anything other than pre-planned demolition. No amount of spin can realistically explain away the absence of commercial jetliner wreckage at the Pentagon. No amount of spin can logically explain away the miles-wide dispersion of airliner debris if Flight 93 was not blown up in the air. Dr. Griffin carefully delineates crucial questions that must be answered directly and honestly, without bias, spin or conflicts of interest. This book is a challenge to the mass media. If the truth about the events of 9/11 remains concealed and ignored, it will be at our—and our nation's—peril."

—Barry R. Komisaruk, Rutgers University
Distinguished Service Professor

"David Ray Griffin hits another one out of the park by taking on the left gatekeepers and the mass media for the lies and cover-up called 'the official story of 9/11/01,' which is the greatest conspiracy theory ever perpetrated on the American public. I highly recommend this book for all thinking Americans."

—Meria Heller, producer and host of the *Meria Heller Show*

DEBUNKING 9/11 DEBUNKING

An Answer to *Popular Mechanics* and Other Defenders
of the Official Conspiracy Theory

David Ray Griffin

OLIVE
BRANCH
PRESS

An imprint of Interlink Publishing Group, Inc.
www.interlinkbooks.com

First published in 2007 by

OLIVE BRANCH PRESS
An imprint of Interlink Publishing Group, Inc.
46 Crosby Street, Northampton, Massachusetts 01060
www.interlinkbooks.com

Library of Congress Cataloging-in-Publication Data
Griffin, David Ray, 1939–
Debunking 9/11 debunking : an answer to Popular mechanics and other defenders of
the official conspiracy theory / David Ray Griffin.
p. cm.
Includes bibliographical references and index.
ISBN 978-1-56656-686-5 (pbk.)
1. September 11 Terrorist Attacks, 2001—Miscellanea. 2. Conspiracies. I. Popular
mechanics. II. Title. III. Title: Debunking nine/eleven debunking.
HV6432.7.G747 2007
973.931—dc22
2007006171

Printed and bound in Canada by Webcom

10 9 8 7 6 5 4 3 2 1

To request our complete 40-page full-color catalog,
please call us toll free at 1-800-238-LINK, visit our
website at **www.interlinkbooks.com**, or write to
Interlink Publishing
46 Crosby Street, Northampton, MA 01060
e-mail: info@interlinkbooks.com

An error does not become truth by reason of multiplied propagation, nor does truth become error because nobody sees it. Truth stands, even if there be no public support. It is self sustained.
—Gandhi

Conspiracy theories are like mushrooms; they grow where there is no light.
—Thomas H. Kean and Lee H. Hamilton, *Without Precedent*

Also by David Ray Griffin

*The New Pearl Harbor: Disturbing Questions About the Bush
Administation and 9/11*

The 9/11 Commission Report: Omissions and Distortions

9/11 and American Empire: Intellectuals Speak Out
(edited with Peter Dale Scott)

Christian Faith and the Truth Behind 9/11

Contents

Acknowledgments viii

Introduction: Conspiracy Theories and Evidence 1

ONE 27
9/11 Live or Distorted: Do the NORAD Tapes Verify
The 9/11 Commission Report?

TWO   95
The Real 9/11 Conspiracy Theory: A Critique of Kean and
Hamilton's *Without Precedent*

THREE   143
The Disintegration of the World Trade Center: Has NIST
Debunked the Theory of Controlled Demolition?

FOUR   207
Debunking 9/11 Myths: A Failed Attempt by *Popular Mechanics*

Conclusion   309

Notes   323
Index   386

Acknowledgments

The 9/11 truth movement is filled with remarkable people, from all walks of life, who are united by a passionate commitment to exposing the falsity of the official theory about 9/11. In writing this book, I have benefited from the generous assistance of a great number of these individuals. My debts to many of them are indicated by my references to their work in this book's endnotes. But I have also received direct help from many of them.

Although I wish I could write a paragraph about each one of them, I can here publicly express my gratitude only by mentioning their names: Daniel Athearn, Elias Davidsson, Kee Dewdney, Eric Douglas, Mark Gaffney, Ed Haas, Ian Henshall, Jim Hoffman, Ken Jenkins, Steven Jones, Michael Meyer, Rowland Morgan, George Nelson, Ralph Omholt, Matthew Ott, Pat Patterson, Russell Pickering, Kevin Ryan, and Chuck Thurston. There are, moreover, four people I must lift up for special thanks because of the extraordinary amount of time they devoted to this project, going far beyond any reasonable call of duty: Matthew Everett, Tod Fletcher, Robin Hordon, and Elizabeth Woodworth.

I also want to express my appreciation to Colin Scoggins. Although he is not a member of the 9/11 truth movement, his willingness to answer a great number of questions greatly aided my understanding of FAA air traffic control in general and the 9/11 actions of controllers at Boston Center in particular. Without his help, combined with that of former controller Robin Hordon, the first chapter would have made little advance on my previous discussions.

In addition, I wish to acknowledge my debt, and that of the 9/11 truth movement in general, to Michel Moushabeck and Pamela Thompson, the publisher and editor, respectively, of Olive Branch Press/Interlink Publishing Group. Without their joint decision back in 2003 to take a chance on a manuscript entitled *The New Pearl Harbor*, it might never have been published, in which case my later 9/11 books would never have been written. One could not imagine, moreover, anyone easier to work with than them and the rest of the team at Interlink.

Finally, I would like to express my inexpressible gratitude to my wife, Ann Jaqua, who in countless ways makes my work possible.

INTRODUCTION

Conspiracy Theories and Evidence

The evidence that 9/11 was an inside job is overwhelming. Most people who examine this evidence with an open mind find it convincing, or at least profoundly unsettling. There are, however, several widely held beliefs that work to prevent people from examining this evidence with, in Richard Falk's phrase, "even just a 30-percent open mind."[1] These beliefs often keep people from examining the evidence at all. I can use myself as a case in point.

My Own Story

Until the spring of 2003, I had not seriously looked at any of the evidence. I was vaguely aware that there were people, at least on the Internet, who were suggesting a revisionist account of 9/11, according to which US officials were complicit. But I did not take the time to find their websites. I was busy writing a history of American imperialism, which I had begun the day after 9/11. Having accepted the official account of the 9/11 attacks, I had also accepted the liberal interpretation thereof, according to which they were "blowback" for US foreign policy, especially in the Arab and Muslim worlds. This interpretation convinced me that the large book on global problems on which I had been working for several years would be incomplete without a separate chapter on American imperialism.

Studying this history probably helped me later change my interpretation of 9/11, because I learned that several of our nation's wars, such as those against Mexico, the Philippines, and Vietnam, had been justified by incidents that, although they were actually created by our own armed forces, were used to claim that we had been attacked. But this awareness did not lead me immediately to conclude that 9/11 had also been orchestrated as a pretext. Although that possibility did cross my mind, I did not take it seriously.

I maintained this mindset even after being introduced, late in 2002, to a professor from another country who said he was quite certain that 9/11 had been an inside job. I remember replying that I did not think the Bush administration—even the Bush administration—would do such a heinous thing. However, I added, I would be willing to look at whatever he considered the best evidence. He directed me to some 9/11 websites, but I did not find them convincing. I do not know if they were bad sites or whether I looked at their evidence with less than a 30-percent open mind.

In any case, I went back to working on American imperialism, assuming 9/11 not to be an instance thereof.

My response was quite different, however, a few months later when another colleague sent a different website, which had an abbreviated version of Paul Thompson's massive 9/11 timeline.[2] Although this timeline was drawn entirely from mainstream sources, it contained hundreds of stories that contradicted one or another aspect of the official account of 9/11. Additional reading then led me to Nafeez Ahmed's *The War on Freedom: How and Why America Was Attacked September 11, 2001*.[3] On the basis of the combined evidence summarized by Thompson and Ahmed, it took me only a short time to realize that there was strong prima facie evidence that the Bush administration had, at the very least, intentionally allowed the attacks to occur. Through additional study, I became aware that some of the strongest evidence indicated that forces within the government must have actually orchestrated the attacks.

Reporting and Evaluating the Evidence

Realizing that this conclusion, if correct, was extremely important—by then the Bush administration had used 9/11 as a basis for attacking Iraq as well as Afghanistan—I wrote *The New Pearl Harbor*, summarizing the evidence that had been gathered by members of the 9/11 truth movement who had opened their minds to it long before I had. Presenting what I called a "strong prima facie case for official complicity,"[4] I argued that this evidence was strong enough to warrant a new investigation if, as then appeared likely, the report of the 9/11 Commission turned out to be a cover-up.

After seeing when it was published in July 2004 that *The 9/11 Commission Report* was even worse than I had anticipated, I wrote *The 9/11 Commission Report: Omissions and Distortions*, in which I pointed out over a hundred instances of deception in the report, many of which were extremely serious. I concluded by stating that the Commission's report, "far from lessening my suspicions about official complicity, has served to confirm them. Why would the minds in charge of this final report engage in such deception if they were not trying to cover up very high crimes?"[5]

Further study reinforced this conviction. Thanks to a conversation with an attorney, Gary Becker, I saw that, given the 9/11 Commission's failure even to try to rebut the prima facie case against the Bush administration, this case could now be considered conclusive. Also, the cumulative argument that the Twin Towers and Building 7 of the World Trade Center were brought down by explosives became even stronger through two developments—an essay by physicist Steven Jones[6] and the release of the 9/11 oral histories given by members of the Fire Department of New York,[7] dozens of which indicated that powerful explosions had occurred in the Twin Towers before and during their collapses. On the basis of these developments, which were discussed in my third book on the subject, *Christian Faith and the Truth Behind 9/11*,[8] I came to consider the evidence for the alternative interpretation of 9/11 strong enough to convince most people, if only they would examine it.

A Former CIA Analyst Examines the Evidence

This contention—that the crucial issue now is simply whether people will expose themselves to the evidence—was illustrated in 2006 by former CIA analyst Bill Christison. In August of that year, he published an essay entitled, "Stop Belittling the Theories About September 11."[9] In a letter to friends explaining why he wrote it, he said: "I spent the first four and a half years since September 11 utterly unwilling to consider seriously the conspiracy theories surrounding the attacks of that day. . . . [I]n the last half year and after considerable agony, I've changed my mind."[10]

Polling the American Public

Although the fact that Christison had been a CIA analyst makes his change of mind especially significant, another measure of the convincing power of the evidence is the sheer number of Americans who by 2006 questioned the official account. A Zogby poll taken that May indicated that 42 percent of the American people believed that "the US government and its 9/11 Commission concealed . . . critical evidence that contradicts their official explanation of the September 11th attacks." Even more significant was the finding that the conviction that no cover-up had occurred was held by only 48 percent. (Ten percent said they were unsure.)[11] This meant that even though virtually all of the mainstream press coverage of 9/11 has supported the official account, less than half the American people are confident that the government and the 9/11 Commission have not covered up evidence contradicting this account.

People can differ, of course, with regard to the kind of evidence they believe is being covered up. Many may think of it as evidence that would merely embarrass the government, not show its complicity in the attacks. More revelatory, therefore, was a Scripps/Ohio University poll in August 2006, which showed 36 percent of the public holding that "federal officials either participated in the attacks on the World Trade Center and the Pentagon or took no action to stop them 'because they wanted the United States to go to war in the Middle East.'"[12]

Until the publication of these polls, the press had evidently considered the 9/11 truth movement a marginal phenomenon, which as such could be ignored. But these polls changed that perception. A story in *Time* magazine, reporting the second poll, wrote: "Thirty-six percent adds up to a lot of people. This is not a fringe phenomenon. It is a mainstream political reality."[13]

A Flurry of Debunking Publications

This new perception was quickly followed in August by four substantial publications intended to reassure those who still believed the official story. Unlike most previous official and semi-official publications, these new writings did not simply affirm the truth of the official account of 9/11. They also explicitly sought to debunk "conspiracy theories" that took issue with this account.

One of these was a *Vanity Fair* essay by Michael Bronner entitled "9/11 Live: The NORAD Tapes."[14] The tapes in question had been used by the 9/11 Commission in 2004 to give a new account of the military's response to the hijackings. The account that had been given in NORAD's timeline of September 18, 2001, which was used as the basis for the military's testimony to the Commission in 2003, had left the military open to the charge that its failure to intercept the airliners resulted from a standdown order. That account also led to the charge that the military had shot down United Flight 93. (I had explained the reasons for these charges in *The New Pearl Harbor*.) The Commission, on the basis of these tapes, constructed a new account, which put all the blame on the FAA. Constructing this new story required accusing the military of having told a false story. Some members of the Commission even suggested that the military told this false story knowingly. But this new story protects the military from the more serious charge of orchestrating, or at least complicity in, the attacks.

Bronner was the journalist to write this story because he was the first one to be given access to these tapes. Why? This may have had something to do with the fact that he was an associate producer of the movie *United 93*, which faithfully portrayed the Commission's new account, according to which the military could not possibly have shot this flight down.

Bronner's essay, in any case, was explicitly intended to refute "conspiracy theories" about the flights in general and United Flight 93 in particular. In one of Bronner's several references to these theories, he cites two questions raised at the first hearing of the 9/11 Commission by its chairman, Thomas Kean— "How did the hijackers defeat the system, and why couldn't we stop them?"—and then says:

> These were important questions. Nearly two years after the attack, the Internet was rife with questions and conspiracy theories about 9/11—in particular, where were the fighters? Could they have physically gotten to any of the hijacked planes? And did they shoot down the final flight, United 93, which ended up in a Pennsylvania field?

Bronner's answer to these questions was "No." The military did not know about the hijackings until after the flights had crashed,[15] so fighters could not have intercepted them and could not have shot down United 93. According to Bronner, the NORAD tapes, by finally revealing the real truth about what happened, shot down the conspiracy theorists.

A second August publication was *Without Precedent: The Inside Story of the 9/11 Commission*, by the men who had served as the commission's chair and vice chair, Thomas Kean and Lee Hamilton. Whereas *The 9/11 Commission Report* never mentioned the existence of theories that challenged the official account, this new book explicitly takes on these "conspiracy theories." Even admitting that the 9/11 Commission as such had been interested in "debunking conspiracy theories," they claim that it succeeded so well that conspiracy theories have now been "disproved by facts."[16] Their book, by confirming Bronner's sensational claim that members of the Commission suspected that the military's previous story had been a lie, helped instill the new story in the public's mind by evoking considerable press coverage.

Whereas Bronner, Kean, and Hamilton sought to debunk alternative theories about the planes, the task of debunking alternative theories about the World Trade Center collapses was taken up by the National Institute of Standards and Technology (NIST). Such theories had not been explicitly discussed in its *Final Report on the Collapse of the World Trade Center Towers*, published in September 2005. But in August 2006, NIST put out a document entitled "Answers to Frequently Asked Questions," which sought to rebut "alternative hypotheses suggesting that the WTC towers were brought down by controlled demolition using explosives."[17] According to a *New York Times* story by Jim Dwyer, "federal officials say they moved to affirm the conventional history of the day because of the persistence of what they call 'alternative theories.'"[18]

Whereas the intent to debunk these alternative theories was made explicit only in the body of each of these first three publications, it was announced in the title of a fourth: *Debunking 9/11 Myths: Why Conspiracy Theories Can't Stand Up to the Facts*. This book, which is an expansion of a *Popular Mechanics* article published in 2005,[19] is not only more explicit but also more ambitious than the other publications. Besides dealing with alternative theories about both the World Trade Center and the failure to intercept the hijacked airliners, its editors, David Dunbar and Brad Reagan, devote chapters to the Pentagon strike and United Flight 93. Of the four August publications, this is the one that is most often cited as proof that the "9/11 conspiracy theorists" are wrong. *Popular Mechanics* was used, for example, as the primary authority on 9/11 by a recent BBC documentary, *The Conspiracy Files: 9/11*, directed and produced by Guy Smith.[20] (Although the BBC has long had a reputation for quality, this show was almost unbelievably bad. I will point out a few of its faults as the occasion arises.)

All four of these publications can be considered official, or at least semi-official, defenses of the government's account of 9/11. *Without Precedent* is written by the chair and vice chair of the 9/11 Commission, which endorsed and even partly created the government's account. NIST is an agency of the US Commerce Department. Bronner's essay was made possible by the privileged access to some NORAD tapes he was afforded by the US military. The *Popular Mechanics* book could arguably be considered a semi-official publication by virtue of the fact that Benjamin Chertoff, a cousin of Homeland Security chief Michael Chertoff, was one of the primary authors of the article from which it is derived (as discussed in Chapter 4). But there are two other, less debatable, bases: Its foreword is written by Republican Senator John McCain and it is endorsed by Condoleezza Rice's State Department as providing "excellent . . . material debunking 9/11 conspiracy theories."[21]

The Present Book

Each chapter of the present book is a response to one of these publications. I show that, although they may seem impressive to people who have only a superficial awareness of the facts about 9/11, their attempts at debunking alternative theories can, through the use of publicly available information, themselves be thoroughly debunked. NIST spokesman Michael Newman has, in fact, admitted that NIST's new document "won't convince those who hold to the alternative theories . . . . It is for the masses."[22] This book can also be read as an explanation, "for the masses," as to why neither NIST's new document nor any of the other three publications is impressive to those of us who, on the basis of familiarity with the relevant facts, hold these alternative theories.

Chapter 1 examines Bronner's *Vanity Fair* article based on the NORAD tapes. This chapter shows that the military's new explanations for its failure to intercept the first three flights, and for why it could not have shot down the fourth flight, are contradicted by too many facts to be accepted as true. This chapter also points out the most significant fact about the change of stories: whether one accepts the old or the new story, US military leaders have lied about 9/11.

Chapter 2 examines Kean and Hamilton's *Without Precedent: The Inside Story of the 9/11 Commission*. This chapter shows that, although Kean and Hamilton correctly describe the characteristics of irrational conspiracy theories, it is the 9/11 Commission's conspiracy theory, not the alternative theory, that embodies these characteristics.

Chapter 3 examines NIST's "Answers to Frequently Asked Questions." It shows that in spite of NIST's reputation as a scientific organization, its attempt to dismiss the alternative hypothesis about the Twin Towers—that they were brought down by explosives—reveals its approach to be thoroughly unscientific.

Chapter 4 examines the *Popular Mechanics* book, *Debunking 9/11 Myths*. It shows that although this book claims to have debunked all the major claims of the 9/11 truth movement, it fails to refute a single one of them. Readers will see that a more accurate title for the book would have been *Perpetuating 9/11 Myths*.

Although readers previously unfamiliar with the debates about 9/11 may find the first chapter somewhat rough going, they should find the second chapter considerably easier. By reading the book as a whole, moreover, readers will be exposed to most of the overall case for the contention that 9/11 was an inside job. In spite of the somewhat difficult nature of the first chapter, therefore, this book can serve as an introduction to the major issues.

Debunking Stories in the Press

The set of official and semi-official writings that came out in August 2006 was not the only flurry of publications that, in response to the growing popularity of the alternative account of 9/11, attempted to debunk that account. Probably because of the coalescence of the shock created by the 9/11 polls and the fact that September 2006 would bring the fifth anniversary of the 9/11 attacks, that summer saw an unprecedented number of debunking stories in the press.

These stories appeared not only in the mainstream but also in the left-leaning press. Indeed, those in the latter were generally more ferocious, apparently because the authors fear that alternative theories about 9/11 discredit the left and distract people from truly important matters.

There is value, in any case, in these debunking stories. They demonstrate that although the four publications of August are considered completely unimpressive within the 9/11 truth community, they have been found quite impressive within the journalistic community. They thereby show the importance of exposing the falsehoods and fallacies in these publications.

These press stories also illustrate three means through which people commonly avoid serious encounter with the evidence provided by the 9/11 movement: a one-sided use of the term "conspiracy theory"; the employment of paradigmatic and wishful thinking; and the acceptance of the assumption that if a document is written by scientists, it must be a scientific document. The remainder of this introduction illustrates how these three methods are used by journalists to avoid serious consideration of facts pointing to the falsity of the official account of 9/11.

Conspiracy Theories: Generic, Rational, and Irrational

In criticisms of the 9/11 truth movement's alternative theory, nothing is more common than the designation of it as a conspiracy theory. This designation takes advantage of the fact that "conspiracy theory" has become such a derogatory term that the claim, "I do not believe in conspiracy theories," is now almost a reflex action. Lying behind the term's derogatory connotation is the assumption that conspiracy theories are inherently irrational. The use of the term in this way, however, involves a confusion.

A conspiracy, according to my dictionary,[23] is "an agreement to perform together an illegal, treacherous, or evil act." To hold a conspiracy theory about some event is, therefore, simply to believe that this event resulted from, or involved, such an agreement. This, we can say, is the generic meaning of the term.

We are conspiracy theorists in this generic sense if we believe that outlaws have conspired to rob banks, that corporate executives have conspired to defraud their customers, that tobacco companies have conspired with scientists-for-hire to conceal the health risks of smoking, that oil companies have conspired with scientists-for-hire to conceal the reality of human-caused global warming, or that US presidents have conspired with members of their administrations to present false pretexts for going to war. We are all, in other words, conspiracy theorists in the generic sense.

We clearly do not believe, therefore, that all conspiracy theories are irrational. Some of them, of course, *are* irrational, because they begin with their conclusion rather than with relevant evidence, they ignore all evidence that contradicts their predetermined conclusion, they violate scientific principles, and so on. We need, in other words, to distinguish between rational and irrational conspiracy theories. Michael Moore reflected this distinction in his well-known quip, "Now, I'm not into conspiracy theories, except the ones that are true."[24]

To apply this distinction to 9/11, we need to recognize that everyone holds a conspiracy theory in the generic sense about 9/11, because everyone believes that the 9/11 attacks resulted from a secret agreement to perform illegal, treacherous, and evil acts. People differ only about the identity of the conspirators. The official conspiracy theory holds that the conspirators were Osama bin Laden and other members of al-Qaeda. The alternative theory holds that the conspirators were, or at least included, people within our own institutions.

In light of these distinctions, we can see that most criticisms of the alternative theory about 9/11 are doubly fallacious. They first ignore the fact that the official account of 9/11 is a conspiracy theory in the generic sense. They then imply that conspiracy theories as such are irrational. On this fallacious basis, they conclude, without any serious examination of the empirical facts, that the alternative theory about 9/11 is irrational.

However, once the necessary distinctions are recognized, we can see that the question to be asked is: Assuming that one of the two conspiracy theories about 9/11 is irrational, because it is contradicted by the facts, is it the official theory or the alternative theory? Once this is acknowledged, the alternative theory about 9/11 cannot be denounced as irrational simply by virtue of being a conspiracy theory. It could validly be called less rational than the official conspiracy theory only by comparing the two theories with the evidence. But journalists typically excuse themselves from this critical task by persisting in the one-sided use of "conspiracy theory," long after this one-sidedness has been pointed out.[25]

For example, Jim Dwyer wrote a *New York Times* story entitled "2 US Reports Seek to Counter Conspiracy Theories About 9/11"[26]—not, for example, "2 US Reports Say Government's Conspiracy Theory Is Better than Alternative Conspiracy Theory." One of those two reports, he pointed out, is a State Department document entitled "The Top September 11 Conspiracy Theories," but he failed to mention that the truly top 9/11 conspiracy theory is the government's own. Then Dwyer, on the basis of this one-sided usage, tried to poke some holes in the alternative theory without feeling a need, for the sake of journalistic balance, to poke holes in the government's theory—because it, of course, is not a conspiracy theory.

Matthew Rothschild, the editor of the *Progressive*, published an essay in his own journal entitled, "Enough of the 9/11 Conspiracy Theories, Already."[27] He was not, of course, calling on the government to quit telling its story. He began his essay by saying:

> Here's what the conspiracists believe: 9/11 was an inside job. Members of the Bush Administration ordered it, not Osama bin Laden. Arab hijackers may not have done the deed. . . . [T]he Twin Towers fell not because of the impact of the airplanes and the ensuing fires but because [of] explosives. . . . I'm amazed at how many people give credence to these theories.

He did *not* have a paragraph saying:

> Here's what the government's conspiracists believe: 19 hijackers with box-cutters defeated the most sophisticated defense system in history. Hani Hanjour, who could barely fly a Piper Cub, flew an astounding trajectory to crash Flight 77 into the Pentagon, the most well-protected building on earth. Other hijacker pilots, by flying planes into two buildings of the World Trade Center, caused three of them to collapse straight down, totally, and at virtually free-fall speed. . . . I'm amazed at how many people give credence to these theories.

Besides failing to have this type of balanced approach, Rothschild described my books as ones in which "Griffin has peddled his conspiracy theory." He gave no parallel description of, say, *The 9/11 Commission Report* as a book in which the government peddled *its* conspiracy theory. Rothschild wrote, "The guru of the 9/11 conspiracy movement is David Ray Griffin." He did not add, "The guru of the government's 9/11 conspiracy theory is Philip Zelikow" (the person primarily responsible for *The 9/11 Commission Report*; see Chapter 2).

In response to the poll indicating that 42 percent of the American people believe that the government and the 9/11 Commission have covered up the truth about 9/11, Terry Allen, in an essay for *In These Times* magazine, explained: "Americans love a conspiracy. . . . There is something comforting about a world where someone is in charge." She did *not* offer this Americans-love-a-conspiracy explanation to account for the fact that 48 percent of our people still believe the official conspiracy theory—according to which evil outsiders secretly plotted the 9/11 attacks. She also ignored the fact that if people's beliefs are to be explained in terms of a psychological need for comfort, surely the most comforting belief about 9/11 would be that our government did not deliberately murder its own citizens.[28] (I, for one, wish that I could believe this.)

This psychological approach was taken even more fully in the aforementioned essay in *Time* magazine. Although it was entitled, "Why the 9/11 Conspiracies Won't Go Away,"[29] the author, Lev Grossman, was not seeking to explain why the government's conspiracy theory won't go away. He did quote Korey Rowe, one of the creators of the popular documentary film *Loose Change*, as saying:

> That 19 hijackers are going to completely bypass security and crash four commercial airliners in a span of two hours, with no interruption from the military forces, in the most guarded airspace in the United States and the world? That to me is a conspiracy theory.

But this did not faze Grossman. He continued to use the term "conspiracy theory" exclusively for the alternative theory.

Then, to explain why *this* conspiracy theory has gained increasing acceptance, rather than going away, he ignored the possibility that its evidence is so strong that, as more and more people become aware of it, they rightly find it convincing. He instead said, "a grand disaster like Sept. 11 needs a grand conspiracy behind it." The question of the quality of the evidence was thereby ignored.

Another problem with Grossman's explanation is that he, like Allen, got it backwards. As Paul Craig Roberts, who had been a leading member of the Reagan administration, has pointed out:

Grossman's psychological explanation fails on its own terms. Which is the grandest conspiracy theory? The interpretation of 9/11 as an orchestrated *casus belli* to justify US invasions of Afghanistan and Iraq, or the interpretation that a handful of Muslims defeated US security multiple times in one short morning and successfully pulled off the most fantastic terrorist attack in history simply because they "hate our freedom and democracy"? Orchestrating events to justify wars is a stratagem so well worn as to be boring.[30]

Roberts also pointed out that the attempt to explain away the 9/11 truth movement in this way would not even begin to explain its leaders:

The scientists, engineers, and professors who pose the tough questions about 9/11 are not people who spend their lives making sense of their experience by constructing conspiracy theories. Scientists and scholars look to facts and evidence. They are concerned with the paucity of evidence in behalf of the official explanation. They stress that the official explanation is inconsistent with known laws of physics, and that the numerous security failures, when combined together, are a statistical improbability.

These are rather obvious facts, to which the "conspiracy theory" label for the movement has apparently blinded Grossman and many other members of the press.

The psychologizing approach to "conspiracy theories," understood one-sidedly, has been fully exemplified in the aforementioned BBC documentary, *The Conspiracy Files: 9/11*. Guy Smith, the director-producer, interviewed only one academic member of the 9/11 truth movement, but this particular member—Professor James Fetzer, a well-published philosopher of science who founded Scholars for 9/11 Truth—was particularly well-suited to discuss the notion of "conspiracy theories," having written an essay on the subject. Fetzer was able to explain to Smith, therefore, the points I have made here—that everyone accepts conspiracy theories in the generic sense, that the official theory about 9/11 is itself a conspiracy theory, and so on. But none of Fetzer's discussion of this issue made it into Smith's documentary. The film instead, using the label "conspiracy theorists" only for people who believe that 9/11 was an inside job, gave time to supporters of the official theory who, demonstrating their skills as amateur psychologists, explained that some people need conspiracy theories as security blankets. Left unmentioned, again, was the fact that if some Americans think what they do about 9/11 because of a need for security, then those people would be more likely to believe that the US government had *not* attacked its own citizens.[31]

This one-sided use of the term "conspiracy theory," combined with the assumption that any theory so labeled is inherently irrational, has created a puzzle for some people, namely: How could otherwise sensible thinkers become conspiracy theorists? One such person is Salim Muwakkil, a senior editor of *In These Times*, who wrote an essay asking, "What's the 411 on 9/11?" After discussing the emergence of the 9/11 truth movement, he said:

> The movement caught my attention when I saw Dr. David Ray Griffin speaking at the University of Wisconsin at Madison on C-SPAN earlier this year. . . . Griffin [is] emeritus professor of Philosophy of Religion at the Claremont School of Theology in California. He has written several well-regarded books on religion and spirituality, co-founded the Center for Process Studies and is considered one of the nation's foremost theologians. I am familiar with his work and regard him as a wise writer on the role of spirituality in society.
>
> So, it was shocking to see him pushing a radical conspiracy theory about 9/11 on C-SPAN. . . . What could have transformed this sober, reflective scholar into a conspiracy theorist?

Stating that Terry Allen, whose essay quoted above was entitled "The 9/11 Faith Movement," had also been puzzled about "what happened to Griffin," Muwakkil evidently accepted her explanation, in which she said: "I think part of it is that he's a theologian who operates on faith."[32] Apparently my own answer as to what happened to me—that I finally looked at the evidence and found it convincing—was ruled out.

The question of how I lapsed into conspiratorial thinking was also raised in another left-leaning magazine, the *Nation*. The occasion was a review of *The New Pearl Harbor* written by former CIA case officer Robert Baer[33] (on whom the "Bob Barnes" character in the film *Syriana*, played by George Clooney, is loosely based).[34] Baer began by saying, "Conspiracy theories are hard to kill." Using this term in a one-sided way, like the previous authors, Baer indicated right off that the alternative conspiracy theory about 9/11 should be killed. He did, however, point out some ways in which the Bush administration, by resisting an investigation of 9/11 and then falsely claiming that Saddam Hussein had been involved, gave this theory traction. Baer also pointed out many reasons to suspect the official story's claim that the attacks were a surprise (for one thing, "bin Laden all but took out an ad in the *New York Times* telling us when and where he was going to attack").

Baer criticized me, however, for having so "easily [leaped] to larger evils, a conspiracy at the top." He then offered his explanation:

> Griffin is a thoughtful, well-informed theologian who before September 11 probably would not have gone anywhere near a conspiracy theory. But the catastrophic failures of that awful day are so implausible and the lies about Iraq so blatant, he feels he has no choice but to recycle some of the wilder conspiracy theories.

I, of course, *had* gone near and even accepted a conspiracy theory on that awful day itself—the government's conspiracy theory. But evidently because it is, in polite company, never called a conspiracy theory, Baer felt no need to explain why I, in spite of being thoughtful and well informed, had held that conspiracy theory for a year and a half. My own explanation is that I was not well informed and hence did not realize that I had passively accepted one of the "wilder conspiracy theories" ever created.

Baer's review, incidentally, came out late in 2004. It would appear that in the intervening period, his suspicions about the official theory have grown. After he, in an interview with Thom Hartmann in 2006, had made a point about 9/11 profiteering ("a lot of people [in the United States] have profited from 9/11. You are seeing great fortunes made—whether they are on the stock market, or selling weapons, or just contractors—great fortunes are being made"), Hartmann asked:

> What about political profit? There are those who suggest that G. W. Bush, and/or Cheney, Rumsfeld, Feith, Perle, Wolfowitz—someone in that chain of command—had pretty good knowledge that 9/11 was gunna happen—and really didn't do much to stop it—or even obstructed efforts to stop it because they thought it would lend legitimacy to Bush's . . . failing presidency.

Baer replied: "Absolutely." To make sure he was clear what Baer was saying, Hartmann asked: "So are you personally of the opinion . . . that there was an aspect of 'inside job' to 9/11 within the US government?" Baer replied: "There is that possibility, the evidence points at it."[35]

If Baer had thereby strayed somewhat from the *Nation*'s stance on 9/11, an able, if somewhat less gentlemanly, replacement was at hand. In September of 2006, the *Nation* published Alexander Cockburn's essay, "The 9/11 Conspiracy Nuts," which was an abbreviated version of a essay that had appeared in Cockburn's own publication, *Counterpunch*.[36] Having no doubt that it is the alternative, not the official, conspiracy theory that is nutty, Cockburn characterizes the members of the 9/11 truth movement as knowing no military history and having no grasp of "the real world." Moreover, he elsewhere quotes with approval a philosopher who, speaking of "the 9/11 conspiracy cult," says that its "main engine . . . is . . . the death of any conception of evidence," resulting in "the ascendancy of magic over common sense [and] reason."[37]

These are strong criticisms, which are easy to throw at the "movement" in the abstract. But do they apply to "the real world," that is, to the intellectual leaders of the 9/11 truth movement? For example, Cockburn refers to me as one of the movement's "high priests." Could anyone—if I may be defensive for a moment—really read my books in philosophy, philosophy of religion, and philosophy of science,[38] all of which involve discussions of epistemology, and conclude that I am devoid of "any conception of evidence"? Could one, in fact, conclude that after reading my 9/11 books?

Moreover, if my 9/11 books are nutty, as Cockburn suggests, then people who have endorsed them must also be nuts. The list of nuts would hence include economist Michel Chossudovsky, former CIA analyst Ray McGovern, British Minister of Parliament Michael Meacher, former Assistant Treasury Secretary Paul Craig Roberts, former Assistant Secretary of Housing Catherine Austin Fitts, journalists Wayne Madsen and Barrie Zwicker, Institute for Policy Studies co-founder Marcus Raskin, former diplomat Peter Dale Scott, international law professors Richard Falk and Burns Weston, social philosopher John McMurtry, theologians John B. Cobb, Harvey Cox, Carter Heyward, Catherine Keller, and Rosemary Ruether, ethicists Joseph C. Hough and Douglas Sturm, writer A.L. Kennedy, media critic and professor of culture Mark Crispin Miller, attorney Gerry Spence, historians Richard Horsley and Howard Zinn, and the late Rev. William Sloane Coffin, who, after a stint in the CIA, became one of the country's leading preachers and civil rights, anti-war, and anti-nuclear activists.

Furthermore, if everyone who believes the alternative conspiracy theory, rather than the official conspiracy theory, is by definition a nut, then Cockburn would have to sling that label at Philip J. Berg, former deputy attorney general of Pennsylvania;[39] Colonel Robert Bowman, who flew over 100 combat missions in Vietnam and earned a Ph.D. in aeronautics and nuclear engineering before becoming head of the "Star Wars" program during the Ford and Carter administrations;[40] Andreas von Bülow, formerly state secretary in the German Federal Ministry of Defense, minister of research and technology, and member of parliament, where he served on the intelligence committee;[41] Lt. Col. Steve Butler, formerly vice chancellor for student affairs at the Defense Language Institute in Monterey, California;[42] Giulietto Chiesa, an Italian member of the European parliament;[43] Bill Christison, formerly a national intelligence officer in the CIA and director of its Office of Regional and Political Analysis;[44] A. K. Dewdney, emeritus professor of mathematics and computer science and long-time columnist for *Scientific American*;[45] General Leonid Ivashov, formerly chief of staff of the Russian armed forces;[46] Captain Eric H. May, formerly an intelligence officer in the US Army;[47] Colonel George Nelson, formerly an airplane accident investigation expert in the US Air Force;[48] Colonel Ronald D. Ray, a highly decorated Vietnam veteran who became deputy assistant secretary of defense during the Reagan administration;[49] Morgan Reynolds, former director of the Criminal Justice Center at the National Center for Policy Analysis and former chief economist at the Department of Labor;[50] Robert David Steele, who had a 25-year career in intelligence, serving both as a CIA clandestine services case officer and as a US Marine Corps intelligence officer;[51] Captain Russ Wittenberg, a former Air Force fighter pilot with over 100 combat missions, after which he was a commercial airlines pilot for 35 years;[52] Captain Gregory M. Zeigler, former intelligence officer in the US Army;[53] all the members of Scholars for 9/11 Truth, Scholars for 9/11 Truth and Justice, Veterans for 9/11 Truth, Pilots for 9/11 Truth, and S.P.I.N.E.: the Scientific Panel Investigating Nine-Eleven;[54] and most of the college and university professors listed under "Professors Question 9/11" on the Patriots Question 9/11 website.[55]

Would Cockburn really want to suggest that these people are "nuts" with "no conception of evidence," no awareness of "military history," and no grasp of "common sense" and "the real world"? Cockburn's absurd charges are valuable, however, because they illustrate just how far the labeling of people as "conspiracy theorists" can lead otherwise sensible people away from the real world, in which many very intelligent and experienced people, who cannot by the wildest stretch be called "nuts," have concluded, on the basis of evidence, that 9/11 was, at least in part, an inside job.

Paradigmatic Thinking, Wishful-and-Fearful Thinking, and the Betrayal of Empiricism

The widespread practice of making judgments about the alternative 9/11 theory without seriously examining the relevant evidence is fostered not only by sloppy thinking about conspiracy theories. It is also aided and abetted by two powerful tendencies of the human mind, which can be called "paradigmatic thinking" and "wishful-and-fearful thinking."[56] Both of these tendencies subvert empiricism, understood here to mean the practice of forming our conclusions on the basis of the relevant empirical evidence.

A paradigm, in the most general sense of the term (which became popular through the influence of Thomas Kuhn[57]), is a worldview. Although the term, when used this way, has generally referred to a scientific-philosophical worldview, it can also indicate a political worldview. Our paradigm or worldview informs our judgments about what is possible and impossible, probable and improbable. Insofar as we are paradigmatic thinkers, our interpretation of new empirical data will be largely determined by our prior judgments about possibility and probability. "Although we may be genuinely motivated by the desire for truth," as I put it elsewhere, "we may become so convinced that our present framework is the one and only route to truth that open-minded consideration of the evidence becomes virtually impossible."[58] Although we may believe ourselves to be empiricists, judging matters on the basis of the facts, our empiricist intentions are subverted by our paradigmatic thinking.

With regard to 9/11, many people believe that the idea that the Bush administration would have deliberately killed thousands of its own citizens is beyond the realm of possibility. Ian Markham, a fellow theologian, wrote in criticism of my first book about 9/11: "When a book argues that the American President deliberately and knowingly was 'involved' in the slaughter of 3000 US citizens, then this is irresponsible."[59] When I suggested to Markham that our differences seemed to depend on "a priori assumptions as to what the US government, and the Bush administration and its Pentagon in particular, would and would not do," Markham replied by saying, "yes, I am operating with an a priori assumption that Bush would not kill 3000 citizens [to promote a political agenda]."[60] On that basis, as I showed in my written response to Markham's critique, he could ignore the empirical evidence suggesting the Bush administration had done just that.[61]

Markham's a priori assumption reflects, incidentally, what is known as "the myth of American exceptionalism," two tenets of which are, in the words of Bryan Sacks, that America is "a uniquely benevolent power that only ever acts defensively in its projection of military power" and that "would not conduct covert action against its own citizens." *The 9/11 Commission Report*, Sacks points out, is structured along the lines of this myth.[62] Given the fact that this myth is deeply inculcated into the American psyche, the majority of Americans, including people in the press, were predisposed to accept the Commission's report without careful scrutiny of its details.

A priori assumptions are, to be sure, necessary. We cannot afford to waste our time examining evidence for alleged occurrences that are logically or physically impossible. We are also generally justified in ignoring claims about occurrences that, while not strictly impossible, would be highly improbable. However, we should also remain aware that our assumptions about probability are fallible, so we should, at least when the issue is momentous, be open to having our assumptions corrected by new evidence.

In the case of the widespread assumption, articulated by Markham, that the Bush–Cheney administration would not have knowingly caused the deaths of thousands of American citizens to further its political agenda, we now know of at least two decisions by this administration that disprove this assumption. We know, for one thing, that this administration lied to get us into the war in Iraq. The Downing Street memos show that "the intelligence and facts [about weapons of mass destruction in Iraq] were being fixed around the policy [of going to war]."[63] Also, the administration's claim that Saddam was seeking uranium from Africa was shown to be a lie.[64] The Americans who have died in Iraq because of these lies now outnumber those who died on 9/11 itself, and they were sent to their deaths not to defend our country but to further the political agenda of the Bush administration.

The second example: A week after 9/11, the Bush administration's EPA issued a statement assuring the people of New York City that the "air is safe to breathe." It specifically said that the air did not contain "excessive levels of asbestos"[65]—even though a *Boston Globe* story a few days earlier had reported "levels of asbestos up to four times the safe level, placing unprotected emergency workers at risk of disease."[66] Later, a volunteer's shirt that had been stored in a plastic bag since 9/11 revealed levels "93,000 times higher than the average typically found in the environment in US cities."[67]

By 2006, 70 percent of the 40,000 Ground Zero workers, according to a study of 10,000 of them (most of whom were young people), had suffered respiratory problems, with a third having reduced lung capacity.[68] Dr. Robert Herbert of Mount Sinai Medical Center, which conducted the study, said that "as a result of their horrific exposures, thousands of World Trade Center responders have developed chronic and disabling illnesses that will likely be permanent."[69] Other studies showed, moreover, that at least 400 cases of cancer had already appeared.[70] Attorney David Worby, who is leading a class-action lawsuit, says that 80 of his clients have already died.[71] That so many cases developed so quickly is alarming, because many types of cancer, such as asbestosis, can take 15 or 20 years to develop. Experts expect the eventual death toll to be in the thousands. According to Worby, "More people will die post 9/11 from these illnesses, than died on 9/11."[72]

One EPA scientist, Dr. Cate Jenkins, later testified that the EPA's statement about the air was not a mistake but a lie.[73] Why did the EPA lie? According to EPA Inspector General Nikki Tinsley, pressure came from the White House, which "convinced EPA to add reassuring statements and delete cautionary ones,"[74] a consequence of which was that workers did not wear protective gear.

We have no a priori basis, accordingly, for assuming that the Bush administration would not have intentionally killed thousands on 9/11. This position has been endorsed by Daniel Ellsberg, who knows something about what U.S. administrations would do. Asked whether an administration would be "capable, humanly . . . of engineering such a provocation," Ellsberg, who served in the administration of Lyndon Johnson, replied: "Yes, . . . I worked for such an administration myself," referring to the fact that Johnson "put destroyers in harm's way in the Tonkin Gulf . . . several times, . . . hoping that it would lead to a confrontation." With regard to the evidence that 9/11 was engineered by the Bush administration, Ellsberg said: "I find . . . parts of it quite solid, and there's no question in my mind that there's enough evidence there to justify a very comprehensive and hard hitting investigation of a kind that we've not seen, with subpoenas, general questioning of people, and raising the release of a lot of documents."[75]

If careful attention to the empirical data can be discouraged by false paradigmatic beliefs, it can equally be forestalled by the tendency generally called "wishful thinking." Wishful thinkers, we say, tend to believe what they wish to be true. But equally powerful is the other side of this tendency, which has been called "fearful thinking."[76] Insofar as we are subject to this tendency, "We tend to reject a priori all those things that we do not want to be true, or at least do not want to be generally believed."[77] The tendency is hence best called wishful-and-fearful thinking. In relation to 9/11, some people have said to me: "I simply refuse to believe your account, because I don't want to live in a country whose political and military leaders would do such a thing."

Although we like to think of ourselves as empiricists, who make our judgments on the facts, we tend uncritically to accept explanations that prevent us from having to accept conclusions that would cause great discomfort. I will give several examples.

Incompetence Is a Better Explanation: Many critics assure their readers that there is no need to examine the evidence for complicity because the entire fiasco was simply another example of the American government's incompetence. Rothschild asks, rhetorically, if "we're supposed to believe that this incompetent Administration, which brought you Katrina, was somehow able to execute this grand conspiracy?"—as if the competence of the US military could be measured by that of FEMA and the Department of Homeland Security. Cockburn says that one reason that members of the 9/11 truth movement are "nuts" is that we have a "preposterous belief in American efficiency," not realizing that "minutely planned operations—let alone responses to an unprecedented emergency—screw up with monotonous regularity" and that the Bush–Cheney administration is one of "more than usual stupidity and incompetence."[78] JoAnn Wypijewski, writing in Cockburn's *Counterpunch*, complains that members of the 9/11 movement "have absolute faith in the military capability of the United States, despite the evidence of Iraq"[79]—evidently forgetting that the strictly military part of the operation was hailed as a brilliant success. Baer told readers that there was no need for my "wacky theories" because everything could be explained by "a confluence of incompetence, spurious assumptions and self-delusion on a grand scale."

One problem with this argument—which Baer, at least, seems to have reconsidered—is that although all of these critics appear to have read *The New Pearl Harbor*, they fail to mention that I devoted an entire chapter to this issue, showing that an incompetence theory becomes a huge coincidence theory, which entails "that FAA agents, NMCC and NORAD officials, pilots, immigration agents, US military leaders in Afghanistan, and numerous US intelligence agencies all coincidentally acted with extreme and unusual incompetence when dealing with matters related to 9/11."[80] Is such a theory really more plausible than the theory that all these failures happened because of coordination?

With regard to Cockburn's suggestion that "F-15s didn't intercept and shoot down the hijacked planes" because of "the usual screw-ups," Robin Hordon, a former FAA air traffic controller, wrote, explicity in response to Cockburn's statement:

> One of the most important elements of our nation's National Air Defense System is the speed, efficiency and timeliness of both launching interceptor fighters and then the steps taken to actually intercept "target" aircraft once airborne. Without such timeliness, there would be no purpose in having such a defense system at all. . . . So, at every problematic point of readiness, over the years, the military and FAA have worked diligently, through practice and experience, to get interceptors airborne and headed for intercept operations as quickly as possible. This has resulted in an amazingly responsive system in which, pilots, flight mechanics, aircraft, airport configurations and NORAD/FAA radar procedures have been honed and developed to save time as measured in seconds. This operation is precise—so Cockburn simply does not know what he's talking about.[81]

The more general point here concerns the nonsensical nature of sweeping generalizations about the efficiency of "the present administration." Besides needing to distinguish between, say, FEMA and the US military, we need, with regard to our armed forces, to distinguish between tasks for which they are highly trained, such as invading other countries, and tasks for which they are poorly prepared, such as *occupying* other countries.

This point is germane not only to the issue of intercepting airplanes but also to the claim that the Bush administration and its military were too incompetent to have organized the 9/11 attacks. The Pentagon regularly organizes military exercises, sometimes called "war games," to practice various possible scenarios. Included in these exercises, as will be discussed later, have been some that were quite similar to those that occurred on 9/11. The failures of FEMA in New Orleans and the failure of US ground troops to quell violence in Iraq have no relevance to the question of whether the Pentagon could have staged the attacks of 9/11.

Still another problem with the claim that the Bush administration and its military were too incompetent to have orchestrated the attacks is that this a priori argument could equally well be used to prove that they could not have organized the military assaults on Afghanistan and Iraq.

Also, if the US government, with its Pentagon, was too incompetent to have orchestrated the attacks, would this not have been all the more true of al-Qaeda? Cockburn seeks to silence this question by calling it "racist," but the issue behind that question involves means and opportunity, not race (see the statement by General Leonid Ivashov, 327n46).

Still another problem with the incompetence theory is that it leaves out a huge amount of the data that needs explaining, such as the vertical collapse of three skyscrapers at virtually free-fall speed. Baer, having mentioned such problems, seemed content to leave them as anomalies, saying, with more than a hint of wishful thinking, "[a]s more facts emerge about September 11, many of Griffin's questions should be answered."

Cockburn, using me to illustrate the "idiocy" of the "9/11 conspiracy nuts," explains that we overestimate the American military's competence because we "appear to have read no military history." Actually, I have read some, and one thing I learned was how common it has been for imperial powers, including the United States, to stage false-flag attacks to provide pretexts for going to war.[82] I have also read Michael Parenti's observation that "policymakers [sometimes] seize upon incompetence as a cover"—a cover that is then "eagerly embraced by various commentators," because they prefer to see incompetence in their leaders "rather than to see deliberate deception."[83] Although this form of wishful-thinking surely does not characterize Cockburn himself, it has probably influenced the acceptance of the incompetence explanation of 9/11 by many other journalists.

Someone Would Have Talked: Another popular argument is that, in Rothschild's words, in any "vast conspiracy . . . [t]here's the likelihood that someone along the chain would squeal." Even this administration— Baer said his experience had taught him— "could never have acquiesced in so much human slaughter and kept it a secret. Especially when so many people would have to have been involved." Although this argument may seem strong at first glance, it becomes less impressive under examination.

This argument is, for one thing, based partly on the belief that it is impossible for big government operations to be kept secret very long. However, the Manhattan Project to create an atomic bomb, which involved some 100,000 people, was kept secret for several years. Also, the United States provoked and participated in a civil war in Indonesia in 1957 that resulted in some 40,000 deaths, but this illegal war was keep secret from the American people until a book about it appeared in 1995.[84] It also must be remembered that if the government has kept several other big operations hidden, we by definition do not know about them. We cannot claim to know, in any case, that the government could not keep a big and ugly operation secret for a long time.

A second reason to question this a priori objection is that the details of the 9/11 operation would have been known by only a few individuals in key planning positions. Also, they would have been people with a proven ability to keep their mouths shut. Everyone directly complicit in the operation, moreover, would be highly motivated to avoid public disgrace and the death penalty. The claim that one of these people would have come forward by now is irrational.

When people suggest that whistleblowers would have come forward, of course, they usually have in mind people who, without being complicit in the operation, came to know about it afterward, perhaps realizing that some order they had carried out played a part in the overall operation. Many such people could be kept silent merely by the order to do so, along with the knowledge that if they disobeyed the order, they would be sent to prison or at least lose their jobs. For people for whom that would be insufficient intimidation, there can be threats to their families.[85] How many people who have expressed certainty about whistleblowers would, if they or their families or their jobs would be endangered by coming forward with inside information, do so?

In any case, the assumption that "someone would have talked," being simply an assumption, cannot provide a rational basis for refusing to look directly at the evidence.

Overwhelming Evidence for al-Qaeda's Responsibility: Another reason for claiming that there is no need to examine the evidence for the alternative theory is that the evidence for al-Qaeda's responsibility is overwhelming. Although this may sound like an empirical argument, it is only quasi-empirical, because it takes a claim of one of the suspects—the Bush administration—as evidence, then uses it as a basis for ignoring the evidence that, according to the 9/11 truth movement, disproves that claim.

This approach has been exemplified by Rothschild, who said that the alternative theory is "outlandish . . . on its face" because "Osama bin Laden has already claimed responsibility for the attack. . . . Why not take him at his word?" Rothschild thereby revealed his ignorance of the fact that there are good reasons to consider all of these "confessions" fabricated. As I point out in Chapter 2, the more famous of the bin Laden confession videos is widely considered a fake.[86] Rothschild was also evidently unaware of the fact that the FBI's page on bin Laden as a "Most Wanted Terrorist" does not list him as wanted for 9/11 and that, when asked why, a FBI spokesman said, "because the FBI has no hard evidence connecting bin Laden to 9/11[87]—a fact that publications such as *Progressive,* one would think, should be discovering and reporting."

It would seem that Rothschild's wish that the 9/11 truth movement would go away—reflected in his angry title, "Enough of the 9/11 Conspiracy Theories, Already"—accounts for his failure to study the movement's evidence sufficiently to learn even such elementary facts. The complaint by Allen and Cockburn that the 9/11 movement is a "distraction" from truly important issues suggests that this form of wishful-and-fearful thinking may be a major factor in many left-leaning journalists' disinclination to look seriously at the evidence.

Fear of Being Labeled: An even more obvious example of wishful-and-fearful thinking, which could explain why few journalists have examined the evidence in an open-minded way, at least in print, has been pointed out by Michael Keefer: "the fear of being mocked as a 'conspiracy theorist' or 'tinfoil hat wearer,' with a consequent loss of public credibility and professional respect." Although Keefer was thinking of writers on the left,[88] this dynamic surely applies to journalists in general, for whom "credibility is everything" (as one often hears).[89]

Salim Muwakkil was apparently influenced by this fear. Reporting that hearing my lecture awakened his "latent skepticism" about the official story, he explained that the collapse of the towers in 2001 had reminded him "of how Chicago's public housing high-rises collapsed vertically into their own foundations following controlled implosions." He then said:

> Inherently skeptical of official dogma, the left has an affinity for alternative explanations, which sometimes makes progressives pushovers for any scammer with a debunking tale to tell. People like Griffin and Brigham Young University physics professor Steven E. Jones, who also believes the towers were toppled by . . . controlled demolition, are not the usual suspects. Their dissent from the official line is more credible because their credentials connote respectability. Griffin stoked my interest because of my respect for his scholarship. But his expertise was in a realm completely unrelated to the knowledge needed to make his theories credible.

At that point, having ignored the fact that Jones' expertise is *not* unrelated to the issue of why the buildings collapsed, Muwakkil continued: "Progressive journalists have an added burden not to be seen as fodder for conspiracists. Sometimes they need a little help." For such help, he reported, he turned to Chip Berlet, whose work is devoted to making sure that "progressives are not duped by conspiracists of any stripe." Muwakkil evidently silenced his latent skepticism about the official story by accepting Berlet's assurance that "Griffin's work [is] 'a lot of . . . armchair guesswork by people who haven't done their homework.'"[90]

Although Muwakkil mentioned that Berlet had made such charges in a critique of *The New Pearl Harbor*, he failed to point out that the website containing Berlet's critique also contains my response,[91] which shows that I had done my "homework" on 9/11 far more thoroughly than had Berlet. (I had originally planned to include this essay in this book, but had to leave it out to keep the size down.) And although the alternative theory is not in the slightest debunked by Berlet's attack, Muwakkil ends his essay by indicating that it *has* been debunked, so that "ongoing skepticism about the official 9/11 story" is fueled solely by "lack of faith in the Bush administration, as well as its pathological aversion to transparency." The fact that the Twin Towers collapsed "vertically into their own foundations," just as had "Chicago high-rises . . . following controlled implosions," had evidently been wiped from Muwakkil's mind.

Scientists and Scientific Explanations

Having looked at two ways in which people, as illustrated by journalists, can avoid confronting the evidence that 9/11 was an inside job, I now look at a third: the assumption that if an explanation is given by scientists, it is a scientific explanation.

In our critical moments, we know that this is not necessarily true. We know that there have been scientists who were willing to prostitute themselves—to fudge the truth for the sake of money, which in some cases might simply mean to keep their jobs. We even know that some scientists have done this with regard to global warming, an issue that threatens the very survival of human civilization. We should be aware, accordingly, that if 9/11 was orchestrated by our own government, there would be scientists on the government's payroll, or on the payroll of companies heavily dependent on government contracts, who would provide false accounts of the collapses of the World Trade Center buildings or the damage to the Pentagon. There is, nevertheless, a widespread tendency to assume that if some explanation is provided by scientists, it must be a scientific explanation. An explanation should be considered scientific, however, only if it exemplifies certain standard criteria.

One criterion, often expressed by speaking of scientific method as involving "inference to the best explanation," is that the explanation has been shown to be superior to the other possible hypotheses. Scientists cannot say: "We assumed that A was the cause of X. We then found a way that A might have caused X. We were happy with this explanation. So we didn't consider hypothesis B, which some other people had suggested." And yet, as shown in Chapter 3, this is exactly the method used by the scientists who wrote the NIST report.

To be sure, scientists can often in practice get away with using that method if their resulting explanation fulfills the most important of all criteria—that the explanation be consistent with all of the relevant evidence. If it is not, then the explanation is said to be falsified. Or, to be more precise, the explanation must at least be consistent with *virtually* all of the evidence: It is usually considered acceptable to have a few "anomalies"—phenomena that, it is assumed, will eventually be shown to be consistent with the theory. But an explanation cannot be considered scientific if it must classify the *majority* of the evidence as anomalous.

In making an inference to the best explanation, in other words, "best" does not mean best from the point of view of our previous beliefs, our hopes and fears, or the political survival of the present administration. It means best in terms of taking account, in a self-consistent and otherwise plausible way, of all of the relevant evidence. Judged in terms of this standard, as we will see, the official 9/11 conspiracy theory is a complete failure.

Because scientists, like everyone else, are subject to paradigmatic and wishful-and-fearful thinking, the scientific method involves another feature: peer review. To be accepted as good science, an explanation must be able to pass muster with fellow scientists having no vested interest in the outcome. It is not clear, however, that any of the official reports about 9/11 have been subjected to such review. And, insofar as critiques of these reports have been proffered by independent scientists, they have been ridiculed as the ravings of "conspiracy theorists" or simply ignored. All offers to debate have been spurned.

In the experimental sciences, there is another criterion: repeatability. If the proffered explanation deals with some result that could in principle be reproduced if the explanation is correct, then the explanation—the theory or the hypothesis—must be tested. One of the many problems with the NIST report on the Twin Towers, as I point out in Chapter 3, is that it ignores this condition.

I distinguished earlier between rational and irrational conspiracy theories. I have here distinguished between scientific and unscientific theories. These two distinctions can, for our present purposes, be treated as interchangeable, because the criteria for rational theories are virtually identical with the criteria for scientific theories.

The main point of this discussion, in any case, is that the official theory about the collapse of the World Trade Center or the damage to the Pentagon cannot be considered scientific (or rational) simply because it has been endorsed by scientists. One reason is that other scientists have given alternative explanations, sometimes in papers that have passed peer review by independent scientists. The competing theories must be judged solely in terms of how well they handle the relevant facts. If one wants to make a rational judgment about 9/11, accordingly, there is no escape from examining the relevant facts. There can be no short-cut to truth by means of appeal to the authority of certain scientists—who may be scientists-for-hire.

Journalists who seek to debunk the alternative theory about 9/11, however, regularly appeal to the official and semi-official reports as if these were neutral, scientific documents. I will illustrate this point by using the essay by Matthew Rothschild, which is the lengthiest of the journalistic debunking attempts.

Having mentioned the claims that both the Twin Towers and Building 7 of the World Trade Center were brought down by explosives, Rothschild says: "Problem is, some of the best engineers in the country have studied these questions and come up with perfectly logical, scientific explanations for what happened." He then cites the FEMA report, which was based on work by the American Society of Civil Engineers (ASCE). He was evidently unaware, however, that the editor of *Fire Engineering* magazine wrote that there was "good reason to believe that the 'official investigation' blessed by FEMA . . . is a half-baked farce that may already have been commandeered by political forces whose primary interests, to put it mildly, lie far afield of full disclosure."[92] Rothschild was also apparently unaware that FEMA, according to a book by *New York Times* reporters, refused to provide the ASCE engineers with "basic data like detailed blueprints of the buildings" and "refused to let the team appeal to the public for photographs and videos of the towers that could help with the investigation."[93] He was also perhaps unaware that the ASCE team reported that its best hypothesis with regard to why WTC 7 collapsed had "only a low probability of occurrence."[94]

Rothschild also appealed to the report put out by NIST, perhaps unaware that NIST is an agency of the Commerce Department and hence of the Bush administration. Given this administration's record of manipulating science (see Chapter 3), there is no reason to assume that NIST's investigation was any less "commandeered by political forces" than was FEMA's. In what criminal trial would a document produced solely by the defendant's staff be accepted, without any chance for rebuttal by the prosecuting attorney, as neutral scientific evidence of the defendant's innocence? One must actually examine NIST's report to see if it is a scientific, rather than a political, document. And, as I show in Chapter 3, it proves to be worse, at least in some respects, than the FEMA report.

Rothschild points out that I had mentioned the oddity that, although the official story claims that the fires caused the towers to collapse by weakening their steel, the South Tower collapsed first, even though it was struck second, so that its fires had less time to heat up the steel. Rothschild rebuts this point by saying: "[NIST's] Final Report . . . notes that ten core columns were severed in the South Tower, whereas only six were severed in the North. And 20,000 more square feet of insulation was stripped from the trusses in the South Tower than the North." The word "notes," however, suggests that NIST based these figures on empirical evidence. As I show in Chapter 3, however, NIST's claims are pure speculation, which, far from being supported by the available evidence, run counter to it. Rothschild assumes, however, that since the NIST team involved scientists and engineers, NIST's published conclusions must be scientific.

With regard to Building 7, Rothschild quoted NIST's initial report, which says: "NIST has seen no evidence that the collapse of WTC 7 was caused by bombs, missiles, or controlled demolition." Did Rothschild think that a report put out by an agency of Bush's Commerce Department could possibly say anything else?

Turning to the Pentagon, Rothschild rebutted alternative theories by quoting the *Popular Mechanics* book and Mete Sozen, one of the authors of the *Pentagon Building Performance Report*, upon which that book relies. In Chapter 4, I show why that official report on the Pentagon and the book by *Popular Mechanics* are unreliable.

With regard to the alternative theory's claim that United Flight 93 "was brought down not by the passengers struggling with the hijackers but by a US missile," Rothschild said: "But we know from cell phone conversations that passengers on board that plane planned on confronting the hijackers." As I show in Chapters 1 and 4, however, the cell phone calls that were allegedly made from this flight, which played a big part in the movie *United 93*, would not have been possible in 2001. As evidence that United 93 could not have been shot down, Rothschild claimed that it had already crashed before NORAD knew what was going on. Basing this claim on Michael Bronner's *Vanity Fair* article about the NORAD tapes, Rothschild showed no awareness of the massive evidence against this claim, which I had summarized in my critique of the 9/11 Commission's report.[95]

On the basis of such appeals to these official and semi-official publications, Rothschild says: "Not every riddle that Griffin and other conspiracists pose has a ready answer. But almost all of their major assertions are baseless. . . . At bottom, the 9/11 conspiracy theories are profoundly irrational and unscientific."

I agree, of course, that there is a 9/11 conspiracy theory that is "profoundly irrational and unscientific." In the pages to follow, however, I show, by means of critiques of these official and semi-official publications, that it is the official 9/11 conspiracy theory that deserves this description.

Postscript: While correcting proofs for this book, I learned that the editor of a left-leaning website had, in explaining why it was not necessary to read anything I had written about 9/11, said that "a professor of theology is not qualified to talk about anything but myths." He apparently failed to see that I should, therefore, be eminently qualified to discuss the official account of 9/11.

ONE

9/11 Live or Distorted: Do the NORAD Tapes Verify
The 9/11 Commission Report?

A significant stir was created in the first week of August 2006 by the publication in *Vanity Fair* of an essay by Michael Bronner entitled "9/11 Live: The NORAD Tapes."[1] Bronner was the first journalist to be given access to these audiotapes, which NORAD had provided, upon demand, to the 9/11 Commission in 2004, excerpts from which were played during its public hearing in June. There was really nothing new in Bronner's article. It simply popularized the position that had been articulated in *The 9/11 Commission Report*, which had appeared in the summer of 2004. But the sensational charge in this report that is highlighted by Bronner's essay had hardly been noticed by the public or the press, due to the size of the Commission's report, the number of issues it covered, and the unsensational way in which this charge was made. This charge was that the story the US military had told from 2001 to 2004 about its response to the hijacked airliners on 9/11 was false. It is called false because it conflicts with the tapes received from NORAD.

The stir created by Bronner's essay was increased by the publication at the same time of *Without Precedent*, a book by Thomas Kean and Lee Hamilton—the chair and vice chair of the Commission, respectively—in which this charge is also made. Bronner's essay makes the charge even more sensational by reporting that at least some members of 9/11 Commission believe that these military leaders had made these false statements deliberately—that they had lied.[2]

In the present chapter, I will first describe the conflicts between what the military had said and what these NORAD tapes imply, explaining why some members of the Commission believe that these conflicts mean that the military had lied. I will then ask whether the conflicts, along with other facts, might more reasonably lead to a different conclusion—that these NORAD tapes present a false story. I will also point out an implication of the 9/11 Commission's report and Bronner's essay that neither of them intended, namely, that regardless of what we conclude about these tapes, we now know that the American military has lied about 9/11.

Conflicts between the NORAD Tapes and the Military's Previous Testimony

The charge that the military gave a false account primarily involves its pre-

2004 claims about the responses of NEADS—the Northeast Air Defense Sector of NORAD (the North American Aerospace Defense Command)—to two flights: AA (American Airlines) Flight 77 and UA (United Airlines) Flight 93. There is also, although Bronner does not deal with it, a serious discrepancy with regard to the military's pre-2004 claims about UA Flight 175. All of these claims are contradicted by the tapes, with "tapes" here meaning not only what Bronner calls "the NORAD tapes," but also what he calls "the parallel recordings from the F.A.A.,"[3] which he used in conjunction with the NORAD tapes. (Excerpts of these FAA tapes were also played at the Commission's June 2004 hearings.)

Here are the earlier claims made by the military—as represented at a 9/11 Commission hearing on May 23, 2003,[4] by Major General Larry Arnold, the commanding general of NORAD's Continental Region, and Colonel Alan Scott, who had worked closely with Arnold—followed by the contradictory information provided by the tapes:

(1) *The military's earlier claim:* When fighter jets at Langley Air Force Base in Virginia were scrambled at 9:24 that morning, they were scrambled in response to word from the FAA that possibly either AA 77 (as implied by Colonel Scott) or UA 93 (as stated by General Arnold) had been hijacked and was headed toward Washington.

What the tapes indicate: NEADS did not learn that AA 77 and UA 93 had been hijacked until after they had crashed. The Langley fighters were instead scrambled in response to "phantom AA 11"—that is, in response to a false report that AA 11 had not struck the World Trade Center and was instead headed toward Washington.

(2) *The military's earlier claim*: Having learned from the FAA about the hijacking of UA 93 at 9:16, NEADS was tracking it and was in position to shoot it down if necessary. (Although the claim about the 9:16 notification is not reflected in NORAD's timeline—which instead has "N/A"—both Arnold and Scott made this claim in their May 2003 testimony.)

What the tapes indicate: NEADS, far from learning of the possible hijacking of UA 93 at 9:16 (at which time it had not even been hijacked), did not receive this information until 10:07, four minutes after UA 93 had crashed. So NEADS could not have had fighter jets tracking it.

(3) *The military's earlier claim*: NEADS was prepared to act on a command, issued by Vice President Cheney, to shoot down UA 93.

What the tapes indicate: There was no command to shoot down UA 93 before it crashed. Cheney was not even aware of the possible hijacking of this flight until 10:02, only one minute before it crashed, and the shootdown authorization was not given by him until many minutes after UA 93 had crashed.

The 9/11 Commission, assuming that the newly released tapes provide the definitive account of NEADS' conversations on 9/11, concluded that

Colonel Scott and General Arnold made false statements. Also, pointing out that these military leaders had reviewed the tapes before giving their testimony, some Commission members, dismissing the idea that they could have simply been confused, concluded that they lied.

The implications of the tapes, assuming their authenticity, are even more sweeping, because the statements by Scott and Arnold reflected the timeline issued by NORAD on September 18, 2001.[5] This document gave the times at which, NORAD then claimed, the FAA had notified it about the four flights and then the times at which NEADS had scrambled fighters in response. Scott, in fact, had prepared this timeline, Bronner reports, in conjunction with Colonel Robert Marr, then the battle commander at NEADS. The implication of the NORAD tapes, therefore, is that virtually the entire account given by NORAD on September 18, 2001—which served as the official story from that date until the issuance of *The 9/11 Commission Report* in July 2004—was false.

The crucial difference between the two accounts is that, according to the earlier one, the FAA, while being unaccountably slow in notifying the military about the possible hijacking of AA 11, UA 175, AA 77, and UA 93, did notify it about all four flights before they crashed. Not only that, they notified the military, at least with regard to the last three flights, early enough that fighter jets could have intercepted them.[6] According to the tapes-based account provided by the 9/11 Commission, by contrast, the military was not notified about the last three flights until after they had crashed. The military, therefore, could not be blamed for failing to stop them.

If this tapes-based timeline is correct, some central claims of the 9/11 truth movement—that the military failed to intercept UA 175 and AA 77 because of a "stand-down order" and then shot down UA 93—are significantly undermined. It is no wonder, then, that one of NORAD's generals, taking the tapes-based story to be the real story, said: "The real story is actually better than the one we told."[7]

If this new story is true, the fact that it puts the military in a much better light has a staggering implication: Everyone in the military—from those in the Pentagon's National Military Command Center (NMCC), under which NORAD operates, to both high-level officers and lower-level employees at NEADS and in NORAD more generally, to pilots and other subordinates—who knew the true course of events, whether from direct experience or from listening to the tapes, kept quiet about the inaccuracies in NORAD's timeline, even though they knew that the true story would put the military in a better light, virtually removing the possibility that it had stood down its defenses. Why would they do this?

Bronner, addressing this issue in terms of the question of why Scott and Arnold apparently lied, says that members of the 9/11 Commission staff to whom he spoke said that "the false story ... had a clear purpose." What was that purpose? It was, according to staff member John Farmer, "to obscure mistakes on the part of the F.A.A. and the military, and to overstate the readiness of the military to intercept and, if necessary, shoot down UAL 93."[8] The motivation to lie, in other words, was to cover up confusion and incompetence. That same motivation is presumably thought to explain why the military as a whole acquiesced in the lie from September 18, 2001, until the 9/11 hearings in June 2004, when General Arnold was confronted with evidence from NORAD's tapes contradicting statements he had made at the hearing in May 2003.

However, although this explanation has been widely accepted, it is not really believable. If our military had been guilty only of confusion and incompetence on 9/11, it would have been strange for its officials, by saying that they had been notified by the FAA earlier than they really had, to open themselves to the charge that they had deliberately not intercepted the hijacked airliners. We are being asked to believe, in other words, that Scott, Arnold, and the others, in telling the earlier story, acted in a completely irrational manner—that they, while being guilty only of confusion and perhaps a little incompetence, told a lie that could have led to charges of murder and treason.

Nevertheless, we must conclude that they acted in this irrational way as long as we accept Bronner's presupposition that the tapes contain "the authentic military history of 9/11."[9] That presupposition has been accepted by stories in the mainstream press, such as a *New York Times* story that refers to what "the tapes demonstrate."[10]

If this presupposition is false, however, the tapes do not demonstrate anything—except that the military, perhaps in collusion with members of the 9/11 Commission, went to extraordinary lengths to fabricate audiotapes that would seem to rule out the possibility that the military and thereby members of the Bush–Cheney administration were complicit in the 9/11 attacks.

But is there any reason to suspect the truth of this alternative hypothesis? Is there any reason to believe that the 9/11 Commission, as well as the military, would have engaged in such deceit? Are there reasons to believe that the story as reflected in the tapes is false? Is there any way in which the tapes could have been altered?

Although to some readers these questions may seem merely rhetorical, the answer to each one is actually "Yes." Let us begin with the question of whether the 9/11 Commission would engage in deceit.

Would the 9/11 Commission Engage in Deceit?
One fact about the Commission that most Americans still do not know is by whom its work was carried out. Although the public face of the

Commission was provided by the ten commissioners led by Thomas Kean and Lee Hamilton, most of the actual research and the writing of reports was carried out by a staff of about 75 people, over half of whom were former members of the CIA, the FBI, the Department of Justice, and other governmental agencies.[11]

Most important, this staff was directed by Philip Zelikow, who was virtually a member of the Bush administration: He had worked with Condoleezza Rice on the National Security Council in the administration of George H. W. Bush; he later co-authored a book with her; then Rice, as National Security Advisor for President George W. Bush, brought Zelikow on to help make the transition from the Clinton to the Bush National Security Council; he was then appointed to the President's Foreign Intelligence Advisory Board; finally, Rice brought him on to be the principal drafter of the Bush administration's 2002 version of the National Security Strategy, which used 9/11 to justify a new doctrine of preemptive (technically "preventive") war, according to which the United States can attack other countries even if they pose no imminent threat.[12] This was hardly the man to be in charge of an investigation that should have been asking, among other things, whether the Bush–Cheney administration, which had benefited so greatly from the 9/11 attacks, was itself complicit in them.

And yet in charge Zelikow was. As executive director, he decided which topics would be investigated by the staff and which ones not. The staff was divided into eight investigative teams and, one disgruntled member reportedly said at the time, seven of these eight teams "are completely controlled by Zelikow." More generally, this staff member said, "Zelikow is calling the shots. He's skewing the investigation and running it his own way."[13] As executive director, moreover, Zelikow was able largely to control what would appear in—and be excluded from—*The 9/11 Commission Report*.

To illustrate how crucial such exclusions could be and also why the Zelikow-led 9/11 Commission cannot be assumed to be above deceit, we can look at a portion of Secretary of Transportation Norman Mineta's testimony at the Commission's hearing on May 23, 2003. Mineta testified that on the morning of 9/11, after arriving at the White House and stopping to see Richard Clarke (the national coordinator for security and counterterrorism), he went down to the Presidential Emergency Operations Center (PEOC) under the White House, where Vice President Cheney was in charge. Mineta then told Vice Chair Lee Hamilton:

> During the time that the airplane was coming in to the Pentagon, there was a young man who would come in and say to the Vice President, "The plane is 50 miles out." "The plane is 30 miles out." And when it got down to "the plane is 10 miles out," the young man also said to the

Vice President, "Do the orders still stand?" And the Vice President turned and whipped his neck around and said, "Of course the orders still stand. Have you heard anything to the contrary?"

When Mineta was asked by Commissioner Timothy Roemer how long this conversation occurred after he arrived, Mineta said: "Probably about five or six minutes," which, as Roemer pointed out, would mean "about 9:25 or 9:26."[14]

This story was very threatening to the account that would be provided in *The 9/11 Commission Report*. According to that account, Cheney did not even enter the PEOC until almost 10:00, "perhaps at 9:58."[15] According to Mineta's testimony, however, Cheney had arrived some time prior to 9:20. Mineta's time is consistent, moreover, with many other reports about Cheney's descent to the PEOC.[16]

Perhaps most amazingly, the Zelikow-led Commission even contradicted Cheney's own account. Speaking on NBC's *Meet the Press* five days after 9/11, Cheney said: "[A]fter I talked to the president, . . . I went down into . . . the Presidential Emergency Operations Center. . . . [W]hen I arrived there within a short order, we had word the Pentagon's been hit."[17] In an interview for a CNN story a year later, Cheney repeated that he was in the PEOC before word about the Pentagon strike, which reportedly occurred at about 9:38, was received.[18]

The fact that Cheney had gone down to the PEOC shortly after the second strike on the World Trade Center was also confirmed by National Security Advisor Condoleezza Rice. On an ABC News television program one year after 9/11, based on interviews by Peter Jennings, Rice said: "[T]he Secret Service came and said, 'you have to leave now for the bunker. The Vice President's already there. There may be a plane headed for the White House. There are a lot of planes that are in the air that are not responding properly,'" after which Charlie Gibson said: "In the bunker, the Vice President is joined by Rice and Transportation Secretary Norman Mineta."[19]

The Commission's time of 9:58 is clearly false and cannot be considered anything other than an outright lie. This illustration by itself shows that nothing the Commission says can be accepted on faith.

An even more important feature of Mineta's testimony, moreover, is that it is in strong tension with the Commission's claim that the military did not know that an aircraft was approaching the Pentagon until 9:36, so that it "had at most one or two minutes to react to the unidentified plane approaching Washington."[20] According to Mineta's account, however, the vice president knew at least ten minutes earlier, by 9:26. Are we to believe that although Cheney knew, the military did not?

Worse yet, Mineta's account could be read as eyewitness testimony to the confirmation of a stand-down order. Mineta himself, to be sure, did not make this allegation. He assumed, he said, that "the orders" mentioned by the young man were orders to have the plane shot down. Mineta's interpretation, however, does not fit with what actually happened, because the aircraft was *not* shot down. Mineta's interpretation, moreover, would make the story unintelligible: If the orders had been to shoot down the aircraft if it entered the forbidden air space over Washington, the young man would have had no reason to ask if the orders still stood. His question made sense only if the orders were to do something unexpected—not to shoot it down.

How did *The 9/11 Commission Report* deal with Mineta's testimony? By simply omitting it from the final report. One can understand such an omission, of course, if the purpose of the Zelikow-led Commission was to protect the Bush administration's account of 9/11. This omission is not, however, consistent with the Commission's purpose as stated by Kean and Hamilton, namely, "to provide the fullest possible account of the events surrounding 9/11."[21]

This omission of Mineta's testimony, as serious as it is, might not be fatal to our overall judgment about *The 9/11 Commission Report*'s reliability if it were an isolated example. As I have shown in a book-length critique, however, this omission is simply one example of a systematic pattern, in which all available evidence that contradicts the official story is systematically omitted or, in some cases, distorted.[22]

For another example, we can look at the Commission's treatment of the alleged hijackers. According to the official story of 9/11, the planes were hijacked by devout Muslims ready to meet their maker. *The 9/11 Commission Report* supports this picture, saying of Mohamed Atta, called the ringleader, that he had become very religious, even "fanatically so."[23] However, stories by *Newsweek*, the *San Francisco Chronicle*, and investigative journalist Daniel Hopsicker had reported that Atta loved cocaine, alcohol, gambling, pork, and lap dances.[24] The *Wall Street Journal* had reported, moreover, that several of the other alleged hijackers had indulged such tastes in Las Vegas.[25] But the 9/11 Commission, simply ignoring these reports, called Atta fanatically religious and professed to have no idea why he and the others met in Las Vegas several times.[26]

The Commission also ignored reports published by the British mainstream press that some of the alleged hijackers were still alive after 9/11. Eleven days afterward, for example, BBC News reported that Waleed al-Shehri, after seeing his photograph in newspapers and TV programs, notified authorities and journalists in Morocco, where he worked as a pilot, that he was still alive.[27] However, *The 9/11 Commission Report*, making no reference to this evidence about al-Shehri (as well as evidence that other alleged hijackers had still been alive after 9/11),[28] not only named al-Shehri as one of the hijackers and reproduced the FBI's photograph of him. It even suggested that al-Shehri stabbed one of the flight attendants shortly before Flight 11 crashed into the North Tower.[29] Whether or not these stories of alleged hijackers who were still alive after 9/11 would hold up after investigation, the Commission clearly should have discussed them.

In the light of these and over a hundred other illustrations provided in my critique of *The 9/11 Commission Report*, we cannot rule out in advance the possibility that the Zelikow-led Commission might have engaged in deceit with regard to the NORAD tapes. When we look closely at the part of the 9/11 Commission's story that is based on these tapes, moreover, we see that there are reasons to conclude that it contains falsehoods. One such reason to believe this is the Commission's portrayal of the FAA's behavior that morning.

Is the 9/11 Commission's Tapes-Based Portrayal of the FAA Believable?

The 9/11 Commission's tapes-based portrayal of the FAA's behavior is doubly problematic: it is intrinsically incredible and it is contradicted by many prior reports, some of which we otherwise have no good reason to question. Bronner suggests that these tapes are embarrassing to the military, showing it to have been very confused and inept on 9/11. The potential embarrassment from this confusion and ineptness is, indeed, said to have led military leaders to give a false account. But in the story told by Bronner and the 9/11 Commission on the basis of the tapes, it is the FAA, not the military, that is portrayed as confused and incompetent. The incompetence is, in fact, so extreme as to strain credulity.

This problem arises because FAA personnel, from top to bottom, are portrayed as repeatedly failing to follow standard procedures on 9/11, even though these men and women are highly competent individuals who, prior to that day, had carried out these procedures regularly.

According to these standard procedures, if an FAA flight controller notices anything about an airplane suggesting that it is in trouble—if radio contact is lost, if the plane does not obey an order, if the plane's transponder goes off, or if the plane deviates seriously from its flight plan—and the controller is unable to get the problem fixed quickly, the military will be contacted, perhaps to see if its radar operators can see something not evident to the civilian radar operators. If the problem cannot then be speedily resolved, the military will be asked to scramble jet fighters to intercept the airplane to find out what is going on. The FAA makes scramble requests routinely—over 100 times a year.[30]

According to the NORAD tapes and the 9/11 Commission, however, the FAA, far from following these procedures on 9/11, did not even come close.

AA Flight 11

According to the tapes, the FAA's Boston Center,[31] which was in charge of AA 11, did not contact the military until 8:38, in spite of the fact that the following events had occurred: At 8:14, the pilot failed to heed an order to climb, after which the controller realized that radio contact had been lost. At 8:21, the transponder signal was lost, and then the plane went radically off course. At 8:25, the controller heard what seemed to be the voice of a hijacker. In spite of these three events, any one of which should have evoked a call to the military, the FAA's Boston Center, according to the tapes, did not call anyone until 8:28. And then, rather than calling the military directly, Boston called the FAA Command Center in Herndon, Virginia, after which Herndon, rather than immediately calling the military, waited until 8:32 and then called FAA headquarters in Washington—which also did not contact the military. Finally, the Boston Center started trying to contact the military directly at 8:34 but did not reach NEADS until 8:38.[32]

Can we really take seriously this account, according to which gross and even criminal negligence was shown by FAA personnel at every level? Is not this portrayal rendered especially unbelievable by the lack of reports that any FAA employees at Boston Center, Herndon, or Washington were fired or even reprimanded for dereliction of duty?

Standard Procedures: The account given by NORAD of Flight 11 in its timeline of September 18, 2001, is the one account that was not significantly modified by the 9/11 Commission. And yet that account provides strong evidence that some kind of stand-down order, canceling standard operating procedures, must have been in place. At 8:14, the flight missed a clearance (meaning it did not obey an order to climb) and went NORDO (meaning that radio contact was lost). The standard procedure would have been for the controller to try to reestablish contact on the regular frequency and then, if that failed, on the emergency frequency, and this is what the controller, Pete Zalewski, reportedly did.[33] If that did not succeed within a few minutes, the controller should have contacted his supervisor (John Schipanni), which he did, and this supervisor should have had NEADS contacted quickly, but this contact allegedly did not occur.

FAA instructions make very clear that controllers are not to wait to make sure there is truly an emergency before contacting the military. In a statement that I had quoted in *The New Pearl Harbor*,[34] these instructions say to controllers:

> Consider that an aircraft emergency exists . . . when: . . . There is unexpected loss of radar contact and radio communications with any . . . aircraft. . . . If . . . you are in doubt that a situation constitutes an emergency or potential emergency, handle it as though it were an emergency.[35]

After seeing my quotation of this passage, Robin Hordon, who was formerly an air traffic controller at the FAA's Boston Center, said: "Certainly that's the way we always handled potential emergencies."[36] He believes, therefore, that Boston should have called NEADS "between 8:18 and 8:20."[37]

If the loss of radio contact for several minutes was considered insufficient for the controller to declare an "in-flight emergency," the fact that Flight 11 went radically off course at 8:21 certainly should have been sufficient. The day after 9/11, MSNBC, discussing the fact that every pilot had to file a flight plan, said:

> If a plane deviates by 15 degrees, or two miles from that course, the flight controllers will hit the panic button. They'll call the plane, saying 'American 11, you're deviating from course.' It's considered a real emergency.[38]

In this case, of course, the controllers had already lost radio contact, so they could not call the plane. But they still should have "hit the panic button" by calling NEADS if they had not already done so. After all, they now had seen two of the main signs that a flight is in trouble.

Also, just before they saw the plane go radically off course, they lost the transponder signal, so they had hit the trifecta, having observed all three of the standard signs that a plane is in trouble. The official story, according to which no one called NEADS even at this time, strains credulity.[39]

It is, moreover, not only former Boston controller Robin Hordon who believes that NEADS should have been contacted at about this time. This belief is shared by Colin Scoggins, who was, and still is, Boston Center's military specialist—sometimes called the military liaison—and who, in fact, plays a major role in Bronner's narrative. He has said:

> A NORDO aircraft prior to 9/11 wasn't a big deal; eventually you would get them back. The thing on 9/11 was an aircraft missed a clearance, was NORDO and lost a transponder, then made a 90-plus-degree turn. It just wasn't right. . . . I would have [called] almost immediately.[40]

Scoggins thereby indicates that he would have called NEADS at 8:21 or 8:22.

When Did the FAA First Contact the Military? Hordon takes it a step further, believing that Boston Center not only should have contacted NEADS this early but actually did so: "When the very first call regarding AA 11 was initiated to any military facility is being covered up," he says.[41] His previously quoted comment that the call should have occurred "between 8:18 and 8:20" is his "educated guess" as to when it actually occurred. He believes this partly because "it's procedure to get another set of eyes on the potential emergency."[42] The standard procedure would have at least led Boston Center, as a first step, to ask "NEADS radar personnel [if they could] see something about AA 11 that perhaps the FAA radar might not be able to see."[43] But he also believes that contact was made around 8:20 because, he says: "I know people who work there [at Boston Center] who confirmed to me that the FAA was not asleep and the controllers . . . followed their own protocols."[44]

These reasons to believe that the military must have been contacted around 8:20 are supported, moreover, by strong evidence that it actually was. Two insiders, Tom Flocco reports, told him that a teleconference initiated by the Pentagon on 9/11 began about 8:20 that morning.

The fact that a teleconference was organized by the NMCC (National Military Command Center) is well known. Richard Clarke reports that, as he was getting ready to set up his own teleconference from the White House after the second tower was hit, the deputy director of the White House Situation Room told him: "We're on the line with NORAD, on an air threat conference call."[45] This would have been a little before 9:15.[46] The 9/11 Commission also discusses this teleconference, pointing out that it was upgraded to "an air threat" conference call after having started as a "significant event" conference call.[47]

The crucial question is: When did this teleconference begin? The 9/11 Commission claims that it did not commence until 9:29. This claim, however, is implausible for several reasons: First, it is not supported by any evidence.[48] Second, the military admits that it had been told of AA 11's hijacking by 8:38; the NMCC surely would not have waited another 50 minutes to start a conference call. Third, the 9:29 claim is also contradicted by Richard Clarke, who reports that he learned about this conference call before 9:15. The fact that it was already being called an "air threat" conference call at that time indicates, moreover, that it had already been going on for some time. For how long? That is the question to which Tom Flocco's reports speak.

NMCC teleconferences would normally have been organized by Brigadier General Montague Winfield, the NMCC's director of operations. But for some reason, he had himself replaced at 8:30 that morning by his deputy, Captain Charles Leidig. It was Leidig, the Pentagon said, who organized the teleconference, so it was he who testified about it to the 9/11 Commission (on June 17, 2004). During this testimony, however, Leidig was apparently not asked to state when the teleconference began.

Flocco, who was at this hearing, reports that he rushed up to Leidig at the end of the session and asked him when, approximately, his phone bridges—another name for a teleconference—had begun. Leidig, according to Flocco, claimed that he could not recall.[49] This claim is unbelievable, however, given the momentous events of that day combined with the fact that it had surely been Leidig's first time to be in charge of such a call, because he had only recently become qualified to stand in for

Winfield.[50] Leidig certainly could have given an approximate time, reporting, say, whether his conference began before or after the strikes on the World Trade Center. The claim that he could "not recall" suggests that the military did not want him to say.

Flocco, in any case, was especially interested in this question, he reports, because a year earlier, at the 9/11 Commission hearing that took place in Washington on May 22, 2003, he had talked with Laura Brown, the deputy in public affairs at FAA headquarters. She told him, he says, that Leidig's phone bridges had begun around 8:20 or 8:25. That answer made sense to Flocco, because it would mean that the conference call had begun shortly after the appearance of signs that AA 11 was in trouble.

However, Flocco then reports: "After returning to her office and conferring with superiors, Brown sent an e-mail to this writer . . . , revising her initial assertions for the commencement of Leidig's phone bridges to around 8:45AM."[51] Flocco clearly believes that Laura Brown's first statement, before her memory had been "refreshed" by superiors, was the truth. (Even her revised time, in any case, contradicts the 9/11 Commission's claim that the NMCC teleconference did not start until 9:29, giving us additional evidence that the Commission is lying.)

Flocco believes the 8:20 starting time not only because of the reasons already given but also because he received the same information from another insider. In July of 2003, just two months after he had talked with Laura Brown, he wrote that "at 8:20AM, . . . according to our conversation with a Department of Transportation source, phone bridges were established linking Secret Service, Defense Department, NORAD, and Transportation Department officials—and others."[52] Flocco reports, moreover, that although the Pentagon made a transcript of the recording of this conference call, this transcript, besides being classified, was subjected to an "executive privilege" review by the White House.[53]

Robin Hordon's conviction that the military was contacted around 8:20 is, therefore, supported not only by Colin Scoggins' statement (that that is when he himself would have initiated the contact) and the statement to Hordon by other personnel at Boston Center (that standard protocols were followed). It is also, according to Tom Flocco, supported by two independent reports—one from Laura Brown of the FAA and one from a source within the Department of Transportation—that the NMCC's teleconference had begun at about 8:20. We have, in other words, good evidence that the FAA had contacted the military about AA 11 approximately 25 minutes before it crashed into the World Trade Center, not merely 9 minutes beforehand, as the 9/11 Commission claims on the basis of the tapes—tapes that contain no communications to or from the NMCC and that, at least as received by Bronner, reportedly do not even begin until 8:26:20.

Hijacking vs. Emergency Protocol: As we have seen, Boston Center should have notified NEADS by 8:21, if not earlier. According to the 9/11 Commission's tapes-based account, however, it did not even try to contact anyone until after 8:25, when the controller for AA 11 heard a voice saying things suggesting that a hijacking was in progress. The FAA controller, who "then knew it was a hijacking," alerted his supervisor, after which Boston Center, "in accordance with the FAA protocol. . . , starting notifying their chain of command that American 11 had been hijacked." What that meant concretely was that "Boston Center called the Command Center in Herndon to advise that it believed American 11 had been hijacked." Herndon then "passed word of a possible hijacking to . . . FAA headquarters," which "began to follow the hijack protocol but did not contact the NMCC to request a fighter escort." No one in the FAA, according to this account, tried to contact the military until Boston Center started trying at 8:34. It first tried to "contact the military through the FAA's Cape Cod facility," then "tried to contact a former alert site in Atlantic City, unaware it had been phased out" (both parts of this sentence, however, are false).[54] Boston Center finally reached NEADS at 8:38.[55]

The most significant feature of this account, Hordon says, is that it, by not having any contact between the FAA and NEADS until after Boston Center had evidence that the plane had been hijacked, puts the emphasis on the "hijack protocol." Why is that important? Because this protocol is very different from the emergency scramble protocol, which would be followed in the conditions discussed earlier: losing radio contact and the transponder signal and/or seeing the plane go radically off course.

Under this emergency protocol, speed is of the essence. Besides the fact that the FAA is to contact the military quickly, the military is set up to scramble fighters and reach the troubled flight quickly. In Hordon's words:

> [T]he NORAD defense system is on call 24/7/365. . . . Therefore, whenever and wherever the need to scramble comes up, the interceptor "launch system" is sitting in waiting for immediate reaction and launch. Interceptors are located in open-ended hangars near the ends of runways, the flight crews are located within a few feet and few moments of climbing on board the fighter, the mechanics keep the aircraft mechanically fit and warm with power sources connected for immediate start-up . . . . This is a highly skilled and highly practiced event. . . . Everyone [concerned is] prepared to launch within a few minutes of the request. . . . The "emergency scramble protocol" [then] calls for the fighter pilots to fly at top speed to intercept the emergency aircraft and immediately pull alongside the aircraft, attempt to assess the emergency, and then to get hold of the pilot.[56]

If standard procedure had been followed, therefore, the FAA would have notified NEADS no later than 8:22, NEADS would have issued the scramble order no later than 8:23, the fighters would have been airborne no later than 8:27, and AA 11 would have been intercepted by 8:37— over nine minutes before the North Tower of the World Trade Center was struck. Even if effecting the protocol had taken several minutes longer, the interception could still have been made.

Why did that not occur? It would appear, argues Hordon, that this is the question the 9/11 Commission and Bronner seek to keep us from asking. The Commission, as we have seen, does not discuss emergency protocol. It does not focus on the question why Boston did not call NEADS at 8:18 or 8:21, when the emergency protocol would have been the only one relevant. By claiming that NEADS was not reached until after the FAA had heard evidence of a hijacking, the Commission could plausibly limit the discussion entirely to the hijacking protocol.

And this protocol, Hordon emphasizes, is very different from the emergency protocol, for several reasons. First, whereas a controller can immediately declare an "in-flight emergency" on the basis of any of the danger signs discussed earlier, assigning a "hijacked" status to a flight is much more difficult and time-consuming. Second, because the response to the hijacking needs to involve the coordinated efforts of the Pentagon's NMCC and the FAA, the military is to be contacted by the hijack coordinator at FAA headquarters in Washington; Boston Center would, accordingly, contact Herndon or FAA headquarters. Third, the fighters, rather than pulling up alongside the hijacked aircraft, would generally follow miles behind it, remaining out of sight. In the words of the 9/11 Commission, "The protocols did not contemplate an intercept. They assumed the fighter escort would be discreet, 'vectored to a position five miles directly behind the hijacked aircraft,' where it could perform its mission to monitor the aircraft's flight path."[57] Fourth, because planes had historically been hijacked to fly to other airports or to negotiate for something, it had been presumed, in the 9/11 Commission's words, that "there would be time to address the problem through the appropriate FAA and NORAD chains of command." For all these reasons, the hijack protocol takes much longer to carry out than does the emergency protocol, which can be carried out within five to ten minutes—and *must* be, because a plane off course is a danger to other air traffic.[58]

Accordingly, by virtually ignoring the in-flight emergency, signs of which began at 8:14 and became very strong at 8:21, in favor of the hijacking, signs of which did not begin until 8:25, the 9/11 Commission took the focus off the question of why the emergency protocol was not carried out in the eleven minutes before there was any indication of a hijacking. The Commission's ignoring of this issue is evident in many places. For example, it cites Colin Scoggins in support of its statement that "in the event of a hijacking. . . , the protocols for the FAA to obtain military assistance from NORAD required multiple levels of notification and approval at the highest levels of government."[59] But it gives no evidence of having solicited his opinion on whether NEADS should have been called at 8:21, before there was evidence of a hijacking. Likewise, the Commission reports that, according to Boston Center operations manager Terry Biggio,

> the combination of three factors—loss of radio contact, loss of transponder signal, and course deviation—was serious enough for him to contact the ROC [Regional Operations Center] in Burlington, Mass. However, without hearing the threatening communication from the cockpit, he doubts Boston Center would have recognized or labeled American 11 "a hijack."[60]

The Commission gives no indication of having asked him why this combination of factors was not sufficient to have called the military.

Having focused entirely on the hijacking protocol, the 9/11 Commission could conclude that "the existing protocol was unsuited in every respect for what was about to happen,"[61] thereby ignoring the fact that there was an emergency protocol, which, if employed, would have worked just fine.

It was only, moreover, by completely eliminating any reference to the emergency protocol that the Commission could make the "existing protocol" (note the singular) seem inadequate to the situation. Hordon says:

> AA 11 was always an in-flight emergency, and only after hearing the cockpit troubles was it considered a "hijack." Therefore, "emergency aircraft protocols" and "hijack protocols" should have been used all throughout the event, and the fastest protocol would be utilized.[62]

The 9/11 Commission could portray the FAA and the military as having followed protocol only by claiming that there was no report to the military until the hijacking report and then treating this as if it were a request for an escort.

Once we are alerted to this issue, we can see that Bronner's tapes-based account does the same thing. Saying that "the military's first notification that something is wrong" does not occur until 8:38, he drives this point home by stating that the "first human voices captured on tape that morning" at NEADS were those of three female technicians discussing a furniture sale ("O.K., a couch, an ottoman, a love seat, and what else. . . ? Was it on sale. . . ? Holy smokes! What color is it?"). Clearly, we can infer, NEADS had not received word of any emergency, even though this was 24 minutes after FAA controllers had lost radio contact with AA 11.

However, if NEADS had received word of this emergency at, say, 8:21, the tapes Bronner received would not have reflected this fact, because, he reports, they do not begin until 8:26:20.[63]

In any case, having begun his "authentic military history" some 23 minutes after the first signs that AA 11 was in trouble, Bronner then tells us that a caller from Boston Center said: "We have a hijacked aircraft headed toward New York, and we need you guys to, we need someone to scramble some F-16s or something." In spite of the urgency of the call—which, pointing out that the hijacked plane was heading toward New York City, asked for fighters to be scrambled—Bronner discusses "standard hijack protocol," saying that the scrambled fighters "are trained to trail the hijacked plane at a distance of about five miles, out of sight." "Hijackers," Bronner adds, "had never actually flown airplanes; it was expected that they'd land and make demands."[64]

By having the FAA–NEADS interaction begin with the report that AA 11 had been hijacked and by ignoring the urgency of the call from Boston Center, Bronner and the 9/11 Commission diverted attention away from the prior and most important question: Why had interceptors not been launched earlier, on the basis of multiple evidence that this plane was experiencing an in-flight emergency?

When Was NEADS Notified About the Hijacking? Having ignored that question, Bronner and the 9/11 Commission then imply that even if NEADS had responded immediately to the report of the hijacking of AA 11, it could not have intercepted this airliner before it hit the North Tower. They do this by saying that although Boston Center learned about the hijacking at 8:25, it did not notify NEADS about it until almost 8:38 (8:37:52), at which time Jeremy Powell, a technical sergeant, answered a call and heard:

> Hi. Boston Center T.M.U., we have a problem here. We have a hijacked aircraft headed toward New York, and we need you guys to, we need someone to scramble some F-16s or something up there, help us out.

Powell then asked, "Is this real-world or exercise?" and was told: "No, this is not an exercise, not a test."[65] From other sources, we learn that Powell then transferred the call to Colonel Dawne Deskins, who, after identifying herself, heard the caller say: "Uh, we have a hijacked aircraft and I need you to get some sort of fighters out here to help us out."[66]

However, the claim that the military was not contacted about the hijacking until 8:38 is contradicted by two ABC specials in 2002. A show entitled "Moments of Crisis" said that, "shortly after 8:30AM, . . . word of a possible hijacking reached various stations of NORAD." And the earlier-mentioned show, based on interviews by Peter Jennings, specified the time at which Deskins received the call as "8:31."[67] Although 8:31 is considerably later than 8:20, it is also considerably earlier than 8:38.

That this call was no later than 8:31 can also be inferred from statements made by Colin Scoggins. According to Bronner's tapes-based account, Scoggins reported to NEADS at 8:40 that AA 11 was "35 miles north of Kennedy now at 367 knots." However, Scoggins, who states that he "made about forty phone calls to NEADS" that day,[68] says that when he made his first call, he reported that the flight was "20 [miles] south of Albany heading south at a high rate of speed, 600 knots."[69] By the time the plane was 35 miles north of JFK, therefore, it had traveled about 90 miles. If we estimate that the plane's average speed was 500 knots and hence 8.3 nautical miles per minute, traversing that distance would have taken almost 11 minutes. Scoggins' first call, therefore, must have occurred at 8:28 or 8:29 (which would mean that, although he says he recalls not getting to the floor until about 8:35, his memory must be mistaken; he admits that he cannot otherwise explain the apparent contradiction).[70] Scoggins says, moreover, that before he arrived on the floor that morning, Joe Cooper, an air traffic management specialist, had phoned NEADS about the hijacking.[71] Cooper's call, therefore, must have occurred at 8:27 or 8:28. However, Cooper's call is the one that, according to the tapes, was received at NEADS by Powell and then Deskins at about 8:38.[72] Something, obviously, is terribly wrong.

This problem is greatly mitigated if we follow the ABC timeline, according to which this call was received by Deskins at 8:31. We then have to assume only that ABC was off by three or four minutes to get that call pushed back to 8:28 or 8:27, so that it could have occurred a minute or two before Scoggins' first call at 8:28 or 8:29.

It would seem, therefore, that the first call from Boston Center to NEADS about the hijacking—ignoring here the question of a still earlier call about the in-flight emergency, which would explain why the NMCC evidently organized a teleconference at 8:20—must have come at least 10 minutes earlier than Bronner and the 9/11 Commission claim on the basis of the tapes.

A call at 8:27 or 8:28 is, moreover, roughly what would be expected if Boston Center called NEADS shortly after 8:25, when controller Pete Zalewski had clear evidence, from hearing the voice of a man with a foreign accent, that AA 11 had been hijacked.

There were, to be sure, conflicting views about what protocol should have been used that day in response to a hijacking. Some of those involved said that Boston Center should indeed have contacted the military directly. One of those was Ben Sliney, who was the Operations Manager at the FAA's Command Center in Herndon. In testimony to the 9/11 Commission, he said: "[T]he protocol was in place that the center that reported the hijacking would notify the military. . . . I go back to 1964, where I began my air traffic career, and they have always followed the same protocol." Boston Center, therefore, would have notified the military directly. Sliney added, moreover, that it was his understanding that "a notification to NORAD [was] made promptly."[73]

However, Monte Belger, who was the FAA's acting deputy administrator, affirmed the hierarchical hijacking protocol, saying: "[T]he official protocol on that day was for the FAA headquarters, primarily through the hijack coordinator, who is a senior person in the security organization, to request assistance from the NMCC if there was a need for DOD assistance."[74]

Given that tension, Scoggins makes a very interesting comment, saying that the official protocol, as articulated by Belger, did not exclude the faster, direct approach articulated by Sliney. He writes:

The Justice department questioned . . . where I got the authority to go directly to NEADS, and [asked] how come I didn't follow the protocol on 9/11. . . . I have a letter of agreement with NEADS . . . , and I have a phone line directly to NEADS; I knew which direction I was going to go right from the beginning. It wasn't my job to call the NMCC; it was [the job of] the FAA Hijack coordinator, who was to be called from our New England ROC [Regional Operations Center], who was called by our OMIC [Operations Manager in Charge], Terry Biggio; we did follow protocol, but I went another route *at the same time*.[75] [Emphasis added.]

Accordingly, Scoggins treated the situation, just as Hordon said would be normal, as an in-flight emergency as well as a hijacking.

If other people at Boston with direct lines to NEADS had the same view as Sliney, Scoggins, and Hordon, then we would expect that someone would have notified NEADS shortly after 8:25.

Scoggins reports, however, that the protocol was delayed a minute or so because the supervisor, John Schipanni, disputed Zalewski's conviction that the plane had been hijacked—a dispute reflected in the movie *United 93*. Scoggins adds, however, that Schipanni did, without great delay, pass the information on to the OMIC, Terry Biggio, who then, according to Scoggins, called the Regional Operations Center. The 9/11 Commission, by contrast, says that Boston Center called Herndon.[76] In any case, it would seem likely that someone, simultaneously, would have called NEADS. (Hordon says: "That is exactly what the Watch Desk team does: they split up the communications responsibilities and get on the phones immediately."[77]) If so, the call would have been made at about 8:28 — which is the time at which Boston Center, according to the Commission, called Herndon. And this, as we saw, was about when Joe Cooper's call to NEADS must have been made. Scoggins, moreover, says he himself contacted NEADS "at the same time" as Biggio was making his call. We have, therefore, multiple lines of evidence pointing to approximately

8:28—rather than 8:38, as the tapes indicate—as the time when Boston Center notified NEADS about the hijacking.

We have, moreover, still additional evidence that the 8:38 time is wrong. Jane Garvey, the head of the FAA, testified that the FAA contacted the military at 8:34.[78] That is, of course, the time at which, according to the 9/11 Commission, someone at the Boston Center—Daniel Bueno, the traffic management supervisor, Scoggins reports—called "the FAA's Cape Cod Facility." However, there are three facilities at Cape Cod: the Otis Air Force Base Tower, the Otis Air National Guard, and Cape TRACON (Terminal Radar Approach Control). Only the latter one—Cape TRACON—is an FAA facility. But Bueno, according to Scoggins, called not only Cape TRACON but also the Otis Tower.[79] The fact that the Otis Tower was reached is shown by the Air Force's book about 9/11, *Air War over America*, which reports that one of the pilots on alert at Otis, Lieutenant Colonel Timothy Duffy, said: "About 8:30, 8:35, . . . I got a phone call from one of the sergeants," who said: "Duffy, you have a phone call from tower. . . . Something about a hijacking."[80]

The 9/11 Commission's claim that Boston Center called only the FAA's facility at Otis is an essential element in its claim that the military was not informed about AA 11 until 8:38. But because Bueno called the Otis Tower, the military was reached at 8:34. Indeed, according to the account in *Air War over America*, the commander of the Otis fighter squadron, Lieutenant Colonel Jon Treacy, phoned NEADS to report the FAA's request for help.

So, even if we ignore the evidence that the military was contacted at around 8:20 and the evidence that it was contacted around 8:28, we have strong evidence that it was contacted at 8:34—four minutes earlier than Bronner and the 9/11 Commission claim. Although this four-minute difference may not seem like much, it would mean that the military was notified about AA 11 at least thirteen minutes, rather than only nine minutes, before the North Tower was struck—which would mean that, if the Otis fighters had been scrambled immediately, they could have made the interception.

Moreover, this call must have come even earlier than 8:34. Duffy, in saying that the call came "about 8:30, 8:35," seemed open to this possibility. And Bueno's call to Otis was earlier than Joe Cooper's call to NEADS,[81] which, as we saw, must have occurred by 8:28. The military at Otis, therefore, must have been contacted by 8:27.

We hence have even more evidence that the tapes do not give "the authentic military history of 9/11."

Why Were the Fighters Not Launched More Quickly? In any case, through the methods discussed thus far, the tapes-based account has dealt with the 24 minutes between 8:14 and 8:38. This account, however, still has a question to answer: Why, even if the notification of the military did not occur until 8:38, were fighters not launched until 8:52?

Part of the answer involves the emphasis on the hijacking protocol. Right after receiving the notification of the hijacking at 8:38, Bronner says, NEADS mission crew commander Major Kevin Nasypany,

> following standard hijack protocol, prepares to launch two fighters from Otis Air National Guard Base, on Cape Cod, to look for American 11. . . . He orders his Weapons Team . . . to put the Otis planes on "battle stations." This means that . . . [t]hey . . . do everything they need to do to get ready to fly short of starting the engines.[82]

Why were the engines not started so that the pilots could take off as soon as possible? The implicit answer to this question, evidently, is that because the hijack protocol was in effect, there was not a great sense of urgency: No use starting the engines until the planes were ready to take off.

Why could they not be scrambled immediately? It certainly was not because the Otis pilots were not ready. Timothy Duffy reports that, after he received the phone call about the hijacking, he contacted the other pilot, Major Daniel Nash, so they were suited up and headed toward their planes when the "battle stations" order came.[83] As this response shows, they were treating the notice as an emergency, which required a rapid response. So what caused the delay?

The problem, we are told, is that although the NEADS technicians were trying to find out "where [AA 11] is, so Nasypany can launch the fighters," they "can't find American 11 on their scopes." Why? One reason, Bronner says, is that "the scopes were so old, . . . strikingly anachronistic compared with the equipment at civilian air-traffic sites."[84]

However, Hordon says, Bronner has confused two very different things: radar scopes and radar targets. Although the FAA did have newer radar scopes, "The radar targets provided were the same quality from the same sources on the old scopes as they would be on the new scopes." And, Hordon adds: "The military has always had the best radars on planet earth, and they have them for national air defenses." By way of emphasizing the absurdity of Bronner's claim, Hordon asks, rhetorically: If scope problems "prevented [military radar technicians] from seeing a Boeing 757," how could they have seen the smaller "invading aircraft" they were ready to spot during the Cold War?[85]

> And since the Cold War [Hordon adds], the military radar systems have been getting exponentially better and better. Certainly they are not getting worse: the old scope–new scope thing is nothing but a fool's tale. The military's radar targets are the best they have ever been.[86]

In previous writings, I had illustrated Hordon's point by referring to the military's statement that one of its systems, called PAVE PAWS, is capable of monitoring a great number of targets simultaneously and "does not miss anything occurring in North American airspace."[87]

Bronner's claim that the military's radar was inferior to the FAA's is clearly false. But it is not his only explanation for why NEADS technicians could not find AA 11. He also says:

> In order to find a hijacked airliner—or any airplane—military controllers need either the plane's beacon code (broadcast from an electronic transponder on board) or the plane's exact coordinates. When the hijackers on American 11 turned the beacon off, . . . the NEADS controllers were at a loss. "You would see thousands of green blips on your scope," Nasypany told me. . . . [W]ithout that information from F.A.A., it's a needle in a haystack.". . . . [M]ore than 3,000 jetliners are already in the air over the continental United States, and the Boston controller's direction—"35 miles north of Kennedy"—doesn't help the NEADS controllers at all.[88]

This portrayal of the situation, Hordon says, is "total hogwash."

NORAD technicians, he explains, do not need "exact coordinates," meaning the plane's latitude and longitude, in order to locate an aircraft. For decades, military and civilian controllers helped each other locate aircraft, with and without transponders, by referring to "well-known navaids, airway intersections, military special use areas, major airports, military bases, and other common points of reference."[89]

Scoggins adds some information here, saying that in the 1990s, the military reduced the use of common reference points. But this reduction did not mean that to locate an airplane with its transponder off, the military controllers needed exact coordinates. Common reference points were still used. "If we needed to reference an aircraft," Scoggins says, "we would give them a fix/radial/distance from the common reference point."[90] This practice is illustrated in Scoggins' account of his attempt to help the NEADS technicians locate Flight 11:

> I was giving NEADS accurate location information on at least 5 instances where AA 11 was yet they could never identify him. . . . I originally gave them an F/R/D, which is a fix/radial/distance from a known location; they could not identify the target. They requested latitude/longitudes, which I gave them; they still could not identify the AA 11. . . . I gave them 20 [miles] South of Albany heading south at a high rate of speed, 600 knots, then another call at 50 South of Albany.[91]

As the military specialist at Boston Center, Scoggins, who had called NEADS often, surely knew what was customary.

Another important point in Scoggins' statement is that he did give exact coordinates (latitude and longitude), but he was still told that NEADS could not locate the flight. It would appear, therefore, that Bronner's excuse, evidently provided by Nasypany, is just that—an excuse, not a genuine reason.

Another dubious part of Bronner's attempt to defend NEADS is his statement that the information (given by Scoggins) that Flight 11 was 35 miles north of JFK "doesn't help the NEADS controllers at all."[92] Having seen this statement, Hordon replied: "In order to believe this, one must believe that the NEADS flight monitors do not know what '35 miles' looks like on their scopes, and that they do not know where the John F. Kennedy International Airport is. Absurd!"[93]

Equally absurd, Hordon says, is Nasypany's statement, quoted by Bronner, about "thousands of green blips," which implies that each controller's scope would be showing all of the air traffic in the United States. In reality, the contiguous United States is broken into three regions, one of which is NEADS, and within NEADS the airspace is broken down into much smaller sections, so that each scope is showing only a small percentage of the planes aloft in the country at any given time.[94] Nasypany's statement was, therefore, clearly designed to mislead.

In any case, the most important falsehood, which is stated by both Bronner and the 9/11 Commission, is that the US military cannot track airplanes that are not sending out a transponder signal. The military still has its traditional (primary) radar, which does not depend upon anything being sent from the aircraft. If aircraft not sending out transponder signals were "invisible" to the military radars, then Soviet bombers coming to attack the United States during the Cold War could have avoided detection by simply turning their transponders off. Surely the US military's defense of the United States was not based on the hope that Soviet pilots would have the courtesy to leave their transponders on!

The question Bronner is answering, to recall, is why fighters were not scrambled as soon as NEADS learned about the hijacking of AA 11. This explanation—that the technicians at NEADS could not locate the aircraft because of inadequate radar—is, as we have seen, preposterous.

But what about the prior claim—that Nasypany could not get the fighters airborne before learning exactly where AA 11 was? After all, he knew approximately where it was and that it was headed south. Why did he not have the pilots—who were, Bronner tells us, "in their jets, straining at the reins"—get airborne and headed in that general direction, then give them the more exact information when it became available? Hordon supports this point, saying:

> Where does it say in any regulations or protocols that the NORAD personnel need to observe the target first? . . . If there is trouble, you go to where a trusted professional says the trouble is, and you begin to "snoop, intercept or search" for that trouble on the way there, then you get real close after you find the target.[95]

Bronner seems to suggest that this would have been unrealistic by claiming that the information NEADS had received was far too vague. All that NEADS knew, Bronner says, was that the plane was "currently somewhere north of John F. Kennedy International Airport."[96] The statement by Scoggins quoted above, however, indicates that this is not true. He says: "I gave them 20 south of Albany heading south at a high rate of speed, 600 knots." If Nasypany needed pretty specific information to launch fighters, that was pretty specific.

Bronner next lets us know, however, that such specific information was not needed to launch. He writes:

> Less than two minutes later [at 8:43], frustrated that the controllers still can't pinpoint American 11 on radar, Nasypany orders [James] Fox to launch the Otis fighters anyway. Having them up, Nasypany figures, is better than having them on the ground, assuming NEADS will ultimately pin down American 11's position.

That is good logic, but it would have been equally good five minutes earlier. Why did Nasypany not use it then, rather than wasting five precious minutes waiting for more exact information? This would have been especially important in light of the fact that the fighters were being sent from Otis, which is about 155 miles—hence about five minutes for F-15s going full speed—from New York City.

Whatever be the answer to that question, the fighters would finally, we would assume, be launched shortly after 8:43. But they were not, we are told, launched until 8:52. Why not? One part of the answer is that the Otis pilots were not given the green light to taxi out to the runway until 8:46. Given the fact that scrambling fighters is a highly rehearsed operation, in which every second counts, why did it take three minutes to go from launch order to green light, when the pilots had long been ready to go? Bronner gives a hint by saying that "Colonel Marr and General Arnold ha[d] approved Nasypany's order to scramble."[97]

By consulting *The 9/11 Commission Report*, we learn that Colonel Robert Marr, the battle commander at NEADS, telephoned Arnold, the head of NORAD's Continental Region, which is headquartered at Tyndall Air Force Base in Florida. Although exactly when Marr supposedly made this call is not clear, the authorization reportedly did not come until 8:46, even though Arnold later claimed that, in order to expedite matters, he said "go ahead and scramble them, and we'll get authorities later."[98]

Did Marr really need to get authorization from Arnold? The 9/11 Commission, arguing that authorization was needed from the top, cited a memo issued June 1, 2001 (about 3 months before 9/11), by the Chairman of the Joint Chiefs of Staff, entitled "Aircraft Piracy (Hijacking) and Destruction of Derelict Airborne Objects." The crucial statement in this document says:

> [T]he NMCC is the focal point within Department of Defense for providing assistance. In the event of a hijacking, the NMCC will be notified by the most expeditious means by the FAA. The NMCC will, *with the exception of immediate responses as authorized by reference d*, forward requests for DOD assistance to the Secretary of Defense for approval.[99] [Emphasis added.]

As the italicized words show, this document does not say, as some interpreters have argued, that all requests to scramble fighters in response to a hijacking had to be approved by the office of the secretary of defense. Such approval is not necessary, these italicized words show, when "immediate responses" are needed. When we look at "reference d," moreover, we find that the requests do not even need to go to the NMCC (a fact illustrated by Arnold's statement, "we'll get the authorities later"). Reference d points back to a 1997 document, Directive 3025.15, which says: "The DoD Components that receive verbal requests from civil authorities for support in an exigent emergency may initiate informal planning and, if required, immediately respond."[100]

NEADS, being a "DoD component" that received a request from a civil authority (the FAA) for what was clearly an "exigent emergency," had the authority to "immediately respond." Marr did not even need to get approval from Arnold.

Having made this argument in my critique of *The 9/11 Commission Report*,[101] I was interested to learn that Scoggins agrees. He says:

> According to FAA Order 7610.4, NEADS has the authority issued by NORAD to launch fighters; they do not have to wait for authority from NORAD. On 9/11, I believe Col. Marr at NEADS would not launch without authority from General Arnold at NORAD; that caused a delay.[102]

Moreover, even General Arnold himself evidently agreed that Marr had the authority. In the 2003 book *Air War over America*, for which Arnold wrote the foreword, there is an account of the response at Otis to Boston Center's call about a hijacked airliner. Reporting that the commander of the fighter squadron at Otis called NEADS to report the FAA's request for help, the book says: "The sector commander would have authority to scramble the airplanes."[103]

However, although Arnold wrote the foreword for a book saying that Marr had the authority to launch, he publicly went along with the fiction that Marr needed to get his permission. Part of the reason for the delay in launching the fighters, Arnold told the 9/11 Commission in 2003, is that when the call from Marr came, he (Arnold) was participating in a video teleconference and did not learn about Marr's call until it was over, at which time, he says, "I was handed a note that we had a possible hijacking at Boston center, and . . . Colonel Bob Marr . . . had requested that I call him immediately."[104] If this is a true account, Marr certainly demonstrated a lack of urgency, not even telling the person who took the call to interrupt Arnold, because he needed to speak with him immediately. When we put this story together with the fact that Marr did not even need Arnold's permission, we seem to have clear evidence of a deliberate attempt to delay the launching of the Otis fighters.

Scoggins certainly considered the delay unusual. In continuing his reflections on it, he said: "They [the military officials] state in several places that they were waiting on a clearance from the FAA. That is false; we asked them on several occasions why the fighters had not launched. It seemed like an eternity."[105]

In spelling out the "several occasions" on which Boston Center called the military to check on the launch, Scoggins first says that, learning that Joe Cooper had already called NEADS, "I asked Bueno to call Otis again and see if they had got a call from NEADS."[106] He later says that, besides calling NEADS many times, "I called Otis at least 3 or 4 times."[107] When I asked whether these calls to Otis were different from the calls he made on "several occasions" to ask why the fighters had not launched, Scoggins replied: "Yeah, I kept going back and forth [between Otis and NEADS]."[108] Scoggins clearly believed that the military's slowness in launching was far from normal.

The waiting probably "seemed like an eternity" to Scoggins partly because, even after the delays discussed already, it took another full six minutes for the Otis fighters to become airborne.

That this long launch time is indeed peculiar, moreover, can be seen by comparing it with standard practice. Hordon's description given above, according to which everyone concerned is "prepared to launch within a few minutes of the request," is consistent with other reports. In a story about alert pilots at Homestead Air Reserve Base in Florida, for example, we read: "Within minutes, the crew chiefs can launch the pilots. . . . 'If needed, we could be killing things in five minutes or less,' said Capt. Tom 'Pickle' Herring."[109] With regard to Otis Air National Guard Base in particular, a story in the *Cape Cod Times*, four days after 9/11, said: "two pilots are on alert 24 hours a day, and if needed, must be in the air within five minutes."[110]

Five minutes is, in fact, rather slow. A NORAD press release in 2000 explained that a command-and-control breakdown "resulted in alert fighters on 5 minute airborne response time instead of 2–3 minute response time."[111] That 2-to-3 minute time to become airborne is consistent, moreover, with the statement on a US Air Force website prior to 9/11, according to which F-15s routinely go from scramble order to 29,000 feet in 2.5 minutes.[112]

If pilots can be high in the sky so quickly after receiving a scramble order, why did it take the Otis pilots a full six minutes simply to get airborne after they were already in their jets, on the runway, "straining at the reins"? How can we avoid inferring that a stand-down, or at least a slow-down, order was in effect?

In sum, the attempt by Bronner and the 9/11 Commission to blame the failure to intercept Flight 11 on the FAA misfires, partly because its defense of the military's role in the failure contains several falsehoods and partly because its portrayal of FAA incompetence is so extreme as to be incredible. As I indicated, moreover, Hordon does not believe this portrayal, being quite certain instead that FAA controllers did notify the military about AA 11 over 20 minutes before it crashed into the North Tower—which means that there would have been plenty of time for it to be intercepted.

However, even if we ignore this likelihood and even the likelihood that the first notification about the hijacking occurred closer to 8:28 than to 8:34, the Otis fighters still could have reached Manhattan before 8:46:40, when the North Tower was struck. As we saw, when the Otis Air Force Base Tower was notified of the hijacking at 8:34, Lt. Colonel Jon Treacy, the commander of the Otis fighter squadron, called NEADS. If this call was made immediately, as it certainly should have been, NEADS could have given the scramble order at 8:35, and the F-15s could have been airborne by 8:40. If they had then traveled full speed—and we have Duffy's declaration that when they did become airborne they went "full-blower all the way"[113]—they would have been going over 1,800 (nautical) miles per hour, which would mean at least 30 miles per minute. The flight from Cape Cod to Manhattan would have, therefore, required only five minutes (not ten minutes, as Bronner claims[114]). Having reached Manhattan by about 8:45, they would have had over a minute to take action. Shootdown authorization could have been given while they were en route.[115]

The first attack on the World Trade Center could have been prevented, therefore, even if the FAA had responded as slowly as the tapes imply. We have seen, moreover, that there are reasons to be suspicious of the account implied by the tapes.

Do the Tapes Give a True Picture? The tapes, Bronner claims, provide "the authentic military history of 9/11." Bronner himself, however, lets us know that that is at best an exaggeration. He says, for example: "Most of [Marr's] conversations on 9/11 are unrecorded: he [for instance] speaks over a secure phone with his superior, Major General Larry Arnold." We have, therefore, no idea what Arnold and Marr said to each other. And that is simply one example. We also do not know what General Richard Myers and Donald Rumsfeld were saying to each other or to subordinates. We do not know what Cheney was saying to Rumsfeld, Myers, and Bush. The tapes also lack any information about communications to and from the NMCC, and this lack is especially vital, because the NMCC, as we saw, is "the focal point within Department of Defense for providing assistance [in the event of a hijacking]." The tapes also tell us nothing about communications to and from NORAD's two facilities in Colorado: the NORAD operations center at Cheyenne Mountain and NORAD headquarters at Peterson Air Force Base. They also do not tell us about any orders issued by the Secret Service. Even if the tapes are authentic, therefore, they do not give us anything close to "the authentic military history of 9/11."

Moreover, although Bronner says that "the truth . . . is all on tape," Hordon does not believe that the tapes even tell the true story of the communications between the FAA and NEADS. Rather, he believes, the tapes were prepared by officials who "cherry picked transmissions," using only those that could be used to support the new story while leaving out everything that contradicted it.[116]

At the FAA's Boston Center, Hordon says, recordings are made of the communications going to and from many, many positions. And, speaking as a person who had been certified in "breaking out transcripts from audio tape recordings," he says:

> If one reads the transcripts, one can see that only a few of the communications that were surely made on any of those "positions" are presented. . . . I believe that there are other, earlier communications to and from any number of sectors . . . to NORAD/NEADS before the times shown. . . . Any of the . . . "control positions" could have been used to contact NORAD, but this would not necessarily be a "formal" notification. . . . When FAA controllers have emergencies, they reach out to the appropriate military facilities to begin the process of providing appropriate assistance. And in the case of such emergencies as the loss of radio, radar and flight path controls as seen on AA 11 and the others, this means that the radar controller, the hand-off controller, or the assistant radar controller can call out to any of these facilities from those different positions. There are a lot of audio tracks that need to be scoured for conversations.[117]

Hordon later estimated that there are "130–150 positions or locations that have either direct 'hot button,' or the less direct dial-up, capabilities to have called NEADS, all of which have a dedicated channel recorded on the huge tape machines" at Boston Center.[118]

Although we have no access to these tapes to see what may have been left out, Scoggins has provided some possible examples. He says that he "made about forty phone calls to NEADS."[119] Only a few of these calls are mentioned in the tapes provided in connection with Bronner's article, and it seems probable that even the "30-some hours" of tapes provided to Bronner did not include some of Scoggins' calls, such as those referred to in Scoggins' statement that "we asked them [NEADS] on several occasions why the fighters had not launched. It seemed like an eternity." Likewise, the call, to be mentioned below, in which he suggested launching fighters from Andrews, Toledo, and Selfridge (as well as Atlantic City) was also probably not included. (If these tapes *were* included, they were not reflected in the accounts provided by Bronner and the 9/11 Commission.)

Erasing or otherwise eliminating tapes from the public record would be an easy way to produce a distorted history of that day. For example, if the FAA first contacted the military around 8:20, then that conversation, in which Boston Center reported an in-flight emergency (not a hijacking), could have simply been eliminated.

Scoggins, incidentally, while not believing that an earlier call was made, agrees that it *might* have been. In response to my question whether it was possible that, unbeknownst to him, someone had contacted the military before he arrived, he said:

> If someone called from the floor it would have been on the hotlines. Those are recorded, . . . but I have never read the full transcript from Boston Center so someone could have called and the 9/11 Commission may not have thought it important; they didn't publish anywhere near all of the stuff that was out there.[120]

Hordon would differ with Scoggins here only on the question of why, if an earlier call was made, the 9/11 Commission did not mention it.

In any case, besides believing that the "NORAD tapes" used by Bronner are products of cherry picking, including erasure, Hordon also suspects that they were doctored, perhaps especially the times of some of the transmissions. He writes:

> When a controller is focused upon such critical situations, he or she does not look at the times of transmissions, conversations or dialogues—too busy. Therefore, it's the audio tapes that would show the actual times of such communications. [But] they all can be "fixed," especially the time-encoding elements.[121]
>
> [O]ne could "write over" the time channel, adjusting it to any time one would want. Or one could transfer all the audio information on particular channels onto another tape that already has a chosen time reference impregnated upon it.[122]

A possible example of this type of doctoring is provided by the two accounts of the first call to NEADS reporting the hijacking of AA 11. According to the tapes that were provided to the 9/11 Commission in 2004, as we saw, this call came at 8:38. According to two ABC shows in 2002, however, this call came at 8:31. If the ABC stories were closer to the truth, Hordon suggests, adjusting the time of this call would have been a simple matter.

With this warning about the tapes, we will now turn to the tapes-based account of the other flights. As we will see, the portrayal of FAA incompetence becomes even more incredible and the conflict with previously reported fact becomes even stronger, thereby increasing the question of the authenticity of the tapes.

UA Flight 175

We are told by the 9/11 Commission, on the basis of the tapes, that although UA Flight 175 veered off course some minutes after 8:42 and its transponder code was changed at 8:47, the flight controller at Boston Center did not notice these changes until 8:51, after which he tried without success to contact the pilot. At 8:55, the Boston controller told a manager in New York Center that she thought UA 175 had been hijacked. This manager then allegedly tried to contact the regional managers but "was told that they were discussing hijacked aircraft . . . and refused to be disturbed." Between 9:01 and 9:02, a New York Center manager called Herndon, saying: "We have several situations going on here. It's escalating big, big time. We need to get the military involved with us." But Herndon did not call the military. Finally, New York Center called NEADS directly—but this was not until 9:03, "at about the time the plane was hitting the South Tower."[123]

Bronner, reporting on what the tapes say about events at New York Center, indicates that it was not until a little after 8:57, when UA 175 made a sudden swing toward Manhattan, that the controllers realized that it had been hijacked. They then, Bronner says, "start speculating what the hijacker is aiming at." It is, accordingly, "not until the last second, literally, that anyone from New York Center thinks to update NEADS."[124]

These accounts of FAA behavior, besides being intrinsically unbelievable, are also in tension with several prior reports.

Contradictory Reports: In its timeline of September 18, 2001, NORAD said that it had been notified about UA 175 by the FAA at 8:43.[125] Can we believe that NORAD officials would have said this—which would mean that NEADS failed to prevent this flight from crashing into the WTC even though it had 20 minutes to do so—if the truth was that the military had not been notified until 9:03? Would that not have been a very irrational lie? The only other explanation would seem to be that these NORAD officials were confused. But can we believe that they would have been so confused about such a major point only a few days after the event?

Also, countless news stories had reported on the FAA's advance notification of NORAD about UA 175. For example, in an August 2002 story, Associated Press writer Leslie Miller, after saying that the FAA had notified NORAD about the possible hijacking of AA 11 at 8:40, wrote:

"[T]hree minutes after that, NORAD was told United Airlines 175 had been hijacked."[126]

Another example involves Captain Michael Jellinek, a Canadian who on 9/11 was overseeing NORAD's headquarters in Colorado. According to this story, which appeared in the *Toronto Star*, Jellinek was on the phone with NEADS as he watched Flight 175 crash into the South Tower. Afterward, he asked NEADS, "Was that the hijacked aircraft you were dealing with?"—to which NEADS said "Yes."[127] If one accepts the new timeline, according to which NEADS did not know about UA 175 until it crashed, this Jellinek story must be regarded as a fabrication. But what motive would Jellinek or the reporter have had for making it up? The 9/11 Commission avoided this question by not mentioning this story.

According to the aforementioned ABC show *Moments of Crisis*, which aired in 2002, Brigadier General Montague Winfield of the NMCC said: "When the second aircraft flew into the second tower, it was at that point that we realized that the seemingly unrelated hijackings that the FAA was dealing with were in fact a part of a coordinated terrorist attack on the United States."[128] Although Winfield did not say how many hijackings he had known about before the second tower was hit, he clearly indicated that he knew about more than AA 11, which is the only one the tapes-based account says he could have known about.

This account, according to which the military did not know about problems with UA 175 until 9:03, when NEADS received a telephone call from the FAA's New York Center, is also contradicted in a Newhouse News Service story by Hart Seely, which says: "At 8:43AM, [Master Sergeant Maureen] Dooley's technicians [at NEADS], their headsets linked to Boston Center, heard of a second plane, United Flight 175, that also was not responding. It, too, was moving to New York."[129] According to this story, which was published early in 2002, NEADS knew by 8:43 that UA 175 might be in trouble.

That account is in tension with Bronner's story, which is oriented around these same women: Maureen "Mo" Dooley and her two technicians, Stacia Rountree and Shelley Watson. According to the tapes, Bronner reports, Rountree, after fielding a call from New York Center at 9:03, exclaims: "They have a second possible hijack!" The presentation suggests that this was the first time that these NEADS technicians had any idea that UA 175 was in trouble. According to Hart Seely's 2002 story, however, they knew already by 8:43 that it was not responding.

We also have contradictory stories about UA 175 that involve the testimony of air traffic controllers. According to Bronner, controllers first realized that UA 175 had been hijacked shortly after 8:57. However, a 2002 NBC show, in which Tom Brokaw interviewed air traffic controllers, gave a very different account. The New York controller for UA 175, Dave

Bottiglia, said that he knew a few minutes after 8:46 that this plane had been hijacked. Shortly thereafter, Brokaw says:

> 8:52AM: It has been six minutes since American 11 hit the north tower. And NORAD—responsible for the defense of North American airspace—is now alerted to a second hijacking. It scrambles two F-15 fighter jets from Otis air force base in Massachusetts to potentially intercept the United plane. But they are more than 150 miles, and some 20 minutes, away.[130]

Brokaw's final sentence presupposes that these fighters would be going only 450 miles per hour. In any case, later in the program, Bob Varcapade, one of the Newark controllers, says about these two F-15s: "If they only could've gotten there a couple minutes earlier. They just missed it."[131] Although this controller portrayed the fighters as much closer than did Brokaw, who repeated the then-official story, they agreed that they were sent to intercept UA 175.

In 2006, MSNBC provided an "updated" version of this program, "America Remembers," in which Brokaw's statement is significantly different. In the new version, Brokaw says:

> 8:53AM: It has been just over six minutes since American 11 hit the north tower. By now, NORAD—responsible for the defense of North American airspace—has scrambled two F-15 fighter jets from Otis air force base in Massachusetts. They streak toward New York—but already they are too late.[132]

In this new version, NORAD is not told about "a second hijacking." The fighters from Otis are no longer scrambled in order to "intercept the United plane." And they are "already . . . too late"—because they, according to the new story, were scrambled to intercept AA 11, not UA 175 (because they had not been notified about the latter flight). However, the original version, which contradicts this new story, can still be viewed. These controllers can, therefore, be seen and heard reporting things that they did and experienced that, according to the new story based on the NORAD tapes, could not have happened.

The new tapes-based story is also contradicted by the previously discussed memo, "FAA Communications with NORAD on September 11, 2001," which was sent to the 9/11 Commission in 2003 by Laura Brown. This memo, to recall, stated:

> Within minutes after the first aircraft hit the World Trade Center, the FAA immediately established several phone bridges that included FAA field facilities, the FAA Command Center, FAA headquarters, DOD [meaning the NMCC in the Department of Defense], the Secret Service. . . . The US Air Force liaison to the FAA immediately joined the FAA headquarters phone bridge and established contact with NORAD. . . .

The FAA shared real-time information on the phone bridges about the unfolding events, including information about loss of communication with aircraft, loss of transponder signals, unauthorized changes in course, and other actions being taken by all the flights of interest.[133]

This memo implies that even if no one from Boston or New York had called the military, both NORAD and the NMCC would have known about UA 175's troubles shortly after 8:47 (given the evidence that the FAA knew about these troubles by 8:40).

The fact that the military was involved in this teleconference was, moreover, confirmed by General Craig McKinley when he testified, along with Scott and Arnold, at the 9/11 Commission hearing on May 23, 2003. Commissioner Richard Ben-Veniste, asking if NORAD "did not have an open line with the FAA at that time," alluded to the information in the memo, saying: "[W]e are advised that there was . . . essentially an ongoing conference where under, in real time, FAA was providing information as it received it, immediately after the first crash into the Towers." McKinley replied: "It is my understanding from talking with both FAA and our supervisors at the Northeast Air Defense Sector [NEADS] in Rome, that those lines were open and that they were discussing these issues."[134] The Pentagon cannot now credibly claim, therefore, that although the FAA knew about the hijacking of UA 175, the military did not.

Still another source of information would have been the NMCC's conference call. Even if we accept Laura Brown's revised statement, according to which it began at about 8:45 (rather than 8:20 or 8:25), the NMCC would have learned through this teleconference about the hijacking of UA 175 almost 20 minutes before it hit the South Tower.

In sum, the claim about UA 175 made by Bronner and the 9/11 Commission—that the military did not know about this flight's troubles until 9:03, when it had already crashed—is strongly contradicted by evidence from many sources. "The truth," Bronner says, "is all on tape." To the contrary, a lot of the truth seems to be have been left off the tapes, at least those that have been made available.

Where Were the Otis Fighters? However, even if this claim of ignorance could be sustained, a most serious question would still remain: Why were the Otis fighters not stationed over Manhattan before 9:03, thereby being in position to prevent the South Tower from being struck?

Those who defend the official story, according to which there was no stand-down order, face one of their most difficult problems here. The F-15s, according to all accounts, were airborne by 8:53. As we have seen, they were, according to pilot Timothy Duffy, going "full-blower all the way," which would mean they could have been over Manhattan by 8:58. A CAP (combat air patrol) could have been established over Manhattan five minutes before UA 175 arrived. (By then, moreover, there could have been no excuse for a failure to have given shootdown authorization.) Why did this not happen?

The 9/11 Commission's story becomes extremely vague here. The Commission simply says:

> Lacking a target, [the Otis fighters] were vectored toward military-controlled airspace off the Long Island coast. To avoid New York area air traffic and uncertain about what to do, the fighters were brought down to military airspace to "hold as needed." From 9:09 to 9:13, the Otis fighters stayed in this holding pattern.[135]

This would be a good candidate for the lamest, most problematic paragraph in *The 9/11 Commission Report* (which would be saying a lot). Although each sentence is problematic, the most problematic is the final one, in which the Commission tells us only what the fighters do from 9:09 on.

The military airspace off Long Island, we are told, is 115 miles from Manhattan,[136] which means that it is only about 40 miles from Cape Cod. If the fighters were airborne by 8:53 and were going at full speed, they would have been there by 8:55. What were they doing from 8:55 until 9:09? The official story, as told by the 9/11 Commission, simply leaves out 13 minutes in the existence of the Otis fighters! This enormous hole in the official story provides strong evidence that it is false.

Bronner's account, which provides more detail, conveys the impression that the officers at NEADS were very concerned to protect the city. Having said that NEADS learned, just as the fighters were becoming airborne, that AA 11 had hit the World Trade Center, Bronner writes: "Someone asks Nasypany what to do with the fighters. . . . Pumped with adrenaline, Nasypany doesn't miss a beat. 'Send 'em to New York City still. Continue! Go!'" Bronner then adds that Nasypany later told him: "I'm not gonna stop what I initially started with scrambling Otis—getting Otis over New York City. . . . If this is a false report, I still have my fighters where I want them to be."[137]

But that, of course, is exactly what did *not* happen. Why?

The next thing we learn is that at almost 9:04, Nasypany says to Marr: "Sir, we got—we've got unconfirmed second hit from another aircraft. . . . Fighters are south of—just south of Long Island, sir."[138] Bronner then explains: "The two F-15s, scrambled from Otis, are now approaching the city."

He does not explain, however, why they are still south of Long Island, rather than already over the city. He does not explain, in other words, how they managed to travel only 40 miles in the eleven minutes between 8:53 and 9:04—which would mean that these F-15s, which are capable of traveling 1,800 miles an hour and hence 20 miles a minute, had covered less than four miles a minute (which would mean they were going under 240 miles per hour).

According to Bronner, however, they were not dawdling. He says that they were "streaking toward Manhattan." He also quotes Major Nash as saying that they were "flying supersonic toward New York and the controller came on and said, 'A second airplane has hit the World Trade Center.'" But if they had left Otis at 8:53 and were "streaking," they would have been over the city before the South Tower was struck, not 100-some miles away. Bronner then gives this explanation of why:

> With both towers now in flames, Nasypany wants the fighters over Manhattan immediately, but the weapons techs get "pushback" from civilian F.A.A. controllers, who have final authority over the fighters as long as they are in civilian airspace.
>   The F.A.A. controllers are afraid of fast-moving fighters colliding with a passenger plane, of which there are hundreds in the area, still flying normal routes.[139]

This is Bronner's explanation for why "[t]he fighters are initially directed to a holding area just off the coast, near Long Island."

This explanation continues the effort to put all of the blame for the success of the second attack on New York on the FAA. Bronner, like the 9/11 Commission before him, quoted a statement by Nasypany in which he says that NEADS needed to convince the FAA to let the military put fighters over Manhattan. In Bronner's material, Nasypany even says that he wants to "make sure this is on tape."[140]

This explanation only works, however, on the assumption that the military did not know that UA 175 was hijacked and headed toward the city. Given the evidence that the military did know this, we can see that the issue of establishing a CAP at that time, before all the known emergencies were taken care of, is a distraction. NEADS should have had the Otis fighters intercept the flight and, if necessary, shoot it down.

Bronner and the 9/11 Commission, to be sure, claim that no shootdown could have occurred because that order could only have come from the president, who was occupied in a classroom in Florida.[141] As I have shown elsewhere, however, authorization from the president is not needed. Even approval from the office of the secretary of defense is not necessary. As the Pentagon document says: "The DoD Components that receive verbal requests from civil authorities for support in an exigent emergency may . . . , if required, immediately respond."[142]

Hordon says, moreover, that this stipulation extends to the pilots. Having made the distinction between emergency and hijack protocol, he says:

> However, make no mistake about this, should the "hijacked aircraft" appear to threaten major populations, or seem to be headed for important military or civilian targets, then the pilots can shoot them down on their own. Shootdown orders are authorized for the pilots to

use under certain conditions, some of them pre-approved by higher ups, and some of them at a moment's notice. . . . If an Otis fighter . . . pilot saw the Boeing descend and head straight for NYC, he would already be considering shooting the aircraft down miles and miles away from NYC. And this is regardless of it being an airliner full of passengers. If the pilot came to the conclusion that AA 11 was going to crash into NYC, or its nuclear plant, I will guarantee that AA11 would have been shot down prior to hitting any buildings.[143]

If this was true of AA 11, it would have been all the more true of UA 175, after the North Tower had already been struck. The South Tower clearly could have been saved.

What, in any case, happened to the Otis fighters? *The 9/11 Commission Report* simply says that at 9:13, they "exited their holding pattern and set a course direct to Manhattan."[144] Why? In the endnotes, we read: "At 9:12:54, the Otis fighters told their Boston Center controller that they needed to establish a combat air patrol over New York, and they immediately headed for New York City."[145] The pilots *told* the controller. At this time, clearly, the planes are following the orders of military, not civilian, controllers. What were the pilots being told by their superiors at NEADS? We do not know. "Because of a technical issue," the 9/11 Commission tells us, "there are no NEADS recordings available of the NEADS senior weapons director and weapons director technician position responsible for controlling the Otis scramble."[146] And yet, Bronner assures us, the tapes give us the "authentic military history of 9/11."

Moreover, even though Nasypany had been presented as extremely concerned to get these fighters over the city, we read that after exiting at 9:13, they arrived in Manhattan at 9:25.[147] No question is raised about why it took these these supersonic fighters twelve minutes to make this 115-mile trip—which would be quite an urgent question if a third airliner had struck Manhattan at, say, 9:20.

In any case, the 9/11 Commission's account of UA 175 shows, perhaps even more clearly than its tapes-based account of AA 11, that the tapes do not give the true story of why the attacks succeeded.

How Many Fighter Jets Were Available? There is, moreover, still another element in Bronner's account that suggests that protecting the nation's cities was far from NEADS' chief concern that day. Bronner says that although Nasypany, after the second tower was hit, wanted to bring up the two alert fighters from Langley Air Force Base "to establish a greater presence over New York," Colonel Marr refused. The reason, Marr later said, was that he would have had all his fighters "in the air at the same time, which means they'd all run out of gas at the same time." By way of explanation, Bronner wrote:

Incredibly, Marr has only four armed fighters at his disposal to defend about a quarter of the continental United States. Massive cutbacks at the close of the Cold War reduced NORAD's arsenal of fighters from some 60 battle-ready jets to just 14 across the entire country. . . . Only four of NORAD's planes belong to NEADS and are thus anywhere close to Manhattan—the two from Otis, now circling above the ocean off Long Island, and the two in Virginia at Langley.[148]

Bronner is here repeating one of the deceptive equations of the official story. The claim that there were only two bases in NORAD's Northeast Sector designated as "alert" bases, which is true, is equated with the claim that these were the only two bases from which NEADS could have drawn ready fighters, which is false.

I have, for example, argued that Andrews Air Force Base, which is next to Washington DC, surely had fighters that could have been employed. In this connection, I have repeated a conversation that Kyle Hence, co-founder of 9/11 CitizensWatch, reported having had with Donald Arias, the chief of public affairs for NORAD's Continental Region. After Hence asked Arias if any alert fighters had been available at Andrews, Arias replied that Andrews was not part of NORAD. When Hence then asked if "there were assets at Andrews that, though not technically part of NORAD, could have been tasked," Arias hung up.[149]

The validity of this distinction has now been confirmed by Colin Scoggins. Saying that there could have been more fighters in the air, he wrote:

> I requested that we take from Atlantic City very early in the AM, not launch from the ground but those already airborne in Warning Area 107 if they were there, which I believe they were. . . . I requested that NEADS launch fighters from Andrews Air Force Base, the DC Guard. They don't have an intercept mission, but they fly every morning as well. I requested that they launch fighters out of Toledo, or Selfridge. I knew none of these had an interceptor mission but that we needed to get planes up in the air. I didn't ask them to launch from Burlington or Syracuse right away because they were away from where the planes were going.[150]

When I asked Scoggins to clarify his statement about Atlantic City, he replied:

> Atlantic City is ANG [Air National Guard] Base. But there are F-16s there, and they schedule every day [in a Warning Area]. Their first mission every day is usually between 8:30AM and 9:00AM. . . . They don't have an intercept mission; it was taken away a long time ago. [But] NEADS could have called them and asked them to cancel their mission and divert.

With regard to Andrews, Toledo, Selfridge, Burlington, and Syracuse, Scoggins replied: "All the same as the above. . . . NEADS' authority doesn't necessarily extend to them, but under the circumstances, they could have grabbed all those aircraft."[151]

Accordingly, rather than having only 4 fighters at his disposal, Marr had at least 16. The 9/11 Commission claimed that calling on them would not have helped, because these "[o]ther facilities, not on 'alert,' would need time to arm the fighters and organize crews."[152] Scoggins, however, says otherwise, and so did a story in *Aviation Week and Space Technology*, which reported that after the second tower was hit: "Calls from fighter units also started pouring into NORAD and sector operations centers, asking, 'What can we do to help?' At Syracuse, N.Y., an ANG commander told Marr, 'Give me 10 minutes and I can give you hot guns.'"[153]

The idea that such a quick response was possible is supported by a story at the time reporting that Hancock Field Air National Guard Base, just outside Syracuse, had F-16s that were "ready to fly in any weather, at a moment's notice."[154]

It would appear, therefore, that Marr could have put four fighters over New York City and some more over the next most likely target, Washington, DC, and still have several in reserve. Why did he not do this?

Hordon, in fact, says that the military should have done even more. Brigadier General Winfield, as we saw, said that when the second tower was struck, he and others in the National Military Command Center realized that there was "a coordinated terrorist attack on the United States."[155] Why, Hordon asks, did they not then declare a "national defense emergency," which would mean reallocating all military resources and establishing a CAP (combat air patrol) over every major city? After all, if it was a surprise attack, they would have had no idea how many cities had been targeted. At one time, in fact, they apparently had reports of eleven hijackings. Why did the military leaders not respond as if the country really was under attack? The very fact that they did not speaks volumes.

AA Flight 77

One of the primary targets of the Commission's tapes-based account, as we have seen, was the military's earlier assertion that it was notified by the FAA at 9:24—not 9:34, as the tapes have it—that AA 77 had possibly been hijacked and appeared to be heading back toward Washington. The Commission, labeling this assertion "incorrect," also called it "unfortunate," because it "made it appear that the military was notified in time to respond."[156] Refuting that notification time, the Commission thereby indicated, was essential to protecting the military from the charge that it had, either through complicity or incompetence, failed to prevent the attack on the Pentagon. The real problem, the Commission claims on the basis of the tapes, was "the FAA's [in]ability to provide the military with timely and accurate information that morning."[157] It was, in other words, entirely the FAA's fault, not at all the military's.

According to the Commission's tapes-based account, the FAA controller in Indianapolis, after seeing Flight 77 go off course at 8:54, lost its transponder signal and even its radar track. However, not knowing about the other hijackings (even though AA 11 had hit the WTC eight minutes earlier), the Indianapolis Center assumed that AA 77 "had experienced serious electrical or mechanical failure," after which it had crashed.[158]

Later, after hearing about the other hijackings and coming to suspect that AA 77 may have also been hijacked, Indianapolis shared this suspicion with Herndon, which at 9:25 shared it with FAA headquarters. But no one called the military, so "NEADS never received notice that American 77 was hijacked."[159] NEADS finally did hear about this flight at 9:34, but even then it learned only that this flight was lost, not that it had been hijacked, and it learned this only by chance, during a NEADS-initiated conversation with the FAA's Washington Center about AA 11.[160]

This story strains credulity and then some. Can anyone really believe that the officials at Indianapolis could have been so utterly stupid and that those at Herndon and FAA headquarters, after knowing that two hijacked airplanes had already crashed into the WTC, would not have told the military that AA 77 might also have been hijacked?

This story, moreover, is challenged by earlier reports. For one thing, contrary to the claim that the Indianapolis Center did not know of previous hijackings, Boston flight controllers, according to stories in the *Guardian* and the *Village Voice* that appeared shortly after 9/11, had at 8:25 notified other regional centers—one of which was Indianapolis—of the hijacking of Flight 11.[161] That this notification was common knowledge was confirmed by the aforementioned NBC program narrated by Tom Brokaw, which said that at 8:30AM, "Boston Center supervisors notify the FAA and other air traffic centers about the hijacking of American Flight 11."[162]

These stories also fit with what Robin Hordon, speaking as a former air traffic controller, says would have happened:

> The system would be notified about a hijacked aircraft . . . . [The notification about AA 11] would be sent out around 8:27–28AM and without doubt the entire air traffic control facility network would be reading and relaying it no later than 8:30AM. This would be the hottest news in a decade. It would fly around the ATC community.[163]

The same view has been expressed, moreover, by General Mike Canavan, former associate administrator for civil aviation security at the FAA. "[A]s soon as you know you had a hijacked aircraft, you notify everyone," he says. "[The notification] gets broadcast out to all the regions."[164]

Accordingly, when the flight controller at Indianapolis saw AA 77 go off course and then lose its transponder signal, he would have immediately suspected that this flight had also been hijacked. In light of this information, the Commission's claim—that he did not notify the military because he assumed that the plane had crashed due to electrical or mechanical failure—is ludicrous.

Also, contrary to the claim that Indianapolis first noticed AA 77's deviation from its flight path at 8:54, NORAD's earlier statement and many news reports said that it went significantly off course for four minutes at 8:46, after which radio contact was lost.[165] It was at that time, therefore, that the Indianapolis flight controller would have become suspicious.

The Commission's tapes-based story is also challenged by the existence of many published reports indicating that officials knew about Flight 77's hijacking some time before the Pentagon was struck. In the FBI section of the Arlington County "After-Action Report" on the Pentagon attack, for example, we read: "At about 9:20AM, the [FBI's] WFO [Washington Field Office] Command Center was notified that American Airlines Flight #77 had been hijacked shortly after takeoff from Washington Dulles International Airport."[166] The 9/11 Commission simply treated all such reports as if they had never been written.

The Commission's new story is challenged, finally, by evidence that the FAA had talked to the military about AA 77 even earlier than 9:24, which was the notification time given on NORAD's September 18 timeline. FAA official Laura Brown's aforementioned memo, after stating that a teleconference was established with the military "within minutes after the first aircraft hit the World Trade Center" (and hence by about 8:50), said that the FAA shared "real-time information" with the military about "all the flights of interest, including Flight 77." Bringing out the full implication of this assertion, she added:

> NORAD logs indicate that the FAA made formal notification about American Flight 77 at 9:24AM, but information about the flight was conveyed continuously during the phone bridges before the formal notification.[167]

In a telephone conversation I had with Laura Brown in 2004, she emphasized this distinction, saying that the formal notification was primarily a formality and hence irrelevant to the question of when the military knew about Flight 77.[168]

Brown's main point, in other words, was that the FAA and the military had been talking about AA 77 long before 9:24. The implication of her memo, therefore, is that although, as Bronner and the 9/11 Commission say, the 9:24 notification time was false, it was false by being too late, not too early.

Brown's account is supported, moreover, by other reports. A *New York Times* story appearing four days after 9/11 began:

During the hour or so that American Airlines Flight 77 was under the control of hijackers, up to the moment it struck the west side of the Pentagon, military officials in a command center on the east side of the building were urgently talking to law enforcement and air traffic control officials about what to do.[169]

Laura Brown's 2003 memo, therefore, reflects information that was available immediately after 9/11.

What did the 9/11 Commission do about Brown's memo? It did discuss it. Richard Ben-Veniste, after reading it into the record, even said: "So now we have in question whether there was an informal real-time communication of the situation, including Flight 77's situation, to personnel at NORAD." He then drove the point home, saying:

> So if the military were apprised, as FAA is now telling us, in real time of what FAA is seeing on its radars, and now focusing specifically on Flight 77, that would mean that someone at NORAD was advised of the deviation from course, which is substantially earlier than the formal notification of hijacking.[170]

The Commission knew, therefore, that this was the FAA's position, and it offered no rebuttal. When *The 9/11 Commission Report* appeared, however, it contained no mention of this memo or its information. The Commission implicitly even claimed in effect that the memo's account could not be true by claiming that the FAA-initiated conference did not begin until 9:20[171]—even though Laura Brown's memo, which was read into the Commission's records, said that it had begun about 8:50. (Her view, incidentally, was independently supported by another high FAA official.[172]) As usual, inconvenient facts were simply eliminated.

If we, however, refuse to ignore all these facts, we have very strong reasons to consider the Commission's tapes-based account of AA 77 false—which would imply that the tapes give an *inauthentic* "military history of 9/11." An examination of the Commission's account of UA 93 will provide additional support for this conclusion.

UA Flight 93

Michael Bronner, who was an associate producer for the film *United 93*, which essentially follows the 9/11 Commission's tapes-based account, focuses heavily on the military's earlier statements about this flight that—assuming the tapes to be accurate—must be false.

When Did the Military Learn? According to one of these earlier statements that are contradicted by the tapes, the military, having learned about the hijacking of UA 93 at 9:16, was tracking it before it crashed. On the basis of the tapes, the 9/11 Commission argues that the military, far from learning about the hijacking of UA 93 at 9:16, did not learn about it until 10:03, when this flight crashed.

This claim involves yet another tale of amazing incompetence by FAA officials. At 9:28, the Commission says, the traffic controller in Cleveland heard "sounds of possible screaming" and noticed that Flight 93 had descended 700 feet, but he did nothing. At 9:32, he heard a voice saying, "We have a bomb on board." On this basis, not being completely brain dead, he finally notified his supervisor, who in turn notified FAA headquarters. But four minutes later, at 9:36, when Cleveland asked Herndon whether the military had been called, Herndon "told Cleveland that FAA personnel well above them in the chain of command had to make the decision to seek military assistance and were working on the issue."[173]

To accept this account, we must believe that the decision to call the military is a momentous, extraordinary one, not a routine one, made regularly. We must also believe that, on a day on which hijacked airliners had already caused much death and destruction, officials at FAA headquarters had to debate whether a hijacked airliner with a bomb on board was important enough to disturb the military. We must believe, moreover, that they were still debating this 13 minutes later at 9:49, when the following conversation between Herndon and FAA headquarters occurred:

> *Command Center:* Uh, do we want to think, uh, about scrambling aircraft?
>
> *FAA Headquarters:* Oh, God, I don't know.
>
> *Command Center:* Uh, that's a decision somebody's gonna have to make probably in the next ten minutes.

The decision, moreover, was obviously that the military should not be disturbed, because another 14 minutes later, at 10:03, when Flight 93 crashed in Pennsylvania, "no one from FAA headquarters [had yet] requested military assistance regarding United 93."[174] To believe the Commission's tapes-based report, in other words, we must believe that FAA officials acted like complete idiots.

Besides the fact that the Commission's new story about UA 93 is intrinsically implausible in the extreme, it is challenged by several inconvenient facts.

One such fact is the emphatic testimony of General Arnold, before the 9/11 Commission in May 2003, that NORAD knew about UA 93's troubles quite early. Having been asked whether 9:24 was the first time NORAD had been informed about AA 77, Arnold replied: "Our focus— you have got to remember that there's a lot of other things going on simultaneously here—was on United 93, which was being pointed out to us very aggressively I might say by the FAA."[175] He later said, "very shortly [after the second tower was struck] we got a call . . . on the United 93 flight being a possible hijacking." (In saying that the FAA was talking to the military "aggressively," he made clear that the FAA was doing its job.)

Another inconvenient fact is the existence of the FAA-initiated teleconference mentioned in Laura Brown's memo. The Commission, as we saw, claims that this teleconference did not start until 9:20 (instead of about 8:50, as her memo indicated), but this claim, even if accepted, would not help the Commission's case with regard to UA 93: It did not crash until 10:03AM, so the time between 9:30 and 10:00 was the crucial period, and Brown's memo said, as we saw, that "[t]he FAA shared real-time information . . . about . . . all the flights of interest." The Commission itself agreed, moreover, that by 9:34, FAA headquarters knew about the hijacking of Flight 93, so it was a "flight of interest." Accordingly, the Commission's tapes-based claim—that the military was not told about the hijacking of UA 93 until it crashed—is flatly contradicted by Laura Brown's memo, which, although it was ignored in the Commission's final report, had been read into its record by Richard Ben-Veniste.

Another inconvenient fact was a videoconference being run from the White House that morning by Richard Clarke, who described this videoconference in his best-selling book, *Against All Enemies*—which came out in 2004 while the hearings were still going on. The FAA was represented in this videoconference by its head, Jane Garvey. And although the Commissioners claimed, absurdly, that they did "not know who from Defense participated,"[176] Clarke had clearly stated that the Pentagon was represented by Secretary of Defense Donald Rumsfeld and General Richard Myers, who on 9/11 had been Acting Chair of the Joint Chiefs of Staff. Clarke had also said that at about 9:35, Garvey reported on a number of "potential hijacks," which included "United 93 over Pennsylvania."[177] Therefore, more than 25 minutes before Flight 93 crashed, according to Clarke, both Myers and Rumsfeld heard from the head of the FAA that Flight 93 was considered a potential hijack.

Still another inconvenient fact is the existence of military liaisons to the FAA, through whom the military, if by no other means, would have known about FAA communications. The existence of such liaisons, besides being mentioned in Laura Brown's memo, was mentioned at a 9/11 Commission hearing in 2004 by Ben Sliney, who, to recall, was the operations manager at the FAA's Command Center in Herndon. Given the 9/11 Commission's later claim that information from the FAA went to Herndon but then was not passed on to the military, his testimony is most interesting. He said:

> Available to us at the Command Center of course is the military cell, which was our liaison with the military services. They were present at all of the events that occurred on 9/11. . . . If you tell the military you've told the military. They have their own communication web. . . . [I]n my mind

everyone who needed to be notified about the events transpiring was notified, including the military.[178]

The point was made again by Monte Belger, the FAA's acting deputy administrator. After Commissioner Bob Kerrey, on the basis of the tapes, said to Belger, in relation to UA 93: "[A] plane was headed to Washington D.C. FAA Headquarters knew it and didn't let the military know," Belger replied:

> I truly do not mean this to be defensive, but it is a fact—there were military people on duty at the FAA Command Center, as Mr. Sliney said. They were participating in what was going on. There were military people in the FAA's Air Traffic Organization in a situation room. They were participating in what was going on.[179]

This testimony by itself destroys the 9/11 Commission's narrative about 9/11, so it is no surprise to learn that these comments were excluded from *The 9/11 Commission Report*.

With regard to UA 93 in particular, this testimony means that if FAA headquarters learned that UA 93 had a bomb on board at 9:32, as the tapes indicate, then the military would have learned about it at that time (if it did not already know). The Commission, while portraying the FAA personnel as incompetent fools who debated endlessly whether "to seek military assistance," ignored the fact, pointed out by Brown, Sliney, and Belger, that military personnel already knew about Flight 93.

Another inconvenient fact is that Secret Service personnel would also have been aware of these FAA communications about UA 93 (and other flights). Laura Brown's memo mentioned that the Secret Service was part of the teleconference established by the FAA. Richard Clarke, reporting that the Secret Service's director told him shortly after 9:30 that radar showed the existence of an aircraft headed toward Washington, explained: "Secret Service had a system that allowed them to see what FAA's radar was seeing."[180] This fact was also revealed inadvertently by Vice President Cheney, who during a television interview five days after 9/11 said, "The Secret Service has an arrangement with the FAA. They had open lines after the World Trade Center was . . ." —at which point Cheney stopped himself before finishing the sentence. In 2006, moreover, Barbara Riggs, who had just retired as deputy director of the Secret Service, said: "Through monitoring radar and activating an open line with the FAA, the Secret Service was able to receive real time information about . . . hijacked aircraft. We were tracking two hijacked aircraft as they approached Washington, D.C."[181]

In the face of such facts, the claim that no one except the FAA knew about the errant airliners is absurd.

With regard to the FBI, moreover, we need not say merely that it must have known about Flight 93's condition. We have information, from mainstream sources, that it actually did know. According to *New York Times* reporter Jere Longman's well-known book about this flight, Deena Burnett, the wife of passenger Tom Burnett, received a call, which she believed to be from him (see the discussion of phone calls from the flight, below). She was told that United Flight 93 had been hijacked and was asked to call the authorities, and by 9:34 she was talking to the FBI.[182] In the NBC show with Tom Brokaw, moreover, flight controller Greg Callahan reported that an FBI agent said he suspected "that this aircraft has now been taken over by hostile forces."[183] We are surely not expected to believe that the FBI, knowing at 9:34 that Flight 93 had been hijacked, would not have informed the military. If it did not, then, as Rowland Morgan says, "the FBI [would need] to explain why it did not alert the US Air Force."[184] But if it did, then why is the US military now agreeing to the 9/11 Commission's contrary claim? Either way, there is a lie at the heart of the official story about Flight 93.

Finally, we have it from Brigadier General Winfield, deputy director for operations at the Pentagon's NMCC, that the military was indeed informed. During the ABC program containing interviews by Peter Jennings, Winfield said: "We received the report from the FAA that Flight 93 had turned off its transponder . . . and was now heading toward Washington, DC."[185]

The combined force of these inconvenient facts disproves—the word is not too strong—the Commission's main claim about UA 93—that "[b]y the time the military learned about the flight, it had crashed."[186] The proof that the tapes-based story is false becomes even stronger when we look at the next disputed question about this flight.

Was the Military Ready to Shoot It Down? Whereas the main problem for the Commission with regard to the first three flights was to explain why the military did not intercept and perhaps shoot them down, its main concern in relation to UA 93 was to refute the claim that the military *had* shot it down. There was, in fact, considerable evidence to support this claim.

Part of this evidence consisted of a rumor to this effect within the military. Major Daniel Nash, one of the F–15 pilots sent to New York City that morning, reported that when he returned to base he was told that a military F-16 had shot down an airliner in Pennsylvania.[187] Susan Mcelwain, a local witness to the crash of UA 93 in Pennsylvania, said that shortly thereafter she received a call from a friend who said that her husband, who was in the Air Force, had called her and said: "I can't talk, but we've just shot a plane down."[188] During General Myers' interview with the Senate Armed Services Committee on September 13, chairman Carl Levin asked him about "statements that the aircraft that crashed in Pennsylvania was shot down."[189]

This rumor was, moreover, seemingly confirmed by reports from people who lived near the spot where the airliner came down—reports of sightings of a small military airplane, of missile-like noises, of debris falling from the airliner miles from its crash site, and of part of one of the engines far from that site.[190]

The Commission, in seeking to refute the claim that UA 93 had been shot down, did not do so by disputing any of this evidence, which it simply ignored. It instead simply constructed a new timeline, based in part on the tapes, which entails that the military could not possibly have shot down UA 93.

This new timeline involves four claims: (1) Cheney, who was known to have issued the shootdown authorization, did not get down to the Presidential Emergency Operations Center until almost 10:00. (2) Since NEADS did not learn that UA 93 had been hijacked until 10:07, it could not have been tracking it.[191] (3) Cheney was not notified about UA 93's hijacking until 10:02[192]—"only," Bronner emphasizes, "one minute before the airliner impacted the ground." (4) Cheney did not give the shootdown authorization until "some time between 10:10 and 10:15."[193]

As we saw in the first section, the first claim is clearly false. Cheney had entered the PEOC before 9:20, when Norman Mineta got there.

The second claim—that NEADS could not have been tracking UA 93—is challenged not only by the evidence, examined above, that the military knew about the hijacking long before it crashed, but also by evidence that UA 93 was, in fact, being tailed by US military fighters. One flight controller, ignoring a general order to controllers not to talk to the media, reportedly said that "an F-16 fighter closely pursued Flight 93."[194] On September 13, General Richard Myers said that fighters were scrambled "on the [airliner] that eventually crashed in Pennsylvania. . . [W]e had gotten somebody close to it."[195] Two days later, Deputy Secretary of Defense Paul Wolfowitz said that "the Air Force was tracking the hijacked plane that crashed in Pennsylvania . . . and had been in a position to bring it down if necessary."[196] Moreover, one of the Air Force pilots who was in the air that morning, Lt. Anthony Kuczynski, has reported that while he was flying an E-3 Sentry (a modified Boeing 707) toward Pittsburgh alongside two F-16s, he was "given direct orders to shoot down an airliner" and would have done so if UA 93 had not crashed before they could intercept it.[197] Kuczynski's testimony agrees, furthermore, with that of Major General Mike J. Haugen of the North Dakota National Guard, who said that the Secret Service had told the North Dakota-based F-16s to "protect the White House at all costs" and that only the crash of Flight 93 "kept us from having to do the unthinkable."[198]

If we believe the Commission's tapes-based account, we must regard all these testimonies as false. But if we cannot do that, we must regard the tapes-based account as false.

The third and fourth claims—that Cheney did not learn of UA 93's hijacking until 10:02 and did not give the shootdown authorization until after 10:10—are challenged by many contrary reports. For example, on the aforementioned ABC television program that aired on the first anniversary of 9/11, Norman Mineta, Karl Rove, and White House photographer David Bohrer all stated on camera that Cheney was deciding what to do about Flight 93, which was known to be heading toward Washington. Bohrer said: "There was a, a PEOC staffer who would keep coming in with updates on Flight 93's progress toward DC." The program then had statements from Cheney, Rice, Andrew Card, and others indicating that the decision to have the plane shot down was made and passed on to the military.[199] The story told by all these people had to be a lie, or a collective delusion, if we accept the truth of Bronner's tape-based account, according to which Cheney had heard nothing about Flight 93 until 10:02.

With regard to the time the shootdown authorization was passed on, the 9/11 Commission claims that Richard Clarke did not receive it from Cheney until 10:25. However, Clarke himself said that he received it 30 to 40 minutes earlier, between 9:45 (when the White House was evacuated) and 9:55 (when Air Force One in Florida took off with the president aboard).[200]

The account given by Clarke and the ABC program was also presented by a CNN program, also aired one year after 9/11, which was based on interviews with Cheney and Josh Bolton, then deputy White House chief of staff. It contained the following account:

> After the planes struck the twin towers, a third took a chunk out of the Pentagon. Cheney then heard a report that a plane over Pennsylvania was heading for Washington. A military assistant asked Cheney twice for authority to shoot it down.
>
> "The vice president said yes again," remembered Josh Bolton, deputy White House chief of staff. "And the aide then asked a third time. He said, 'Just confirming, sir, authority to engage?' And the vice president—his voice got a little annoyed then—said, 'I said yes.'" ... "I think there was an undertone of anger there. But it's more a matter of determination. You don't want to let your anger overwhelm your judgment in a moment like this," Cheney said.[201]

Brigadier General Montague Winfield, during the ABC show with Peter Jennings, confirmed the Clarke–Cheney–Bolton account while adding that the military had actually received shootdown authorization. Winfield reported that he and others in the NMCC had heard from the FAA that the plane was headed toward Washington, then said:

The decision was made to try to go intercept Flight 93. . . . The Vice President [said] that the President had given us permission to shoot down innocent civilian aircraft that threatened Washington, DC. We started receiving reports from the fighters that were heading to . . . intercept. The FAA kept us informed with their time estimates as the aircraft got closer and closer. . . . At some point, the closure time came and went, and nothing had happened, so you can imagine everything was very tense in the NMCC. . . . It was about, you know, 10:03 that the fighters reported that Flight 93 had crashed.[202]

Immediately afterward, Cheney, who was also being interviewed, said: "Eventually of course, we never fired on any aircraft." Even if that point were granted, however, Winfield stated, contrary to the tapes-based account, that the military, being informed by the FAA, had fighter jets closing in on UA 93 with permission to shoot it down. (We have here a prime illustration of the absurdity of the idea that the "authentic military history of 9/11" could be written without having records of the communications to and from the NMCC.)

That the shootdown authorization was actually transmitted to pilots was stated during the same interview by Colonel Marr. After receiving the order, he reports, he "passed that on to the pilots. United Airlines Flight 93 will not be allowed to reach Washington, DC."[203]

Both Marr and Larry Arnold, moreover, gave more complete accounts in the US Air Force book about 9/11, *Air War over America*. Arnold, reporting that they were tracking UA 93 even before it turned around— meaning before 9:36—states: "we watched the 93 track as it meandered around the Ohio–Pennsylvania area and started to turn south toward D.C."[204] Marr, reporting that the shootdown authorization was received that early, said: "we received the clearance to kill if need be. In fact, Major General Arnold's words almost verbatim were: 'We will take lives in the air to save lives on the ground.'"[205] Leslie Filson, the author of this Air Force account, concludes her discussion with these words:

> The North Dakota F-16s were loaded with missiles and hot guns and Marr was thinking about what these pilots might be expected to do. "United Airlines Flight 93 would not have hit Washington, D.C.," Marr says emphatically. "He would have been engaged and shot down before he got there." Arnold concurs: "I had every intention of shooting down United 93 if it continued to progress toward Washington, D.C."[206]

According to the Air Force's official account in 2003, then, the military knew before 9:36 that UA 93 was in trouble; it was tracking it; and it was planning to shoot it down.

Arnold has, moreover, continued to maintain the truth of that account, even after the appearance of the movie *United 93*, on which Bronner worked. In a statement about this movie, Arnold said:

> The movie trailer said the military was not notified of UAL 93 until 4 minutes after it had crashed. That is not true as we were notified a short time before it crashed.[207] . . . I advised Col. Marr to intercept UAL 93 and have pilots divert it away from DC; secondly, to fire warning shots if it didn't respond; and thirdly to shoot it down if all else failed. . . . Bob Marr has consistently said that he passed that information to the pilots.[208]

This whole account, to be sure, is said by Bronner and the 9/11 Commission to be false, since it disagrees with the story suggested by the tapes. As we have seen, however, the list of people who had to have been lying, if the story on the tapes is true, extends far beyond Colonel Scott and General Arnold, on whom Bronner focuses. It also includes David Bohrer, Josh Bolton, Andrew Card, Colonel Marr, General Richard Myers, and General Montague Winfield. Bronner explicitly accuses the vice president of lying about this matter. Having quoted Cheney's statement—made, Bronner says, with "dark bravado"—that the order to a pilot "to shoot down a plane full of Americans is . . . an order that had never been given before." Bronner then adds, "And it wasn't on 9/11, either."[209]

Bronner, admitting that many people had said that the military was ready to shoot the plane down, says: "The recordings tell a different story." That is certainly true. However, if we think it unlikely that all of these people were lying about UA 93, then the fact that the tapes tell a different story provides more evidence that they, besides providing a very limited window into the military history of 9/11 (one that does not include the people cited in the previous paragraph), have also been altered. According to the tapes, for example, Nasypany at 10:10 announces the answer he has received from higher officials to his question: "Negative. Negative clearance to shoot."[210]

Positive clearance, as we have seen, had been given at least 20 minutes earlier. I turn now to the other issue that has led to the charge of widespread lying.

Phantom Flight 11

The concept of a "phantom Flight 11"—the name given to the nonexistent plane that, according to the tapes, was thought by the FAA and NORAD to be heading toward Washington—is absolutely crucial to the 9/11 Commission's new story. It is so important because of the well-entrenched report that fighters were scrambled from Langley Air Force Base at 9:24 (becoming airborne at 9:30). As we saw earlier, the original NORAD timeline indicated that the Langley fighters were scrambled in response to word from the FAA at 9:24 that AA 77 had possibly been hijacked and appeared to be heading back toward Washington. General Arnold, in his 2003 testimony to the Commission, gave a different account, saying that the fighters were really scrambled in response to word about UA 93. The

9/11 Commission, insisting that the military did not learn about either flight until after 9:30, needed an alternative explanation for the Langley scrambles. The tapes provide this alternative explanation: phantom AA 11.

Although the tapes-based story of phantom 11 is undoubtedly convenient, the question is whether it is true. An examination of this story—which, thanks to Bronner's article, is now available in more detail than it was in *The 9/11 Commission Report*—will provide reasons to doubt its truth.

At 9:21 (34 minutes after Flight 11 had crashed into the World Trade Center), according to Bronner's account, NEADS received word from Colin Scoggins that AA 11, rather than having hit the WTC, was actually still aloft and headed toward Washington. As to how this false idea came about, Scoggins reportedly told Bronner that while he was monitoring a conference call between FAA centers, "word came across—from whom or where isn't clear—that American 11 was thought to be headed for Washington." The problem evidently started, to quote Bronner's paraphrase of Scoggins' statement,

> with someone overheard trying to confirm from American whether American 11 was down—that somewhere in the flurry of information zipping back and forth during the conference call this transmogrified into the idea that a different plane had hit the tower, and that American 11 was still hijacked and still in the air.

Then, after talking to a supervisor, Scoggins "made the call and said [American 11] is still in the air and it's probably somewhere over New Jersey or Delaware heading for Washington, D.C."[211]

This message then, according to the 9/11 Commission, went to the NEADS mission crew commander (Kevin Nasypany), who issued a scramble order to Langley. So, the Commission claims, the Langley jets were scrambled in response to "a phantom aircraft," not "an actual hijacked aircraft."[212]

This new story, however, is riddled with problems. One problem is the very idea that this mistake could have been made. The traffic controllers at Boston Center were reportedly very clear about the fate of AA 11. According to a story in the *Christian Science Monitor* two days after 9/11, flight controllers said that they never lost sight of this plane.[213] Flight controller Mark Hodgkins later told ABC News: "I watched the target of American 11 the whole way down."[214] *New York Times* and Newhouse News stories reported that as soon as the Boston flight controllers heard that a plane had hit the WTC, they knew that it was AA 11, because they had been tracking it continuously since it had begun behaving erratically.[215] Scoggins should have known all of this. How, then, could any conversation have "transmogrified" into "the idea that a different plane had hit the tower, and that American 11 was still hijacked and still in the air"?

Another problem in this story is the claimed inability to determine the person in the FAA who originated the idea that AA 11 was headed toward Washington. Bronner, paraphrasing Scoggins, says, "word came across — from whom or where isn't clear." This conversation, however, should be contained on the FAA's tapes, and nowadays the identities of people can be determined with great precision from their voices. Since the FAA must have tapes with the voices of all its personnel who get involved in teleconferences, the claim that this alleged person's identity could not be determined seems suspiciously convenient, as this way no one needs to take the blame.

In addition to the inherent implausibility of the story, another problem is that prior to 2004, phantom AA 11 had never been mentioned in any official reports. As the Commission itself said, this story "was not recounted in a single public timeline or statement issued by the FAA or Department of Defense."[216] It was, for example, not in the US Air Force's official report, *Air War over America*, the foreword for which was written by General Arnold. If this extraordinary episode, which led NORAD to send fighters on a wild goose chase, really happened, is the fact that it is not mentioned in this report not puzzling? We can perhaps understand that the FAA would not have wanted to publicize such an embarrassing mistake. But what motivation would the military have had for keeping silent about it?

That said, however, we need to distinguish between two questions about the idea that Flight 11 was still aloft after the North Tower was struck. One question, already answered in the negative, is whether this idea was contained in any official reports. Another question, however, is whether the idea had ever been publicly mentioned by FAA or NORAD officials prior to 2004. And the answer to this question is yes. It was mentioned, very briefly, in the ABC News program with interviews by Peter Jennings. In that program, aired one year after 9/11, Dawne Deskins said that not long after the North Tower had been hit: "They [Boston air traffic controllers] told us that they showed the American Airlines Flight 11 was still airborne. So now, we're looking at this, well if, if an aircraft hit the World Trade Center, who was that?"[217]

Even though this report came a full year after 9/11, we can take it as confirmation for the truth of Bronner's claim, based on Scoggins' statements, that confusion had developed at the Boston Center "over whether the plane that hit the tower really was American 11."[218]

However, assuming that this really occurred, would that mean that the 9/11 Commission's claims about phantom Flight 11 are true? Not necessarily, because we here need to distinguish between some other questions.

One question is whether someone at the FAA's Boston Center (Scoggins) and someone at NEADS came to think that AA 11 might have still been in the air. A very different question is whether that belief is what led the Langley fighter jets to be scrambled.

With regard to this latter question, we also need to distinguish between what Scoggins believes happened and what really happened. Having corresponded with Scoggins, I am convinced that he believes that the Langley fighters were scrambled because of his communication to NEADS that AA 11 was still airborne. But his belief does not mean this is what really happened. Not being privy to all the communications between Boston and NEADS or to the communications involving the military officers who would have made the decision, he has no basis for saying that NEADS, which was so dreadfully slow in scrambling fighters in response to the real AA 11, immediately did so in response to the phantom version. Scoggins may simply be among the people who have been deceived by the new story.

The ABC program on which Dawne Deskins reported having received the message from Scoggins certainly gave no basis for concluding that this message led to the scrambling of the Langley fighters. Right after her question— "if an aircraft hit the World Trade Center, who was that?"—the narrator said: "Whoever it is, Colonel Deskins knows she needs to call NORAD operations in Florida, to inform the public affairs officer, Don Arias." Deskins then says: "And his reaction to me at that point was; my God, my brother works in the World Trade Center, and I said well, you have to go call your brother." That, according to news reports about this conversation, was Arias's reaction to her statement, "We think the aircraft that just hit the World Trade center was American Airlines Flight 11."[219] There is no indication, therefore, that Deskins passed on the idea that Flight 11 might still be in the air. Moreover, even though Deskins was one of the people interviewed for this ABC program, there is no suggestion in the script that the Langley fighters were scrambled because of a belief that AA 11 was still airborne.

Indeed, the original story—that these fighters were scrambled to go after AA 77—was stated in a story that appeared only four months after 9/11 in which Deskins played a major role, being heavily quoted. In this story, we read:

> 9:24AM: FLIGHT 77
> A third plane, American Airlines Flight 77 from Washington to Los Angeles, changed course and stopped responding.
> Instantly, Rome scrambled fighter jets from the nearest air base, Langley in Virginia.[220]

The same thing is said in the 2002 NBC program narrated by Tom Brokaw. At 9:30, Brokaw says, "Flight 77 has been out of contact with controllers in Indianapolis for more than 20 minutes. Fighter jets are dispatched to track the flight."[221]

Prior to the appearance of the NORAD tapes in 2004, accordingly, there is considerable evidence that the Langley jets were scrambled in response to a report about Flight 77 and no evidence, apparently, that they were scrambled in response to phantom Flight 11. And it is hard to imagine why, if the latter were the truth, the military would have concealed this fact.

It is theoretically possible, to be sure, that this was the truth but that the military, rather than deliberately concealing it, simply forgot about it. This was General Arnold's claim at the Commission's hearing in June 2004, at which he was berated for having failed to mention phantom 11 in his 2003 testimony to the Commission—a failure that, the Commission complained, led him to give a false report about AA 77. Commissioner Richard Ben-Veniste asked:

> General Arnold. Why did no one mention the false report received from the FAA that Flight 11 was heading south during your initial appearance before the 9/11 Commission back in May of last year? . . . [I]s it not a fact that the failure to call our attention to the . . . the notion of a phantom Flight 11 continuing from New York City south . . . skewed the official Air Force report, . . . which does not contain any information about the fact that . . . you had not received notification that Flight 77 had been hijacked? . . . [S]urely by May of last year, when you testified before this commission, you knew those facts.

Arnold's reply was that he "didn't recall those facts in May of last year."[222]

But if those alleged facts were real facts, this reply would be beyond belief. According to the Commission's new story, AA 11, UA 175, and AA 77 struck their targets—and UA 93 would have struck its target were it not for heroic passengers—because NORAD, under Arnold's command, failed to intercept them. And this failure, which would forevermore sully his legacy, was really the fault of the FAA, which repeatedly failed to notify NORAD about the hijackings. On top of all this, the one time that Arnold's NORAD did get fighters scrambled in time to intercept a flight, they were sent after a phantom. Arnold would have surely been furious about this stupid error on the FAA's part. And yet 20 months later, he claimed that he "didn't recall those facts." Assuming that those "facts" truly were facts, Bronner and the commissioners would be right to be skeptical about Arnold's claim not to recall.

The idea that Arnold could have forgotten such facts is made even more difficult by the details of the new official story. According to Bronner and The 9/11 Commission Report, at 9:22, just after Rountree and Dooley had heard from Scoggins that AA 11 was still in the air, Nasypany said to Marr: "O.K. American Airlines is still airborne—11, the first guy. He's heading toward Washington. O.K., I think we need to scramble Langley right now." Then, according to Bronner: "Arnold and Marr approve scrambling the two planes at Langley, along with a third unarmed trainer, and Nasypany sets the launch in motion."[223]

According to this story, in other words, Nasypany told Marr that AA 11, which they had thought had crashed into the World Trade Center 36 minutes earlier, was still in the air and headed toward Washington. Marr then told Arnold about this astounding turn of events and got his approval to launch the Langley fighters. If this really occurred, the idea that Arnold could have soon forgotten this episode is beyond belief.

Bronner, moreover, gives still another reason for doubting that Arnold could have forgotten. After the first mention of phantom AA 11 on the NORAD tapes, Bronner says:

> Over the next quarter-hour, the fact that the fighters have been launched in response to the phantom American 11—rather than American 77 or United 93—is referred to six more times on [one] channel alone. How could Colonel Scott and General Arnold have missed it [in 2003] in preparing for their 9/11-commission testimony?[224]

So, even if Arnold and Scott had for some reason forgotten the phantom 11 episode, their memories would have been jogged by listening to the tapes. Accordingly, if the tapes provide "the authentic military history of 9/11," as Bronner says, then we are led with him to conclude that Arnold and Scott—along with many other military and political leaders—must have lied in 2003.

FAA Competence and Incompetence

But do the tapes really present an authentic picture of what occurred? One major reason to doubt this, we saw earlier, is that the 9/11 Commission has proven itself willing to conceal and distort facts. Another reason for skepticism is the fact that the FAA's incompetence as portrayed by the tapes is too extreme to be believed. The task that the FAA allegedly failed to perform repeatedly that day—asking the military to scramble fighters because of some possible problem with an airplane—is one that the FAA had long been carrying out regularly. Can we really believe that virtually everyone—from the flight controllers to their supervisors and managers to the personnel in Herndon and FAA headquarters—suddenly became completely incompetent to perform their tasks?

This allegation becomes even more unbelievable when we reflect on the fact that the FAA successfully carried out an unprecedented operation that day: grounding all the aircraft in the country. The Commission itself says that the FAA "execut[ed] that unprecedented order flawlessly."[225] Is it plausible that FAA personnel, on the same day that they carried out an unprecedented task so flawlessly, would have failed so miserably with a task that they had been performing regularly?

Still another reason to doubt the authenticity of the tapes-based account of phantom AA 11 is that the tapes-based account of the four real flights have all proved to be false. Why should we expect this one to be any different?

Is the Alleged Motive to Lie Credible?

The new tapes-based story also raises the question, touched on earlier but requiring further discussion, whether we can really believe that Scott, Arnold, and other military officials would have told the particular lies with which they have been charged. If the tapes are authentic, there is no escape from the conclusion that they did, because the claim that they had simply been confused about all these matters is not believable. But what if the charge of lying is equally incredible?

The charge leveled by John Farmer, as we saw, is that these officers lied "to obscure mistakes on the part of the F.A.A. and the military, and to overstate the readiness of the military to intercept and, if necessary, shoot down UAL 93." Bronner, using his own wording, suggests that the motive was "to downplay the extent of the confusion and mis-communication flying through the ranks of the government."[226] We can, to be sure, understand that military officials might have been tempted to cover up mistakes and incompetence on their own part. According to the tapes, however, it was the FAA that was guilty of virtually all the confusion and incompetence. Would military officials have lied to protect the FAA?

This problem is expressed, in fact, in Bronner's article. Reporting that Farmer had accused Arnold and others of lying, Bronner said that Farmer could not understand why they would have felt a need to do this: "The information they got [from the FAA] was bad information, but they reacted in a way that you would have wanted them to. The calls [they made] were the right ones."[227] This picture creates a big problem for the Farmer–Bronner charge. If the NORAD officials, given the information they had received from the FAA, made the right decisions, what possible motivation would they have had to lie? Are we supposed to believe that, after the FAA had repeatedly given the military late and false information, military officials fudged the truth for the FAA's sake?

Even more unbelievable is the fuller scenario we are expected to buy. If the military had told the truth, according to this scenario, the public would have known that the FAA had failed to inform the military about flights 175, 77, and 93 until after they had crashed. There could, therefore, have been no suspicion that the military had been responsible for the success of the attacks on the South Tower and the Pentagon and for shooting down the plane that crashed in Pennsylvania. Nevertheless, we are supposed to believe, NORAD invented a false timeline that could lead people to suspect that the military was responsible for those events. This would mean that military officials, to protect themselves and primarily the FAA from the charge of confusion and incompetence, invented a lie that would expose themselves to the charge of murder and treason. This would have been a completely unmotivated, even irrational, lie. Not one of us could imagine even being tempted to tell such a lie.

Let us return, in particular, to the charge that Arnold, Scott, and the military in general lied by not mentioning phantom Flight 11—that is, by failing to point out that the Langley jets had been scrambled in response to the FAA's false information that AA 11 was still aloft and headed toward Washington. If this was really the truth, why would these military men have deliberately failed to point this out? Surely not to protect Scoggins and other FAA personnel, with whom the military would have been furious for, on top of everything else that day, giving it that false report. And surely not to protect itself, because upon receiving the false report, it quickly had fighters airborne. (The fighters did, to be sure, allegedly head out to sea instead of toward Washington, but that problem existed whether they were scrambled in response to AA 77 or phantom AA 11.)

Besides having no motivation to keep silent about the phantom Flight 11 mixup, the military officials would have had every reason to tell it instead of the story they did tell. The story told by NORAD's old timeline—that the Langley fighters were scrambled in response to the FAA's notification at 9:24 about AA 77—opened NORAD to the charge that it had had time to intercept this flight before it got to the Pentagon. (Recall the 9/11 Commission's statement that this story had been "unfortunate," because it "made it appear that the military was notified in time to respond."[228]) But the story about phantom Flight 11 lets the military off the hook, putting all the blame on the FAA. If the story about phantom Flight 11 were true, it would have been completely irrational for the military not to have talked about it.

Is it not more plausible that the reason no one in the military had mentioned that the Langley fighters were scrambled in response to phantom Flight 11 is that this story was a late invention? The 9/11 Commission, as we saw, does not believe Arnold's statement that when he testified in 2003, he did not remember the phantom Flight 11 episode. The Commission does not believe him because Arnold and other officers, when preparing to give testimony in 2003, listened to NORAD's tapes, and when these tapes were played for the Commission in 2004, they contained abundant evidence that the Langley fighters had been scrambled in response to a false report about AA 11. But if in 2003 the tapes did not yet have dialogue on them supporting that view, there would be no mystery about why Scott and Arnold did not "remember" this episode and also why no one else in the military had ever mentioned it.

However, if that is the case, so that Scott, Arnold, and others are being falsely charged on the basis of the Commission's tapes-based new story, why do they not just say so? Why have they publicly accepted the new story, thereby publicly agreeing that their previous testimony was incorrect? There are several possible reasons.

One reason is simply military discipline. Even in retirement, military officers would be very reluctant to challenge an official story being promulgated by the Pentagon, especially on an issue as important and potentially explosive as the military's response on 9/11.

Also, Scott, Arnold, and other officers would have to go along with the new tapes-based story, even while knowing it to be false, if the story contained in NORAD's earlier timeline was itself a lie. And, as we have seen in our discussions of the four flights, there is much evidence that it was. This story simply could not withstand scrutiny, because even if the FAA had given notification as late as NORAD had claimed in its timeline of September 18, 2001, the fighters could still have intercepted the airliners. This point was effectively argued by early members of the 9/11 truth movement (whose findings were summarized in my first book on 9/11, *The New Pearl Harbor*).[229] The whole purpose of the 9/11 Commission's revisions was to have an account that would be immune to those criticisms.

Accordingly, there was, even before the 9/11 Commission's tapes-based account, good reason to believe that the story told by Scott, Arnold, and the NORAD timeline was a lie.

If that is the case, then it is understandable that Scott and Arnold would go along with the new story, even if it causes some embarrassment to them and the military in general. Knowing that both accounts are false, they would not challenge the latter in the name of the former, thereby opening them both up to public scrutiny.

The third and surely most decisive reason why these officers would go along with the new story is that, insofar as the press and the public accept it, the military as a whole will avoid the charge of having been criminally complicit or even terribly incompetent. Scott, Arnold, and the other officers accused of lying, recognizing that someone needs to serve as scapegoats for the sake of this greater good, would understandably go along with the role assigned to them—except for insisting that they were not deceitful, merely confused and forgetful.[230]

The fact that the officers accused of lying have not publicly challenged the new tapes-based story, therefore, does not count against the conclusion that the tapes must have been distorted.

How Could False Tapes Have Been Produced?

That conclusion can be sensibly held, of course, only if someone would have had the motivation, means, and opportunity to produce distorted tapes.

Any doubt about sufficient motivation can be quickly dismissed. If the 9/11 attacks were orchestrated or at least deliberately allowed by the

Bush–Cheney administration and its Pentagon, then the motivation to cover up this murderous and treasonous act, which has increased military spending by hundreds of billions of dollars, would be unlimited. No expenditure of time and money would be considered too great.

Although that is obvious, the question of the means to produce altered tapes may seem less so. The tapes have evidently seemed authentic to people who have listened to them. The voices of the main players in the drama are clearly recognizable. If these people did not say in real time everything that is presently on the tapes, how could they now be heard saying these things?

Cherry Picking and Time Alteration

I previously mentioned three methods, suggested by Robin Hordon, by which the tapes could have been made to tell a false story. One method would involve "cherry picking": out of the thousands of hours of tapes available, the agents creating the tapes would have selected those conversations that could be used to construct the desired account. All the tapes that have contrary information would be suppressed, perhaps even erased.

Hordon says, as we saw, that the so-called NORAD tapes contain only a few of the recordings that would have been made of communications going to and from Boston Center that morning. "There is," he says, "an FAA source of information, conversation and tapes that is most likely a thousand times more voluminous than what has been provided so far."[231] What has been provided, moreover, does not include communications from some of the most important positions. For the most part, the tapes only contain recordings of communications involving junior staff of the NEADS facility. It cannot be presumed that these communications give a complete or even accurate picture of what was going on. As Bronner himself points out, we do not have Marr's side of his conversations with Nasypany. As the 9/11 Commission admits, we do not have the instructions given to the fighter pilots by their military controllers. And we certainly do not have recordings of Marr's conversations with Arnold. We also do not have recordings of any conversations that occurred between FAA headquarters and the NMCC. It cannot simply be assumed, therefore, that the "NORAD tapes" given to Bronner provide an accurate portrayal of the most crucial communications for writing "the authentic military history of 9/11."

Besides using cherry-picked recordings, the producers of the tapes could have further distorted the truth by doctoring some of the ones selected for use. Hordon, given his strong belief that someone at the Boston Center notified NEADS about AA 11 long before the military claims, emphasizes that altering the times on the tapes would have been especially easy:

Doctoring these tapes would pose very few difficulties whatsoever. Either one could "write over" the time channel, adjusting it to any time one would want. Or one could transfer all the audio information on particular channels onto another tape that already has a "chosen" time reference impregnated upon it.[232]

Moreover, if some of the elements in the new story, such as evidence that the Langley fighters were in fact launched in response to phantom Flight 11, could not be produced by cherry picking and simple doctoring but required outright fabrication, there were two ways in which needed statements could have been produced.

Inserting Scripted Statements

The simplest way to produce new elements would have been to write scripts for certain key players, record them making those scripted statements, then insert these recorded statements into the tapes. A prime candidate for this type of fabrication would be the statement on the tapes in which Major Nasypany said to Colonel Marr: "O.K. American Airlines is still airborne—11, the first guy. He's heading toward Washington. O.K., I think we need to scramble Langley right now." Another prime candidate would be Nasypany's statement at 10:10 (some 20 minutes after Richard Clarke says that he received and passed on the shootdown authorization): "Negative: Negative clearance to shoot." Inserting these and other needed statements into the tapes would have been a very simple matter, as long as the people whose statements were needed were willing to participate in the deception.

It is possible, however, that those who produced the tapes felt that statements were needed by various people who had not been conscious participants in the plot. Many such people would likely not be willing to participate in the cover-up and, the producers of the tapes might well have thought, should not even be entrusted with knowledge of what had really happened on 9/11. If statements on the tapes from such people were desired, the needed technology was at hand.

Voice Morphing

I refer to the fairly new technology of "voice morphing" (which is one of the forms of digital morphing, with others being video and photo morphing). This technology has been available for several years, as shown in a 1999 *Washington Post* article by William Arkin.[233] As an example of what was already possible at that time, Arkin described a demonstration in which General Carl Steiner, former commander-in-chief of the US Special Operations Command, was heard making a statement that began: "Gentlemen! We have called you together to inform you that we are going to overthrow the United States government." In another demonstration, the voice of Colin Powell was heard to say: "I am being treated well by my captors." Neither Steiner nor Powell had ever uttered those statements. They were complete fabrications.

What is required to produce such fabrications? "By taking just a 10-minute digital recording of [anyone's] voice," Arkin reported, voice morphing experts can "clone speech patterns and develop an accurate facsimile," causing people to appear to have said things that they "would never otherwise have said." Although earlier voice morphing techniques required cutting and pasting, often producing robotic intonations, the new software "can far more accurately replicate the way one actually speaks."[234]

This new technology, developed in the Los Alamos National Laboratory, can be used equally by Hollywood and by military and intelligence agencies. "For Hollywood, it is special effects. For covert operators in the US military and intelligence agencies, it is a weapon of the future." One agency interested in this weapon, Arkin reports, is "the Information Operations department of the National Defense University in Washington, the military's school for information warfare."

Referring to what the military calls PSYOPS, meaning psychological operations, Arkin explains that these operations "seek to exploit human vulnerabilities in enemy governments, militaries and populations." But voice morphing, I would add, could equally well be used as a weapon to exploit human vulnerabilities in a government's own population. The "human vulnerabilities" in the US population could include the public's ignorance of such technologies plus its tendency to trust its political and military leaders and to reject "conspiracy theories."

Arkin, saying that video and photo manipulation had already "raised profound questions of authenticity for the journalistic world," teaching it that "seeing isn't necessarily believing," points out that the addition of voice morphing means that "hearing isn't either." Or at least it shouldn't be. Surely, given the existence of this technology plus the manifold problems in the 9/11 Commission's story based on the NORAD tapes, our media should be questioning the authenticity of these tapes.

If the means existed to doctor the tapes, what about the opportunity? This is also no problem. The NORAD tapes were under the military's control all the time. Of course, given the fact that when Arnold, Scott, and others listened to the tapes in 2003, they apparently did not hear many of the things that are on the tapes now, the editing process might not have begun until some time in 2003—perhaps after some members of the 9/11 Commission realized that the story NORAD had been telling since 2001 was not good enough to defend the military against the charge of complicity in the attacks. But because excerpts of the tapes were not played in public until the Commission's hearing on June 17, 2004—over a year after the hearing at which Arnold and the others first testified—there would have been plenty of time to get the tapes modified.

However, it might be objected, although the modification of the NORAD tapes can be thus explained, it is quite otherwise with the FAA tapes—to which Bronner referred as "parallel recordings," thereby indicating that they agreed with the NORAD tapes. Excerpts from these tapes were also played at that hearing in 2004. We can suppose, indeed, that any skepticism about the authenticity of the NORAD tapes would have been overcome by the fact that the FAA tapes agreed with them. Could anyone believe that the FAA, knowing that it had done its job properly and that only the military had fouled up, would have doctored its own tapes to exonerate the military by making itself look completely incompetent?

That would indeed be a good rhetorical question if the FAA's tapes had been in its own possession all the time. But that was evidently not the case. In the telephone conversation I had with Laura Brown in 2004, she told me that immediately after 9/11, the FAA was required to turn over all its records from that day to the FBI. Although it was not unusual, she added, for the FAA to turn over its records after a major disaster, they were normally turned over to the National Transportation Safety Board. This time, however, they had to be turned over to the FBI.[235] It was, moreover, not only the tapes from FAA headquarters that were taken by the FBI. A *Christian Science Monitor* story two days after 9/11, referring to tapes made at Boston Center, said: "Those tapes are now presumed to be in the hands of federal law-enforcement officials, who arrived at the flight-control facility minutes after Flight 11 crashed into the World Trade Center."[236] (Is this not suspiciously just?) There would have been plenty of time and opportunity, therefore, for the FBI or some other intelligence agency to doctor the FAA's tapes.

In the following chapter, moreover, I show that we have very strong evidence that the FAA's chronology from 9/11 has been doctored to make it agree with the 9/11 Commission's new story. If its chronology has been doctored for this purpose, then its tapes needed to be doctored. And if they were doctored in those respects, there is reason to suspect that they were doctored to bring them into conformity with the doctored NORAD tapes.

In light of this information plus the voice morphing techniques that have been available to intelligence agencies since at least 1999, the agreement between the NORAD and the FAA tapes that have been made public poses no problem for the fabrication hypothesis.

United 93 Telephone Calls: A Prior Example?

There is reason to believe, moreover, that voice morphing had already been used at least once before in the process of creating the official story about the 9/11 attacks. I refer to the alleged telephone calls made by passengers on United Flight 93 before it crashed in Pennsylvania.

At least nine of these calls were reportedly made on cell phones. Given the fact that there were at most only two alleged cell phone calls from the other three flights combined, UA 93 has been called the "Cellphone Flight."[237] There is reason to believe, however, that these calls were fabricated. Given the cell phone technology at the time, the alleged calls from cell phones (as distinct from seat-back phones) would apparently have been impossible.

In the system that then existed, a cell phone had to reach and then complete an electronic "handshake" with the nearest cellsite. The handshake took at least eight seconds. Then if the cell phone, being in a moving automobile or a low-flying airplane, moved into a new cell, the call had to be "handed off" to a new cellsite, and this process, which could take several seconds, often resulted in dropped calls.

Given that system, the claim that cell phone calls were successfully made from Flight 93 faces two problems. One problem involved altitude. For a cell phone call to be made from an airplane, the phone had to reach a cellsite on the ground; otherwise the phone would indicate "no signal." But if the plane was too high, the cell phone could not make contact with a cellsite or, if it did manage to make contact, it could not maintain it long enough to complete a call.

Experiments to test the possibility of the alleged calls were undertaken by the Canadian science writer A. K. Dewdney, a former professor of mathematics and computer science known to readers of *Scientific American* as the long-time author of a regular column. On the basis of experiments with various kinds of cell phones in a single-engine plane, he reached the following conclusions: Successful calls were for the most part possible only under 2,000 feet. Between 2,000 and 8,000 feet, they were highly unlikely. Above 8,000 feet, they were extremely unlikely. At 20,000 feet, Dewdney concluded, "the chance of a typical cell phone call making it to ground and engaging a cellsite there is less than one in a hundred. . . . [T]he probability that two callers will succeed is less than one in ten thousand." The likelihood of nine successful calls at that altitude, he says, would be "infinitesimal," which in operational terms, he added, means "impossible."[238]

In later experiments, he found that in a twin-engine airplane, there was an even lower and more definite cutoff point. In the single-engine aircraft, "The success rates [had] decayed from 75 percent at 2,000 feet to 13 percent at 8,000." But in the twin-engine aircraft, "The success rate decayed from 95 percent at 2,000 feet to 44 percent at 5,000 feet, 10 percent at 6,000 feet, and 0 percent at 7,000." This finding supported his earlier hypothesis that "[t]he larger the mass of the aircraft, the lower the cutoff altitude." The implication would be that in a large airliner, the absolute cutoff altitude would be even lower. This conclusion, he adds, "is very much in harmony with many anecdotal reports . . . that in large passenger jets, one loses contact during takeoff, frequently before the plane reaches 1000 feet altitude."[239] Dewdney's later experiments give him reason to be even more confident of his earlier assertion that cell phone calls from airliners flying above 30,000 feet would have been "flat out impossible."[240]

This conclusion creates an enormous problem for the official story, because UA 93, according to the 9/11 Commission, was at 34,300 feet when "the passengers and flight crew began a series of calls from GTE airphones and cellular phones." Shortly thereafter, moreover, an air traffic controller "observed United 93 climbing to 40,700 feet."[241] The likelihood that even one of those alleged cell phone calls would have gotten through was, therefore, close to zero. There was simply no possibility whatsoever that *nine* of the alleged cell phone calls could have been successful.

Flight 93's altitude was, moreover, only part of the problem. Also problematic was its speed, which would have been in the range of 500 miles per hour.

As we saw, it took several seconds for a cell phone to complete an electronic "handshake" with a cellsite, then a few more seconds for it, when moving from one cell to another, to be "handed off" to the new cell site. A cell phone in an airplane going 500 miles per hour would generally have been moving from cellsite to cellsite too quickly for these transactions to have been completed.

The twofold problem faced by the claim about Flight 93's cell phone calls was stated succinctly in 1999 by an airline pilot, who wrote: "The idea of being able to use a cell phone while flying is completely impractical. Once through about 10,000 feet, the thing is useless, since you are too high and moving too fast (and thus changing cells too rapidly) for the phone to provide a signal."[242] (Additional evidence supporting this claim will be provided in Chapter 4.)

The new technology that would make such calls possible was successfully tested only in 2004. These new cell phones employ a completely different system. Antennas in the front and rear of the cabin transmit the calls to a cellular base station on the plane known as a "pico cell," which then transmits the calls via a satellite to the worldwide terrestrial phone network.[243] QUALCOMM Inc., which developed this system, announced on July 15, 2004, that it and American Airlines had completed a successful demonstration flight. "Through the use of an in-cabin third-generation (3G) 'picocell' network," the company announced, "passengers on the test flight were able to place and receive calls as if they were on the ground." An American Airlines vice-president added that "commercial availability of cell phone use in flight is approximately 24 months away."[244] This new technology would have hardly been hailed as such a breakthrough if cell phone calls from airliners had already been possible, as suggested by the movie *United 93*.

It might be thought, of course, that even if the cell phone calls were not genuine, the calls from the seat-back phones—which were GTE Airfones— might have been. However, the content of some of these calls (as well as that of some of the alleged cell phone calls) makes their authenticity unlikely. In the most notorious case, a man claiming to be Mark Bingham called Bingham's mother, Alice Hoglan. When she answered, he said: "Mom, this is Mark Bingham." Have any of us, even in the most stressful situation, identified ourselves to our own mother by giving our last name? This, at least, would have been very strange for Mark Bingham, who was close to his mother and called often. His formality would have been even stranger in light of the fact that the call had originally been answered by Alice's sister-in-law, who had told her that Mark was on the phone, so that when Alice took the phone, she said, "Hi, Mark." Is it believable that her son, especially after that, would have said, "Mom, this is Mark Bingham"?

The remainder of the call, moreover, provides nothing to assure us that the call was authentic. "Mark Bingham" next said: "I'm on a flight from Newark to San Francisco. There are three guys aboard who say they have a bomb." His mother then asked, "Who are these guys, Mark?" After a pause, the caller said: "Do you believe me? It's true." After which she said, "I do believe you, Mark. Who are these guys?" After a long pause, the line went dead.[245]

Given the caller's failure to respond to any questions, we might assume this to have been a pre-recorded statement. If it had been pre-recorded, however, the "Mark Bingham" goof would surely have been corrected. Also, some of the other alleged calls did contain a little genuine interaction.

But these two facts present no problem, given the existence, since at least the mid-1990s, of voice transformers. Dewdney, explaining how they work, writes:

> One speaks into a microphone, the sound pattern is digitized and, in real time the computer within the device produces a signal that is reconstituted as sound, a voice that can be entirely different from your own. Everything you say will be spoken by the synthesized voice and with . . . the specific "sound" of a particular person's voice.

We can thus understand how callers might have been able to interact— albeit in limited ways—with the people who were called. In a discussion of how the fake phone calls could have been orchestrated, Dewdney writes:

> On the fateful day the calling operation would take place in an operations

center, basically a sound studio that is equipped with communication lines and several telephones. An operations director displays a scripted sequence of events on a screen so that the voice operators know what stage the "hijacking" is supposed to be at. All calls are orchestrated to follow the script. . . . To supplement the calls with real sound effects, an audio engineer would have several tapes ready to play. The tapes, which portray mumbled conferences among passengers or muffled struggles, replete with shouts and curses, can be played over any of the phone lines, as determined by the script, or simply fed as ambient sound into the control room. Trained operators with headsets make the actual calls, talking into voice changers that have been adjusted to reproduce the timbre of voice for every passenger designated to make [telephone] calls.[246]

Each operator, Dewdney further suggests, would have been given personal profiles, both of the individuals they are to impersonate and the ones they are to call. These profiles would include pet names for spouses, information on whether the couple had children and, if so, how they referred to them ("the kids"), and so on. This information could have been acquired in various possible ways, such as intercepting a couple's phone calls.

Additional support for this explanation is provided by reading the transcripts of the "Flight 93" calls in light of Dewdney's hypothesis. Many of the transcripts, in addition to the one from "Mark Bingham," make more sense on the supposition that the caller was an impersonator.[247]

Most of us, to be sure, cannot imagine being willing to make such calls to spouses or other relatives of the passengers, even if we were in the military and were ordered to do so, so we may find it hard to believe that any of our fellow citizens would so such a thing. But we also cannot imagine being willing to participate in the murder of thousands of people in the Twin Towers and over a hundred people at the Pentagon, and yet the evidence, as we will see in later chapters, implies that some of our fellow citizens did participate in these murders. By comparison with those acts, participation in deceptive phone calls, which did not involve directly killing people, would surely have been less difficult.

In any case, if voices were morphed to produce apparent telephone calls from UA 93 (a hypothesis for which further evidence will be presented in Chapter 4), this gives us additional reason to suspect that the NORAD and FAA tapes have been altered by means of such technology. Also, given the fact that Bronner was involved in the production of *United 93*, in which cell phone calls play a major role, the fact that his article raises no question about the authenticity of the tapes provides no evidence against this hypothesis.

The trial of Zacarias Moussaoui, who had been accused of being complicit in the 9/11 attacks, was concluded in 2006 just as this movie was released, probably giving it a big boost at the box office. But this trial also involved a development that, had it become widely known, would have been a big embarrassment for the movie. A reporter wrote:

> In the back of the plane, 13 of the terrified passengers and crew members made 35 air phone calls and two cell phone calls to family members and airline dispatchers, a member of an FBI Joint Terrorism Task Force testified Tuesday.[248]

So when the government was in court, where its claims might have been challenged, it was not willing to risk having to defend the claim that nine or more cell phone calls had been made from Flight 93, most of which would have been from six miles up. It suddenly reduced the claim to only two calls. (Although the report did not state which alleged calls the FBI was still ready to defend, they were probably the last-made alleged calls, when the plane's altitude might have been low enough that the calls could arguably have gone through.)

In line with this reduction is the fact that, although the evidence submitted by the prosecution included telephone company records of various calls made by various alleged terrorists, it did not include any phone company records of any of the alleged calls from the airplanes.[249]

We have here another case where the government has implicitly admitted that it had long been lying. The claim that nine or more cell phone calls were made from UA 93 had been made repeatedly. It had been widely publicized in films about this flight (including the film with which Bronner was involved). For the government to retract this claim in 2006 involved an implicit admission that it had been supporting a lie for five years.

For our present purposes, the main implication is that the government has covertly admitted that most of the alleged cell phone calls on Flight 93 could not have occurred. This admission implies that these calls must have been fabricated. And if those calls were fabricated, why should we not assume that the Airfone calls, in which the same kinds of things were said, were also fabricated?

But Would All Those People Participate in a Lie?

I have been using the evidence that the telephone calls from Flight 93 were fabricated as support for the hypothesis that the NORAD and FAA tapes as described by Bronner have been altered. There is, to be sure, a rather obvious objection to this hypothesis: If these tapes have been altered, then many military and FAA personnel would know this. Surely at least some of them would speak up? Surely not everyone would be willing to be complicit in such an enormous fraud by remaining silent?

However—and this could turn out to be the most important implication of the new story—it is now established beyond doubt that members of both the FAA and the military are capable of such deceit and complicity. On the one hand, if the new story is true, then many people in both the FAA and the military knew the old story to be false and yet supported it—whether actively or by their silence—from 2001 to 2004. On the other hand, if the new story is false, then many people in both the FAA and the military know this and yet have supported it—whether verbally or merely by not challenging it—since the publication of *The 9/11 Commission Report* in July 2004. Given Bronner's portrayal of some of the people at NEADS, to be sure, it is not pleasant to think of them as consciously participating in an enormous lie. But we have no choice, because if the new story is true, then they were complicit in an enormous lie between 2001 and 2004. And if so, we have no reason to believe they would not support, or at least go along with, a new, improved lie.

On the basis of this awareness, it could be argued that there is really no need for the suggestion that the tapes were altered by means of voice morphing. If the FAA and military personnel have been involved in a complicity of silence about the tapes, there was no need to morph their voices. Those who were fabricating the tapes could have simply ordered the various people to read the new lines that had been written for them.

That is, to be sure, possible. But there is a big difference, at least for basically honest people, between actively participating in a fraud and merely remaining silent—under orders—about one. Many people who would do the latter would not do the former. It would seem more likely, therefore, that if the tapes were doctored, voice morphing technology was used, at least in some instances.

Also, only a small portion of the many hours of tapes made available to the 9/11 Commission and Bronner have been made public. If some people's voices were morphed without their knowledge, they would likely never know this.

There is no need, in any case, to settle this question in advance of an investigation. All that is needed at this stage is awareness that the government agents would have had both the means and the opportunity, as well as the motivation, to produce fraudulent tapes.

Conclusion

Motivation for producing fraudulent tapes would have been provided by the American public's growing rejection of the government's conspiracy theory in favor of the alternative view, according to which 9/11 was an inside job. The effectiveness of these tapes in undermining this alternative conspiracy theory is suggested by a *New York Times* editorial, which begins:

> No topic investigated by the 9/11 Commission hatched more conspiracy theories than the failure of American air defense systems to intercept any of the four planes that had been hijacked by terrorists. That makes [Bronner's *Vanity Fair* essay and Kean and Hamilton's *Without Precedent*]

particularly welcome. . . . [These reports show that there] was absolutely no evidence that any air defenders deliberately stood aside to let the terrorists have their way . . . , as conspiracy theories have suggested.[250]

The effectiveness of these publications in getting the new story accepted is illustrated by the remainder of the *Times* editorial, which says:

The Federal Aviation Administration . . . failed miserably in its duty to alert the military. . . . However, the F.A.A. did tell the military, erroneously, that a plane that had already hit the World Trade Center was still headed south toward Washington. As a result, the military scrambled two planes to chase a ghost. . . .

And for all the bravado surrounding the "shoot down" order issued by Vice President Dick Cheney during the crisis, the order reached Norad too late to be of any use. . . .

After the fact, military officials gave false testimony that exaggerated their readiness to protect the nation's capital. They indicated that the F.A.A. had alerted the military more promptly than it actually had, that fighter jets were scrambled to protect Washington from real planes rather than to chase the ghost flight, and that the military was tracking—and ready to shoot down—a plane that it did not even know had been hijacked and that had already crashed in Pennsylvania.

[If it is determined that] these false statements were [not] made deliberately, . . . someone will still have to explain why the military . . . could not come up with the real story until the 9/11 commission forced it to admit the truth.

As can be seen, the new story is swallowed hook, line, and sinker. There is no mention of the fact that this new story is riddled with problems or of the possibility that the tapes, first played publicly almost three years after the event, might have been doctored. There is no puzzling about what could have motivated military officials to say that "the F.A.A. had alerted the military more promptly than it actually had." From the perspective of the *Times* and the mainstream media more generally, all these things must be true, because they are on the tapes.

A more plausible interpretation, I suggest, is that these tapes have been produced by a combination of cherry picking and various kinds of doctoring, perhaps including voice morphing—which would mean that this "weapon of the future" in the arsenal of specialists in psychological warfare has been successfully employed "to exploit human vulnerabilities" in the US population, including the US press.

I will conclude by returning to the significance of the 9/11 Commission's charge, made on the basis of the new story, that the military had previously lied about 9/11. Many commentators who have mentioned this fact have assumed, with the *New York Times*, that this charge is a big embarrassment to the military, which would not "come up with the real story until the 9/11 commission forced it to admit the truth." What is really going on, however, is that the military is briefly suffering a little embarrassment, experienced primarily by a few scapegoats, for the sake of the new story, which, if accepted, almost fully removes the basis for suspicion of guilt—for treason and murder—from everyone in the military. It does not *fully* remove this suspicion, because of remaining problems, most notably the failure to respond quickly to the notice about AA Flight 11, the incoherencies in story about the Otis fighters, and the sending of the Langley fighters out to sea. But this story at least comes much closer to getting the military off the hook.

The new story is hence best seen as the military's replacement of its old story with a better one. Remember: the military freely gave these tapes to Bronner, knowing that he would write a story that, given its sensational charge that the military had lied, was sure to get a lot of attention. This suggests that any embarrassment caused to the military by having this new story widely known is far overshadowed by the benefits.

Seen in this light, the now established fact that the military has lied about 9/11 has a perhaps unforeseen implication—that there is no good reason to take the military's new story on faith. For if the military was lying to us between 2001 and 2004, we have no basis for trusting what it says now. To appreciate this point, it is important to get the logic of the situation right. The truth of the new story would imply the falsity of the old story. But the falsity of the old story would not imply the truth of the new story. They could both be false. And if the previous story, which only poorly absolved the military from suspicion, was a lie, should we not suspect that the new story, which more fully absolves it, is an even bigger lie?

This implication will not be seen, to be sure, as long as one accepts the narrative promulgated by the 9/11 Commission and repeated by the *Times*—that the military had to be "forced" to tell this story, to its great embarrassment, by the 9/11 Commission. But once we see that this is the military's new story, which it used the 9/11 Commission to tell (albeit perhaps with some coaching from this Zelikow-led body), then we have reason not to accept this new tale without examining its inherent implausibility, its conflict with prior reports, and the possibility of cherry-picked and fraudulently produced tapes. When this tale is examined with those questions in mind, I have suggested, there are many, many reasons to consider it a lie.

One cannot reasonably claim, therefore, that the NORAD tapes, even in conjunction with the FAA tapes, debunk the claim that there was a military stand down on 9/11. This issue will be further pursued in the following chapter.

TWO

The Real 9/11 Conspiracy Theory:
A Critique of Kean and Hamilton's *Without Precedent*

The appearance of Bronner's essay in *Vanity Fair* occurred almost simultaneously with the publication of *Without Precedent: The Inside Story of the 9/11 Commission*, coauthored by Thomas H. Kean and Lee H. Hamilton, the commission's chair and vice chair. Much of this book is about the 9/11 Commission's new story about NORAD and the FAA. Whether the timing was planned or merely coincidental, this double-barreled approach served to implant this new story in the public mind much more widely than had *The 9/11 Commission Report* itself.

According to Kean and Hamilton, conspiracy theories about 9/11 had grown up primarily because of problems in the previous story about the planes, which the military had been telling since September 18, 2001, when NORAD put out its timeline. By getting those problems cleared up, they claim, the new story overcomes the basis for those theories. The first purpose of this chapter is to show the falsity of this claim. The second and more general purpose of this chapter, reflected in its title, is to show that although Kean and Hamilton correctly describe the main faults of irrational, anti-scientific conspiracy theories, their criticisms apply most of all to the government's own conspiracy theory, which their Commission defended.

Trying to Debunk the Stand-Down Theory

Although the new Kean–Hamilton book, insofar as it deals with substantive matters, simply reaffirms, for the most part, the claims of *The 9/11 Commission Report*, there is one major difference. In that earlier book, there was no mention of the existence of alternative theories about 9/11, according to which it was an inside job, orchestrated by forces within the Bush–Cheney administration and its Pentagon. In *Without Precedent*, by contrast, Kean and Hamilton not only refer to the existence of such theories; they even admit that the Commission had been interested in "debunking conspiracy theories."[1]

Although they mention several such theories, including the theory that the Pentagon was hit by a missile instead of Flight 77,[2] they focus almost entirely on the theory that, they say, exists "[a]t the core of several prominent conspiracy theories," namely, "the notion that the military had foreknowledge or warning of the attacks, and had issued a 'stand down' order on 9/11, thus permitting the attacks to occur."[3]

This theory arose, they say, because of the inaccurate story told not only by the FAA but also by the military in its timeline of September 18, 2001, in its book *Air War over America*, and in its testimony to the Commission in 2003.[4] Although Kean and Hamilton speak of the stand-down theory with contempt, calling it "bizarre" and "irrational,"[5] they admit that, given the story told by the FAA and the military, the theory had a good basis.

> [I]f the military had had the amount of time they said they had . . . and had scrambled their jets, it was hard to figure how they had failed to shoot down at least one of the planes. . . . In this way, the FAA's and NORAD's inaccurate reporting after 9/11 created the opportunity for people to construct a series of conspiracy theories that persist to this day.[6]

The point that Kean and Hamilton are at pains to make, however, is that these theories should no longer persist, because the 9/11 Commission resolved the problems.

> Through our statements and hearings, we had cleared up inconsistencies in the FAA and NORAD accounts of 9/11—inconsistencies that had fed so many bizarre theories. Those who chose to continue believing conspiracy theories now had to rely solely on imagination, their theories having been disproved by facts.[7]

The basis for allegedly clearing up these inconsistencies was, as Bronner emphasized, the tapes that the Commission received from NORAD and the FAA. The reason for calling certain statements by FAA and NORAD officials false was that they disagreed with these tapes.[8] The tapes, unlike people, are infallible: "The tape recordings . . . from the day were extremely important—they provided a real-time record of what was happening that enabled our staff to relive the day, instead of relying solely on people's memory or their hurried notes of what took place."[9] That is the Kean–Hamilton claim.

As shown in the previous chapter, however, we cannot simply assume that the tapes actually provide a "real-time record." We must ask whether the tapes contain things that suggest that they have been doctored. To employ an extreme example: If the tapes contained the voice of President Eisenhower, most of us would assume that they had been doctored, no matter how strongly those who provided the tapes insisted that they were fully authentic. Once this principle is established—that the authenticity of the tapes must be evaluated in terms of the plausibility of their content—we must ask: How radically can the tapes diverge from people's memories and still be considered entirely authentic? Surely there must be some limit.

And yet, the divergences are very radical. "For United Airlines Flight 175," say Kean and Hamilton on the basis of the tapes, "NORAD had no advance notification."[10] However, as we saw in the previous chapter, the officers who wrote NORAD's September 18 timeline evidently remembered that the FAA had notified NORAD about the hijacking of this plane at 8:43 (twenty minutes before the South Tower was struck), and NORAD's Captain Michael Jellinek and some technicians at NEADS evidently knew about the hijacking before the crash.

The tapes also indicate that there was no notification about AA 77 until after the strike on the Pentagon. But it was ingrained in the military's institutional memory that it had received formal notification about this flight at 9:24, and Laura Brown's memo, incorporating the FAA's institutional memory, said that the FAA had been talking to the military about this flight even earlier. (This memo was discussed and read into the 9/11 Commission's record by Richard Ben-Veniste, who said: "So now we have in question whether there was an informal real-time communication of the situation, including Flight 77's situation, to personnel at NORAD."[11] However, *Without Precedent* follows the precedent of *The 9/11 Commission Report* by not mentioning it.)

The tapes also indicate that the military did not know about UA 93's hijacking until after it had crashed. But according to Richard Clarke's memory, recorded in his *Against All Enemies*, FAA head Jane Garvey, while participating in Clarke's videoconference in which both Donald Rumsfeld and General Richard Myers were also participating, identified "United 93 over Pennsylvania" as a "possible hijack" at about 9:35, hence almost 30 minutes before its crash time.[12] Moreover, many members of the military, including Myers, General Larry Arnold, Brigadier General Montague Winfield, and Colonel Robert Marr, reportedly remembered that they were in position to shoot this flight down. This same memory was reportedly shared by Deputy Secretary of Defense Paul Wolfowitz and even Vice President Cheney. Yet Kean and Hamilton want us to believe that all these men, telling essentially the same story, were either mistaken or lying.

Besides insisting that we must declare, on the basis of the tapes, that all these things that all these people reportedly thought they remembered did not really happen, Kean and Hamilton also insist, like Bronner, that we must believe that something that evidently no one in the military remembered actually did happen. That is, as we saw in the previous chapter, the tapes indicate that the Langley fighters, which were airborne at 9:30, were scrambled not in response to AA 77, as NORAD had said, but in response to phantom AA 11. But, Kean and Hamilton quote *The 9/11 Commission Report* as acknowledging, "this response to a phantom aircraft [American 11] was not recounted in a single public timeline or statement issued by FAA or Department of Defense."[13]

Kean and Hamilton even provide evidence that some people, after hearing the tapes, did not remember things the way the tapes present them. When General Arnold was asked at a 9/11 hearing why he had not reported that the Langley fighters had been scrambled in response to the false report that AA 11 was still aloft and headed toward Washington, he replied that the information supplied by the 9/11 Commission had "helped us [the military] reconstruct what was going on." He did not say: "Now that I've been reminded of what really happened, I remember." Then, after Richard Ben-Veniste said: "General Arnold, surely by May of last year, when you testified before this commission, you knew those facts," Arnold replied: "I didn't recall those facts in May of last year."[14] He did not add: "But now I do." Kean and Hamilton have unwittingly, therefore, supplied evidence that the new timeline was constructed out of whole cloth, not out of authentic records of 9/11.

Kean and Hamilton are fond of using the word "irrational" or some synonym for people who doubt the official version of the events. But given all the contradictions between the tapes and people's memories, would it be rational to maintain faith in the authenticity of the tapes? Would it not be more rational, especially given the other factors discussed in the previous chapter, to suspect that it is the tapes that give a false account?

Furthermore, as we saw, the rationality of this suspicion is strengthened by the implausibility of the charge, made according to Bronner by some members of the 9/11 Commission staff, that the story told by the military from 2001 to 2004 was a lie. Kean and Hamilton, while not as blunt, support this interpretation. Besides reporting that "the staff front office" said that NORAD's behavior "bordered on willful concealment," they say: "Fog of war could explain why some people were confused on the day of 9/11, but it could not explain why all of the after-action reports . . . and public testimony by FAA and NORAD officials advanced an account of 9/11 that was untrue."[15] This is an indirect way of saying that these officials must have been lying. But, as we have seen, such behavior on the part of military officials would be completely inexplicable. We can understand that, if FAA officials had fouled up as badly as the Commission's new story implies, they might have been tempted to fudge the truth. But whereas the 9/11 Commission's new story gets the military almost fully off the hook, the military's previous story made it seem as if the military must have stood down its defenses or else acted in extremely incompetent ways. Kean and Hamilton themselves say, as we saw, that "if the military had had the amount of time they said they had . . . , it was hard to figure how they had failed to shoot down at least one of the planes." If the new story were the truth, it would have been wholly irrational for the military to have told the earlier story. Kean and Hamilton, while calling the stand-down theory "irrational," fail to reflect on the fact that it is their own theory that is truly irrational.

One cannot say, therefore, that the stand-down theory has been "disproved by facts."

What about Other Conspiracy Theories?

Kean and Hamilton, moreover, make a more sweeping claim: that their Commission had used facts to disprove all 9/11 conspiracy theories.[16] But this, as I showed in *The 9/11 Commission Report: Omissions and Distortions*, is a goal they do not even approach. I will give a few examples.

Kean and Hamilton dismiss as "absurd" the theory that something other than American 77 hit the Pentagon. The only basis they give for this judgment is the claim that the 9/11 Commission staff "told the story of American Airlines Flight 77 in such detail—with radar tracking, air traffic control conversations, calls from the plane, and a timeline of the flight's movements—that it simply was not credible to advance a theory that anything but American Flight 77 crashed into the Pentagon."[17]

None of that alleged evidence, however, can survive scrutiny. I show the problems with the alleged "calls from the plane" in Chapters 1 and 4. There are no "air traffic control conversations" with anyone on this plane after radio contact was lost about 40 minutes before the Pentagon was struck. And there is no evidence that the aircraft picked up by radar near Washington was AA 77, so the latter part of the resulting "timeline," in which the aircraft is headed back toward Washington, cannot be known to be the timeline for AA 77. As former controller Robin Hordon emphasizes, after AA 77 went off the FAA radar screens before 9:00AM, positive radar contact was never reestablished and, in fact, could not have been reestablished, in the absence of the transponder signal, without the cooperation of the pilot.[18] This fact undermines the claim of Colonel Alan Scott, who summarized the timeline for the 9/11 Commission, that AA 77 "appears back in radar coverage" at about 9:10. In fact, Scott himself, saying that "the FAA controllers now are beginning to pick up primary skin paints on an airplane," admits that "they don't know exactly whether that is 77."[19]

As we saw in the previous chapter, moreover, the Commission's story about Flight 77, besides being inherently implausible, is also challenged by previous reports and by Laura Brown's memo.

Even aside from these problems, furthermore, *The 9/11 Commission Report* failed to address other reasons for doubting that the Pentagon was struck by AA 77, such as the implausibility of the idea that Hani Hanjour, who could barely fly a small plane, could have piloted a Boeing 757 through the 330-degree downward spiral that was, according to the radar, taken by the aircraft that hit the Pentagon; the implausibility of the idea that Hanjour, even if he had been capable of this maneuver, would have gone out of his way to hit the Pentagon's west side, given the fact that Rumsfeld and the top brass were in the east side; and the fact that according to both photographs and eyewitnesses, neither the damage nor the debris suggested that the Pentagon had been hit by a giant airliner.

(The only problem the Commission dealt with was that of Hani Hanjour's competence, and it did so by making contradictory statements, acknowledging at places that he was a "terrible pilot," who as late as July 2001 was so incompetent even in a small airplane that an instructor refused to go up with him a second time,[20] then saying elsewhere that Hanjour was assigned to hit the Pentagon because he was "the operation's most experienced pilot."[21]) Kean and Hamilton continue to ignore all these problems in their new book.

They also continue to avoid all the problems involved in the official theory of the collapse of the World Trade Center buildings. They ignore the fact that steel-frame buildings had never, prior to the three alleged cases on 9/11, suffered total collapse from any cause except pre-set explosives. They ignore the fact that the collapses of these buildings manifested many characteristics, such as coming straight down and at virtually free-fall speed, that are typical features of planned implosions. And, relying on the theory that the Twin Towers were brought down by the impacts of the airplanes plus the resulting fires, Kean and Hamilton ignore, as did *The 9/11 Commission Report*, the fact that WTC 7, which was not hit by a plane, also collapsed. (They speak only of the collapse of "the towers."[22])

Still another thing that has led critics to regard 9/11 as an inside job was the behavior of Bush's Secret Service detail that morning. As Kean and Hamilton point out, one of the central questions raised by the 9/11 families was: "Why was President Bush permitted by the Secret Service to remain in the Sarasota elementary school where he was reading to children?"[23] The point of this question was that once it was clear, after the second strike on the World Trade Center at 9:03, that terrorists with hijacked airplanes were going after high-value targets, the Secret Service— if this was indeed a surprise attack—should have assumed that a hijacked airliner was bearing down on the school at that very moment. They should have immediately rushed the president to a safe location. Instead, they let him remain at the school for another 30 minutes, even allowing him to make a televised address to the nation, thereby letting any interested terrorists know that he was still there.

Kean and Hamilton provide no answer to this question. Perhaps they assumed that it had been answered in *The 9/11 Commission Report*. But it had not. As I pointed out in my critique of that book, the Commission's total response to this question was contained in one sentence: "The Secret Service told us they were anxious to move the President to a safer location, but did not think it imperative for him to run out the door."[24] For the Commission to accept that answer, I pointed out, was to accept the idea that "these highly trained Secret Service agents were . . . more concerned about appearances than about the possibility that a hijacked airliner might crash into the school, killing the president and everyone else, including themselves."[25] The answer accepted by the Commission, in other words, was wholly implausible. The only plausible explanation for the Secret Service's behavior seems to be that it knew that the school would not be attacked.

Also relevant is the fact that the White House later put out a different account. About a year after 9/11, Andrew Card, the White House chief of staff, was quoted as saying that after he told the president about the second attack on the World Trade Center, Bush "excused himself very politely to the teacher and to the students" and left the classroom within "a matter of seconds."[26] Although this revisionist revealed the White House's awareness of the problematic nature of Bush's having remained in the classroom, the Commission did not address this issue.

Given the Commission's failure to address any of these problems in the official story, the truly absurd claim is that all the reasons for suspecting the government's complicity in the 9/11 attacks were removed by the 9/11 Commission.

The Real "Conspiracy Theory"

Thus far, I have followed, without comment, Kean and Hamilton's practice with regard to the term "conspiracy theories," using it exclusively for theories that reject the official account of 9/11 in favor of some version of the view that the attacks were orchestrated, or at least deliberately allowed, by forces within the US government.

But that, of course, is a prejudicial use of the term, because the government's own theory, which the 9/11 Commission supported, is also a conspiracy theory. As pointed out in the introduction, a conspiracy is simply "an agreement to perform together an illegal, treacherous, or evil act." According to the official account, the 9/11 attacks resulted from a secret agreement between Osama bin Laden and other members of al-Qaeda, principally Khalid Shaikh Mohammed and the 19 Arab Muslims said to have hijacked the four airliners. The official account is, accordingly, a conspiracy theory, differing with the alternative theory only on the identity of the conspirators.

Given the fact that the theory supported by Kean and Hamilton is a conspiracy theory—it is, in fact, the original conspiracy theory about 9/11—their practice of using the term "conspiracy theorists" exclusively for people who hold the alternative conspiracy theory is confused at best, dishonest at worst. It is dishonest if they, being aware that they themselves are also conspiracy theorists about 9/11, nevertheless use the term in their one-sided way to take advantage of the negative connotations the terms "conspiracy theory" and "conspiracy theorists" have for most people in our culture.

In any case, whatever the reasons for their one-sided usage, a proper employment of these terms would require that they always be preceded by identifying adjectives. Because Kean and Hamilton consider the theory that 9/11 was an inside job to be irrational,[27] they could speak of that view as the "irrational conspiracy theory" while calling their own view the "rational conspiracy theory."

Of course, although this usage would bring a gain in both clarity and honesty, it would mean that Kean and Hamilton would no longer be able to score points against their critics simply by calling them "conspiracy theorists." They would have to show that their own conspiracy theory is actually more rational.

Given various statements they make, however, they should not consider this a significant disadvantage. Besides describing versions of the alternative theory as "far-fetched," "irrational," "absurd," and "loony,"[28] Kean and Hamilton explain their use of these terms by making, more or less explicitly, five charges against those whom they portray as irrational conspiracy theorists: (1) These conspiracy theorists begin with their conclusion, then marshal evidence to support it, rather than beginning with the facts and allowing their theory to emerge therefrom. (2) They continue to hold theories that are "disproved by facts."[29] (3) They "have no interest in any evidence that does not adhere to their views."[30] (4) They uncritically accept any reputed evidence, no matter how suspect, that can be used to bolster their theory. (5) They have "disdain for open and informed debate."[31]

If these attitudes and practices have indeed been used to construct the various alternative conspiracy theories but not the conspiracy theory supported by the 9/11 Commission, then Kean and Hamilton should have no trouble showing the latter to be the more rational theory.

Unfortunately for them, however, they have thereby provided a perfect description of the attitudes and practices that lay behind the construction of the 9/11 Commission's conspiracy theory. The remaining five sections of this chapter will be devoted to supporting this claim. I will show, in other words, that given Kean and Hamilton's criteria for calling an account a "conspiracy theory," it is the 9/11 Commission's account that is the real 9/11 conspiracy theory.

Beginning with the Conclusion

Kean and Hamilton talk a lot about their determination to begin with the facts, not with a theory. They say:

> The starting point for our report was that it would focus on the facts. We were not setting out to advocate one theory or interpretation of 9/11 versus another. Our purpose was to fulfill our statutory mandate, gathering and presenting all of the available and relevant information.[32]

Indeed, Kean and Hamilton say, "the term 'go to the facts' became something of a joke within the commission."[33] The real joke, however, is the claim that they began with the facts rather than with their conclusion. Their own account shows the opposite to have been the case.

Having explained that, after choosing Phillip Zelikow to be the executive director, they accepted his view that the Commission would do its work by means of "a staff organized around subjects of inquiry,"[34] they then say: "When we set up our staff teams, we assigned the subject of 'al Qaeda' to staff team 1," assigning to team 1A the task of "tell[ing] the story of al Qaeda's most successful operation—the 9/11 attacks."[35]

If that does not provide a text-book example of starting with a theory, what would? As the 9/11 Commission was fully aware—any possible doubt about this is removed by *Without Precedent*—there were, broadly speaking, two theories: (1) the official theory, according to which 9/11 was orchestrated and carried out solely by al-Qaeda, and (2) the alternative theory, according to which 9/11 was orchestrated or at least consciously permitted by forces within our own government. The Commission simply began with the first theory, ignoring the second one. As I wrote elsewhere:

> Many readers of *The 9/11 Commission Report* have assumed that it indeed played the role of an impartial jury, simply evaluating the evidence for the competing conspiracy theories and deciding which one was more strongly supported.
>
> In reality, however, the Commission took the role of the prosecution. Simply assuming the truth of the Bush administration's account of 9/11, the Commission devoted much of the report to Osama bin Laden, al-Qaeda, and the 19 alleged hijackers, as if their responsibility for the attacks were unquestionable.[36]

Kean and Hamilton, far from denying the claim that the Commission "took the role of the prosecution," confirm it, saying:

> Often, the truth about a criminal conspiracy comes out in the trial of the conspirators, where the public is presented with evidence and witness testimony. This time, though, there would be no trial: the nineteen perpetrators were dead, victims of their own atrocities. So we directed our team 1A to approach their task as if putting together the case against the conspirators.[37]

Now, as everyone who watches TV crime shows is aware, attorneys for the prosecution do not impartially weigh all the relevant evidence, presenting in court all the evidence that counts against, as well as all the evidence that supports, the guilt of the accused. They present only the evidence that they have discovered—or perhaps fabricated—that would support a guilty verdict. The task of challenging this evidence and presenting exculpatory evidence—which might include evidence that the crime was committed by someone else—is left to the defense attorney. The 9/11 Commission, however, did not appoint anyone to play the role of attorney for the defense. Accordingly, the public was presented only with evidence pointing to al-Qaeda's responsibility for the 9/11 attacks. If some of this evidence was fabricated, moreover, there was no one to challenge its authenticity.

To illustrate the one-sidedness of the evidence that would be presented by this prosecutorial approach, we can use Kean and Hamilton's statement that "[t]he starting point would be Usama Bin Ladin's February 1998 fatwa instructing his followers to kill Americans, military and civilian."[38] This was a good starting point, given the Commission's goal, because a prosecuting attorney, to get a conviction, must show that the accused had the motive, means, and opportunity to commit the crime in question, and it is often wise, for psychological purposes, to begin with the motive. Describing the 1998 fatwa issued by bin Laden and Ayman al-Zawahiri, the Commission wrote: "Claiming that America had declared war against God and his messenger, they called for the murder of any American, anywhere on earth," as the duty of all Muslims. Entitling this part of its report "A Declaration of War," the 9/11 Commission wrote that bin Laden saw himself as organizing "a new kind of war to destroy America and bring the world to Islam."[39]

The 9/11 Commission was thereby able, in its prosecutorial role, to portray bin Laden and his Muslim followers as having a plausible motive: they had declared war on America because America, in their eyes, had declared war on Allah and Islam.

Excluded Evidence

However, what if there had been attorneys for the defense, who would have argued that the Bush–Cheney administration, besides having had far more means and opportunity to carry out the attacks than did al-Qaeda, also had a more powerful motive? Would there have been any evidence to which they might have pointed? Yes, indeed.

They could have pointed out that a movement known as neoconservatism, which included Dick Cheney, Donald Rumsfeld, Richard Perle, and Paul Wolfowitz, had expressed interest in establishing a global Pax Americana, the first all-inclusive empire in history; that in 1992, Cheney, before ending his tenure as secretary of defense, had Wolfowitz write a draft of the Defense Planning Guidance, which has been called "a blueprint for permanent American global hegemony"[40] and Cheney's "Plan . . . to rule the world"[41]; that the main points in this document were reaffirmed in a 2000 document entitled *Rebuilding America's Defenses*, written by a neoconservative think tank called Project for the New American Century (PNAC); that the stated requirements for the Pax Americana included a huge increase in military spending, a technological transformation of the military to reorient it around computer-guided weapons (including weapons in space), and a revised doctrine of preemptive war that would allow America to attack other nations even if they posed no imminent threat. The defense attorneys for al-Qaeda could also have pointed out that many of the leading neocons, including Rumsfeld and Wolfowitz, had been wanting to take over Iraq and its oil since the early 1990s and that the Bush–Cheney administration had in July 2001 reportedly indicated that it would attack Afghanistan "by the middle of October."[42]

Perhaps most important, these attorneys could have pointed out, Zbigniew Brzezinski had suggested in 1997 that the American public would support "imperial mobilization," through which America could retain its primacy by taking control of the oil-rich region of Central Asia (which includes Afghanistan), only in the event of "a truly massive and widely perceived direct external threat"—just as the American public had been willing to support "America's engagement in World War II largely because of the shock effect of the Japanese attack on Pearl Harbor."[43] These defense attorneys could then have pointed out that *Rebuilding America's Defenses*, perhaps inspired by Brzezinski's argument, suggested that the process of transforming the US military in the desired direction was "likely to be a long one, absent some catastrophic and catalyzing event—like a new Pearl Harbor."[44] They could have further pointed out that, besides the fact that 9/11 was widely compared with Pearl Harbor, it was also said to have presented "opportunities" by Bush, Rice, and Rumsfeld, with the latter saying that 9/11 created "the kind of opportunities that World War II offered, to refashion the world."[45]

Would not any neutral jury, having heard the prosecution and then the defense, have concluded that the Bush–Cheney administration, which was heavily populated with members of PNAC, had, at the very least, motives as strong as those attributed to Osama bin Laden and his al-Qaeda followers? But, of course, the jury—the American public—was not allowed to hear any attorneys for the defense. Accordingly, although we were told about what Kean and Hamilton call "Bin Ladin's murderous ideology,"[46] we were not allowed to hear whether the Bush–Cheney administration might have been staffed by people with an at least equally murderous ideology.

In one sense, the fact that the 9/11 Commission began with a theory is in itself not objectionable, because a purely Baconian method, which looks at the relevant evidence before forming any hypothesis whatsoever, is not really possible. We can decide what counts as "relevant evidence" only in light of some hypothesis. The problem is that the Commission also systematically excluded the main competing hypothesis from consideration, thereby ignoring all evidence that might support it, and this *is* objectionable, being a violation of intellectual and ethical standards common to scientists, historians, and courts of law.

Those who read Kean and Hamilton carefully can, in fact, see that this completely one-sided approach was built into the Commission's mandate. In their preface to *The 9/11 Commission Report*, they had said that their mandate was to investigate "facts and circumstances relating to the terrorist attacks of September 11, 2001." Their aim, they said, was "to provide the fullest possible account of the events surrounding 9/11."[47] In the present book, however, they add a nontrivial qualification, saying that they had the task of "gathering and presenting all of the available and relevant information *within the areas specified by our mandate*" (emphasis added).[48] What exactly was that mandate? "The law creating the 9/11 Commission," they inform us, "allowed for us to ascertain, evaluate, and report on the evidence developed by all relevant governmental agencies regarding the facts and circumstances surrounding the attacks."

So they were not, as they had suggested in the preface to *The 9/11 Commission Report*, to provide all the 9/11-related facts and circumstances whatsoever. They were to provide only the evidence about these facts and circumstances that had been developed *by governmental agencies*. What was the chance that any governmental agencies during the Bush–Cheney administration would have provided evidence suggesting that forces within this administration had orchestrated or at least deliberately permitted the attacks? About zero. What was the chance that these agencies would provide evidence supporting the administration's interpretation of 9/11? About 100 percent. So the 9/11 Commission's conclusions were virtually implicit in its mandate.

Zelikow as Executive Director

If there was need for any further guarantee that the Commission would support the conspiracy theory about 9/11 promulgated by the Bush–Cheney administration, this was provided by Kean and Hamilton's choice of Philip Zelikow to be the Commission's executive director—a choice they made, they admit, "with little consultation with the rest of the commission." It would appear, in fact, that the only other commissioner involved was Slade Gorton, who had recommended Zelikow.[49] In their preface to *The 9/11 Commission Report*, Kean and Hamilton said that they had "sought to be independent, impartial, . . . and nonpartisan."[50] In the present book, they reaffirm that they had been determined to be "nonpartisan and independent."[51] Had those truly been central concerns, however, they certainly would not have had their commission run by Zelikow, who was essentially a member of the Bush–Cheney administration.

That this description is no exaggeration can be seen by reviewing some of Zelikow's history. He had worked with Condoleezza Rice on the

National Security Council (NSC) in the administration of the first President Bush. When the Republicans were out of office during the Clinton administration, Zelikow and Rice wrote a book together. Then when Rice was named national security advisor for the second President Bush, she had Zelikow help make the transition to the new NSC, during which time he, according to Richard Clarke, received warnings about al-Qaeda.[52]

"But," claim Kean and Hamilton, "we had full confidence in Zelikow's independence. . . . He recused himself from anything involving his work on the NSC transition." Kean and Hamilton thereby pretend that Zelikow's association with Rice and the Bush administration more generally would have been a problem only with regard to discussions in which he was directly involved—as if the main problem were not that he was politically, personally, and ideologically intertwined with the Bush administration. For the 9/11 Commission to have been "independent" would have been for it to be independent from all the organizations that might have been responsible—whether through incompetence, carelessness, or complicity—for the success of the 9/11 attacks. To dramatize the degree to which Zelikow's role on the Commission compromised its independence, we can imagine the outcry that would have been evoked if an al-Qaeda sympathizer had been made the Commission's executive director.

Because of his background, Kean and Hamilton admit, "Zelikow was a controversial choice. . . . Democratic commissioners other than Lee [Hamilton] were wary of Zelikow's appointment. The 9/11 families questioned his ability to lead a tough investigation." This ridiculously anemic description of the 9/11 families' opposition to Zelikow is partially rectified in a later statement, in which Kean and Hamilton admit that "[t]he 9/11 families, and the FSC [Family Steering Committee] in particular, had accused him of conflict of interest because of his past relations with Condoleezza Rice."[53] Even this statement, however, does not begin to reflect the vehemence of the FSC's opposition to Zelikow. Here is part of what they said in a press release of March 20, 2004:

> It is apparent that Dr. Zelikow should never have been permitted to be Executive Staff director of the Commission. . . . It is abundantly clear that Dr. Zelikow's conflicts go beyond just the transition period. . . . The Family Steering Committee is calling for: 1. Dr. Zelikow's immediate resignation. . . . 4. The Commission to apologize to the 9/11 families and America for this massive appearance of impropriety.[54]

Nevertheless, although Kean and Hamilton portray themselves as having the support of the 9/11 families,[55] they dismissed the FSC's call for Zelikow's removal.

The importance of Zelikow's role as executive director could hardly be exaggerated. The statement by the FSC says: "As Executive Staff

Director his job has been to steer the direction of the Commission's investigation." Kean and Hamilton themselves make clear Zelikow's centrality, saying that "Zelikow drove and organized the staff's work."[56] Presupposed by this statement is the fact that the Commission's staff, composed of some 75 members, was organized by Zelikow into various teams, to each of which he gave a topic to investigate. Zelikow had enormous power, therefore, to determine what the Commission would investigate—and, therefore, what it would *not* investigate. Zelikow was, moreover, evidently not reluctant to exercise his power to shape the Commission's results. As one disgruntled member of the staff reportedly said at the time, "Zelikow is calling the shots. He's skewing the investigation and running it his own way."[57]

Zelikow also had great power to determine the shape and contents of the final report. He provided its "overarching vision" and, with the aid of his former coauthor Ernest May, prepared the outline, which he presented to the staff, assigning "different sections and subsections of it to individual staff members."[58] Finally, Zelikow's role as executive director gave him enormous power to determine what would be included in, and hence deleted from, the final report. For example, although various members of the Commission's staff wrote the first drafts of the various chapters, May tells us, revised drafts were then produced by the "front office," which was headed by Zelikow.[59] Zelikow's power was likely so great, in fact, that the Commission's report, rather than being called the Kean–Hamilton Report, as it often is, or even the Kean-Zelikow Report, as I previously suggested, should simply be called the Zelikow Report. In any case, the importance of Zelikow's power to shape the Commission's final report will become clearer in the following sections. First, however, we need to look at two more episodes in Zelikow's career—episodes that make even more serious the question of why he was chosen to be the Commission's executive director.

Zelikow and NSS 2002: One of the benefits that the Bush–Cheney administration derived from 9/11 was the ability to announce the new doctrine of preemptive warfare mentioned earlier. A little known fact— perhaps because it has been carefully concealed after Zelikow was chosen to be executive director of the 9/11 Commission[60]—is that Zelikow was the primary author of the document in which this new doctrine was made official US policy.

This new doctrine—which came to be known as the "Bush doctrine"—was articulated in the president's address at West Point in June 2002 (when the administration started preparing the American people psychologically for the attack on Iraq). Having stated that, in relation to the "new threats," deterrence "means nothing," Bush said: "If we wait for threats to fully materialize, we will have waited too long." Our security, therefore, "will require all Americans . . . to be ready for preemptive action."[61]

This new doctrine was then articulated in *The National Security Strategy of the United States of America* for 2002 (NSS 2002),[62] published later that year. According to James Mann in *Rise of the Vulcans*, a first draft had been produced by Richard Haass of the State Department. But Condoleezza Rice, who had the responsibility for getting this document written, wanted "something bolder." She therefore "ordered the document be completely rewritten" and "turned the writing over to her old colleague . . . Philip Zelikow."[63]

The result was a document that, on the basis of 9/11, declared that American behavior would no longer be constrained by the basic principle of international law as embodied in the charter of the United Nations. This is the principle that one country cannot launch a preemptive attack upon another country unless it has certain knowledge that an attack on itself from that other country is imminent—too imminent to be taken to the UN Security Council. NSS 2002, in seeking to justify this new doctrine, said:

> Given the goals of rogue states and terrorists, the United States can no longer rely on a reactive posture . . . . The inability to deter a potential attacker, the immediacy of today's threats, and the magnitude of potential harm that could be caused by our adversaries' choice of weapons, do not permit that option. We cannot let our enemies strike first.[64]

Clearly stating that the United States is now giving itself the right to attack another country even without certain knowledge that an attack from that country is imminent, NSS 2002 says:

> The greater the threat, . . . the more compelling the case for taking anticipatory action to defend ourselves, even if uncertainty remains as to the time and place of the enemy's attack. To forestall or prevent such hostile acts by our adversaries, the United States will, if necessary, act preemptively.[65]

The covering letter, signed by the president, spells out even more clearly the idea that there need be no imminent threat, saying that with regard to "our enemies' efforts to acquire dangerous technologies," America will, in self-defense, "act against such emerging threats before they are fully formed."[66]

Although the United States had in practice often violated the principle of international law that it has now formally renounced, the novelty and importance of this formal renunciation should not be underestimated. As Stefan Halper and Jonathan Clarke point out: "Never before . . . had any president set out a formal national strategy doctrine that included preemption."[67]

If it had been widely known that Philip Zelikow had been the primary author of NSS 2002, his selection as executive director would surely have aroused far more protest, especially in light of the following three points.

First, 9/11 allowed the agenda of the neoconservatives to become official US policy. This point is not controversial: Stephen Sniegoski, writing from the left, says that "it was only the traumatic effects of the 9/11 terrorism that enabled the agenda of the neocons to become the policy of the United States of America."[68] Halper and Clarke, writing from the perspective of Reagan conservatives, say that 9/11 allowed the "preexisting ideological agenda" of the neoconservatives to be "taken off the shelf . . . and relabeled as the response to terror."[69]

Second, Zelikow, in using 9/11 to get the new doctrine of preemption turned into official US policy, was using 9/11 to advance the neocon agenda. This statement is also not controversial. For example, Max Boot, a well-known neocon, has described NSS 2002 as a "quintessentially neo-conservative document."[70]

Third, Zelikow was then put in charge of directing the work of the 9/11 Commission, which should have been asking, among other things, whether the Bush–Cheney administration might have wanted the attacks to occur.

In light of these three points, it is no surprise that the items mentioned above under "excluded evidence"—such as the neoconservative agenda and PNAC's reference to the benefit that could come from "a new Pearl Harbor"—were excluded. With Zelikow in charge, the 9/11 Commission provided a classic example of putting a fox in charge of investigating the foxes.

Zelikow and Catastrophic Terrorism: The choice of Zelikow to direct the 9/11 Commission becomes even stranger—on the assumption that the Commission was supposed to seek the truth about 9/11—in light of an essay he co-authored in 1998 on "catastrophic terrorism." In this essay, which suggests that he had been thinking about the World Trade Center and a new Pearl Harbor several years prior to 2001, Zelikow and his coauthors say:

> If the device that exploded in 1993 under the World Trade Center had been nuclear. . . , the resulting horror and chaos would have exceeded our ability to describe it. Such an act of catastrophic terrorism would be a watershed event in American history. It could involve loss of life and property unprecedented in peacetime and undermine America's fundamental sense of security, as did the Soviet atomic bomb test in 1949. Like Pearl Harbor, this event would divide our past and future into a before and after. The United States might respond with draconian measures, scaling back civil liberties, allowing wider surveillance of citizens, detention of suspects, and use of deadly force.[71]

Is this not a remarkable statement? Besides the fact that it, like Brzezinski's book the year before (1997) and the PNAC document two years later (2000), speaks of a new catastrophe as having effects comparable to those of Pearl Harbor, it also imagines the new catastrophe as an attack on the World Trade Center. Moreover, this statement by Zelikow and his coauthors (one of whom, John Deutch, had been the director of the CIA in 1995–1996) predicts with great accuracy the effects of the new catastrophe: the division into "before and after" (the contrast between a pre-9/11 and a post-911 mindset has become one of mantras of the Bush administration) and the government's response with "draconian measures," namely, "scaling back civil liberties, allowing wider surveillance of citizens, detention of suspects, and use of deadly force."

Would it not be interesting if we were to learn that those who orchestrated the attacks of 9/11 were able to put one of their own— someone who at least had foreknowledge of the attacks—in charge of carrying out the official investigation into these attacks?

Even apart from this possibility, however, Zelikow's intimate relation with the Bush–Cheney administration, especially his role in the drafting of NSS 2002, should lead to an investigation of exactly how his selection came about. Kean and Hamilton tell us that he was recommended by one of the Republicans on the Commission, Slade Gorton. But why did Gorton make this recommendation? Kean and Hamilton mention that Gorton had worked with Zelikow on two previous commissions, and it is possible that he recommended Zelikow simply because he had been impressed with his work. But it is also possible, for all we know, that someone within the White House, such as Condoleezza Rice, Karl Rove, or Dick Cheney, suggested to Gorton that he make this recommendation. It could also be the case, given Kean and Hamilton's proven tendency to tell less than the full truth about many matters, that they were directly pressured to choose Zelikow.

That supposition would, at least, make sense of three otherwise puzzling features of this choice: the previously discussed fact that, although Kean and Hamilton clearly wanted to keep the support of the 9/11 families, they retained Zelikow in spite of the Family Steering Council's very strong objections; the fact that Hamilton was the only one of the Democratic commissioners who was not "wary of Zelikow's appointment"; and the fact that, as Kean and Hamilton report, Zelikow was the only candidate they seriously considered.[72] Why, for such an exceedingly important position, would they not have made their choice after considering a large number of candidates?

Insofar as an irrational conspiracy theory is one that is accepted prior to examining the relevant facts, the 9/11 Commission's conspiracy theory provides an extreme case, partly because of the choice of Zelikow to direct the Commission's investigations. I turn now to the second feature of irrational conspiracy theories identified by Kean and Hamilton.

Adherence to Theories Disproved by Facts

In the first two sections, I mentioned various facts that, according to defenders of the alternative conspiracy theory, contradict the official theory. The 9/11 Commission has failed to show that these facts do not contradict the official story.

The Commission has clearly done the best job with the charge that it tried the hardest to debunk—the charge that the military's failure to intercept the airliners could only be explained in terms of a stand-down order. In the previous chapter, I have shown, to be sure, that the 9/11 Commission did not prove that there was no stand-down order; far from it. But I also recognize that people can find the tapes quite compelling and that the case against the tapes-based story is very complex, involving elements that many readers may regard as too complex and "conspiratorial" to be plausible. I recognize, therefore, that if the stand-down issue is considered in itself, in isolation from the other problems in the official account, some people might feel that the official story has not been disproved.

The situation is quite otherwise, however, when we turn to the behavior of Bush and his Secret Service detail that morning. The 9/11 Commission, as we saw, did nothing to rebut the claim that this episode disproves the official theory's claim that the attacks were a surprise. In holding that the attacks were a surprise, the 9/11 Commission is holding a view that can reasonably be claimed to be "disproved by facts."

Likewise with the strike on the Pentagon. As we saw, there are many facts, not one of which the Commission even attempted to rebut, that contradict the official story. The Commission is again holding a theory that is arguably "disproved by facts."

This is even more clearly the case in relation to the collapses of the Twin Towers and Building 7 of the World Trade Center. In the physical sciences, the best way to be labeled irrational is to argue for the occurrence of an absolutely unique event—one that has never happened before and that can never be replicated. And yet the official story claims that on 9/11, three steel-frame high-rise buildings suffered total collapse because of fire and externally caused damage, even though prior to 9/11 not a single steel-frame high-rise building had ever suffered total collapse from any cause other than pre-set explosives. Also, no experiment to see whether fire and externally produced damage could induce total collapses has been performed or even proposed. Accordingly, the claim that three such collapses just happened to occur on 9/11 remains a claim in conflict with one of the basic principles of the scientific method.

Moreover, the fact that the collapse of each building was total is only one of the features that the official theory cannot explain. The collapses had at least a dozen features that can be explained, and arguably only explained, on the assumption that explosives were used—unless, that is, one is willing to accept an explanation that violates elementary laws of physics.

One such feature is that the buildings came down at virtually free-fall speed. *The 9/11 Commission Report* even mentioned this fact in passing, saying that the "South Tower collapsed in 10 seconds."[73] The Commission accepted the "pancake" theory, according to which the floors above the hole created by the impact of the airliner fell on the floor below, breaking the floor free from vertical columns to which it was connected. This then started a chain reaction, so that the floors "pancaked" all the way down.

This theory faced severe problems, one of which was that it could not explain the fact that the collapses were total. If the floors had broken loose from the vertical columns, those columns should have still been standing; the 110-story columns in the Twin Towers should not have collapsed into a pile of rubble only a few stories high. A second problem with this theory is that it, as physicist Steven Jones points out, violates "the Law of the Conservation of Momentum, one of the foundational laws of physics." In explaining this point, Jones writes: "as upper-falling floors strike lower floors, including intact steel support columns, the fall must be significantly impeded by the impacted mass. . . . How do the upper floors fall so quickly, then, and still conserve momentum in the collapsing buildings? This contradiction is ignored by the 9/11 Commission."[74]

Jones' point is that, assuming that explosives were not used to destroy the lower floors, each floor, with all its steel and concrete, would have—assuming that the pancake theory were otherwise even possible—offered resistance to the mass of material falling on it. Let us assume that the delay would have been very slight, so that the collapses would have proceeded at the rate of two floors per second. The South Tower was struck at about the 80th floor, so the pancaking would have involved approximately 80 floors. At two floors per second, the pancaking would have taken 40 seconds. And yet the 9/11 Commission admitted that the South Tower collapsed in about 10 seconds. In endorsing the pancake theory, therefore, Kean and Hamilton's 9/11 Commission endorsed a theory that was irrational in the sense of contrary to a well-established law of physics.

The extreme irrationality of their theory, according to which the buildings were not brought down by explosives, becomes even more apparent when we look at other features of the collapses—such as the production of molten metal, the pulverization of most of the concrete into tiny particles, and other features discussed in the next chapter—that can only be explained through the use of explosives. The official theory about the collapses of the buildings will surely go down, therefore, as the most irrational, anti-scientific theory ever widely accepted in the modern world.

The 9/11 Commission did not admit these problems, let alone resolve them. It even failed to mention the fact that WTC 7 collapsed, perhaps because the previously published FEMA report admitted that the best explanation it could come up with—on the assumption, of course, that explosives were not used—had "only a low probability of occurrence."[75] Moreover, the situation was no better with regard to WTC 7 by the time Kean and Hamilton published *Without Precedent*. Although they would doubtless claim that the National Institute of Standards and Technology (NIST) has given a satisfactory explanation of the collapse of the Twin Towers (even though this is not true, as explained in the following chapter), NIST, at the time *Without Precedent* was published, had still not issued a report on the collapse of WTC 7. The claim that this building could have collapsed in the way it did only through the use of explosives had, therefore, remained unrefuted for five years. Nevertheless, Kean and Hamilton, having no basis for denying that the official theory of the collapse of WTC 7 had been "disproved by facts," reaffirmed that theory.

Moreover, once it is accepted that the World Trade Center buildings were destroyed by explosives, the conclusion that this destruction was an inside job is an obvious inference, for several reasons: Members of al-Qaeda could not have gotten access to the buildings for all the hours it would have taken to plant the explosives, whereas there is no difficulty in explaining how home-grown terrorists could have gotten such access, especially after we learn that Marvin Bush (the president's brother) and Wirt Walker III (Marvin and George's cousin) were principals in a company that provided security for the World Trade Center (with Walker being the CEO from 1999 until January 2002).[76] This is one of the many relevant facts that the 9/11 Commission did not tell the American public.

Also, al-Qaeda demolition experts surely would not have had the courtesy to ensure that these huge buildings came straight down. They would have instead made them topple over sideways, as this, besides being far easier, would have been far more destructive to lower Manhattan.

All the evidence, therefore, supports the notion that the destruction of the World Trade Center was an inside job. Once this is seen, moreover, it becomes clear that the military's failure to intercept the airliners must have been orchestrated in advance. Why? Because the Twin Towers were wired to begin collapsing from high up, near the places they were struck by the airplanes. The idea, in other words, was to be able to claim that the buildings collapsed because they were hit by the planes. It was essential to the entire operation, therefore, that planes would strike the buildings. There could be no chance that the airliners might be intercepted and shot down.

Once this is realized, it is easier to see through the 9/11 Commission's new story, according to which the first three flights were able to hit their targets not because of a military stand down but because of incredibly incompetent behavior on the part of FAA officials. The new story contains so many implausible elements and contradicts so many previous reports because it is a wholly false account, fabricated to conceal the fact that a stand-down order had been issued. Taken in connection with the destruction of the World Trade Center, therefore, we can add the 9/11 Commission's new theory about the FAA and NORAD to the elements in the official story that are "disproved by facts."

To believe the official story about 9/11 is, accordingly, to affirm a completely irrational conspiracy theory.

Ignoring Evidence Contradicting One's Theory

A third characteristic of people on the "loony left" who hold "heinous conspiracy theories assigning culpability for 9/11 to the Bush administration," say Kean and Hamilton, is that they "have no interest in any evidence that does not adhere to their views."[77] Looking aside from the fact that many people who believe 9/11 was an inside job are conservatives, not members of the left,[78] Kean and Hamilton have again stated the opposite of the truth.

The 9/11 truth movement, which assigns culpability for 9/11 to the Bush–Cheney administration, has engaged in vigorous debate—both internal debate, in which some members dispute the evidence being used by other members for some particular theory (such as what struck the Pentagon or what exactly was used to destroy the WTC buildings), and external debate with people who hold the official theory. As a result of these discussions, in which members are sometimes confronted with evidence with which they had been unfamiliar, they sometimes change their minds about some dimension of the particular theory they had held.

I can, moreover, cite my first book about 9/11, *The New Pearl Harbor*, as an example that contradicts the Kean–Hamilton charge that those of us who claim that 9/11 was an inside job have no interest in evidence in tension with our views. After providing a prima facie case for the conclusion that the Bush administration had orchestrated 9/11, I devoted six pages to facts that present difficulties for that conclusion.[79]

However, although Kean and Hamilton's third characteristic of irrational conspiracy theorists does not apply to the leading members of the 9/11 truth movement, it does apply, and strongly so, to the 9/11 Commission.

Part of the basis for this claim was provided in the previous chapter, where I pointed out several examples of the 9/11 Commission's proclivity for simply ignoring evidence that contradicted its account of 9/11. For example:

—Claiming that the FAA had not notified the military about UA 175, AA 77, and UA 93 until after they had crashed, the Commission ignored Laura Brown's memo, which indicated otherwise, even though this memo had been discussed and read into the Commission's record by Richard Ben-Veniste.

—Claiming that it did not know who from the Defense Department participated in Richard Clarke's video conference, the Commission ignored the clear statement in Clarke's *Against All Enemies*—which became a national bestseller while the Commission was in session—that the participants were Donald Rumsfeld and General Richard Myers. (Although Kean and Hamilton mention the fact that Clarke contradicted Condoleezza Rice,[80] they do not point out that he also contradicted them.)

—Seeking to construct a new timeline to prove that UA 93 could not have been shot down by the military, the Commission ignored evidence not only that fighter jets had been in position to shoot it down but also that it had, in fact, been shot down.

—Claiming that Vice President Cheney did not enter the bunker under the White House until almost 10:00—"perhaps at 9:58"[81]—the Commission simply ignored the testimony, given at a Commission hearing by Secretary of Transportation Norman Mineta, that Cheney was already in the bunker at 9:20, when Mineta arrived.[82] (Although I exposed this omission of Mineta's contradictory testimony in my book on the Commission's report, Kean and Hamilton repeat their claim about Cheney's arrival time in their new book,[83] thereby demonstrating continued disdain for evidence that contradicts their story.)

—Claiming that no one knew that an aircraft was approaching the Pentagon until 9:36, the 9/11 Commission ignored Mineta's testimony that Cheney was informed of this fact no later than 9:26. (In the present book, in which Kean and Hamilton are at pains to undermine the idea that there was a stand-down order, they continue to ignore Mineta's report, which is best interpreted as eyewitness testimony to the fact that a stand-down order was in effect.)

—Claiming that Richard Clarke did not receive the shootdown authorization from Cheney until 10:25, the Commission ignored Clarke's own testimony, according to which he received it at least 35 minutes earlier, by 9:50.[84]

Several more examples of evidence contradicting its story that the Commission simply ignored have been provided in the present chapter:

—All the facts contradicting the claim that the Pentagon was struck by Flight 77 under the control of Hani Hanjour.

—Richard Clarke's testimony that, during his videoconference in which Rumsfeld and Myers were participating, Jane Garvey of the FAA reported on UA 93 as a possible hijack about 30 minutes before it crashed.

—All the facts that contradict the official theory about the collapses of the World Trade Center buildings.

—The very fact that WTC 7 collapsed.

—The fact that the principals of the company in charge of security at the World Trade Center included a brother and a cousin of President Bush.

Still more examples of the Commission's tendency simply to ignore evidence that conflicted with its account were provided in my book, *The 9/11 Commission Report: Omissions and Distortions*. Here are a few examples:

—The report that Osama bin Laden, who already was America's "most wanted" criminal, was treated in July 2001 by an American doctor in the American Hospital in Dubai and visited by the local CIA agent.[85]

—A report that at a meeting in Berlin in July 2001, US representatives said that because the Taliban refused to agree to a US proposal that would allow a pipeline project to go forward, a war against them would begin by October.[86]

—Evidence that key members of the Bush administration, including Donald Rumsfeld and his deputy Paul Wolfowitz, had been agitating for a war with Iraq for many years.[87]

—The statement by Larry Silverstein, the owner of WTC 7, that while he and the fire department commander were discussing this building, they decided to "pull it."[88]

—The fact that the steel from the WTC buildings was quickly removed from the crime scene and sold before it could be analyzed for evidence of explosives.[89]

—The fact that film from various security cameras could presumably answer the question of what really hit the Pentagon.[90]

—Evidence presented in *The 9/11 Commission Report* and elsewhere that contradicted Myers' claim, endorsed by the Commission, that NORAD had not recognized the possibility that terrorists might use hijacked airliners as missiles.[91]

—Mayor Rudy Giuliani's statement that he had received advance word that the World Trade Center was going to collapse.[92]

To bring out fully how important such omissions could be, I will use the last-mentioned example. Kean and Hamilton admit that they did not ask Giuliani many things they should have, saying: "The questioning of Mayor Giuliani was a low point in terms of the commission's questioning of witnesses at our public hearings. We did not ask tough questions." Indeed, they admit: "Each commissioner opened his or her questioning with lavish praise." Kean himself had begun his questioning by saying, "New York City on that terrible day in a sense was blessed because it had you as a leader," and Hamilton had concluded by saying, "It's important that I simply express to you my appreciation."[93]

However, although it is good that Kean and Hamilton admitted their commission's failure in this case, the "tough questions" they acknowledged that they should have raised were limited to questions about radios and other matters related to the failure to communicate information that might have saved the lives of employees and firefighters in the towers. As important as those questions were, the toughest questions would have involved Giuliani's statement that he knew, prior to the collapse of either tower, that a collapse was coming. Talking on ABC News about his temporary emergency command center at 75 Barkley Street, Giuliani said: "We were operating out of there when we were told that the World Trade Center was gonna collapse, and it did collapse before we could get out of the building."[94]

Given the fact that, prior to 9/11, nothing other than explosives had ever brought down a steel-frame high-rise building, this is a remarkable statement. The firemen who reached the 78th floor of the south tower certainly did not believe that it was going to collapse. Even the 9/11 Commission said that to its knowledge, "none of the [fire] chiefs present believed that a total collapse of either tower was possible."[95] So on what basis would someone have told Giuliani that "the World Trade Center was gonna collapse"?

The most reasonable answer, given all the evidence that the towers were brought down by explosives—which will be discussed more fully in the following chapter—is that someone knew that explosives had been set and were about to be discharged.

We now know from the 9/11 oral histories recorded by the FDNY, moreover, that Giuliani is not the only one who was told that a collapse was coming. At least four of the testimonies indicate that shortly before the collapse of the south tower, the Office of Emergency Management (OEM) had predicted the collapse of at least one tower.[96] The director of OEM reported directly to Giuliani.[97] So although Giuliani said that he and others "were told" that the towers were going to collapse, it was his own people who were doing the telling. The main question the 9/11 Commission should have asked Giuliani was why people in his office were convinced that "the World Trade Center was gonna collapse," given the fact that there was no historical precedent to support that conviction.

Furthermore, if the Commission had interviewed firefighters, rather than simply praising them while not allowing them to tell their stories, they could have learned that the foreknowledge of the South Tower's collapse was even more widespread. Fire Chief Joseph Pfeifer, in his 9/11 oral history, gave this statement about what he observed in the lobby of the North Tower, where a command post had been set up: "[R]ight before the south tower collapsed, I noticed a lot of people just left the lobby, . . . high-level people in government, everybody was gone, almost like they had information that we didn't have."[98] An interview with Giuliani together with Chief Pfeifer might have been most interesting.

As these examples show, the 9/11 Commission was guilty in spades of the fault that Kean and Hamilton (rightly) consider one of the primary characteristics of irrational conspiracy theorists: simply ignoring evidence that does not fit their theory.

That, moreover, is not the only way to mistreat evidence. Unscrupulous conspiracy theorists often distort it. And, as I indicated by subtitling my critique of the Commission's report "Omissions and Distortions," the Commission used distortion as well as omission to try to conceal the fact that its account of 9/11 was in tension with various established facts.

The fact that the Commission sometimes distorted evidence is important. If its only way of dealing with evidence suggesting that 9/11 was an inside job was to ignore it, we might assume that the Commission was simply unaware of such evidence. However, as I pointed out in a prior book, "The fact that the Commission sometimes engaged in [distortion] shows that it was not averse to trying to rebut such evidence."[99] I have long assumed, in fact, that whenever the Commission feared it could not convincingly rebut such evidence, it simply ignored it, but that when it thought it could rebut it, perhaps by distorting it more or less subtly, it would do so. In their new book, Kean and Hamilton partly confirm this assumption, saying: "If, in the course of our inquiry, we could address or knock down a particular conspiracy theory, we did so."[100] They do not, of course, admit that they tried to knock down such theories by distorting the evidence on which they were based. But that they engage in distortion can be seen by looking at a couple of examples mentioned in their new book.

One example involves the fact that there was "an unusually high volume of trades on the parent companies of American and United Airlines." Although some people have concluded from this fact that the traders must have had foreknowledge of the attacks, Kean and Hamilton assure us that the trades "were demonstrably part of a legitimate and innocuous trading strategy" and hence "unrelated to the attacks."[101]

The Commission, however, did not provide evidence to support this conclusion. Its primary claim was that "[a] single US-based institutional investor with no conceivable ties to al Qaeda purchased 95 percent of the UAL puts."[102] The implicit syllogism behind this conclusion, as I have pointed out, was the following:

—The attacks of 9/11 were planned and executed solely by al-Qaeda.

—No other person or agency had any role in, or even advance knowledge of, the attacks.

—The purchaser of the put options on United Airlines stock had no connection with al-Qaeda.

—Therefore the purchaser could not have had any advance knowledge of the attacks.[103]

The Commission's argument, accordingly, was perfectly circular: Taking as unquestionable the assumption that the attacks were planned and executed solely by al-Qaeda, with no help from US officials or anyone else, they concluded that if purchasers did not get advance information about the attacks directly from al-Qaeda, they did not get advance information, period. The Commission hence reached its conclusion by begging the question, which is precisely whether people other than agents of al-Qaeda were involved in planning the attacks.

A second example of distortion involves the issue of whether the FAA had informally told the military about the hijacking of AA Flight 77 considerably before the Pentagon was struck—even earlier than the formal notification time of 9:24 given in NORAD's timeline—as Laura Brown's memo said. One opportunity for this informal notification to have occurred would have been Richard Clarke's videoconference, which, he indicates in *Against All Enemies*, began at about 9:15 and involved Jane Garvey of the FAA and both Donald Rumsfeld and General Richard Myers of the Pentagon. The 9/11 Commission claimed that Clarke's videoconference did not begin until 9:25 and expressed doubt that it was "fully under way before 9:37, when the Pentagon was struck."[104] However, the evidence that this conference really began by 9:15, as Clarke says, is extremely strong. (For one thing, Mineta, as both Clarke and Mineta himself report, stopped in to see Clarke after the videoconference had started, prior to going down to the PEOC, which he reached by 9:20.)[105]

The evidence is very strong, therefore, that the 9/11 Commission's claim to the contrary is a lie, intended to protect its claim that the military had no idea about Flight 77's hijacking before the Pentagon was struck. The 9/11 Commission bolstered its claim about the 9:25 starting time by citing the FAA chronology from 9/11.[106] Part of the distortion of the evidence here would, accordingly, involve doctoring the FAA's chronology—which, according to Laura Brown (as I reported in the previous chapter), had been turned over to the FBI right after 9/11.

There is abundant evidence, therefore, that the third defect of irrational conspiracy theorists pointed out by Kean and Hamilton—their tendency to ignore evidence that contradicts their theories, either by distorting or simply omitting it—is supremely exemplified by their own 9/11 Commission.

Uncritical Acceptance of Dubious Evidence

"One issue that had been seized upon by conspiracy theorists," write Kean and Hamilton, "was that the FAA and NORAD had not followed their protocols on 9/11." Because Kean and Hamilton claim (wrongly) that their Commission had explained away this problem, their statement implies that irrational conspiracy theories involve a fourth defect: Their proponents uncritically accept reputed evidence that, when critically scrutinized, does not really support their theories. Although the example used by Kean and Hamilton does not really provide a case in point, the tendency to which they refer is certainly a defect. But it is the official theory, supported by the 9/11 Commission, that is the principal exemplar of this defect.

We already looked, in the first section of this chapter, at one example of how the Commission supported a major element of its conspiracy theory by uncritically accepting evidence that it should have considered suspect—namely, by (publicly) accepting the NORAD and FAA tapes as giving an accurate picture of what happened on 9/11. (I ignore the question of whether, while some members of the Commission were duped, others participated in the duping.) I will here give two more examples.

Al-Qaeda's Responsibility
Another major element in the Commission's conspiracy theory is, of course, its (public) acceptance of "the notion that the attacks were the work of al Qaeda." This notion is, Kean and Hamilton assure us, supported by "overwhelming evidence." But let us see whether this evidence can survive scrutiny.

Recovered Passports: Part of this evidence, according to Kean and Hamilton, consists of "the four hijacker passports that were recovered— two from the wreckage of United Airlines Flight 93, one that was picked up at the World Trade Center before the towers collapsed, and one from a piece of luggage that did not make it from the hijackers' connecting flight onto American Airline Flight 11."[107] All of these alleged discoveries are highly suspect.

With regard to the passport allegedly found at the World Trade Center, Kean and Hamilton say that it was "picked up . . . before the towers collapsed." One problem with this story, which involved the passport of alleged Flight 11 hijacker Satam al-Sugami (not Mohamed Atta, as widely reported), is that it has come in two versions. According to the first version, the passport was found after the Twin Towers had collapsed. This story was quickly recognized as being very implausible. As a story in the *Guardian* said, "the idea that [this] passport had escaped from that inferno unsinged would [test] the credulity of the staunchest supporter of the FBI's crackdown on terrorism."[108]

Perhaps not surprisingly, that version was replaced by a second one, which was provided by CBS the following January, according to which the passport was found "minutes after" the attack.[109] This second version, which is the one supported by Kean and Hamilton, is perhaps thought to be less implausible. But even this idea—that after AA 11 crashed into the North Tower and ignited a huge fire, a passport belonging to one of the five hijackers would have escaped from the cabin and the building and fallen safely to the ground—is quite far-fetched (to use one of Kean and Hamilton's words).

Perhaps even more far-fetched is the claim that the passports of two hijackers on UA 93, along with one of the red bandanas they were allegedly wearing, were found at the crash site. According to the official story, as we will see in Chapter 4, this plane, because it crashed while flying downward at 580 miles per hour, went completely into the ground. This theory explained why people who came to the site unanimously reported not seeing any part of the plane, not even the tail. Nevertheless, we are told, the authorities found one of the hijacker's red bandanas, undamaged, and the passport of Ziad Jarrah, said to have been flying the plane. So we are supposed to believe that although Jarrah's body, being in the cockpit, was thrust dozens of feet into the ground, his passport, presumably in his pocket, flew out of the cockpit and, along with one of the bandanas, landed intact on the surface of the ground. This is, incidentally, one of the pieces of nonsense in the official story that is told as sober truth by Guy Smith's BBC documentary, *The Conspiracy Files: 9/11*. (With regard to Kean and Hamilton's statement that two passports were found at this site: Susan Ginzburg, the 9/11 Commission's chief counsel, did testify that the passport of Saeed al-Ghamdi was also found; but it was never produced.)[110]

Atta's Luggage: I turn now to the passport allegedly found in "a piece of luggage that did not make it from the hijackers' connecting flight onto American Airline Flight 11." The official story is that on September 11, Mohamed Atta and another alleged hijacker, Abdullah al-Omari, drove a rented Nissan Altima from Boston up to Portland, Maine, stayed overnight, then took a commuter flight back to Boston the next morning in time to catch AA Flight 11, but that Atta's luggage did not get loaded onto Flight 11 because the commuter flight was too late. Authorities later allegedly discovered in this luggage various incriminating materials—such as flight simulation manuals for Boeing airplanes, a copy of the Quran, a religious cassette tape, a note to other hijackers about mental preparation—and also Atta's passport and will.[111]

But this story is riddled with problems. First, there was, as even the 9/11 Commission points out, a full hour between the arrival of the commuter flight and the departure of Flight 11,[112] so there is no explanation as to why his bags would have been left behind.

Second, why would Atta, who was already in Boston, have gone up and stayed overnight in Portland, hence making it necessary to take an early morning commuter flight back to Boston on September 11? Commuter flights are often delayed. Would Atta, allegedly the "ringleader" of the hijackers, have risked blowing the whole operation, for which he had been preparing for well over a year, by doing such a thing? The 9/11 Commission admitted that it had no answer as to why Atta and al-Omari went to Portland.[113] In the present book, Kean and Hamilton, perhaps seeking to overcome this embarrassment, report that an FBI agent suggested that Atta and al-Omari took the flight from Portland to avoid having "five Arab men all arriving at Boston's Logan Airport at once for Flight 11."[114] It apparently did not occur to Kean, Hamilton, and this FBI agent that this problem could have been avoided far less dangerously by simply having the five Arab men arrive in separate cars.

A third problem with this story of Atta's baggage is that Atta surely would not have taken his will on a plane that he was going to crash into the World Trade Center, creating a fiery inferno in which all his belongings would be burned up.

The Kean–Hamilton adjective "far-fetched" is not adequate for this story; it requires their term for the most outrageous conspiracy theories: absurd.

We can make sense of Atta's Portland trip, however, if we assume that it was set up by someone partly so that Atta's luggage with the incriminating contents would be "found" and partly to provide an opportunity for the security video frames showing Atta and al-Omari at the Portland airport to be taken—photos that "were flashed round the world and gave a kick start to the official story in the vital hours after the attacks," partly because they were widely thought to have been taken at Boston's Logan airport rather than at Portland. (There were, in fact, no photos of them at Boston's Logan airport, which, as a major international airport, was surely better equipped with security cameras than was Portland's airport.)[115]

Atta and the ISI: This hypothesis—that Atta went to Portland under orders from someone—would fit with reports about Atta and Pakistan's intelligence agency that those supporting the official account about 9/11 have tried to hush up. According to one report, conveyed by the *Wall Street Journal*, General Mahmoud Ahmad, the head of Pakistan's ISI (Inter-Services Intelligence), ordered $100,000 to be wired to Mohamed Atta.[116] This was a "damning link," as Agence France Presse called it, given the close relations that had long existed between the ISI and the CIA.[117] One could speculate that the CIA used the ISI to funnel money to Atta.

The embarrassment for the US government was made even worse by the report that ISI chief Ahmad was in Washington the week prior to 9/11, spending most of his time meeting with CIA chief George Tenet (but also meeting with officials in the Pentagon, the National Security Council, and the State Department).[118] This meeting between the US and Pakistani intelligence chiefs was made even more remarkable by the fact that Ahmad Shah Masood, the charismatic leader of the Northern Alliance in

Afghanistan, was assassinated on September 9, the very day the Tenet–Ahmad meetings came to an end. This could, of course, be simply a coincidence, and it was treated as such by the 9/11 Commission, which said that Masood was killed by "al Qaeda assassins."[119] The Commission failed, however, to mention a Reuters story reporting that the Northern Alliance claimed that the assassination by the al-Qaeda agents was sponsored by the ISI.[120] (The reason this may be important is that US interests were served by the death of Masood. Not only was he a charismatic leader who would have probably headed up a post-Taliban government after the US bombing of Afghanistan [which had been planned prior to 9/11]; he was also supporting Argentina's bid to build an oil-and-gas pipeline through Afghanistan, thereby opposing Unocal, which was backed by the United States. I have explained this more fully elsewhere.[121])

A potentially "damning link" might have been revealed if the fact of ISI chief Ahmad's presence in Washington the week before 9/11 had become widely known, especially if this fact had been connected to the report that Ahmad's ISI had wired money to Atta. It would not be surprising, therefore, to learn that the Bush administration attempted to suppress the story. Michel Chossudovsky has drawn attention to a White House transcript suggesting that such an attempt was in fact made.

Chossudovsky first points out that the following interchange occurred between a reporter and Condoleezza Rice during her press conference on May 16, 2002:

> QUESTION: Are you aware of the reports at the time that the ISI chief was in Washington on September 11th, and on September 10th, $100,000 was wired from Pakistan to these groups in this area? And why he was here? Was he meeting with you or anybody in the administration?
>
> MS. RICE: I have not seen that report, and he was certainly not meeting with me.

This transcript of the press conference was issued by the Federal News Service. However, Chossudovsky then points out, the White House version of this transcript begins thus:

> QUESTION: Dr. Rice, are you aware of the reports at the time that (inaudible) was in Washington on September 11th. . . ?

This version of the transcript, which does not contain the information that the person being discussed was "the ISI chief," was the version provided by the White House to the news media. It was, for example, the version reported on the CNN show "Inside Politics" later that day.[122]

This effort at suppression by the White House was evidently successful, because to this day few Americans seem to realize either that General Ahmad was present in Washington the week of 9/11 or that he reportedly ordered $100,000 to be wired to Mohamed Atta. Americans certainly did not learn these facts from the 9/11 Commission, in spite of its stated effort to provide "the fullest possible account of the events surrounding 9/11." The closest the Commission came to reporting General Ahmad's remarkable presence in Washington during that remarkable week was to mention that on September 13, Deputy Secretary of State Richard Armitage met with "the visiting head of Pakistan's military intelligence service, Mahmud Ahmed."[123] For all the reader would know, General Ahmad had come to Washington only after 9/11, perhaps to offer help.

The Commission's failure here becomes even more significant in light of evidence that the ISI may have transferred as much as $325,000 to Atta.[124] If this is correct, it would mean that Pakistan—America's major Asian ally in the war on terror—provided most of the $400,000 to $500,000 that the Commission believed the 9/11 operation to have required.[125] This would be quite an oversight.

The Commission, to be sure, follows up that estimate with the statement that "we have seen no evidence that any foreign government— or foreign government official—supplied any funding." But that appears clearly to be a lie. A *Los Angeles Times* story, based on interviews with Bob Kerrey and other members of the 9/11 Commission in June 2004, reported that these members reported that the Commission had uncovered "extensive evidence" of assistance to al-Qaeda by both Pakistan and Saudi Arabia. The reporter added that "the bipartisan commission is wrestling with how to characterize such politically sensitive information in its final report, and even whether to include it."[126] The resulting decision, obviously, was not only to omit this information but also to lie about it.

Alleged Hijackers as Patsies: As this exploration of the apparent link between Atta and Pakistan's ISI shows, the available evidence about the alleged hijackers not only fails to support the official theory; it also lends support to an alternative theory, which suggests that Atta and the others were patsies. The money funneled to Atta combined with his otherwise inexplicable trip to Portland suggests that he was, at least to some extent, a willing patsy.

The idea that Atta was simply paid to play his role in the 9/11 drama is also consistent with the evidence, reported in the previous chapter, that conflicts with the 9/11 Commission's image of Atta as "fanatically" religious. This image of Atta and the other alleged hijackers as devout Muslims, ready to meet their maker, was essential to the Commission's characterization of them as a "cadre of trained operatives willing to die."[127] That characterization of them would have been much less believable if the Commission had mentioned the reports that Atta loved gambling, cocaine, alcohol, pork, and lap dances, and if they also mentioned the *Wall Street Journal*'s report, in an editorial entitled

"Terrorist Stag Parties," that several of the other men had similar appetites, which they sometimes indulged in Las Vegas.[128] This information fits much better with the hypothesis that these young men were being paid to play out a role—a role that would not require them to commit suicide.

Of course, we will surely need to wait until there is a genuinely independent and thorough investigation of 9/11 to learn exactly what role Atta and the other men played in the plan (and also if, as considerable evidence suggests, there were two men going by the name of "Mohamed Atta"[129]). But we already have enough information to conclude that the official story about their role on 9/11 is extremely dubious at best.

Security Videos: One apparent role for Atta and al-Omari, we have seen, was to get a photo of themselves taken in Portland. Another alleged hijacker evidently had a similar role. On July 21, 2004, the same day as *The 9/11 Commission Report* was published, a video was distributed worldwide as corroboration of the official story by the Associated Press. The caption reads: "Hijacker Khalid al-Mihdhar . . . passes through the security checkpoint at Dulles International Airport in Chantilly, Va., Sept. 11 2001, just hours before American Airlines Flight 77 crashed into the Pentagon in this image from a surveillance video." This would appear to be the video mentioned in a note of *The 9/11 Commission Report*, which refers to "Metropolitan Washington Airport Authority videotape, Dulles main terminal checkpoints, Sept 11 2001." So this video is presumably part of the "overwhelming evidence" of al-Qaeda responsibility for 9/11 to which Kean and Hamilton would appeal.

However, as Rowland Morgan and Ian Henshall point out, "a normal security video has time and date burned into the integral video image by proprietary equipment according to an authenticated pattern, along with camera identification and the location that the camera covered. The video released in 2004 contained no such data." Accordingly, in spite of what the AP told the world, there was no evidence that this video was taken on September 11 or even at Dulles.[130] Moreover, as Jay Kolar has shown, as part of his devastating examination of official evidence for the alleged hijackers, there are several other facts that challenge the authenticity of the Dulles video, including the fact that the man on the video said to be Hani Hanjour "does not remotely resemble Hanjour."[131]

Phone Calls: Another part of the "overwhelming evidence" of al-Qaeda's responsibility to which Kean and Hamilton might appeal is suggested by their reference to "the phone calls placed to and from passengers on United 93."[132] That is, they could say that phone calls from passengers on this and other flights provided ample evidence that the planes had been hijacked by Arab Muslims. However, as we saw in the previous chapter, the alleged cell phone calls most certainly did not occur, given their technological impossibility in 2001. And if the alleged cell phone calls were fabricated, the same is surely true of the alleged calls from the seat-back phones.

19 Dead Men: At this point, Kean and Hamilton, even if they would grant that the types of evidence discussed above are at least dubious, would most likely say that it still remains true that after 9/11, as they put it, "[t]he nineteen perpetrators were dead."[133] Their meaning, of course, is that the 19 men who were identified as the hijackers by the FBI were dead. That, however, remains a claim for which no publicly verifiable evidence was ever provided. We have, for example, been given no proof that the remains of any of these men were found at any of the crash sites (I discuss the Pentagon site in Chapter 4).

The claim that all of the named nineteen men are dead is, moreover, a claim that was contradicted by reports in the British press. For example, a story by David Bamford on BBC News eleven days after 9/11 reported that Waleed al-Shehri notified authorities and journalists in Morocco, where he was working as a pilot, that he was still very much alive. In Bamford's words:

> The FBI named five men with Arab names who they say were responsible for deliberately crashing American Airlines Flight 11 into the World Trade Center. One of those five names was Waleed Al-Shehri, a Saudi pilot who had trained in the United States. His photograph was released by the FBI, and has been shown in newspapers and on television around the world. That same Mr. Al-Shehri has turned up in Morocco, proving clearly that he was not a member of the suicide attack. He told Saudi journalists in Casablanca that he has contacted both the Saudi and American authorities to advise them that he had nothing to do with the attack. He acknowledges that he attended flight training school at Dayton [sic] Beach in the United States, and is indeed the same Waleed Al-Shehri to whom the FBI has been referring.[134]

A day later, a story in the *Telegraph* by David Harrison reported that several other alleged hijackers were still alive.[135]

It is possible, of course, that the 9/11 Commission might have been able to explain away all the problems created by these stories in such a way that its basic claim—that the airliners had been hijacked by members of al-Qaeda—could have been salvaged. (One of the men discussed by Harrison, for example, turned out to be a case of mistaken identity.[136]) But *The 9/11 Commission Report* made no attempt to do this. It simply repeated the FBI's report about the 19 men, even reproducing their photographs. With regard to Waleed al-Shehri in particular, the Commission speculated that he stabbed one of the flight attendants shortly before Flight 11 crashed into the North Tower.[137]

The official story about the hijackers is also thrown into serious doubt by the discovery of overwhelming evidence that Ziad Jarrah, the man said to have piloted the hijacked UA 93, had a double.[138] The official story is made even more dubious by the fact that although "Jarrah's family has indicated they would be willing to provide DNA samples to US researchers, . . . the FBI has shown no interest thus far."[139]

If one of the marks of a conspiracy theory in the pejorative sense is that it uncritically employs evidence that has been shown to be dubious, the 9/11 Commission's conspiracy theory stands condemned by Kean and Hamilton's own criterion.

Osama bin Laden's Role: However, they might reply, even if there are doubts about the identity of the hijackers, surely there can be no doubt about the main element in the case for al-Qaeda's responsibility: the fact that the 9/11 attacks were authorized by Osama bin Laden. To the contrary, however, there are good grounds for doubt even on this basic point.

Shortly after 9/11, Secretary of State Colin Powell promised to provide a white paper providing proof that the attacks had been planned by bin Laden, but this paper was never produced. British Prime Minister Tony Blair did provide such a paper, which was entitled "Responsibility for the Terrorist Atrocities in the United States." But it began with the admission that it "does not purport to provide a prosecutable case against Usama Bin Laden in a court of law."[140] Also, although the Taliban said that it would hand bin Laden over if the United States presented evidence of his involvement in 9/11, Bush refused.[141]

This failure to provide proof was later said to be unnecessary because bin Laden, in a video allegedly found in Afghanistan late in 2001, admitted responsibility for the attacks. This "confession" is now widely cited as proof. As I mentioned in the introduction, however, this video is widely thought to be far from definitive, with some people even calling it a fabrication. "It's bogus," says Professor Bruce Lawrence, who is widely regarded as the leading academic bin Laden expert in America and who adds that, according to informants within the US intelligence community's bin Laden units, everyone there knows that the video is a fake.[142]

The most damning lack of evidence for bin Laden's involvement, however, comes from the agency that, according to Kean and Hamilton, was the most cooperative with the Commission's investigation. If one looks up "Usama bin Laden" on the FBI's web page for Most Wanted Terrorists, one will find that he is wanted for bombings of US embassies in Dar es Salaam, Tanzania, and Nairobi and that he is "a suspect in other terrorist attacks throughout the world." But one would—at least as this book was going to press—not find any mention of 9/11. Puzzled by this, Ed Haas, the author of the Muckraker Report, contacted FBI headquarters to ask why. Rex Tomb, chief of investigative publicity for the FBI, replied:

"The reason why 9/11 is not mentioned on Usama Bin Laden's Most Wanted page is because the FBI has no hard evidence connecting Bin Laden to 9/11."[143] (This statement suggests that this department of the FBI did not find any of the bin Laden "confession videos" convincing.)

Many people will, of course, find this shocking. But is it not equally shocking that Kean and Hamilton, while ridiculing other conspiracy theories as employing dubious evidence, do not even mention the FBI's admission, which has long been implicitly present on its website, that it has no hard evidence that bin Laden had anything to do with 9/11? It cannot be claimed, incidentally, that the 9/11 Commission was not aware of the fact that the FBI's page on bin Laden does not mention 9/11. In February 2004, the Family Steering Committee submitted a number of questions for the Commission to ask President Bush, one of which was: "Please comment on the fact that UBL's profile on the FBI's Ten Most Wanted Fugitives poster does not include the 9/11 attacks."[144]

False-Flag Operation: We have, in any case, two hypotheses about the alleged hijackers. According to the government's hypothesis, the 9/11 attacks were actually carried out by these 19 men, under orders from the al-Qaeda leaders, most importantly Osama bin Laden. A big problem for this hypothesis is to account for the fact that all the evidence for it seems, when scrutinized, to dissolve.

According to the alternative conspiracy theory that is accepted by most of the 9/11 truth movement, 9/11 was an example of a government false-flag operation, in which evidence is planted in order to convince a nation that it has been attacked by the very people that the government had already decided to attack. For example, when the Japanese in 1931 wanted to take over Manchuria, they blew up their own railroad tracks near Mukden, then blamed the Chinese. When the Nazis wanted to crack down on Communists and Social Democrats, they set fire to the Reichstag and blamed the Communists. Then when the Nazis were ready to invade Poland, they had Germans dressed as Poles stage a series of attacks on German sites near the border with Poland. When the United States during the Cold War wanted to prevent leftist parties in Western European countries such as France, Italy, and Belgium from coming to power through democratic elections, the CIA and the Pentagon used right-wing organizations to carry out terrorists attacks that, thanks to planted evidence, were blamed on Communists and other leftists.[145]

On the basis of the hypothesis that 9/11 was also a false-flag operation, we can explain both why there was so much prima facie evidence that the attacks were carried out by members of al-Qaeda but also why none of this evidence—the NORAD tapes, the passports, the security video frames, the evidence reportedly found in Atta's luggage, the phone calls from passengers, the bin Laden confession video—will stand up under scrutiny. This false-flag hypothesis, by being able to explain all this evidence in a way that is consistent with all the other evidence about 9/11 that can survive scrutiny, is clearly far more adequate than the official hypothesis.

Reliance on Third-Hand Evidence

We are looking at ways in which the 9/11 Commission's conspiracy theory draws on suspect evidence. The first example was the Commission's use of dubious—probably planted—evidence to support its claim that al-Qaeda was responsible for the attacks. I turn now to a type of evidence that is so obviously dubious that Kean and Hamilton even admit it.

The greatest difficulty they had in getting access to people and information they needed, they report, was "obtaining access to star witnesses in custody . . . , most notably Khalid Sheikh Mohammed, a mastermind of the attacks, and [Ramzi] Binalshibh, who helped coordinate the attacks from Europe."[146] Kean and Hamilton explain why getting such access was essential:

> These and other detainees were the only possible source for inside information about the plot. If the commission was mandated to provide an authoritative account of the 9/11 attacks, it followed that our mandate afforded us the right to learn what these detainees had to say about 9/11.[147]

This was a right, however, that they were not given and that they in the end did not even demand. After CIA director Tenet turned down their initial request for access to the "more than one hundred detainees," they narrowed their request to "only seven key detainees," but this request was also denied. They then offered a compromise:

> [The Commission's] interrogators could be blindfolded on their way to the interrogation point so that they would not know where they were. . . . [They would not] interrogate the detainees themselves [but would instead] observe the interrogation through one-way glass [so that they] could at least observe the detainee's demeanor and evaluate his credibility. Or our staff could listen to an interrogation telephonically, and offer questions or follow-up questions to the CIA interrogator through an earpiece.[148]

But this compromise was also rejected.

Accordingly, believing strongly that they needed at least this much access because otherwise they "could not evaluate the credibility of the detainees' accounts," they considered going public with their demand. However, "[t]he Bush administration pleaded with us not to take the issue public." And so, evidently assuming that the Bush administration made this plea not because it had anything to hide but only, as it claimed, because it "did not want to risk interrupting the interrogation of these detainees [by the CIA], which was important to US efforts to obtain intelligence to thwart attacks, capture terrorists, and save American lives," the Commission "decided not to take the issue public."[149]

It instead accepted Tenet's best offer: the CIA would appoint a "project manager," through whom "we could submit questions and follow-up questions." But this procedure meant, as Kean and Hamilton point out, that "they were receiving information thirdhand—passed from the detainee, to the interrogator, to the person who writes up the interrogation report, and finally to our staff in the form of reports, not even transcripts." The Commission "never even got to meet with the people conducting the interrogations."[150]

The implications were serious, as Kean and Hamilton admit, saying: "We . . . had no way of evaluating the credibility of detainee information. How could we tell if someone such as Khalid Sheikh Mohammed . . . was telling us the truth?"[151] With regard to Khalid Sheikh Mohammed— usually referred to simply as "KSM"—the Commission was completely at the mercy of the CIA. The CIA could have simply made up anything that it thought would bolster the official account of 9/11, then claimed that this alleged fact was learned during an "interrogation of KSM"—a phrase that occurs ad nauseam in the notes to The 9/11 Commission Report, especially the notes for the all-important Chapter 5, "Al Qaeda Aims at the American Homeland."

In spite of these severe problems, Kean and Hamilton assure us that it all worked out: "we did get access to the information we needed; our report . . . draws heavily on information from detainees, notably Khalid Sheikh Mohammed and Ramzi Binalshibh." Now Kean and Hamilton's statement may be true in the sense that they got "the information [they] needed" to portray the attacks as having been authorized by bin Laden. But if the question is whether they got the information that they would have needed to give a true account of 9/11, they, by their own admission, can have no such confidence. For all they know (assuming the truth of what they have told us), KSM might not have made a single statement attributed to him.

In light of this awareness—that every claim in The 9/11 Commission Report that is attributed to KSM (or to Ramzi Binalshibh or any other alleged detainee) is a third-hand claim that must be considered suspect— let us look at a string of assertions made by the Commission:

> Khalid Sheikh Mohammad [was] the principal architect of the 9/11 attacks. . . . KSM arranged a meeting with Bin Ladin in Tora Bora [and] presented the al Qaeda leader with a menu of ideas for terrorist operations. . . . KSM also presented a proposal for an operation that would involve training pilots who would crash planes into buildings in the United States. This proposal eventually would become the 9/11 operation. . . . Bin Ladin

... finally decided to give the green light for the 9/11 operation sometime in late 1998 or early 1999. . . . KSM reasoned he could best influence US policy by targeting the country's economy. . . . New York, which KSM considered the economic capital of the United States, therefore became the primary target. . . . Bin Ladin summoned KSM to Kandahar in March or April 1999 to tell him that al Qaeda would support his proposal. . . . Bin Ladin wanted to destroy the White House and the Pentagon, KSM wanted to strike the World Trade Center. . . . Bin Ladin also soon selected four individuals to serve as suicide operatives.[152]

If one turns to the endnotes to find the source of these bits of information, one finds in every case: "interrogation(s) of KSM."[153]

The implication, of course, is that everything the Commission tells us about al-Qaeda's intent to attack America is suspect. Incredibly, Kean and Hamilton, in their new book, admit this, saying that when they could not corroborate the reports attributed to KSM or other detainees—which was surely the case in most instances—"it was left to the reader to consider the credibility of the source—we had no opportunity to do so."[154] They, in other words, had no way of knowing whether any of the statements in the indented material above is true.

Theories that reject the notion that 9/11 was orchestrated by al-Qaeda are irrational, Kean and Hamilton charge, because that notion is supported by "overwhelming evidence." Once this evidence is carefully scrutinized, however, it turns out to be quite underwhelming. We can perhaps understand, therefore, why the FBI knows that it has no "hard evidence" connecting Osama bin Laden with the attacks of 9/11.

Disdain for Open and Informed Debate

As we have seen, the first four defects attributed by Kean and Hamilton to irrational conspiracy theorists—meaning those "assigning culpability for 9/11 to the Bush administration"—are actually exemplified by the conspiracy theorists making up the 9/11 Commission: The Commission began with its conclusion; it affirmed many ideas that are disproved by facts; it either ignored or distorted facts that contradict its theory; and it uncritically accepted dubious facts. I turn now to the fifth defect that Kean and Hamilton attribute to irrational conspiracy theorists: a "disdain for open and informed debate."

As one who holds a theory "assigning culpability for 9/11 to the Bush administration," I must say that of all the charges leveled by Kean and Hamilton, this one is the most hilarious. Members of the 9/11 truth movement have been seeking open and informed debate about 9/11, while members of the Bush administration, the 9/11 Commission, and other official agencies have shown disdain for such debate. They will never meet us in a public forum, such as an auditorium or a radio or TV talk show, where we could have a back-and-forth debate. For a long time, they simply ignored our evidence and arguments. More recently, they have taken to issuing *ex cathedra* statements in books and magazines and on websites. Members of the 9/11 movement read their statements and sometimes offer point-by-point responses (as in the present book). But the members of the Bush administration, the 9/11 Commission, or other official agencies that have dealt with 9/11 will not respond in turn to our arguments—except perhaps to dismiss them as "absurd" or "nutty."

A particularly striking example of this refusal to debate has been reported by Ed Haas on his Muckraker Report website. Haas had a telephone conversation with Michael Newman, spokesman for the Public and Business Affairs department of the National Institute of Standards and Technology (NIST), which has provided the official report on the collapse of the Twin Towers. Haas, after pointing out that "more than half of all Americans now believe the US government has some complicity if not culpability regarding 9/11"—a fact that Newman did not dispute—suggested that "a possible method to reconcile the division in the United States between the government and its people" might be to have a series of televised debates between the scientists who worked on the NIST report and scientists who question its plausibility. Before he could get his suggestion fully out, Haas reports, he "was abruptly interrupted and told that none of the NIST scientists would participate in any public debate."[155]

Newman's response was especially interesting in light of the fact that earlier in the discussion, Newman had compared those who reject the government's account of the collapses with people who believe in Bigfoot and a flat earth. If Newman truly believes that NIST's account is accurate and that people who reject it are so irrational, would he not be confident that NIST's scientists could show them up for the fools they are and thereby bring to an end the growing skepticism about the government's account?

NIST, moreover, is not the only official defender of the official conspiracy theory with disdain for open debate. This fact was brought out through another attempt by Haas to organize a debate. His first step was to obtain an agreement from seven members of Scholars for 9/11 Truth to participate in a national (televised) debate about 9/11 that would take place in Charleston, South Carolina, on September 16, 2006. These members included an attorney, a former member of the US Air Force, and professors of physics, mechanical engineering, economics, philosophy of science, and philosophy of religion (myself). This would not seem to be a group of people so lacking in intelligence and status that to debate them would be demeaning to public officials. Not one of them, to my knowledge, believes that the earth is flat or has gone searching for Bigfoot. In any case, Haas, having this team ready to debate, proceeded to invite the thirteen scientists responsible for the NIST report on the Twin Towers plus the ten members of the 9/11 Commission, including, of course, Kean and Hamilton.

Not a single one of these invitees accepted. The NIST scientists did not even respond. After Haas sent several more invitations to them, he received a message from Newman saying: "The project leaders of the NIST World Trade Center investigation team respectfully decline your invitations to participate in the National 9/11 Debate on September 16, 2006." Haas then asked Newman if there was a better date or location, to which Newman sent an e-mail reply saying: "The members of the NIST WTC Investigation Team has [sic] respectfully declined your invitation to participate in the National 9/11 Debate. A change in venue or date will not alter that decision."[156] Whether this response represented a disdain for debate or some other attitude—such as *fear* to debate—it certainly represented a *refusal* to debate.

Also, in light of the fact that *Popular Mechanics* has become somewhat of a semi-official defender of the official story about 9/11, Haas also sent invitations to James B. Meigs, the editor-in-chief of *Popular Mechanics* (which in March 2005 published "9/11: Debunking the Myths"), and to Brad Reagan and David Dunbar, the editors of the book version published in 2006, *Debunking 9/11 Myths*. In his letter of invitation, Haas, besides pointing out that all expenses would be covered, added:

> I have noted that *Popular Mechanics* is now touting itself as the final answer that debunks 9/11 myths. The question now is will the people behind and responsible for the book titled *Debunking 9/11 Myths*, people such as yourself, stand firmly behind your work and participate in the National 9/11 Debate?

This letter was sent August 24, 2006. As of March 1, 2007, Haas had received no reply from any of these men.[157]

With regard to Kean and Hamilton, it should be observed that had they accepted the invitation, they would have had the opportunity to debate me and other members of what they call the loony left. When asked on talk shows whether they would be willing to debate me and other members of the 9/11 truth movement, they have said "no" on the grounds that they would not want to "lend credibility" to our views. But if they really believe that we are "loony" and "irrational" and hold views that are "absurd," then they would surely be confident that they could demonstrate this in a public debate, thereby destroying whatever credibility we may have. Kean and Hamilton's refusal to debate is more plausibly explained, I suggest, by their knowledge that it is their own conspiracy theory, not ours, that cannot be defended in "open and informed debate."

Conclusion

In a self-congratulatory discussion, Kean and Hamilton suggest that although their commission was "set up to fail," they nevertheless succeeded.[158] As to the meaning of "success," they evidently meant that they put out a report that "the broad majority of the American people could accept."[159] Most Americans probably assumed that the Commission was working with a somewhat more ambitious criterion of success, such as: to discover and report the truth about what happened on 9/11.

Be that as it may, was *The 9/11 Commission Report* a success even by Kean and Hamilton's standard? Evidently not. A Zogby Poll taken in May 2006 indicated that 42 percent of the American public believes that the government and the 9/11 Commission have covered up evidence contradicting the official account. Only 48 percent, moreover, said that they were confident that there had *not* been a cover-up.[160] So, far from being accepted by a "broad majority" of the American people, the Commission's report is evidently not even accepted by a *bare* majority.

Kean and Hamilton also measure their success partly by the fact that they "had the support of an extraordinary outside group: the 9/11 families." Although they admit that the Commission's relations with the families "were up and down, and sometimes very difficult," they suggest that the families continued to support the Commission: "Their public voice did not waver." Kean and Hamilton also say that their book "was a bestseller" because "it answered people's questions."[161] However, did the Commission, by answering the questions of the 9/11 families, retain their support? A film about the 9/11 families, *9/11: Press for Truth*, suggests that it did not. Near the end of the film, one of the family members, Monica Gabrielle, says: "What we're left with after our journey are no answers. . . . I've wasted four years of my life." Another family member, Bob McIlvaine, says: "I'm so pissed off at this government, because of this cover-up."[162]

Kean and Hamilton suggest one more criterion of success by saying: "As for conspiracy theorists, it is hard to say how many minds we changed."[163] I personally know of no one whose mind was changed by *The 9/11 Commission Report*. Reading through the customer reviews for it on amazon.com, moreover, I did not find anyone saying that his or her mind had been changed by it.

Reading through these reviews in historical order, in fact, suggests that increasingly fewer people accept the *Report*. In 2004, the year the *Report* appeared, the reviews were overwhelmingly positive, with most reviewers awarding the book five stars. However, in 2005 and 2006, as the public became increasingly aware of the facts revealed by the 9/11 truth movement, the reviews became increasingly negative, one-star reviews. On the day I was writing this paragraph, for example, the five most recent reviews had these headings: "Whitewash. A rewrite of history"; "An Absolute Travesty—Deliberately Misleading"; "A perfect example of the US administration 'creating its own reality'"; "The Omission and Distortion Report"; and "Fiction. More lies per square inch than the Warren Commission Report."

Insofar as minds have changed about 9/11, the change all seems to go in the other direction. Millions of people who once believed the official story have come to doubt it, as the 2006 Zogby poll indicated, or even to accept the view that the government was complicit in the attacks, as indicated in a Scripps/Ohio University poll later that same year. According to this poll, as we saw in the introduction, 36 percent of the American people think it likely that "federal officials either participated in the attacks on the World Trade Center and the Pentagon or took no action to stop them 'because they wanted the United States to go to war in the Middle East.'"[164] The very "conspiracy theory" that Kean and Hamilton sought to debunk is already accepted by over a third of the American population.

The fact that all of the conversions about 9/11 go in only one direction, away from the official story, is an important test of truth. If the official story were true, we would expect that people, as they received more and more information about various aspects of the story, would become increasingly convinced of its truth, or that, if they had doubted its truth, would come to embrace it. But this apparently does not occur. As people learn more and more facts about 9/11, they tend to reject the official story in favor of the alternative conspiracy theory. This one-way direction of the intellectual conversions suggests that the evidence for the alternative theory is stronger than that for the official theory.

Appendix: My Ersatz Interview of Lee Hamilton

Neither Thomas Kean nor Lee Hamilton, as I indicated above, have agreed to participate in the National 9/11 Debate. I doubt, moreover, whether I will ever have the chance to discuss the 9/11 Commission's report with either of them in a public setting. In 2006, however, Hamilton was interviewed for a television program on the Canadian Broadcasting Corporation.[165] This interview was conducted by a man who, having read some of my writings,[166] asked many of the questions I would have asked. This exchange can, therefore, be considered my ersatz interview of Lee Hamilton, whose responses are quite revealing.

Cell Phone Calls

One question raised by the interviewer, Evan Solomon, involved the alleged cell phone calls from United Flight 93. Solomon first pointed out that this plane's flight path shows that "it flew well over 10,000 feet—

30,000, 40,000 feet—from about 9:30 onward." He then said: "one allegation . . . is: cell phones don't work above 10,000 feet, so how could people get on their cell phone on a plane and phone their relatives?"

Hamilton replied: "I'm no expert on that. I've been told cell phones work—sometimes—above 10,000 feet, and as high as 30,000 feet. So it may have been that some of the calls went through and some didn't, I just don't know."

So, although the official story would necessarily be false if these cell phones calls were not genuine, Hamilton simply says he's no expert—meaning he did not see it as part of his duty as vice chair of the 9/11 Commission to become well informed about this issue, even though the Commission's report states, as historical fact, that several cell phone calls were made from UA 93. Hamilton then adds that he has "been told" that cell phones sometimes work "as high as 30,000 feet," even though he had just been asked about 40,000 feet, which was appropriate because the Commission's report said that the plane was at 40,700 during the period many of the calls would have been made.[167]

We can assume from Hamilton's response that the question of the possibility of these calls was not something that was discussed during the Commission's deliberations. So, although some people have said that such calls must be possible because the 9/11 Commission thought so, Hamilton's response provides no basis for such confidence.

The ISI Payment to Mohamed Atta

Referring to "the Pakistani Secret Service, called the ISI," Solomon said: "there's some allegations and evidence to show that they paid Mohamed Atta $100,000. The reason this is important is: who funded the people who conducted the attacks, the terrorist attacks? What did the Commission make of payment from the ISI to Mohamed Atta of $100,000?" Hamilton replied: "I don't know anything about it." Solomon then asked: "Did the Commission investigate any connection between ISI, Pakistani intelligence, and . . . ," to which Hamilton, interrupting before the question could be completed, replied: "We may have but I don't recall it."

Solomon's question is obviously highly important. If the ISI paid Atta $100,000, this could suggest that Pakistan, America's alleged ally, had funded a terrorist plot against this country. Or, given the fact that the ISI had long been closely related to the CIA, this story, which our government has not refuted, could suggest that the CIA had helped orchestrate 9/11. Hamilton's reply, however, implies either that the Commission did not discuss this matter or that, if it did, Hamilton found the discussion so unimportant that he did not remember it.

Mineta's Testimony and Cheney's Descent

Solomon, asking about when "Vice President Dick Cheney . . . went down to the protective bunker," said: "[T]here was some suggestion that the Secretary of Transport[ation], [Norman] Mineta, testified in front of the Commission that he in fact talked to Dick Cheney at 9:20AM . . . That was eventually omitted from the final report. Can you tell us a bit about what Secretary of Transport[ation] Mineta told the Commission about where Dick Cheney was prior to 10AM?" Hamilton replied: "I do not recall." When Solomon started to ask a follow-up question, Hamilton said: "Well, we think that Vice President Cheney entered the bunker shortly before 10 o'clock."

Later in the interview, Hamilton said, "I do not know at this point of any factual error in our report." Yet he had here been confronted with what is arguably the most obvious and important factual error in *The 9/11 Commission Report*. In my book-length critique of this report, I filled four pages with evidence, which included Mineta's testimony, that the Commission's claim that Cheney did not reach the bunker until shortly before 10AM was a lie. And yet Hamilton could "not recall" Mineta's testimony and then, when reminded of it, simply reaffirmed the Commission's claim.

This exchange shows, as clearly as anything could, that *The 9/11 Commission Report* cannot be trusted. It also provides strong evidence that Hamilton's claims not to remember cannot be believed. He was the one doing the questioning when Mineta reported on the young man who came in repeatedly to tell Vice President Cheney that an aircraft was approaching, and Hamilton began his questioning of Mineta by saying: "You were there [in the PEOC] for a good part of the day. I think you were there with the Vice President." And Mineta's exchange with Timothy Roemer, during which it was established that Mineta had arrived there at about 9:20, came immediately afterward.[168]

The Time of the Shootdown Authorization

Solomon, having noted that Richard Clarke, in his book *Against All Enemies*, said that he had received authorization from Dick Cheney to shoot down Flight 93 at about 9:50AM, said: "In the Commission's report, it said the authorization didn't come from Dick Cheney until 10:25, and Richard Clarke's testimony . . . isn't mentioned in the Commission's. . . . Why didn't you mention that?" Hamilton replied: "Look, you've obviously gone through the report with a fine-toothed comb, you're raising a lot of questions. . . . All I want from you is evidence. You're just citing a lot of things, without any evidence to back them up, as far as I can see."

Solomon, however, *had* cited evidence—the report that Atta had received $100,000 from the ISI; Norman Mineta's statement about seeing

Cheney in the underground bunker 40 minutes before the Commission said Cheney got there; and testimony contained in the book by Richard Clarke, who on 9/11 had been the national coordinator for security and counterterrorism. If this is not evidence that counts against the official story, what would be? In any case, Solomon's question was simply why the 9/11 Commission's report did not include these things. When he tried to clarify that this was his question, the following exchange ensued:

> Hamilton: I don't know the answer to your question.
>
> Solomon: I guess part of the reason is. . . .
>
> Hamilton: I cannot answer every question with regard to 9/11. I can answer a good many of them, but I can't answer them all.
>
> Solomon: I guess, Mr. Hamilton, I don't think anyone expects you to have all the answers. . . .
>
> Hamilton: Well, you apparently do, because you have asked me questions of enormous detail from a great variety of sources. You want me to answer them all—I can't do it (laughs).

Hamilton's anger here perhaps reflects the fact that he had unexpectedly found himself in precisely the kind of situation he had tried to avoid: a televised interview in which he was being asked questions by a journalist who was aware of some of the serious problems in the Commission's report and not afraid to bring them up—a situation in which Hamilton had never been placed by American journalists.

Zelikow's Staff and the Commissioners

I said earlier that Hamilton's responses in this interview were quite revealing. What they reveal is that he did not know enough about 9/11 or even his own Commission's work to have been significantly responsible for the content of its report. The same is surely all the more true of Thomas Kean.[169] This realization, that neither Kean nor Hamilton knew enough to have been primarily responsible for the 9/11 Commission's report, supports my earlier suggestion that this report should be seen primarily as the product of the 9/11 staff's director, Philip Zelikow. This suggestion is further supported by Hamilton's response to Solomon's next question.

Saying that his real question was whether "the Commission considered . . . what made it into the report," Solomon added: "[T]his being the . . . most extensive document that the public has, there are questions as to what made it in and what you heard, and what you didn't." Hamilton replied: "A lot of things that came to the attention of staff did not come to the attention of the Commission. Some of the things did come to the attention of the Commission, and we didn't put 'em in, or at least we put 'em in at a lower level. But many of the things did not come directly to my attention." Hamilton repeated this admission in another context.

Saying that evidence about a particular issue raised by Solomon was not brought to the Commission, so far as he knew, he added: "[S]taff filtered a lot of these things, so not necessarily would I know."

The degree to which Hamilton seemed unaware of some very basic things, both about relevant facts and about the Commission's work and its final report, is further shown by his responses to questions about the World Trade Center, which will prepare us for the following chapter.

The World Trade Center Collapses

With regard to the Twin Towers, Hamilton said that the Commission, having looked very carefully, found no evidence that the buildings were brought down by explosives. Instead, he said: "What caused the collapse of the buildings, to summarize it, was that the super-heated jet fuel melted the steel super-structure of these buildings and caused their collapse." Members of the 9/11 truth movement have pointed out that jet-fuel fires cannot get anywhere close to hot enough to melt steel. They have then been criticized by *Popular Mechanics* and other defenders of the official conspiracy theory—as we will see in the following chapters—for having invented a straw-man argument to tear down. No one, these defenders of orthodoxy declare, ever claimed that jet-fuel fire could melt steel. We see, however, that this belief was still held, five years after 9/11, by the vice chair of the supposedly authoritative 9/11 Commission.

Solomon, evidently knowing more about this than Hamilton, then pointed out that fire had never caused steel-frame buildings to collapse, "because steel doesn't melt at temperatures that can be reached through a hydrocarbon fire. . . . [T]here are countless cases of other buildings that have been on fire that have not collapsed." Hamilton replied: "But not on fire through jet fuel, I don't think you have any evidence of that." Hamilton thereby showed that he did not understand that there is nothing special about jet fuel—that it is essentially kerosene—so that a jet-fuel fire is just an ordinary hydrocarbon fire, devoid of magical properties.

From Hamilton's response here, we can infer that the Commission had no discussion of elementary scientific facts relevant to the question of why the Twin Towers collapsed. Hamilton's response would probably be that this question was being handled by the National Institute of Standards and Technology (NIST), to which the Kean–Hamilton book once refers.[170] The 9/11 commission, however, was supposed to be telling us who was responsible for the 9/11 attacks. How could they answer that question if they did not have enough scientific knowledge to make an informed judgment on whether buildings could have possibly been brought down by the airplane impacts and the ensuing fires?

Hamilton revealed himself to be even more ignorant in relation to WTC 7. Solomon asked: "[W]hy didn't the Commission deal with the collapse of Building 7, which some call the smoking gun?" Hamilton replied: "Well, of course, we did deal with it."

This is amazing. One of the main criticisms of the Commission's report has been its failure even to mention the collapse of this building. In my critique of the report, for example, I wrote:

> The Commission avoids another embarrassing problem—explaining how WTC 7 could have collapsed, also at virtually free-fall speed—by simply *not mentioning the collapse of this building*. Building 7 of the WTC was 47 stories high, so it would have been considered a giant skyscraper if it had been anywhere other than next to the 110-story Twin Towers. But the collapse of such a huge building was not even considered worthy of comment by the Commission.[171]

If Hamilton had regarded the Commission as a truth-seeking body, and if he hoped that its report was devoid of "factual errors," he surely would have been motivated to read some critiques of it. Had he done so, he could hardly have avoided coming across passages such as this. And yet he evidently believed that the Commission's report had discussed the collapse of WTC 7. Solomon later came back to the question, during which the following exchange occurred:

> Solomon: You said that the Commission Report did mention World Trade Center Building 7 in it . . . . It did mention it or it didn't?
>
> Hamilton: The Commission reviewed the question of the Building 7 collapse. I don't know specifically if it's in the Report, I can't recall that it is, but it, uh. . . .
>
> Solomon: I don't think it was in the report.
>
> Hamilton: OK, then I'll accept your word for that.
>
> Solomon: There was a decision not to put it in the report?
>
> Hamilton: I do not recall that was a specific discussion in the Commission and we rejected the idea of putting Building 7 in, I don't recall that. So I presume that the report was written without reference to Building 7 at all, because all of the attention . . . was on the Trade tower buildings.

However, although Hamilton had not been sure whether the Commissioners had discussed Building 7 in their report, he did suggest that they did not consider its collapse a great mystery: "[W]ith regard to Building 7, we believe that it was the aftershocks of these two huge buildings in the very near vicinity collapsing."

In 2003, a friend told me that she had heard it said that Building 7 came down because of being destabilized by ground tremors caused by the collapse of the Twin Towers. I replied that this was absurd—that even an extremely powerful earthquake could not have caused a collapse of this type—total, symmetrical, straight down, and at virtually free-fall speed. It is quite amazing to learn that one of the exponents of this absurd theory is the vice chair of the 9/11 Commission, who has been involved in the production of two major books claiming that there is no doubt about al-Qaeda's sole responsibility for the destruction of the World Trade Center.

In the following chapter, we will see if NIST was able to come up with better answers to why, if these buildings were not brought down by explosives, they collapsed—and in the way they did.

THREE

The Disintegration of the World Trade Center: Has NIST Debunked the Theory of Controlled Demolition?

The National Institute of Standards and Technology, often simply called NIST, was given the task of providing the definitive explanation of why three buildings of the World Trade Center—WTC 1 and 2 (the Twin Towers) and WTC 7—collapsed on 9/11. In June 2005, NIST issued a draft of its final report on the Twin Towers.[1] This document evoked serious and substantial critiques, the most extensive being Jim Hoffman's "Building a Better Mirage: NIST's 3-Year $20,000,000 Cover-Up of the Crime of the Century."[2] In September 2005, NIST issued its *Final Report on the Collapse of the World Trade Center Towers*, which contained a half-page response to a few criticisms.[3] This brief response did not begin to answer the serious questions that had been raised. Finally, on August 30, 2006—almost a year later and just two weeks before the fifth anniversary of 9/11—NIST issued a document entitled "Answers to Frequently Asked Questions."

In the present chapter, I will show that NIST, besides even failing to acknowledge some of the most serious questions, gave entirely unsatisfactory answers to those it did acknowledge.

Readers previously unaware of the problems in NIST's position will probably be less shocked by its performance in this document if they are aware that NIST was no more independent of the White House than was the 9/11 Commission. NIST's name—National Institute of Standards and Technology—could easily suggest that it is an independent organization, with no political connections. And NIST itself, in explaining why it was given the task of carrying out this investigation, says in the "Fact Sheet" for its WTC investigation: "Since NIST is not a regulatory agency and does not issue building standards or codes, the institute is viewed as a neutral, 'third party' investigator."[4]

However, even if it is indeed viewed this way by uninformed people, there is in reality nothing "neutral" or "third party" about it with regard to the question of whether 9/11 was an inside job. NIST is an agency of the US Department of Commerce. The first page of NIST's final report, therefore, contains the name of Carlos Gutierrez, Bush's secretary of commerce. And all of NIST's directors are Bush appointees.[5] NIST's final report and its "Answers to Frequently Asked Questions" must, therefore, be viewed as products of the Bush administration.

The content of these documents will also be less surprising insofar as readers are aware of the Bush administration's record with regard to science. Already in 2003, the editor of *Science* spoke of growing evidence that the Bush administration has undermined the scientific integrity at federal agencies by "invad[ing] areas once immune to this kind of manipulation."[6] Later that year, the minority staff of the House Committee on Government Reform published a document entitled "Politics and Science in the Bush Administration." It described "numerous instances where the Administration has manipulated the scientific process and distorted or suppressed scientific findings."[7] In 2004, a statement accusing the Bush administration of engaging in "distortion of scientific knowledge for partisan political ends" was signed by 62 renowned scientists; by December 2006, this statement had been signed by over 10,000 scientists, including 52 Nobel Laureates and 63 recipients of the National Medal of Science.[8] If agencies of the Bush administration would produce flawed scientific analyses to promote the administration's agenda on issues such as the environment and Iraqi weapons of mass destruction, as these studies show, then it would hardly be surprising that a Bush administration agency would produce a scientifically flawed report to rebut evidence that this administration was responsible for treason and mass murder.

We do not, of course, like to think that scientists would prostitute themselves to support immoral and illegal causes. However, the record—from scientists who denied a link between smoking and cancer to scientists who have denied the reality of human-caused global warming—shows otherwise. Becoming a scientist does not, unfortunately, immunize people from common human motives and emotions, such as greed, ambition, and cowardice, that sometimes lead normally decent human beings to do indecent things.

These considerations should not, of course, lead anyone to prejudge the NIST documents. They must be evaluated on their own merits. But these considerations should lead us to study NIST's writings carefully and ask if they explain the destruction of the World Trade Center buildings in a way that is adequate to the relevant evidence. As I pointed out in the introduction, we should not simply assume that, because these documents are produced by scientists working for an agency called the National Institute of Standards and Technology, they must be scientifically sound. That judgment must be made on the basis of actually studying them. (What we will find, to anticipate, is that although some of the scientists did excellent work, there is often a great discrepancy between their results and the conclusions stated in NIST's final report and its "Answers to Frequently Asked Questions.")

With these prefatory comments, I turn to this latter document. Although it contains fourteen questions, the most important elements in

NIST's answers can be organized under six questions: (1) Why did the airplanes cause so much damage to the Twin Towers? (2) How did the impact damage from the airplanes help induce collapse? (3) How did the fires help induce collapse? (4) Why did the towers actually collapse? (5) What about the evidence for controlled demolition? (6) Why has NIST not issued a report on WTC 7? (Note: As the title of this chapter indicates, these buildings did not collapse; they disintegrated. However, because NIST claims that the buildings "collapsed," I use this term when discussing its theory.)

Why Did the Airplanes Cause So Much Damage?

As NIST acknowledges, "a document from the Port Authority of New York and New Jersey . . . indicated that the impact of a . . . Boeing 707 aircraft. . . would result in only local damage which could not cause collapse." If so, then "why did the impact of individual 767s cause so much damage?"[9]

NIST's first response to this question is to claim that "NIST investigators were unable to locate any documentation of the criteria and method used in the impact analysis and, therefore, were unable to verify the assertion that [such a collision] 'could not cause collapse.'"

However, assuming the truth of NIST's claim, its failure to find any documentation for the method and criteria used in the impact analysis says absolutely nothing about the quality of that analysis. NIST does, to be sure, try to cast doubt on this quality with the following statement:

> The capability to conduct rigorous simulations of the aircraft impact, the growth and spread of the ensuing fires, and the effects of fires on the structure is a recent development. . . . [T]he technical capability available . . . to perform such analyses in the 1960s would have been quite limited in comparison to the capabilities brought to bear in the NIST investigation.

However, to whatever extent this statement might be true, it provides no reason to believe that the earlier analysis would have been as defective as it must have been if we are to draw the desired inference. To do this, we would need to believe that although that earlier analysis said that the impact of a Boeing 707 would cause only local damage, the truth is that the impact of a plane that size would cause the entire building to collapse.

Or, to be more precise, such a total collapse, NIST wants us to believe, would be caused if the airplane was a little bigger: NIST points out that "a Boeing 767 aircraft . . . is about 20 percent bigger than a Boeing 707." Having made that statement, NIST then says: "The massive damage was caused by the large mass of the aircraft [and] their high speed and momentum." As this statement shows, NIST recognizes that the plane's destructive force would depend on its speed as well as its size. And yet, in comparing a 767 with a 707, it points out only that the 767 "is about 20 percent bigger." The reader is clearly being led to draw the conclusion that a 767 would cause more damage than a 707.

Would that conclusion follow if we took into consideration speed as well as weight? Evidently not. According to one analysis:

> The Boeing 707 and 767 are very similar aircraft, with the main differences being that the 767 is slightly heavier and the 707 is faster. . . . In all the likely variations of an accidental impact with the WTC, the Boeing 707 would be traveling faster. In terms of impact damage, this higher speed would more than compensate for the slightly lower weight of the Boeing 707. [So] if the twin towers were designed to survive the impact of a Boeing 707, then they were necessarily designed to survive the impact of a Boeing 767.

Another author, quantifying the comparison, has written:

> The kinetic energy released by the impact of a Boeing 707 at cruise speed is . . . 4.136 billion ft lbs force. . . . The kinetic energy released by the impact of a Boeing 767 at cruise speed is 3.706 billion ft lbs force. [So] under normal flying conditions, a Boeing 707 would smash into the WTC with about 10 percent more energy than would the slightly heavier Boeing 767. That is, under normal flying conditions, a Boeing 707 would do more damage than a Boeing 767.[10]

The difference between the impacts of the Boeing 767s on 9/11 and the impact of the 707 envisaged in the report from the 1960s would, in fact, be even greater, because the Boeing 767s that hit the North and South Towers were said to be traveling at 440 and 540 mph, respectively, whereas the report from the 1960s spoke of a 707 traveling at 600 mph.[1]

NIST's deceptive statement has, accordingly, done nothing to explain why the towers would not have withstood the impact of the 767s.

NIST's deceptiveness is also apparent in another method it employs to cast doubt on its critics. These critics, it says, have asked: "If the World Trade Center (WTC) towers were designed to withstand multiple impacts by Boeing 707 aircraft, why did the impact of individual 767s cause so much damage?" NIST then says that the aforementioned document by the Port Authority of New York and New Jersey "indicated that the impact of a [single, not multiple] Boeing 707 aircraft was analyzed during the design stage of the WTC towers." In adding the bracketed words, NIST implied that critics, in saying that an authoritative source had stated that "the towers were designed to withstand multiple impacts by Boeing 707 aircraft," were making a false claim.[12]

But that statement had indeed been made by someone who could speak with authority. In a pre-9/11 documentary, *World Trade Center: A Modern Marvel*, Frank De Martini, who had been the on-site construction manager for the World Trade Center, said of one of the towers:

The building was designed to have a fully loaded 707 crash into it, that was the largest plane at the time. I believe that the building could probably sustain multiple impacts of jet liners because this structure is like the mosquito netting on your screen door—this intense grid—and the plane is just a pencil puncturing that screen netting. It really does nothing to the screen netting.[13]

So, whereas the Port Authority had said that the impact of a single Boeing 707 would cause only local damage, De Martini said that this would also be true if there were multiple impacts.

De Martini's judgment was, moreover, in line with that of other authorities. John Skilling, who was responsible for the structural design of the Twin Towers, said in 1993 (after the bombing of the World Trade Center) that his analysis showed that if one of these buildings were to suffer a strike by a jet plane loaded with jet-fuel, "there would be a horrendous fire" and "a lot of people would be killed," but "the building structure would still be there."[14] Leslie Robertson, who was a member of Skilling's firm (Worthington, Skilling, Helle and Jackson) when the Twin Towers were built, has said that they were designed to withstand the impact of a Boeing 707.[15]

The fact that NIST did not quote any of these statements—either in this document or in its original report—suggests that NIST has been engaged in propaganda rather than objective reporting. NIST has, in any case, done nothing to blunt the force of the rhetorical question it set out to answer: "If the World Trade Center (WTC) towers were designed to withstand multiple impacts by Boeing 707 aircraft, why did the impact of individual 767s cause so much damage?" The implication of this question is, of course, that the destruction of the Twin Towers must have been due to something other than the impact of the airplanes.

NIST would have us believe, to the contrary, that it has shown that "the structural damage to the towers was due to the aircraft impact and not to any alternative forces," such as pre-set explosives.[16] This thesis can be sustained, of course, only if NIST shows that this aircraft-caused structural damage plus the resulting fires could by themselves account for the total collapses of the towers. But it does not.

How Did Impact Damage Help Induce Collapse?

NIST introduces its account of the role of the impact damage in a response to the following frequently asked question: "How could the WTC towers have collapsed without a controlled demolition since no steel-frame, high-rise buildings have ever before or since been brought down due to fires?" Those who have raised this question have done so after articulating the point, made in the previous section, that the impact of the airplanes would have been insignificant, from which it follows that the official theory must rely almost entirely on fire.

However, NIST, to emphasize its thesis that the impact of the airplanes would *not* have been insignificant, attacks the question as inappropriate, saying: "The collapse of the WTC towers was not caused either by a conventional building fire or even solely by the concurrent multi-floor fires that day." Instead, the airplanes' impacts played a major role because they "severed and damaged support columns, dislodged fireproofing insulation coating the steel floor trusses and steel columns, and widely dispersed jet fuel over multiple floors." As a result, "the subsequent unusually large, jet-fuel ignited multi-floor fires weakened the now susceptible structural steel."

NIST then gives its answer to the question of why, given the fact that no steel-frame high-rise building had ever before suffered total collapse except by means of controlled demolition, the Twin Towers collapsed without the help of explosives. (Note that this is the real question implicit in NIST's formulation.) NIST's answer is: "No building in the United States has ever been subjected to the massive structural damage and concurrent multi-floor fires that the towers experienced on Sept. 11, 2001."[17]

This statement is correct. In 1945, to be sure, a B-25 bomber struck the Empire State Building at the 79th floor, creating a hole 18 feet wide and 20 feet high, after which "[t]he plane's high-octane fuel exploded, hurtling flames down the side of the building and inside through hallways and stairwells all the way down to the 75th floor."[18] But the B-25, being much smaller than a 767, would not have caused as much structural damage.

However, although NIST's statement is accurate, it does not answer the question that NIST is supposed to be addressing, namely: How could the towers have suffered total collapse? The mere fact that no previous steel-frame high-rise building in which there have been multi-floor fires had suffered this much—such "massive"—structural damage does not explain how this combination of impact damage and fire could have, in these cases, caused total collapse. For one thing, very few buildings have been hit by large airplanes, so it is not surprising that the damage to the Twin Towers is unprecedented. For us to believe that the destruction of the towers was in fact caused by this combination, NIST would need to convince us that the damage to each building was so massive and the fire in each one so big and hot that this combination could do something that was previously thought impossible. We will examine the question of the fires in later sections. For now, we are asking whether the structural damage, while admittedly unprecedented, could have been sufficient to do what NIST claims.

According to NIST's new document, the airplanes, with their "large mass" and high speed, "severed the relatively light steel of the exterior columns on the impact floors."[19] In a slightly longer statement, NIST says that "the impact of the planes severed and damaged support columns [and] dislodged fireproofing insulation coating the steel floor trusses and steel columns."[20] Because these statements are very vague, we need to look at NIST's final report itself to see what is being claimed. This report, discussing WTC 1 (the North Tower), says that the structural and insulation damage was estimated to be:

> 35 exterior columns severed, 2 heavily damaged.
> 6 core columns severed, 3 heavily damaged.
> 43 of 47 core columns stripped of insulation on one or more floors.

For WTC 2 (the South Tower), the estimates were:

> 33 exterior columns severed, 1 heavily damaged.
> 10 core columns severed, 1 heavily damaged.
> 39 of 47 core columns stripped of insulation on one or more floors.[21]

This account raises two questions. First, assuming these estimates to be plausible, just how "massive" would the damage have been? Second, are these estimates really plausible? Let us look first at the alleged damage to the columns.

The North Tower had 240 perimeter (exterior) columns, so, given NIST's estimate, 205 of them would *not* have been severed.[22] Also, because there were 47 core columns, 41 of them would *not* have been severed. And so, as MIT professor Thomas Eagar had written in a major scientific journal before NIST put out its report, these effects would have been insignificant, because "the number of columns lost on the initial impact was not large and the loads were shifted to remaining columns in this highly redundant structure."[23]

Even stronger statements can be found in reports in *Engineering News-Record* in 1964. Explaining that "[t]he World Trade Center towers would have an inherent capacity to resist unforeseen calamities," these reports said that "live loads on these [perimeter] columns can be increased more than 2000% before failure occurs" and that "one could cut away all the first-story columns on one side of the building, and part way from the corners of the perpendicular sides, and the building could still withstand design live loads and a 100-mph wind force from any direction."[24]

In light of these considerations, the estimated damage to the columns, relative to the size of the buildings, would not have been especially "massive."

An equally serious problem is the plausibility of NIST's estimates, which were based, as architect Eric Douglas emphasizes, entirely on computer simulations.[25] This problem of plausibility is especially serious with regard to the South Tower. NIST estimates, as we have seen, that 10 core columns were severed. As Jim Hoffman points out, this estimate, which entails that the South Tower suffered far more core damage than did the North Tower (in which only 6 core columns are said to have been severed), is highly problematic for two reasons.

First, the core columns were thicker on the lower floors, where they had more weight to support. The core columns at the South Tower's 80th floor, which was its impact zone, would have been considerably thicker than the core columns at the North Tower's impact zone, the 95th floor, making them more difficult to sever.[26]

The second problem arises from the fact that, whereas the North Tower was struck straight on, so that the plane would have been headed toward its core, the South Tower, as video evidence shows, was struck near the right corner, with the result that the right engine exited the building without significant obstruction. (One of the many misleading features of Guy Smith's BBC documentary, *The Conspiracy Files: 9/11*, was that to support its claim that core columns could have been broken, it showed a simulation of an airliner striking a tower in the very center, thereby giving a completely false impression of the South Tower impact.) In fact, only the plane's left wing and engine would have been able to do any damage to the core.[27] But the wing, being made of aluminum and having already encountered the perimeter columns, would probably not have been able to sever any of the much thicker core columns. As Eric Douglas points out, moreover, NIST itself said that an engine could sever one column at most.[28]

If it seems that only one of the South Tower's core columns might have been broken, where did NIST get the figure of 10? As Douglas emphasizes, it got its figures from computer simulations. In coming up with estimates, it would begin, in the words of NIST's own scientists, with "a 'base case' based on a best estimate of all input parameters." But it would also provide "more and less severe damage estimates based on variations of the most influential parameters."[29] Then NIST would choose the most severe estimates. Why? "NIST selected the more severe cases because, and only because," Douglas says, "they were the only ones that produced the desired outcome."[30] They were needed, in other words, to produce collapse. With regard to the core columns in the South Tower, NIST estimated that from three to ten columns were broken, then chose the most severe estimate, because only with ten core columns severed would the tower, in the computer simulation, collapse.[31]

In any case, assuming that each airplane actually severed some core columns in both towers, there would have been fewer columns severed in the South Tower, not more. The damage to this tower would, in other words, have been even less "massive" than the damage to the North Tower, and yet it came down after less time.

Let us turn now to the other element in the alleged structural damage, the stripping of insulation from the core columns. NIST claims that this occurred on six floors of the South Tower. Even if that could be believed (see below), it would mean that the insulation would have remained intact on 104 of the building's 110 floors. NIST's own simulations indicated that "none of the columns with intact insulation reached temperatures over 300C," which means that "the temperature . . . would not have increased to the point where they would have experienced significant loss of strength."[32] This consideration does not bode well for NIST's theory that column failure, due to softening of stripped core columns by the fires, led to the total collapse of each building.

Still another problem with NIST's theory is how we are to imagine that the plane, while severing or heavily damaging only 9 core columns in the North Tower, could have stripped the insulation from 43 out of 47 of them.

To be sure, knowing that the NIST report was written by scientists and engineers who are—NIST's "factsheet" informs us—"world-renowned experts in analyzing a building's failure and determining the most probable technical cause,"[33] we might assume that these men and women had some precise method for making this determination. However, former Underwriters Laboratories executive Kevin Ryan, being curious about this method, discovered that NIST's "test for fireproofing loss, never inserted in the draft reports, involved shooting a total of fifteen rounds from a shotgun at non-representative samples in a plywood box. Flat steel plates were used instead of column samples."[34]

Besides the fact that—to a layman like myself anyway—this seems a most unscientific method for answering the question, there was, Ryan points out, "simply no energy available to cause fireproofing loss. . . . NIST's tests indicate that 1 MJ of energy was needed per square meter of surface area to shear the fireproofing off. For the areas in question . . . , the extra energy needed would be several times more than the entire amount of kinetic energy available to begin with." To make matters worse, Ryan adds: "Previous calculations by engineers at MIT had shown that all the kinetic energy from the aircraft was consumed in breaking columns, crushing the floors and destroying the aircraft itself."[35]

NIST's method for then calculating how much insulation was stripped off was equally arbitrary. In a document explaining the criteria for determining this, we find that if the debris from the impact of the airplane damaged any room furnishings on a given floor, then NIST assumed that the fire protection on the entire floor was dislodged.[36] It made this assumption, moreover, even though the core columns were insulated with gypsum board, rather than (or in addition to) the much derided SFRM (sprayed fire resistive material).[37]

Many people have evidently taken the conclusions of the NIST report on faith, assuming that sound scientific methods were used. However, the more closely we examine the way NIST reached its conclusions and how it answers questions about them, the less such faith seems warranted.

How Did the Fires Help Induce Collapse?

I turn now to the other central claim in NIST's theory—the claim that "the subsequent unusually large, jet-fuel ignited multi-floor fires weakened the now susceptible structural steel."[38] The statement that the fires were "unusually large" can be taken as NIST's shorthand way of claiming that the fires were extraordinary in the ways that would be necessary for them to weaken the structural steel in the towers.

Steel is an excellent conductor of heat. If heat is applied to one portion of a steel beam, that portion will not be quickly heated up to the temperature of the flame, because the heat will quickly be diffused throughout the beam. Also, if that beam is connected to another one, the heat will be dispersed to that second beam. And if those two beams are interconnected with hundreds of other beams, the heat will be diffused throughout the entire network of beams. Accordingly, for fire in such a situation to heat up even one portion of one of these beams to its own temperature, it could not be simply a localized fire, directly affecting only a few of these beams. It would have to be a very large fire, directly affecting a large number of beams. Moreover, even if it was large enough to be directly affecting (say) 20 percent of the beams, it would need to be a very long-lasting fire, because one beam could not be heated up to the temperature of the fire until the whole interconnected set of beams was heated up considerably, and that would take time.

Each of the 110-story Twin Towers contained about 90,000 tons (180 million pounds) of steel. All of this steel, in the form of (vertical) columns and (horizontal) beams and trusses, was interconnected, so that each piece was interconnected with the remainder. Accordingly, for the fires in the towers to have heated up the steel enough to weaken it, the fires would have needed to be (1) hot enough, (2) big enough, and (3) long-lasting enough. These three conditions set the challenge for NIST's account, which stands or falls with the plausibility of its claim that "multi-floor fires weakened the . . . structural steel." Let us see how it fares with these three conditions.

Were the Fires Hot Enough?

NIST seeks to refute the claim that "[t]emperatures due to fire don't get hot enough for buildings to collapse."[39] It begins its attack on this claim by phrasing it thus: "How could the steel have melted if the fires in the WTC towers weren't hot enough to do so?" It easily refutes this claim by saying: "In no instance did NIST report that steel in the WTC towers melted due to the fires." It elaborates on this point by saying that whereas "[t]he melting point of steel is about 1,500° Celsius (2,800° Fahrenheit), ... NIST reported maximum upper layer air temperatures of about 1,000° Celsius (1,800° Fahrenheit)."[40] NIST thereby implied that critics of its final report, on the basis of ignorance of elementary facts about fire and steel, had misrepresented that report.

However, the idea that the towers collapsed because fire melted the steel has been refuted by critics of the official account only because it was originally put forward by defenders of that account. For example, an early BBC News special quoted Hyman Brown, who had been the construction manager for the Twin Towers, as saying: "steel melts, and 24,000 gallons of aviation fluid melted the steel." Chris Wise, a structural engineer, was quoted as saying: "It was the fire that killed the buildings. There's nothing on earth that could survive those temperatures with that amount of fuel burning. . . . The columns would have melted."[41] When critics of the official account argue that fire cannot melt steel, they are responding to such claims by defenders of the official account, which have misinformed the public. NIST is misleading, therefore, in implying that its critics have faulted it for claiming that the fire caused the steel to melt. No such charge will be found, for example, in the critiques by Hoffman and Steven Jones.[42]

In any case, NIST, having dealt with that red herring, still had the task of showing that the fires could have been hot enough to weaken the towers' steel sufficiently to cause them to collapse, a task not nearly so easy. NIST attempts to show this by suggesting that the fires, having reached temperatures of 1,000°C (1,800°F), heated crucial sections of the steel up to that temperature. "[W]hen bare steel reaches temperatures of 1,000 degrees Celsius," NIST tells us, "it softens and its strength reduces to roughly 10 percent of its room temperature value."[43] Although NIST does not quite say that this is what happened, it clearly tries to lead the reader to believe that it is saying this. And insofar as this claim is implied, it is an empirically unsupported claim. NIST reports that its metallographic analysis of recovered steel found "no evidence that any of the samples had reached temperatures above 600°C [1,112°F]"—and this is a statement about recovered steel of every type, not simply steel from core columns.[44]

With regard to the temperature, NIST at one point speaks in passing of "jet-fuel ignited multi-floor fires (which reached temperatures as high as 1,000° Celsius [1,800° Fahrenheit])."[45] If this claim is taken to mean that the fires in the building were burning at this temperature, it would be completely implausible. To see why, we can look at a statement from MIT's Thomas Eagar (who, as a defender of one version of the theory that the buildings were brought down by fire, can hardly be suspected of deliberately underestimating how hot the fires would have been). Eagar wrote:

It is argued that the jet fuel burns very hot, especially with so much fuel present. This is not true. . . . The temperature of the fire at the WTC was not unusual. . . . In combustion science, there are three basic types of flames, namely, a jet burner, a pre-mixed flame, and a diffuse flame.... A fireplace is a diffuse flame burning in air, as was the WTC fire. Diffuse flames generate the lowest heat intensities of the three flame types. . . . The maximum flame temperature increase for burning hydrocarbons (jet fuel) in air is, thus, about 1000°C [about 1832°F] . . . . But it is very difficult to reach [even] this maximum temperature with a diffuse flame. There is nothing to ensure that the fuel and air in a diffuse flame are mixed in the best ratio.[46]

And, as Eagar pointed out, the fact that the towers were emitting black smoke was a sign that the fires in the towers, far from having the best ratio of fuel and oxygen, were oxygen-starved fires. He estimated that the fires were "probably only about 1,200° or 1,300°F [648 or 704°C]."[47] Accordingly, if NIST were claiming that the fires were burning at 1,800°F [1,000°C], this claim would be obviously false.

However, what the NIST report actually says is that the fires "reached temperatures as high as 1,000° Celsius [1,800° Fahrenheit])." In what is probably meant to be a more precise statement, the new NIST document says that "NIST reported maximum upper layer air temperatures of about 1,000° Celsius (1,800° Fahrenheit) in the WTC towers."[48] Jim Hoffman, explaining that this statement is deceptive even if perhaps technically correct, writes:

Temperatures of 800°C to 1,100°C (1472°F to 2012°F) are normally observed only for brief times in building fires, in a phenomenon known as flashover. Flashover occurs when uncombusted gases accumulate near the ceilings and then suddenly ignite. Since flame consumes the pre-heated fuel-air mixture in an instant, very high temperatures are produced for a few seconds. . . . The first section of the [NIST] Report describing the fires deceptively implies that 1,000°C (1,832°F) temperatures (rarely seen in even momentary flashovers) were sustained.[49]

To make this deceptive statement plausible, NIST, moreover, resorts to additional deceptive language, saying: "Normal building fires and hydrocarbon (e.g., jet fuel) fires generate temperatures up to about 1,100° Celsius (2,000° Fahrenheit)."[50] If we take the word "normal" here to mean "normal types of fires," such as building fires and other hydrocarbon fires, and if we see that the statement says only that such fires can generate temperatures *up to* "1,100° Celsius (2,000° Fahrenheit)," we can again see that what NIST says is technically accurate—or, rather, only an exaggeration of about 100°C (168°F): Eagar, as we saw, said that diffuse hydrocarbon fires can at best—that is, with a perfect mixture of air and fuel—reach 1,000°C (1,832°F).

However, the term "normal" could easily be taken to mean "normally," in which case the statement would mean that building and hydrocarbon fires normally reach these temperatures. And if the importance of the phrase "up to" is missed, readers could easily assume that it is normal for such temperatures to be sustained for a long period of time. By creating this impression in the reader's mind, NIST would make the idea that the fires in the towers were burning at 1,000°C [1,832°F] seem plausible.

This interpretation of "normal" would, however, involve a gross distortion of the truth. Eagar, having pointed out that fuel and oxygen are seldom mixed in the ideal ratio to produce the highest possible temperatures, added: "This is why the temperatures in a residential fire are usually in the 500°C to 650°C [932–1202°F] range."[51] Any suggestion that building fires and other hydrocarbon fires regularly burn at temperatures of 1,000°C [1,832°F] would, therefore, be overstating the case by 350° to 500°C [730 to 900°F]. Once we realize that ordinary fires normally do not exceed 650°C [1,202° F], we can see that insofar as NIST is suggesting that the fires in the towers were burning at 1,000°C [1,832°F], this suggestion could be plausible only if these were truly extraordinary fires, having not only a lot of highly combustible fuel but also a virtually perfect mix of fuel and oxygen.

The impression that the fires had lots of highly combustible fuel is created by speaking repeatedly of the jet fuel. Besides referring several times to "jet-fuel ignited fires," NIST says that "the impact of the planes . . . widely dispersed jet fuel over multiple floors," leading to "unusually large, jet-fuel ignited multi-floor fires."[52] And in one place, rather than speaking of "jet-fuel ignited fires," NIST speaks simply of "jet fuel fires."[53] However, much of the jet fuel was burned up quickly in the enormous fireballs that were produced when the planes hit the buildings, and the rest, as even Shyam Sunder, the lead investigator for the NIST study, said, "probably burned out in less than 10 minutes."[54] According to NIST's final report itself, in fact, "The initial jet fuel fires themselves lasted at most a few minutes."[55]

This acknowledgment would in itself make difficult any claim that the fires in the towers were extraordinarily hot, because the fires, after being initially ignited, would have had to depend entirely on office materials and furnishings, such as paper, desks, and carpets, and it is unlikely that fires based on such fuels would come anywhere close to the highest temperatures possible for hydrocarbon fires. In any case, these fires could have been extraordinarily hot only if they had an ideal mixture of fuel and oxygen.

However, as Thomas Eagar acknowledged, the fires were producing large quantities of black smoke, indicating that they were oxygen-starved.

This brings us to another of NIST's "frequently asked questions," namely:

> If thick black smoke is characteristic of an oxygen-starved, lower temperature, less intense fire, why was thick black smoke exiting the WTC towers when the fires inside were supposed to be extremely hot?[56]

In NIST's "answer" to this question, it says:

> Nearly all indoor large fires, including those of the principal combustibles in the WTC towers, produce large quantities of optically thick, dark smoke. This is because, at the locations where the actual burning is taking place, the oxygen is severely depleted and the combustibles are not completely oxidized to colorless carbon dioxide and water.[57]

I put the word "answer" in scare quotes to draw attention to the fact that although the statement gives the impression of disagreeing with the point of the question—that because black smoke was coming out, the fire was oxygen-starved and hence not terribly hot—NIST does not actually disagree. NIST agrees that "at the locations where the actual burning [was] taking place, the oxygen [was] severely depleted." As James Fetzer says:

> This is a nice example of conceding a point while denying that you have conceded it. The billowing black clouds of smoke were indicative of oxygen deprived fires, which were burning at temperatures way below those that could be attained under ideal conditions . . . . This undercuts the whole NIST account, since if the fires were burning at temperatures far, far below those required to even weaken, much less melt, steel, then it cannot be the case that the steel weakened . . . as an effect of those fires.[58]

NIST, of course, does not draw this conclusion, since it does not admit that it has conceded the point. But insofar as it did in fact concede it, what is the real point of its statement?

This point is apparently implicit in the first sentence, which says: "Nearly all indoor large fires . . . produce large quantities of optically thick, dark smoke." The purpose of this technically correct but deceptive statement is evidently to suggest that, since all large indoor fires produce black smoke, the fact that the WTC fires were producing black smoke is no reason to think that these were not the hottest building fires of all time. NIST does not, however, actually say this. It says merely that nearly all large indoor fires produce black smoke, and that is correct. But some large indoor fires have, as Hoffman points out, "produced bright emergent orange flames," because they were not oxygen starved and were, accordingly, hotter.[59]

NIST has done nothing, therefore, to undermine Eagar's judgment that the fires were "probably only about 1,200° or 1,300°F [648° or 704°C]."[60]

There are reasons to believe, moreover, that the fires were not even that hot. For example, in some other high-rise building fires, the fires were hot enough to break windows. Photographs and videos of the towers while they were burning, however, provide no evidence that their fires were breaking windows.[61] It would seem, therefore, that the fires in the towers were probably down in what Eagar calls the normal range for residential fires, namely, the "500°C to 650°C [932–1202°F] range."

This inference from outer appearances is supported, moreover, by data provided by NIST's own studies. Some of these data were revealed in a letter of November 11, 2004, from Kevin Ryan, while he was still an executive at Underwriters Laboratories (UL), to Frank Gayle, who was leading the team addressing the steel forensics of NIST's investigation of the WTC failures. Ryan had become alarmed when he saw that the advance summary of the NIST report seemed to contradict the findings of Gayle's team and thereby to reflect badly on UL, which had certified the steel used in the towers. Ryan's letter to Gayle contained the following passage:

> The results of your recently published metallurgical tests seem to . . . support your team's August 2003 update . . . , in which you were ready to "rule out weak steel as a contributing factor in the collapse" . . . . Your comments suggest that the steel was probably exposed to temperatures of only about 500°F (250°C), which is what one might expect from a thermodynamic analysis of the situation.
>
> However the summary of the new NIST report seems to ignore your findings, as it suggests that these low temperatures caused exposed bits of the building's steel core to "soften and buckle." Additionally this summary states that the perimeter columns softened, yet your findings make clear that "most perimeter panels (157 of 160) saw no temperature above 250°C."

The evidence to which Ryan referred even made it into NIST's final report, which said that its scientific studies found that of the 16 perimeter columns examined, "only three columns had evidence that the steel reached temperatures above 250°C [482°F]." It reported, moreover, that it found no evidence that any of the core columns had reached even that temperature.[62]

What did NIST do this with evidence? It simply gave an excuse for ignoring it, saying that it "did not generalize these results, since the examined columns represented only 3 percent of the perimeter columns and 1 percent of the core columns from the fire floors."[63] That only such a tiny percent of the columns was available was due, of course, to the fact that government officials had most of the steel immediately sold and shipped off. In any case, NIST's findings on the basis of this tiny percent of the columns are far from irrelevant, because they are the only scientific evidence available as to the temperatures reached by steel columns in either tower. Accordingly, any speculation that some of the core columns reached much higher temperatures would be just that—pure speculation backed up by no empirical evidence.

This fact did not, however, prevent NIST from engaging in such speculation and then passing it off as scientific fact. NIST claims that the columns in the core had been greatly weakened by fires that had reached 1,000°C (1,832°F). Because of the conductivity of steel, to be sure, it is true that if some core columns were heated up to 250°C [482°F], we can reasonably assume that the fire itself (the air temperature) was considerably hotter. But there would appear to be no reason to think that it went beyond what we earlier saw to be the normal range for building fires, namely, the 500°C to 650°C [932–1202°F] range.

NIST's claim about the temperature in the core, besides being unsupported by empirical evidence, even runs counter to the available evidence. As Hoffman points out, the core "had very little fuel; was far from any source of fresh air; . . . [and] does not show evidence of fires in any of the photographs or videos."[64] We would assume, therefore, that the fires in the core would be cooler, not hotter, than the perimeter fires that were getting fresh air.

In any case, the crucial fact is that NIST's own scientists reported finding no evidence that the fire heated any steel column above 250°C [482°F]. This fact renders largely irrelevant NIST's (equally unsupported) claim that the planes stripped fireproofing from some of the core columns, thereby allowing their steel to be directly exposed to the fire. "[S]tructural steel," reports Thomas Eagar, "begins to soften around 425°C [797°F]."[65] Accordingly, far from having evidence that any of the steel reached the temperature at which it would have softened sufficiently to lose 90 percent of its strength, we have no evidence that any of the steel even reached the temperature—425°C [797°F]—at which it would have begun to soften. The steel in the Twin Towers could have been directly exposed to fires of 250°C (482°F) all day without even beginning to weaken.

This discrepancy pointed out by Ryan—between the claims in NIST's final report and the scientific study carried out by NIST's own scientists—has been noticed by other researchers. Mark Gaffney reports, in fact, that seeing "the disparity between the NIST's research and its conclusions" left him in a state of "mild shock."[66]

In any case, things become even worse for NIST's theory when we turn to the question of the size and duration of the fires.

Were the Fires Sufficiently Big and Long-Lasting?

As we saw earlier, for a fire to be truly extraordinary—so extraordinary that we might believe that it could, for the first time ever, produce the total collapse of a steel-frame high-rise building—it would have to be not only hot enough to heat up the steel to the point where it would lose much of its strength, but also both big enough and long-lasting enough to compensate for the fact that steel is an excellent conductor of heat. The fires in the towers were neither.

With regard to size, NIST, as we saw, claims that the fires were "unusually large." It also suggests that there was a "raging inferno" in each tower.[67] The evidence, however, counts against this claim, especially with regard to the South Tower, which collapsed only 56 minutes after it was struck. The point of impact was between floors 78 and 84, so the fire should have been largest in this region. And yet Brian Clark, a survivor, said that when he got down to the 80th floor, "You could see through the wall and the cracks and see flames . . . just licking up, not a roaring inferno, just quiet flames licking up and smoke sort of eking through the wall."[68] A similar account was given by a fire chief who, having reached the 78th floor, reported finding only "two isolated pockets of fire."[69]

So, even if one were to accept NIST's unfounded speculation that the fires in the towers burned at 1,000°C (1832°F), the fires in the South Tower, besides being limited to only a few floors of this 110-story building so that most of its steel was not exposed to fire, were not even big enough to heat up some of the steel quickly to anywhere near that temperature. Such steel temperatures could have been reached only with a fire that endured for a very long time. But it was here that NIST faced its greatest challenge, because the fire in neither tower lasted very long before the building came down. The North Tower came down 102 minutes after it was struck, the South Tower after only 56 minutes. That could not possibly have been long enough—even if one granted, for the sake of argument, NIST's claim that the fires were very hot.

The crucial claim that NIST knows it must support, if its account is to seem even prima facie plausible, is implied by its previously quoted statement that, "when bare steel reaches temperatures of 1,000° Celsius [1,832° Fahrenheit], it softens and its strength reduces to roughly 10 percent of its room temperature value." The crucial statement in leading the reader to infer that this really happened comes in the next sentence, namely: "Steel that is unprotected (e.g., if the fireproofing is dislodged) can reach the air temperature within the time period that the fires burned within the towers."[70] With regard to the South Tower, this would mean within 56 minutes.

The reader is supposed to infer, accordingly, that steel in the South Tower from which the fireproofing had been stripped could have reached the temperature of 1,000°C (1,832°C) within 56 minutes. That inference would be absurd, even if the fires had been as big and hot as NIST suggests, because of the enormous amount of interconnected steel in the

South Tower: some 90,000 tons. It would have taken a very long time for even some of that steel to have been heated up to the temperature of the fire itself, even if the fire was directly connected with 25 percent of the steel. It is absurd to suggest that this could have occurred in 56 minutes.

The new NIST document, however, does not actually make this claim. It merely says: "Steel that is unprotected (e.g., if the fireproofing is dislodged) can reach the air temperature within [56 minutes]." And that is perfectly true, if one has in mind a fairly small piece of steel, unconnected with any other pieces of steel. It could reach the temperature of the air surrounding it within 56 minutes. Note that NIST's statement says nothing about the actual air temperature. It also does not say that any actual piece of steel in the South Tower—which of course would have been interconnected with all the rest of the steel in that building—could have reached the air temperature of the rooms in which the fire was burning the hottest. The NIST document does not claim, therefore, that some of the steel in the South Tower actually reached the temperature of 1,000°C (1,832°F). But that is the inference that the document, with its deceptive language, is leading the reader to make.

NIST uses still another form of deception to lead the reader to make the next necessary inference, namely, that the steel, if unprotected by fire-proofing, would within 56 minutes have "soften[ed] and [had] its strength reduce[d] to roughly 10 percent of its room temperature value," thus making it ready to buckle if subjected to additional pressure. The deception to which I refer comes in NIST's answer to the following question:

> Since . . . the temperature of jet fuel fires does not exceed 1,800° Fahrenheit and Underwriters Laboratories (UL) certified the steel in the WTC towers to 2,000° Fahrenheit for six hours, how could fires have impacted the steel enough to bring down the WTC towers?

To rebut the premise of this question, NIST wrote: "UL did not certify any steel as suggested. . . . That the steel was 'certified . . . to 2000° Fahrenheit for six hours' is simply not true."[71]

NIST's statement is technically correct but again deceptive. It is technically correct because Underwriters Laboratories, as Kevin Ryan has pointed out, certified the steel to 2,000°F (1,093°C) only for the times stipulated by the New York City code at the time, "which required fire resistance times of 3 hours for building columns, and 2 hours for floors."[72]

The statement about certification for 6 hours had been erroneously made by a member (not Ryan) of the 9/11 truth movement. By choosing that statement to rebut, NIST distracted attention from the important fact—a fact threatening to NIST's suggestion that the steel columns could have lost virtually all their strength within 56 minutes—that the steel had been certified to withstand temperatures of 2,000°F (1,093°C) for three hours. In fact, as Ryan has pointed out, UL's CEO, Loring Knoblauch, declared in a letter in December 2003 that the "steel clearly met [the test] requirements and exceeded them." Knoblauch's statement suggests that the steel was perhaps capable of enduring 2,000°F fires for at least four hours without being significantly weakened. In any case, Knoblauch also seemed to imply that the results of the tests had been listed in the UL Fire Resistance Directory at the time.[73]

In any case, NIST, not content with that deception, went on to claim that, "in fact, in US practice, steel is not certified at all; rather structural assemblies are tested for their fire resistance rating in accordance with a standard procedure such as ASTM E 119."[74] As philosopher of science James Fetzer has written: "This response trades upon an equivocation. If UL certified 'assemblies' whose principal components are steel, then the claim that UL had certified the steel is justified."[75]

NIST's equivocation on this point may, incidentally, have come from Underwriters Laboratories, which—as revealed by former employee Kevin Ryan (who was fired after he allowed his letter to Frank Gayle to become public)—has worked closely with NIST in making misleading statements and even telling outright lies. In describing an e-mail conversation he had with Tom Chapin, the manager of UL's Fire Protection division, Ryan says:

> Chapin . . . made the misleading claim that UL does not certify structural steel. But even an introductory textbook lists UL as one of the few important organizations supporting codes and specifications because they "produce a Fire Resistance Index with hourly ratings for beams, columns, floors, roofs, walls and partitions tested in accordance with ASTM Standard E 119."[76] He [Chapin] went on to clarify that UL tests assemblies of which steel is a component. This is a bit like saying "we don't crash test the car door, we crash test the whole car."[77]

UL's duplicity is further shown by the fact that although Knoblauch, its CEO, had written at the end of 2003 that UL had tested the steel (as we saw earlier), Underwriters Laboratories told the press in November 2004—after the letter from Ryan to NIST's Frank Gayle was made public—that there was "no evidence" that any firm had tested the steel used in the WTC buildings. A newspaper account of Ryan's firing said: "UL vehemently denied last week that it ever certified the materials," then quoted UL spokesman Paul Baker as saying: "UL does not certify structural steel, such as the beams, columns and trusses used in World Trade Center."[78] But Ryan's letter to Gayle had said:

> As I'm sure you know, the company I work for certified the steel components used in the construction of the WTC buildings. . . . We know that the steel components were certified to ASTM E 119. The time temperature curves for this standard require the samples to be exposed

to temperatures around 2000°F for several hours. And as we all agree, the steel applied met those specifications.[79]

Ryan's letter was not challenged by Gayle.

That UL's statement, made through Baker, was a lie—in the sense of a statement made with the intent to deceive—is also shown by an announcement, on NIST's website, of an award to UL "for the testing of the steel joist-supported floor system of the Word [sic] Trade Center towers under the fire conditions prescribed in ASTM E 119." This contract was awarded, to be sure, in August of 2003, so it does not show that UL had tested the steel at the time the towers were being built. The announcement, however, goes on to say:

> UL provides conformity assessment services for a wide range of products, equipment and construction materials, including determination of fire resistance ratings. Fire ratings are based upon the test method and acceptance criteria in ANSI/UL 263 (ASTM E 119 and NFPA 251), "Fire Tests of Building Construction and Materials."

This 2003 statement therefore contradicts Baker's statement, made in 2004, that "UL does not certify structural steel."

As this history shows, NIST's claim that the steel in the Twin Towers had not been certified is more than misleading; it is a lie. It is, of course, a lie that is essential to NIST's position, according to which steel columns in the South Tower failed after being exposed to fire for 56 minutes. Even if there had been enormous fires burning at 1,832°F (1,000°C), as NIST suggests, these fires would not have caused the steel columns to lose most of their strength within 56 minutes, given the fact that the steel was certified to withstand even hotter fires (2000°F; 1093°C) for at least three times that long.

NIST has done nothing, therefore, to mitigate the absurdity inherent in the claim, required by its defense of the official theory, that core columns in the South Tower could have been heated up to the point where they lost 90 percent of their strength within 56 minutes.

The absurdity of the official theory becomes even clearer if we compare the fires in the towers with fires in some other steel-frame high-rises. In 1988, a fire in the First Interstate Bank Building in Los Angeles raged for 3.5 hours and gutted five of this building's 62 floors, but there was no significant structural damage.[80] In 1991, a huge fire in Philadelphia's One Meridian Plaza lasted 18 hours and gutted eight of the building's 38 floors, but, said FEMA's report on this fire, although "[b]eams and girders sagged and twisted . . . under severe fire exposures . . . , the columns continued to support their loads without obvious damage."[81] In Caracas in 2004, a fire in a 50-story building raged for 17 hours, completely gutting the building's top 20 floors, and yet the building did not collapse.[82] Unlike the fires in the WTC towers, moreover, the fires in these buildings were hot enough to break windows.

Another important comparison is afforded by a series of experiments run in Great Britain in the mid-1990s. The purpose of these experiments was to see what kind of damage could be done to steel-frame buildings by subjecting them to extremely hot, all-consuming fires that lasted for many hours. FEMA, having reviewed those experiments, said: "Despite the temperature of the steel beams reaching 800–900°C (1,500–1,700°F) in three of the tests. . . , no collapse was observed in any of the six experiments."[83] The temperatures here, it should be stressed, are not merely air temperatures. They are the temperatures actually reached by the steel, and they approach the temperatures that, according to NIST's speculations, were reached by some core columns in the towers.

These comparisons bring out the absurdity of NIST's claim that the towers collapsed because the planes knocked the fireproofing off the steel columns. Fireproofing provides protection for only a few hours, so the steel columns in the buildings in Philadelphia and Caracas would have been directly exposed to raging fires for over 10 hours, and yet they did not buckle. NIST claims, nevertheless, that the steel in the South Tower buckled because a little of it was directly exposed to flames for 56 minutes.[84]

NIST's account becomes even more preposterous when we note another detail ferreted out by Kevin Ryan. NIST estimates that it took the fire 10 to 20 minutes after the airplane's impact to reach the area where, it believes, the South Tower failed, and 50 to 60 minutes to reach the North Tower's failure zone. If so, the fires in each case would have had only about 45 minutes to do what bigger and hotter fires had not been able to do in 17 or 18 hours.[85] So the idea that the fires caused any structural failure is absurd.

What Actually Caused the Towers to Collapse?

At this point, to be sure, NIST would probably remind us that according to its account, the buildings were caused to collapse not from the fires alone, but from the fires combined with the effects of the airplane impacts. And, NIST would add, my account has not yet addressed a critical part of its theory involving these impact effects. The difference between the Twin Towers and these other buildings, NIST would say, is that the lower floors of the towers, after their steel had been weakened, suffered a tremendous downward force from the floors above. I turn now to this part of NIST's theory, which is supposed to explain why the towers, after they were damaged by the airplane impacts and weakened by the resulting fires, actually collapsed.

In its final report, NIST suggested that the towers suffered "progressive collapse," a phenomenon that occurs, it said, when "a building or a significant portion of a building collapses due to disproportionate spread of an initial local failure."[86] By thus giving it a name (which it used 15 times), NIST implied that the collapses of the towers belonged to a general class. It thereby suggested that such collapses are more or less regular occurrences. It further suggested this by saying that after the conditions for collapse initiation were reached, "collapse became inevitable."[87]

However, as Hoffman points out, this suggestion was deceptive, because there are "no examples of total progressive collapse of steel-framed buildings outside of [the alleged cases of] 9/11/01." Further explaining the importance of this point for a document that is supposed to be scientific, Hoffman says: "The fact that there is not a single example of total top-down progressive collapse outside of the alleged examples of the Twin Towers makes it entirely unscientific to presuppose that the alleged phenomenon was operative here."[88]

Another problem was that NIST, after devoting large amounts of space, often with great quantitative analysis, to much less important matters, devoted very little space to, and provided absolutely no quantitative analysis in, its section entitled "Collapse Analysis of the Towers." Hoffman registered the following complaint:

> That section is nine mostly redundant pages with the primary account of the theories for the North and South Towers occupying only three and four paragraphs. These accounts have virtually no quantitative detail, which contrasts with the scores of pages describing plane impact modeling and fire tests and modeling.[89]

NIST's new document, perhaps in response to Hoffman's critique, acknowledges the fact that "[a] key critique of NIST's work lies in the complete lack of analysis supporting a 'progressive collapse' after the point of collapse initiation." The lack of any quantitative analysis, however, is not remedied in the NIST's new document. It simply makes vague statements such as the following:

> Based on [its] comprehensive investigation, NIST concluded that the WTC towers collapsed because [after the planes caused damage, the fires] significantly weakened the floors and columns with dislodged fireproofing to the point where floors sagged and pulled inward on the perimeter columns. This led to the inward bowing of the perimeter columns and failure . . . , initiating the collapse of each of the towers.[90]

To get a little clearer idea of NIST's theory, one must return to its final report, which says that the sagging floors caused the perimeter columns to become unstable and then this instability increased the gravity load on the core columns, which by then had been weakened by the (allegedly) very hot fires, and that this combination of factors produced "global collapse."[91]

As I mentioned earlier, NIST's theory also says that this global collapse was initiated by downward pressure. This element is mentioned in NIST's new document's statement that the fire "weaken[ed] the structure to the point that the towers could not resist the tremendous energy released by the downward movement of the massive top section of the building at and above the fire and impact floors."[92] In other words, as we saw earlier, when the planes impacted the buildings, they severed not only many of the perimeter columns but also some of the core columns and damaged still others. Given this destruction of several core columns and then the softening by fire of many others (from which the insulation had been stripped), these columns soon "buckled" under the weight of the floors above. Then when the weight of all those floors above the point of impact fell on the floors below, the collapse of the entire tower followed.

To call this theory problematic would be an understatement. One problem is simply the fact that NIST's "theory" is a bare assertion. There is no explanation of why the core columns would "buckle" or even what this might mean. How, for example, could each tower's 287 columns have collapsed into a pile of rubble only about seven stories high?

A second problem is that, as we have seen, there is no evidence that the fires were anywhere near hot enough or big enough to weaken the steel columns, let alone soften them up so much that they would lose virtually all their strength. And yet if the columns buckled all the way down, NIST's theory would seem to entail that the columns of the South Tower were heated up to 1,832°F (1,000°C) all the way from the impact zone (about the 80th floor) to the ground in 56 minutes—a completely impossible theory. (NIST would probably deny that its theory entails this, yet without this assumption, how does NIST's theory even begin to account for the breaking or buckling of the massive core columns in the lower floors?)

But perhaps the most incredible part of NIST's theory is its attempt to deal with one of the stubborn facts that simply could not be ignored: the fact that the towers came down at virtually free-fall speed.

This had been a difficulty for the "pancake" theory developed by Thomas Eagar and endorsed by the 9/11 Commission. According to that theory, the floors above the impact floor broke loose from the core and perimeter columns and fell on the floor below, causing it in turn to break loose, after which all these floors caused the next one to break loose, and so on, all the way down. Besides its inherent implausibility and its inability to explain why all the columns, at least the core columns, were not still standing, this theory was also challenged by the law of the conservation of momentum. The upper floors could not have fallen through the lower floors as if they, with all their steel and concrete, would have offered no more resistance than air. Even if the pancaking had been otherwise conceivable, each floor would have arrested the downward momentum, if only slightly. Even if we suppose, as we did in the case of the South Tower earlier, that each floor would have taken a half second to collapse, that would mean the collapse of the 90 floors below the North Tower's impact zone would have taken 45 seconds. And yet the North Tower came down in about 11 seconds. So the pancake theory could not be true.

NIST's progressive collapse theory faces essentially the same problem, as NIST acknowledges in stating one of its frequently asked questions: "How could the WTC towers collapse in only 11 seconds (WTC 1) and 9 seconds (WTC 2)—speeds that approximate that of a ball dropped from similar height in a vacuum?"[93]

In beginning to answer this question, this new document quotes a statement from NIST's final report, which says that these collapse times show that

> the structure below the level of collapse initiation offered minimal resistance to the falling building mass at and above the impact zone. The potential energy released by the downward movement of the large building mass far exceeded the capacity of the intact structure below to absorb that energy through energy of deformation.
>
> Since the stories below the level of collapse initiation provided little resistance to the tremendous energy released by the falling building mass, the building section above came down essentially in free fall, as seen in videos.[94]

Up to that point, NIST has offered no explanation. It has simply stated what happened. NIST's entirely true statement that the lower floors "provided little resistance" would be compatible with the alternative theory, according to which the lower floors were removed by explosives.

It could appear, however, that an explanation is offered by NIST's next statement:

> [T]he momentum (which equals mass times velocity) of the 12 to 28 stories (WTC 1 and WTC 2, respectively) falling on the supporting structure below (which was designed to support only the static weight of the floors above and not any dynamic effects due to the downward momentum) so greatly exceeded the strength capacity of the structure below that it (the structure below) was unable to stop or even to slow the falling mass.[95]

NIST might here seem to be claiming that because the structure at any given level "was designed to support only the static weight of the floors above," it was not strong enough to offer any resistance when the upper floors fell on them, because their momentum—a product of their tremendous mass multiplied by their velocity—was overwhelming.

If read carefully, however, the statement does not actually say this. It first simply makes a statement about what the lower part of the structure was designed to support. (This statement is, incidentally, not true, because the structure was actually designed with great redundancy, so that it would support many times the weight of the floors above. But we can here ignore this point for the sake of argument.) NIST's statement then simply says that the momentum of the falling upper floors "so greatly exceeded the strength capacity of the structure below that it (the structure below) was unable to stop or even to slow the falling mass." Instead of reading this as a statement about the strength of the lower structure prior to 9/11, we could read it as merely saying that once the building started to collapse, the structure below had no strength to stop or even slow the material falling down from above. And this was obviously true—because, one might suppose, explosives had been used to destroy its strength.

But the task of NIST, of course, was to convince readers that the towers came down at virtually free-fall speed even though explosives were not used. It must, therefore, count on readers to take its statement as saying that although the lower structure was still fully intact when the upper floors fell on it, this lower structure was "unable to stop or even to slow the falling mass." And with this interpretation, NIST's account is, as Hoffman says, "absurd," because it "requires us to believe that the massive steel frames of the [lower structure of the] towers provided no more resistance to falling rubble than [would] air."[96]

Let us discuss this in terms of the North Tower. Its total weight was about 500,000 tons (one billion pounds). The impact occurred at about the 95th floor, so the upper portion, which (supposedly) fell on the lower structure, would have consisted of only 16 floors. Also the structure at this height had relatively little weight to bear compared with the structure lower down, so the steel columns in these upper floors were quite thin compared with the columns in the lower floors, which became increasingly massive toward the base. This means that the upper 16 floors surely constituted less than fifteen percent of the building's total weight, meaning less than 65,000 tons.

NIST, speaking of "the tremendous energy released by the downward movement of the massive top section of the building," would have us believe that these upper 16 floors of the North Tower, having fallen only one story and hence having little velocity and hence momentum, would not have been stopped or even slowed down by hitting the lower part of the structure, with its more than 435,000 tons. This idea would surely be a candidate for the most absurd idea ever articulated in modern times in a supposedly scientific document. It is similar to suggesting that if a sports car going 30 miles per hour ran into the rear of a huge truck stopped at a traffic light, the car would simply continue at the same speed, pushing the truck ahead of it.

One of the formal weaknesses of NIST's explanation is that it is, as

Hoffman complains, "unsupported by any calculation." From merely the simple calculations in the previous paragraph, however, one can see why NIST would have wanted to avoid all quantitative analysis.

Scottish mechanical engineer Gordon Ross, while not having the $20,000,000 available to NIST, has provided the kind of quantitative analysis that is absent in its documents. Ross's technical essay shows, moreover, the essential correctness of the intuitive analysis contained above. Having calculated both the velocity (8.5 meters per second) and the kinetic energy (2.1 GJ) of the 16 upper floors after falling a story (3.7 meters), Ross concluded that the impact would absorb so much energy that "vertical movement of the falling section would be arrested . . . within 0.02 seconds after impact."[97] Ross's quantitative analysis, accordingly, reveals just how absurd is NIST's scenario, according to which the vertical movement would continue down through the remaining 90 floors.

NIST, moreover, added another absurdity in order to deal with one more feature of the collapses, as it described them. It said that the towers collapsed at "speeds that approximate that of a ball dropped from similar height in a vacuum (with no air resistance)." This means that the towers came down faster than free-fall speed through the air. It is not clear from the videos that this is actually true, incidentally, since the dust clouds so obscure our vision that it is difficult to tell exactly how fast the towers came down. But since these were the speeds that NIST accepted (11 seconds for the North Tower, 9 seconds for the South), it had to account for them. It at least appeared to do so by saying, after its statement that the lower structure was unable to slow the falling mass: "The downward momentum felt by each successive lower floor was even larger due to the increasing mass."

Here again, it is not clear exactly what NIST means. To explain why the towers fell faster than a ball dropped from the top of the towers would have fallen, NIST would need to mean that the velocity of the falling matter increased as it progressed downward. But this would violate the law of the conservation of momentum, according to which each floor, with its inertial mass, would have decreased the velocity of the falling matter (assuming, for the sake of discussion, that NIST's theory is otherwise possible). This would especially be the case given the fact, as electrical engineer Sean Glazier has pointed out, that "the floors and columns that the upper floors were impacting were progressively sturdier than the floors above."[98] (Glazier's point is that although the floors themselves were presumably all the same, the columns supporting the lower floors were progressively thicker.)

However, what NIST actually says is that the momentum increased because, according to its theory, each successive floor was added to the body of falling material, increasing its mass. And, since momentum is the product of mass times velocity, the momentum would be increased even if the velocity decreased—if, at least, the increased mass in each case more than compensated for the decreased velocity.

It is possible that NIST deliberately crafted this ambiguous wording so that the statement could be interpreted differently by different audiences. On the one hand, NIST could hope that the general public, not distinguishing between velocity and momentum, would think it had explained why the towers fell faster than free-fall speed through the air. On the other hand, if NIST were to be challenged by fellow scientists (perhaps in a court case bringing charges against the NIST scientists for participating in the cover-up of a crime), it could point to the second interpretation, which is at least arguably defensible.

In any case, NIST's theory of the destruction of the towers is absurd, as we have seen, for a variety of reasons. Some of those reasons involve the vast discrepancies between what NIST's theory requires from the airplane impacts and the fires and what the evidence actually suggests. In the present section, however, we have seen that, even if NIST's unfounded speculations about these matters were granted, its theory of why the buildings came down would still be absurd, partly because it conflicts with basic principles of physical science.

As if all these problems were not enough, moreover, NIST's account is contradicted by evidence, available in photographs and videos, of what actually happened. NIST's account depends, as we have seen, on the idea that the collapse was finally triggered by "the tremendous energy released by the downward movement of the massive top section of the building." NIST refers repeatedly to the "falling building mass" or simply the "falling mass." However, as mechanical engineer Judy Wood says, with reference to photographs of the top of the South Tower when it starts to come down:

> [A]s we can observe, the building disintegrated and there was no block of material. . . . Given that the building disintegrated from the top down, it is difficult to believe there could be much momentum to transfer. . . . After being pulverized, the surface-area/mass is greatly increased and the air resistance becomes significant. . . . [T]his pulverized material can[not] contribute any momentum as it 'hangs' in the air and floats down.[99]

This pulverization is also emphasized by Steven Jones. In videos and photographs of the onset of the destruction of the South Tower, Jones points out,

> We observe that approximately 30 upper floors began to rotate as a block, to the south and east. They began to topple over, as favored by the Law of Increasing Entropy. . . . But then—and this I am still puzzling over—this block turned mostly to powder in mid-air! How can we understand this strange behavior, without explosives? This is a remarkable, amazing phenomenon, and yet the US government-funded reports [including the NIST's] failed to analyze it.[100]

Chuck Thurston, in an essay pointing out that the towers did not really collapse—they instead exploded—writes:

> At the onset of destruction for each Tower, we do see the top part of each building begin to fall, and this, no doubt, is what gives the initial impression that a collapse is taking place. In both cases, however, this upper block of floors somehow quickly disintegrates and is lost in the growing cloud of dust and debris. There are no intact portions of either building that survive the wave of destruction that moves down each Tower.[101]

Accordingly, even if all the previously mentioned problems in NIST's theory did not exist, this theory would be rendered irrelevant simply by the fact that it depends on a claim—that the lower structure of each building was impacted by "the massive top section of the building"—that can be seen to be false simply by looking at the available videos and photographs, which show that the top section was pulverized.

Tweaked Computer Models

The scientists on NIST's WTC study team would have, of course, been aware that their conclusions were scientifically unsupported. They evidently decided, therefore, to rest their case on another basis, mentioned above by Eric Douglas: computer simulations. As Kevin Ryan has explained:

> [W]e should examine what NIST did with the results of its physical tests, which had failed to support its conclusions. Did NIST perform more tests, at least to prove its key argument that much of the fireproofing on the steel in the Twin Towers popped off due to the impact of the airliners? No, it did not. Instead, NIST put together a black box computer model that would spit out the right answers. This black box model was driven by initial parameters that could be tweaked. When the parameters that had initially been considered "realistic" did not generate results that "compared to observed events," NIST scientists performed their final analysis using another set of parameters they called "more severe."[102] When they were finished, their model produced video graphics that would enable anyone to see the buildings collapse without having to follow a train of logic to get there.[103]

Steven Jones discusses this same feature of NIST's theory. Saying that "[t]he computerized models of the Twin Towers in the NIST study . . . are less than convincing," Jones quotes the following statement from NIST's final report:

> The Investigation Team then defined three cases for each building by combining the middle, less severe, and more severe values of the influential variables. Upon a preliminary examination of the middle cases, it became clear that the towers would likely remain standing. The

less severe cases were discarded after the aircraft impact results were compared to observed events. [Again, the "observed events" are the collapses of the buildings.] The middle cases . . . were discarded after the structural response analysis of major subsystems were compared to observed events.[104]

Jones then adds: "The NIST report thus makes for interesting reading. The less severe cases based on empirical data were discarded because they did not result in building collapse! But one must 'save the hypothesis,' so more severe cases were tried and the simulations tweaked, as the NIST report admits," a claim that Jones supports by quoting the following statement (the bracketed phrase is by Jones):

> The more severe case . . . was used for the global analysis of each tower . . . . To the extent that the simulations deviated from the photographic evidence or eyewitness reports [that complete collapse occurred, for example], the investigators adjusted the input. . . . Thus, for instance, . . . the pulling forces on the perimeter columns by the sagging floors were adjusted.[105]

Jones then comments: "How fun to tweak the model like that, until one gets the desired result! But the end result of such tweaked computer hypotheticals is, of course, not compelling."[106]

Ryan, describing an episode that occurred while he worked at Underwriters Laboratories, illustrates just how shamelessly NIST tweaked data to make its model work.

> Underwriters Laboratories performed . . . tests to establish the fire resistance of models of the WTC floor assemblies. The results were that . . . the floors barely sagged—only about 3 inches, despite the use of double the known floor load and two hours of fire exposure (i.e. over twice the duration of fires known to have existed in the failure zones). NIST then added this 3 inch sag to their computer model, and . . . it suddenly became 42 inches of extreme sagging. . . . Without a doubt, one rarely finds more shameful and obvious examples of the distortion of science.[107]

Jones and Ryan have thereby, along with Eric Douglas and Mark Gaffney, pointed out one of the main reasons that NIST's report cannot be considered an example of good science. In Gaffney's words, "computer models are no better than the quality of input and the accuracy of the programmer's assumptions."[108] In Douglas's words:

> [A] fundamental problem with using computer simulation is the overwhelming temptation to manipulate the input data until one achieves the desired results. Thus, what appears to be a conclusion is actually a premise. We see NIST succumb to this temptation throughout its investigation. . . . [T]hroughout the simulations, NIST tweaked the input until the buildings fell down.[109]

In other words, NIST's reasoning was, as Gaffney points out, perfectly circular.[110] Its scientists began with the conclusion that the buildings collapsed because of the impact of the planes plus the ensuing fire. They thereby "knew" that these were the sole causes, because they "knew" that there were no pre-set explosives going off. They were, from that perspective, justified in putting in sufficient impact and fire damage to cause the simulated buildings to collapse.

A Thoroughly Unscientific Hypothesis

Besides being unscientific by virtue of contradicting empirical facts, contravening basic scientific laws, and manipulating data, NIST's theory of "progressive total collapse" cannot even be considered a scientific hypothesis in the purely formal sense. Hoffman, explaining why, says:

> [T]here is no historical or experimental basis for believing that collapse events near the tops of the towers could progress all the way down the towers' vertical axes to produce total collapses. Lacking such a basis, the core assumption of NIST's theory is unscientific.

Hoffman's point is that in the experimental (as distinct from the historical) sciences, a hypothesis cannot be considered a scientific hypothesis if it posits an absolutely unique event: one that has never occurred before and that cannot be experimentally replicated. But there is no previous example—in spite of NIST's deceptive language intended to suggest otherwise—of a steel-frame high-rise building's suffering a progressive total collapse without the aid of explosives. And there has been no attempt to confirm NIST's theory experimentally.

It might be thought, to be sure, that performing the needed experiments would be too expensive to be practicable. But this is not so. The experimenters could simply choose some steel-frame high-rises with similar designs (having both core and perimeter columns) that are already scheduled for demolition. Then some old Boeing 767s that need to be replaced could be flown by remote control into the buildings. If the impact and the resulting fires fail to induce total collapse, the experiment could be repeated several times.

Against the objection that these experiments would be too expensive, it can be pointed out that the wars that have been justified by the official theory of the 9/11 attacks have already cost several hundred billion dollars, with some economists estimating that the final price tag for the war in Iraq alone will be between one and two trillion dollars. Surely it would be worth a few million to test the definitive explanation of the central feature of the official theory about 9/11, which has provided the basis for the whole "war on terror."

Furthermore, Jim Hoffman has pointed out,[111] the idea could be tested much more simply by building a miniature model of one of the towers. If the alleged phenomenon of top-down progressive collapse could occur in the towers, then it should be replicable in a model that is identical except for being much smaller.

In any case, given NIST's claim that collapse became inevitable once the planes and fires had done their work, it should enthusiastically support this proposal to test its hypothesis.

In reality, of course, NIST will not support this proposal and no experiment will be done, because both NIST and the government know that the official theory is false. They know that the buildings were brought down by explosives in the procedure known as "controlled demolition." But NIST, of course, publicly had to deny that this is what happened. I turn now to its treatment of this issue.

What About Controlled Demolition?

Two of the questions it has frequently been asked, NIST acknowledges, are these:

—Why did NIST not consider a "controlled demolition" hypothesis with matching computer modeling and explanation?

—Did the NIST investigation look for evidence of the WTC towers being brought down by controlled demolition? Was the steel [for example] tested for explosives or thermite residues?[112]

NIST's twofold answer to these questions was that (1) it "found no corroborating evidence for alternative hypotheses suggesting that the WTC towers were brought down by controlled demolition using explosives planted prior to Sept. 11, 2001" and that (2) it did not look for such evidence—a point that was made by saying that "NIST did not test for the residue of [thermite or other explosives] in the steel." Now, given the second part of the answer, the first part is certainly no surprise. As Fetzer points out: "To assert that NIST 'found no corroborating evidence' for alternative accounts, such as controlled demolition, would be significant only if NIST had actually looked for evidence that might support alternative accounts."[113]

How does NIST justify not even considering the hypothesis of controlled demolition? By means of a threefold argument.

Other Hypotheses Obviated by NIST's Account?

NIST's first and most important argument is that there is "conclusive evidence" for its own account, so there was simply no need to explore any alternative hypothesis. In NIST's words:

NIST's findings ... do not support the "controlled demolition" theory since there is conclusive evidence that: the collapse was initiated in the impact and fire floors of the WTC towers and nowhere else, and the time it took for the collapse to initiate (56 minutes for WTC 2 and 102 minutes for WTC 1) was dictated by (1) the extent of damage caused by the aircraft impact, and (2) the time it took for the fires to reach critical locations and weaken the structure to the point that the towers could not resist the tremendous energy released by the downward movement of the massive top section of the building at and above the fire and impact floors.[114]

We have seen, however, that NIST's own theory, far from being based on "conclusive evidence," is based on unfounded speculation, tweaked computer models, and hypotheses that contradict basic scientific principles. So NIST's own theory certainly does not provide a good a priori reason to ignore evidence for a theory that is not afflicted with such defects.

Must Controlled Demolitions Be Bottom-Up Affairs?
In giving its second argument for ignoring the hypothesis of controlled demolition, NIST writes: "Video evidence ... showed unambiguously that the collapse progressed from the top to the bottom." The implicit argument here could be stated thus:
—Controlled demolitions necessarily begin at the bottom.
—The Twin Towers began collapsing from the top.
—Therefore these collapses were not instances of controlled demolition.

The only problem with this syllogism is that the first premise is false. In most controlled demolitions in which the buildings come down, to be sure, a collapse of the building begins at the bottom. It is not true, however, that this is the only way to make a building come down. As Steven Jones says:

Unlike WTC 7, the Twin Towers appear to have been exploded "top-down" rather than proceeding from the bottom—which is unusual for controlled demolition but clearly possible, depending on the order in which explosives are detonated.[115]

The general point here is that experts can, by determining the placement and timing of the explosives, make a building come down in about any way desired. As Mark Loizeaux, the head of Controlled Demolition, Inc., has said, "by differentially controlling the velocity of failure in different parts of the structure, you can make it walk, you can make it spin, you can make it dance."[116] (This point is brought out in 911 Mysteries: Demolitions.)

As Hoffman has pointed out, moreover, there would have been a good reason for having the destruction of the towers begin near the top:

NIST implies that the top-down order of destruction of the Twin Towers weighs against the controlled demolition theory. However, as part of a psychological operation, the controlled demolition of the Twin Towers would be designed to support a false narrative of events (that the plane crashes caused the collapses) so of course the events were engineered to have the destruction start around the crash zones.[117]

The faulty premise in NIST's reasoning has been pointed out in Chuck Thurston's aforementioned essay, which is entitled "Explosion or Collapse?" This premise is the very idea that the towers "fell" or "collapsed." As Thurston points out: "'Falling' and 'collapsing' are both categories for gravity-driven events." Given that premise, it can seem self-evident that, if the buildings had been brought down by explosives, the collapse would have needed to start from the bottom. "Collapse," however, is the wrong category for describing how the towers were destroyed.

> [T]he word "collapse" means: "to cave or fall in or give way . . . . But, if one considers all the evidence, it quickly becomes apparent that the Towers didn't cave in, fall or give way—they were systematically and progressively exploded from the top down, starting from the impact zone in each Tower.[118]

NIST's argument can appear convincing to some people, therefore, only because NIST has misdescribed the destruction of the towers.

No Evidence of Explosions?

NIST's third reason for dismissing the hypothesis of controlled demolition is that "there was no evidence (collected by NIST, or by the New York Police Department, the Port Authority Police Department or the Fire Department of New York) of any blast or explosions in the region below the impact and fire floors."[119]

This statement, passed over quickly by the average reader, might be taken to mean that there was no evidence of explosions of any type. Thus interpreted, the statement would be a candidate for the most obviously false statement in the document. I have, for example, published an essay entitled "Explosive Testimony," which includes dozens of testimonies about explosions in the Twin Towers,[120] and most of these even meet NIST's criterion of having been "collected by the Fire Department of New York" (FDNY), because they are contained in the 9/11 oral histories of fire fighters and emergency medical workers recorded by the FDNY a few months after 9/11.[121] A subsequent study by Graeme MacQueen, moreover, reported that of the 503 members of the FDNY whose oral histories have been made available, 118 members—only 31 of whom had been quoted in my essay—refer to the occurrence of explosions in the towers.[122] Any denial that evidence of such explosions exists would, therefore, be contradicted by a vast amount of evidence.

What NIST's statement actually says, however, is only that the FDNY (and other mentioned agencies) had found no evidence of *explosions below the floors that were impacted and/or on which there were fires*. NIST's implicit point seems to be that if explosions occurred on the impact and fire floors, they could be explained as resulting from the airplane impact and/or the fire. Explosions, in other words, would be evidence that explosives had been set in advance only if these explosions occurred "in the region below the impact and fire floors." But this statement is doubly problematic.

One problem is that NIST's statement is unduly restrictive. Explosions on floors that were above the impact floors and devoid of fire would also provide strong evidence for pre-set explosives.

A second problem with NIST's statement is that evidence about explosives, to be considered authentic, should not be restricted to evidence "collected by NIST, or by the New York Police Department, the Port Authority Police Department or the Fire Department of New York." Testimonies reported by journalists and other reliable authors should also be included.

NIST's claim, revised to remove these two restrictions on evidence, would read: "there was no evidence collected by reliable sources of any blast or explosions in the regions above or below the impact and fire floors." How would this claim survive encounter with the facts? Not very well.

Explosions Above the Impact and Fire Floors: There are many reports of explosions above the impact and fire floors of the South Tower. For example, Fire Department Captain Dennis Tardio said: "I hear an explosion and I look up. It is as if the building is being imploded, from the top floor down, one after another, boom, boom, boom."[123] Chief Frank Cruthers said: "There was what appeared to be at first an explosion. It appeared at the very top, simultaneously from all four sides, materials shot out horizontally. And then there seemed to be a momentary delay before you could see the beginning of the collapse."[124] *Wall Street Journal* reporter John Bussey said: "I . . . looked up out of the [WSJ] office window to see what seemed like perfectly synchronized explosions coming from each floor. . . . One after the other, from top to bottom, with a fraction of a second between, the floors blew to pieces."[125]

Explosions Below the Impact and Fire Floors: NIST's claim does not even stand up in relation to the region below the impact and fire floors. With regard to the North Tower, employee Teresa Veliz reported that as she was making her way down the stairs from the 47th floor, "There were explosions going off everywhere. I was convinced that there were bombs planted all over the place and someone was sitting at a control panel pushing detonator buttons. . . . I didn't know where to run."[126] Genelle

Guzman, the last survivor to be rescued from the rubble, reports that when she got down to the 13th floor some 20 minutes before the North Tower came down, she heard a "big explosion" and "[t]he wall I was facing just opened up, and it threw me on the other side."[127] Firefighter Louie Cacchioli, after reaching the 24th floor, said that he "heard this huge explosion that sounded like a bomb [and] knocked off the lights and stalled the elevator."[128] Fire Captain Karin Deshore said:

> Somewhere around the middle of the [North Tower of the] World Trade Center, there was this orange and red flash coming out. Then this flash just kept popping all the way around the building and that building had started to explode. The popping sound, and with each popping sound it was initially an orange and then a red flash came out of the building and then it would just go all around the building on both sides as far as I could see. These popping sounds and the explosions were getting bigger, going both up and down and then all around the building.[129]

With regard to the South Tower, firefighter Kenneth Rogers said: "[T]here was an explosion in the south tower. . . . I kept watching. Floor after floor after floor. One floor under another after another and when it hit about the fifth floor, I figured it was a bomb, because it looked like a synchronized deliberate kind of thing."[130]

Some of the witnesses reported, moreover, that the "collapse" of the South Tower began lower than the impact and fire floors. Timothy Burke, for example, reported that while he was watching flames coming out of the South Tower, "the building popped, lower than the fire." He later heard a rumor that "the aviation fuel fell into the pit, and whatever floor it fell on heated up really bad, and that's why it popped at that floor." At the time, however, he said, "I was going oh, my god, there is a secondary device because the way the building popped. I thought it was an explosion."[131] This same twofold observation was made by firefighter Edward Cachia, who said: "As my officer and I were looking at the south tower, it just gave. It actually gave at a lower floor, not the floor where the plane hit. . . . [W]e originally had thought there was like an internal detonation, explosives, because it went in succession, boom, boom, boom, boom, and then the tower came down."[132]

Some witnesses reported evidence of explosions still lower. For example, Stephen Evans, a New York-based correspondent for the BBC, said: "I was at the base of the second tower . . . that was hit. . . . There was an explosion. . . . The base of the building shook. . . . [T]hen there was a series of explosions."[133] Assistant Fire Commissioner Stephen Gregory said:

> I thought . . . before . . . No. 2 came down, that I saw low-level flashes . . . Lieutenant Evangelista . . . asked me if I saw low-level flashes in front of the building, and I agreed with him because I . . . saw a flash flash flash . . . [at] the lower level of the building. You know like when they

demolish a building, how when they blow up a building, when it falls down? That's what I thought I saw.[134]

Back in the North Tower, some witnesses reported explosives even further down, in the basements. Janitor William Rodriguez reported that he and others felt an explosion below the first sub-level office at 9AM, after which co-worker Felipe David, who had been in front of a nearby freight elevator, came into the office with severe burns on his face and arms yelling, "explosion! explosion! explosion!"[135] Rodriguez's account has been corroborated by José Sanchez, who was in the workshop on the fourth sub-level. Sanchez said that he and a co-worker heard a big blast that "sounded like a bomb," after which "a huge ball of fire went through the freight elevator."[136]

Engineer Mike Pecoraro, who was working in the North Tower's sixth sub-basement, said that after an explosion he and a co-worker went up to the C level, where there was a small machine shop. "There was nothing there but rubble," said Pecoraro. "We're talking about a 50 ton hydraulic press—gone!" They then went to the parking garage, but found that it was also gone. Then on the B level, they found that a steel-and-concrete fire door, which weighed about 300 pounds, was wrinkled up "like a piece of aluminum foil." Having seen similar things after the terrorist attack in 1993, Pecoraro was convinced that a bomb had gone off.[137] (Testimony about explosions by Pecoraro and many other witnesses can be seen in the film *911 Mysteries: Demolitions*.)

In light of these testimonies, it is interesting that Mark Loizeaux, head of Controlled Demolition, Inc., has been quoted as saying: "If I were to bring the towers down, I would put explosives in the basement to get the weight of the building to help collapse the structure."[138]

If there were indeed explosions in the basements, they would likely have caused the ground to shake. Many people, in fact, reported feeling vibrations. According to the official account, any such vibrations would have been caused by material from the collapsing towers hitting the ground. But the testimony of some witnesses suggests that they felt shaking before the buildings started to come down. Medical technician Lonnie Penn said that just before the collapse of the South Tower, "I felt the ground shake, I turned around and ran for my life. I made it as far as the Financial Center when the collapse happened."[139] Fire patrolman Paul Curran said that he was standing near the North Tower when, "all of a sudden the ground just started shaking. It felt like a train was running under my feet. . . . The next thing we know, we look up and the tower is collapsing."[140] FDNY Lieutenant Bradley Mann saw both buildings come down. "Shortly before the first tower came down," he said, "I remember feeling the ground shaking. I heard a terrible noise, and then debris just started flying everywhere. People started running." Then, after they returned to the area, "we basically had the same thing: The ground shook again, and we heard another terrible noise and the next thing we knew the second tower was coming down."[141]

Contrary to what NIST suggests, accordingly, there is abundant evidence of explosions both below and above the impact and fire zones, and most of this evidence was even collected by the FDNY, one of the agencies NIST indicated it would trust. The fact that NIST itself evidently did not collect such information is probably best understood as another example of the fact, mentioned by Fetzer, that NIST would not find what it did not look for. NIST's apparent lack of interest in such testimony has been reported, incidentally, by one of the people quoted above, William Rodriguez, who has said:

> I contacted NIST . . . four times without a response. Finally, [at a public hearing] I asked them before they came up with their conclusion . . . if they ever considered my statements or the statements of any of the other survivors who heard the explosions. They just stared at me with blank faces.[142]

It is clear, in any case, that NIST's third reason for not considering the hypothesis of controlled demolition—that "there was no evidence (collected by [reliable sources]) of any blast or explosions in the region below the impact and fire floors"—is contradicted by a huge body of evidence. I turn now to NIST's fourth reason, which survives a comparison with the available evidence no better.

No Other Evidence of Controlled Demolition?
NIST's fourth and final stated reason for ignoring the hypothesis of controlled demolition, hence for not examining whether the recovered steel contained tell-tale signs of explosives, is that, in addition to there being no evidence for explosions, there is also no other credible evidence for the controlled demolition hypothesis.

It should be recognized that NIST's willingness to discuss such evidence involved a significant advance. In its final report, it had defined its task in such a circumscribed way that most of the evidence for controlled demolition was ruled out in advance. That is, while claiming to have described and explained the destruction of each tower, it merely offered an account of "the sequence of events from the instant of aircraft impact to the . . . time at which the building . . . was poised for collapse." Although, for the sake of "brevity," NIST said, it referred to this sequence as the "probable collapse sequence," it admitted that this sequence "does not actually include the structural behavior of the tower after the conditions for collapse initiation were reached."[143] Having defined its task in such a restricted way, NIST could ignore the various features of this "structural behavior" that are common features of controlled demolitions.

NIST's new document moves beyond this self-imposed restriction by discussing some of the phenomena to which advocates of the controlled demolition hypothesis appeal. NIST discusses only a few such phenomena in this document and its discussion of these is very inadequate. But the very fact that it has discussed them is significant for two reasons. First, it has thereby admitted that such phenomena are relevant for choosing between its hypothesis and that of controlled demolition. Second, it has opened itself to the question of why it discussed only a few such phenomena.

The answer to the second question would appear to be that NIST decided to discuss those phenomena, mentioned by various advocates of the controlled demolition hypothesis, for which it thought it could give a plausible explanation—plausible, at least, for the general reader—while ignoring the phenomena for which it realized it could not provide even the appearance of a plausible explanation. I will, in any case, look at NIST's explanations of the phenomena it mentioned, then draw attention to various phenomena that it simply ignored.

The Speed of the Collapses: As we have already seen, although NIST tried to refute the claim that the controlled demolition hypothesis is proved by the free-fall speed of the collapses, NIST's effort here failed ridiculously.

"Puffs of Smoke": In response to a question—"Weren't the puffs of smoke that were seen, as the collapse of each WTC tower starts, evidence of controlled demolition explosions?"—NIST says that "the falling mass of the building compressed the air ahead of it—much like the action of a piston—forcing smoke and debris out the windows as the stories below failed sequentially."[144] There are at least four problems with this explanation.

One problem lies in the very description of these horizontal ejections, sometimes called "squibs," as "puffs of smoke." This description begs the question, which is whether the material ejected was simply smoke from the fires or whether it included pulverized concrete produced and ejected by powerful explosives.

A second problem with NIST's explanation is that it does not match some of the eyewitness descriptions of the collapses. For example, firefighter James Curran said: "When I got underneath the north bridge I looked back and . . . I heard like every floor went chu-chu-chu. . . . [E]verything was getting blown out of the floors before it actually collapsed."[145] If material was being blown out from floors before those floors collapsed, then the ejections cannot be explained as resulting from the collapse.

A third problem with NIST's explanation is that it does not do justice to the nature of the squibs themselves, especially their rapidity and other features shared in common with puffs of stuff that can be observed in videos of controlled demolitions. This issue will be further discussed in the section on WTC 7.

A fourth problem with NIST's explanation, according to which the top floors were exerting tremendous pressure on the lower floors like a giant piston coming down, is contradicted by the visual data. Referring to the same phenomenon discussed above by Judy Wood and Steven Jones, James Fetzer says that NIST's account "might have been true if the floors had actually collapsed as the government maintains, but they were blown up from the top down."[146]

Seismic Spikes: Another question NIST chose to tackle was: "Why were two distinct spikes—one for each tower—seen in seismic records before the towers collapsed? Isn't this indicative of an explosion occurring in each tower?" NIST's reply reads:

> The seismic spikes for the collapse of the WTC Towers are the result of debris from the collapsing towers impacting the ground. The spikes began approximately 10 seconds after the times for the start of each building's collapse and continued for approximately 15 seconds. There were no seismic signals that occurred prior to the initiation of the collapse of either tower. The seismic record contains no evidence that would indicate explosions occurring prior to the collapse of the towers.[147]

Whether NIST is correct about this is something I cannot judge. Some students of the collapses who accept the controlled demolition theory believe that the seismic evidence shows that there were pre-collapse explosions.[148] Others do not.[149] As this difference of opinion shows, although good seismic evidence for such explosions would certainly strengthen the case for the controlled demolition hypothesis, such evidence is not essential to this case.

Molten Metal in the WTC Basements: NIST also decided to take on the problem of molten metal. "Why," NIST admits it was frequently asked, "did the NIST investigation not consider reports of molten steel in the wreckage from the WTC towers?"[150] It is interesting that NIST uses the term "reports," as if the existence of molten metal might be in doubt. Indeed, John L. Gross, one of NIST's main scientists, has in a public presentation challenged the idea that "there was a pool of molten steel," saying: "I know of absolutely no . . . eyewitness who has said so."[151]

The existence of molten metal has, however, been reported by people whose word surely cannot be doubted. Mark Loizeaux, president of Controlled Demolition, Inc., which was involved in the clean-up operation, said that several weeks after 9/11, when the rubble was being removed, "hot spots of molten steel" were found "at the bottoms of the elevator shafts of the main towers, down seven [basement] levels." Peter Tully, president of Tully Construction, which was also involved in the clean-up, said that he saw pools of "literally molten steel" at the site.[152] Leslie Robertson, a member of the engineering firm that designed the Twin Towers, said: "As of 21 days after the attack, the fires were still burning and molten steel was still running."[153] William Langewiesche, the only journalist who had unrestricted access to Ground Zero, wrote of descending to "areas where underground fires still burned and steel flowed in molten streams." Captain Philip Ruvolo, a firefighter involved in the recovery effort, said (in a video available on the Internet), "You'd get down below and you'd see molten steel, molten steel, running down the channel rails, like you're in a foundry, like lava."[154]

Some of the witnesses spoke specifically of steel beams. Charlie Vitchers, a construction superintendent said, "There were cherry-red pieces of steel sticking out of the ground. It was almost like being in a steel-manufacturing plant," and Bobby Gray, a crane operator, said, "I remember pulling columns up that were cherry red. Especially at night, that was incredible to see. A 30-foot column carried high above the ground would be cherry red."[155] Greg Fuchek, vice president of a company that supplied some of the computer equipment used to identify human remains, reported that "sometimes when a worker would pull a steel beam from the wreckage, the end of the beam would be dripping molten steel."[156] And there were still more witnesses.[157]

The existence of the molten metal is very well known, partly because Steven Jones' famous essay begins with this issue. After quoting several people who reported "observations of molten metal in the basements of all three buildings," Jones added:

> [S]ome six weeks after 9/11, the observed surface of the metal was still reddish-orange. This suggests that there was a large quantity of a metal with fairly low heat conductivity and a relatively large heat capacity. It is, therefore, more likely to be iron or steel than aluminum.[158]

Given the fact that the fires in the Twin Towers, even if they had been as hot as NIST claims, could not account for molten iron or steel, it is not surprising that many people asked why NIST had not investigated the reports of molten metal. NIST begins its answer with an amazing set of statements—so amazing that I had to read them several times before I could believe that NIST had really written such things. Here are those statements, with my comments interspersed:

> NIST investigators and [other] experts . . . found no evidence that would support the melting of steel in a jet-fuel ignited fire in the towers prior to collapse.[159]

Comment: Surely that point is not at issue. The whole question is why, since fire could *not* have melted steel, there was molten steel (or iron) under the rubble. As Jones had said:

> This [NIST] report admits that the fires were insufficient to melt steel beams. That admission raises the obvious question: Where, then, did the molten metal come from? All of the official reports—the FEMA Report,

The 9/11 Commission Report, the NIST Report—have failed to tackle this mystery. Yet the presence of molten metal is a significant clue to what caused the Towers and WTC 7 to collapse.[160]

NIST, however, claims otherwise, saying:

> The condition of the steel in the wreckage of the WTC towers (i.e., whether it was in a molten state or not) was irrelevant to the investigation of the collapse since it does not provide any conclusive information on the condition of the steel when the WTC towers were standing.[161]

This was the statement that really made me rub my eyes. How could the existence of steel in a molten condition be irrelevant, since it would be very strong evidence that the steel columns had been cut by explosives? Jones reports that he has asked numerous scientists and engineers whether there are "any examples of buildings toppled by fire, or any reason other than deliberate demolition, that show large pools of molten metal in the rubble," but that "no examples have emerged."[162]

Accordingly, contrary to NIST's statement that molten steel in the basements would "not provide any conclusive information on the condition of the steel when the WTC towers were standing," we can reasonably infer that it provides decisive information about the condition of some of the steel while the towers were still standing but were about to collapse.

Another reason why the claim about irrelevance is absurd is explained by James Fetzer, writing from his perspective as a philosopher of science:

> The presence of molten metal in the subbasements three, four, and five weeks later cannot be "irrelevant" to the NIST explanation of the "collapse," since it was an effect of that event. If the NIST cannot explain it, then the NIST's account is incomplete and fails to satisfy a fundamental requirement of scientific reasoning, known as the requirement of total evidence, which states scientific reasoning must be based upon all of the available relevant evidence.[163]

NIST, however, believed that it did not need to offer an explanation, because it had conclusively shown that the collapses were caused without the use of explosives. In its own words:

> NIST considered the damage to the steel structure and its fireproofing caused by the aircraft impact and the subsequent fires when the buildings were still standing since that damage was responsible for initiating the collapse of the WTC towers.[164]

We have here a perfectly circular argument: NIST articulated its theory. Critics responded that this theory did not explain the molten metal. NIST replied that the molten metal was irrelevant because it plays no role in NIST's theory, which accounts for the collapses entirely in terms of impact damage and fire.

Nevertheless, after having declared the molten metal irrelevant, NIST says that, if there *was* molten metal in the wreckage, it could be explained without resort to explosives:

> Under certain circumstances [NIST claims] it is conceivable for some of the steel in the wreckage to have melted after the buildings collapsed. Any molten steel in the wreckage was more likely due to the high temperature resulting from long exposure to combustion within the pile than to short exposure to fires or explosions while the buildings were standing.

Another incredible statement. A diffuse hydrocarbon fire, under the most ideal conditions, could never get much above 1,832°F (1,000°C). Steel does not begin to melt until 2,800°F (1,538°C). Would any scientist not employed to defend the government's conspiracy theory seriously suggest that combustion in an oxygen-starved pile of rubbish could produce temperatures almost 1,000°F hotter than the world's hottest forest fire? And yet that is what these NIST scientists, to defend this theory, have done.

And, Jones points out, they have done so in a purely speculative—that is, unscientific—manner. In the experimental sciences, to repeat, a claim, to count as a scientific claim, must be supported either by experimental evidence or historical precedent. Jones, while not rejecting NIST's speculation out of hand, says:

> It would be interesting if underground fires could somehow produce molten steel, but then there should be historical examples of this effect, since there have been many large fires in numerous buildings. But no such examples have been found. It is not enough to argue hypothetically that fires could possibly cause all three pools of molten metal. One needs at least one previous example.[165]

NIST provides no such example and yet presents its theory as scientific, apparently hoping that readers will assume that, since the theory is put out by scientists, it must be scientific.

Although NIST evidently thought that it could refute the idea that these three phenomena—the rapidity of the collapses, the squibs, and the molten metal—provide good evidence for the controlled demolition hypothesis, it could not. Even more damaging to NIST's theory, however, are various phenomena suggestive of controlled demolition that it did not even mention. Its very failure to mention them, in fact, suggests that the NIST scientists felt they would be unable to provide explanations that were plausible as well as politically acceptable. An examination of these phenomena will show why these scientists might have felt this. I will discuss nine such phenomena.

Total (Global) Collapse: As photographs of the site show, the towers, which had been 110 stories high, ended up as piles of rubble about seven stories high. How was that possible, given the fact that each tower, in addition to its 240 perimeter columns, had 47 core columns, which were massive steel box columns?[166]

This fact provided one of the major problems for the pancake theory, articulated by Thomas Eagar and endorsed by the 9/11 Commission. According to that theory, as we have seen, the floor that was just above the impact zone broke loose from the perimeter and core columns and crashed down on the floor just below the impact zone, causing it to break loose and fall on the next floor down, after which the floors "pancaked" all the way down. But if that is what had happened, the 47 core columns would still have been standing (even if, as the theory had it, the loss of support from the floors had caused the perimeter columns to fall down). This fact is illustrated, amazingly, in a graphic animation of the collapses of the towers shown in the BBC documentary, *The Conspiracy Files: 9/11*. This graphic clearly shows the core columns remaining standing as the floors break lose sequentially and crash to the ground. Guy Smith, the director-producer, was evidently oblivious to the problem. The 9/11 Commission, in any case, solved this problem by simply denying the existence of the 47 core columns, saying: "The interior core of the buildings was a hollow steel shaft, in which elevators and stairwells were grouped."[167]

NIST distanced itself from this theory, saying in answer to one of its questions: "NIST's findings do not support the 'pancake theory' of collapse. . . . [T]he floors did not fail progressively to cause a pancaking phenomenon." According to NIST's theory, collapse occurred not because the floors became disconnected from the columns but because they "remain[ed] connected to the columns and pull[ed] the columns inwards."[168]

However, even if NIST's new theory could explain how collapse of some sort resulted, it would still not explain why it was a total (or what NIST calls "global") collapse. NIST seems to suggest that, whereas the pancake theory would have left the columns, at least the core columns, standing, its own theory explains why they all fell down. But it does not. Each tower had 240 columns around its perimeter and 47 columns in its core, each one of which was about 1,400 feet long. All these columns were broken into many pieces. Indeed, reported Jim Hoffman after studying various photos of the collapse site, much of the steel seemed to be "chopped up into . . . sections that could be easily loaded onto the equipment that was cleaning up Ground Zero."[169] That observation is especially interesting in light of the statement by Controlled Demolition, Inc., in its publicity: "Our DREXS™ systems . . . segment steel components into pieces matching the lifting capacity of the available equipment."[170] My point here, of course, is that the controlled demolition theory could account for the post-collapse condition of the steel columns.

For example, a consultant for Controlled Demolition has said of RDX, one of the commonly used high explosives, that it slices steel like a "razor blade through a tomato."[171]

But how would NIST account for the fact that the steel columns were broken into fairly short pieces? According to Hoffman's judgment based on an aerial image, most of the pieces seemed to be between 24 and 48 feet long, with only a few over 50 feet.[172] But let us be generous, for the sake of argument, and suppose that most of the pieces were about 60 feet long. This would mean that each of the columns had to be broken into over 20 sections. NIST's theory would have to entail, therefore, that the downward pressure from the upper floors caused each of the 287 columns to break in 20 places. NIST's theory about the sagging floors and insulation-stripped columns applies only to a few floors, so even if it could explain why the stories above the collapse zone fell on the story below, it would not explain how the steel columns in the lower stories would have broken into pieces. This problem would be greatest with regard to the lowest floors, in which the steel box columns were at least 36 by 16 inches and about 4 inches thick on each side. NIST's theory does not even begin to explain how occurrences 80 or 90 stories higher could have caused these lower portions of the columns, which would not have even been significantly heated up, to break into pieces.

NIST's theory, insofar as it is supposed to explain total collapse, is a total failure. It does no better, moreover, with the next feature.

Vertical, Symmetrical Collapse: The most important thing in a controlled demolition of a tall building that is close to other buildings is that it come straight down, into, or at least close to, its own footprint, so that it does not harm the other buildings. Achieving this result, especially with a very tall building, is no easy matter. As Mark Loizeaux, the president of Controlled Demolition, has explained, "to bring [a building] down . . . so . . . no other structure is harmed," the demolition must be "completely planned," using "the right explosive [and] the right pattern of laying the charges."[173]

If the 110-story Twin Towers had fallen over, they would have caused an enormous amount of damage to buildings covering many city blocks. But the towers came straight down, rather than falling over. And this was cause for surprise, as illustrated by the reaction of structural engineer Joseph Burns, a partner in the Chicago firm of Thornton–Thomasetti Engineers. Saying that he was "in absolute shock over the whole thing," he exclaimed: "It just came straight down. I've seen buildings collapse like that, but they are buildings set for demolition."[174]

This vertical nature of the collapse of each tower, being obvious from the videos, is something NIST clearly needed to explain. But it did not. Here is its description of how the collapse of the North Tower was initiated:

The impact damage to the exterior walls and to the core resulted in redistribution of severed column loads. . . . Under the high temperatures and stresses in the core area, the remaining core columns with damaged insulation were thermally weakened and shortened, causing the columns on the floors above to move downward. . . . [Loads were redistributed] to the perimeter walls. . . . The long-span sections of the 95th to 99th floors on the south side weakened with increasing temperatures and began to sag. . . . As the fires intensified on the south side, the floors there sagged. . . . The sagging floors . . . pulled inward on the south perimeter columns, causing them to bow inward. . . . The bowed south wall columns buckled and were unable to carry the gravity loads. Those loads shifted to the adjacent columns . . . , but those columns quickly became overloaded as well. In rapid sequence, this instability spread all the way to the east and west walls. . . . The downward movement of [the section of the building above the impact zone] was more than the damaged structure could resist, and global collapse began.[175]

That is virtually the entire account. Besides not explaining why the collapse was global (total), it does not explain why it was vertical.

The main problem is that for the buildings to have come straight down, as Hoffman has pointed out, "All 287 columns would have to have weakened to the point of collapse at the same instant."[176] That is, even if NIST's theory could explain why all 287 columns broke into many pieces, it could not explain why all 287 columns broke on, say, the 90th floor of the North Tower at the same time, why they then all broke simultaneously on the 85th floor, why they then all broke simultaneously on the 80th floor, and so on. Unless something at least close to such simultaneous breaking had occurred, the collapse would not have been symmetrical and hence not straight down.

NIST again did not explain a very obvious feature of the collapses. The fact that it did not even try suggests that it, knowing that it could not explain it, simply had to hope that most readers would not notice. In any case, although this feature of the collapse cannot be explained by NIST's theory, it can readily be explained by the controlled demolition theory. It is, therefore, another part of the evidence for the truth of this theory.

Pulverization and Dust Clouds: Still another feature of the collapses that NIST's theory does not explain is the twofold fact that virtually everything in the towers except the steel—all the concrete, the desks, the computers, the windows, and so on—was pulverized, and that huge dust clouds arose.

Referring to the first of these facts, Hoffman reports that "nearly all of the non-metallic constituents of the towers were pulverized into fine powder."[177] That observation, incidentally, is not controversial. It was also made by Colonel John O'Dowd of the US Army Corps of Engineers. "At the World Trade Center sites," he told the History Channel, "it seemed like everything was pulverized."[178] Likewise, Bobby Gray, the crane operator who was quoted earlier, said:

> I don't remember seeing carpeting or furniture. You'd think a metal file cabinet would make it, but I don't remember seeing any, or phones, computers, none of that stuff. . . . [E]ven in areas that never burned we didn't find anything. It was just so hard to comprehend that everything could have been pulverized to that extent. How do you pulverize carpet or filing cabinets?[179]

The extent of the pulverization is further suggested by a Mount Sinai Medical Center environmental healthy study, carried out in relation to rescue workers who developed lung problems, according to which the pulverized dust contained "trillions upon trillions of microscopic shards of glass."[180]

Only because of this pulverization of virtually everything except the steel could the towers have ended up as piles of rubble only a few stories high. Otherwise each pile of rubble would have contained close to 400,000 tons of concrete stacked up.

This fact creates another enormous problem for NIST'S theory, according to which the only energy available was the gravitational energy. Although this energy would have been sufficient to break most of the concrete into fairly small pieces, it would not have been close to sufficient to pulverize most of the concrete and other non-metallic contents of the buildings into extremely tiny particles.

One result of this pulverization was the formation of giant dust clouds. This is a common feature of collapses produced by explosives, as can be seen in videos of controlled demolitions of structures such as Seattle's Kingdome and the Reading Grain Facility, which are available on the Web. The dust clouds produced at the Twin Towers differ only by being much bigger, which is what could have been predicted, given the fact that these buildings were much larger, so they would have required more powerful, and a greater number of, explosives.[181]

The difficulty the dust clouds created for NIST's theory, according to which the only available energy was gravitational, is made especially clear by the fact that, according to Hoffman's calculation, simply the expansion of the North Tower's dust cloud—ignoring the energy needed to slice the steel and pulverize the concrete and other materials—would have required at least ten times the gravitational energy available.[182]

Another problem not addressed by NIST is that gravitational energy is wholly unsuited to explain the production of these dust clouds. This is most obviously the case in the first few seconds of the collapses. In Hoffman's words: "You can see thick clouds of pulverized concrete being ejected within the first two seconds. That's when the relative motion of the top of the tower to the intact portion was only a few feet per second."[183] Jeff King, who was trained as an engineer, says, in the same vein: "[A great amount of] very fine concrete dust is ejected from the top of the building very early in the collapse. . . [when] concrete slabs [would have been] bumping into each other at [only] 20 or 30 mph."[184]

The importance of King's point can be appreciated by juxtaposing it with the claim by Shyam Sunder, NIST's lead investigator, that although the clouds of dust created during the collapses of the Twin Towers may create the impression of a controlled demolition, "it is the floor pancaking that leads to that perception."[185] This is a surprising remark, since NIST has distanced itself from the pancake theory developed by Thomas Eagar and endorsed by the 9/11 Commission, according to which the floors broke loose from the columns. Its new document, saying that "NIST's findings do not support the 'pancake theory' of collapse," states that its account of "inward bowing required the sagging floors to remain connected to the columns and pull the columns inwards."[186] Nevertheless, as Sunder's statement shows, NIST's account still involves a type of pancaking in a more general sense, according to which the upper parts of the building sequentially came down on the lower ones. This dynamic, according to NIST, began at the floor beneath the holes created by the impacts of the airliners, and NIST, as we saw earlier, used this idea to explain what it called "puffs of smoke" coming out of the lower floors. But as King points out, this theory cannot handle the fact, as revealed by the photographs and videos, that dust clouds were created far above the points of impact.

As with the previous phenomena, something that cannot be explained by NIST's theory fits perfectly with the theory of controlled demolition.

Horizontal Ejections of Pieces of Steel: From reading the "frequently asked questions" that NIST has acknowledged receiving, one might think that the only feature of the collapses suggestive of horizontal energy was the occurrence of squibs. Whereas many people might find plausible NIST's interpretation of these phenomena—that they were "puffs of smoke" ejected as the floors collapsed—NIST would surely have much greater difficulty providing a plausible interpretation, consistent with its non-explosive theory of the collapses, of the fact that, as photos and videos reveal, "Heavy pieces of steel were ejected in all directions for distances up to 500 feet, while aluminum cladding was blown up to 700 feet away from the towers."[187] Since the time at which Don Paul and Jim Hoffman wrote that statement, moreover, evidence has come forth showing that some of the steel from the North Tower landed close to 600 feet away.[188]

According to NIST's theory, the only energy available was gravitational energy, which is strictly vertical, causing matter to fall straight down. It is hard to imagine what could account for the horizontal ejections of extremely heavy pieces of steel, except very powerful explosives. It is not surprising, therefore, that NIST, in responding to questions that have been raised about its theory, did not mention these ejections, preferring to pretend that the only horizontal ejections were the squibs. (These ejections and most of the other phenomena discussed here are shown in *911 Mysteries: Demolitions*.)

Sulfidation of Steel: A journal published by Worcester Polytechnic Institute (WPI) stated early in 2002 that "metallurgical studies on WTC steel brought back to WPI reveal that a novel phenomenon—called a eutectic reaction—occurred at the surface, causing intergranular melting capable of turning a solid steel girder into Swiss cheese." WPI materials science professors Ronald Biederman and Richard Sisson, the journal added, confirmed the presence of eutectic formations "by examining steel samples under optical and scanning electron microscopes." The journal emphasized the significance of this discovery by reminding readers that "steel—which has a melting point of 2,800° Fahrenheit—may weaken and bend, but does not melt during an ordinary office fire."[189] Another WPI professor, Jonathan Barnett, specifically pointed out that fire and structural damage "would not explain steel members in the debris pile that appear to have been partly evaporated in extraordinarily high temperatures."[190]

The journal further suggested the significance of the discovery by pointing out the presence of sulfur in this eutectic reaction, saying: "the presence of oxygen, sulfur and heat caused iron oxide and iron sulfide to form at the surface of structural steel members. This liquid slag corroded through intergranular channels into the body of the metal, causing severe erosion and a loss of structural integrity."[191] This point is especially significant because, as Steven Jones has pointed out, sulfur is a common ingredient in explosives.[192]

The WPI journal, while not mentioning the possible use of explosives, did describe the damage to the metal in a way that would seem hard to explain if explosives had not been used, saying:

> The significance of the work on a sample from Building 7 and a structural column from one of the twin towers becomes apparent only when one sees these heavy chunks of damaged metal. A one-inch column has been reduced to half-inch thickness. Its edges—which are curled like a paper scroll—have been thinned to almost razor sharpness. Gaping holes—some larger than a silver dollar—let light shine through a formerly solid steel flange. This Swiss cheese appearance shocked all of the fire-wise professors, who expected to see distortion and bending—but not holes.[193]

As shown by the reaction of these "fire-wise professors"—WPI at the time had a Fire Protection Engineering program, which in 2005 became a full-fledged department[194]—this was a truly shocking discovery. The *New York Times* called it "perhaps the deepest mystery uncovered in the investigation."[195]

The first official report on the collapses of the World Trade Center, put out by FEMA, reported this discovery, saying that steel samples recovered from one of the towers as well as WTC 7 were "rapidly corroded by sulfidation." FEMA also, to its credit, appropriately called for further investigation of this finding.[196] Anyone who assumes that the NIST investigation was a truth-seeking enterprise will naturally assume that it would have carried out this investigation. The results of this investigation would have been reported, they will assume, in the section of NIST's report headed "Learning from the Recovered Steel."[197] However, besides not reporting on any such investigation, NIST did not even mention the discovery of the evaporation and sulfidation. NIST apparently did not want people thinking about "the deepest mystery uncovered in the [WTC] investigation."

North Tower Antenna Drop: Another problem noted by FEMA is that videos show that "the transmission tower on top of the [North Tower] began to move downward and laterally slightly before movement was evident at the exterior wall. This suggests that collapse began with one or more failures in the central core area of the building."[198] This drop was also mentioned in a *New York Times* story by James Glanz and Eric Lipton, which said: "Videos of the north tower's collapse appear to show that its television antenna began to drop a fraction of a second before the rest of the building. The observations suggest that the building's steel core somehow gave way first."[199]

In the supposedly definitive NIST report, however, we find no mention of this antenna drop. This is another convenient omission, since the most plausible, and perhaps only possible, explanation would be that the core columns had been sliced by explosives. This antenna drop, which can easily be seen on videos,[200] is especially problematic for NIST, Jim Hoffman explains, because of a feature of the tower's construction known as the "hat truss." This was, in Hoffman's words, "a lattice of large diagonal I-beams that connected the perimeter walls to the core structure between the 107th floor and roof." This hat truss had several functions: "[It] strengthened the core structure, unified the core and perimeter structures, and helped to support the large antenna mounted atop the North Tower."[201]

It was precisely because it had these multiple functions that the antenna drop creates an insuperable problem for NIST. On the one hand, the hat truss is essential to NIST's account of the "probable collapse sequence," because NIST "blames the hat truss for transferring 'column instability' between the core structures and the perimeter walls."[202] On the other hand, "[t]he hat truss would have assured that the façade and antenna drop in unison."[203] We can perhaps understand, therefore, why one can find no mention of the antenna drop in NIST's discussion of the collapse of the North Tower.

South Tower Tipping and Disintegration: If the North Tower's antenna drop was inexplicable from the perspective of NIST's theory, the South Tower's collapse contained an even stranger anomaly. The uppermost floors—above the level struck by the airplane—began tipping toward the corner most damaged by the impact. According to the law of the conservation of momentum, this block of approximately 34 floors should have fallen to the ground far outside the building's footprint. "However," observe Don Paul and Jim Hoffman, "as the top then began to fall, the rotation decelerated. Then it reversed direction [even though the] law of conservation of angular momentum states that a solid object in rotation will continue to rotate at the same speed unless acted on by a torque."[204]

And then, in the words of Steven Jones quoted earlier, "this block turned mostly to powder in mid-air!" This disintegration stopped the tipping and allowed the uppermost floors to fall straight down into, or at least close to, the building's footprint. As Jones asked, "How can we understand this strange behavior, without explosives?"[205]

Of course, someone might well ask, would even the explosives theory allow us to understand behavior this strange? Here we need only remind ourselves of the previously quoted statement by Mark Loizeaux, the head of Controlled Demolition:

> [B]y differentially controlling the velocity of failure in different parts of the structure, you can make it walk, you can make it spin, you can make it dance . . . . We'll have structures start facing north and end up going to the north-west.[206]

Obviously, explosives can also blow up an entire section of a building, causing it to turn to powder. Once again, something that is inexplicable in terms of the official theory becomes a matter of course if the theory of controlled demolition is adopted.

I turn now to two more facts that, while not about the collapses themselves, may be relevant to the real explanation of how they occurred.

Removal of the Steel: Although, as we have seen, a little steel was recovered, making its examination possible, it was very little. Virtually all of the steel—99.7 percent of it, meaning about 90,000 tons[207]—was removed and sold to scrap dealers, who put most of it on ships to Asia,[208] before it could be properly examined. The Science Committee of the House of Representatives complained that the "lack of authority of investigators to impound pieces of steel for examination before they were recycled led to the loss of important pieces of evidence."[209] Generally, removing any evidence from the scene of a crime is a federal offense. But in this case, federal officials allowed the removal to proceed, and quickly.[210]

This removal evoked protest. On Christmas Day, 2001, the *New York Times* said: "The decision to rapidly recycle the steel columns, beams and trusses from the WTC in the days immediately after 9/11 means definitive answers may never be known."[211] The next week, *Fire Engineering* magazine said: "We are literally treating the steel removed from the site like garbage, not like crucial fire scene evidence. . . . The destruction and removal of evidence must stop immediately."[212]

However, Mayor Bloomberg, defending the decision to dispose of the steel, said: "If you want to take a look at the construction methods and the design, that's in this day and age what computers do. Just looking at a piece of metal generally doesn't tell you anything."[213] But that is not true. An examination of the steel could have revealed whether it had been sliced by explosives. If much more steel had been examined, investigators might have found dozens or even hundreds of pieces with sulfidation or other tell-tale signs of explosives.

If NIST's primary purpose had been scientific investigation in order to determine the true cause of the destruction of the World Trade Center, it surely would have pointed out that its investigation was greatly handicapped by the removal of the steel, which could reasonably be interpreted as an attempt by authorities to cover up crucial evidence. But the NIST scientists—not surprisingly when we recall that they were working on behalf of the Bush–Cheney administration's Commerce Department—did not even mention this removal, although it was surely the most massive destruction of evidence in history.

WTC Security: The suggestion that explosives might have been used raises the question of how anyone wanting to place explosives in the towers could have gotten through the security checks. NIST could have helped the public imagine a possible answer to this question if it had informed them that from 1999 until January of 2002, President Bush's cousin Wirt Walker III was the CEO of a company—now called Stratesec but then called Securacom—that helped provide security for the World Trade Center; and that from 1993 to 2000, during which the company installed a new security system, Marvin Bush, the president's brother, was one of the company's directors.[214]

In reading NIST's final report and its answers to frequently asked questions, however, one will not find any mention of this interesting coincidence, although it had been widely discussed in critiques of the official account of the destruction of the WTC.

NIST claimed that it "found no corroborating evidence for alternative hypotheses suggesting that the WTC towers were brought down by controlled demolition using explosives planted prior to Sept. 11, 2001." How exactly that statement should be interpreted is not clear: NIST might have simply meant that it found no such evidence because it did not look for it. Or NIST might have meant that it was already aware of such evidence, so there was no need to find it. But this statement should not, in any case, be taken to mean that no such evidence exists. There is, as we have seen, an abundance of such evidence: the squibs, the molten metal, the evaporation and sulfidation of steel, the pulverization of concrete, the dust clouds, the horizontal ejection of steel beams, the South Tower tipping and disintegration, the North Tower antenna drop, and the fact that the collapses were total, vertical, symmetrical, and occurred at virtually free-fall speed. NIST's theory cannot explain any of these features, let alone all of them.

At the heart of all these problems is the fact, mentioned earlier, that NIST has misdescribed the destruction of the towers. Although I have, in order to discuss NIST's theory, been using its term "collapse," that is a misnomer. The towers, as Thurston has emphasized, did not collapse. Rather, to repeat Thurston's description, "they were systematically and progressively exploded from the top down, starting from the impact zone in each Tower." Once this is recognized, all the features to which NIST's collapse theory cannot do justice create no problem: they are what would be expected.

What about WTC 7?

The final question on NIST's list is: "Why is the NIST investigation of the collapse of WTC 7 . . . taking so long to complete?" Here is its answer:

> When NIST initiated the WTC investigation, it made a decision not to hire new staff to support the investigation. After the June 2004 progress report on the WTC investigation was issued, the NIST investigation team stopped working on WTC 7 and was assigned full-time through the fall of 2005 to complete the investigation of the WTC towers. With the release and dissemination of the report on the WTC towers in October 2005, the investigation of the WTC 7 collapse resumed. Considerable progress has been made since that time. . . . It is anticipated that a draft report will be released by early 2007.[215]

The answer, in other words, is that NIST did not have sufficient time to complete the report, because its staff was too small.

Why was its staff too small? Because when NIST began the WTC investigation, "it made a decision not to hire new staff to support the investigation." On what basis did it make such an amazing decision? We are not told. NIST appears to believe that, although the American taxpayers ponied up over $20,000,000 to pay for NIST's investigation, we were not entitled to know why it did not hire sufficient staff to complete the job in a reasonable period of time.

The fact that the report was not available by the fifth anniversary of 9/11 is completely unacceptable, given the overwhelming importance of the issue. From the perspective of the official interpretation of the attacks on the World Trade Center, the collapse of WTC 7, which was not hit by a plane, has clearly been the most puzzling occurrence. And yet the official interpretation of what happened on 9/11 has been used to justify wars in two countries, which have cost hundreds of billions of dollars and caused hundreds of thousands of deaths. From a scientific, a moral, and a public policy point of view, finding an answer to the puzzle of why WTC 7 collapsed was of the greatest importance. The effort to find this answer should not have been put on hold for over a year.

It might be assumed that NIST failed to hire additional staff because of insufficient funds. But NIST, we should recall, is an agency of the US Commerce Department and hence an agency of the US government. Does anyone seriously doubt that if President Bush had asked Congress for an additional $10 million in tax dollars to expedite NIST's work, Congress would have provided it?

If NIST's delay in putting out a report on WTC 7 cannot be explained by either lack of importance or lack of funds, we are led to wonder what the real reason might have been. And once that question is raised, a likely answer suggests itself: NIST, realizing that its explanation of the collapse of this building would be more obviously implausible than its explanation of the collapses of the Twin Towers, decided, or was ordered, to delay this report as long as possible.

Regarding this explanation as likely, of course, presupposes that NIST feared that it could not issue an explanation that would be widely accepted as plausible. And there are, indeed, reasons to think this, all of which involve the fact that giving a plausible non-demolition explanation of the collapse of WTC 7 is even more difficult than for the Twin Towers.

Prior Recognition of WTC 7's Special Difficulty

The special difficulty of explaining this collapse has been recognized from the beginning. A *New York Times* story that appeared about two and a half months after 9/11 focused on the collapse of WTC 7. Although the author, James Glanz, supported the official line, according to which the building "suffered mightily from the [out-of-control] fire that raged in it," he also pointed out that "experts said no building like it, a modern, steel-reinforced high-rise, had ever collapsed because of an uncontrolled fire." Glanz also quoted a man in charge of structural engineering at a prominent architectural firm who said that "within the structural engineering community, [Building 7] is considered to be much more important to understand [than the Twin Towers]," because they have no answer to the question, "why did 7 come down?"[216]

This perception—that the collapse of WTC 7 is even more difficult to explain than that of the Twin Towers—was supported by the report issued by FEMA in 2003. Its authors, after describing a sequence of events that might conceivably have led to the collapse of WTC 7, added that this scenario had "only a low probability of occurrence."[217]

The 9/11 Commission Report also acknowledged the difficulty of explaining this collapse by silence—that is, by simply not mentioning it. This was clearly a major omission in a report that, according to its preface, was written "to provide the fullest possible account of the events surrounding 9/11." WTC 7 was a huge building, which in most locations would have been the biggest building in the city, even the state. Its collapse was remarkable, however, primarily because it apparently demonstrated, contrary to the universal conviction prior to 9/11, that large steel-frame buildings could collapse from fire alone, even without having been struck by an airplane. This apparent demonstration should have meant that building codes and insurance premiums for all steel-frame buildings in the world needed to be changed. And yet the 9/11 Commission, in preparing its 571-page report, did not devote a single sentence to this historic event. Given the 9/11 Commission's behavior with regard to other matters (as discussed in the previous chapter), a reasonable supposition is that the Commission, having seen that FEMA had no plausible explanation for this collapse, decided it was simply best not to mention it and hope that most readers, including members of the press, would not notice or at least would not comment. And the press did not disappoint.

The idea that WTC 7 was perceived by defenders of the official account as presenting an especially difficult problem is also suggested by the fact that there appears to have been a concerted effort to keep the collapse of this building from being widely known. Since the day of 9/11 itself, although videos of the collapses of the Twin Towers have been played on mainstream television countless times, the collapse of WTC 7 has seldom been shown. The very fact that the 9/11 Commission did not mention it could also be interpreted as part of the effort to keep awareness of it down. And if there has been such an effort, it has been quite successful. A Zogby poll taken in May 2006, almost five years after 9/11, showed that only 52 percent of the population were aware that WTC 7 had collapsed.[218] NIST itself has apparently engaged in obfuscation about the collapse of WTC 7. In its website "Fact Sheet," NIST says that one of its primary objectives is to determine "why and how the World Trade Center buildings 1, 2, and 7 collapsed after the initial impact of the aircraft"—thereby perhaps suggesting to unknowing readers that WTC 7, like WTC 1 and 2, was struck by an airplane.[219]

Be that as it may, it was NIST that, following the failures of FEMA and the 9/11 Commission, was given the ultimate responsibility for performing this admittedly difficult task: to provide an account of WTC

7's collapse that would not contradict the Bush administration's conspiracy theory, according to which the attacks on the WTC were carried out entirely by al-Qaeda terrorists—a theory entailing that the collapse of WTC 7 had to result from the airplane strikes on WTC 1 and 2. There are good reasons to believe that NIST will be unable to do much better than its predecessors.

Challenges WTC 7 Presents to NIST

The most obvious problem is that WTC 7 was not hit by an airplane. Accordingly, NIST, in explaining the collapse of this building, cannot use any of the three main claims it employed to explain the collapse of each of the Twin Towers—namely, that (a) the airplane's impact stripped fireproofing from the steel, that (b) the airplane's explosion and jet fuel started very big fires, and that (c) the airplane, by severing several columns, caused the section of the building above the impact zone to fall down on the lower section, providing the final trigger for "global collapse."

Being unable to employ any of these ideas, NIST will evidently need to rely entirely on fire damage plus external damage caused by debris from the towers. It is far from obvious that such an explanation could even appear to be plausible.

NIST's task—to debunk the claim that WTC 7 was brought down by explosives—is made even more difficult by several other factors.

One factor is that whereas the collapse of each tower started near the top, allowing NIST to claim that these collapses could not have been controlled demolitions, the collapse of WTC 7 began at the bottom, like classic examples of the type of controlled demolition known as "implosion," in which the building implodes and folds in on itself, forming a quite small pile of rubble.[220] Even the FEMA report on WTC 7 admitted this, saying: "The collapse of WTC 7 had a small debris field as the facade was pulled downward, suggesting an internal failure and implosion."[221]

The collapse of WTC 7, moreover, had many other standard characteristics of planned implosions. The collapse began suddenly and then the building came straight down at virtually free-fall speed. This collapse produced squibs, dust clouds, molten metal, and even sulfidized steel. If, therefore, the collapse of WTC 7 was not a planned implosion, it was a perfect imitation.

But could the idea that it was a perfect imitation of a planned implosion—which is what NIST will have to claim—be even remotely plausible? According to ImplosionWorld.com, a website about the demolition industry, an implosion is "by far the trickiest type of explosive project, and there are only a handful of blasting companies in the world that possess enough experience . . . to perform these true building implosions."[222] Can anyone really believe that a combination of fire and externally caused damage would have just happened to produce the kind of collapse that can be reliably produced by only a few demolition companies in the world?

To see more fully how implausible such a claim would be, let us look more closely at some of the features of WTC 7's collapse.

First, this collapse was total. Although this building was dwarfed by the Twin Towers, it was nevertheless, as emphasized earlier, a huge building. As stated in the aforementioned *New York Times* story about the collapse of WTC 7, had the Twin Towers not come down, the collapse of this building would have been "a mystery that . . . would probably have captured the attention of the city and the world."[223] One of the biggest elements of this mystery is how this 47-story building's 81 columns—24 core and 57 perimeter columns—could have collapsed into a very compact pile of rubble without being sliced by explosives. (Interesting here is a statement made by Stacey Loizeaux, daughter of Controlled Demolition's president Mark Loizeaux, in a 1996 interview. Describing the preparatory work for bringing down a building, she said: "Depending on the height of the structure, we'll work on a couple different floors—usually anywhere from two to six. The taller the building, the higher we work. We only really need to work on the first two floors, because you can make the building come down that way. But we work on several upper floors to help fragment debris . . . , so all the debris ends up in small, manageable pieces."[224])

Equally mysterious is how the collapse could have been almost perfectly symmetrical, so that the building came straight down. All 81 columns would have had to collapse at the same time. Even if fires could somehow cause column failure, fires spread unevenly (asymmetrically) throughout a building could not produce this kind of symmetrical failure. As Steven Jones has written: "The likelihood of near-symmetrical collapse of WTC 7 due to random fires (the 'official' theory)—requiring as it does near-simultaneous failure of many support columns—is infinitesimal."[225]

Another mystery is how a fire-induced collapse, even if possible, could have occurred at virtually free-fall speed (about 6.6 seconds). Although NIST's theory as to why the Twin Towers came down at free-fall speed is thoroughly implausible, even scientifically impossible, it is at least a theory. But what possible theory could NIST scientists put out with a straight face to explain how WTC 7 came down at this speed, just as if explosives had been used?

The molten metal underneath WTC 7 is, if anything, even more problematic for NIST's scientists, because they cannot claim that it was somehow produced by the planes.

And then there are those pieces of steel that, according to Jonathan Barnett, appeared to be partly evaporated. Barnett was speaking of WTC 7 when he said that, even if a combination of fire and structural damage could explain why the building collapsed, it could not explain those pieces of steel in the debris pile.[226]

Furthermore, according to Steven Jones, the squibs that are visible in videos of WTC 7's collapse are too similar to squibs produced by planned implosions to be dismissed as puffs of smoke produced by pancaking floors. Referring to some videos of the collapse of WTC 7,[227] he wrote:

[H]orizontal puffs of smoke and debris, sometimes called "squibs," emerge from the upper floors of WTC 7, in regular sequence, just as the building starts to collapse. The upper floors have evidently not moved relative to one another yet, from what one can observe on the videos. In addition, the timing between the puffs is less than 0.2 seconds, so air-expulsion due to collapsing floors, as suggested by defenders of the official account,[228] is evidently excluded. Since this is near the initiation of the collapse, free-fall time for a floor to fall down to the next floor is significantly longer than 0.2 seconds: the equation for free fall yields a little over 0.6 seconds.[229] The official reports lack an explanation for these squibs.

However, the presence of squibs proceeding up the side of the building is common when pre-positioned explosives are used, as can be observed on several videos at the Website for Implosion World.[230]

As Jones' account shows, it would be particularly difficult for NIST to claim that all of WTC 7's squibs were produced by collapsing smoke-filled floors.

Finally, as with the Twin Towers, there were reports, even if not nearly as many, of explosions. One emergency medical worker said:

We were watching the building actually 'cause it was on fire . . . and . . . we heard this sound that sounded like a clap of thunder. . . . turned around—we were shocked to see that the building was ah well it looked like there was a shockwave ripping through the building and the windows all busted out. . . . [A]bout a second later the bottom floor caved out and the building followed after that.[231]

Another report came from Peter DeMarco, a *New York Daily News* reporter, who said:

At 5:30PM there was a rumble. The building's top row of windows popped out. Then all the windows on the thirty-ninth floor popped out. Then the thirty-eighth floor. Pop! Pop! Pop! was all you heard until the building sunk into a rising cloud of gray.[232]

Still another report came from Michael Hess, New York City's corporation counsel, who had been in the building's emergency management center on the 23rd floor. During an interview, he said: "Another gentleman and I walked down to the 8th floor, where there was an explosion, and we've been trapped with smoke all around us for an hour and a half."[233]

Given all these mysteries, from the total collapse through the explosions, we can see that the scientists at NIST would consider the task of formulating a plausible account of the collapse of WTC 7, while maintaining that it was not caused by explosives, to be a task of utmost difficulty.

The Very Appearance of this Collapse

NIST's task is made even more difficult by the fact that, besides objectively having many standard features of a planned implosion, the collapse of WTC 7, when seen on a video, immediately appears to be a controlled demolition to people who have previously seen such operations. For example, Dan Rather, showing a video of the collapse of WTC 7 on CBS News the evening of 9/11, said that it was "reminiscent of those pictures we've all seen too much on television before when a building was deliberately destroyed by well-placed dynamite to knock it down." (Although the collapse of WTC 7 has, as mentioned earlier, seldom been shown on mainstream television since then, it can be viewed on various websites and DVDs.[234])

The collapse of WTC 7 looks like a planned implosion, moreover, not only to laypeople like Dan Rather but also to the trained eyes of professionals. This fact was recently demonstrated in Holland. Danny Jowenko, who has been in the demolition business for 27 years and has his own company, was interviewed for a Dutch TV program investigating 9/11 theories. With the camera running, he was shown videos, from various angles, of the collapse of WTC 7, but without being told what the building was (he had previously been unaware that any building other than the Twin Towers had come down on 9/11). In commenting on the collapse, he said: "It starts from below. . . They have simply blown away columns. . . . A team of experts did this. . . .This is controlled demolition." When he was then told that this building collapsed on September 11, seven hours after the Twin Towers, he was incredulous, asking repeatedly whether the interviewer was sure. When Jowenko was finally convinced, he said: "Then they've worked very hard." Later, after examining the evidence more extensively, he said: "This is professional work, without any doubt. These boys know very well what they do."[235]

Danny Jowenko is, moreover, not the only expert in Europe to state this conclusion (which can be expressed in Europe with somewhat less danger of reprisal than in the US). Two professors of structural engineering at Switzerland's most prestigious university, the ETH Swiss Federal Institute of Technology in Zurich, have also expressed this conclusion. Professor emeritus Hugo Bachmann has said: "In my opinion WTC 7 was with the utmost probability brought down by controlled demolition done by experts." Jörg Schneider has said: "WTC 7 was with the highest probability brought down by explosives." Likewise, Heikki Kurttila, an accident analyst for the Finnish National Safety Technology Authority, has concluded his technical analysis with this statement:

> The observed collapse time of WTC 7 was 6.5 seconds. That is . . . half a second shorter than the falling time of an apple when air resistance is taken into account. . . . The great speed of the collapse and the low value of the resistance factor strongly suggest controlled demolition.[236]

Two More Unique Features of This Collapse

Besides the fact that WTC 7 was not hit by a plane and that its collapse looked just like a planned implosion, there were two other unique features about its collapse that increase the difficulty of defending the official conspiracy theory.

One of these features is that although there was foreknowledge of all three WTC collapses, the foreknowledge of WTC 7's collapse was more widespread and of longer duration than that for the Twin Towers. The information we have about foreknowledge of the collapse of the South Tower would be consistent with the supposition that this knowledge was acquired only shortly in advance. It can be supposed, therefore, that someone saw something going on in the South Tower that led Mayor Giuliani's Office of Emergency Management to infer that the building was going to collapse. The 9/11 oral histories reveal, however, that the fact that WTC 7 was going to collapse was known several hours in advance.

It was evidently again Giuliani's Office of Emergency Management that had the foreknowledge. Captain Michael Currid, the president of the Uniformed Fire Officers Association, said that some time after the collapse of the Twin Towers, "Someone from the city's Office of Emergency Management" told him that WTC 7 was "basically a lost cause and we should not lose anyone else trying to save it," after which the firefighters in the building were told to get out.[237] A collapse zone was then established some "five or six hours" before the building collapsed, according to Fire Chief Frank Fellini. "We hung out for hours waiting for 7 to come down," reported firefighter Vincent Massa.[238]

This information creates an additional difficulty for the official theory, which NIST must defend. Given the fact that fire and external damage had never caused a steel-frame high-rise building to collapse, why would people in Giuliani's office have concluded around noon that WTC 7 was going to collapse? Although the Twin Towers had just come down, the fact that these buildings had been hit by airplanes, whereas WTC 7 had not, could well have seemed relevant. Also, there were, in addition to the Twin Towers, five buildings in the WTC complex, some of which were pounded by debris from the towers much more heavily than was WTC 7, and yet evidently only the latter was expected to collapse. This unique expectation is explainable, and arguably only explainable, on the supposition that someone in the Office of Emergency Management knew that there were explosives in WTC 7 that were going to be set off.[239]

A second unique feature of the collapse of WTC 7 follows from the first: Because everyone was removed from the building several hours in advance, no one was killed when it actually did collapse. This fact undermines the reason that was given for the rapid removal of the steel: the claim that some of the victims might still be alive in the rubble, so the steel needed to be removed to aid the search-and-rescue mission. This rationale might have seemed plausible for the Twin Towers (although, in fact, the last of the 20 people rescued from the rubble—Genelle Guzman, mentioned earlier—was rescued shortly after noon on September 12[240]), but it could not be applied to the WTC 7 site. Nevertheless, the removal of the steel from that site proceeded just as quickly. This fact supports the notion that the real reason for the unprecedented destruction of evidence was to cover up an unprecedented crime.

What Will NIST Say about WTC 7?

In light of all these problems, what is NIST's report on WTC 7 likely to say? Given the limited possibilities plus what NIST has already said,[241] the report will probably say that the collapse was caused by fires, alleged to be very big and hot, plus severe structural damage to the building caused by steel falling from at least one of the Twin Towers.

We can be quite certain, in other words, that NIST will not seriously explore evidence that the building was brought down by explosives. Some indication that this line of thought has been ruled out in advance is provided by NIST's statement about awarding a contract to Applied Research Associates (ARA)—which provided analysis of the aircraft impact on the Twin Towers—to provide an analysis of WTC 7's collapse. According to NIST's statement, ARA's "detailed floor analyses will determine likely modes of failure for Floors 8 to 46 due to failure of one or more supporting columns."[242] Besides seeming to imply that NIST told ARA in advance what its analysis must conclude, the restriction to floors 8 to 46 is especially interesting in light of the statement by Stacey Loizeaux of Controlled Demolition, quoted earlier, that "[w]e only really need to work on the first two floors, because you can make the building come down that way." As Ed Haas, after quoting these statements, has written: "So why isn't ARA being asked by the government to conduct analysis of the entire WTC-7 structure from the basement level to the top floor?"[243]

In any case, assuming that NIST is committed to providing a non-explosive explanation, it will have to rely solely on big, hot fires and severe structural damage. But both will be highly problematic. To begin with the former: any case made for big and hot fires will be contradicted by both testimonial and photographic evidence.

Some first responders on the scene indicated that there were fires on only a few floors. For example, medical technician Decosta Wright said: "I think the fourth floor was on fire." As he and others saw the firefighters just standing around, "we were like, are you guys going to put that fire out?"[244] Chief Thomas McCarthy said: "[T]hey were waiting for 7 World Trade to come down. . . . They had . . . fire on three separate floors . . . , just burning merrily. It was pretty amazing, you know, it's the afternoon in lower Manhattan, a major high-rise is burning, and they said 'we know.'"[245]

Some of the members of the FDNY, to be sure, claimed that WTC 7 had become a towering inferno. Chief Daniel Nigro spoke of "very heavy fire on many floors."[246] Harry Meyers, an assistant chief, said that "[w]hen the building came down it was completely involved in fire, all forty-seven stories."[247] That claim was also made by firefighter Tiernach Cassidy, who said: "[WTC 7] was fully engulfed. . . . [Y]ou could see the flames going straight through from one side of the building to the other."[248]

One way to decide which of these conflicting accounts to believe is to use a common principle employed by historians in situations of this type, where some members of an organization or movement say things that support its official line, while other members say things that contradict it. All other things being equal, historians give greater credence to the latter. To see why, we can use the present case. The official story, which the FDNY, as an agency of the City of New York, had to support, was that WTC 7 had huge fires. If this claim was not true, we can imagine several reasons why some members of the FDNY, testifying about three months after the fact, would have nevertheless made the claim—reasons such as loyalty to the organization, fear of reprisal from superiors, and so on. But if, on the contrary, WTC 7 was indeed, as Assistant Chief Harry Meyers said, "completely involved in fire, all forty-seven floors," it would be hard to imagine why any members of the department would have said otherwise. The testimony of those who said there was fire on only a few floors must, therefore, be considered more credible. (They perhaps contradicted the official line because they were unaware of this line, or because no pressure was put on them to support it, or because they simply felt the need to tell the truth.)

This conclusion would have to be reconsidered, to be sure, if the photographic evidence supported the view that WTC 7 had become a towering inferno by the time it collapsed. But this is not the case. All the photographs and videos suggest that the fires in this building were small, not very hot, and limited to a few floors. A photograph of the north side of this building taken by Terry Schmidt at about 3:15, hence only about two hours before the building came down, supports Chief Thomas McCarthy's testimony, showing fires on only three floors of this 47-story building.[249] So if the south side, which faced the towers, had fires on many other floors, they were not, contrary to Tiernach Cassidy's claim, extensive enough to be seen from the other side of the building.

The empirically based conclusion that the fires in this building were even smaller than those in the towers is, moreover, just what should be expected, given the absence of an airplane explosion and jet fuel to get a big fire started.

NIST could, to be sure, claim that the fires became really big only after Schmidt's photograph was taken. But if this were true, we would expect that, given all the photographers and videographers at the WTC site that afternoon, pictures of WTC 7 as a towering inferno would be plentiful. But, far from having such pictures and videos, we have videos of the building when it begins collapsing showing it *not* to be engulfed in flames. We also have the testimony of *New York* magazine reporter Mark Jacobson, who says of the building a few minutes before it collapsed: "It wasn't a 47-story building that was engulfed in flames. The whole building wasn't on fire. . . . There was a lot of fire coming out of a few floors."[250]

Another problem with the claim about a late-blooming fire would be that, if the fires did not really get going until about 3:30, they would have had only two hours to cause damage. And yet the fireproofing was supposed to be good for two hours and then, after it was gone, the unprotected steel was certified for another three hours. Given the fact that raging fires that have gone on for over sixteen hours in steel-frame high-rises have not produced even partial collapse, the idea that a two-hour fire could somehow produce a total collapse is completely implausible.

Of course, given the outrageous claims that NIST has made with regard to the Twin Towers, these problems are not likely to deter it from claiming that WTC 7 collapsed partly because its fires were extremely big, hot, and long-lasting. One route open to it is to follow the FEMA report by suggesting that the diesel fuel in the building somehow caught fire and created raging fires. To be sure, FEMA, while noting that "the total diesel fuel on the premises contained massive potential energy," frankly admitted that "the best hypothesis" it could come up with as to how this fuel caught fire and then caused structural collapse had "only a low probability of occurrence."[251] NIST scientists, however, have proven themselves more imaginative in estimating probabilities.

These scientists may also find a way to argue that, even without an airplane impact, the fireproofing insulation was missing from some of the steel columns, perhaps coincidentally at just those places where NIST's computer simulations will imply that the fires would have been hottest.

As indicated earlier, moreover, NIST will probably not rely on fire alone but will also argue that the physical damage to the building was much greater than previously thought, with falling steel beams from the Twin Towers doing damage analogous to that caused to the towers by the airplane impacts. Indeed, NIST's lead investigator, Shyam Sunder, has already said about WTC 7: "On about a third of the face to the center and to the bottom—approximately 10 stories—about 25 percent of the depth of the building was scooped out." NIST has also pointed out that there was damage to this building's upper stories and southwest corner that FEMA's report missed.[252]

However, although this combination of structural damage, missing insulation, and raging fires will probably be the best NIST can do, it could not begin to explain the collapse of WTC 7. Damage to one side of the building plus asymmetrical fires could not explain the symmetrical, straight-down collapse. As Hoffman, on the basis of NIST's preliminary reports on the collapse of WTC 7, has said:

> Even if one accepts all of NIST's claims about extensive structural damage to WTC 7, and its claims about fires on several different floors, its collapse scenario is not remotely plausible. The alleged damage was asymmetric, confined to the tower's south side, and any weakening of the steelwork from fire exposure would also be asymmetric. Thus, even if the damage were sufficient to cause the whole building to collapse, it would have fallen over asymmetrically—toward the south. But WTC 7 fell straight down, into its footprint.[253]

Moreover, raging fires and externally produced structural damage could not explain how steel columns 47 stories high collapsed into a small pile of rubble no more than three stories high or how the building came down at virtually free-fall speed. This combination of fire and structural damage also could not account for the dust clouds, the squibs, the molten metal, and the partly evaporated steel. But scientists employed by the Bush administration's NIST, who have already proven themselves undeterred by either laws of science or lack of historical precedence, will probably suggest otherwise.

The mainstream press and even much of the left-leaning press will, moreover, probably again let them get away with it, dismissing any challenges to NIST's account as based on wild conspiracy theories. This attitude is truly remarkable.

When we combine the fact that the collapse of WTC 7 immediately appears to be a controlled demolition with the twofold fact that all prior collapses of steel-frame high-rise buildings have been produced by explosives and that the collapse of WTC 7 has many features in common with planned implosions, the view that it was a planned implosion should be the natural assumption. The burden of proof should be placed on any claim that WTC 7 was brought down by something other than explosives, because this is the wild, empirically baseless hypothesis devoid of historical precedent, which is just the kind of hypothesis that one expects from irrational conspiracy theorists.

However, the fact that the conspiracy theory being supported by this wild, scientifically and historically baseless speculation is the government's own is, for some reason, thought to justify turning things upside down. In this topsy-turvy framework, those whose theory is consistent with science, the empirical facts, and all historical precedent are ridiculed as nutty conspiracy theorists while those who articulate a wildly speculative theory, which contradicts all prior experience, several laws of science, and numerous empirical facts, are considered the sober, sensible thinkers, whose pronouncements can be trusted without examination.

We can hope, if not expect, that when NIST finally produces its report on WTC 7, this situation will have changed.

Conclusion

As I pointed out in the introduction, if an investigation is to be considered scientific, it must examine the possible hypotheses, then settle on the one that is best in terms of accounting for the relevant data. By its own admission, however, the NIST study did not do this. It did not consider the hypothesis of controlled demolition. Rather, it assumed from the outset the truth of the government's theory, then tried to offer an explanation as to how the impact of the airplanes plus the ensuing fires could have brought the buildings down.

That this was indeed NIST's approach was confirmed, reports Michael Green, in a conversation he had with Ronald Hamburger, one of the structural engineers who contributed to the NIST report. Green asked: "Was your group given the task of explaining how the Towers collapsed, based on the assumption that the collapse was caused solely by the damage from the impact of the airplanes and the subsequent fire?" Hamburger replied, simply, "yes." After receiving this answer plus listening to a lecture by this engineer, Green, who is a philosopher as well as a clinical psychologist, concluded:

> Mr. Hamburger does not give us science. He gives us politics wrapped in science, bracketed by science, but not science. The question of what caused the Towers and WTC7 to collapse was never addressed by NIST, no more than NIST addressed the question "Do pigs fly?" Rather, NIST addressed the question, "On the assumption that pigs fly, how do they do it?"[254]

To carry out the analogy more fully on the basis of the earlier discussion of computer simulations, we could imagine a team of scientists using simulations to show that pigs could, in fact, fly. To do this, they hollow out the pigs' bones, eliminate most of their body fat, and give them enormous ears that flap like wings. When asked why they put in such unrealistic data, they reply: "Otherwise, the pigs could not fly."

FOUR

Debunking 9/11 Myths:
A Failed Attempt by *Popular Mechanics*

In March 2005, *Popular Mechanics* magazine, which is owned by Hearst Magazines, published an article entitled "9/11: Debunking the Myths."[1] This attempt at debunking critics of the official 9/11 conspiracy theory was itself thoroughly debunked by various members of the 9/11 truth movement, including Jim Hoffman and Jeremy Baker, the latter of whom said, "if this absurdly flawed attempt to discredit the 9/11 truth movement is an example of PM's research skills and technical expertise, I'm definitely not building that tree house on page 87."[2] I myself called it a "spectacularly bad article," adding that "*Popular Mechanics* owes its readers an apology for publishing such a massively flawed article on such an important subject."[3]

However, far from apologizing, *Popular Mechanics* in 2006 published a somewhat revised and expanded version of this essay as a book, entitled *Debunking 9/11 Myths: Why Conspiracy Theories Can't Stand Up to the Facts.*[4] And this book, apart from correcting a few of the flaws in the article, is no better. Its errors are especially important because, besides the fact that this book is easily the most widely read of the four documents examined here, its ideas have been spread even further by Guy Smith's BBC documentary, *The Conspiracy Files: 9/11*, which treated *Popular Mechanics* as the primary authority about 9/11.

Senator John McCain's Foreword
The book's many problems begin in its foreword, written by Senator John McCain. Although obtaining McCain's endorsement was probably regarded as a great coup by *Popular Mechanics*, his foreword does nothing to create an expectation that Baker's characterization of the original article—"a train wreck of disinformation and as conspicuous a propaganda ploy as one could imagine"[5]—will not apply to the book version.

The propagandistic nature of McCain's own statement is illustrated by his one-sided use of the term "conspiracy theorist" to apply only to people who reject the government's own conspiracy theory about 9/11. Although the whole purpose of the book he is endorsing is to defend this conspiracy theory, he praises the book for "reject[ing] . . . conspiracy."[6]

McCain rightly points out that a major problem with conspiracy theorists in the pejorative sense is that they "chase any bit of information, no matter how flimsy, and use it to fit their preordained conclusions." But then he praises the *Popular Mechanics* book, as if it followed his dictum that people should reach their conclusions about 9/11 by using "the methods of science."[7] But it presupposes the conclusions of NIST and the 9/11 Commission, which, as we have seen, violate the scientific criteria of repeatability and adequacy to all the relevant evidence.

McCain also complains that "[p]olitical extremists peddle [conspiratorial] explanations that support their ideologies."[8] But then McCain himself illustrates how the official theory has been used to support the Bush administration's post-9/11 ideology, according to which America the Good was attacked by evil Muslims—the ideology used to justify the so-called war on terror. On 9/11, McCain says, America was subjected to

> a savage atrocity, an act so hostile we could scarcely imagine any human being capable of it. . . . But as 19 men showed the world their worst, we Americans displayed what makes our country great: courage and heroism, compassion and generosity. . . . [W]e were attacked not for a wrong we had done, but for who we are—a people united in a kinship of ideals.[9]

Given the twofold fact that Americans are so good and the 9/11 attacks were so evil "that we can scarcely imagine any human being" capable of them, McCain is especially incensed by the fact that what he calls the "9/11 conspiracy movement" makes "ugly, unfounded accusations of extraordinary evil against fellow Americans."[10] McCain, however, levels these accusations against Osama bin Laden and "the 19 men," evidently having no trouble imagining that non-American Muslims are capable of such extraordinary evil.

McCain, having no doubt about how truly evil they are compared with how good we are, adds:

> Osama Bin Laden and his ilk have perverted a peaceful religion, devoting it not to the salvation of souls but to the destruction of bodies. They wish to destroy us, to bring the world under totalitarian rule according to some misguided religious fantasy. Our cherished ideals of freedom, equality, and religious tolerance stand in their way.[11]

McCain does not, of course, remind readers that the military forces of our overwhelmingly Christian nation have destroyed far more bodies in Iraq in the past three years than al-Qaeda has anywhere in the world during its entire existence. Nor does he mention that the Project for the New American Century (PNAC), with which many members of the Bush administration have been affiliated, articulated a plan for a Pax Americana that, to other peoples, looks like a plan for totalitarian rule of the planet. McCain thereby provides a perfect illustration of what he says about "political extremists," namely, that they "peddle [conspiratorial] explanations that support their ideologies."

To be sure, McCain, if he were to admit that the official account of 9/11 is itself a conspiracy theory, would surely insist that it differs from the conspiracy theory he is attacking by virtue of being based on the facts. Saying (rightly) that "[a]ny explanation for the tragedy of 9/11 must start and end with the facts," McCain claims that "the evidence for Al Qaeda's central role in the 9/11 attacks is overwhelming."[12] As we have seen in previous chapters, however, that evidence is quite underwhelming. And McCain, although he says that any acceptable theory about 9/11 must "start and end with the facts," fails to inform his readers of the fact that the FBI does not include 9/11 among the crimes for which bin Laden is wanted—because, as its chief of investigative publicity has said, "the FBI has no hard evidence connecting Bin Laden to 9/11."[13] McCain also, of course, does not refer to any of the other facts that cast doubt on the official story about al-Qaeda's role in 9/11.

Instead of acknowledging that the alternative conspiracy theory is based on evidence—both lack of evidence for al-Qaeda's central role in 9/11 and abundant evidence for the Bush administration's central role in it—McCain employs a psychological explanation:

> We want to believe that 19 men could not murder our citizens, destroy our grandest buildings, and terrorize our country. . . . We would like to think that there was something . . . hidden, more sophisticated, something as grand as the lives so easily destroyed.[14]

One problem with this psychological explanation is that most people who now accept the alternative theory did not do so until a year or more after 9/11, having previously accepted the official story. If they eventually came to accept this alternative theory because of a psychological need for a grander theory, why did it take so long for this need to manifest itself? A second problem, which is even more serious, is that even if this need does exist in the American psyche, it is surely outweighed by a far stronger need: to believe that our own government would not attack and deceive us. Insofar as wishful-and-fearful thinking plays a role in determining whether Americans accept the official or the alternative conspiracy theory, the wish to believe that American leaders would not do such a heinous thing surely shapes far more beliefs than does any feeling that the official theory is simply not grand enough.

In any case, having described the conspiracy theories he attacks as grand, he informs us that "the truth is more mundane." Referring to philosopher Hannah Arendt's description of "the banality of Nazi evil," McCain says that the people who orchestrated the 9/11 attacks "were also ordinary, uninteresting men with twisted beliefs."[15] This is a point on which both sides agree. They disagree only about the identity of these men.

In one passage, McCain does acknowledge, implicitly, that the official account of 9/11 is itself a conspiracy theory, as he says that those who accept the alternative theory, having been "unsatisfied with the ordinary truth," have "concocted stories more fanciful, more conspiratorial."

The two theories are, however, equally conspiratorial. The fact that the alternative theory sees the conspirators as members of the Bush–Cheney administration and its Pentagon does not make it more conspiratorial than the official theory, according to which the conspirators were members of al-Qaeda. What McCain must mean, therefore, is simply that the official theory is "more mundane," the alternative theory "more fanciful."

But do those descriptions really match the two theories in the way he suggests? On the one hand, what could be more fanciful than the official theory, according to which 19 young men, following a plan authorized in Afghanistan, prepared for their operation without being detected by any of our many intelligence organizations, defeated the most sophisticated defense system in history, caused the total collapse of three steel-frame high-rise buildings by crashing planes into two of them, and then crashed another plane into what is surely the most well-defended building on the planet? If such a story had been taken to Hollywood, would it not likely have been rejected as too fanciful?

On the other hand, what is more mundane than an imperial power planning a false-flag operation to drum up support for a military adventure? As I mentioned earlier, the Japanese army created such an incident at Mukden in 1931 when it wanted an excuse to attack Manchuria; the Nazis created such an incident in 1939 when they were ready to attack Poland; the Pentagon's Joint Chiefs of Staff created various scenarios for such an incident in 1961, to be called "Operation Northwoods," that would, in their words, "provide justification for US military intervention in Cuba";[16] and in 1964 the US government fabricated tales about an incident in the Gulf of Tonkin to justify an attack on North Vietnam.[17]

It would seem, therefore, that if the more mundane, less fanciful explanation is more likely to be true, as McCain suggests, then it is the alternative theory that, on this a priori basis, we should expect to be true.

This point is reinforced by McCain's observation that one characteristic of false conspiracy theories is that they ascribe to alleged conspirators "powers wholly out of proportion to what the evidence suggests."[18] McCain intends this criticism to apply to theories that ascribe such powers to the US government. But surely, if the question is which organization—the US government or al-Qaeda—was more capable of planning and carrying out the attacks, there is no comparison. The US military, with an annual budget of hundreds of billions of dollars and the most advanced military and intelligence technology on the planet, easily had the capacity to orchestrate this operation. It is the idea that al-Qaeda was capable of outwitting this military's defense system and pulling off all the other amazing feats that involves ascribing "powers wholly out of proportion to what the evidence suggests." The idea that al-Qaeda had such powers has seemed credible to a large (but shrinking) percentage of the American population only because of the media's refusal to expose the fancifulness of the tales spun by the White House, the Pentagon, FEMA, NIST, and the 9/11 Commission.

Another misplaced contrast between the two conspiracy theories is implied by McCain's statement that the alternative theory "exploits the public's anger and sadness." Yet surely a fact about 9/11 on which there is widespread agreement is that the Bush administration exploited the emotions produced by the attacks to get both public and congressional support for policies—including attacks on Afghanistan and Iraq, huge increases in military spending, violations of Geneva conventions regarding prisoners, and serious restrictions on civil rights, such as habeas corpus— that would have been otherwise impossible. What exploitation of post-9/11 emotions by the 9/11 truth movement could remotely compare?

Still another accusation made by McCain is that the movement advocating the alternative theory further "shakes Americans' faith in their government." If by this he means that we shake Americans' faith in the Bush–Cheney administration, then, yes, that is what we want to do and we are glad that McCain thinks we are succeeding. If this administration engineered the 9/11 attacks to get support for its pre-established policies, as we believe, then further shaking Americans' faith in this administration, so it will no longer be given a blank check to carry out its nefarious and destructive policies, is a good thing. But if McCain means the American government in a broader sense, then one thing that is shaking many people's faith in it is its refusal to authorize a truly independent investigation of the problems in the official story about 9/11. McCain himself could have done something to restore this faith if he—as a leading Republican member of the US Senate—had worked to authorize an investigation of 9/11 not controlled by the Bush–Cheney administration.

Instead, McCain has further shaken informed people's faith in the US Congress by endorsing this piece of propaganda put out by *Popular Mechanics*, which embodies the very features McCain excoriates: It "ignore[s] the methods of science"; it uses "any bit of information, no matter how flimsy," that will bolster its "preordained conclusion"; and it "ignore[s] the facts that are present in plain sight." Contrary to McCain's claim, PM's book does not "disprove [the alternative] conspiracy [theory]"—as I will show.

The Story Behind PM's Treatment of 9/11
This book, in one of its many self-congratulatory claims, says on its back cover: "With more than 100 years of expertise in science and technology,

Popular Mechanics is ideally equipped to research the evidence behind [charges that the US government orchestrated the attacks of 9/11]." Readers previously familiar with *Popular Mechanics* (PM) were thereby led to believe that this book on 9/11 was put out by people whose expertise and trustworthiness had been demonstrated over the previous decades. This same impression was created by Guy Smith's BBC documentary, which said: "*Popular Mechanics* is an American institution, a no-nonsense, nuts-and-bolts magazine, writing about technology since the days of Henry Ford and the Wright Brothers."

However, in the months just prior to the publication of the article on which this book is based, a radical change in PM's personnel was orchestrated by the president of Hearst Magazines, Cathleen P. Black. As reporter Christopher Bollyn pointed out, Black is married to Thomas E. Harvey, who has worked for the CIA, the Department of Defense, and the US Information Agency.

Bollyn, describing this Black-orchestrated change at *Popular Mechanics* as "a brutal take-over," wrote: "In September 2004, Joe Oldham, the magazine's former editor-in-chief, was replaced by James B. Meigs. In October, a new creative director replaced PM's 21-year veteran who was given ninety minutes to clear out of his office." In each of the following six months, Bollyn further reported, three or four more people were similarly dismissed.[19] Accordingly, the suggestion that this book about 9/11 reflects PM's long tradition of expertise is misleading.

Bollyn also unearthed another fact relevant to the credibility of PM's writing about 9/11: that 25-year-old Benjamin Chertoff, who described himself as the "senior researcher" for the article, is a cousin of the new head of Homeland Security, Michael Chertoff. Bollyn then wrote an essay entitled "9/11 and Chertoff: Cousin Wrote 9/11 Propaganda for PM." The Hearst Corporation, Bollyn charged, had hired young Chertoff to work on an article supporting the very interpretation of 9/11 that had led to the creation of the department now headed by his older cousin.[20]

As Bollyn learned, this familial relationship seemed to be something that neither Benjamin Chertoff nor PM wanted to advertise. When young Chertoff was asked by Bollyn if he was related to Michael Chertoff, he replied, "I don't know," then said that all further questions should be put to PM's publicist. Bollyn then called Benjamin Chertoff's mother. When asked whether her son was related to the new secretary of Homeland Security, she reportedly replied: "Yes, of course, he is a cousin."

From editor-in-chief Meigs' "Afterword" to the book, however, a reader would assume that there was some doubt about this. After commenting about "the odd coincidence that Benjamin Chertoff, then the head of the magazine's research department, has the same last name as the then newly appointed head of the Department of Homeland Security,

Michael Chertoff," Meigs wrote: "Christopher Bollyn phoned Ben's mother, who volunteered that, yes, she thinks Michael Chertoff might be a distant cousin." Confidence in Meigs' reportorial honesty is hardly inspired by this transmutation—of "yes, of course" into "yes, she thinks" and of "he is a cousin" to "[he] might be a distant cousin." Besides mentioning the conversation between Bollyn and Benjamin Chertoff's mother, Meigs himself says: "it's possible that Ben and Michael Chertoff are distantly related."[21]

Meigs' expression of doubt is amazing. He is claiming that he and his crack staff were in a few months able to discover all the central truths about 9/11—why the planes were not intercepted, why the World Trade Center buildings came down, what really hit the Pentagon, and what really happened to UA Flight 93—and yet they were not able to find out for sure whether a member of their own team was related to the director of Homeland Security!

Meigs does, however, say that there is one thing about the two men of which he is certain: "Ben and Michael Chertoff have never spoken."[22] The point of this denial is, of course, to rule out the suspicion that Michael Chertoff had anything to do with PM's 9/11 article, perhaps encouraging his younger cousin to work on it and even giving advice. If true, this would have suggested, as Bollyn inferred, that PM was consciously serving as an agent of Bush administration propaganda.

Whatever be the truth, it appears that PM took every possible step to avoid having this charge leveled against its book. Whereas Benjamin Chertoff had described himself as the magazine article's senior researcher and his name was prominently displayed at the head of the list of reporters who worked on it, his name is not on the book's cover as one of its editors. His name is not even listed under either "reporters/writers" or "researchers," or anywhere else on the book's technical page. Indeed, the only mention of his name, prior to the Afterword, occurs in the "Acknowledgments" section, where he is thanked—even though he had been head of the research department when the article was put out—only as one of many "members of the original reporting team." Probably no one, reading only this book, would think of it as being heavily indebted to a man related to the director of Homeland Security.

In any case, whether the book was actually written at the behest of the government, it is clearly perceived by the government as a reliable exponent of the official story. A US State Department document entitled "The Top September 11 Conspiracy Theories," after having repeatedly recommended *Popular Mechanics'* article, says that PM's book "provides excellent additional material debunking 9/11 conspiracy theories."[23]

The Book's Claims About Itself

Although the history behind *Debunking 9/11 Myths* may justifiably make readers wary, the important question is whether the book does what it claims. In its introduction, the editors say that the "book aims . . . to answer the questions raised by the [alternative] conspiracy theorists."[24] Or, in a more complete formulation, the book has (1) analyzed the "most common" or "key" claims of the alternative conspiracy theorists, has (2) shown, "[i]n every case," these key claims "to be mistaken," and has (3) shown this by means of "facts," which "can be checked."[25]

It is important for readers, in evaluating PM's claims to success, to understand that it has here correctly stated what it must do to defend the official story about 9/11. That is, it must show that every one of the key claims made by the leading critics of the official story is false. Why? Because each of these claims challenges one of the essential claims of the official story. If even one of those essential claims is disproved, then the official story as such is thrown into doubt. Critics do not need to show the falsity of every essential element in the official account; they need to show only the falsity of one such element. Psychologically, of course, these critiques will be more persuasive if they show several of the official story's essential elements to be false. Logically, however, critics need to show only one of these elements to be false.

The logic is exactly the opposite for attempts to debunk the case *against* the official theory. This case cannot be undermined by refuting merely *some* of the claims used in this case. Insofar as this case consists of claims that challenge essential elements of the official theory, this case is not undermined by showing only some of them to be false or at least unproven. They must *all* be refuted. Accordingly, the authors of *Debunking 9/11 Myths* have correctly stated the threefold task they would have to perform in order to defend the official theory: they would need to (1) deal with all the key claims made by critics of the official story and (2) show every one of them to be a false myth by (3) presenting facts that can be checked.

As we will see, however, the authors of this book do not even fulfill the first of these requirements. Far from dealing with all the key claims of the 911 truth movement, the authors appear to have dealt with only those claims they thought they could appear to debunk in the eyes of the general reader. Although they claim that alternative conspiracy theorists "ignore all but a few stray details they think support their theories," this statement better describes the approach of the authors of *Debunking 9/11 Myths*.

With regard to the second and third requirements, these authors, besides simply ignoring many of the key claims of the 9/11 truth movement (thereby failing to defend many essential elements in the official conspiracy theory), do not even successfully debunk the key claims they choose to discuss. And, far from trying to do so by means of facts that can be checked, readers find in the book's endnotes that the authors have relied primarily on personal interviews, which cannot be checked. Moreover, on those occasions when the authors do cite written documents—such as *The 9/11 Commission Report*, with its 571 pages— they give no page numbers. They have thereby made it difficult or, in most cases, impossible for readers to check their alleged facts.

I will carry out my examination of PM's attempted debunking of the 9/11 truth movement's conspiracy theory by examining the book's four sections: "The Planes," "The World Trade Center," "The Pentagon," and "Flight 93."

Stylistic Note: Because *Debunking 9/11 Myths* came about as a joint effort by many members of the staff of *Popular Mechanics*—some of whom, like Benjamin Chertoff, presumably worked only on the magazine article from which the book derived—I do not, in discussing the book, refer to the book's editors, David Dunbar and Brad Reagan, as if they were solely or even primarily responsible for the book's contents. Rather, I recognize the book's multiple authorship by referring to "PM's authors" or, alternatively, to *Popular Mechanics*, or simply PM.

The Planes

The book's first section is devoted to defending the "widely accepted account that hijackers on September 11, 2001, commandeered and crashed four commercial aircraft into the World Trade Center, the Pentagon, and the countryside of southwestern Pennsylvania."[26] This defense, however, gets off to an unpromising beginning. Saying that this widely accepted account "is supported by reams of evidence," the authors illustrate this claim with "passengers' in-flight phone calls" and "the very basic fact that those on board never returned home." Given the cell phone technology of 2001, as we have seen, the claims about the phone calls are dubious at best. And how in the world would the fact that the passengers did not return home support the official theory over the alternative theory (since the passengers could have been killed in any number of ways)? Of course, PM's statement is technically correct, since it does not claim that the "reams of evidence" supporting the official story are of good quality.

In any case, this section of PM's book begins by employing two of its authors' favorite devices: highlighting unrepresentative positions to illustrate the views of alternative conspiracy theorists and implying guilt by association. In this particular case, the PM authors illustrate alternative views by describing two theories that are held by only a tiny percentage of the 9/11 truth movement. They then inform us that one of these "first appeared on a Web site [that] also promotes revisionist histories of the Holocaust."[27] PM uses this technique in spite of the fact that in Meigs'

Afterword, the discussion of Bollyn's exposure of the relationship between Benjamin and Michael Chertoff is headed "Guilt by Association."

In any case, our PM authors, saying that "all the theories concerning 9/11 aircraft . . . rest on the same small set of factual claims or assumptions," proceed to examine a few of these, beginning with:

The [Alleged] Hijackers' Flying Skills

Although PM fails to insert the word "alleged" in its heading of this topic, it does at least state the claim of alternative theorists in a fair way: "A group of men with no professional flight experience could not have navigated three airplanes across hundreds of miles and into building targets with any accuracy." They illustrate this claim, however, by quoting "an unattributed January 2006 article on www.aljazeera.com" and actor Charlie Sheen,[28] as if this claim had not been made by any pilots, such as Russ Wittenberg and Ralph Omholt, who are quoted below. PM thereby illustrates one of its tactics: giving the impression that all "experts" support the official theory and that the alternative theory is supported solely by "conspiracy theorists" devoid of expertise in the relevant fields.

Although the PM authors admit that the alleged hijackers "were not highly skilled pilots," they offer reasons for concluding that "it's not surprising that they operated the planes with some degree of competence."[29] To see how they moved from the first point to the second, let us examine their discussion of Hani Hanjour, called in The 9/11 Commission Report—which the PM authors use as their authority on this matter—"the operation's most experienced pilot."[30]

Saying that although the men were not highly skilled "they were not complete amateurs," the authors report that in Arizona between 1997 and 1999, "Hanjour earned both his private pilot's license and commercial pilot's license," and that in late 2000, after having spent time in Saudi Arabia, he was "back in Arizona for refresher training on small commercial jets and for Boeing 737 simulator training."[31]

PM's account here leaves out two facts contained in The 9/11 Commission Report: that Hanjour's instructor in 1999 reportedly called him a "terrible pilot" and that Hanjour, while he was in Saudi Arabia, was refused admission to a civil aviation school. (This refusal suggests that his problems in the United States were not due almost entirely, as PM seems to imply, to his poor English.) Even more important, PM's account could lead the reader to believe that Hanjour's "commercial pilot's license" was for "small commercial jets" and that he received refresher training on such jets in 2000. The 9/11 Commission Report, however, says: "Hanjour began refresher training. . . . He wanted to train on multi-engine planes, but had difficulties because his English was not good enough. The instructor advised him to discontinue."[32] There is no indication, in other words, that Hanjour had any training in small commercial jets.

The PM authors next, while admitting that Hanjour "was repeatedly encouraged to quit because of his subpar English and poor performance," accentuate the positive, saying that "he finished simulator training in March 2001."[33] They also tell us that Hanjour and Jarrah "requested and subsequently took training flights down the Hudson Corridor," thereby implying that these men's abilities had improved. But vital information from *The 9/11 Commission Report* was left out. Because Jarrah was deemed "unfit to fly solo," the Commission's report tells us, "he could fly this route only with an instructor." And Hanjour? "[H]is instructor declined a second request because of what he considered Hanjour's poor piloting skills."[34] In other words, Hanjour, "the operations's most experienced pilot," was evidently a worse pilot than Jarrah.

Having left out these little details, the PM book's next sentence says that "Hanjour also took a training flight over Washington D.C."[35] This statement involves two deceptions. First, whereas *The 9/11 Commission Report* mentioned that Hanjour did this only after switching to another flying school, the PM authors, having failed to tell us that Hanjour's instructor at the previous school had refused to go up with him again, left out Hanjour's change of school. Second, PM's statement that Hanjour flew "over Washington D.C." seems designed to suggest that he would have become familiar with the Pentagon area. The 9/11 Commission, however, said merely that the flight allowed him "to fly near Washington, D.C."

All of these omissions and changes are, to be sure, small, but their cumulative effect is to lead readers to believe that Hanjour was more prepared for flying an airliner into the Pentagon than even the 9/11 Commission suggested.

The PM authors, besides granting, if only partly, that Hanjour was a poor pilot, also admit that "none of the hijacker pilots [as they continue to call the four men] had ever flown a commercial-size airline jet and had logged far fewer than the 1,500 hours required for FAA airline pilot's licenses." They suggest, however, that these liabilities were overcome by four things.

The first one is that the men "were, in fact, certified pilots."[36] Our PM authors, however, fail to tell us that doubts have been raised about Hanjour's license. A story in the *Washington Post* a month after the attacks said: "Federal Aviation Administration records show [Hanjour] obtained a commercial pilot's license in April 1999, but how and where he did so remains a lingering question that FAA officials refuse to discuss."[37] A later CBS story reported that the JetTech flight school in Phoenix had reported Hanjour to the FAA at least five times "because his English and flying skills were so bad . . . they didn't think he should keep his pilot's license." The school's manager, Peggy Chevrette, even said: "I couldn't believe he had a commercial license of any kind with the skills that he had."[38] A *New York Times* story said:

> Hani Hanjour . . . was reported to Federal Aviation Administration in February 2001 after instructors at Pan Am International Flight Academy in Phoenix found his piloting skills so shoddy and his grasp of English so inadequate that they questioned whether his pilot's license was genuine.[39]

(This was the same school: Pan Am owned the JetTech flight school.) These stories reported, moreover, that an FAA inspector declared Hanjour's license to be legitimate and even "'did not observe any serious issue' with Hanjour's English, even though University of Arizona records show he failed his English classes with a 0.26 grade point average." The *Times* story ended with a quotation from a former employee of the flight school who was "amazed that [Hanjour] could have flown into the Pentagon" because "[h]e could not fly at all."

From these three stories, we can infer that if Hanjour was, as the PM authors say, "a certified pilot," he should not have been.

The second factor aiding the "hijacker pilots," PM says, is that "the equipment they encountered in the Boeing cockpits on September 11 was similar to the simulators they had trained on in the months before the attacks."[40] It is not clear, however, that Hanjour even did much simulator training. According to the simulator manager at a school where Hanjour came to train in 1998, "He had only the barest understanding what the instruments were there to do." Then, after using the simulator a few times, he "disappeared like a fog."[41] The *Times* story, speaking of Hanjour's simulator training in 2001, said:

> Ultimately, administrators at the school told Mr. Hanjour that he would not qualify for the advanced certificate. But [an] ex-employee said Mr. Hanjour continued to pay to train on a simulator for Boeing 737 jets. "He didn't care about the fact that he couldn't get through the course," the ex-employee said.[42]

It could appear that Hanjour was there only so that people could later say that he had trained on a Boeing airliner simulator.

In any case, a third reason why Hanjour and the other pilots succeeded, the PM authors suggest, is that the planes were already in flight, so "[a]ll they [the pilots] had to do was pretty much point and go." And, fourth, the men probably used portable GPS (Global Positioning System) units, in which case they would have needed "only to punch the destination coordinates into the flight management system and steer the planes while looking at the navigation screen."[43]

However, although PM quotes one flight instructor in support of points three and four, other experts indicate that the story about Hanjour is completely implausible. Stan Goff, a former Special Forces master sergeant who also taught military science at West Point, said that the idea that Hanjour's simulator training could have given him the ability to fly a large airliner through US airspace is "like saying you prepared your teenager for her first drive on I-40 at rush hour by buying her a video driving game."[44] Russ Wittenberg, who flew large commercial airliners for 35 years after serving in Vietnam as a fighter pilot, says that men who could barely handle a Piper Cub could not have flown "big birds" such as Boeing 757s and 767s. Recalling that when he moved up from Boeing 727s to Boeing 737s, 757s, and 767s, which have highly sophisticated computerized systems, he needed considerable training before he could fly them, he said: "For a guy to just jump into the cockpit [of one of these planes] and fly like an ace is impossible."[45]

However, even if we were to think that Hanjour, who had never before flown anything larger than a single-engine plane, could have, on the basis of simulator training alone, flown a Boeing 757 for several hundred miles back to Washington, DC, what about the claim that he was able to execute the maneuver allegedly made by Flight 77 in order to hit Wedge 1 of the Pentagon? Many critics of the official story about the Pentagon consider this its most implausible element. Goff, after citing several features in the official story about 9/11 that he considers absurdities, says that "the real kicker" is the idea that Hanjour, who could barely fly a small plane,

> conducts a well-controlled downward spiral, descending the last 7,000 feet in two-and-a-half minutes, brings the plane in so low and flat that it clips the electrical wires across the street from the Pentagon, and flies it with pinpoint accuracy into the side of this building at 460 nauts.[46]

Wittenberg agrees, saying that even he, with 35 years of commercial jetliner experience, could not, in a Boeing 757, have "descended 7,000 feet in two minutes, all the while performing a steep 270 degree banked turn before crashing into the Pentagon's first floor wall without touching the lawn." And if he himself could not have done it, Wittenberg says, it would have been "totally impossible for an amateur who couldn't even fly a Cessna to maneuver the jetliner in such a highly professional manner."[47] According to the recently released information from the flight data recorder, incidentally, the actual trajectory involved a 330-degree downward spiral in which the aircraft descended 8,000 feet in 3 minutes and 40 seconds[48] — a modification that, if anything, makes the feat even more inconceivable for a poor pilot.

How do the PM authors deal with this problem? In their book's introduction, as we saw, they had assured us that they would "answer the questions raised by the [alternative] conspiracy theorists."[49] The impossibility of Hanjour's having performed this maneuver is clearly one of the central questions that have been raised. It was raised, for example, in Nafeez Ahmed's first 9/11 book, *The War on Freedom*, and in mine, *The New Pearl Harbor*, both of which quoted Goff's statement.[50] But *Debunking 9/11 Myths*, far from answering this question, simply ignores it. In its only discussion of the period of time in question, it says that because Hanjour flew most of the route on autopilot, "He steered the plane manually for only the final eight minutes of the flight."[51] *Only* for this period, during which the impossible was allegedly performed in a 757 by a man who could barely fly a tiny plane!

The PM authors like to claim that their case is supported by experts. But for their entire section on the "hijackers' flying skills," they quote only one flight instructor, and he speaks only to the issue of whether the hijackers could have pointed their planes toward their targets, not to the issue of whether Hanjour could have flown the trajectory allegedly taken by Flight 77 in its final minutes. Why did the PM authors not quote any Boeing 757-qualified pilots on this question? The reason is probably that they knew that they would get answers only like that of Russ Wittenberg, quoted above, or Ralph Omholt, a former (captain-qualified) 757 pilot, who has written: "The idea that an unskilled pilot could have flown this trajectory is simply too ridiculous to consider."[52]

PM's treatment of this issue—simply ignoring the oft-raised question of Hanjour's ability to fly this trajectory—helps us see the real meaning of its assertion that, "[i]n every case we examined, the key claims made by conspiracy theorists turned out to be mistaken."[53] The book could appear to make good on this assertion, even to readers not well informed about the facts (at whom their book is aimed), only by limiting the claim to "every case we examined," then not examining the most difficult cases— those they knew they could not even appear to debunk.

Because the official story fails if even one of its central features cannot be defended, the authors of *Debunking 9/11 Myths*, by implicitly admitting that they cannot debunk the claim that Hanjour could not have flown Flight 77 into the Pentagon, have implicitly admitted that the official story about 9/11 is indefensible. I could, accordingly, end my examination of this book here. I will, nevertheless, continue in order to show that this is far from the only key claim made by critics of the official story that the PM book has failed to debunk. I will, however, pause momentarily to look at its treatment of two peripheral issues.

Peripheral Issues

The PM writers claim, as we have seen, to have debunked the "most common" or "key" claims made by critics of the official story. However, besides not dealing with many of these key claims, they also devote several pages of their 112-page text to claims that are peripheral, being held by only a small portion of those who have publicly criticized the official account. One of these—discussed by PM in a section called "Where's the Pod?"[54]—is the claim that the aircraft that hit the South Tower of the World Trade Center had an object under the fuselage that would not be on a Boeing 767, appearing instead to be a "military pod," which might be a bomb or a missile.

The treatment of this issue by the PM authors is problematic, as they were evidently unable even to present the claim in a neutral way. They refer to "video footage shot just before Flight 175 hit the South Tower," when the question at issue is whether the aircraft was indeed UA Flight 175. In any case, the authors attempt to rebut the claim that this aircraft featured a military pod and therefore was not Flight 175. I will not comment on this attempt, however, because even if it is deemed successful, the pod-claim is not considered by most members of the 9/11 truth movement to be a central feature of the case against the official story.

The book's next section discusses a statement made during an interview on Fox News by, it says, "Marc Birnbach, a freelance videographer," who said, shortly after an airplane hit the South Tower: "It definitely did not look like a commercial plane. I didn't see any windows on the sides." (The man's name is usually spelled "Mark Burnback," but since PM says it interviewed him and also puts a third spelling ["Bernback"] in scare quotes, I assume that the book got the spelling correct.) PM was again unable to state the issue in a neutral way, heading the section "Flight 175's Windows," as if anyone doubted that UA Flight 175 had windows. I will, in any case, not discuss PM's debunking of the claim that the aircraft that hit the South Tower had no windows, because it is even more peripheral than the claim about pods.

However, although PM's debunking of these two peripheral claims, even if successful, is *logically* irrelevant, the authors probably count on its being *psychologically* effective. That is, they probably count on most of their readers not realizing that the task of debunking the official account of 9/11 is different in kind from the task of debunking the claims made by its critics, so that a different logic applies. The logic of the official theory is suggested by the chain metaphor, according to which a chain is only as strong as its weakest link: If even one of the essential elements of the official story is disproved, the whole story is thrown into doubt.[55] The argument against the official story, however, involves a different logic. It is a cumulative argument, comprised of dozens of arguments, many of which are independent of the rest. Insofar as each of these is directed at one of the essential claims of the official story, only one of them needs to be successful in order to disprove that story.

To clarify, let us assume, arbitrarily, that the official story about 9/11 consists of 100 essential elements and that the 9/11 truth movement's consensus case against this story takes aim at 50 of these elements. The movement's cumulative argument against the official account would, in other words, consist of 50 key claims. To defend the official account, the defenders would need to debunk all 50 claims made by its critics. Debunking only 20 would not do the job, because 30 essential elements of the official story would remain undefended. This is the logic of the case.

The psychology, however, can work in a very different way. If the defenders of the official story appear to have debunked 20 key claims of the 9/11 truth movement, this may lead some readers to conclude that all of this movement's claims could be similarly debunked. Moreover, the debunkers, to achieve this psychological victory, need not limit themselves to key claims of the 9/11 movement. They can mix in some peripheral claims, call them key claims, and then debunk them (while ignoring some genuinely key claims, such as that Hani Hanjour could not have flown a plane in the way the official story alleges). This tactic could be especially effective if used at the beginning of the argument, thereby suggesting from the outset that the arguments against the official story are weak. It is noteworthy, therefore, that these two peripheral arguments are confronted in the second and third sections of the book's first chapter. (In the original article, in fact, they were the very first arguments presented.)

In any case, with these reflections on the logical irrelevance but psychological importance of PM's treatment of these peripheral arguments, I turn now to the question of why the airliners, if they were really hijacked, were not intercepted by the US military—an issue that is easily in everyone's top 10 list of reasons for doubting the official story.

No Stand-Down Order

The claim to be debunked in PM's section headed "No Stand-Down Order" is the contention that no military jets intercepted the airliners because, in the words of www.standdown.net, "Our Air Force was ordered to Stand Down on 9/11."[56] The PM authors' method of debunking this claim is simply to repeat many assertions made in *The 9/11 Commission Report*—without, of course, pointing out that those assertions have been undermined in my critique, *The 9/11 Commission Report: Omissions and Distortions*.

I am uncertain why the PM authors make no mention of my book, given their stated intention to "answer the questions raised by [alternative] conspiracy theorists." They clearly know that I am one of those theorists, as they cite my first book on the subject, *The New Pearl Harbor*. Why do they not cite my second book, which is generally considered the major critique of *The 9/11 Commission Report*? One possibility is that they were unaware of it. If that is the case, however, they can hardly present themselves as definitive defenders of the official story, ones who have shown "the key claims made by [alternative] conspiracy theorists . . . to be mistaken." The only other explanation is that, although they were aware of my book, they decided not to inform their readers of it and thereby the many questions it raises concerning the 9/11 Commission's explanation of the military's failure to intercept. Such deliberate withholding of relevant information would, of course, be even more damning than mere ignorance. In either case, PM's method—simply repeating the 9/11 Commission's account as authoritative without responding to serious questions that have been raised about it—shows that *Debunking 9/11 Myths* cannot be taken as a reliable guide.

Having made this general point, I will now mention the specific claims of *The 9/11 Commission Report* that are repeated by the PM authors, then indicate the nature of my responses and give (in the notes) the location of those responses in my critique of the Commission's report so that interested readers can consult them. (Unlike the PM authors, I do present "facts [that] can be checked.")

Only 14 Fighters on Alert: The PM authors begin their attempt to debunk the stand-down claim by stating this "fact":

> On September 11, only 14 fighter jets were on alert in the contiguous 48 states. Several jets were scrambled in response to the hijackings, but they were too late to affect the day's terrible outcomes.

Unfortunately for PM's credibility, its authors reveal here that they have not comprehended the nature of the 9/11 Commission's new story, which says that no fighters were scrambled in response to any of the hijacked airliners. According to this new story, as we saw in Chapter 1, the military did not even know that Flights 175, 77, and 93 were hijacked until after they crashed, and although a scramble order had been issued in relation to Flight 11, the fighter jets did not actually take off until this flight was crashing into the North Tower of the World Trade Center. The only fighters that were actually sent to intercept a plane, according to this new story, were sent after a nonexistent plane, phantom Flight 11.

The PM authors, in saying, "Several jets were scrambled in response to the hijackings, but they were too late," are still telling NORAD's earlier story, which the 9/11 Commission repeatedly declared "incorrect" and, as we have seen in Chapters 1 and 2, now even consider a lie. It is amazing that *Popular Mechanics*, having not studied the 9/11 literature sufficiently to understand this basic change in the official story, would set itself up as an authority.

In any case, the 9/11 Commission did, even while telling a new tale in which the question of how many fighters were on alert is largely irrelevant, repeat NORAD's claim that it had only seven bases in the continental United States with fighter jets on alert, only two of which—Otis in

Massachusetts and Langley in Virginia—were available to NEADS, the sector of NORAD in which all the 9/11 activity occurred.

However, as we saw in Chapter 1, although this claim is technically correct, it is misleading insofar as it is taken to mean those were the only two bases from which fighters could have been scrambled. As Colin Scoggins pointed out, although the bases at Atlantic City, Toledo, Selfridge, Burlington, and Syracuse were not designated as alert sites, they do have fighters that fly training missions every day and could have been tasked. And there is also good reason to believe that, although Andrews Air Force Base was not one of NORAD's alert sites, it did keep fighters on alert at all times.

Our PM authors, in discussing this question, write: "As the base nearest the nation's capital, didn't it have fighters on constant alert? The answer is no." In support of this assertion, they quote Chris Yates, the aviation security editor and analyst for *Jane's Defence Weekly*, as saying: "There was no reason to. . . . The US homeland had never been attacked previously in this way—apart from Pearl Harbor."[57]

No reason to have fighters on alert? This base has long had the primary responsibility of protecting the nation's capital, as indicated by a National Guard spokesman who said, the day after 9/11: "Air defense around Washington is provided mainly by fighter planes from Andrews Air Force Base in Maryland near the District of Columbia border."[58] As I wrote in an essay published in December 2005: "Can anyone seriously believe that Andrews, given the task of protecting the Pentagon, Air Force One, the White House, the houses of Congress, the Supreme Court, the US Treasury Building, and so on, would not have fighters on alert at all times?"[59] This essay was published on the same website (911Truth.org) that, one month later, published an essay of mine that is cited in *Debunking 9/11 Myths*. Why, if its authors were dedicated to answering the questions raised by members of the 9/11 truth movement, did they not respond to this question, rather than simply quote Yates' incredible assertion that there was no reason for Andrews to have any fighters on alert?

Even more important, why did these authors ignore all the evidence given in *The 9/11 Commission Report: Omissions and Distortions* that Andrews did in fact maintain fighters on alert prior to 9/11 (so that they would have been alert on 9/11 itself unless a special order had been given to the contrary)?

Part of this evidence was the fact that the US military's own website indicated that several fighter jets were kept on alert at Andrews at all times. According to this website, the "mission" of the District of Columbia Air National Guard (DCANG) was "to provide combat units in the highest possible state of readiness." The Marine Fighter Attack Squadron 321, which flew "the sophisticated F/A-18 Hornet," was said to be supported by a reserve squadron providing "maintenance and supply functions necessary to maintain a force in readiness." The 121st Fighter Squadron of the 113th Wing, equipped with F-16s, was said to provide "capable and ready response forces for the District of Columbia in the event of natural disaster or civil emergency."[60]

The PM authors quote Sergeant Sean McEntee, "public affairs specialist for the 113th Wing," as seeming to say that although "[t]he job of [its] F-16s is to control the airspace around the capital [in] national capital emergencies," that has been the case only since 9/11. McEntee's statement does not actually say this. It says only that a particular operation—the Department of Homeland Security's Operation Noble Eagle—"was set up after 9/11. It didn't exist at the time." Obviously this particular operation did not exist, because the Department of Homeland Security did not exist. But the PM authors use McEntee's statement to imply that prior to 9/11, the 113th Fighter Wing did not have the task of protecting the nation's capital. As usual, preferring oral quotations to written documentation, they simply ignore the documentation provided by the military's own website. Like other conspiracy theorists that John McCain complained about, "they ignore the facts that are present in plain sight."[61]

In any case, the military, which claimed after 9/11 that no fighters had been on alert at Andrews,[62] had altered the document on its website, from which I quoted above, that had indicated otherwise. The DCANG website as of April 19, 2001, said that DCANG's "mission" was "to provide combat units in the highest possible state of readiness."[63] By September 13, 2001, this document had been replaced with one saying that DCANG's mission was to "[b]e the premier State Head Quarters in the Air National Guard" and that its "vision" was "[t]o provide peacetime command and control and administrative mission oversight to support customers, DCANG units, and NGB in achieving the highest state of readiness."[64] Given this alteration, DCANG no longer said that it maintained forces of its own in the "highest possible state of readiness." It merely hoped to help various groups—including DCANG units, to be sure, but also customers—"achiev[e] the highest state of readiness." With DCANG units put on the same level as "customers," the phrase "highest state of readiness" no longer implied being on constant alert for scramble orders.

Further evidence that the claim that no fighters were on alert at Andrews is a lie was provided by the conversation, reported in Chapter 1, between Donald Arias, chief of public affairs for NORAD's Continental Region, and Kyle Hence of 9/11 Citizens Watch.

That Andrews and perhaps other bases around Washington kept fighters on alert was suggested on 9/11 by former Secretary of Defense Casper Weinberger. During an interview on Fox News, he said: "The city

[Washington] is ringed with Air Force bases and Navy bases and the ability to get defensive planes in the air is very, very high." Referring to a situation in which the area over Washington is designated a no-fly zone, he said that "any planes that can't identify themselves that get into that are to be shot down."[65]

In sum, the claim that there were no fighters on alert at Andrews is both a priori implausible and a posteriori (empirically) contradicted. *Debunking 9/11 Myths* has done nothing here to debunk the claim that, if the Pentagon was hit by a commercial airliner, this would have required a military stand-down order.

Communication Breakdowns: A second reason for the failure to intercept, say our PM authors, was "a series of communication breakdowns among government officials."[66] What they mean is made clear in their next paragraphs, which repeat the 9/11 Commission's claims about incredible incompetence by virtually everyone in the FAA, from the air traffic controllers to their managers to the Command Center in Herndon to FAA headquarters in Washington.

As I pointed out, however, such complete incompetence by the FAA is implausible. Why? Besides the fact that this incompetence was evidently manifested only on 9/11, it was said to have been manifested only in relation to a task that the FAA had been carrying out regularly, namely, notifying the military whenever some airplane seemed to be in trouble. It was not manifested when the FAA was given a task it had never carried out before: landing all the aircraft in the country. The FAA "execut[ed] that unprecedented order flawlessly," the 9/11 Commission noted. "Is it not strange," I asked, "that the FAA personnel carried out that unprecedented task so flawlessly and yet failed so miserably with the tasks they had been performing on a regular basis?"[67]

Besides making this a priori argument, I provided a variety of evidence, from multiple sources, that contradicts the Commission's claim that the FAA failed to notify the military about the probable hijackings of Flights 175, 77, and 93 until after they had crashed. Having reported this evidence in Chapter 1 of the present book, I will here summarize it (although only in relation to Flights 175 and 77, saving that about Flight 93 for my discussion of PM's chapter devoted to that flight).

With regard to UA Flight 175, this evidence includes the fact that, according to NORAD's timeline of September 18, 2001, the FAA notified NORAD at 8:43; the fact that Captain Michael Jellinek, who was overseeing NORAD's headquarters in Colorado that day, was reportedly on the phone with someone at NEADS as they both watched Flight 175 crash into the South Tower, after which the person at NEADS replied in the affirmative when Jellinek asked, "Was that the hijacked aircraft you were dealing with?"; and the fact that Laura Brown of the FAA reported in a memo to the 9/11 Commission that immediately after the North Tower was hit, the FAA established a teleconference in which it shared with the military "real-time information . . . about . . . all the flights of interest," which would have included Flight 175.[68]

With regard to AA Flight 77, the evidence includes the fact that according to the timeline created by NORAD right after 9/11, the FAA notified NORAD about this flight at 9:24; the fact that Laura Brown's memo, after saying that the FAA in its teleconference had shared information about "all flights of interest," specifically added, "including Flight 77" (noting that although formal notification was not made until 9:24, "information about the flight was conveyed continuously during the phone bridges before the formal notification"); and the fact that a *New York Times* story four days after 9/11 reported that from the time AA 77 was hijacked until the Pentagon was struck, "military officials in [the National Military Command Center in the Pentagon] were urgently talking to law enforcement and air traffic control officials about what to do."[69]

Rather than discuss any of this publicly available information, our PM authors seek to support the 9/11 Commission's claim about the FAA's failure to communicate by quoting, as if it were significant, a statement by Major Douglas Martin, a former public affairs officer for NORAD, according to which the FAA "had to pick up the phone and literally dial us."[70] This statement might be significant if the FAA had failed to do this, as the 9/11 Commission alleges. But the evidence summarized above, about which the PM authors were either inexcusably ignorant or else deceitfully silent, shows otherwise.

Moreover, Martin's statement, besides being insignificant, is not even accurate, for three reasons. First, besides calling the military to inform it about particular flights, the FAA can also establish teleconferences, as we have seen, through which it has ongoing conversations with the military about one or more flights. Second, as I emphasized in Chapter 1, there were military liaisons between the FAA and the military, so that as soon as the FAA knew something, the military knew it. Third, the point of saying that the FAA had to "literally dial" NORAD is evidently to say that it is a time-consuming process. This might be true if Martin is referring to calling "NORAD" in the sense of NORAD headquarters in Cheyenne. But all the FAA controllers that day would have been calling NEADS (NORAD's northeastern sector), and for this purpose they have many "hot button" lines. Someone at the Boston Center can be speaking to someone at NEADS within a second or two.[71]

Still another problem in the account given by the PM authors is that, in seeking to explain why the FAA (allegedly) failed to contact the military, they say that under the protocols in place at the time, "a controller's concerns that something was amiss had to ascend through multiple layers at the FAA and the Department of Defense before action could be taken." In spelling out these "multiple layers," they say:

> In the case of a hijacking, a controller would alert his or her supervisor, who contacted another supervisor, who confirmed suspicion of hijacking and informed a series of managers, all the way to the national ATC Command Center in Herndon, Virginia, which then notified FAA headquarters in Washington. . . . If the [FAA's hijack coordinator] confirmed the incident as a hijacking, he or she would contact the Pentagon to request a military escort aircraft from the National Military Command Center (NMCC). . . . The NMCC then would request approval from the office of the secretary of state. If given, the order for a military escort would be relayed to NORAD, which would then order [the nearest air force base with fighters on alert] to scramble fighters.[72]

According to this Byzantine protocol, as described by our PM authors, it would take nine steps to get planes scrambled.

On the very next page, however, they reveal that it was not necessary to go through all these layers. They report that after the Boston flight controller for AA Flight 11 concluded that it had been hijacked, he consulted his supervisors, after which "Boston Center bypassed the prescribed protocol and contacted NORAD's Northeast Air Defense Sector (NEADS)," after which "[t]wo F-15s were immediately ordered to battle stations at Otis Air Force Base." A little later, moreover, the PM authors, still following *The 9/11 Commission Report*, say that "the New York Center called NEADS directly to report that Flight 175 had been hijacked."[73] In each of these cases, in other words, at least four of the nine allegedly necessary steps were bypassed. The PM authors, like the 9/11 Commission before them, evidently reported these direct communications from air traffic controllers to NEADS without realizing that they contradicted their claim that the protocol was impossibly complex.[74]

The problem here is that although the PM authors begin by discussing "a controller's concerns that something was amiss," they immediately equate something's being amiss with a hijacking and hence go into a description of the hijacking protocol. The Boston controllers, as we saw in Chapter 1, also exercised the emergency protocol, in which they, using their hot button lines, contacted NEADS directly.

Another problem with PM's statement is its claim that if the FAA asks the Pentagon's NMCC to send planes after a hijacked airliner, "The NMCC would request approval from the office of the secretary of state." This requirement would truly be bizarre. We can probably assume, however, that when "research editor Davin Coburn . . . scrutinized the text for accuracy,"[75] he simply failed to notice that someone had written "secretary of state" when he or she should have written "secretary of defense."

Even thus corrected, however, the statement is false. The PM authors do, for a change, cite a written document for support,[76] but this document does not support their claim. As we saw in Chapter 1, this document's crucial passage says that in the cases where "immediate responses" are needed, the requests do not need to go through the office of the secretary of defense.

Why would the PM authors tell their readers that the Pentagon document they cite says what it clearly does not? The explanation can only be ignorance, carelessness, or dishonesty; they have again proven themselves unreliable guides.

In the book's introduction, its editors say: "We simply checked the facts."[77] But their method of ascertaining the "facts" consists mainly of repeating the claims of the Zelikow-led 9/11 Commission, as if it had been some neutral fact-finding body, while ignoring all questions that have been raised about the accuracy of that commission's report.

They continue this method with regard to the question of whether the Langley fighters were scrambled in response to the FAA's report about Flight 77 or about phantom Flight 11. Ruling out the first possibility, our authors say that the military "did not know Flight 77 was missing,"[78] thereby simply ignoring all the evidence, some of which I have just summarized, that the military had received information from the FAA about Flight 77. As to what really happened, they write: "At 9:30AM, two Langley F-16s took off, although the pilots mistakenly believed they were on the lookout for Flight 11, unaware that it had already crashed into the World Trade Center." Stating this claim as if it were an unquestioned "fact," they simply ignore all the evidence I had presented against this idea (which is summarized in Chapter 1).

Ignoring Mineta's Testimony: The PM authors, we have seen, illustrate John McCain's complaint that some conspiracy theorists, in seeking to support their preordained conclusions, "ignore the facts that are present in plain sight." A particularly clear example of this involves their claim that no one in Washington knew that an aircraft was approaching the Pentagon. They make this claim by simply repeating the 9/11 Commission's story, saying:

> At 9:32AM, controllers at Washington Dulles International Airport spotted an inbound plane and relayed the information to the Secret Service. . . . Once controllers at Boston Center realized that an unidentified aircraft was closing in on Washington, the F-16s [from Langley] were ordered to return to the D.C. area. . . . The fighters were still 150 miles east of the capital when Flight 77 hit the Pentagon at 9:37AM.[79]

As I reported in my critique of the Commission's report, this story left out a vital piece of contradictory evidence, namely, Secretary of Transportation

Norman Mineta's testimony, given to the Commission in an open hearing. Although this testimony has already been quoted in Chapter 1, I will repeat it here for convenience. Under questioning from Lee Hamilton, Mineta, reporting what he heard in the Presidential Emergency Operations Center under the White House, said:

> During the time that the airplane was coming in to the Pentagon, there was a young man who would come in and say to the Vice President, "The plane is 50 miles out." "The plane is 30 miles out." And when it got down to "the plane is 10 miles out," the young man also said to the Vice President, "Do the orders still stand?" And the Vice President turned and whipped his neck around and said, "Of course the orders still stand. Have you heard anything to the contrary?"

During an exchange between Mineta and Commissioner Timothy Roemer, it was established that Mineta had arrived at 9:20 and that this exchange with the young man occurred at "about 9:25 or 9:26."

Accordingly, Cheney and those with him, which included members of the Secret Service, knew at least 11 minutes before 9:37 that an unidentified aircraft was approaching Washington. Secretary of Defense Rumsfeld's spokesman, in explaining why the Pentagon was not evacuated before it was struck, claimed that "[t]he Pentagon was simply not aware that this aircraft was coming our way."[80] The 9/11 Commission claimed that there was no warning about an unidentified aircraft heading toward Washington until 9:36 and hence only "one or two minutes" before the Pentagon was struck at 9:38.[81] Mineta's testimony, however, shows that there would have been plenty of time to have the Pentagon evacuated, with the result that 125 lives—primarily young members of the Army and the Navy—would have been saved.

Mineta's testimony is available on the Web in transcript form.[82] Also available are videos of his conversation with Hamilton and Roemer.[83] This evidence is, therefore, rather literally "in plain sight." And yet *Debunking 9/11 Myths*, like *The 9/11 Commission Report*, simply ignores it.

Of course, these authors, seeking to debunk the claim that there was a stand-down order on 9/11, needed to omit Mineta's report. Because of the importance of this point to the present discussion, I will here simply repeat the argument given in Chapter 1:

> Mineta's account could be read as eyewitness testimony to the confirmation of a stand-down order. Mineta himself, to be sure, did not make this allegation. He assumed, he said, that "the orders" mentioned by the young man were orders to have the plane shot down. Mineta's interpretation, however, does not fit with what actually happened: The aircraft was not shot down. Mineta's interpretation, moreover, would make the story unintelligible: If the orders had been to shoot down the aircraft if it entered the forbidden air space over Washington, the young

man would have had no reason to ask if the orders still stood. His question made sense only if the orders were to do something unexpected—*not* to shoot it down.

We can understand, therefore, that the PM authors, if they were to appear in the eyes of unknowing readers to achieve their purpose, had to conceal Mineta's testimony from them.

This understanding, however, must drive us to conclude that we cannot rely on *Debunking 9/11 Myths* to provide the evidence relevant to deciding the truth about 9/11. It would seem, in fact, that a more accurate title for PM's book would have been *Perpetuating 9/11 Myths*. This conclusion will be confirmed, moreover, by our examination of additional matters related to the stand-down question, one of which involves the official theory's claim about transponders.

Turned Off Transponders: The PM authors, giving another reason why the planes were not intercepted, write:

> One of the first steps the hijackers took after seizing control of the four aircraft was to turn off the jets' transponders. At the time of the hijackings, there were 4,500 planes in the skies over the continental United States. Without transponder data . . . , controllers were forced to search for the missing aircraft among all the identical radar blips.[84]

This statement is riddled with falsehoods.

In the first place, the PM authors give the impression that, because the hijacked airliners' transponders were turned off, air traffic control (ATC) had to try to find them in a field of identical blips. Indeed, PM's magazine article had explicitly said this, writing:

> Why couldn't ATC find the hijacked flights? When the hijackers turned off the planes' transponders, which broadcast identifying signals, ATC had to search 4500 identical radar blips crisscrossing some of the country's busiest air corridors.

However, as I pointed out in Chapter 1, the radar scopes cover only a limited local region. No controller would have thousands of blips on his or her screen. PM's book version takes account of this fact by saying that "each controller [is] responsible for varying numbers of planes in his or her sector." The authors thereby protect themselves from the charge of stating an outright falsehood, while still suggesting the original claim to the unknowing reader.[85]

A second problem involves the claim about "identical blips." The FAA's radar scopes receive data from both primary and secondary radar. The primary radar employs rebounding radio waves to produce the blip. The secondary radar receives from the plane's transponder its altitude and 4-digit code number, which appear on the radar scope next to the blip. So, the blips of the four hijacked airliners would *not* have been identical with any of the other blips, because only they would have been devoid of the transponder data.

In the third place, the transponder for UA 175 went off for only 30 seconds. It then came back on with "a signal that was not designated to any plane on that day. . . , [thereby] allow[ing] controllers to track the intruder easily."[86]

In the fourth place, shortly after AA 77's transponder signal was lost, the flight was also lost to primary radar. So there was no "blip" until much later, when a high-speed primary target, which according to the official story was AA 77, is seen moving toward Washington.

Furthermore, the blips appeared sequentially, rather than simultaneously, according to the times given by the 9/11 Commission. Flight 11 had already crashed into the North Tower by the time (8:47) that Flight 175's transponder went off momentarily. By the time Flight 93's transponder quit transmitting (9:41), Flight 77 was history. This fact, however, did not prevent Guy Smith's BBC documentary from stating, on Davin Coburn's authority, that the military was unprepared because "a passenger airliner hadn't been hijacked in the U.S. since 1979, and now there were four at once."

Besides the fact that the loss of the transponder signals would not have had a paralyzing effect on air traffic controllers, this loss would have made little difference to military radars. The 9/11 Commission, to be sure, had suggested otherwise. In explaining why NORAD had failed to intercept Flight 11, in spite of being notified about its hijacking nine minutes before it crashed, the Commission said:

> Because the hijackers had turned off the plane's transponder, NEADS personnel spent the next minutes searching their radar scopes for the primary radar return. American 11 struck the North Tower at 8:46. Shortly after 8:50, while NEADS personnel were still trying to locate the flight, word reached them that a plane had hit the World Trade Center.[87]

As I've written elsewhere,[88] it is absurd to suggest that the loss of transponder signal makes it impossible for the US military to track planes: Was the US military's defense of the homeland during the Cold War based on the assumption that Soviet pilots would have the courtesy to leave their transponders on?

The founder of Pilots for 9/11 Truth has recently made the same point. Responding to PM's claim (made on a radio show by PM editor-in-chief James Meigs) that the planes could not be tracked because their transponders had been turned off, this experienced pilot pointed out that that view would lead to the absurd conclusion that, if an enemy country sent bombers into our country with their transponders off, we would not be able to track them. Even if a plane has its transponder off, he said, it can be "monitored like a hawk."[89]

Although the PM authors should have been able to find dozens of people in the military who could have told them this, they endorsed the 9/11 Commission's absurd claim that the loss of transponder signals would make the hijacked airliners virtually invisible to the military. For the final paragraph of their "No Stand-Down Order" section, they simply quote the Commission's summary explanation of why the planes were not intercepted, which begins: "In sum, the protocols in place on 9/11 for the FAA and NORAD to respond to a hijacking presumed that the hijacked aircraft would be readily identifiable and would not attempt to disappear"[90]—as if the loss of transponder signals would cause planes to disappear from the military's radar system.

Finally, the transponder issue is a double-edged sword. One of the major problems in the official story, according to which hijackers took control of the cockpits, is why none of the eight regular pilots in the four planes used the transponder to "squawk" the standard code to signal a hijacking. Punching this code (7500) into the transponder would take only a second, and yet, we are told, none of the pilots did this during the scuffles. On UA Flight 93, the 9/11 Commission says, the pilots are heard declaring "Mayday" and shouting: "Hey get out of here—get out of here—get out of here."[91] So, according to the official story, there was plenty of time to notify ground control of the attempted hijacking, but not one pilot did so. This "failure" casts doubt on the whole hijacking story, many critics of the official conspiracy theory have pointed out. And yet the PM authors do not mention it.

An Unprecedented Challenge? Besides falsely suggesting that the FAA flight controllers had to search for the hijacked airliners in a vast sea of blips, the PM authors also say that they faced an "unprecedented" challenge: "Without direct communication from either the pilots or the hijackers, the FAA, for the first time in its history, had to guess how to respond."[92]

But this is nonsense. The most fundamental issue, as we saw in Chapter 1, is why, according to the official story, the military was not contacted by the FAA's Boston Center until 17 minutes after AA 11 had shown all the standard signs of an in-flight emergency—including the most serious one: going radically off course. The protocol for air traffic controllers is very clear, saying that if the problems cannot be quickly resolved, the military is to be contacted.

The FAA personnel did not, accordingly, need "to guess how to respond." They simply needed to follow their standard operating procedures—which, as we saw in Chapter 1, they evidently did.

In any case, the PM authors, perhaps nervous about putting much weight on the transponder argument, rely primarily on another one.

The "Looking Outward" Defense: Having said that "the terrorists thwarted the FAA by turning off the transponders," *Debunking 9/11 Myths* says: "As for NORAD's more sophisticated radar, it ringed the continent, looking outward for threats, not inward." Citing no documents to support this astounding claim, our authors again simply quote Major Martin as saying: "When you look at NORAD on September 11, we had a ring of radar all around both [Canada and the United States]. It was like a donut. There was no coverage in the middle. That was not the threat."[93]

However, insofar as there is any truth to the donut comparison, the "middle" would refer to the middle of the United States, not the middle of NORAD's northeast sector, where all the action occurred on 9/11. It appears that our PM authors have deliberately obscured this distinction.

Also, if we look to see what high-ranking NORAD officials said, we find that they were tracking hijacked planes in the middle of NORAD's northeast sector. As I pointed out in Chapter 1, both Colonel Robert Marr and General Larry Arnold wrote that NORAD had been tracking UA Flight 93, with Arnold saying: "we watched the 93 track as it meandered around the Ohio–Pennsylvania area and started to turn south toward D.C."[94]

Also, in Colonel Alan Scott's timeline testimony to the 9/11 Commission, he said, referring to 8:53AM of 9/11, "we are now picking up the primary radar contacts off of the F-15s out of Otis."[95] The military radar was, in other words, picking up very small planes flying out of Cape Cod.

The claim, repeated by PM, that NORAD's radar was "looking outward" evidently originated with General Richard Myers, who in 2004 told the 9/11 Commission:

> [O]ur military posture on 9/11, by law, by policy and in practice, was focused on responding to external threats, threats originating outside of our borders. . . . [W]e were clearly looking outward. We did not have the situational awareness inward because we did not have the radar coverage.[96]

In one of the rare instances in which the Commission did not let a witness get away with nonsense, Jamie Gorelick said:

> [I]f you go back and you look at the foundational documents for NORAD, they do not say defend us only against a threat coming in from across the ocean, or across our borders. It has two missions, and one of them is control of the airspace above the domestic United States, and aerospace control is defined as providing surveillance and control of the airspace of Canada and the United States.

Myers then tried more nonsense, claiming that the Posse Comitatus law prevents the military from being "involved in domestic law enforcement," at which point Gorelick, who had previously been general counsel for the Department of Defense, explained: "Posse Comitatus says, you can't arrest people. It doesn't mean that the military has no authority . . . to defend the United States from attacks that happen to happen in the domestic United States."[97]

Although Gorelick's point was surely that Myers' claim—that NORAD had had a strictly external posture—was incredible, the Commission, when it wrote its report, took Myers' statement as a truthful account of NORAD's actual posture, saying:

> NORAD's mission . . . to defend the airspace of North America . . . does not distinguish between internal and external threats; but because NORAD was created to counter the Soviet threat, it came to define its job as defending against external attacks. . . . America's homeland defenders faced outward. . . . . [NORAD's] planning scenarios occasionally considered the danger of hijacked aircraft being guided to American targets, but only aircraft that were coming from overseas.[98]

The PM authors have, therefore, accurately stated the 9/11 Commission's claim. As usual, however, they did not compare the claim of these conspiracy theorists with independently researched fact. They did not refer the reader to my critique of the 9/11 Commission's report, in which I quoted the Gorelick–Myers confrontation. They simply accepted the Commission's claim as fact. They next do the same with another Commission claim.

The "Unprepared-for-this-Scenario" Defense: Appealing to the authority of Chris Yates—the expert who said there was no reason to have fighters on alert at Andrews—our authors say that "US civilian and military officials had [not] prepared for" the kind of hijacking scenario that would end "in what we saw on that day." Rather, these officials were prepared only for hijackers who would be "making a political statement [and] a bunch of demands [so that] eventually the aircraft would land somewhere." They were not prepared for "a suicide hijacking designed to convert the aircraft into a guided missile."[99]

The PM authors are here again following the 9/11 Commission, which claimed: "The threat of terrorists hijacking commercial airliners within the United States—and using them as guided missiles—was not recognized by NORAD before 9/11."[100] Our authors remain silent, however, about a wealth of facts that contradict this claim of the official conspiracy theory, some of which I had cited in my critique of the Commission's claim.

Part of this evidence consists of reports that were cited in *The 9/11 Commission Report* itself, such as these:

> In early 1995, Abdul Hakim Murad—Ramzi Yousef's accomplice in the Manila airliner bombing plot—told Philippine authorities that he and Yousef had discussed flying a plane into CIA headquarters. In August of [1998], the intelligence community had received

information that a group of Libyans hoped to crash a plane into the World Trade Center.

In 1998, [Richard] Clarke chaired an exercise [that] involved a scenario in which a group of terrorists commandeered a Learjet on the ground in Atlanta, loaded it with explosives, and flew it [on a suicide mission] toward a target in Washington, D.C.

After the 1999–2000 millennium alerts, . . . Clarke held a meeting of his Counterterrorism Security Group devoted largely to the possibility of a possible airplane hijacking by al-Qaeda.

In early August 1999, the FAA's Civil Aviation Security intelligence office summarized the Bin Ladin hijacking threat. . . . [T]he paper identified a few principal scenarios, one of which was a "suicide hijacking operation."[101]

As I also pointed out,[102] the Commission's claim ("The threat of terrorists hijacking commercial airliners within the United States—and using them as guided missiles—was not recognized by NORAD before 9/11") is further undermined by reports that the Commission failed to mention, such as the following:

In 1993, a panel of experts commissioned by the Pentagon suggested that airplanes could be used as missiles to bomb national landmarks. In 1994, one of these experts wrote in *The Futurist* magazine: "Targets such as the World Trade Center not only provide the requisite casualties but, because of their symbolic nature, provide more bang for the buck. In order to maximize their odds for success, terrorist groups will likely consider mounting multiple, simultaneous operations with the aim of overtaxing a government's ability to respond."[103]

In 1995, Senator Sam Nunn, in *Time* magazine's cover story, described a scenario in which terrorists crash a radio-controlled airplane into the US Capitol Building.[104]

In 1999, the National Intelligence Council said in a special report on terrorism: "Suicide bombers belonging to al-Qaeda's Martyrdom Battalion could crash-land an aircraft packed with high explosives . . . into the Pentagon, the headquarters of the Central Intelligence Agency (CIA), or the White House."[105]

In October 2000, Pentagon officials carried out an emergency drill to prepare for the possibility that a hijacked airliner might be crashed into the Pentagon.[106]

At 9:00 on the morning of 9/11, the National Reconnaissance Office, which draws its personnel from the military and the CIA, had planned to simulate the accidental crashing of an airplane into its own headquarters, four miles from Dulles Airport.[107]

The falsity of the 9/11 Commission's claim, parroted by *Popular Mechanics*, is further shown by some reports that were not mentioned in my critique of the 9/11 Commission's report:

In 2004, former FBI director Louis Freeh told the 9/11 Commission that in 2000 and 2001, planning for events designated "National Special Security Events" involved the possible "use of airplanes . . . in suicide missions."[108]

In a 2004 story entitled "NORAD Had Drills of Jets as Weapons," *USA Today* said: "In the two years before the Sept. 11 attacks, the North American Aerospace Defense Command conducted exercises simulating what the White House says was unimaginable at the time: hijacked airliners used as weapons to crash into targets and cause mass casualties. One of the imagined targets was the World Trade Center." NORAD, in confirming that such exercises had been run, said: "These exercises tested track detection and identification; scramble and interception; hijack procedures; [and] internal and external agency coordination." Although NORAD claimed that "[t]he planes in the simulation were coming from a foreign country," *USA Today* noted that "there were exceptions . . . , including one operation . . . that involved planes from airports in Utah and Washington state that were 'hijacked.'"[109]

As abundantly shown by this evidence (more of which will be presented in discussing PM's treatment of the Pentagon strike), the idea that the US military was not prepared for the kind of hijackings that reportedly occurred on 9/11 is one of the official conspiracy theory's myths that had already been debunked when *Popular Mechanics* began its study of 9/11. Rather than informing its readers of this fact, however, it has used its influence to perpetuate the myth.

Military Intercepts

In its final effort to debunk the idea that on 9/11 a stand-down order had been issued (which was not rescinded until shortly before the downing of Flight 93), PM disputes the 9/11 truth movement's claim that NORAD's fighter jets routinely intercepted planes and usually did so in a matter of minutes. PM's contrary "fact" is that, "In the decade before 9/11, NORAD intercepted only one civilian plane over North America: golfer Payne Stewart's Learjet in October 1999."[110]

No "Routine" Interceptions: One impediment to their claim was a *Boston Globe* article, quoted in *The New Pearl Harbor*, in which the author, Glen Johnson, reported that NORAD spokesman Mike Snyder, speaking a few days after 9/11, said that NORAD's fighters, in Johnson's paraphrase, "routinely intercept aircraft."[111] To rebut this claim, our authors do not cite any documentary evidence. They simply say: "When contacted by *Popular Mechanics*, spokesmen for NORAD and the FAA clarified their remarks by noting that scrambles were routine, but intercepts were not—especially over the continental United States."[112] But these alleged "spokesmen" remain anonymous, a fact suggesting that PM could not find anyone in either NORAD or the FAA willing to have his or her name associated with this claim. PM has not really, therefore, undermined the statement made by NORAD spokesman Mike Snyder, a few days after 9/11, that NORAD makes interceptions routinely.

The idea that interceptions occur regularly has not, of course, been based solely or even primarily on Snyder's statement. It has also been based on reports that fighters have been scrambled about a hundred times a year. A 2001 story in the *Calgary Herald* reported that NORAD had scrambled fighters 129 times in 2000; an Associated Press story by Leslie Miller in 2002 referred to NORAD's "67 scrambles from September 2000 to June 2001."[113] By extrapolation, one can infer that NORAD had scrambled fighters about a thousand times in the decade prior to 9/11. This figure makes it very hard for *Popular Mechanics*, by claiming that most scrambles do not result in interceptions (a claim made by Benjamin Chertoff during a radio show debate with me when he was still a PM spokesperson), to claim that only one civilian plane had been intercepted in North America during the decade before 9/11. As I argued in print, this claim could be true "only if in all of these cases, except for the Payne Stewart incident, the fighters were called back to base before they actually intercepted the aircraft in question. . . , a most unlikely possibility."[114]

PM's solution to this problem is to argue not only that interceptions are rare but also that scrambles are—at least scrambles within the continental United States. But this solution faced a problem: Major Douglas Martin, who on other issues has been quoted in support of PM's position, was the person who had been quoted in Leslie Miller's Associated Press story about NORAD's "67 scrambles from September 2000 to June 2001." Martin himself had implied, in other words, that NORAD had been scrambling jets about 100 times a year. PM tries to neutralize this statement by saying:

> However, the Knight-Ridder/Tribune News Service produced a more complete account, which included an important qualification. Here's how the Knight-Ridder story appeared in the September 28, 2002, edition of the *Colorado Springs Gazette*: "From June 2000 to September 2001 [sic],[115] NORAD scrambled fighters 67 times but not over the continental United States. . . . Before September 11, the only time officials recall scrambling jets over the United States was when golfer Payne Stewart's plane veered off course and crashed in South Dakota in 1999."
>
> Except for that lone, tragic anomaly, all NORAD interceptions from the end of the Cold War in 1989 until 9/11 took place in offshore Air Defense Identification Zones (ADIZ). . . . The planes intercepted in these zones were primarily being used for drug smuggling.[116]

There are several problems with this response. Two of them involve inconsistencies in PM's argument. For one thing, PM is supposed to be defending its claim that in the decade prior to 9/11 there had been only one interception "over North America," but the qualification in this Knight-Ridder story speaks only of "the continental United States." The PM authors have thereby ignored Canada, that other North American country that is protected by NORAD, and Alaska. A second inconsistency is that, after having emphasized the distinction between scrambles and interceptions, the PM authors then conflate them. We can, however, set aside these inconsistencies in order to focus on more serious problems.

First, given the fact that the Knight-Ridder story not only appeared several months after the AP story but also appeared in a newspaper in Colorado Springs, near NORAD headquarters, it could be disinformation put out to provide the basis for exactly the case that PM is now making — that NORAD's failure to intercept the airliners on 9/11 was not a failure to do something that it had been doing routinely.

Second, given this possibility, PM's description of the Knight-Ridder story as a "more complete account" begs the question, because of the possibility that it is a distortion, rather than simply a more complete account, of the truth. An indication that it does involve distortion, moreover, is provided by the fact that Martin, in illustrating the increased number of scrambles after 9/11, said: "In June [2002], Air Force jets scrambled three times to intercept small private planes that had wandered into restricted airspace around the White House and around Camp David." These clearly were over the continental United States. If the Knight-Ridder qualification were true, we would expect Martin to have said: "After 9/11, not only have there been more interceptions, but now some of them are within the continental United States." But there is no indication in the AP story that he made any such statement. Also, although PM interviewed Martin in 2004, it gives no sign that he endorsed the Knight-Ridder qualification.

A third problem with PM's defense is that, even if it were true that all the interceptions had been offshore instead of over American or Canadian soil, that would do little to defend the military against the charge that it had stood down on 9/11. The issue at hand is whether the military had regularly intercepted planes. It matters not whether these interceptions were over the land or over the water.

A fourth problem is the existence of reports that fighter jets had indeed intercepted civilian planes quite regularly in the decades prior to 9/11. I had quoted, for example, a 1998 document warning pilots that any airplanes persisting in unusual behavior "will likely find two [jet fighters] on their tail within 10 or so minutes."[117] Also, the above-cited story in the *Calgary Herald*, which reported that NORAD had scrambled fighter jets 129 times in 2000, also said: "Fighter jets are scrambled to babysit suspect aircraft or 'unknowns' three or four times a day. Before Sept. 11, that happened twice a week."[118] Twice a week would be about

100 times per year, and "babysitting" is not what jets would do with planes suspected of smuggling drugs into the country.

A fifth problem for PM's claim—that in the decade before 9/11, all of NORAD's interceptions except one were offshore and primarily involved drug smuggling—is a 1994 report from the General Accounting Office, which strongly contradicts this claim. It said:

> Overall, during the past 4 years, NORAD's alert fighters took off to intercept aircraft (referred to as scrambled) 1,518 times. . . . Of these incidents, the number of suspected drug smuggling aircraft averaged . . . less than 7 percent of all of the alert sites' total activity. The remaining activity generally involved visually inspecting unidentified aircraft and assisting aircraft in distress.[119]

In the period from 1989 through 1992, according to this account, NORAD made an average of 379 interceptions per year, 354 of which "involved visually inspecting unidentified aircraft and assisting aircraft in distress," not intercepting planes suspected of smuggling drugs. Besides the fact that 1992 was part of "the decade before 9/11," it is doubtful that the pattern of interceptions would have changed radically after that.

With regard to NEADS in particular, Colonel John K. Scott, the commander from March 1996 to June 1998, said: "We probably 'scramble' fighters once a week. When unknowns come up you have to make the decision to launch or not."[120]

PM has clearly not, therefore, debunked the idea that NORAD routinely intercepted planes over the continental United States. The question remains, therefore, why this routine activity did not occur on 9/11.

No Interceptions "Within Minutes": "Some conspiracy theorists," the PM authors say, "mistakenly believe the Stewart case bolsters their argument that fighters can reach wayward passenger planes within minutes."[121] In attempting to refute this belief, they argue that, because of a crossing of a time zone, Stewart's plane was not really intercepted within 19 minutes, as widely believed, but an hour and 19 minutes. Be that as it may (I have elsewhere suggested that the documents are too confused to make a firm judgment[122]), the important issue is whether, prior to 9/11, scrambled fighters regularly intercepted aircraft within minutes.

There is evidence that they did. Above, I quoted a 1998 document stating that fighters commonly intercept aircraft "within 10 or so minutes." Also, in a 1999 story, a full-time alert pilot at Homestead Air Reserve Base (near Miami) was quoted as saying, "If needed, we could be killing things in five minutes or less."[123]

These reports suggest that unless there had been a stand-down order on 9/11, any hijacked airliners would have been intercepted within 10 minutes or so. This contention is supported by former Air Force Colonel

Robert Bowman, who was an interceptor pilot before becoming head of the "Star Wars" program during the Ford and Carter administrations. He has said:

> If our government had merely done nothing—and I say that as an old interceptor pilot and I know the drill, I know what it takes, I know how long it takes, I know what the procedures are . . . —if our government had merely done nothing and allowed normal procedures to happen on that morning of 9/11, the twin towers would still be standing and thousands of Americans would still be alive.[124]

No Armed Fighters on Alert: The PM authors argue at the end of their section on military intercepts—evidently intending this as their knockout punch—that between the end of the Cold War and 9/11, the US did not even keep armed fighters on alert. To support this astounding claim, our authors again cite no documentary evidence. They do not even quote anyone from the US military. They rely entirely on a statement from former Senator Warren Rudman (R, NH), who was quoted in Glen Johnson's 2001 *Boston Globe* article as saying:

> We don't have capable fighter aircraft loaded with missiles sitting on runways in this country. We just don't do that anymore. . . . [T]o expect American fighter aircraft to intercept commercial airliners . . . is totally unrealistic and makes no sense at all.[125]

However, although this quotation concludes PM's section on intercepts, it is far from the final word in Johnson's article. Rather, the very next paragraphs say:

> Otis offers something close to that posture, however. Its 102d Fighter Wing is equipped with 18 F-15 Eagles, twin-engine, supersonic, air-to-air combat aircraft. . . .
> The planes, which can fly at more than twice the speed of sound, . . . [have] responsibility for protecting Boston, New York, Philadelphia, and Washington . . . .
> To complete that mission, *the unit has two armed and fueled aircraft ready to fly around the clock, each day of the year*, a unit spokeswoman said.[126] [Emphasis added]

So much for PM's knockout punch. And so much, once again, for its reportorial honesty.

The falsity of PM's claim is also evident from other sources. For example, Major Steve Saari, an alert pilot at Tyndall Air Force Base, has been quoted as saying: "In practice, we fly with live missiles."[127] Captain Tom "Pickle" Herring, an alert pilot at Homestead Air Reserve Base near Miami, has been quoted as saying: "[W]e have weapons on our jets. We need to be postured such that no one would dare threaten us."[128]

Failing with all its claims, *Debunking 9/11 Myths* has done nothing to debunk the idea that the 9/11 attacks succeeded because there had been a stand-down order.

The World Trade Center

Popular Mechanics next attempts to refute the 9/11 truth movement's claim that the Twin Towers and WTC 7 "were brought down intentionally—not by hijacked airplanes, but by . . . controlled demolition."[129] It makes this attempt primarily by appealing to the NIST report. Having already seen, in the previous chapter, that this report does not stand up to scrutiny, one could reasonably infer that PM's attempt to defend the official conspiracy theory will also fail. We should, nevertheless, examine what PM's authors have to say, to see if they have perhaps done better than NIST in debunking the controlled demolition theory.

Continuing their ploy of suggesting that all "experts" support the official account while only loony "conspiracy theorists" support the alternative theory, the PM authors, in introducing the controlled demolition claim, do not mention any of the physicists, engineers, or philosophers of science who have made it. They instead mention a Danish writer who thinks that the controlled demolition of the Twin Towers was "part of a wide-ranging plot by the Freemasons to create a New World Order" and that "the Apollo moon landings were a hoax."

They then mention that the controlled demolition hypothesis is also endorsed by Morgan Reynolds, former chief economist at the US Department of Labor. But they evidently think that Reynolds, emeritus professor at Texas A&M University, was sufficiently discredited by the fact that (then) Texas A&M president Robert Gates "released a statement noting that Reynolds did not keep an office on the campus and characterizing the professor's comments as 'beyond the pale.'"[130]

In any case, our authors, continuing their effort to discredit their opposition, begin their next paragraph with these words: "Though Reynolds and a handful of other skeptics cite academic credentials to lend credence to their views. . . ."[131] Although I am not quite sure how many skeptics these authors can hold in one hand, "a handful" suggests merely a few, perhaps a dozen. However, the website "Professors Question 9/11" has well over 100 names,[132] and they, moreover, constitute only a fraction of the active members of the 9/11 truth movement having academic credentials. (For example, several of the contributors to three recent anthologies of scholarly critiques of the official story are not professors.[133])

In any case, the important part of the statement is the next part, which says, "not one of the leading [alternative] conspiracy theorists has a background in engineering, construction, or related fields."

An obvious problem with this statement is that the PM authors, in writing their article and now their book, have become "leading conspiracy theorists" for the other side but evidently do not have academic degrees in "engineering, construction, or related fields." I would not, however, use that as an argument against their book. To be a credible, responsible defender of either the official or the alternative theory about the WTC collapses, one need not have a degree in physics, engineering, or any other technical field. What one needs is the ability to read with comprehension, to evaluate evidence, and to draw logical conclusions from that evidence. Our entire judicial system depends on the ability of laypeople—judges and jury members—to evaluate the testimony of competing experts.

Of course, as that statement indicates, it is necessary for those who challenge the official conspiracy theory to be able to appeal to experts in fields relevant to the question of why the buildings collapsed, and one of those fields is physics. The 9/11 truth movement includes several people with advanced degrees in physics, one of whom, Steven Jones, is among the leading critics of the official theory. The movement also includes chemists, engineers, computer scientists, mathematicians, architects, pilots, former military officers, politicians, and people with expertise in political science and military intelligence, all of which are relevant to the question at hand (see pages 14–15).

The PM authors, however, try to convince their readers that all the experts are on their side. Having implied that there are no experts who support the controlled demolition theory, they then say that the collapses of the WTC buildings have been studied by "hundreds of experts from academic and private industry, as well as the government," after which they assert:

> The conclusions reached by these experts have been consistent: A combination of physical damage from the airplane crashes—or, in the case of WTC 7, from falling debris—and prolonged exposure to the resulting fires ultimately destroyed the structural integrity of all three buildings.[134]

But this statement is doubly misleading. On the one hand, virtually all of the "experts" who have reached—or at least publicly endorsed—the government's theory have been working on behalf of government agencies (such as FEMA and NIST) and/or for private industries that are dependent on government funding. On the other hand, the 9/11 truth movement can appeal to a growing number of experts, including Holland's Danny Jowenko, Switzerland's Hugo Bachmann and Jörg Schneider, and Finland's Heikki Kurtilla (all mentioned in the previous chapter), who reject the official theory. The debate between the two theories cannot, therefore, be settled by appeal to authority. It must be settled by appeal to the evidence.

The Empire State Building Accident

True to form, the PM authors begin their examination of the evidence for the collapses by tackling a "claim" that is peripheral, even invented. They say: "Some conspiracy theorists point to the bomber crashing into the Empire State Building as proof that commercial planes hitting the World Trade Center could not bring down the towers."[135] I have never seen or heard anyone offer this as a proof. PM implies, by quoting a statement from a long-time member of the 9/11 truth movement, Peter Meyer, that he did so. Meyer, to be sure, said that the fact that "the Empire State Building [did not collapse after it] was hit by a B-25 bomber" proved something. But what it proved was that although "a heavy plane hitting a skyscraper would deliver a 'tremendous shock,' . . . it doesn't follow that the building must therefore collapse." He said, in other words, that a big plane hitting a skyscraper would not necessarily cause it to collapse. That is very different from saying what the PM authors accuse him of saying, namely, that the Empire State Building accident proves that an airplane strike could not possibly cause a skyscraper to collapse. This is elementary logic: To say "X would not necessarily cause Y" is not the same as saying "X could not possibly cause Y."

Now, it may be true that a plane crashing into one of the towers could not have caused it to collapse, and Meyer may believe it, as I do. But he did not say that the crash into the Empire State Building proved it, and neither would I. I do believe, as Meyer does, that the 1945 crash into the Empire State Building is relevant to the question at issue,[136] since it does disprove the view, evidently held by some people, that any skyscraper hit by a large airliner would collapse. But to say it is relevant in this sense is very different from saying that it disproves the official theory.

In any case, the PM authors, having created this straw-man argument, proceed to use the comparison between the WTC and the Empire State Building strikes to suggest that Boeing 757s crashing into the Twin Towers would necessarily have caused them to collapse, and this for two reasons. On the one hand, the 757s that hit the towers were ten times as heavy, carried ten times as much fuel, and were going over twice as fast as the B-25 that struck the Empire State Building. On the other hand, the Twin Towers were "more fragile" than the Empire State Building.

Although the comparison between the planes is accurate, it is somewhat misleading, because a comparison, to be meaningful, would need to discuss the size, speed, and fuel load of each plane *relative to the size of the building* it struck, and WTC 1 and 2 were much bigger than the Empire State Building. We can set aside that problem, however, in order to focus on PM's claim that the towers were relatively fragile.

The authors support this claim by saying that each tower's "dense interior core of steel and concrete . . . shared load-bearing responsibilities with a relatively thin exterior shell of 14-inch-square box columns."[137] This statement gives the impression that the perimeter of each tower had little steel. But although the perimeter box columns were indeed "relatively thin," they were only thin *relative to the core columns*, which were massive. Compared with many other steel columns, these 14-inch-square box columns would have been relatively thick. Moreover, these perimeter columns could be relatively thin, compared with the core columns, because there were so many more of them: 240 compared with 47. Accordingly, the fact that the core columns "shared load-bearing responsibilities" with these perimeter columns does not mean that the exterior part of the towers was inadequately supported.

The PM authors next suggest that the engineers, in constructing the towers, perhaps forgot to think about the fact that any planes hitting the towers would have fuel that would start big fires. They quote Leslie Robertson, called "[John] Skilling's chief colleague in the WTC project," as saying: "We . . . designed for the impact of [a Boeing 707]. The next step would have been to think about the fuel load, and I've been searching my brain, but . . . I don't know if we considered the fire damage that would cause."[138] However, perhaps Robertson, instead of simply searching his brain, should have searched to see what Skilling said. At least the PM authors should have done this, because, although they present Robertson as "Skilling's chief colleague in the WTC project," Skilling was the one in charge. Robertson was at the time a junior member of the firm (Worthington, Skilling, Helle, and Jackson). And Skilling, as I pointed out in Chapter 3, *had* thought about the fire damage, saying that if one of the towers were to be hit by a plane loaded with jet-fuel, "there would be a horrendous fire" and "a lot of people would be killed," but "the building structure would still be there."[139]

In any case, PM then, in its effort to convey the impression that the collapses were not surprising, went to extreme lengths by quoting engineer Jon Magnusson, who reportedly said: "Ninety-nine percent of all [modern] high-rises, if hit with a large-scale commercial aircraft, would collapse immediately. . . . Not just collapse, but collapse immediately."[140] The point of the statement is to say that, compared with most modern high-rises, the Twin Towers were pretty good, because they did not collapse immediately. But, regardless of the purpose of the statement, one can only wonder why PM would undermine whatever credibility it still had with its readers, at this point in the book, by quoting with approval such an absurd statement. One problem with it is that if a steel-frame high-rise were to collapse immediately upon being struck, even before the fire did any damage, the designers and builders would surely be charged with gross negligence. Are we supposed to believe that they would be so reckless?

In the introduction to this chapter, I quoted Jeremy Baker's statement that the magazine article that was expanded into this book was "as conspicuous a propaganda ploy as one could imagine." That the book is indeed propaganda, in the negative sense of the term, is illustrated by its choice of statements from experts to quote. One example is its quotation of Robertson but not of Skilling. Another example is its quotation of Magnusson's statement but not MIT professor Thomas Eagar's statement that "the number of columns lost on the initial impact was not large and the loads were shifted to remaining columns in this highly redundant structure."[141] Also passed over was the well-known statement by Frank De Martini, the on-site construction manager, who said nine months prior to 9/11 that either of the towers "could probably sustain multiple impacts of jet liners."[142]

Widespread Damage

The PM authors next try to debunk the claim that damage in the buildings prior to their collapse shows that explosives were going off. As usual, these authors attribute this claim to a source that can easily be discredited—in this case, a website posting by an anonymous writer who puts a lot of words in all capital letters. Against this writer's claim—that the damage to the ground-floor lobbies could not have been caused by the impact of the planes 80 or 90 floors above and the ensuing fires—the PM authors seek to impress readers with statistics: "the 10,000-page NIST report" was based on a "three-year study," which involved interviews "with more than 1,000 survivors and witnesses." Having thoroughly impressed us with these figures, they point out that this report concluded that the planes "sliced through the utility shafts in both towers' cores, creating conduits for burning jet fuel," with the result that the lobbies were affected by "excess jet fuel ignited by the crash pouring down the elevator shafts."[143] But this position presupposes, implausibly, that the jet fuel would not have been largely burned up before it reached the lobby 80 or 90 floors below.

Finally coming to the question of explosives, the PM authors devote only a page and a half to it. This brief treatment, moreover, deals solely with the question of whether members of the 9/11 truth movement have twisted the words of firefighter Louie Cacchioli. To imply that they have, PM quotes Cacchioli's correction to a story in *People* magazine, which had quoted him as having said that a bomb went off. Cacchioli later insisted, PM reports, that he said only, "It sounded like a bomb."[144] So, yes, *People* magazine evidently misquoted him. But did members of the 9/11 truth movement?

My own quotations from Cacchioli were taken from an article by Greg Szymanski, who had interviewed him in July 2005. Early in the article, Szymanski says: "Cacchioli was upset that *People* Magazine misquoted him, saying 'there were bombs' in the building when all he said was he heard 'what sounded like bombs' without having definitive proof bombs were actually detonated." Accordingly, a year before PM reported this correction, Greg Szymanski of the 9/11 truth movement had already reported it in a widely read article.[145] Szymanski went on, however, to report many more things that Cacchioli told him, some of which clearly indicated that at the time, Cacchioli had believed that explosives were going off.

I used some of these quotations from Cacchioli in an article, "Explosive Testimony: Revelations about the Twin Towers in the 9/11 Oral Histories," which was originally posted at 911Truth.org. These quotations show that Cacchioli, while never saying definitely that there were bombs in the building, reported that he saw and heard things that did suggest that there were. Here was my paragraph about this testimony:

> Firefighter Louie Cacchioli, after entering the north tower lobby and seeing elevator doors completely blown out and people being hit with debris, asked himself, "how could this be happening so quickly if a plane hit way above?" After he reached the 24th floor, he and another fireman "heard this huge explosion that sounded like a bomb [and] knocked off the lights and stalled the elevator." After they pried themselves out of the elevator, "another huge explosion like the first one hits. This one hits about two minutes later . . . [and] I'm thinking, 'Oh. My God, these bastards put bombs in here like they did in 1993!'"[146]

It is, therefore, clearly not a distortion of Cacchioli's words to say that he reported believing at the time that explosives were going off. Also, to say that Cacchioli thought this at the time does not imply that he believed it later. As I said with regard to Brian Dixon, another witness who reported that he at the time thought explosives were going off: "Like many others, Dixon indicated that he later came to accept the official interpretation."[147]

In any case, even if the PM authors had shown that the 9/11 truth movement had twisted Cacchioli's words, that would have done little to counter the testimony pointing to explosions in the Twin Towers by firefighters and others at the scene. My essay "Explosive Testimony," to which the PM authors refer (but without discussing its contents or even giving its title), quotes from such testimonies by 41 people—27 firefighters, 5 emergency medical workers, 4 WTC employees, and 5 journalists, including a journalist from the BBC and two from the *Wall Street Journal*. Why did the PM authors ignore all these testimonies? This essay also refers the reader to the 9/11 oral histories recorded by the Fire Department of New York a few months after 9/11, and these histories, as Graeme MacQueen has reported, contained 118 testimonies suggesting that explosives had been going off in the towers.[148] The PM authors, rather than simply saying that "NIST investigators spoke with more than 1,000 survivors and witnesses," should have asked why NIST did not interview these 118 people and then report their testimonies. Better yet, PM could itself have quoted some of these testimonies, rather than simply trying to discredit the use of Cacchioli's testimony. That is what writers truly intent on stating "the facts" would do.

Such writers would have also done other things differently. The PM authors refer to the documentary film by the Naudet brothers, *9/11*, seeking to use it to support their position. But they fail to mention the well-known clip from this film, which, as I reported in "Explosive Testimony," contains the following exchange, in which two firemen are describing their experiences to other firemen.

> Fireman 1: "We made it outside, we made it about a block . . . ."
>
> Fireman 2: "We made it at least two blocks and we started running."
> He makes explosive sounds and then uses a chopping hand motion to emphasize his next point: "Floor by floor it started popping out . . . ."
>
> Fireman 1: "It was as if they had detonated—as if they were planning to take down a building, boom boom boom boom boom . . . ."
>
> Fireman 2: "All the way down."[149]

Moreover, had the PM authors been interested in reporting the facts, they could have quoted other witnesses who said similar things, such as firefighter Edward Cachia, who said with regard to the beginning of the collapse of the South Tower, "we originally had thought there was like an internal detonation, explosives, because it went in succession, boom, boom, boom, boom, and then the tower came down,"[150] or firefighter Thomas Turilli, who said "it almost sounded like bombs going off, like boom, boom, boom, like seven or eight."[151] But PM does not quote these or any of the dozens of other witnesses who reported such things.

"[Every] firefighter contacted by *Popular Mechanics*," our authors tell us, "accepts that the combination of jet impacts and fire brought down the WTC buildings." But they do not tell us how many they contacted, so this statement is meaningless. Also, they do not quote Auxiliary Lieutenant Fireman Paul Isaac's statement, which I quoted, that "many other firemen [besides me] know there were bombs in the buildings, but they're afraid for their jobs to admit it because the 'higher-ups' forbid discussion of this fact."[152]

Melted Steel

When *Popular Mechanics* dealt with the issue of "melted steel" in its magazine article, it set up the claim to which it would respond this way:

> "We have been lied to," announces the Web site AttackOnAmerica.net. "The first lie was that the load of fuel from the aircraft was the cause of structural failure. No kerosene fire can burn hot enough to melt steel."

The posting is entitled "Proof Of Controlled Demolition At The WTC."

The PM article then debunked this claim by saying: "experts agree that for the towers to collapse, their steel frames didn't need to melt, they just had to lose some of their structural strength—and that required exposure to much less heat."

Jim Hoffman, pointing out in his well-known critique of PM's magazine article that it depended heavily on "straw man" arguments, wrote:

> The article implies that skeptics' criticism of the official account that fires weakened the towers' structures is based on the erroneous assumption that the official story requires that the fires melted the steel. In fact the fire-melts-steel claim was first introduced by apologists for the official story.[153]

When PM published its book, nevertheless, it simply repeated this same straw-man argument and rebuttal, word for word.[154]

The real issue, in any case, is whether the point on which the "experts" are said to agree— "that for the towers to collapse, . . . they just had to lose some of their structural strength"—is true. To support this claim, the PM authors evidently felt a need to resort to various types of deception.

They begin by saying: "Jet fuel burns at 1,100 to 1,200° Celsius (2,012 to 2,190° Fahrenheit)."[155] This statement is quite surprising, given the fact that virtually everyone else says that the temperature of hydrocarbon fires burning in the air is much lower. In the previous chapter, for example, I quoted MIT's Thomas Eagar as saying: "The maximum flame temperature increase for burning hydrocarbons (jet fuel) in air is . . . about 1,000°C [about 1,832°F]."[156] A clue to the reason for the discrepancy is provided by a note at the back of the book, in which the PM authors say they are referring to "the gas temperature, which is measured just next to the flame, as opposed to the flame temperature."[157] This suggests, Jim Hoffman says, that they may be speaking of "compartment fires," which "can effectively trap heat," so that "temperatures of 1,200°C are possible."[158]

But even if so, he adds, their statement is doubly misleading. On the one hand, the fires at issue—those in the Twin Towers—were not compartment fires, in which the heat, being contained, can build up to 1,200°C (2,190°F). On the other hand, they were diffuse-flame fires, meaning that the fuel and air were not pre-mixed (as they are in a gas stove). And, as Eagar has pointed out, "it is very difficult to reach [even 1000°C (1832°F)] with a diffuse flame," because "[t]here is nothing to ensure that the fuel and air in a diffuse flame are mixed in the best ratio." Accordingly, it is doubly misleading for the PM authors to suggest that the jet-fuel fires in the Twin Towers would have been burning at 1,200°C (2,190°F).

PM's statement is also deceptive in another way—by suggesting that the temperature at which jet fuel burns is even relevant to the question of how hot the fires in the towers were. As the authors themselves admit a page later, all the jet fuel would have been burned up within 10 minutes.[159]

They try to handle this problem by saying, on the authority of another expert, that "the resulting infernos were intensified by the . . . rugs, curtains, furniture, and paper." Does PM really mean to suggest that once the jet fuel was gone, the fires would have become more intense by virtue of being fed by these materials instead of the jet fuel? That would be absurd—especially given the fact that the NIST's final report itself said that the combustibles in each location would have burned up within twenty minutes.[160]

Then the PM authors, becoming even more misleading, say:

> The NIST report states that pockets of fire hit 1,000° Celsius (1,832° Fahrenheit). . . . At 980° Celsius (1,800° Fahrenheit), [steel] retains less than 10 percent [of its strength].[161]

There are several problems with this statement.

First, to say that "pockets of fire hit" 1,000°C is not to say that the air temperature was actually that high in any pockets for more than a few seconds. As mentioned in the previous chapter, the temperature in such pockets can get this high only briefly, when a "flashover" occurs, and these momentary events would not be relevant to the question of how hot the steel in those pockets might have become. With regard to the sustained temperature, Thomas Eagar estimated, given the fact that the fires were putting out black smoke, that the fire was burning at a temperature of only about 648 to 704°C (1,200 to 1,300°F).

Second, PM conflates air temperature with the completely different issue of steel temperature. Given the conductivity of steel and the enormous amount of interconnected steel in the towers, as we saw in the previous chapter, fire could have brought some of the steel up to its own temperature only if it had been a very big and long-lasting fire, but the fires in the towers were neither.

Third, by pointing out that steel loses 90 percent of its strength if it is heated up to 980°C (1,800°F), the PM authors imply that some of the steel in the towers was actually heated up to this temperature. But for that to be true, the fire itself would have had to be at least that hot, which it clearly was not. Also the NIST report, which the PM authors usually take as authoritative, says that its scientists found no evidence that any of the steel had reached temperatures above 600°C (1,112°F).[162] Even more significant, in light of the fact that the crucial issue is how hot the core columns became, is NIST's admission that it found no evidence that any core column had reached the temperature of 250°C (482°F).[163]

It is hard to imagine anything more deceptive, accordingly, than PM's intent to lead readers to believe that the core columns were heated up to 980°C (1,800°F). An exaggeration of over 700° Celsius (1,300° Fahrenheit) would be quite an exaggeration. And yet the PM authors, without actually making this claim, evidently felt that their readers needed to believe it, if they were to accept PM's NIST-based claim that after some of the core columns were severed by the airplane strikes, "the remaining core columns softened and buckled."[164]

There is deception, as well, in the PM authors' claims about the effects of the airplane strikes. They say, for example, that the planes "hit the buildings and plowed into their centers," whereas the plane that struck the South Tower hit a corner and was aimed away from the center. PM also says, "NIST believes a great deal of the fireproofing insulation was likely knocked off the surviving columns," without giving any idea of how much "a great deal" is and not mentioning that, since the planes plowed into only a few floors, the insulation on over 95 percent of the floors would not have been affected. Our authors also say, "NIST found that the impact stripped fireproofing insulation from trusses that supported 80,000 square feet of floor space,"[165] and the word "found" makes it sound as if NIST had made an empirical discovery. As I reported in the previous chapter, however, Kevin Ryan learned that NIST came up with its estimates by firing shotgun rounds at steel plates in a plywood box.

PM extended its deception by again quoting Jon Magnusson, who had earlier said that most modern high-rise buildings, if hit by an airliner, would collapse immediately. This time he claimed that when the planes struck, "they damaged the structure, so they took out the towers' redundancy, their ability to balance overload."[166] This statement is contradicted by Thomas Eagar's statement, quoted above, that "the number of columns lost on the initial impact was not large and the loads were shifted to remaining columns in this highly redundant structure."[167] It is also contradicted by articles in *Engineering News-Record* in 1964 stating that the Twin Towers would remain stable even if one fourth of their columns were lost and if loads on the perimeter columns were increased by 2,000 percent.[168]

Although the discussion under the heading "Melted Steel" in PM's book simply repeats, for the most part, the discussion in its magazine article, the book does add a discussion of another issue, which it introduces with a question from physicist Steven Jones: Since "the building fires were insufficient to melt steel beams," as the government reports admit, "then where did the molten metal pools come from?"[169]

In response, the PM authors resort to the same incredible debris-pile argument used by NIST, saying that there are "experts" who

> note that the debris pile sat cooking for weeks, with the materials at the bottom of the pile getting increasingly hot because the fires were confined and lost minimal heat to the atmosphere. As a result, the fires could have easily reached temperatures sufficient to melt steel.[170]

We are asked to believe, in other words, that fires at the bottom of piles, where there is virtually no oxygen, would get hotter than fires on the surface—1,000° hotter, no less.

Also, showing again their fondness for circular argumentation, the PM authors support this claim by pointing out that "the fires were still burning more than two months after the tower collapses," as if this fact were not one of the signs, according to Jones and other critics of the official theory, that explosives must have been used.

Another problem with the PM authors' claim here, aside from its prima facie absurdity, is that although they cite Jones' essay, they ignore his rebuttal to the debris-pile argument. Jones said, as I pointed out in the previous chapter, that a purely speculative argument cannot count as a scientific hypothesis. "[I]f underground fires could somehow produce molten steel," Jones wrote,

> there should be historical examples of this effect, since there have been many large fires in numerous buildings. But no such examples have been found. It is not enough to argue hypothetically that fires could possibly cause all three pools of molten metal. One needs at least one previous example.[171]

Did the PM authors fail to mention Jones' rebuttal because they had no answer to it?

In any case, one of the "experts" to which the PM authors refer is the ever-helpful Jon Magnusson. He is quoted as saying that the existence of molten metal under the debris is "in and of itself . . . nowhere near the physical evidence that there must have been explosives. That's a leap."

According to Magnusson and our PM authors, in other words, it is *not* a leap to say that the fires in the debris field melted the steel, even though there is no known case of this having happened, even when the fires had been much bigger, hotter, and longer lasting than the fires in the Twin Towers. But it *would* be a leap to say that the molten metal proves that explosives were used, even though the use of explosives is the standard way of quickly heating up steel beyond its melting point.

Perhaps because of understandable nervousness about the debris-pile argument, the PM authors turn to an even more desperate argument: perhaps there was no molten metal to explain. For this argument, they quote a professor who said: "The photographs shown to support melting steel ... show materials that appear to be other than steel," such as "glass with unmelted steel rods in it. Glass melts at much lower temperatures than steel."[172]

But why did the PM authors quote this statement? Were they unaware that the evidence for molten metal in the debris pile consists not only of photographs but also of eyewitness testimony, including testimony from experts? Were they unaware of Leslie Robertson's statement that "21 days after the attack, ... the molten steel was still running"?[173] Surely not, because they refer to Steven Jones' article, in which this statement is quoted. But then why did they not inform their readers of this statement by Robertson, whom they were happy to quote on another topic? They also quote Mark Loizeaux several times, but they remain silent about his statement that "hot spots of molten steel" were found "at the bottoms of the elevator shafts of the main towers, down seven [basement] levels."[174] In any case, given the existence of these testimonies and many others, such as journalist William Langewiesche's statement that "steel flowed in molten streams,"[175] PM's attempt to cast doubt on the reality of molten metal in the debris has done nothing but discredit itself.

Puffs of Dust

The PM authors next seek to undermine the claim that the squibs, or puffs of dust, that were ejected horizontally from the buildings provide evidence of explosions. Not much time need be devoted to their account, since it simply repeats NIST's account, the inadequacy of which was shown in the previous chapter. PM's discussion does, however, contain some note-worthy features.

One such feature is that it brings out, more clearly than did NIST's own discussion, the apparent contradiction between NIST's new theory of the collapses, which rejects the "pancake" theory, and its explanation of the squibs, which presupposes it. Here is PM's explanation:

> Once each tower began to collapse, the weight of all the floors above the collapsed zone bore down with pulverizing force on the highest intact floor. Unable to absorb the massive energy, that floor would fail, transmitting the forces to the floor below, allowing the collapse to progress downward through the building in a chain reaction. Engineers call the process pancaking. ... [T]he Twin Towers were mostly air. As they pancaked, all that air—along with the concrete, drywall, and other debris pulverized by the force of the collapse—was ejected with enormous energy.[176]

PM even quotes the statement by Shyam Sunder, NIST's lead investigator, that this effect is caused by "the floor pancaking."

As we saw in the previous chapter, however, NIST now says: "NIST's findings do not support the 'pancake theory' of collapse. ... [T]he floors did not fail progressively to cause a pancaking phenomenon." As NIST explained, it holds that collapse occurred not because the floors became disconnected from the columns but because they "remain[ed] connected to the columns and pull[ed] the columns inwards."[177]

The PM authors themselves endorsed NIST's new theory, saying, "The floors outside the impact zone, which are believed to have remained intact, began to sag from the heat, pulling [the core] columns inward."[178]

It may be, then, that the PM authors have actually accomplished something valuable. In the course of failing to articulate a coherent theory of the collapses of the Twin Towers, they have made it evident, more than it was in NIST's own documents, that NIST also does not have a coherent theory. While denying the pancake theory in some contexts, it affirms it in others.

PM's Treatment of Buzant, Loizeaux, and Romero

Our authors also unwittingly contradict NIST in their discussion of Zdenek Bazant whom they had asked about a criticism, made by Jones, of a paper Bazant had co-authored with Yong Zhou on why the WTC buildings collapsed.[179] Jones had argued that this paper was fatally flawed by its assumption that the steel columns were exposed to temperatures above 800°C (1,472°F). In his reply, Bazant said: "Today it is clear that the temperatures were much lower." He even suggested that they may have been "less than 400°C." Bazant went on to claim that this difference was unimportant for his analysis. Be that as it may, it involves a huge contradiction with NIST's analysis (as distinct from its empirical data), according to which steel was exposed to fires of 1,000°C (1,800°F). Bazant's statement—that the fire may have been less than 400°C—also contradicts the impression, which PM tries to create, that some of the steel was heated up to 980°C (1,800°F). Did PM's right hand not know what its left hand was doing?

Although that attempt to undermine Jones' credibility misfired, the PM authors try again by quoting Mark Loizeaux as saying (in the jargon of his profession): "The explosives configuration manufacturing technology [to bring down those buildings] does not exist."[180] But our authors do not explain how this statement is consistent with Loizeaux's statement, quoted elsewhere: "If I were to bring the towers down, I would put explosives in the basement to get the weight of the building to help collapse the structure."[181] How could he have done that if the technology did not exist?

The contradiction is especially profound given Loizeaux's statement, paraphrased by PM, that the biggest charges that are commercially available cannot cut through steel that is more than three inches thick.[182] The steel of the core columns in the basement, where Loizeaux would have put explosives, was at least four inches thick. So the statement about the biggest charges that are "commercially available" must be deceptive. Unless Loizeaux's statement was just a lie, it implies the existence of charges that are available to some organizations, such as perhaps the US military and friendly demolition companies, that would have been capable of cutting the columns in the WTC basements, where he said he would have placed the charges.

Another matter discussed by our authors is what I have called "The Van Romero Episode."[183] On 9/11 , a story in the *Albuquerque Journal* quoted Romero as saying that the Twin Towers must have been brought down by explosives.[184] Ten days later, the same journal published a story stating that Romero "says he now believes there were no explosives in the World Trade Center towers."[185] There was widespread speculation within the 9/11 truth movement that Romero—who has been a very successful lobbyist for Pentagon contracts for his employer, the New Mexico Institute of Mining and Technology—changed his public stance for business reasons, not because he had really changed his mind. Perhaps to counter that accusation, Romero even came to deny that he had changed his mind, as illustrated by his statement to PM: "I was misquoted in saying that I thought it was explosives that brought down the buildings. I only said that that's what it looked like."[186]

But was Romero misquoted? The PM authors do not enable its readers to check this out, because they do not mention the first *Albuquerque Journal* story. Instead, before quoting Romero's claim that he was misquoted, these authors say only that Romero is "prominently referenced by many Internet investigators," thereby creating the impression that he had been misquoted by conspiracy theorists on the Internet.

However, if the PM authors had been honest reporters, they would have pointed out that in the first *Albuquerque Journal* story, written by Olivier Uyttebrouck, Romero was quoted as having said: "My opinion is, based on the videotapes, that after the airplanes hit the World Trade Center there were some explosive devices inside the buildings that caused the towers to collapse." Also, saying that the collapse of the buildings were "too methodical" to be the chance result of the airplane impacts, Romero added: "It would be difficult for something from the plane to trigger an event like that."[187] Romero was hardly misquoted.

Why is the truth about the Van Romero episode significant? Because it shows that one of the world's experts—the kind of people the PM authors like to pretend are all on their side—immediately, upon seeing the collapses of the Twin Towers, said that they had to have been produced by explosives. That this is significant is shown by the fact that Romero and the PM authors now try to conceal it.

Seismic Spikes and Other Phenomena

PM concludes its discussion of the Twin Towers by disputing the claim that spikes shown on seismographs point to the occurrence of pre-collapse explosions. I have nothing to add to the comments I made about this issue in Chapter 3.

However, the fact that the PM authors dealt with this topic, as well as with squibs and reports of molten metal in the debris, is significant, because it suggests that, when they thought they could debunk claims that certain phenomena point to the occurrence of explosions, they tried. What then, are we to make of all the phenomena suggestive of explosions that they do not try to debunk—that they, indeed, even fail to mention? One defense of this failure might be that they were unaware of these phenomena. But if so, they should not have set themselves up as authorities. This ignorance-based defense would be implausible, in any case, because Jim Hoffman, in his well-known critique of PM's magazine article, had provided a list of such phenomena that the article had ignored:

> The towers fell straight down through themselves maintaining vertical symmetry.
> The towers' tops mushroomed into vast clouds of pulverized concrete and shattered steel.
> The collapses exhibited demolition squibs shooting out of the towers well below the zones of total destruction.
> The collapses generated vast dust clouds that expanded to many times the towers' volumes—more than occurs in typical controlled demolitions.
> The towers came down suddenly and completely, at a rate only slightly slower than free-fall in a vacuum.
> The explosions of the towers were characterized by intense blast waves that shattered windows in buildings 400 feet away.
> The steel skeletons were consistently shredded into short pieces that could be carried easily by the equipment used to dispose of the evidence.
> Eyewitnesses reported explosions before and at the outset of the collapses.[188]

As can be seen, only one of these phenomena, the existence of squibs, was added when PM revised and expanded its article into the book.

A scientific theory about some occurrence, such as the origin of life, the emergence of consciousness, or the collapse of the Twin Towers, cannot legitimately be considered true unless it can do justice to the various features of that occurrence. PM has declared that the government's theory, according to which the collapses were caused by the airplane impacts and the ensuing fires, is true and that, therefore, the controlled demolition theory is wrong. But it has failed to show how its theory can do justice to most of the phenomena to which advocates of the other theory appeal.

It is hard to avoid the conclusion, moreover, that these authors did not even try to explain many of these phenomena because they knew they could not. As already discussed, they surely know about the various testimonies about explosions in the towers, and yet they do not mention them. They show that they also know that the collapses occurred at virtually free-fall speed, mentioning that "[t]he South Tower collapsed in a span of about 10 seconds, while the North Tower fell in about 12 seconds."[189] But they offer no explanation as to how this could have occurred, especially given the massive steel columns in the core of each building.

Far from seeking to explain all these phenomena, the PM authors even seek to deny some of them, at least implicitly. We already saw their suggestion that the molten metal in the rubble might have really been glass. Also, when they had an occasion to mention the vast dust clouds, they did not do so. This occasion arose when they reported that, according to Mark Loizeaux, "if explosives had been placed on the upper floors, they would have generated significantly more dust and debris than mere 'puffs.'"[190] This is an outlandish statement, since the most impressive feature of videos and photographs of the collapses of the towers is the generation of enormous dust clouds when the upper floors begin to collapse—or, more accurately, when they begin to disintegrate. The PM authors could have corrected Loizeaux here, pointing out that something *did* generate "significantly more dust and debris than mere 'puffs.'" But then these authors would have needed to explain how the combination of fire and gravitational energy could have generated all this dust and debris—far more than had been generated during the collapse of any previous structure. So they remain silent, thereby implicitly denying the existence of these enormous dust clouds.

This deliberate suppression of relevant evidence shows once again that the aim of *Popular Mechanics* was not to discover and state the truth about 9/11 but simply to confirm, for uninformed readers, the truth of the official story.

WTC 7

Even though, as we saw in the previous chapter, NIST had released only a preliminary report on WTC 7 when *Popular Mechanics* put out its book, the PM authors were ready to treat this preliminary report as definitive. Disputing the claim of "conspiracy theorists" that this building was brought down by controlled demolition, our authors say that although its collapse was "initially puzzling to investigators," they "now believe the building failed from a combination of long-burning fires in its interior and damage caused from the North Tower's collapse."[191]

The new element in the NIST hypothesis is that "WTC 7 was far more compromised by falling debris than the FEMA report indicated." No longer, therefore, can critics refute the official explanation by pointing out that "there were no other examples of large fire-protected steel buildings falling because of fire alone." The main damage, as we saw in the previous chapter, is said to be on the south face, where "approximately 10 stories" were "scooped out."[192]

The other element in this explanation, the "long-burning fires," may have been supplied by fuel tanks in the building "for up to seven hours."[193] What do our authors do about the fact that none of the photos or videos show any big, long-lasting fires? They say: "The fifth floor did not have any windows, so pictures of the building prior to collapse do not provide clues to the severity of the fire there."

Our authors evidently believe that an argument from ignorance is better than no argument at all. Arguments from ignorance are, of course, generally considered illegitimate, because they would permit people to argue almost anything on the basis of no evidence whatsoever.

The most serious problem with this theory, however, is that it is completely inadequate to the empirical facts. Damage to one face of the building plus small fires on a few floors—plus perhaps really big fires on the fifth floor—could not explain why the building collapsed into a debris pile only three stories high, as this would have required the 81 columns of this 47-story-high columns to break into several pieces simultaneously. This damage and fire could not explain why the building came down at virtually free-fall speed. They could not explain the squibs, the molten metal, or the sulfidized steel. The official theory, in other words, cannot explain why, if this was not an example of controlled implosion, it was a perfect imitation thereof. The arguments for these points, having been made in the previous chapter, need not be repeated here.

Let us instead reflect on the fact that although these various points constitute a powerful cumulative argument for the controlled demolition of WTC 7, the PM authors are content to dismiss this idea by saying:

> [T]he NIST report is definitive on this account. The preliminary report states flatly: "NIST has seen no evidence that the collapse of WTC 7 was caused by . . . controlled demolition."

The fact that these authors are willing to take a preliminary report as "definitive" shows once again that they are determined, regardless of evidence, to reject the idea that WTC 7 could have been brought down by explosives. This fact is made even clearer when we take this statement together with another one, in which they say:

> Sunder says it appears the fires worked in conjunction with the damage from debris to weaken the building's structure, but NIST has not determined whether one or the other was the primary instigator of the collapse.[194]

So even though NIST, at the time the PM book was written, had not yet settled on a theory about the building's collapse, the PM authors wrote as if they knew that it was caused by some combination of fire and debris damage, with no aid from explosives.

PM research editor Davin Coburn stated this conclusion confidently in Guy Smith's BBC documentary, *The Conspiracy Files: 9/11*. In response to the statement that the collapse of WTC 7 "does look exactly like a controlled demolition," Coburn replied:

> I understand why people may think that . . . , but when you learn the facts about the way the building was built and about the way in which it supported itself and the damage that was done by the collapsing towers that preceded it, the idea that it was demolition simply holds no water.

That response was evidently good enough for Smith, whose narrator then explained that the building collapsed because it, in addition to being damaged by debris from the towers, became a "raging inferno." This occurred, Smith's narrator added, because "the sprinkler system didn't work," because "the water supply to the building was knocked out when the Twin Towers came down, so there was "no way to put the fire out." If Smith was relying on Coburn for this information, then the PM research editor had again not done his homework. As stories that appeared shortly after 9/11 reported, three fireboats pumped water to the WTC site from the Hudson River. One of those boats, the John J. Harvey, reportedly "can pump 16,000 to 20,000 gallons of water a minute," which is "the equivalent of 15 [fire] engines drafting water." In any case, NIST, citing "FDNY first-person interviews," says: "[W]ater was never an issue at WTC 7, since firefighting was never started in the building."[195]

Although PM portrays itself as taking a scientific approach to 9/11, the extreme difference between its method and the scientific method cannot be exaggerated. The scientific method requires that when there is more than one hypothesis to explain some phenomenon, the alternative hypotheses are to be evaluated in terms of their capacity to do justice to all the relevant facts. If Hypothesis A can do justice to all the relevant facts while Hypothesis B can do justice to only some of them, then, unless there is a third possible explanation, Hypothesis A must be accepted, even if we, for some reason or another, had a prior attachment to Hypothesis B. NIST and *Popular Mechanics*, however, take a completely different approach, saying, in effect: "We are committed to the truth of Hypothesis B. So we are going to construct the best theory we can on this basis, even if it means that we must suggest scientifically incredible ideas and engage in special pleading and arguments from ignorance to explain some of the facts and must completely ignore some of the other facts. We will not genuinely consider Hypothesis A, because we have (nonscientific) reasons for ruling it out."

If this is indeed their method, trying to argue with them would be futile. However, pointing out that this does seem to be their method may help readers realize that their claim to being scientific is contradicted by their actual approach.

Be that as it may, PM concludes this chapter by dealing with the notorious statement of Larry Silverstein, the owner of WTC 7, that he, while talking with the fire department commander about this building, suggested that they "pull it." PM seeks to debunk the claim that this statement, made in a PBS documentary,[196] constituted a confession that WTC 7 was brought down with explosives. The PM authors, citing Silverstein's own later statement, say that he was talking about pulling the squadron of firefighters from the building.[197]

There are good reasons to be puzzled about the "pull it" statement. Why would Silverstein, who was hoping to receive several billions in insurance money on the assumption that the buildings had been brought down by terrorists, have publicly admitted that WTC 7 was brought down by explosives at his suggestion? Also, Silverstein's statement, taken as referring to a decision to bring the building down, could not be completely true, insofar as it suggests that the decision was made only at that moment, because preparing the building for demolition would have taken considerable time. There are, accordingly, reasons to be cautious about concluding that Silverstein's statement constituted a confession.

Nevertheless, the statement does seem to refer to having the building brought down, because Silverstein's alternative interpretation is unconvincing. Let us look again at his original statement: "I said, 'We've had such terrible loss of life, maybe the smartest thing to do is pull it.' And they made that decision to pull and we watched the building collapse."[198]

The claim that the "it" in "pull it" refers to the squadron of firefighters does not seem plausible, especially given the second sentence.[199] Silverstein's later explanation is, at the very least, not a natural one.

PM argues, however, that "pull it is not slang for controlled demolition." They support this claim by citing several experts, including Mark Loizeaux, and then saying: "Firefighters contacted by *Popular Mechanics* confirm that pull it is a common firefighting term for removing personnel from a dangerous structure."[200] Unfortunately for these claims, a member of the 9/11 truth movement took the initiative to call Loizeaux's company, Controlled Demolition, Inc. Reaching the receptionist, the caller asked, "if you were in the demolition business and you said the, the term 'pull it,' I was wondering what exactly that would mean?" After asking the caller to hold for a moment, the receptionist returned and said, "'Pull it' is when they actually pull it down."[201]

Popular Mechanics on *The O'Reilly Factor*

The PM authors claim to have written a scientific, not a political, document. This claim was the theme of a conversation in 2006 between editor-in-chief James Meigs and Bill O'Reilly on the latter's Fox News show, *The O'Reilly Factor*. Saying that "*Popular Mechanics* magazine . . . is debunking these [9/11] conspiracy theories using scientific evidence," O'Reilly asked Meigs about the "myth" that the "World Trade Center towers fell too quickly." Meigs said:

> Well, they didn't. . . . [O]ne of the things that comes up a lot in these conspiracy theories is kind of a cartoon version, how we think things ought to have happened. Well, no one had ever seen a 100-plus story building collapse to the ground before. And so the idea that it was going to tip over like a big tree or something was based on just a hunch, as opposed to science.

This exchange, in which Meigs claimed to speak for science even though he had ignored the question (which concerned the speed of the collapses), was later followed by this comforting discussion of the scientific nature of PM's conclusions:

> O'Reilly: So there's absolutely no evidence . . . that anything happened that was stunning to the analysts who, after the fact, examined it, correct?
>
> Meigs: That's exactly right.
>
> O'Reilly: All right, so it's all scientifically proven that A led to B, led to C.
>
> Meigs: Right.
>
> O'Reilly: No miraculous things or any of that. . . . Now you're not a political magazine. . . , right?
>
> Meigs: And these aren't political questions.
>
> O'Reilly: No, these are scientific questions, right?
>
> Meigs: Facts are facts. Facts don't have politics.[202]

Although facts do not have political agendas, people who discuss facts often do. And everything about the PM authors' discussion of the destruction of the World Trade Center suggests that their entire effort was carried out to support the politically acceptable conclusion that the destruction occurred without the aid of explosives. The claim that "it's all scientifically proven that A led to B, led to C," so that there is nothing "miraculous" or even "stunning" about the collapses, is just that—a claim. It is a claim, moreover, that runs counter to all the (apolitical) facts.

The Pentagon

The PM authors next attempt to defend the official account of what happened at the Pentagon. They do this in two ways: presenting positive evidence for the claim that the Pentagon was struck by Flight 77 under the control of al-Qaeda hijackers, and refuting evidence that, according to critics, contradicts this claim. But their attempt does not succeed. The primary problem is that they simply fail to discuss the strongest arguments against the government's claim. They also fail to undermine some other reasons for concluding that the government has been hiding the truth about what happened at the Pentagon on 9/11.

To understand PM's strategy, we must realize that the government's central claim—that the Pentagon was struck by Flight 77 under the control of al-Qaeda hijackers—is a composite claim, composed of two elements: (1) the Pentagon was struck by Flight 77 and hence a Boeing 757; (2) when Flight 77 struck the Pentagon, it was being piloted by al-Qaeda hijacker Hani Hanjour. PM's strategy is to focus on the first claim, citing evidence that supports it and disputing arguments against it, while ignoring the problems involved in the second claim.

In discussing PM's attempt to defend the official story about the Pentagon strike, I will first discuss its defense of the claim that the Pentagon was struck by Flight 77. I will then show that, even if this defense could be considered successful, it would not defend the official story about the Pentagon strike, because it has ignored the problems in the second part of the government's composite claim. I will then point out two more factors suggesting that government officials have been concealing the truth about the attack on the Pentagon. In carrying out this critique, I will refer most often to Russell Pickering's website, Pentagon Research.[203]

Much of the controversy about the attack on the Pentagon, which killed 125 Pentagon employees, has revolved around the claim that the Pentagon was struck by AA Flight 77. And most of the controversy about this claim has centered on the question of whether the aircraft that struck the Pentagon was, like Flight 77, a Boeing 757. The PM authors devote most of their chapter on the Pentagon to arguing, contrary to the claim that "a missile or a different type of plane smashed into the Pentagon," that it was a Boeing 757 and, in particular, Flight 77.

I will look first at their positive evidence for this claim, then at their attempt to debunk evidence that has been said to refute it. Some of this positive evidence is intended simply to support the claim that the striking aircraft was a Boeing 757, while some of it is meant to show that it was Flight 77 in particular.

Support for the Boeing 757 Claim

In support of the claim that the aircraft was a 757, PM relies entirely on eyewitness testimony, claiming that "hundreds of witnesses saw a Boeing 757 hit the building."[204] But PM provides no evidence that there were hundreds of such witnesses, and it ignores various problems that have been raised about the evidentiary value of the testimony that does exist. Critics setting out to debunk PM's claims about the weight of the witness testimony could do so with little difficulty.[205]

One witness is structural engineer Allyn E. Kilsheimer, who arrived at the crash site that afternoon. Arguing against the claim that what hit the Pentagon was a missile, Kilsheimer said:

> It was absolutely a plane. . . . I picked up parts of the plane with the airline markings on them. . . . I held in my hand the tail section of the plane, and I stood on a pile of debris that we later discovered contained the black box. . . . I held parts of uniforms from crew members in my hands, including body parts. Okay?[206]

But this is hardly "okay." Besides the fact that few people, aside from pathologists, would pick up body parts, the tail section of a Boeing 757 is over 20 feet long and quite heavy.

Moreover, when *Popular Mechanics* quoted Kilsheimer's statement in its magazine article back in 2005, he reportedly said, "and I found the black box." Various critics pointed out, however, that the (two) black boxes were found, according to the official story, by two firefighters three days later.[207] At what school of journalistic ethics did the PM authors learn that, if part of a statement you have quoted from one of your star witnesses turns out to be false ("I found the black box"), you may simply change that part of the statement (to "I stood on a pile of debris that we later discovered contained the black box")?

This modification is especially interesting in light of PM's James Meigs complaint that few of the documents put out by alternative conspiracy theorists "handle factual material with enough care to pass muster at a high-school newspaper."[208] Once again, the official conspiracy theorists are found to illustrate the very sins of which they accuse their opponents.

Another witness cited by PM is retired Army officer Frank Probst, who was working on the renovation. Supporting the idea that an American airliner came toward the Pentagon very close to the ground, Probst claimed that it was flying so low that he dove to the ground for fear that it might hit him.[209] In part of his testimony not quoted by PM, Probst even said that one of the plane's engines passed by him "about six feet away."[210] Dave McGowan, who has studied the effects of wind turbulence from large airliners, says that if a Boeing 757 going several hundred miles an hour had come this close to Probst, he would have been a victim, not a witness.[211]

Another eyewitness quoted by PM is Don Mason, a Pentagon employee. Mason, whose credibility is already undermined by the fact that he supports Probst's story, reported seeing, while stuck in traffic just west of the Pentagon, an airliner clip three light poles during its approach.[212]

This claim, that the plane en route to the Pentagon hit five light poles at the Washington Boulevard overpass—three with one wing, two with the other—has been an important part of the evidence that a Boeing 757, or in any case an airplane with a wingspan of at least 100 feet (the distance between the light poles on the two sides of the road), really did strike the Pentagon. PM's support of this claim includes photographs of the five poles, which were knocked over.[213]

Serious questions about the credibility of this claim have long been raised.[214] But videotaped testimony has recently been presented that, if reliable, would make the claim even more dubious than it was before.

The official story depends on the idea that the aircraft that hit the Pentagon flew past the south side of the nearby Citgo gas station (now called the Navy Exchange). Only if this is true could the plane have hit the light poles and then struck the Pentagon at the angle that would lead to the so-called exit hole in the C-ring (to be discussed below). However, Pentagon police officer William Lagasse, who was at the Citgo station, has always maintained that he was on the starboard side of the airplane, which would mean that the plane passed on the north side of the Citgo station. Supporters of the official story were able to dismiss Lagasse's statement by assuming that he had simply confused starboard and port.

Now, however, Lagasse and three other eyewitnesses have all stated on camera that the airplane definitely passed on the north side of the station.[215] One of these witnesses is Chadwick Brooks, another police officer at the Pentagon. The other two are Robert Turcios, an employee at the station, and Edward Paik, an auto mechanic at a nearby shop. Assuming their testimony to be true, it would have been impossible for the airplane to have clipped the light poles at the Washington Boulevard overpass. For this to have happened, as Richard Stanley and Jerry Russell have explained (in an essay entitled "The Quantum Flight Path?"), the plane would have needed to make a quantum leap from one trajectory to another.[216]

All three of these men, in harmony with their testimony that the plane passed on the north side of the station, say that they did not see the plane strike any light poles, even though one of them, Brooks, had earlier said that he did.

This testimony is, moreover, supported by an animation, prepared by the National Transportation Safety Board on the basis of the Flight Data Recorder, of the flight path of the aircraft—alleged to be Flight 77—that approached the Pentagon. It shows the flight path as being to the north of the flight path portrayed in the animation put out by the 9/11 Commission. Also, according to the analysis of this NTSB animation carried out by Pilots for Truth, the flight path, besides being to the north of the trajectory that would have been needed to hit the light poles, was also too high.[217]

This testimony, besides throwing into doubt the testimony of Don Mason and the other people who claimed to have seen the light poles clipped, suggests something even more important: that the five light poles were staged to provide evidence for the official story. If so, then we must suspect that other evidence for the official story was also planted. If any of the evidence is demonstrably planted, in fact, we must doubt the truth of the entire story.

Support for the Flight 77 Claim

In any case, in spite of PM's failure to do so, let us assume, for the sake of discussion, that several credible people did report seeing the Pentagon struck by a Boeing 757 with American Airline markings. This fact would not, by itself, prove that this plane was Flight 77.

This distinction must be made not only, as we saw in Chapter 2, because there is no evidence that the radar target seen approaching the Pentagon was AA 77, which was lost from radar some 40 minutes earlier. It must also be made because one of the Pentagon's false-flag techniques, we now know, is to use planes painted to fool eyewitnesses. One source of this knowledge is the now notorious "Operation Northwoods" document, in which the Pentagon's joint chiefs of staff in 1962 presented a number of operations that could be used as pretexts to invade Cuba. One of the operations was described thus:

> It is possible to create an incident which will demonstrate convincingly that a Cuban aircraft has attacked and shot down a chartered civil airliner enroute from the United States. . . .
>
> An aircraft at Eglin AFB would be painted and numbered as an exact duplicate for a civil registered aircraft belonging to a CIA proprietary organization in the Miami area. At the designated time the duplicate would be substituted for the actual civil aircraft and would be loaded with selected passengers, all boarded under carefully prepared aliases. The actual aircraft would be converted to a drone.
>
> The drone aircraft and the actual aircraft will be scheduled to allow a rendezvous south of Florida. From the rendezvous point the passenger-carrying aircraft will descend to minimum altitude and go directly into an auxiliary field at Eglin AFB where arrangements will have been made to evacuate the passengers and return the aircraft to its original status. The drone aircraft meanwhile will continue to fly the filed flight plan. When over Cuba the drone will be transmitting on the international distress frequency a "MAY DAY" message stating he is under attack by Cuban MIG aircraft. The transmission will be interrupted by destruction of the aircraft which will be triggered by radio signal.[218]

We also know that such an idea might have occurred to the Bush administration, thanks to the release of a memo from a meeting between Bush and British Prime Minister Tony Blair on January 31, 2002, according to which Bush, discussing ways to get a UN resolution to justify war against Iraq, said: "The US was thinking of flying U2 reconnaissance aircraft with fighter cover over Iraq, painted in UN colours. If Saddam fired on them, he would be in breach."[219]

It would not, of course, occur to the PM authors to mention the possibility that a deception of this type might have been involved in the attack on the Pentagon. They do, however, present two types of evidence intended to show that the plane that hit the Pentagon was not simply a Boeing 757 but Flight 77 in particular: phone calls and DNA tests.

Alleged Phone Calls from AA 77: With regard to the phone calls, the PM authors say that "at least two passengers—Renee May and Barbara Olson, wife of US Solicitor General Ted Olson—phoned family members to let them know that their plane had been hijacked."[220] We can ignore the detail, evidently missed by PM's fact checkers, that Renee May was a flight attendant, not a passenger.[221] But we cannot ignore the fact that she reportedly called her mother on her cell phone and that this, as we saw in Chapter 1, would have been impossible in 2001.[222] (In the later section on Flight 93, I will discuss PM's attempt to refute this claim.)

We also cannot ignore the fact, unmentioned by the PM authors, that the information about Barbara Olson came from Ted Olson, that he was working for the Bush–Cheney administration, and that he testified before the Supreme Court that there are situations in which "government officials might quite legitimately have reasons to give false information out."[223] Also unmentioned by PM is the fact that Ted Olson gave contradictory statements about how his wife had made the call. Three days after 9/11, he said on one TV show that she must have called from the airplane phone and, on another show, that she used a cell phone. On September 14, Tony Mauro, the Supreme Court correspondent for American Lawyer Media, published an account that said, "She was calling on her cell phone from aboard the jet."[224] Six months later, Olson had settled on his first answer, saying during an interview for the London *Telegraph* that, "calling collect," she "us[ed] the phone in the passengers' seats."[225] He later produced Department of Justice telephone accounts purportedly showing that there were two reverse-charge calls from Flight 77's Airfone number about 9:20AM on September 11, 2001.

However, one of the things revealed in Rowland Morgan and Ian Henshall's *9/11 Revealed* is that AA's 757s (unlike UA's 757s) were not equipped with seat-back phones. Morgan and Henshall report: "A call by us to American Airlines' London Office produced a definitive statement from Laeti Hyver that [AA's] 757s do not have Airfones. This was confirmed by an e-mail from AA in the US."[226] Although this e-mail correspondence was not printed in their *9/11 Revealed* or in Morgan's *Flight 93 Revealed*, in which it is also mentioned,[227] they have made it available for my use in this book.

This correspondence began in 2004 with a letter to American Airlines asking, "Are 757s fitted with phones that passengers can use?" A reply, signed "Tim Wagner, AA Spokesman," said: "American Airlines 757s do not have onboard phones for passenger use." Because Wagner's answer might have meant that there were phones for crew use, which Barbara Olson might conceivably have borrowed, another letter was sent, asking, "are there any onboard phones at all on AA 757s, i.e., that could be used either by passengers or cabin crew?" Wagner's response said: "AA 757s do not have any onboard phones, either for passenger or crew use. Crew have other means of communication available."[228]

This information fits, moreover, with what can be found on the American Airlines website headed "Onboard Technology." Under "Inflight Satellite Phones," it reads: "Turn flight time into quality time by arranging meetings, calling your broker or calling home. Worldwide satellite communications are available on American Airlines' Boeing 777 and Boeing 767 aircraft almost anytime while flying over North America and worldwide."[229] The Boeing 757 is not mentioned.

Accordingly, given the evidence that Barbara Olson could not have called from Flight 77 using either a cell phone or a seatback phone, we have very good evidence that the call to Ted Olson, like the call to Renee May's parents, was fabricated—unless, of course, he simply made up the story, then produced doctored DoJ telephone records.

The DNA Evidence: With regard to the DNA evidence, the PM authors write: "All but five of the 189 people who died on the aircraft and in the Pentagon were later identified through DNA testing. (The five hijackers were positively identified.)"[230] As evidence, they cite a report of November 16, 2001, from the "Armed Forces Institute of Pathology." But it does not support their claim.

According to Dr. Andrew Baker's summary of this report (which had the total number of victims as 188, rather than 189, as given by *Popular Mechanics* and many other sources), there were 183 bodies with sufficient remains to be submitted to DNA analysis, but there were only "178 positive identifications." Although Baker says that "[s]ome remains for each of the terrorists were recovered," this was merely an inference from the fact that there were "five unique postmortem profiles that did not match any antemortem material provided by victims' families." The fact that this conclusion—that these unmatched remains were those of "the five hijackers"—was merely an inference was stated more explicitly in a *Washington Post* story, which said: "The remains of the five hijackers have been identified *through a process of exclusion*, as they did not match DNA samples contributed by family members of all 183 victims who died at the site" (emphasis added).[231]

PM's claim that the hijackers were "positively identified," therefore, appears to be untrue. Indeed, the alleged hijackers could have been positively identified only if DNA samples had been obtained from their relatives, but this evidently was not done. Why not? The FBI could easily have located relatives. And these relatives, most if not all of whom did not believe their own flesh and blood had been involved in the attacks, would have surely been willing to supply the needed DNA. (Indeed, as I mentioned in Chapter 2, the family of Ziah Jarrah, accused of being the pilot of Flight 93, offered to supply DNA.) PM does not, however, point this out.

In any case, this lack of positive identification of the alleged hijackers is consistent with the fact that the autopsy report, which was released in response to an FOIA request from Dr. Thomas Olmsted, contains no Arab names.[232] All the autopsy report really says, in any case, is that there were five bodies whose DNA did not match that of any of the known Pentagon victims or any of the crew members or regular passengers on Flight 77.

However, defenders of the official story might reply, the autopsy report, by identifying crew members and passengers on Flight 77, verified the fact that it was Flight 77 that crashed into the Pentagon. That would be true, however, only if we had independent evidence, not provided by the FBI or the Pentagon, that the bodies of the crew and passengers were really found in the Pentagon wreckage. But we have no such evidence.

As Russell Pickering reports, the FBI immediately took complete control of the Pentagon crash site and did not allow the press to get very close. And although Dr. Marcella Fierro, the chief medical examiner of Virginia, pointed out that it was her office's responsibility to carry out the autopsies, the FBI insisted that the autopsies be done by the Armed Forces Institute of Pathology at Dover Air Force Base. Also, when the bodies arrived at the Dover Institute, they were brought by the Army and accompanied by the FBI.[233] Therefore, although the remains of 189 (or 188) bodies were evidently delivered to the Dover Institute with word that they had all come from the Pentagon, we have no independent evidence that all of them, as distinct from the remains of only the 125 Pentagon employees, were actually brought from that site. The radiology report from the Dover Institute, for example, says:

> [S]pecimens ranging from relatively intact bodies to small body-part fragments were received from the Pentagon site. Unfortunately, many specimens were received as body parts, often unrecognizable from their gross appearance and mixed with debris from the site. Each specimen designated for processing had an identification number assigned by the Federal Bureau of Investigation that linked it to its recovery location at the scene.[234]

So, although the authors of this document evidently assumed that all the human remains they received had come "from the Pentagon site," some of the remains could have been mixed with debris from the site en route. The authors of the document had only the word of the FBI and military personnel who brought the remains that they all came from the Pentagon site.

There were, moreover, places where this mixing could have occurred. The victims of the Pentagon attack were taken to a temporary morgue in the Pentagon's north parking lot loading dock. They were then trucked to Davison Army Airfield at Fort Belvoir, then flown by helicopter to Dover. "FBI agents rode in the trucks, participated in the escort, and accompanied the remains during the flight to preserve the chain of custody."[235] For all we know, therefore, human remains from two different sites could have been combined by FBI and military personnel before they were brought to Dover.

But the PM authors, taking the position that the government's story about 9/11 is true, assume, circularly, that information given to the public by the FBI can be taken at face value without examination.

Having looked at PM's positive evidence for the Flight 77 claim, I turn now to its attempt to debunk evidence that has seemed to many critics to count against this claim. This evidence includes the FBI's refusal to release information.

Lack of Expected Debris
One claim that PM seeks to debunk is that the crash site did not contain the debris that would have been present after the crash of a Boeing 757.

Probably the first televised eyewitness report of this type was by CNN Pentagon correspondent Jamie McIntyre, who said: "From my close-up inspection, there's no evidence of a plane having crashed anywhere near the Pentagon. . . . There are no large tail sections, wing sections, fuselage, nothing like that anywhere around."[236] Seeking to minimize the importance of McIntyre's statement, the PM authors declare: "Today, we know why very little wreckage was visible from McIntyre's vantage point: Flight 77 didn't crash near the Pentagon. It crashed into the Pentagon."[237]

This interpretation, however, is based on the false assumption that McIntyre's "vantage point" was the media area in front of the Citgo gas station, from which the interview was taped. He in reality was talking about his "close-up inspection" of the area around the strike zone.[238]

McIntyre was not, to be sure, denying that a plane had struck the Pentagon. His statement was made in response to someone's observation that the airplane appeared to crash short of the Pentagon. McIntyre responded by saying that there was no evidence for the view that it landed near the Pentagon, after which he added: "The only site is the actual site of the building that's crashed in." And at that site, he said, he "could see parts of the airplane that crashed into the building." Thus far, his statement supported the official view.

But he then said that all he saw were "very small pieces of the plane . . . The biggest piece I saw was about three feet long." He later added that all the pieces "are small enough that you can pick up in your hand. There are no large tail sections, wing sections, fuselage, nothing like that anywhere around."[239]

An examination of the available photographs produces the same verdict. Pilot Ralph Omholt, for example, writes: "There was no particular physical evidence of the expected 'wreckage.' There was no tail, no wings."[240]

A common response by those who believe that Flight 77 did hit the Pentagon is that, if the wreckage was not outside, it must have been inside. At a Pentagon briefing the next day, however, county fire chief Ed Plaugher, who had been in charge of putting out the fire, was asked whether anything was left of the airplane. He replied that there were "some small pieces . . . but not large sections . . . . [T]here's no fuselage sections and that sort of thing." At a Pentagon press conference three days later, Lee Evey, who headed up the renovation project, said that the evidence of the aircraft is "not very visible. . . . None of those parts are very large. . . . You don't see big pieces of the airplane sitting there extending up into the air."[241]

April Gallop, a member of the Army who, along with her two-month-old son, was seriously injured, has said in an interview:

> I was located at the E ring. . . . And we had to escape the building before the floors, debris etcetera collapsed on us. And I don't recall at any time seeing any plane debris. . . . I didn't know it was a plane until I was informed at the hospital. If I wasn't informed I would have never believed it. I walked through that place to try to get out before everything collapsed on us . . . . Surely we should have seen something.[242]

Although journalists were not allowed inside the Pentagon, Judy Rothschadl, a documentary producer, for some reason "was granted immediate access to the crash site." She reported: "There weren't seats or luggage or things you find in a plane."[243] Also ABC's John McWethy has reported that an army two-star general, a friend of his, took him inside (with his press badge turned over "so it would look like it was an official badge that had been blown by the wind"). In describing what he saw, he said:

> It was a scene of destruction. . . . It was the kind of scene I had seen . . . in combat situations during the war in Kosovo and other places. . . . I had to do it very quickly and circumspectly . . . . But I got in very close, got a look early on at the bad stuff. I could not, however, see any plane wreckage.[244]

With regard to the plane, McWethy added: "it was well inside and had been, basically, vaporized." But that was merely his inference or what he had been told.

This idea that the plane was vaporized, because the fires inside the Pentagon were so hot, was used by some early defenders of the official theory to explain away the absence of debris indicative of a 757.[245] However, besides the fact that hydrocarbon fires do not get anywhere close to the temperature needed to vaporize metal, this claim was wildly incompatible with the assertion that the bodies of the plane's occupants were later identified by their DNA.

A second effort to defend the official view has been to claim that the allegedly missing airplane parts were indeed present within the Pentagon. Various photos do reveal wheel and engine components that some interpreters say are 757 parts.[246] PM carries on this approach, even appealing to the flimsy little piece of metal on the Pentagon lawn photographed by Mark Faram, calling it "a small piece of Flight 77's fuselage."[247] This could be seen as a rather literal illustration of John McCain's charge that "conspiracy theorists chase any bit of information, no matter how flimsy," that they can use to "fit their preordained conclusions."

However, an empty Boeing 757 weighs well over 100,000 pounds. Dave McGowan, in light of this fact, says: "Even if all of the photos did actually depict debris from a 757, and if all that debris was actually found inside the Pentagon, then a few hundred pounds of Flight 77 has been accounted for." The official story, therefore, "cannot account for . . . 99.9% of the wreckage."[248] Even if defenders of the 757 story argue that the aircraft debris within the Pentagon would have weighed several thousand pounds, not just a few hundred, the problem would still remain.

How do the PM authors try to debunk the claim that this absence of 757 debris disproves the official theory? Evidently aware that they have a very weak argument, they spend most of the section talking about other things: Thierry Meyssan's missile hypothesis, his misinterpretation of Mike Walter's statement about a "cruise missile with wings," eyewitnesses who said they saw an American airliner, the (alleged) cell phone calls, and the (alleged) DNA identifications of the (alleged) hijackers. When they finally get around to the question of the debris, they begin by conceding the empirical facts, saying: "It is true that after the crash, only pieces of the plane were recovered: the landing gear, bits of the fuselage, and the flight data recorder, among others." But, they say:

> Much of the airliner was pulverized due to the combination of mass and velocity. . . . "The plane disintegrated on itself," says Paul Mlakar, a senior research scientist with the US Army Corps of Engineers, who was team leader for the *Pentagon Building Performance Report.*[249]

There are, however, many problems with this explanation.

For one thing, in NIST's account of the Twin Towers, which PM endorses, the "mass and velocity" of the planes is used to make the opposite argument: that they would sever not only the perimeter steel columns but also the massive core columns. Here, by contrast, the mass-and-velocity argument is used to explain why the plane, hitting a building with much less steel, would itself disintegrate. Is this not special pleading?

Even more seriously, PM's purported explanation is nothing but a mere assertion. PM holds itself up as the defender of the scientific method. And yet we have not even the hint of a quantitative analysis of what kind of energy it would take to cause an airliner to disintegrate. Although they appeal to the authority of "senior research scientist" Paul Mlakar, he offers no scientific analysis. He merely gives an analogy: The plane's hitting the Pentagon was "like taking a Coke can and smashing it against the wall. The back and the front become one."[250]

As a scientist, Mlakar would know that smashing a Coke can does not reduce its weight. So why has no one reported finding a 100,000-pound piece of steel and aluminum in the wreckage?

Having seen that PM has not answered the debris problem, let us see if it does better with other problems.

Big Plane, Small Hole

One of the most widely publicized arguments against the official theory is that although it entails that virtually all of a Boeing 757 went inside the Pentagon, the hole created in the Pentagon's façade is too small for this claim to be plausible. This objection has been supported by Major General Albert Stubblebine, who during the Cold War was in charge of the US Army's Imagery Interpretation for Scientific and Technical Intelligence. Stubblebine has said:

> I measured pieces of Soviet equipment from photographs. It was my job. I look at the hole in the Pentagon and I look at the size of an airplane that was supposed to have hit the Pentagon. And I said, "The plane does not fit in that hole." So what did hit the Pentagon? . . . What's going on?[251]

The PM authors would no doubt reply that Stubblebine's query presupposed the false view, based on some widely circulated photographs, that the hole was only about 16 feet in diameter. The more accurate view, they would say, is the official view, supported by photographs, that beneath the small hole there was a hole approximately 90 feet wide, which was obscured by water from fire hoses in most of the photographs. Citing the *Pentagon Building Performance Report*, the PM authors write: "When Flight 77 hit the Pentagon it created a hole in the exterior wall of the building approximately 90 feet wide."[252]

However, although that is indeed the official view, the photographs supporting it are far from unambiguous. PM comes closer to describing this "hole" by calling it a "messy 90-foot gash," but even this suggests something more continuous than what we see in the photographs.[253] The PM authors acknowledge this fact by quoting one expert as saying that "a jet doesn't punch a cartoonlike outline into a concrete building upon impact."[254] Another problem is that some of the remaining structure appears to be bending outward, suggesting that the damage was caused by a blast from inside. Still another problem is the fact that this gash is at ground level, and it is hard to imagine how a Boeing 757, with its engines extending beneath its wings, could have struck the Pentagon so low without damaging the lawn and destroying the large spools in front of the damaged area on the ground floor.

In any case, let us assume, for the sake of argument, that this gash was really created by the striking aircraft. This agreement would somewhat mitigate the problem for the 757 theory, but it would not remove it. The PM authors state the remaining problem thus: "Why wasn't the initial hole as wide as a 757's 124-foot, 10-inch wingspan?"

"For one thing," they reply, "both wings were damaged before striking the Pentagon façade." Relying primarily on the testimony of Frank Probst—the man who claimed that one of the 757's engines passed within six feet of him—they say that "the right wing smash[ed] into a portable 750 kilowatt generator . . . and the left engine [struck] a ground-level external vent." They also appeal to the claim, mentioned earlier, that the 757's wings clipped three light poles. On this twofold basis, they suggest that "the outer portions of both wings sheared off in the precrash collisions."[255]

The PM authors evidently did not realize that, in claiming that the wings sheared off before the Pentagon was struck, they had contradicted their earlier admission that no big airplane pieces were found (because the whole plane was pulverized). If a 757, which has 125-foot wingspan, created a hole only 90 feet wide because the ends of its wings were sheared off, then there should have been two 17-foot wingtips on the lawn. But Jamie McIntyre, it will be recalled, said that he saw no aircraft parts more than 3 feet long.

In addition to claiming that the wings were sheared off, PM claims, as we have seen, that "a jet doesn't punch a cartoonlike outline into a concrete building upon impact," thereby contradicting their previous point, which was that the 757's sheared wings explain why it punched a 90-foot rather than a 125-foot outline into the Pentagon's façade. PM, in any case, supports this new claim by appeal to Purdue University engineer Mete Sozen (one of the authors of the *Pentagon Building Performance Report*), who based this conclusion on a computer simulation.[256]

This simulation reportedly showed that when Flight 77 hit reinforced-concrete columns, the plane's exterior crumpled up "like a sausage skin" and that the remainder of the plane "flowed into the structure in a state closer to a liquid than a solid mass." Just as computer simulations worked miracles in relation to the Twin Towers, they seem to have done the same at the Pentagon—although in the former case they explained why an airplane would cause so much damage, in the latter case, why so little. In the Pentagon miracle, the basic premise, fed into the computer, seems to be that "the mass of [a 757 airplane] is mostly fluid fuel." But Flight 77, with its passengers, cargo, and fuel, would have weighed close to 150,000 pounds. Only about 36,000 pounds of that would have been due to its 5,000 gallons of "fluid fuel." How could Sozen have made such a claim?

When one turns to the website for the Purdue simulation experiments to which Sozen is referring and for which he was the team leader, one finds, at the outset of the description of the experiments, this statement:

> A basic hypothesis, informally confirmed with engineers knowledgeable in this subject, is that the bulk of the impact damage is due to the body of fuel in the wing and center tanks. Most of the aircraft structure is light-weight, low-mass, and relatively low strength, with the exception of the wheel undercarriage.[257]

Is this not an extraordinary statement? Although Sozen and his colleagues give a wildly counterintuitive hypothesis—that most of the impact damage would have been due to the fuel, even though it would have constituted only about 25 percent of the plane's mass—they provide no support except to say that it was "informally confirmed" with some engineers. We are, moreover, not told who these engineers were, leaving us to suspect that no engineers were willing to associate their names with this hypothesis.

Nevertheless, this unsupported, counterintuitive hypothesis formed the basis for the simulation experiments carried out by Sozen's team, the first of which was: "A single body of fluid hits a single column. The purpose of this simulation is to understand the response of a reinforced concrete column subjected to high-speed impact of the fuel in the aircraft tanks." What possible relevance would this experiment have to the theory in question, which is that the columns were hit by a 150,000-pound steel-and-aluminum airplane going several hundred miles per hour?

The arbitrariness of Sozen's team's hypothesis about the aircraft that hit the Pentagon becomes even more obvious when we turn to their computer simulations of the attack on the North Tower of the World Trade Center. Here they say:

> From our modeling of the aircraft crash into the Pentagon building, we knew that a critical issue in defining the damage was the modeling of the fuel in the aircraft. Much of the mass of the aircraft is provided by the fuel; in this case about 27%.[258]

So whereas in the Pentagon case, "the bulk" of the damage is due to the fuel, in the WTC case, only "much" of the mass is provided by the fuel, and "much" is defined as only "about 27%." Why the difference? Can we avoid the suspicion that it is because in the case of the Pentagon, Sozen's group needed to explain why the plane caused so little damage, while in the case of the North Tower, they had to explain why it caused so much?

In any case, the Sozen team, rather than following the scientific procedure of applying general explanatory principles to this particular situation, has created a purely ad hoc hypothesis to explain why the 757 created so little damage (just as NIST's theory of "progressive global collapse" is a theory with no exemplifications either before or after 9/11).[259] In appealing to the Purdue simulations, therefore, the PM authors have not provided a scientific explanation.

The Hole in the C-Ring

Another much-discussed problem for the official theory is the fact that a round hole, about 9 feet in diameter, was created in the Pentagon's C-ring in Wedge 2, 310 feet from the impact zone at about the place a projectile continuing the attacking aircraft's trajectory would have hit. (Although the aircraft struck Wedge 1, it struck at an angle, so that by the time it reached the third of the Pentagon's five rings—the C-ring—it would have crossed into Wedge 2. Readers unfamiliar with the Pentagon may want to consult some photographs.[260]) How could this hole have been created by a 757? The official explanation at the beginning was that it was made by the plane's nose. For example, Lee Evey, the program manager for the Pentagon Renovation Project, said: "The plane actually penetrated through the . . . E ring, D ring, C ring. . . . The nose of the plane just barely broke through the inside of the C ring, so it was extending into A-E Drive a little bit."[261] Evey's claim that the nose was seen was also made by Donald Rumsfeld, who said: "I'm told the nose is—is still in there." The claim that the hole was caused by the nose was made in all the early official reports.[262]

However, the nose of a 757 is very fragile. The nose of Flight 77, even if it could have gone through the outer (E-ring) wall, with its steel-reinforced concrete, and then made its way through the concrete columns and interior walls inside the building, could not have punched out a large hole in the C-ring wall, with its steel mesh and 8 inches of brick. Thierry Meyssan, as I pointed out in *The New Pearl Harbor*, used this problem as one of his main arguments in favor of the idea that the Pentagon was instead struck by a missile—the type used to pierce bunkers.[263]

How do our PM authors deal with this problem? They begin by attributing the claim of the critics—that the hole in the C-ring could not possibly have been made by the nose of a 757—to an obscure website promising to bridge "science and shamanism." This is a good tactic, of course, if the goal of the PM authors is to avoid informing their readers of the best websites about the Pentagon.

In any case, they then say: "In fact, the hole was not made by . . . the nose of Flight 77 pushing through the building's interior. . . ."[264] They thereby give unknowing readers the impression that critics of the official theory, besides being focused on bridging science and shamanism, do not even understand the official story. As Pickering emphasizes, however, "[t]he Secretary of Defense, the building construction manager, a Pentagon spokesperson, and the only three official reports that mention it all attribute the cause of the hole to the nose of a 757–200." If the PM authors were honest, therefore, they would not have implied that critics of the official story were confused. They would have explained that defenders of the 757 theory, having realized that their original explanation of the C-ring hole was too ridiculous to be maintained, simply quit giving that explanation.

PM offers a new explanation, namely, that although "the less dense items, including the shell of the plane . . . , essentially disintegrated upon impact," the impact "created a hole through which the heavier, denser items could continue forward into the building." Accordingly, the plane's landing gear, being "one of the heaviest and most dense parts of the plane, . . . flew farther than any other item . . . and was responsible for puncturing the wall in Ring C."[265] But this explanation, like most of PM's explanations, is problematic. One problem is that it is hard to imagine how both things can be true: that even though the plane's shell "disintegrated upon impact," it "created a hole" in the heavily reinforced wall.

A second problem is that PM seems to offer the landing gear explanation on its own authority. Its authors give the impression that this explanation was provided by the *Pentagon Building Performance Report*, stating that its team leader, Paul Mlakar, said he saw the landing gear almost 300 feet inside the building.[266] This report does indeed claim that the landing gear was found at this location. But it does not suggest that the landing gear created the hole in the C ring; indeed, it offers no explanation as to what created the hole.[267] Evidently the PM authors, believing that some other explanation was needed now that the original explanation had proven too obviously ridiculous to maintain, took it upon themselves to offer one. If this is their idea of how scientific explanations are given, perhaps their magazine's name should be changed to *Populist Mechanics*.

In any case, a second problem is created by the fact that, if the C-ring hole was 310 feet from the point of impact, as the Mlakar report says, while the landing gear was only 300 feet away,[268] then this landing gear, after punching a hole completely through the C-ring wall, had to bounce back 10 feet, a physical impossibility.

A third problem is created by the claim, which PM takes over from the *Pentagon Building Performance Report*, that the flight data recorder "was found almost 300 feet inside the building."[269] This claim creates a problem because it contradicts what was publicly reported. A *Newsweek* story in 2003 reported that before 4AM three days after the attack, two firefighters,

> were combing through debris near the impact site. Peering at the wreckage with their helmet lights, the two spotted . . . two odd-shaped dark boxes, about 1.5 by 2 feet long. They'd been told the plane's "black boxes" would in fact be bright orange, but these were charred black. . . . They cordoned off the area and called for an FBI agent, who in turn called for someone from the National Transportation Safety Board (NTSB) who confirmed the find: the black boxes from AA Flight 77.[270]

To report this story is not to say that it is true. Indeed, those who reject the idea that the Pentagon was struck by Flight 77 have always been suspicious of this story of the very early morning discovery, thinking it likely that the black boxes had been planted. What this story does show, however, is that there are two official accounts about the flight data recorder: the account, given in the *Pentagon Building Performance Report*[271] and echoed by *Popular Mechanics*, that it was found 300 feet from the crash site, and the account, given by the two firefighters and evidently confirmed by the NTSB, that it was found, along with the other black box, near the impact site.

Strangely, the PM authors in effect endorse both accounts. While explicitly endorsing the view that the flight data recorder was found 300 feet from the crash site, they also implicitly endorse the other view by quoting Allyn Kilsheimer's statement that while he was at the crash site, picking up body parts and other things, he "stood on a pile of debris that . . . contained the black box."

In any case, besides the fact that the official story, as defended by *Popular Mechanics*, contains this contradiction about the flight data recorder, it also contains the change of stories about what caused the hole in the C-ring. Officials first said that it was caused by the 757's nose, with Evey and Rumsfeld both reporting that the nose could be seen just beyond the C-ring wall (although Terry Mitchell, chief of the Defense Press Office's Audio-Visual Division, said, perhaps indiscreetly: "They suspect that this was where a part of the aircraft came through this hole, although I didn't see any evidence of the aircraft down there"[272]). After that explanation was widely ridiculed, defenders of the official story simply quit explaining the origin of this hole. How can we help but believe that these officials are trying to hide the truth about what really happened? And, given the fact that our PM authors do not even mention these contradictions, how can we take them as trustworthy guides?

In any case, besides being rendered dubious by these contradictions, PM's account of the C-ring hole faces a much more serious objection: that the hole could not have been created by either a 757's nose or its landing gear. Russell Pickering, referring to photographs showing no damage to the B-ring wall, which is across the 40-foot driveway from the C-ring wall with the hole in it, asks rhetorically:

> If any solid part of an aircraft survived after traveling through this structure. . . , [h]ow did it break such a clean hole and then decelerate in the space of 40 feet so as not to even chip the opposing "B" ring wall?[273]

Michael Meyer, a mechanical engineer who has worked with explosives, has said that "[t]he C-Ring exit hole carries a unique signature, which can only be explained by something other than a 757 impact." After explaining why the hole cannot be explained by the Pentagon's "nose-cone" theory or Purdue's "circle of energy" theory, he suggests a more likely possibility. Explaining that a "shaped charge" consists of "high explosives formed in a very specific geometry so that the explosive force is extremely focused," he says that the C-ring hole may well have been "caused by a shaped charge warhead or device," because "[t]he hole is circular," like a typical shaped charge warhead, and "[t]he hole is cleanly cut, . . . as would be expected from the extremely localized and focused energy from the shaped charge warhead."[274]

This is the kind of information one would expect to have learned from authors writing for a magazine called *Popular Mechanics*. But they merely say that the hole was made by the landing gear, without giving any explanation as to how it could have caused the kind of hole in question. With regard to PM's theory, Meyer says:

> A huge problem with the landing gear impact theory is that bricks on the outer wall . . . are cut, while the bricks on the inner wall are intact. How could the bricks have been cut in what appears to be a circle, if the underlying bricks, on the impact side of the wall, are not broken . . . ? Tensile loads transmitted through the brick and mortar wall would require the underlying bricks to be displaced to have the outer bricks broken. Even aside from that problem, the landing gear theory could not explain why the bricks were cut in a circular pattern.[275]

In any case, Pickering, making a different suggestion, says that there is a weapon—"already in the possession of the military and something readily concealable and deployable"—called a Rapid Wall Breaching Kit, which can create a hole virtually identical with the C-ring hole.[276]

Why Pentagon officials would have deliberately created this hole is another question.[277] But the evidence—that an explosive charge and only an explosive charge is capable of creating such a hole—seems to imply that they did. Contrary to *Popular Mechanics*, therefore, the hole in the C-ring provides strong evidence that the official story about what happened at the Pentagon on 9/11 is untrue.

The FBI's Refusal to Release Videos

Additional evidence that government officials have been concealing the truth is provided by the fact that shortly after the Pentagon strike, the FBI confiscated videos from security cameras at a nearby hotel and the Citgo gas station across the highway. The fact that both the FBI and the Pentagon refused to release these and other videos, even after FOIA requests were made, led critics of the official conspiracy theory to charge that the videos must show that whatever hit the Pentagon was not an American Airlines Boeing 757. In 2002, some still-frame shots were leaked, and in May 2006, some videos, said to be all the videos from the Citgo security cameras, were released.[278] However, they show nothing, as the PM authors admit, but "a blur followed by a massive explosion," so they did nothing to undermine the charge.[279] The PM authors, however, make a couple of attempts to do so.

One attempt is to argue that the released pictures show nothing except blurs because the security cameras were set at a slow rate (one frame per second), and that this is "almost always" done in order to conserve storage space. "As a result," our authors conclude, "it is unlikely that the recording system of any nearby security camera would be set at a rate high enough to capture the speeding plane with decent resolution."[280]

Although that might be true, the claim that it is true is speculation. John McCain in the Foreword told us that "*Popular Mechanics* stands for an old-fashioned approach to facts. It relies on . . . evidence . . . and rejects speculation."[281] So why do PM's authors here rely on speculation instead of demanding to see the empirical evidence?

This evidence, moreover, is much greater than they let on. Although they speak of "other videos, reportedly seized by the FBI from businesses near the Pentagon,"[282] they surely know that the Department of Justice has admitted to the existence of no less than 85 of these.[283] Is it really likely that not a single one of the still unreleased videos has a clear image of the strike on the Pentagon? CNN's Jamie McIntyre has suggested otherwise. In May of 2006, he said that "there are at least 80 other tapes that the government is holding onto. We're told that they don't really show much, but sources have told us that at least one of the tapes from a security camera at a nearby hotel may have captured the plane in the air."[284]

Why does PM, with its "old-fashioned approach to facts," not join the chorus of voices demanding that all these videos be released, so that we can see for ourselves what they do and do not show, rather than offering a speculative explanation as to why seeing the videos would probably not be helpful?

PM's second attempt at damage control is to try to suggest that whereas the released footage did not prove the official theory's claims, it "also failed to live up to the hopes of conspiracy theorists," who have claimed that the government had "withheld the footage because it contained unequivocal proof that a missile or noncommercial aircraft had hit the building."[285] The point seems to be that the empirical evidence fails to support both views equally. But this is a silly argument. We have been shown virtually none of the empirical evidence. The release of a few blurry frames from two security cameras, even assuming that they are from 9/11/01 (the slides released in 2002 were stamped "Sept. 12, 5:37PM"[286]), says nothing about what would be seen if all 85 videos were released in their entirety. Nothing has been done, therefore, to undermine the contention that the government has failed to release these videos because they contain information the government wants to remain hidden.

The FBI's Removal of Evidence

The PM authors write: "Within minutes of the crash, FBI agents arrived on the scene and began collecting the debris. . . . Many conspiracy theorists point to this as further evidence of a cover-up." Here is PM's answer:

> [A]irline accident experts say that is standard protocol. . . . Just as the police wouldn't leave a murder weapon lying around in the grass . . . , investigators commonly collect aircraft debris as quickly as possible to preserve the integrity of the evidence.[287]

This answer is, however, doubly problematic.

For one thing, PM blurs the issue of "standard protocol." It is indeed standard protocol for the FBI to become the lead investigative agency when a crash site is determined to be a crime scene, but for it to conceal evidence is not standard protocol. PM portrays the FBI as having collected the debris to "preserve the integrity of the evidence." As Omholt points out, however: "The pieces are not photographed in place, nor documented, for a true forensic investigation—they are just collected."[288]

Also, PM fails to report on what was done after the FBI finished picking up pieces of debris. As Omholt shows with photographic evidence, the entire lawn was then covered with dirt and gravel, with the result that any remaining forensic evidence was literally covered up.[289]

Where's the Fire?

Another problem for the official theory is that the crash evidently did not create the kind of fire that should have been created by the crash of a 757 carrying 5,000 gallons of fuel. There was an initial fireball, to be sure, but it was very localized and lasted only a few seconds. Photos do show that there were fires in the early minutes.[290] But these photos show nothing like the intense, jet-fuel-fed fires that occurred in the first few minutes after the strikes on the Twin Towers. Also, Pickering, describing a video made by Bob Pugh, which began about seven minutes after the attack, says:

"The most evident aspect of this video is the lack of fire and firefighting activity at the impact site."[291] Omholt, on the basis of photographs, says:

> There are no firemen with shiny aluminized protective hoods donned, prepared to penetrate a jet fuel fire, in a rescue attempt. . . . There is no suggestion of an aircraft crash and the expected fuel fire. . . . An aircraft full of fuel, crashing at 300 Knots will not experience a delay in the full burning of its fuel . . . . [T]he fire—what little there is—comes from the second-floor windows. What happened to all that fuel which is supposed to be spilled on the ground floor? There is no evidence of any prominent fire in the natural channel for something as volatile as jet fuel.[292]

Although the PM authors do not explicitly acknowledge the fire problem, they do speak to it in the context of explaining that the entrance hole was so small because the ends of the wings were broken off.

> [T]he damage to the wings . . . minimized the destruction in another important way . . . . [A]n estimated 80 percent of the plane's 5,324 gallons of fuel was stored in the wings, at least one fifth of which never entered the building . . . . [M]ost of the fuel ignited upon impact: the large fireball outside the building burned off about 700 gallons of fuel. This obviously lessened the amount of fire damage to the interior. And, the fuel that did enter the building traveled a maximum of 310 feet along the ground floor . . . and burned there.[293]

However, even if we accept PM's assertions about the wings and the fireball, there would have been about 3,800 gallons of jet fuel to feed an immediate fire of great intensity on the ground floor. But neither the photographs nor Bob Pugh's video shows such a fire. There is again a disconnect between the official theory and the empirical evidence.

We also have here another case of special pleading by those who defend the official theory about 9/11. When dealing with the WTC buildings, they insist that jet-fuel fires would be sufficiently big, hot, and destructive to cause enormous steel columns to buckle. But when dealing with the Pentagon, which was purportedly hit by an airplane of roughly the same size, they write as if the lack of evidence for a fire of similar destructiveness should be of no concern.

The Lack of a Seismic Signal

Still another kind of evidence counting against the claim that the Pentagon was struck by a Boeing 757, and hence Flight 77, is the fact that it alone of the four crash sites, according to the official reports, did not have a strong enough signal for seismologists to determine the time of impact. Won-Young Kim and Gerald Baum, who were asked by the Army to see if they could ascertain the time of the attack, wrote:

We analyzed seismic records from five stations in the northeastern United States, ranging from 63 to 350 km from the Pentagon. Despite detailed analysis of the data, we could not find a clear seismic signal. Even the closest station . . . did not record the impact. We concluded that the plane impact to the Pentagon generated relatively weak seismic signals.[294]

As we will see below, moreover, they were able to ascertain the time of the crash of UA Flight 93 into a soft field in Pennsylvania. If that crash generated a clear seismic signal, why would not the crash of a Boeing 757 going several hundred miles into a reinforced building not do so? The PM authors do not mention this problem.

The Claim about Hani Hanjour

As we have seen, the PM authors have failed to offer a credible defense of the claim that the Pentagon was struck by Flight 77. I turn now to the fact that they have also failed to support the official story about the Pentagon against charges that would be even more difficult to debunk—as is suggested by the fact that they do not even try. These charges involve the latter part of the official story's composite claim, namely, that (1) the Pentagon was struck by Flight 77 (2) under the control of al-Qaeda hijacker Hani Hanjour. This latter claim—that Flight 77 was under the control of Hani Hanjour—involves two problems. These problems are so severe, in fact, that even if PM had made a stronger case for the 757 theory, as have some genuine researchers,[295] it would not have thereby defended the official theory.

One of these objections, which was discussed in the first section, is that Hani Hanjour, according to experts, could not have flown the trajectory said to have been taken by the aircraft that hit the Pentagon. Even if a truly superb commercial jet pilot could have flown this trajectory in a 757, Hani Hanjour had never flown a commercial jet and could barely fly a single-engine plane. I above quoted pilot Russ Wittenberg's statement that it would have been "totally impossible for an amateur who couldn't even fly a Cessna" to have "descended 7,000 feet in two minutes, all the while performing a steep 270 degree banked turn before crashing into the Pentagon's first floor wall without touching the lawn."[296] I also quoted pilot Ralph Omholt's statement, "The idea that an unskilled pilot could have flown this trajectory is simply too ridiculous to consider."[297]

This problem by itself proves the falsity of the official story. The government has insisted that it was definitely Flight 77, with Hani Hanjour at the controls, that struck the Pentagon. It has, as we saw, assured us that DNA tests have confirmed the identity of the passengers, the crew, and (by a process of elimination) the hijackers. The official story stands or falls, therefore, with the claim that Hanjour was piloting the plane when it crashed into the Pentagon. But that claim cannot possibly be true. Hence, the official story falls.

If the official story about the Pentagon strike falls, moreover, the official story about 9/11 as a whole falls. It is astounding, to be sure, that the perpetrators would have made the aerial acrobatics of a completely incompetent pilot an essential part of the official story. But they did. And thus far they have gotten away with it, thanks to the failure of the press and the Congress to focus on the impossibility of this part of the official story. If the question, however, is not the story's success but its truth, then we must conclude that the official story is false.

That leaves the question, of course, of what really happened at the Pentagon. Various possibilities have been suggested. One possibility would be that the striking aircraft was not even a Boeing 757 but a remotely-controlled smaller military aircraft of some sort or a cruise missile. This theory would provide a simple explanation for the apparent lack of sufficient damage and debris and the FBI's destruction of evidence and failure to release the videos. This theory would also, by holding that the attacking aircraft had a military transponder, explain how it could have approached the Pentagon without being shot down or even challenged.

Another possibility would be that what hit the Pentagon was not Flight 77 but a remotely controlled Boeing 757 painted to look like it. This account would be consistent with the testimonies that a 757 hit the Pentagon.

Still another possibility, consistent with the view that the aircraft really was a 757 and even Flight 77, would be that there was a technological override, so that the plane's fate was taken out of the hands of everyone on board. This theory, besides getting rid of the need for a suicidal pilot (whether Hani Hanjour or someone else), could possibly also explain how a 757 could have executed the amazing maneuver needed to strike Wedge 1 at almost ground level.

Yet another possibility, which could be combined with any of the above, is that some of the damage was done by explosives within the Pentagon (as Barbara Honegger has suggested[298]).

And still other ideas have been proposed. However, to disprove the official story about the Pentagon strike, it is not necessary to explain what really happened. That would be the task of a genuine investigation. Investigators with subpoena power and the authority to threaten criminal prosecution could learn quickly enough what really happened. To show the need for such an investigation, it is sufficient to show that the official story is false. And that is shown by the inability of Hani Hanjour to have piloted Flight 77 into the Pentagon.

This part of the official story is also sufficient by itself to prove one more thing: the complete untrustworthiness of *Debunking 9/11 Myths*. This untrustworthiness is shown by the fact that the PM authors, while discussing a wide range of issues regarding the Pentagon, do not even mention the issue of whether Hanjour had the ability to have executed the 330-degree downward spiral, even though this issue has been raised by virtually all investigators who have questioned the official conspiracy theory about the Pentagon strike, which includes investigators who believe that the Pentagon was hit by a Boeing 757.[299] Once again we see the hollowness of PM's claim that it set out to "answer the questions raised by conspiracy theorists." It consistently ignored the most difficult questions.

Why Strike Wedge 1?

Another difficult question ignored by the PM authors is why al-Qaeda hijackers, who were allegedly brilliant enough to outfox the world's most sophisticated defense system, would have chosen to strike Wedge 1. There are six reasons why this would have been a completely irrational decision.

First, Wedge 1 was the only part of the Pentagon that was being renovated—with steel-reinforced concrete, blast-resistant windows, fire-resistant Kevlar cloth, and a new sprinkler system—to make it less vulnerable to terrorist attacks. This renovation was, in fact, virtually complete: By amazing coincidence, it had been scheduled to be completed the very next day (although in reality the work would not have been completed until later that week). The strike on the Pentagon, therefore, caused far less damage than would have an attack on any of the other four wedges. The fact of the Pentagon's renovation, moreover, had been public knowledge for three years, and would have been obvious to anyone casing the building for a terrorist attack. Why would foreign terrorists, presumably wanting to inflict as much damage as possible on America's chief symbol of military power, have crashed their plane into the section in which the least damage would be caused?

Second, these terrorists would also presumably have wanted to kill as many Pentagon employees as possible. And yet, because the renovation had not yet been completed, Wedge 1 was still only sparsely occupied. As a result, only 125 Pentagon employees were killed. The death toll would surely have been much higher, probably in the thousands, if any other part of the Pentagon had been struck. Why would foreign terrorists wanting to kill members of the US armed forces have chosen the part of the Pentagon where the fewest would be killed?

Third, Wedge 1, and only Wedge 1, presented an obstacle course for an attacking airplane. Because of its location by a highway with elevated signs and also because of the control tower for the Pentagon's heliport, the plane, as Pickering points out, "would have had to change altitude after narrowly missing the VDOT 125-foot radio antenna on Columbia/Pike, then dip down and level out in a relatively short distance in order to strike where [it] did without touching the lawn." Because of the renovation, furthermore, there were many large objects on the lawn. In fact, according to reports, the plane's wings struck some lamps, a cyclone fence, a generator trailer, a mobile home, and still more things before striking the building. Any of the other wedges, by contrast, would have provided an obstacle-free approach path. Why would they have chosen the only one that presented an obstacle course?

Fourth, why would they, in fact, have chosen to hit any of the side walls? The Pentagon's roof provided a 29-acre target, which even a poor pilot might have hit, and a plane crashing down through the roof of a highly occupied section would have caused enormous death and destruction.

Fifth, given the fact that they were flying through the most restricted airspace in the United States, the hijackers should have feared that they would be intercepted and shot down by fighter jets. And yet executing the downward spiral required their plane to be aloft for at least three additional minutes. Why would they have taken this extra risk, through which the whole mission might have failed?

Sixth, al-Qaeda terrorists would surely have wanted to strike the offices of the secretary of defense and the Pentaton's top brass. But these offices are in Wedge 4 close to Wedge 3, which is on the opposite side of the Pentagon—as far from the strike zone as possible. Why would al-Qaeda terrorists have planned to strike the Pentagon in a location that would guarantee the safety of Rumsfeld and the top brass?[300]

These reasons why the decision to hit Wedge 1 would have been irrational are summarized by Pickering in the following statement, in which he asks what might have led Hani Hanjour to make such a decision:

> So, you're nervously flying a 757-200 for the first time. Years of planning have gone into the operation. Your goal is to strike a deep blow to the heart of America and inflict as much damage as possible. You have no idea when military intercept is coming . . . . You're in the most restricted airspace in America and your target is in sight. The heavily trafficked airspace around Reagan International happens to be clear. The Pentagon is in your sights. Instead of diving straight in, you do a perfect 330 degree spiral with military precision that a seasoned 757 pilot would find challenging. You descend 8,000 feet taking an additional 3 minutes and 35 seconds to do so. You focus on an obscure corner of the Pentagon buried in shadow. You pass on the more destructive option of continuing your maneuver into the unobstructed front of the building where the brass resides. You skip the devastating option of diving straight into the roof . . . in order to strike the only recently blast reinforced wall at the least occupied wedge of the Pentagon. You chose the most difficult and least damaging option available?[301]

How does PM deal with these problems, which show that the decision to strike Wedge 1 would have been completely irrational, if this was a decision made by al-Qaeda? It does not even try. And yet these are problems on which there is consensus among critics of the official theory about the Pentagon, including those who accept the view that it was struck by Flight 77 or at least a Boeing airliner. Accordingly, even if we assume, for the sake of discussion, that PM has successfully defended the claim that Flight 77 hit the Pentagon, it has not defended the government's conspiracy theory about the Pentagon.

Anticipation and Aftermath: Two Additional Problems

Before concluding this critique, I will point out two more facts, left unmentioned by our PM authors, that suggest that the official story about the Pentagon is a lie. One of these problems involves the period prior to 9/11; the other, the period afterward.

Government officials have claimed, as we have seen, that they had not anticipated the use of hijacked airliners as weapons to attack buildings, so the military was "unprepared for the transformation of commercial aircraft into weapons of mass destruction."[302] We have also seen, however, that this claim is false, because the military had scheduled various training exercises involving the crash of airliners into various high-profile buildings, and some of these exercises involved attacks by hijacked airliners.

Those buildings included the Pentagon. In October 2000, the military held a mass casualty exercise involving a mock crash of a commercial airliner into the Pentagon.[303] In April 2001, the joint chiefs of staff held a worldwide exercise, called Positive Force, to deal with the government's preparedness to keep operating after an attack on the United States. One of the proposed (albeit reportedly not accepted) scenarios involved a terrorist group that would hijack a commercial airliner and fly it into the Pentagon.[304] In May 2001, two medical clinics in the Pentagon held a training exercise involving a scenario in which a hijacked 757 was crashed into the Pentagon.[305] And in August 2001, the Pentagon held a mass casualty exercise involving the evacuation of the building after it was hit by an airplane. General Lance Lord, head of US Air Force Space Command, later said that on 9/11, thanks to this practice just a month earlier, "our assembly points were fresh in our minds." He then added: "Purely a coincidence, the scenario for that exercise included a plane hitting the building."[306]

A crash into the Pentagon by an airliner had, accordingly, clearly been anticipated. The PM authors, in failing to tell their readers about this anticipation, left out vital information. These authors also left out important information about something that happened—or rather something that did not happen—after 9/11.

These authors, as we saw, defended the FBI's removal of aircraft debris from the Pentagon lawn as necessary "to preserve the integrity of the evidence."[307] They thereby implied that the FBI would be using this evidence to determine what happened so that it could issue a report. And the National Transportation Safety Board stated on its website that the FBI, which had taken the lead role in the investigation of the Pentagon attack, would be issuing a report on it. But the FBI's report consists of a single web page, which contains the photos of five men—Hani Hanjour and the other four alleged hijackers—preceded by the following:

American Airlines # 77
Boeing 757
8:10AM Departed Dulles for Los Angeles
9:39AM Crashed into Pentagon[308]

This is all that the FBI, which insisted on taking charge of the Pentagon investigation, has reported about it.[309]

Or at least this is all that it has explicitly reported. The FBI has implicitly told us one more thing through the fact that its web page on "Usama bin Laden," as a "most wanted terrorist," does not mention 9/11 as one of the crimes for which he is wanted. Indeed, as I mentioned in Chapter 2, Rex Tomb, the FBI's Chief of Investigative Publicity, spelled out this message explicitly, saying that 9/11 is not mentioned "because the FBI has no hard evidence connecting Bin Laden to 9/11."[310] Does this statement, taken together with the photos on the FBI's one-page report on the Pentagon attack, mean that the FBI has hard evidence that the alleged hijackers were involved in 9/11 but not that they were working for bin Laden?

In any case, given the controversy about what happened at the Pentagon, we can only wonder about the reasons for the FBI's failure to issue a real report. As retired Air Force Colonel George Nelson, who had specialized in the investigation of aircraft mishaps, has explained, if the aircraft that struck the Pentagon was a Boeing 757, "it would be a simple matter to confirm that [it was]." This is because every plane has many "time-change parts," which must be changed periodically because they are crucial for the safety of flight. Each time-change part has a distinctive serial number. By identifying some of those numbers, investigators can determine the make, model, and registration number of the crashed aircraft. Moreover, Nelson emphasizes, most of these parts are virtually indestructible, so an ordinary fire resulting from an airplane crash could not possibly "destroy or obliterate all of those critical time-change parts or their serial numbers."[311]

Accordingly, even without the videos, the FBI could have known what struck the Pentagon within hours after the attack. The fact that it has issued no report containing this information suggests that it has something important to hide.

Also, the fact that the PM authors do not discuss the FBI's failure to issue a report suggests that they are assisting the cover-up. Given their access to people involved with the investigation, they surely could have learned that a positive identification of the striking aircraft could have been made on the basis of the serial numbers of the time-change parts. Given PM's professed love of empirical facts, why would it, while suggesting that none of the videos may provide a positive identification of the aircraft, fail to mention this alternative, even more certain, means of identification?

Conclusion

As we have seen, PM has not presented convincing evidence that the Pentagon was struck by Flight 77 or even a Boeing 757. It has not answered the objections to this claim based on insufficient fire, impact damage, and debris. It has not provided a plausible explanation for the hole in the C-ring. It has not shown why we should find unsuspicious the FBI's destruction of evidence and refusal to release videos. It has not mentioned the reasons to doubt that Hani Hanjour piloted a Boeing 757 into Wedge 1. Nor has it mentioned the falsity of the claim that an attack on the Pentagon was unexpected, or the failure of the FBI, which controlled every aspect of the investigation, to issue a report, including a positive identification of the striking aircraft. It is hard to imagine how PM's attempt in this chapter—to debunk the claim that the Pentagon strike was an inside job—could have failed more thoroughly.

Flight 93

In dealing with UA Flight 93, the PM authors seek to debunk the claim that "the US government shot down the plane and then covered it up."[312] In making this attempt, they take the same approach used in their previous chapters: discussing some allegations, including peripheral ones, that can be debunked, at least apparently, while ignoring evidence less susceptible to even the appearance of refutation.

The F-16 Diversion

Giving a peripheral allegation pride of place, the PM authors begin their chapter by taking on the claim that Flight 93 was shot down by an F-16 piloted by "Major Rick Gibney." This claim came about through a two-step process: A retired Army colonel, Donn de Grand-Pre, claimed during a radio interview to know the pilot who shot the flight down, saying that he was a member of a North Dakota Air National Guard unit known as the Happy Hooligans; then one website identified the pilot as "Major Rick Gibney." Even though this is clearly not one of the 9/11 truth movement's crucial claims (my books, for example, contain neither Donn de Grand-Pre's nor Rick Gibney's name), the PM authors devote three pages—almost one fifth of their chapter—to it. They perhaps hoped their readers would not notice that after they had debunked this particular claim, they had not yet done anything to undermine the more general thesis they had set out to debunk, namely, that "the US government shot down the plane and then covered it up."

Appealing to the 9/11 Commission's Claim about NORAD's Ignorance

To refute this claim, the PM authors simply appeal to *The 9/11 Commission Report* as authoritative.

> As to whether another fighter could have shot down the plane, the 9/11 Commission report is clear that no shoot-down order was in place for Flight 93, due to garbled communication between the various agencies. When the flight crashed, NORAD was still unaware the plane had been hijacked.[313]

In their introduction, however, the editors of *Debunking 9/11 Myths* said that they were going to confront the claims of the conspiracy theorists with the facts. It turns out, however, that what they really do is simply confront claims made by advocates of the alternative conspiracy theory with claims made by defenders of the official conspiracy theory, then treat the latter as "facts" while simply ignoring all the evidence that contradicts those alleged facts.

In *The 9/11 Commission Report: Omissions and Distortions*, I showed that there is abundant evidence that the Commission's claim is not true. Since some of this evidence was discussed in the first chapter of the present book, I will here simply summarize it.

FAA Communication: With regard to the claim that "garbled communication" prevented the military from learning about Flight 93 until after it crashed, there is in fact strong evidence that the FAA had indeed reported the hijacking of this flight to the military long before it crashed. This evidence includes Richard Clarke's statement that during his video conference, Jane Garvey had reported, in the video presence of both Donald Rumsfeld and General Richard Myers, that the "potential hijacks" included "United 93 over Pennsylvania."

Military Tracking of Flight 93: As I mentioned in Chapter 1, the evidence that the military was fully aware of this flight also includes the fact that many authorities—including General Myers, Deputy Secretary of Defense Paul Wolfowitz, Brigadier General Montague Winfield of the Pentagon's NMCC, and Colonel Robert Marr of NEADS—said that the military had been tracking the flight before it crashed.

Does *Debunking 9/11 Myths* refute this reported evidence? No, it simply says: "According to the 9/11 Commission's report, 'NORAD did not even know the plane was hijacked until after it had crashed.'"[314] That is indeed what the 9/11 Commission claims. But the actual facts show otherwise.

Shootdown Authorization: The facts also show that the military, besides tracking Flight 93, had received authorization to shoot it down. General Montague Winfield, in discussing the decision to intercept Flight 93, said that the vice president had told the NMCC's conference call that the president "had given us permission to shoot down innocent civilian aircraft that threatened Washington, DC."[315] General Larry Arnold said: "I had every intention of shooting down United 93 if it continued to progress toward Washington, D.C."[316] Colonel Robert Marr, besides writing, "we received the clearance to kill if need be,"[317] said that after receiving the shootdown order, he "passed that on to the pilots." And Lt. Anthony Kuczynski reported that he and the two F-16s accompanying him were "given direct orders to shoot down an airliner."[318]

How do our PM authors handle the question of the shoot-down authorization? Deceptively. They say:

> The earliest written confirmation of President Bush's shoot-down order . . . came at 10:20AM when White House press secretary Ari Fleischer . . . recorded that the president had issued the directive. That was 17 minutes after Flight 93's demise.

That is quite likely true. The question at issue, however, is not when the shootdown authorization was first confirmed in writing but when it was first given.

As we have seen, moreover, General Arnold, General Winfield, Colonel Marr, and Lt. Kuczynski all said that they had received the authorization before Flight 93 crashed. Moreover, although the Commission claims that Richard Clarke did not receive the shootdown authorization from Cheney until 10:25, Clarke's own discussion in *Against All Enemies* indicates that he received it some time between 9:45 and 9:55.[319] This is an enormous amount of relevant evidence for *Popular Mechanics*, with its claim that it "simply checked the facts," to have left out.

Still another relevant fact unmentioned by the PM debunkers is the question of who first gave the shootdown authorization—President Bush or Vice President Cheney. Part of the reason PM's statement about written confirmation is deceptive is that it ignores this question, simply pretending that the authorization could not have been given before the president gave it. This is another place where *The 9/11 Commission Report*, in spite of all its omissions and distortions, is a model of honesty in comparison with *Debunking 9/11 Myths*. After reporting that the vice president had said that he had received the shootdown authorization from the president during a telephone call made shortly after he entered the shelter conference room (PEOC), the Commission wrote:

[T]here is no documentary evidence for this call. . . . Others nearby who were taking notes, such as the Vice President's chief of staff, Scooter Libby, who sat next to him, and Mrs. Cheney, did not note a call between the President and Vice President immediately after the Vice President entered the conference room.[320]

Besides quoting this statement in my book on the 9/11 Commission's report, I also pointed out that according to *Newsweek* magazine, this statement was a "watered down" version of an earlier draft, which had reflected the fact that "some on the commission staff were . . . highly skeptical of the vice president's account." That earlier draft, which evidently expressed more clearly the belief that the vice president and the president were lying, was reportedly modified after vigorous lobbying from the White House.[321]

This issue is sensitive because a shootdown authorization can come only from the National Command Authority, which belongs to the president and the secretary of defense (including his authorized subordinates). The vice president could have legally issued the order only if the president had been incapacitated or incommunicado.

In any case, the PM authors, having ignored the above evidence— which shows that the US military, besides knowing about Flight 93's situation, was in position to shoot it down and had received authorization to do so—try to refute the claim that the flight was actually shot down. They do this by disputing several claims used to support the contention that it was.

The White Jet

According to one of these claims, "Flight 93 was shot down by a mysterious white jet." As the PM authors report, "At least six eyewitnesses say they saw a small white jet flying over the crash area almost immediately after Flight 93 went down."[322] Although the FBI claimed that this was a private jet that had been asked to descend to the crash scene, critics replied that the descent from 34,000 feet, which was the private jet's reported altitude, would have required far too long.

PM, defending the idea that it was indeed a private jet, says that it belonged to VF Corporation and that, according to a VF official, it had been flying at an altitude of only about 3,000 or 4,000 feet. However, the claim that it had been flying at over 30,000 feet, far from being invented by critics of the official story, was made by the FBI.[323] Are we supposed to prefer the statement of a corporate official, made in 2006 during an interview with *Popular Mechanics*, to the statement made at the time by the FBI?

A second problem is that even if the private jet had to descend only 3,000 to 4,000 feet, the witnesses, as PM admitted, said that they saw the white jet "almost immediately" after the crash. For example, Dennis

Decker and Rick Chaney say: "As soon as we looked up [after hearing the crash], we saw a midsized jet [painted white with no identifying markings] flying low and fast. It appeared to make a loop or part of a circle, and then it turned fast and headed out."[324]

A third problem is that the claim that the white plane was a corporate jet was evidently the FBI's second story. According to Susan Mcelwain, who reported that the white jet flew about 40 or 50 feet above her head: "The FBI came and talked to me and said there was no plane around. Then they changed their story and tried to say it was a plane taking pictures of the crash 3,000 feet up."[325]

A fourth problem is that, as the British *Independent* put it, "with F-16s supposedly in the vicinity, it seems extraordinarily unlikely that, at a time of tremendous national uncertainty when no one knew for sure whether there might be any more hijacked aircraft still in the sky, the military would ask a civilian aircraft that just happened to be in the area for help."[326] This story is made even more unlikely by the fact that at 9:45, the FAA had ordered all civilian aircraft to land as soon as possible.[327] Would the FAA have asked for help from a pilot who had disobeyed this order?

A fifth problem is that Susan Mcelwain and some other witnesses reported seeing the white jet before the crash as well as afterward.[328]

A sixth problem is that evidently "[t]here is not a single eyewitness who observed a white jet descending several minutes after the crash."[329]

The idea that the white jet was a military plane has, accordingly, clearly not been debunked.

Cell Phone Calls

The PM authors next take on the claim that the cell phone calls supposedly made from Flight 93 must have been faked. They quote Michel Chossudovsky's statement that "given the prevailing technology in September 2001, it was extremely difficult, if not impossible, to place a wireless cell call from an aircraft traveling at high speed above 8,000 feet."[330] Also referring to mathematics and computer science professor A. K. Dewdney (the Canadian professor whose writings I employed on this issue in the first chapter), they quote his statement, based in part on his own experiments, that "cell-phone calls from commercial aircraft much over 8,000 feet are essentially impossible, while those below 8000 feet are highly unlikely."[331] (The PM authors, however, omit the rest of Dewdney's statement, which reads "down to 2,000, where they become merely unlikely." Dewdney, accordingly, did not deny that successful calls could occur between 2,000 and 8,000 feet and he certainly did not deny that calls under 2,000 feet could quite likely be completed.)

The PM authors, stating the "fact" to counter the claim that the alleged calls could not have been authentic, write: "While not exactly reliable, cell-phone calls from airplanes were possible in 2001—even from extremely high altitudes." To support this remarkable counter-claim, they, as usual, cite no written documents, but rely solely on interviews—in this case, interviews in 2006 with two industry representatives. Rick Kemper of CTIA, the Wireless Association, is quoted as saying that cell phone calls at 35,000 feet are "entirely possible," and Paul Guckian of QUALCOMM is quoted as saying that at 30,000 or 35,000 feet, "[some] phones would still get a signal. . . . At some point above that—I would estimate in the 50,000-foot range—you would lose the signal." The PM authors then write, triumphantly: "Flight 93 never flew higher than 40,700 feet."[332]

They then argue that the reason people have not been regularly making cell phone calls from cruising altitude is not because such calls were impossible but only because they were dangerous: they could "interfere with planes' navigation and communication systems," and they could "be picked up by multiple cell towers on the ground," thereby causing confusion in the system and hence "dropped calls across the network." However, although PM is certainly right to say that these two dangers had been widely discussed before 9/11, it provides no evidence from pre-9/11 days that these were the only reasons why cell phone calls could not be made at cruising altitude. PM has provided, in other words, no evidence that such calls were possible from a strictly technological point of view at the time of the 9/11 attacks.

The fact that PM could find two industry spokesmen who would make such claims after 9/11 is not especially impressive. After all, if these men accept the official 9/11 story, which includes cell phone calls being successfully made at cruising altitude, then they would need to believe that such calls had been possible. Thus, based on the sound principle that the fact that X occurred proves that X was possible, they may have adjusted their prior ideas as to the altitudes at which cell phones would work. Another possible explanation for their claims is that they may, as representatives of their organizations, have felt obliged to support the official story about 9/11. If one looks up CTIA, for example, one finds that it represents the wireless industry, "in a constant dialogue with policy makers in the Executive Branch, in the Federal Communications Commission [and] in Congress," and "works closely with the Department of Homeland Security."[333]

Be that as it may, the testimony from these two men is contradicted by other experts. For example, CTIA's Rick Kemper based his statement that cell phone calls at 35,000 feet are "entirely possible" on the fact that "cell sites have a range of several miles."[334] But AT&T spokesperson Alexa Graf, explaining why cell phone systems are not designed for calls from high altitudes, said: "On land, we have antenna sectors that point in three directions—say north, southwest, and southeast. Those signals are radiating across the land." Insofar as "those signals do go up," that is "due to leakage."[335] Her statement implies that Kemper's statement, in suggesting that cellsite signals go vertically as far as they go horizontally, is false.

Further evidence that the testimony by Kemper and Guckian is not representative is provided by a story in the *Travel Technologist*, published one week after 9/11, which said:

> [W]ireless communications networks weren't designed for ground-to-air communication. Cellular experts privately admit that they're surprised the calls were able to be placed from the hijacked planes. . . . They speculate that the only reason that the calls went through in the first place is that the aircraft were flying so close to the ground.[336]

This false assumption, that the planes must have been flying at very low altitudes, was indeed expressed by experts. Another early story said: "Brenda Raney, Verizon Wireless spokesperson, said that . . . the planes were flying low when people started using their phones."[337]

For all these reasons, therefore, PM, by simply finding two industry spokespersons who support their extraordinary claim, have not provided much evidence for it.

The PM authors could have made a more impressive case by carrying out some experiments to disconfirm the conclusions of Dewdney's experiments. Given PM's connections and financial resources, such experiments should have been easy to arrange. Why then did they not carry out and report the results of such experiments, thereby exemplifying their professed preference for facts over speculation?

Or why did PM's authors not at least quote some people who, having carried out some informal experiments, found that the cell phones available in 2001 could indeed operate above 30,000 feet? Some people other than Dewdney did, in fact, report having carried out such experiments. One airline pilot, in response to Dewdney's article about his experiments, wrote in a letter to him:

> I have repeatedly tried to get my cell phone to work in an airplane above 2–3,000 feet and it doesn't work. My experiments were done discreetly on [more than] 20 Southwest Airlines flights between Ontario, California and Phoenix, Arizona. My experiments match yours. Using sprint phones 3500 and 6000 models, no calls above 2,500 feet, a "no service" indicator at 5,000 feet (guestimate).

Another person wrote:

> I was travelling between two major European cities, every weekend, when the events in the US occurred. [Being] puzzled by the reports that numerous passengers on board the hijacked planes had long conversations with ground phone lines, using their mobile phones. . . , I

... left [my mobile phone] on to see if I could make a call happen. First of all, at take off, the connection disappears quite quickly . . . . I would estimate from 500 meters [1,500 feet approx.] . . . . I have done this experiment for over 18 months, ruling out weather conditions, location or coincidence. In all this time the behaviour was the same: making a phone call in a plane is unrealistic and virtually impossible.[338]

This report illustrates Dewdney's conclusion that, according to many anecdotal reports, "in large passenger jets, one loses contact during takeoff, frequently before the plane reaches 1,000 feet altitude."[339]

The fact that the PM authors, knowing Dewdney's work, did not report any experiments contradicting such testimonies suggests that they could find none—especially experiments showing that cell phones worked above 30,000 feet.

There is still another approach the PM authors could have taken that would have been more impressive than quoting a couple of industry spokesmen in 2006. They could have cited some pre-9/11 documents saying that cell phone calls from over 30,000 feet were possible. The fact that they cite no such documents suggests that there were none to be found.

Moreover, in addition to the fact that post-9/11 statements by Kemper and Guckian would in principle be insufficient support for PM's claim, these statements, when closely examined, do not actually support the claim. Guckian says only that at cruising speed, some phones would "still get a signal." He does not say that *all*, *most*, or even *many* cell phones would still get a signal. Also, being able to get a signal is far from the same thing as being able to complete a call. Being able to complete a call, moreover, is not the same as being able to remain connected long enough for a conversation to occur. Guckian's statement does not, therefore, really support the contention that the alleged cell phone calls from Flight 93 could have occurred.

Kemper says only that cell phone calls from 35,000 feet were "entirely possible." Even if this were true—that is, that it would have been possible for a cell phone call to have been completed from that altitude—this would not imply the plausibility of the claim that approximately 10 cell phone calls from Flight 93 were completed. This point can be clarified in terms of Dewdney's suggestion, made at an early point in his experiments, that at 20,000 feet "the chance of a typical cell phone call making it to ground and engaging a cellsite there is less than one in a hundred." This mathematics professor then pointed out that this statement would imply that "the probability that two callers will succeed is less than one in ten thousand." The probability that three calls would succeed, therefore, would be less than one in a million, and so on, until by the time we got to nine calls—the best estimate of the number of successful cell phone calls that were supposedly made from UA 93[340]—the probability would be virtually zero. By not addressing this question of probability, Kemper's statement does not actually support PM's contention that the alleged multiple cell phone calls on UA 93 could really have occurred.

The statement from Kemper quoted by PM, moreover, says of a connection at cruising altitude: "It's not a very good connection, and it changes a lot, and you end up getting a lot of dropped calls because you're moving through cell sites so fast." That statement, for more than one reason, does not support the authenticity of the alleged cell phone calls from Flight 93.

In the first place, most of the connections were reportedly quite good.[341]

In the second place, the alleged calls do not fit Kemper's statement that "you end up getting a lot of dropped calls because you're moving through cell sites so fast." The PM authors do acknowledge this "handoff" problem (which I discussed in the first chapter), saying that although the cellsite network "routinely manages handoffs at car speeds," it "struggles to make the high-speed handoffs required when the customer is in an airplane traveling more than 400 miles per hour."[342] The authors then attempt to show that the network was "struggling" with the UA 93 calls by saying that "[t]he calls that did connect were brief" and that "[t]here is also evidence of calls cutting off, such as passenger Andrew Garcia, whose call ended after he uttered his wife's name."[343]

This attempt, however, fails. Garcia's call was the exception, not the rule: Most of the reported cell phone calls ended because the callers hung up, not because they were cut off. All of the calls from "Tom Burnett," for example, lasted as long as the caller wanted them to last. And the call by "Elizabeth Wainio" lasted eleven minutes.[344] The only struggle here, therefore, is that by the PM authors to convince us that the calls fit Kemper's statement about the difficulty of high-speed handoffs.

These authors also suggest that "[t]he plane's generally low altitude . . . may have contributed to the cell calls going through."[345] But according to *The 9/11 Commission Report*, which PM generally takes as authoritative, the plane was between 34,300 and 40,700 feet when most of the calls were made,[346] and this is not, in this context, a "low altitude." For cell phone use in 2001, a low altitude—low enough to make it even remotely possible that these calls could have occurred—would have been under 10,000 feet.

PM's last stab at showing the alleged calls to have been authentic is to report that when Lorne Lyles, the husband of flight attendant CeeCee Lyles, received a call, "Her name registered in the family's caller ID readout."[347] The PM authors evidently assumed that most readers would take this fact as proof that the call actually came from her cell phone. However, authors writing for a magazine called *Popular Mechanics* would surely know that this is no proof at all, because there are devices that allow caller ID numbers to be faked. On the Internet, for example, one can find an ad that says, "FoneFaker—Call Recorder and Voice Changer Service with Caller ID Spoofing," after which one reads: "Record any call you make, fake your Caller ID and change your voice, all with one service you can use from any phone."[348] Is *Popular Mechanics* unaware of this technology? Or did its authors simply choose not to tell its readers?

They, in any case, have done nothing to undermine the conclusion reached in Chapter 1—that the alleged cell phone calls from UA 93 were faked. And, as I pointed out there, in 2006 the FBI reduced its count of cell phone calls completed from this flight down to two, which probably means the two calls made the latest and hence from the lowest altitude. If so, the FBI and the Department of Justice would no longer be claiming that cell phone calls from cruising altitude are possible. The same year that PM sought to support the government's claim about high-altitude cell phone calls, the government silently withdrew this claim.

The Wreckage

Testimonies about the site where Flight 93 supposedly crashed are unanimous about one surprising point: It did not look like a crash site. To give a few examples. Jon Meyer, a television reporter, said:

> There was just a big hole in the ground. All I saw was a crater filled with small, charred plane parts. Nothing that would even tell you that it was the plane. . . . You just can't believe a whole plane went into this crater. . . . There were no suitcases, no recognizable plane parts, no body parts.[349]

Scott Spangler, a photographer for a nearby newspaper, said: "I didn't think I was in the right place. . . . I was looking for anything that said tail, wing, plane, metal. There was nothing."[350] Paul Bomboy, a paramedic, said that his first thought upon arriving at the site was: "It is just plain weird. Where is the plane?. . . . [T]here weren't normal things going on that you would have expected. When a plane crashes, there is a plane and there are patients."[351] Jeff Phillips, who worked at a nearby auto wrecking shop, said:

> The crater was . . . just a spot that had a little fire on it. . . . [W]e were looking around and wondered where the airplane was. . . . There was no plane to be found, just spray cap size parts everywhere. Almost nothing was recognizable. The only thing we saw that was even remotely human was half a shoe that was probably ten feet from the impact area.[352]

Pat Madigan of the Pennsylvania State Police said that when he arrived:

My first thought at the site was, "Where is the plane crash?" There was a hole in the ground, the trees were burnt, and there was smoke everywhere. But when I looked at the pit, . . . I thought, at first, that it was a burn pit for the coal company. Then one of the firemen said that this was where it went in. I was amazed because it did not, in any way, shape, or form look like a plane crash. You think . . . you would see recognizable plane parts. But at the pit, there was nothing that looked like a plane. There were some parts in the trees and in the wooded area. But they weren't very big parts.[353]

Coroner Wally Miller said that when he arrived at the site, it looked "like someone took a scrap truck, dug a 10-foot ditch and dumped all this trash into it."[354]

The PM authors do not dispute the truth of this testimony. They instead say, "Most of the aircraft was obliterated on impact, shattering into tiny pieces that were driven as much as 30 feet into the earth." They then cite an NTSB investigator who "says that this is a typical outcome when a plane hits the ground at high speed." And, according to the PM authors, Flight 93 certainly did this: After turning sharply to the right and rolling onto its back in its final moments, Flight 93 "collided with the Shanksville field at approximately 580 miles per hour, traveling . . . at a steep, but not vertical, angle."[355]

This claim is taken from *The 9/11 Commission Report*, which also said that this descent began at 10:02:23 and ended with the crash at 10:03:11, which would mean that the plane was flying downward at high speed for its final 48 seconds.[356] But where did the Commission learn the speed and angle of the plane's downward descent? There is a note for the paragraph in which this assertion is made, but it merely says that the quotations from the hijackers were derived from the cockpit voice recorder. The Commission provides no support for its claims about the plane's descent. These claims, moreover, are in conflict with the available evidence.

The figure of 580 mph differs radically from the estimates at the time by "law enforcement authorities" and "the National Transportation Safety Board and other experts," according to whom the plane was only going between 200 and 300 mph.[357]

The claim that the plane was in a high-speed nose dive for its final 48 seconds is, moreover, contradicted by several eyewitnesses. For example, auto worker Terry Butler, after reporting that the plane was flying low to the ground, said that it "banked to the right and appeared to be trying to climb to clear one of the ridges, but it . . . then veered behind a ridge."[358] Tim Thornsberg said: "It came in low over the trees and started wobbling. Then it just rolled over and was flying upside down for a few seconds . . . and then it kind of stalled and [did] a nose dive over the trees."[359]

The testimony of eyewitnesses, therefore, undermines PM's claim that the absence of wreckage and bodies at the crash site was due to the plane having disintegrated into tiny pieces that were driven deep into the ground, because this testimony contradicts the Commission's claim that the plane was in a high-speed nose dive.

There are additional reasons, moreover, to doubt the truth of the 9/11 Commission's account of Flight 93's final minutes.

When Did Flight 93 Crash—10:03 or 10:06?

One reason is that the time the Commission gives for the plane's crash, 10:03:11, was supported by no one except NORAD (which had simply put the time at 10:03[360]). Everyone else said that the crash occurred at about 10:06. This time was given, for example, by two stories that appeared on September 13 in the *Pittsburgh Post-Gazette*, one of which said:

> Early news reports put the crash time at 10:06. The Federal Aviation Administration said yesterday it turned over to the FBI a radar record of United Airlines Flight 93's route. The data traced the Boeing 757-200 from its takeoff from Newark, N.J., to its violent end at 10:06AM, just outside Shanksville.[361]

This time was also given by other Pennsylvania newspapers. One of these reported that "people in Shanksville and the surrounding farm fields . . . saw or heard the jetliner go down at roughly 10:06."[362] Another newspaper reported that Cleveland Air Traffic Control reported losing track of Flight 93 at 10:06.[363]

Besides the fact that the 10:06 time was given by the FAA, Pennsylvania newspapers, and local residents, it was later confirmed in a US Army-authorized study by seismologists Won-Young Kim of Columbia University's Lamont-Doherty Earth Observatory and Gerald R. Baum of the Maryland Geological Survey. Their report put the exact time of the crash at 10:06:05.[364]

Although this report should have settled the issue, the 9/11 Commission disputed it, saying:

> The 10:03:11 impact time is supported by previous National Transportation Safety Board analysis and by evidence from the Commission's staff's analysis of radar, the flight data recorder, the cockpit voice recorder, infrared satellite data, and air traffic control transmissions.[365]

However, the Commission gives no reference for the alleged "National Transportation Safety Board analysis" and Mary Schiavo, a former inspector general of the Transportation Department, said: "We don't have an NTSB investigation here."[366] Moreover, all the other alleged evidence is based on "the Commission's staff's analysis" and, as we have seen in previous chapters, this Zelikow-directed staff has not proven itself worthy of our trust.

The Commission, in arguing that the Kim-Baum seismic study is not reliable, says:

[T]he seismic data on which [the two authors of the seismic study] based this estimate are far too weak in signal-to-noise ratio and far too speculative in terms of signal source to be used as a means of contradicting the impact time established by the very accurate combination of FDR, CVR, ATC, radar, and impact site data sets. These data sets constrain United 93's impact time to within 1 second, are airplane- and crash-site specific, and are based on time codes automatically recorded in the ATC audiotapes for the FAA centers and correlated with each data set in a process internationally accepted within the aviation accident investigation community.[367]

But this argument, while it might at first glance appear impressive, is simply a string of assertions. No evidence that could be confirmed is cited. As Jim Hoffman reports: "All of the sources that the Report cites to support its claim of a crash time of 10:03 are apparently unavailable for public inspection . . . . The 'FDR, CVR, ATC, radar, and impact site data sets' cited by the Report all remain unavailable to the public."[368] We again simply have to accept the word of the Zelikow Commission.

When we look at the actual seismic study, moreover, it seems far less "speculative" than the Commission suggests. Kim and Baum, who were asked to do studies for all four crashes, said that only the signal from the crash into the Pentagon was too weak for a definite time to be determined. For the crash of UA 93, they examined the seismic records from four stations near the crash site. Whereas the signal-to-noise ratio for two of these was very low (about 1:1), it was about 2.5:1 at one of the stations (SSPA). Kim and Baum concluded:

Although seismic signals across the network are not as strong and clear as the WTC case . . . , three component records at station SSPA . . . are quite clear. . . . [From these records] we infer that the Flight 93 crashed around 14:06:05 (UTC) (10:06:05 EDT).[369]

It appears, therefore, that the Commission was engaging in wishful-reading.

The Commission's final argument is to claim, citing an e-mail from Won-Young Kim to the Commission, that "one of the study's principal authors now concedes that 'seismic data is not definitive for the impact of UA 93.'"[370] The Commission, however, does not quote any more of the letter, so we do not know with what qualifications Kim may have made this concession. Also, we do not know what kind of pressure may have been exerted on him. In any case, the Commission adds: "see also Won-Young Kim, 'Seismic Observations for UA Flight 93 Crash near Shanksville, Pennsylvania during September 11, 2001,' July 5, 2004."

But the Commission does not tell us how we are supposed to "see" this alleged document. It cannot, as Hoffman points out, be found on the Web.[371] It is also not included in the list of publications available at Kim's own website[372] — a fact suggesting that, if the paper exists, it is not one of which Kim is especially proud.

Moreover, even if the Commission was able to persuade Kim to state publicly that the seismic data are not definitive, it was evidently unable to wring any such concession from the other principal author of the study, Dr. Gerald Baum. This failure is surely more significant than the concession from Kim — which in any case fell short of endorsing the 10:03 time. And neither Kim nor Baum has disowned their study, so it remains the definitive report of the time that Flight 93 crashed.

This report is endorsed, furthermore, by award-winning seismologist Terry Wallace, who at the time directed the Southern Arizona Seismic Observatory and is now in a leadership role at the Los Alamos National Laboratory.[373] Wallace, who according to journalist William Bunch is widely considered the leading expert on the seismology of man-made events, reportedly said to Bunch, "The seismic signals are consistent with impact at 10:06:05 plus or minus two seconds." He then added, "I don't know where the 10:03 time comes from."[374]

It evidently came from a need on the part of NORAD and the 9/11 Commission to have the crash appear to have happened three minutes earlier than it really did. Why did they have such a need?

Why Would NORAD and the 9/11 Commission Prefer 10:03?

One likely reason for the preference for the earlier crash time is that, according to all public reports, the Flight 93 cockpit voice recorder (CVR) contains, after 10:02, no voices but only engine noise and a wind-like sound and then goes completely silent at 10:03:11, with no sound of impact. The report that the plane did not crash until 10:06 implied that, in addition to the minute in which nothing is heard but engine and perhaps wind-like noise, there was a three-minute period between the end of the tape and the impact. This problem was popularized by a William Bunch story entitled "Three-Minute Discrepancy in Tape: Cockpit Voice Recording Ends Before Flight 93's Official Time of Impact."[375] Changing the impact time to 10:03 got rid of this gap, leaving only the more manageable problems of why the voices go silent before the tape runs out and why the sound of the impact is not recorded.

This explanation implies, of course, that the authorities, not wanting the truth to be known, simply erased the final three (or four) minutes, at least on the tapes that would be played for members of the public. Moreover, we have evidence, beyond that provided by the facts just discussed, that the tapes have indeed been doctored. This evidence consists of contradictions in the Commission's account of what is said in the final moments—contradictions within this account and contradictions between this account and what family members reported after the tape was played for them.

Although family members, when finally permitted by the FBI to hear the CVR tape, were not allowed to record it or even take notes,[376] they evidently agreed on what was said at the end. About 70 family members "listened to the tape through headphones while transcripts, including English translations of Arabic words, were displayed on screens."[377] Those who commented afterward reportedly agreed that passengers managed to enter the cockpit and that, after some scuffling, they heard voices saying "roll it" and "pull it up" or "lift it up" or "turn up." There was "a final rushing sound," after which the tape went silent.[378] The tape could be interpreted to mean that the passengers had entered the cockpit and taken control of the plane.

According to the 9/11 Commission, by contrast, the passengers did not enter the cockpit. And the reported dialogue was very different. At 10:00:08, the Commission says:

> Jarrah asked, "Is that it? Shall we finish it off?" A hijacker responded, "No. Not yet. When they all come, we finish it off." The sounds of fighting continued outside the cockpit. . . . Jarrah stopped the violent maneuvers at about 10:01:00 and said, "Allah is the greatest! Allah is the greatest!" He then asked the hijacker in the cockpit, "Is that it? I mean, shall we put it down?" to which the other replied, "Yes, put it in it, and pull it down."
>
> The passengers continued their assault and at 10:02:23, a hijacker said, "Pull it down! Pull it down!" The hijackers . . . must have judged that the passengers were only seconds from overcoming them. The airplane headed down; the control wheel was turned hard to the right. The airplane rolled onto its back, and one of the hijackers began shouting "Allah is the greatest. Allah is the greatest." With the sounds of the passenger counterattack continuing, the aircraft plowed into an empty field in Shanksville . . . , at 580 miles per hour.[379]

If all that was on the tape when the family members heard it, how could they have thought that the passengers had gotten inside the cockpit? How could they have thought that the passengers were saying "pull it up" when the hijackers were saying "pull it down"? Surely the tape described by the Commission in 2004 was different from the tape heard in 2002 by the family members.

Why did the later account differ from the earlier one? Rowland Morgan suggests that it might have involved anticipatory self-protection by the government in case the military shootdown of the flight became known: "the US Air Force would not be found to have shot down an airliner that had just been saved by righteous American citizens."[380]

Suspicion about the tape's authenticity is also raised by an internal contradiction in the 9/11 Commission's account. It says that when the aircraft crashed, the "passenger counterattack [was still] continuing." But it also says that while the plane was heading down at high speed, "the control wheel was turned hard to the right" and then "[t]he airplane rolled onto its back." As one commentator asked, rhetorically: "[I]s it physically possible to continue the counterattack given the violent movements of the airplane? It should even be impossible in a plane that's going to crash head on and rolling on its back to remain standing on one's feet."[381]

These contradictions reinforce the conclusion that the 9/11 Commission's account, on which our PM authors rely, is completely unreliable.

The Engine

One especially important part of the claim about the wreckage that PM sought to debunk is the claim that "[o]ne of Flight 93's engines was found 'at a considerable distance from the crash site,'" meaning "more than a mile . . . , suggesting that the plane was coming apart prior to impact." That an engine broke loose has been seen as especially significant because this is the kind of damage "a heat-seeking missile would do to an airliner."

The truth, says PM, is that "[a] fan from one of the engines was recovered in the catchment basin of a small pond downhill from the crash site," about 300 yards, hence "less than a fifth of a mile," from the impact crater.[382] Stating that the plane was diving "at a steep, but not vertical, angle," the PM authors quote an NTSB official as saying that "high-mass items like the engine fan would be expelled [and] thrown in the direction the plane was traveling." They then quote an airline accident expert as saying, "When you have very high velocities, 500 miles per hour or more, . . . it would only take a few seconds [for something] to bounce up and travel 300 yards."[383] In this way, our authors suggest, they have put to rest the claim that a detached engine provides evidence that Flight 93 had been shot down.

However, all they have done is to oppose the earlier reports with claims that they label "facts." The twofold claim that what was found was merely a fan and that it was only 300 yards from the crash site—downhill at that—is attributed solely to interviews with FBI agents. But the claim that it was a portion of the engine weighing a ton and that it was 2,000 yards (hence more than a mile) from the crash site was made by a highly respected British newspaper, the *Independent*, which added that this fact was "confirmed by the coroner Wally Miller." This same claim was made by another British newspaper, the *Daily Mirror*.[384]

Also Jim Svonavec, whose company provided excavation equipment, reportedly said that the engine was recovered "at least 1,800 feet into the woods."[385] Moreover, Lyle Szupinka, the state police officer who is quoted by PM as saying that one of the engines was found "at a considerable distance from the crash site," also added: "It appears to be the whole engine."[386] Whether or not it actually was the whole engine, Szupinka's testimony suggests that it was more than simply a fan.

In any case, the combined testimony of these sources indicates that a very heavy portion of the engine was found about a mile away. Why should PM expect us to doubt this combined testimony, from sources with no ax to grind, on the basis of statements made to PM interviewers in 2006 by FBI spokespersons, whose job it would be, if the military did bring down the plane, to cover up this fact?

Debris at Indian Lake and Elsewhere

The claim that Flight 93 was shot down has also been based partly on the fact, reported by residents in the area, that debris presumed to be from the airplane fell far from the crash site, suggesting that the plane had been "holed" by a missile. According to a statement in a Pittsburgh newspaper quoted by PM,

> Residents and workers at businesses outside Shanksville . . . reported discovering clothing, books, papers, and what appeared to be human remains. . . . Others reported what appeared to be crash debris floating in Indian Lake, nearly six miles from the immediate crash scene.[387]

PM seeks to debunk this argument by contending that there were a couple of errors in statements made by some of its advocates. Having found a website—as usual, not one of the major 9/11 sites—that had said that the wind could not have blown the debris to Indian lake, PM claims that this website had the wind direction wrong. (Many students of this crash do, however, reject the official view of the wind direction, which PM simply presupposes.) And against those who say that the debris could not have blown six miles in a few minutes, PM says that although Indian Lake is 6 miles from the crash site by car, it is "less than 1.5 miles . . . as the crow flies," which, it suggests, is "easily within range of debris blasted skyward by the explosion from the crash." It then quotes an NTSB official's statement that "there was no pre-impact stress to the airplane."[388] However, besides not asking how this official could possibly have reached this conclusion, PM has won its apparent victory only by ignoring a massive amount of evidence that does not fit its theory.

The Debris Field: One problem is that, although PM suggests that the debris was scattered at most 1.5 miles from the crash site, the debris field was reportedly much more extensive. Roger Bailey, a member of the Somerset Volunteer Fire Department, reported that he and another man "walked the whole debris field" and that "[i]t went a long ways, maybe two miles."[389] According to a Pittsburgh newspaper, the plane actually left "a trail of debris five miles long."[390] At least three newspapers, moreover, said that debris was found in New Baltimore, which was over a mountain ridge more than eight miles from the crash.[391]

And, most interestingly, Brian Cabell of CNN reported that the FBI "cordoned off a second area about six to eight miles away from the crater." He then asked: "Why would debris from the plane—and they identified it specifically as being from this plane—why would debris be located 6 miles away?"[392]

Items Wind Would Not Carry: A second problem faced by PM's theory involves the nature of some of the items found at a distance from the crash site. PM's theory seems to entail that all the debris that was very far from the crash site had to be light and feathery enough to have been carried there by the wind. However, a newspaper story partially quoted by PM said that people outside Shanksville "reported discovering clothing, books, papers, and what appeared to be human remains. Some residents said they collected bags-full of items to be turned over to investigators."[393] Also Roger Bailey, who walked with his colleague for perhaps two miles, said: "We kept finding pieces of a gray type of sheeting that they put over the airplane frame and then put the fiberglass over top of it. We saw . . . fiberglass and mail. . . . I guess there was 5,000 pounds of mail on board."[394] According to a story in the *Pittsburgh Tribune-Review*, Indian Lake Marina employee John Fleegle, describing debris that had washed ashore the next morning, "said there was something that looked like a rib bone amid pieces of seats, small chunks of melted plastic and checks."[395]

All of these reports were simply ignored by our PM authors, as they were in Guy Smith's documentary, *The Conspiracy Files: 9/11*, which treated *Popular Mechanics* as authoritative. Speaking from Indian Lake as if it were the only place where debris was reportedly found, Smith's narrator informed viewers that the debris from Flight 93 consisted entirely of "scraps of paper and insulation that had blown here on the wind."

Instant Confetti: Still another problem for PM's theory is that for wind to carry tiny pieces of debris very far would take time, but witnesses reported seeing debris start falling almost immediately after the crash. Carol Delasko, another Indian Lake Marina employee, reported that she, having heard the explosion and seen the fireball, "ran outside moments later." Seeing what "looked like confetti raining down all over the air above the lake," she thought that someone must have blown up a boat on the lake.[396]

Seeing Debris from the Airliner: Even more inconvenient for PM's theory is the fact that, as a Reuters story put it, "local media have quoted residents as speaking of . . . burning debris falling from the sky."[397] One of those local media outlets was the *Pittsburgh Tribune-Review*, which wrote, "Residents of nearby Indian Lake reported seeing debris falling from the jetliner as it overflew the area shortly before crashing."[398] According to another story in the same newspaper, Indian Lake residents reported that before the jetliner crashed, it started "falling apart on their homes." A state trooper said: "People were calling in and reporting pieces of plane falling." Local resident Jim Stop reported that while he was fishing, the plane flew over him and "he could see parts falling from the plane."[399]

Sounds Suggestive of a Shootdown

Whereas PM's treatment of the debris evidence is wholly inadequate, as we have seen, its treatment of another type of relevant testimony—reports of sounds suggestive of a shootdown—is completely nonexistent. An examination of this testimony provides still further evidence that the US military did indeed shoot down Flight 93.

Tom Fritz reported that after hearing a sound that "wasn't quite right," he looked up and saw the plane going down, adding: "When it decided to drop, it dropped all of a sudden, like a stone."[400] Laura Temyer said that after she heard an airplane pass overhead: "I heard like a boom and the engine sounded funny. . . . I heard two more booms— and then I did not hear anything. . . . I think the plane was shot down."[401] Linda Shepley told a Pittsburgh television station on 9/11 that she heard a loud bang, then saw the plane bank to the side before crashing.[402] Another witness said that after hearing a high-pitched, screeching sound, she saw the plane make a sharp, 90-degree downward turn and crash.[403]

Some people, two of whom had been in the military, said they heard a missile-like sound. Barry Lichty, the mayor of Indian Lake Borough, said that while he and his wife were watching television, "We heard this loud roar above the house that sounded like a missile. We both ducked. Shortly thereafter, we heard an explosion and felt a tremor." He later added: "You have to understand that Flight 93 came from the west and did not come over my house. I don't know what we heard."[404] Ernie Stull, the mayor of Shanksville, said: "I know of two people . . . that heard a missile. . . . This one fellow's served in Vietnam and he says he's heard them, and he heard one that day."[405]

Reports that the Plane Was Shot Down

At least two people in the area reported hearing, from people who should have been in a position to know, that the airliner was indeed shot down. Laura Temyer, who was quoted above, said that people she knew in state law enforcement told her that the plane was shot down and that the debris field was so wide because decompression had sucked objects out of the aircraft.[406] Susan Mcelwain, who reported seeing the white jet, said that within hours of the crash, she received a call from a friend who reported that her husband, who was in the Air Force, had called and said: "I can't talk, but we've just shot a plane down."[407]

These reports coincide with other reports that the plane was shot down. As we saw in Chapter 1, one of the Otis F-15 pilots, Major Daniel Nash, reported that when he returned to base after flying over New York City, he was told that a military F-16 had shot down an airliner in Pennsylvania.[408]

On Christmas Eve 2004, during his surprise trip to Iraq, Secretary of Defense Donald Rumsfeld, in an apparent slip, referred to "the people who attacked the United States in New York, shot down the plane over Pennsylvania and attacked the Pentagon."[409]

Evidence of a more explicit nature was provided in February of 2005 by Paul Cellucci, Washington's envoy to Canada. Seeking to convince Canada that, as part of NORAD, it should support the US effort to create a missile defense shield, Cellucci told his Toronto audience that a Canadian was in charge of NORAD on 9/11 when it, under orders from President Bush, scrambled military jets to shoot down a hijacked aircraft headed for Washington.[410]

When these testimonies are added to the evidence, provided earlier, that the military was in position to shoot the plane down, the evidence that it actually did so is very strong.

It must be added, however, that there is not, in the information reported above, implicitly a coherent account of what really happened. For one thing, the eyewitness reports of an at least largely intact airliner flying near the ground before it crashed do not fit with the description of the crash site as devoid of any sign of a wrecked airliner. Another problem is that the reports of an airliner flying over Indian Lake seem to describe a plane coming from the east, whereas UA 93 was coming from the northwest.[411] The existence of two airliners could, to be sure, explain why there were evidently two crash sites, miles apart. But unless there is a genuine investigation, it will probably be impossible to figure out what really happened. We do know enough, however, to say that the official story is false. *Debunking 9/11 Myths* has done nothing to undermine that conclusion.

Conclusion

I began this book by saying, "The evidence that 9/11 was an inside job is overwhelming." In the ensuing chapters, I showed this to be the case in the course of demonstrating that various recent attempts to defend the official conspiracy theory have failed. However, if the evidence truly is overwhelming, why do polls show that 48 percent of the American public still believe that no cover-up has occurred? Why do only 36 percent of the American people believe that the government orchestrated the attacks or at least deliberately allowed them to occur? Why is the number not 75 percent? (We can ignore the 25 percent who seem completely immune to evidence, still believing, for example, that Saddam Hussein was responsible for 9/11.) Why is the fact that 9/11 was an inside job not part of our public knowledge?

The responsibility lies primarily with the press, both the mainstream press and much of the left-leaning press. Far from pointing out the many problems in the official conspiracy theory, the press has accepted that theory uncritically while attacking those who have tried to bring these problems to the attention of the American people. In saying that the press has accepted the official theory uncritically, I mean that it has done so with no independent examination of the relevant facts to see if that theory can really explain them.

In the introduction to this book, I pointed out several of the reasons for this failure of empiricism, and hence of investigative reporting, on this issue: a one-sided employment of the term "conspiracy theory," paradigmatic thinking, wishful-and-fearful thinking, and the assumption that documents produced by scientists would ipso facto be scientific documents. In relation to this latter tendency, I showed that journalists who have attacked the 9/11 truth movement have often done so by appealing to official and semi-official documents intended to bolster the official theory and debunk the alternative theory.

At that time, my interest was simply to show the importance of a critical examination of these documents by pointing out that they had been widely accepted by the press. However, now that these documents have been shown to be unworthy of trust, I will use the press's appeal to them to illustrate how abysmal its discussion of alternative views about 9/11 has been. Although my tone will be negative, my purpose is positive: to call on the press to become more responsible in its treatment of the 9/11 controversy.

The coverage has been so poor primarily because journalists, being ignorant of the facts and too willing to believe that the government would not have orchestrated the attacks, have simply treated the official and semi-official reports about 9/11 as if they were neutral, scientific reports, which can be trusted as sources of accurate information.

For example, Terry Allen, whose *In These Times* essay entitled "The 9/11 Faith Movement" was quoted in the introduction, assures her readers that "the facts [do not] support the conspiracists' key charge that World Trade Center buildings were destroyed by pre-positioned explosives." As her evidence for this claim, she says:

> Structural engineers found the destruction consistent with fires caused by the jet liner strike; that temperatures need not actually melt the steel but that expansion and other fire-related stresses would account for compromised architectural integrity.[1]

She is obviously referring to the NIST report. So, in an article in which she accused the 9/11 truth movement of being based on faith, she takes on faith a report issued by an agency of the Bush administration's Commerce Department.

Allen, to be sure, might retort that she was not taking anything on faith. "I spent months as a researcher conducting a fact-by-fact dissection of a few key aspects of [the alternative] hypothesis," she tells us. But her article suggests that she did not learn very much. She reveals, for example, no awareness of any problems in NIST's claim that it has explained why the towers collapsed, even though, as we saw in Chapter 3, it did not explain how these 110-story buildings ended up as a pile of rubble only a few stories high, which means that each tower's 287 steel columns had to be broken into many pieces. NIST did not explain why the buildings came straight down, even though these symmetrical collapses could have occurred only if, at many successive levels, all 287 columns had been broken simultaneously. NIST did not explain how these collapses occurred at virtually free-fall speed, even though this would have been possible only if the lower floors had been offering no resistance to the upper floors. NIST also did not explain why virtually everything except the metal was pulverized, why segments of steel weighing several hundred thousand pounds were thrown out horizontally hundreds of feet, and why there was molten metal in the rubble.

In spite of showing no awareness of any of these problems, Allen seems quite confident in her ability to speak with authority, saying that it is "relatively easy" to undermine the "individual 'facts'" employed by the 9/11 truth movement. She says, for example:

> Many conspiracists offer the collapse of WTC Building 7 as the strongest evidence for the kind of controlled demolition that would prove a plot. Although not hit by planes, it was damaged by debris, and suffered fires eventually fueled by up to 42,000 gallons of diesel fuel stored near

ground level. Griffin cited as evidence of government complicity that the building's sprinkler system should have, but didn't, put out the fires. But the theologian did not know and had not considered that the collapse of the towers had broken the area's water main.

This statement, however, is problematic in four respects.

First, Allen implies that because the diesel fuel caught fire, the building was engulfed in flames. However, the idea that diesel fuel caught on fire is pure speculation, not known fact. The photographic evidence does not, in any case, support the claim that the building was engulfed in fire. She could have seen that her suggestion was wrong simply by looking at a few photographs.

Second, there is no reason to believe that, even if the building had been engulfed in fire, the fire could have caused a collapse, especially one that perfectly mimicked a planned implosion.

Third, Allen conveys the impression that the case, or at least my case, for the controlled demolition of WTC 7 rests significantly on the claim that the building's sprinkler system would have put out the fires unless it had been sabotaged. However, the standard arguments for the controlled demolition WTC 7, which were discussed in Chapters 3 and 4, do not include anything about the sprinkler system. In my own previous discussions, in particular, one will find no mention of the sprinkler system.[2]

Fourth, Allen assumes that because the water main was broken, no water was available. As we saw in Chapter 4, however, that is not true, because fireboats were pumping great quantities of water from the river.[3]

Allen's "relatively easy" undermining of the claim that WTC 7 was brought down by explosives consists, in other words, of unfounded presuppositions plus a red herring, which diverts attention from the real reasons why the collapse of WTC is widely thought to provide the strongest evidence that 9/11 was an inside job. This may be cunning journalism, but it is not good journalism.

Allen also seeks to demonstrate her debunking ability in relation to the widespread use of Larry Silverstein's "pull it" statement to support the idea that WTC 7 was brought down by explosives. Allen says that she could find no use of "pull a building" to refer to intentional destruction. The reporter, unlike the member of the 9/11 truth movement cited in Chapter 4, evidently did not think about calling the receptionist at Controlled Demolition, Inc. At any rate, Allen then says:

> An alternative explanation would be that given the lack of water and the number of injured and missing firefighters, the NYFD decided to pull workers from Building 7 to concentrate on search and rescue at the fallen towers.

However, besides the fact that there was no "lack of water," there was also no fire fighting. According to NIST, as we saw in Chapter 4, "water was never an issue at WTC 7 since firefighting was never started in the building."[4] Firefighting was not started because the firefighters were pulled out of the building at about noon, after word was received from Mayor Giuliani's Office of Emergency Management (as we saw in Chapter 3) that this building was going to collapse. Allen could have learned this from my essay, "The Destruction of the World Trade Center,"[5] or from the same source I used, the 9/11 oral histories recorded by the Fire Department of New York. These sources would also have let her know that these firefighters, rather than being sent to "concentrate on search and rescue at the fallen towers," simply stood around, behind lines designating the expected "collapse zone," waiting for the building to collapse.[6]

If Allen had not been so certain that she could easily debunk the claims of the 9/11 truth movement, she might have asked the most important question about this story: Given the fact that WTC 7 was not hit by a plane, that the available photographs show no large fires, and that fire had never caused a steel-frame high-rise to collapse, why did someone in Giuliani's office declare that WTC 7 was going to collapse some five hours before it actually did? This question is made even more important by the fact that, at this writing, Giuliani is running for president.

Alexander Cockburn's treatment of the 9/11 truth movement's case against the government is equally poor. Cockburn says, as we saw in the introduction, that this movement's members are devoid of "any conception of evidence" and have accepted "magic over common sense." With those charges in mind, let us look at what Cockburn says about the collapses of the WTC buildings.

Although he admits that the buildings fell rapidly, he says that the collapses did not require "pre-placed explosives." Why not? "High grade steel," Cockburn explains, "can bend disastrously under extreme heat."[7] Cockburn, in other words, believes that the fire, by bending the steel on a few floors of these huge buildings, caused them to collapse symmetrically, at virtually free-fall speed, into piles of rubble only a few stories high. If that is not magic, it will do until the real thing comes along.[8]

Another problem with the "9/11 conspiracy nuts," Cockburn says, is that "their treatment of eyewitness testimony . . . is whimsical. . . . [T]estimony that undermines their theories . . . is contemptuously brushed aside." What, however, does Cockburn do with the testimonies that explosions were going off in the Twin Towers? He says: "People inside who survived the collapse didn't hear a series of explosions." This is quite amazing. As I had reported in my essay "Explosive Testimony" (which was published both on the Internet and in a book before Cockburn's essay appeared), that is exactly what some survivors reported.

For example, North Tower employee Teresa Veliz said that, while she was making her way downstairs:

> There were explosions going off everywhere. I was convinced that there were bombs planted all over the place and someone was sitting at a control panel pushing detonator buttons. . . . There was another explosion. And another. I didn't know where to run.[9]

Sue Keane, a police officer who was in the North Tower, said:

> [An explosion] sent me and . . . two firefighters down the stairs. . . . I can't tell you how many times I got banged around. Each one of those explosions picked me up and threw me. . . . There was another explosion, and I got thrown with two firefighters out onto the street.[10]

Testimony also came from Sal D'Agostino and Bill Butler, two firefighters who were on the tenth floor of the North Tower. "[T]here were these huge explosions—I mean huge, gigantic explosions," D'Agostino said. "It was like a train going two inches away from your head: bang-bang, bang-bang, bang-bang," Butler added.[11]

It is, moreover, not simply the testimony of people who had been in the buildings that should matter. There were journalists, police officers, and over 100 members of the Fire Department of New York outside the towers who reported phenomena suggestive of explosions.

Were these testimonies "contemptuously brushed aside" by Cockburn? Or was he merely ignorant of them—even though checking Google for "testimonies of explosions in the World Trade Center" would have brought up almost 300,000 items? In either case, Cockburn should not have been accepted as a reliable authority on 9/11 by the editor of the *Nation*.

It would appear, however, that this magazine does not require that essays attacking the 9/11 truth movement demonstrate knowledge of the facts about 9/11. This was again illustrated a few months later, when the *Nation* published, as its cover story, an essay by Christopher Hayes entitled "9/11: The Roots of Paranoia."[12] As this title suggests, Hayes states that the 9/11 truth movement, being based on delusional beliefs, reflects the "paranoid style in American politics."

Not denying that conspiracies do occur, Hayes says that "the problem is continuing to assert the existence of a conspiracy even after the evidence shows it to be virtually impossible." Evidence to prove something "virtually impossible" would, of course, need to be very powerful evidence. However, rather than presenting any such evidence, Hayes merely says:

> In March 2005 *Popular Mechanics* assembled a team of engineers, physicists, flight experts and the like to critically examine some of the Truth Movement's most common claims. They found them almost

entirely without merit. To pick just one example, steel might not melt at 1,500 degrees, the temperature at which jet fuel burns, but it does begin to lose a lot of its strength, enough to cause the support beams to fail.

And then, as if he had just provided a truly devastating blow, Hayes says: "And yet no amount of debunking seems to work." This is the only evidence Hayes provides for his claim that the 9/11 truth movement's beliefs are delusional. And yet he can consider this fact about steel to be strong support for the official theory only if he, like Allen and Cockburn, accepts an essentially magical explanation of the collapses.

Hayes' statement about the buildings also reveals his unawareness of some elementary facts, such as the crucial distinction between fire temperature and steel temperature, the fact that the jet fuel would have burned up within ten minutes, and the fact that fire has never caused steel-frame high-rises to collapse. Hayes was, in fact, apparently so unfamiliar with the 9/11 literature that he did not realize, writing late in 2006, that *Popular Mechanics* had, earlier that year, expanded its article into a book.

In spite of his unfamiliarity with the issues and literature, however, Hayes felt authorized to assure his readers that the 9/11 truth movement's theories "are wrongheaded and a terrible waste of time."

This tendency of journalists to declare the 9/11 truth movement misguided, without having the knowledge to speak on the subject, is also illustrated in Jim Dwyer's *New York Times* story mentioned in the introduction,[13] which reported on NIST's publication of its "Answers to Frequently Asked Questions." Dwyer, while raising none of the dozens of questions that need to be raised about the official conspiracy theory, said that "enormous obstacles" confront the alternative theory's claim that the buildings were brought down by explosives. In stating one of those alleged obstacles, evidently taken straight from NIST's "Answers," Dwyer proclaimed: "Controlled demolition is done from the bottom of buildings, not the top, to take advantage of gravity, and there is little dispute that the collapse of the two towers began high in the towers." However, as we saw in Chapter 3, although this is the normal procedure, it is not the only possible one. Also unmentioned by Dwyer is the fact that the collapse of Building 7, besides otherwise perfectly exemplifying a standard controlled implosion, did start from the bottom.

It was, however, in relation to the issue of molten metal that Dwyer most fully displayed his ignorance of crucial facts. Pointing out that Steven Jones had argued that "the molten [metal] found in the rubble was evidence of demolition explosives because an ordinary airplane fire would not generate enough heat,"[14] Dwyer gave the final word to the director of Protec, a demolition monitoring firm, who said that "if there had been any molten steel in the rubble, it would have permanently damaged any excavation equipment encountering it."

We have here an extreme example of the tendency to favor a priori arguments over empirical evidence. As we saw in Chapter 3, the testimony to the existence of molten metal in the rubble is so strong as to put the issue completely beyond doubt. In one of these statements, moreover, Greg Fuchek said, "sometimes when a worker would pull a steel beam from the wreckage, the end of the beam would be dripping molten steel."[15] Evidently this worker's crane was not "permanently damaged." Dwyer was writing a story for the *New York Times*, which likes to think of itself as having the highest standards of excellence. But he apparently did not check to see if the evidence supported Jones rather than the man from Protec—even though a Google search for "molten metal at Ground Zero" would have turned up over 300,000 items, many of which contain the testimonies of the people quoted in Chapter 3, such as Peter Tully, Mark Loizeaux, and Leslie Robertson.

Similar ignorance of relevant facts is reflected in Matthew Rothschild's story in the *Progressive*, "Enough of the 9/11 Conspiracy Theories, Already,"[16] which was discussed in the introduction. As I pointed out, Rothschild's rebuttal of the claim that the World Trade Center buildings were brought down by explosives consisted of saying: "Problem is, some of the best engineers in the country have studied these questions and come up with perfectly logical, scientific explanations for what happened." In that discussion, I merely pointed out the problematic nature of accepting on faith a report produced by an agency of the Bush administration. Now, however, following our critical examination of NIST's claims, we can see how fully problematic this faith is.

Obviously impressed by NIST's claims about its own thoroughness, Rothschild quotes its statement about how many experts worked on its report, how many people were interviewed, and how many videos, photographs, and documents were studied, and then says:

> [NIST] concluded that a combination of the crash and the subsequent
> fires brought the towers down: "In each tower, a different combination
> of impact damage and heat-weakened structural components contributed
> to the abrupt structural collapse."

That is his rebuttal to all the evidence presented by members of the 9/11 truth movement: NIST says they are wrong, so they are wrong. The logic implicit in his argument is:

—The government did not cause the collapse of the WTC buildings.
—Therefore the official report, put out by an agency of Bush's
Commerce Department, would have no motive to conceal the truth.
—We can, therefore, believe the NIST report.
—The NIST report says that the collapses were caused solely by the
damage caused by the impacts plus the ensuing fires.

—Therefore, those who say otherwise are wrong.

Perfectly logical. And, of course, perfectly circular.

Besides not doing any independent checking about whether the NIST report adequately explains the facts—Rothschild does not even mention the problems in explaining how molten metal and total, straight-down collapses at virtually free-fall speed were produced—he has apparently not even examined photographs of the Twin Towers at the onset of their collapses. On the basis of these photographs, which show that huge clouds of dust were being ejected, I had asked: "What other than explosives could turn concrete into powder and then eject it horizontally 150 feet or more?"[17] Rothschild quoted this question, then rebutted it by quoting Gene Corley as saying:

> That is simply the air pressure being pushed down. . . . Once the collapse started, then you had roughly a twenty-story building and roughly a thirty-story building acting as a very large mass to push everything down. The air pressure gets quite something, and the windows on the lower floors break, and you see puffs of smoke coming out of them.

As this attempted rebuttal shows, Rothschild confused two very different phenomena. He was referring to the so-called squibs, many of which do occur in the lower floors. But my statement was about the huge dust clouds created near the tops of the buildings at the very onset of the collapses. I had made this clear by quoting Jeff King's statement about "how much very fine concrete dust is ejected from the top of the building very early in the collapse" and also by saying: "when the towers started to collapse, they did not fall straight down. . . . They exploded."

The fact that Corley's explanation could not account for the phenomenon to which I was referring should have been even clearer to Rothschild by virtue of my statement immediately after the sentence he quoted, in which I said: "And if it be suspected that the dust simply floated out, some of the photographs show that rather large pieces of the tower were also thrown out 150 feet or more."[18] (NIST, of course, made no attempt to explain this phenomenon.)

Turning to WTC 7, Rothschild says: "This is a favorite of the conspiracy theorists, since the planes did not strike this structure." Rothschild, like Allen, assures his readers that this is no problem. Why? Because "the building did sustain damage from the debris of the Twin Towers." He then quotes *Popular Mechanics*' quotation of NIST lead investigator Shyam Sunder's statement that, "On about a third of the face to the center and to the bottom—approximately ten stories—about 25 percent of the depth of the building was scooped out." Then, as if he had just said something very impressive, Rothschild adds: "What's more, the fire in the building lasted for about eight hours, in part because there were fuel tanks in the basement and on some of the floors."

Besides thereby revealing himself to be unaware of the photographic and testimonial evidence, which shows that the building was not consumed by fires for eight hours, Rothschild was evidently also ignorant of all the other issues we examined in Chapters 3 and 4, such as the difficulty of this damage from fire and debris producing a symmetrical collapse at virtually free-fall speed. He also showed no signs of reflecting on the fact that although buildings 3, 4, 5, and 6 were damaged much more severely by falling debris from the towers than building 7, they did not collapse.

The remainder of Rothschild's essay consists of more of the same. With regard to each problem raised about the official story by the 9/11 truth movement, Rothschild rebuts it by appealing to official or semi-official documents. With regard to the allegation that United Flight 93 was shot down rather than crashing during a struggle between passengers and hijackers, for example, Rothschild says: "But we know from cell phone conversations that passengers on board that plane planned on confronting the hijackers." He seems oblivious to the question of whether such calls were possible in 2001. Then, referring to what "Michael Bronner has shown in his August article for *Vanity Fair*," Rothschild says that before NEADS could figure out whether it had orders to shoot the flight down, the plane had already crashed "in a field in Pennsylvania at 10:03AM."

On the basis of such appeals to authority, Rothschild concludes: "Not every riddle that Griffin and other conspiracists pose has a ready answer. But almost all of their major assertions are baseless." Again, his logic is perfectly circular:

—The alternative conspiracy theorists believe the government was responsible.

—But the government's reports and other studies that support them say that the government's conspiracy theory of 9/11 is accurate.

—Therefore the major assertions of the alternative theorists are baseless.

But Rothschild can draw this conclusion because he, like the previous journalists we have examined, is apparently unaware of a wide range of rather elementary facts that contradict the official account.

The fact that these journalistic critiques of the 9/11 truth movement are based on such unawareness tempts me, on behalf of the movement, to say to these journalists: *We refuse to let our knowledge, however limited, be informed by your ignorance, however vast.*[19]

In any case, Rothschild, besides calling the 9/11 truth movement's major assertions baseless, goes even further, saying:

At bottom, the 9/11 conspiracy theories are profoundly irrational and unscientific. It is more than passing strange that progressives, who so revere science on such issues as tobacco, stem cells, evolution, and global warming, are so willing to abandon science and give in to fantasy on the subject of 9/11.

But that, of course, is exactly what the 9/11 truth movement is saying to Rothschild, Cockburn, Allen, Hayes, and all other progressive thinkers who, on this issue, accept a conspiracy theory that, as I have shown, is completely irrational and dependent on unscientific explanations.

The failure of the progressive or left-leaning press to deal responsibly with the issues raised by the 9/11 truth movement is not, to be sure, the primary reason why much of the American public is still ignorant of basic facts that, at the very least, cast doubt on the truth of the official account of what happened on 9/11. The blame for this ignorance rests more on the mainstream press, from which most Americans still get most of their information about national and international issues. Even though Americans increasingly get information about such issues from alternative sources, as has obviously happened in relation to 9/11, an issue cannot become part of the public discussion in this country unless it is covered by the mainstream press. The fact that the truth about 9/11—that it was an inside job—is not part of our public knowledge is primarily, therefore, the fault of the mainstream press, not the left-leaning press. Nevertheless, the fact that the most prominent left-leaning publications have ignored or even attacked the 9/11 truth movement has made it easier for the mainstream press to do the same than would otherwise have been the case.

Although the left-leaning press has probably had several motives for its dismissal of the 9/11 truth movement, its most commonly expressed one is the charge that this movement's claims constitute a distraction from the real crimes of the Bush administration, both at home and abroad. This charge generally seems to be based on two assumptions: first, that a thorough examination of the facts would prove the 9/11 truth movement's claims to be baseless; and second, that members of this movement focus so single-mindedly on 9/11 that they ignore far more deadly crimes, such as the war in Iraq, the curtailment of constitutional rights in the United States, the increasing gap between rich and poor, and global warming.

However, the falsity of both of these assumptions is illustrated by former CIA analyst Bill Christison. As I pointed out in the introduction, when he, after having been "utterly unwilling to consider seriously the conspiracy theories surrounding the [9/11] attacks" for four and a half years, finally did examine the facts, he concluded that the official story was obviously false. Then, having reached this conclusion, he also concluded that this issue, far from being a distraction, was "more important than any other issue."[20] If the charge that 9/11 was a fraud is true, Christison says, then this fraud involves a much greater crime against the American people and people of the world than any other charges of fraud connected to the run-up to the invasion of Iraq in March 2003. . . . [A]fter all, the events of 9/11 have been used by the administration to justify every single aspect of US foreign policy in the Middle East since September 11. It is a charge that is more important also because it affects the very core of our entire political system.[21]

Speaking of more general reasons to expose the truth about 9/11, Christison quoted Webster Tarpley's statement that, "We must deprive [the 9/11 myth's perpetrators] of the ability to stampede and manipulate hundreds of millions of people [with their] . . . cynically planned terrorist events."[22]

I myself have used the notion of "myth," understood as "an orienting and mobilizing story [with] religious overtones," to explain the importance of exposing the falsity of the official story about 9/11.

[T]his story, serving as a national religious Myth, has been used to justify two wars, which have caused many tens of thousands of deaths; to start a more general war on Islam, in which Muslims are considered guilty until proven innocent; to annul and violate civil rights; and to increase our military spending, which was already greater than that of the rest of the world combined, by hundreds of billions of dollars, partly so that weapons can be put into space.[23]

Elsewhere, in a response to Cockburn's charge that the alternative conspiracy theory is a distraction from truly important matters,[24] I said:

The idea that America was attacked by foreign terrorists on 9/11 has been used to justify the war in Iraq and virtually every other way in which the United States has made the world an uglier, more dangerous place since 9/11. It has also been used to distract attention from the problem of global warming, which is the really serious threat to human civilization. The official conspiracy theory about 9/11, in other words, is the true distraction.[25]

Lying behind this claim was the following argument, which I made in an earlier book:

[One] destructive consequence of the attacks was their use to focus the public and Congressional mind almost exclusively on terrorism, thereby distracting it from the ecological crisis, which is arguably the overarching issue of our age. For the first time in history, one species, our own, is on a trajectory that, if not radically altered, will soon bring our planet's life, at least in its higher forms, to an end. The preeminent issue of our day, therefore, should be whether human civilization can learn to live in a way that is sustainable. Politicians, scientists, educators, and the mass media should be united in working to this end. With the demise of the Cold War, it appeared—partly because the fact of global warming was becoming increasingly obvious—that this issue might start to get the attention it had long deserved.

But the violence of 9/11, along with the official narrative thereof, distracted our primary attention away from the relation between humanity and nature and forced it back to human-vs.-human issues. Given the fact that much valuable time has been lost since the attacks— time that might have been used to slow global warming before it is too late—this dimension of 9/11 may turn out to be the most destructive.[26]

The ways in which the official account of 9/11 has been used to exacerbate and even create problems are rather obvious. Mark Danner, for example, has pointed to the way in which 9/11 has been used by the Bush–Cheney administration to justify a "state of exception," in the sense discussed by Giorgio Agamben, under which the US president increasingly operates without the constraint of law, whether international or constitutional.[27] Once the left-leaning press examines the evidence and learns that 9/11 must have been an inside job, it should have little trouble making an about-face, henceforth portraying the exposé of 9/11 as a key, perhaps the central key, to changing American and global policies for the better.

The possibility of an about-face on the part of the mainstream press is another matter, for several reasons. One is that the corporate owners of the mainstream media and the elite class more generally have been benefiting financially from the global "war on terror" for which 9/11 has served as the pretext. As Robert Baer pointed out in a statement partially quoted in the introduction, "a lot of people [in the United States] have profited from 9/11. You are seeing great fortunes made—whether they are on the stock market, or selling weapons, or just contractors—great fortunes are being made." Members of this class will be disinclined to kill a goose that continues to lay golden eggs.

An even more serious impediment to the exposure of the truth about 9/11 exists if, as has been suggested,[28] some members of this elite class not only are benefiting from 9/11 but were involved in the planning for the event itself and the subsequent cover-up. Such members of the elite class would naturally be reluctant to sanction an exposé that, if it went far enough, would expose their own complicity.

Even apart from such considerations, the elite class, both in the United States and the world more generally, may fear that exposing the truth about 9/11 might, by producing a crisis of confidence in the institutions of the world's most powerful nation, lead to a global economic meltdown.

This could indeed occur. But insofar as this is a concern, we can only hope that at least a significant portion of the global elite who control media outlets will be susceptible to the following argument:

Although the threat of a global economic collapse is real, such a collapse would be temporary and certainly would not bring human civilization to an end. But unless the trajectory of human civilization is changed quickly and drastically, we will likely have a global ecological collapse within the present century. This ecological collapse could be brought on quickly, through a "nuclear winter" caused by even a small exchange of nuclear weapons, or more slowly, through runaway global warming. The United States government has long been the major impediment to a solution to both of these threats. Since 9/11, the United States government has become even more dangerous, ridiculing global warming while practicing an extreme version of double standards in relation to nuclear technology: denying to enemies even the right to develop nuclear energy while planning to strengthen its own arsenal of nuclear weapons and even to position them in space. Apart from a revelation of the truth about 9/11, there is little chance that the present trajectory of US policy, with its threat to the survival of civilization itself, will change. Even a change of administrations will probably result only in minor changes, apart from a revelation of the truth about 9/11, because the present mythology about 9/11 will be used to justify continuing to focus on relationships between human beings rather than on the relationship of human civilization as a whole to the natural world as a whole—the ecosphere on which we are entirely dependent.

Moreover, even though the revelation about global economic collapse might indeed trigger a global economic crisis, it might just as well work in the opposite direction. American prestige is already at an all-time low in the world. Confidence in our government and media have already been shaken. If other countries were to see America revealing the ugly truth about 9/11 as part of a more general effort to return honesty and transparency to government, their confidence in America's institutions might be strengthened.

It is possible that the corporate owners of the mainstream press, recognizing the strength of these arguments, may be led to let their newspapers, magazines, and radio and television networks reveal the truth about 9/11, thereby enabling a radical change of course (as well as bringing renewed respect to the mainstream media).

Unfortunately, however, this is unlikely, at least unless the media are forced into making the revelations by the Democrats, who could use their new control of the House and the Senate to begin the unraveling of the official story through public hearings.

However, the Democratic leadership itself will, for various reasons, probably be reluctant to take up this issue, unless considerable pressure is brought to bear.

One form of pressure would be a large-scale effort, involving letter-writing campaigns, rallies, and a huge march on Washington to make this issue part of the public discussion and persuade the Democratic leadership to deal with it.

Effective pressure could also be brought to bear by a jury composed of highly respected European citizens. Such a jury would take testimony from members of the 9/11 truth movement, on the one hand, and from members of NIST, the 9/11 Commission, and any members of the US government, including the US military, who would be willing to defend the official account of 9/11, on the other hand. This jury would then issue its conclusion to the people of the world in general and the US press and Congress in particular.

The presupposition here is, of course, that this jury, if composed of citizens free of conflicts of interest, would conclude that 9/11 had indeed been an inside job. The 9/11 truth movement has no doubt that this would be the case. Our only question is whether anyone could be found to defend the official account. If not, however, that in itself would be revealing.

Additional pressure could be exerted by similar juries in Canada and other parts of the world. The official story about 9/11 has led to negative effects in the world as a whole. So the effort to expose the falsity of this official story should finally be a worldwide effort.

Although the effort to expose the truth about 9/11, which has been going on now for over five years, will remain an uphill battle in the United States, the Democratic control of the House and the Senate provides at least a ground for hope. This is the time for the 9/11 movement to make its biggest effort. We have, after all, a world to save.

NOTES

Abbreviations used in the notes

AFAQs NIST (National Institute of Standards and Technology). "Answers to Frequently Asked Questions." 30 August 2006 (http://wtc.nist.gov/pubs/factsheets/faqs_8_2006.htm).

Bronner Michael Bronner. "9/11 Live: The NORAD Tapes," *Vanity Fair* August 2006 (www.vanityfair.com/politics/features/2006/08/norad 200608).

Clarke Richard A. Clarke. *Against All Enemies: Inside America's War on Terror*. New York: Free Press, 2004.

D9/11M David Dunbar and Brad Reagan, eds. *Debunking 9/11 Myths: Why Conspiracy Theories Can't Stand Up to the Facts*. New York: Hearst Books, 2006.

ISO David Ray Griffin and Peter Dale Scott, eds. *9/11 and American Empire: Intellectuals Speak Out*. Northampton, MA: Olive Branch Press, 2006.

9/11CR *The 9/11 Commission Report: Final Report of the National Commission on Terrorist Attacks Upon the United States*, Authorized Edition. New York: W. W. Norton, 2004.

NISTFR NIST. *Final Report on the Collapse of the World Trade Center Towers*. September 2005 (http://wtc.nist.gov/NISTNCSTAR1 CollapseofTowers.pdf). As the url indicates, the more complete abbreviation for this document is NIST NCSTAR 1; for the explanation, see ch. 3, note 28.

NPH David Ray Griffin. *The New Pearl Harbor: Disturbing Questions About the Bush Administration and 9/11*. Northampton, MA: Olive Branch Press, 2004.

O&D David Ray Griffin. *The 9/11 Commission Report: Omissions and Distortions*. Northampton: Olive Branch Press, 2005.

oral hist Oral histories of 9/11 were made available at a *New York Times* website (http://graphics8.nytimes.com/packages/html/nyregion/20050812_WTC_GRAPHIC/met_WTC_histories_full_01.html).

WP Thomas H. Kean and Lee H. Hamilton, with Benjamin Rhodes. *Without Precedent: The Inside Story of the 9/11 Commission*. New York: Alfred A. Knopf, 2006.

1 Richard Falk, "Foreword" to NPH, vii.

2 This is Fred Burks's website wanttoknow.info.

3 Nafeez Mosaddeq Ahmed, *The War on Freedom: How and Why America Was Attacked September 11, 2001* (Joshua Tree, CA: Tree of Life Publications, 2002).

4 NPH xxiii.

5 O&D 291.

6 Steven E. Jones, "Why Indeed Did the WTC Buildings Collapse?" This essay was at first available only on the Internet. It was later published in ISO, 33–62. A slightly revised version (under the title "Why Indeed Did the World Trade Center Buildings Completely Collapse?") was published in the *Journal of 9/11 Studies* 3 (September 2006) (www.journalof911studies.com).

7 See the "oral hist" under Abbreviations, above.

8 David Ray Griffin, *Christian Faith and the Truth Behind 9/11: A Call to Reflection and Action* (Louisville: Westminster John Knox, 2006), ch. 2, "Explosive Testimony: Revelations about the Twin Towers in the 9/11 Oral Histories," and ch. 3, "The Destruction of the World Trade Center: Why the Official Account Cannot Be True."

9 Bill Christison, "Stop Belittling the Theories About September 11," www.dissidentvoice.org, 14 August 2006 (www.dissidentvoice.org/Aug06/Christison14.htm).

10 "Letter from Bill Christison to Friends," E-mail sent about 14 August 2006.

11 Zogby International, "A Word about Our Poll of American Thinking toward the 9/11 Terrorist Attacks," Zogby International, 24 May 2006 (www.zogby.com/features/features.dbm?ID=231). For an interpretation, see "Zogby Poll Finds Over 70 Million Voting Age Americans Support New 9/11 Investigation," 911Truth.org, 21 May 2006 (www.911truth.org/article.php?story=200605 220220 41421).

12 Thomas Hargrove and Guido H. Stempel III, "Anti-Government Anger Spurs 9/11 Conspiracy Belief," NewsPolls.org, Scripps Survey Research Center at Ohio University, 2 August 2006 (http://newspolls.org/story.php?story_id=55). The title of the story, incidentally, is the pollsters' inference, not a conclusion supported by the answers.

13 Lev Grossman, "Why the 9/11 Conspiracies Won't Go Away," *Time* 3 September 2006.

14 Bronner 262–285.

15 As I explain in Chapter 1, this claim is made only about the second, third, and fourth flights. The 9/11 Commission let stand NORAD's claim about AA Flight 11, according to which the military did know about it beforehand but not in time to intercept it.

16 WP 102, 268.

17 AFAQs, answer to question # 2.

18 Jim Dwyer, "2 US Reports Seek to Counter Conspiracy Theories About 9/11," *New York Times* 2 September 2006 (www.911review.com/reviews/nyt/markup/02conspiracy.html). Dwyer, incidentally, refers to two reports, the second being "The Top September 11 Conspiracy Theories," which is on the US State Department's "Identifying Misinformation" website (http://usinfo.state.gov/

media/misinformation.html). I have not, however, responded to this document, because it merely contains bullet-point summaries of the standard government line on various issues.

19 "9/11: Debunking the Myths," *Popular Mechanics* March 2005.

20 *The Conspiracy Files: 9/11* was broadcast 18 February 2007, by BBC 2. The documentary can be viewed at www.911blogger.com or on YouTube (www.youtube.com/watch?v=vR3aNMLkahc).

21 US Department of State, Identifying Misinformation, "The Top September 11 Conspiracy Theories," 25 October 2006 (http://usinfo.state.gov/media/misinformation.html).

22 Quoted in Jim Dwyer, "2 US Reports Seek to Counter Conspiracy Theories About 9/11."

23 *The American Heritage Dictionary of the English Language* (The American Heritage Publishing Co., 1969).

24 Michael Moore, *Dude, Where's My Country?* (New York: Warner Books, 2003), 2. I quoted this quip in NPH xxiv.

25 I had a prominent discussion of this issue, under a heading with "Conspiracy Theories" in scare quotes, at the end of the introduction to NPH. But the issue is not acknowledged in any of the stories discussed here that mention this book.

26 See note 19.

27 Matthew Rothschild, "Enough of the 9/11 Conspiracy Theories, Already," *Progressive* 18 September 2006 (www.alternet.org/story/41601/).

28 Terry Allen, "The 9/11 Faith Movement," *In These Times* 11 July 2006 (www.inthesetimes.com/site/main/article/2702). In *9/11 Modus Operandi*, a recent novel by Hal Sisson (Ontario, Canada: Global Outlook, 2007), a newspaper man, referring to the incongruity created in our minds by evidence that our government, which is supposed to protect us, has instead attacked us, says the powers that be "provide us with a cover story which subconsciously reinforces our belief system in a government which serves and protects us, even though the same story ignores the facts and disregards certain evidence" (241–42). Sisson derived this notion from Barrie Zwicker, *Towers of Deception: The Media Cover-Up of 9/11* (Gabriola Island, BC: New Society, 2006), 117–22.

29 Lev Grossman, "Why the 9/11 Conspiracies Won't Go Away," *Time* 3 September 2006.

30 Paul Craig Roberts, "Five Years After and We Still Don't Know," Information Clearing House, 7 September 2006 (www.informationclearinghouse.info/article 14874.htm).

31 Fetzer's essay, "Thinking About 'Conspiracy Theories': 9/11 and JFK," is contained in James H. Fetzer, *The 9/11 Conspiracy: Experts and Scholars Speak Up for Truth* (Peru, IL: Open Court, 2007). Fetzer's statement that he discussed the notion of "conspiracy theories" with Guy Smith is contained in an e-mail of 20 February 2007.

32 Salim Muwakkil, "What's the 411 on 9/11?" *In These Times* 21 December 2005. Had Terry Allen been interested in whether this was a plausible explanation, she could have, by checking my writings, learned that I have a very different understanding of theology than she evidently assumes. I have argued against the type of theology that uses the "method of authority" in favor of the method of

"settling questions of truth and falsity on the basis of common experience and reason—that is, by reasoning on the basis of experience that is at least potentially common to all people" (Griffin, *Two Great Truths: A New Synthesis of Scientific Naturalism and Christian Faith* [Louisville: Westminster John Knox Press, 2004], 62). Allen, however, evidently felt confident of her own understanding of how theologians operate.

33 Robert Baer, "Dangerous Liaisons," *Nation* 27 September 2004 (www.thenation.com/docprem.mhtml?i=20040927&s=baer). My response, "With Enemies Like This. . .," was eventually published by the *Nation* on 13 December 2004 (www.thenation.com/doc/20041213/letter).

34 The film itself was partly based on two books by Baer, *See No Evil* and *Sleeping with the Devil*.

35 "Thom Hartmann Interviews Robert Baer," transcript provided at 911Blogger.com, 9 June 2006 (www.911blogger.com/2006/06/former-cia-member-robert-baer-comments.html).

36 Alexander Cockburn, "The 9/11 Conspiracy Nuts," *Nation* 25 September 2006 (www.thenation.com/doc/20060925/cockburn); "The 9/11 Conspiracy Nuts: How They Let the Guilty Parties of 9/11 Slip Off the Hook," *Counterpunch* 9/10 September 2006 (www.counterpunch.org/cockburn09092006.html).

37 Cockburn, "The Conspiracists, Continued—Are They Getting Crazier?" *Free Press* 16 September 2006 (www.freepress.org/columns/display/ 2/2006/ 1433). As this book was about to go to press, George Monbiot, a left-leaning professor of political science in England who is also a *Guardian* columnist and a best-selling author, published two essays in which he repeated many of Cockburn's points, including the charge that members of the 9/11 truth movement believe in magic. He also used the same kind of abusive language, referring to members of the movement as "morons" and "idiots" and to me in particular as the movement's "high priest." See George Monbiot, "A 9/11 Conspiracy Virus Is Sweeping the World, But It Has No Basis in Fact," *Guardian* 6 February 2007 (www.guardian.co.uk/comment/story/0,,2006529,00.html), and "9/11 Fantasists Pose a Mortal Danger to Popular Oppositional Campaigns," *Guardian* 20 February 2007 (www.guardian.co.uk/commentisfree/story/0,,2017006,00.html). I have replied in "Morons and Magic" (online).

38 See, besides *Two Great Truths*, also *Physics and the Ultimate Significance of Time: Bohm, Prigogine, and Process Philosophy* (Albany: SUNY Press, 1986); *The Reenchantment of Science: Postmodern Proposals* (Albany: SUNY Press, 1995); *Unsnarling the World-Knot: Consciousness, Freedom, and the Mind-Body Problem* (Berkeley & Los Angeles: University of California Press, 1998); *Religion and Scientific Naturalism: Overcoming the Conflicts* (Albany: SUNY Press, 2000); *Reenchantment without Supernaturalism: A Process Philosophy of Religion* (Ithaca: Cornell University Press, 2001); *Two Great Truths: A New Synthesis of Scientific Naturalism and Christian Faith* (Louisville: Westminster John Knox Press, 2004); and *Whitehead's Radically Different Postmodern Philosophy: An Argument for Its Contemporary Relevance* (Albany: SUNY Press, 2007).

39 Philip J. Berg, Esq., "Resolution Calling for an 'Independent International September 11th Truth Commission,'" ThePetitionSite.com (www.thepetitionsite.com/ takeaction/795812120?ltl=1166126877). Berg and all of the other people mentioned here are included on Alan Miller's helpful website, Patriots Question 9/11 (http://patriotsquestion911.com).

40 See Dr. Robert Bowman, "The Impossibility of the Official Government Story" (http://video.google.com/videoplay?docid=-6900065571556128674), and "Retired Air Force Col: They Lied To Us About The War And About 9/11 Itself," 27 October 2005 (www.benfrank.net/blog/2005/10/27/oil_mafia_treason).

41 Andreas von Bülow, *Die CIA und der 11. September. Internationaler Terror und die Rolle der Geheimdienste* (Piper, 2003). See also "Michael Meacher and Andreas Von Bülow Express Their Serious Doubts About 9/11" (http://video.google.com/videoplay?docid=8274552561914055825).

42 On June 5, 2005, Butler wrote in a letter to a local newspaper: "President Bush knew about the impending attacks on America. He did nothing to warn the American people because he needed this war on terrorism." See Jerry Isaacs, "Air Force Officer Delivers Blistering Excoriation of Bush: Says Bush Is Responsible for September 11th Attacks," Rense.com, 11 August 2003 (www.rense.com/general40/ecor.htm).

43 See Chiesa's preface (in Italian) to Philip J. Berg and William Rodriguez, *Il documentato atto d'accusa del guardiano delle Twin Towers* (Rome: Editori Riuniti, 2006); available at www.giuliettochiesa.it/modules.php?name=Sections&op=viewarticle&artid=468. See also *The Infinite War* (Modena, Italy: Yema, 2005), translation by Robert Elliot of *La Guerra Infinita* (Rome: Feltrinelli, 2002).

44 Christison's statement was quoted earlier.

45 A. K. Dewdney, "The Cellphone and Airfone Calls from Flight UA93," Physics 911, 9 June 2003 (http://physics911.net/cell phoneflight93.htm).

46 See General Leonid Ivashov, "International Terrorism Does Not Exist," 2 January 2006 (www.physics911.net/ivashov.htm), in which he says: "Only secret services . . . have the ability to plan, organize and conduct an operation of such magnitude. . . . Osama bin Laden and 'Al Qaeda' cannot be the organizers nor the performers of the September 11 attacks. They do not have the necessary organization, resources or leaders."

47 Captain Eric H. May, "911 and Non-Investigation" (http://mujca.com/captain.htm).

48 George Nelson, "Impossible to Prove a Falsehood True: Aircraft Parts as a Clue to Their Identity," Physics 911, 23 April 2005 (www.physics911.net/georgenelson.htm).

49 Colonel Ray, who has called the official story "the dog that doesn't hunt," says that the evidence suggests that "the conspiracy theory advanced by the administration" is not true. See Paul Joseph Watson, "Former Reagan Deputy and Colonel Says 9/11 'Dog That Doesn't Hunt,'" Knowledge Driven Revolution, 29 June 2006 (www.knowledgedrivenrevolution.com/Articles/200607/ 20060701_911_Ray.htm).

50 Morgan Reynolds, "9/11, Texas A&M University, and Heresy," in ISO, 101–16.

51 Steele has said: "I am forced to conclude that 9/11 was at a minimum allowed to happen as a pretext for war." Review of Webster Tarpley, *9/11 Synthetic Terror: Made in the USA*, 7 October 2006 (www.amazon.com/9-11-Synthetic-Terror-First/dp/0930852311/sr=1-1/qid=1165894073/ref=pd_bbs_sr_1/002-515 8292-7064018?ie=UTF8&s=books).

52 Captain Russ Wittenberg, "The Government Story They Handed Us about

9/11 is Total B.S. Plain and Simple," 17 July 2005 (www.arcticbeacon.com).

53 "Statement of Capt. Gregory M. Zeigler, Ph.D., US Army, Former US Army Intelligence Officer, 19 September 2006" (http://patriotsquestion911.com/Zeigler%20Statement.html).

54 Scholars for 9/11 Truth (http://911scholars.org); Scholars for 9/11 Truth and Justice (http://stj911.com); Veterans for 9/11 Truth (http://v911t.org); Pilots for 9/11 Truth (http://pilotsfor911truth.org); S.P.I.N.E. (http://physics911.net).

55 Professors Question 9/11 (http://patriotsquestion911.com/professors.html).

56 I have employed these terms in relation to discussions of the mind-body problem in David Ray Griffin, *Unsnarling the World-Knot: Consciousness, Freedom, and the Mind-Body Problem* (Berkeley and Los Angeles: University of California Press, 1998), ch. 2, "Paradigmatic and Wishful-and-Fearful Thinking."

57 Thomas Kuhn, *The Structure of Scientific Worldviews*, second ed. (Chicago: University of Chicago Press, 1970). This use of "paradigm" to refer to a worldview was only one of several ways in which Kuhn used the term.

58 Griffin, *Unsnarling the World-Knot*, 11.

59 Ian Markham, "Did Bush Cooperate with Terrorists? Making Conspiracy Theories Respectable Can Be Dangerous," *Zion's Herald* November/December 2004 (www.zhonline.org/archives/Nov2004_perspective2.html).

60 E-mail from Ian Markham, 24 March 2005.

61 David Ray Griffin, "Response to Markham," in *Conversations in Religion and Theology* 3/2 (November 2005), 217–36, in a section entitled "Current Conversations," which included Markham's original critique of NPH. Both essays are posted, under the title "Two Theologians Debate 9/11: David Ray Griffin and Ian Markham," on the website for Scholars for 9/11 Truth (www.scholarsfor911truth.org/ArticleTwoSpeak02May2006.html).

62 Bryan Sacks, "Making History: The Compromised 9-11 Commission," in Paul Zarembka, ed., *The Hidden History of 9-11-2001* (Amsterdam: Elsevier, 2006), 223–60, at 225.

63 David Manning, "The Secret Downing Street Memo: Secret and Strictly Personal—UK Eyes Only," *Sunday Times* (London) 1 May 2005 (www.timesonline.co.uk/article/0,,2087-1593607,00.html). For discussion, see Ray McGovern, "Proof the Fix Was In," Antiwar.com, 5 May 2005 (www.antiwar.com/mcgovern/index.php?articleid=5844), or Greg Palast, "Impeachment Time: 'Facts Were Fixed,'" BuzzFlash, 4 May 2005 (www.buzzflash.com/analysis/05/05/ana05013.html). For a more extended discussion, see Mark Danner, *The Secret Way to War: The Downing Street Memo and the Iraq War's Buried History* (New York: New York Review of Books, 2006).

64 See Col. W. Patrick Lang (ret.), "Drinking the Kool-Aid: Making the Case for War with Compromised Integrity and Intelligence," and Ray McGovern, "Sham Dunk: Cooking Intelligence for the President," in D. L. O'Huallachain and J. Forrest Sharpe, eds., *Neoconned Again: Hypocrisy, Lawlessness, and the Rape of Iraq* (Vienna, Va.: IHS Press, 2005), 249–75 and 277–305, respectively.

65 EPA, Press Release, 18 September 2001 (www.epa.gov/wtc/stories/headline_091801.htm).

66 Gareth Cook and Tatsha Robertson, "Another Worry: Asbestos Dust Poses Threat to Rescue Crews," *Boston Globe* 14 September 2001.

67 "9/11 Ground Zero Volunteer Saves Asbestos-Laden Shirt," *Medical News*

Today 14 April 2006 (www.medicalnewstoday.com/medicalnews.php? newsid= 41603).

68 Anthony DePalma, "Illness Persisting in 9/11 Workers, Big Study Finds," *New York Times* 6 September 2006 (www.nytimes.com/2006/09/06/ nyregion/06health.html?ex=1315195200&en=aaf1bba2e01bc497&ei=5088&p artner=rssnyt&emc=rss).

69 "Ground Zero Workers Not Protected By Federal Officials," *Medical News Today* 9 September 2006 (www.medicalnewstoday.com/ healthnews.php? newsid=51498).

70 Kristen Lombardi, "Death by Dust: The Frightening Link between the 9-11 Toxic Cloud and Cancer," *Village Voice* 28 November 2006 (http://villagevoice.com/news/0648%2Clombardi%2C75156%2C2.html). This essay is also posted at www.911truth.org/article.php?story=20061204132809573.

71 "Dust and Disease," *News Hour with Jim Lehrer* (PBS) 21 November 2006, available on YouTube as "'60 Percent of Ground Zero Workers Sick" (www.youtube.com:80/watch?v=2bA57ObvVLc). Six months earlier, at the time of a previous report ("Autopsy Confirms NYPD Detective Died as a Result of Rescue and Recovery Work at Ground Zero," News Inferno, 12 April 2006 [www.newsinferno.com/archives/1075]), Worby's lawsuit said that 41 people had died.

72 "Dust and Disease."

73 "Insider: EPA Lied About WTC Air," *CBS News* 8 September 2006 (www.cbsnews.com/stories/2006/09/08/earlyshow/main1985804.shtml).

74 EPA Office of Inspector General, "EPA's Response to the World Trade Center Collapse," 21 August 2003, Executive Summary and Chapter 2 (www.mindfully.org/Air/2003/EPA-WTC-OIG-Evaluation21aug03.htm); discussed in "White House Edited EPA's 9/11 Reports," by John Heilprin, Associated Press, *Seattle Post-Intelligencer* 23 August 2003 (http://seattlepi.nw source.com/national/136350_epa23.html). On the failure to wear protective gear, see "Ground Zero Workers Not Protected."

75 Kevin Smith and Alex Jones, "Updated: Pentagon Papers Author Daniel Ellsberg Says 9/11 Deserves Further Investigation," Infowars, 19 July 2006 (www.infowars.com/articles/terror/pentagon_papers_author_gov_maybe_did_911. htm).

76 Susan Haack, "Double-Aspect Foundherentism: A New Theory of Empirical Justification," *Philosophy and Phenomenological Research* 53/1 (March 1993): 116n8.

77 Griffin, *Unsnarling the World-Knot*, 11.

78 Cockburn, "The 9/11 Conspiracy Nuts."

79 JoAnn Wypijewski, "Conversations at Ground Zero: How Far We Have Fallen," *Counterpunch* 28 November 2006 (www.counterpunch.org/ jw11282006.html).

80 NPH 145.

81 E-mail from Robin Hordon, 20 December 2006.

82 See my "False-Flag Operations, 9/11, and the New Rome: A Christian Perspective," in Kevin Barrett, John B. Cobb Jr., and Sandra Lubarsky, eds., *9/11 and American Empire: Christians, Jews, and Muslims Speak Out* (Northampton: Olive Branch Press, 2006), or "9/11 and Prior False-Flag Operations," ch. 1 of

my *Christian Faith and the Truth Behind 9/11* (Louisville: Westminster John Knox Press, 2006).

83 Michael Parenti, *The Terrorism Trap: September 11 and Beyond* (San Francisco: City Lights, 2002) 93–94.

84 Audrey R. Kahin and George McT. Kahin, *Subversion as Foreign Policy: The Secret Eisenhower and Dulles Debacle in Indonesia* (Seattle: University of Washington Press, 1995).

85 For examples of the kinds of intimidation and retaliation that are used on people blowing the whistle on governmental wrongdoing of a much less serious nature than the orchestration of 9/11, see David Rose, "An Inconvenient Patriot," *Vanity Fair* September 2005 (available at www.informationclearinghouse.info/article9774.htm).

86 See "The Fake bin Laden Video" (www.whatreallyhappened.com/osamatape.html), as well as the statement by Bruce Lawrence in Chapter 2.

87 Ed Haas, "FBI says, 'No Hard Evidence Connecting Bin Laden to 9/11,'" Muckraker Report, 6 June 2006 (www.teamliberty.net/id267.html).

88 Michael Keefer, "Into the Ring with Counterpunch on 9/11: How Alexander Cockburn, Otherwise So Bright, Blanks Out on 9/11 Evidence," 911Truth.org, 6 December 2006 (www.911truth.org/article.php?story=20061206104001101).

89 The question of why the media have supported the official conspiracy theory about 9/11, in spite of the overwhelming evidence for the alternative theory, is a complex issue, which would require a separate book. Fortunately, one such book has already been written: Barrie Zwicker's *Towers of Deception: The Media Cover-Up of 9/11* (Gabriola Island, BC: New Society, 2006). See especially ch. 3, "Truth is Hidden in Plain Sight: 2001 Tricks for Avoiding the Obvious."

90 Muwakkil, "What's the 411 on 9/11?"

91 "Response to Chip Berlet's Review of *The New Pearl Harbor*," PublicEye.org, 1 May 2004 (www.publiceye.org/conspire/Post911/dubious_claims.html).

92 Bill Manning, "Selling Out the Investigation," *Fire Engineering* January 2002 (www.globalresearch.ca/articles/MAN309A.html).

93 James Glanz and Eric Lipton, *City in the Sky: The Rise and Fall of the World Trade Center* (New York: Times Books/Henry Holt, 2004) 330.

94 See FEMA, World Trade Center Building Performance Study, ch. 5, sect. 6.2, "Probable Collapse Sequence."

95 O&D, ch. 15.

CHAPTER ONE: 9/11 LIVE OR DISTORTED

1 Bronner 262–285.

2 The impact of Bronner's essay was increased by the availability of snippets from these tapes, which could be accessed from the online version of the article, to be played on TV and radio news reports about the article.

3 Bronner 282.

4 9/11 Commission Hearing, 23 May 2003 (www.9-11commission.gov/archive/hearing2/9-11Commission_Hearing_2003-05-23.htm).

5 "NORAD's Response Times," news release by the North American Aerospace Defense Command, 18 September 2001 (www.standdown.net/noradseptember182001pressrelease.htm).

6 The 9/11 Commission did not challenge NORAD's statement about AA Flight 11, according to which the FAA notified the military about its hijacking at 8:40, only about seven minutes before it struck the North Tower (see "NORAD's Response Times"). The 9/11 Commission was, in fact, more generous to the FAA, saying that it had notified NEADS at 8:38, meaning that there were still about nine minutes before Flight 11 would strike the North Tower.

7 Bronner 264.

8 Bronner 285.

9 Bronner 264.

10 Philip Shenon, "New Tapes Disclose Confusion Within the Military on Sept. 11," *New York Times* 3 August 2006 (www.nytimes.com/2006/08/03/us/03norad.html).

11 O&D 282–95.

12 James Mann, *Rise of the Vulcans: The History of Bush's War Cabinet* (New York: Viking, 2004) 316, 327–31.

13 These statements are quoted in Peter Lance, *Cover Up: What the Government Is Still Hiding About the War on Terror* (New York: Harper-Collins/ReganBooks, 2004) 139–40.

14 9/11 Commission Hearing, 23 May 2003. YouTube has Mineta's exchanges with Hamilton (http://www.youtube.com/watch?v=V7Vs7KnlpXU) and Roemer (http://www.youtube.com/watch?v=6Z2c8IkemYI). One objection to Mineta's testimony has been that he began by saying: "When I got to the White House, it was being evacuated." Because Richard Clarke suggested that the evacuation did not begin until about 9:45, after the strike on the Pentagon (Clarke 7-8), it could be argued that Mineta was wrong about his time of arrival. However, during a live broadcast at 9:52, CNN correspondent John King reported that the evacuation had begun slowly "about 30 minutes ago" but that "in the last 10 minutes or so, the people who came out . . . were told and ordered by the Secret Service to run" (The White House Has Been Evacuated," CNN September 11, 2001); this story was recently reprinted in "Mineta's Testimony Confirmed," George Washington's Blog, March 4, 2007 (http://georgewashington.blogspot.com/2007/03/minetas-testimony-confirmed.html). Clarke was evidently not aware of the slower evacuation that had been going on some 20 minutes prior to the rushed evacuation. In any case, Clarke confirms Mineta's statement that he saw Clarke at about 9:15 and that Cheney was then already in the PEOC: Shortly before Mineta arrived, Clarke reports, Condoleezza Rice said: "I'm going to the PEOC to be with the Vice President" (5, 4).

16 See O&D 241–44.

17 "The Vice President Appears on *Meet the Press* with Tim Russert," Camp David, Maryland, 16 September 2001 (www.whitehouse.gov/vicepresident/news-speeches/speeches/vp20010916.html).

18 In an account given for CNN a year later, Cheney said that after the second World Trade Center tower was hit (at 9:03) and he had telephoned the president, "My [Secret Service] agent all of a sudden materialized right beside me and said, 'Sir, we have to leave now.' He grabbed me and propelled me out of my office, down the hall, and into the underground shelter in the White House." The CNN report then said: "After the planes struck the twin towers, a third took a chunk out of the Pentagon. Cheney then heard a report that a plane over Pennsylvania was heading for Washington." ("Cheney Recalls Taking Charge from the Bunker,"

CNN.com/Inside Politics, 11 September 2002 [http://archives.cnn.com/2002/ALLPOLITICS/09/11/ar911.king.cheney/index.html]).

19 "9/11: Interviews by Peter Jennings: ABC News, 11 September 2002 (http://s3.amazonaws.com/911timeline/2002/abcnews091102.html).

20 9/11CR 27, 34. Another problem with this claim is that the Commission itself says: "At 9:34, Ronald Reagan Washington National Airport advised the Secret Service of an unknown aircraft heading in the direction of the White House" (9/11CR 9). It does not explain why, if this is true, the military did not know about this flight until 9:36.

21 9/11CR xvi.

22 O&D.

23 9/11CR 160.

24 *Newsweek* 15 October 2001; *San Francisco Chronicle* 4 October 2001; Daniel Hopsicker, *Welcome to Terrorland: Mohamed Atta and the 9/11 Cover-up in Florida* (Eugene, OR: MadCowPress, 2004).

25 "Terrorist Stag Parties," *Wall Street Journal* 10 October 2001 (www.opinionjournal.com/best/?id=95001298).

26 9/11CR 248.

27 David Bamford, "Hijack 'Suspect' Alive in Morocco," BBC News 22 September 2001 (http://news.bbc.co.uk/1/hi/world/middle_east/1558669.stm).

28 See David Harrison, "Revealed: The Men with Stolen Identities," *Telegraph* 23 September 2001 (www.telegraph.co.uk/news/main.jhtml ?xml=/news/2001/09/23/widen23.xml).

29 9/11CR 5.

30 According to a 2001 story, NORAD scrambled fighters 129 times in 2000 (Linda Slobodian, "NORAD on Heightened Alert: Role of Air Defence Agency Rapidly Transformed in Wake of Sept. 11 Terrorist Attacks," *Calgary Herald* 13 October 2001; available at http://911research.wtc7.net/cache/planes/ analysis/norad/calgaryherald101301_scrables.html). According to an Associated Press story in 2001, the military scrambled fighters 67 times between September 2000 and June 2001; see Leslie Miller, "Military Now Notified Immediately of Unusual Air Traffic Events," Associated Press, 12 August 2002 (http://911research.wtc7.net/ cache/planes/analysis/norad/020812ap.html). According to a 1994 report by the US General Accounting Office, moreover, NORAD had scrambled fighters 1,518 times during the previous four years, which would have been an average of 379 times per year (www.fas.org/man/gao/ gao9476.htm).

31 This facility, in spite of its name, is in Nashua, New Hampshire.

32 9/11CR 18–20.

33 Mark Clayton, "Controllers' Tale of Flight 11," *Christian Science Monitor* 13 September 2001 (www.csmonitor.com/2001/0913/p1s2-usju.html); Tom Brokaw in "America Remembers: The Skies Over America," NBC 11 September 2002 (www.jonhs.net/911/skies_over_america.htm).

34 NPH 4.

35 The FAA's *Aeronautical Information Manual: Official Guide to Basic Flight Information and Air Traffic Control (ATC) Procedures* (www.faa.gov).

36 E-mail from Robin Hordon, 27 December 2006.

37 E-mail from Hordon, 18 December 2006.

38 Bob Arnot, "Cockpit Security, Quick Response Not in Evidence Tuesday,"

MSNBC 12 September 2001 (http://s3.amazonaws.com/911timeline/2001/msnbc091201.html).

39 The unbelievable nature of the official story is (unintentionally) made even clearer by the earlier cited NBC show, "America Remembers: The Skies Over America," in which Tom Brokaw interviewed several controllers. Pete Zalewski, the Boston controller who was in charge of AA 11, said that after it went NORDO, he tried "to call that aircraft 12 times." Then at 8:20 or 8:21, after the transponder goes off and the flight abruptly changes course, Lino Martin, another controller who is now watching the flight, says: "I'm thinking, 'Well, maybe there's really something wrong. First there's no radio, now we lost this transponder.'" But he apparently does not think about having NEADS called. Zalewski then said: "I very quietly turned to the supervisor and I said, "Would you please come over here? I think something is seriously wrong with this plane." So the supervisor, John Schipanni, was alerted, but he also evidently did not think that NEADS should be called. Tom Roberts, another controller, reported that they then tried to see if the pilots from another flight could talk to the pilots of AA 11, after which Brokaw says: "But that too, fails. There is still no reply—the silence increasingly ominous as the jet [is] now drastically off course . . . . Controllers are scrambling to . . . create a safe zone around the runaway plane, moving every other flight in the area out of the way, from the ground, all the way up to 35,000 feet." So although the silence was "ominous" and the flight was clearly creating huge problems, no one suggested asking the military to help. The account becomes even more absurd after 8:24. Zalewski says that after hearing a foreign voice, which "sounded almost Middle Eastern, . . . I immediately . . . knew it was a hijack. . . . I immediately stood up and yelled at the supervisor, 'John, get over here immediately right now.'" John Shipanni, the supervisor, evidently had wandered off, not thinking that the situation, in which the plane was drastically off course and had been out of radio and transponder contact for several minutes, demanded his constant supervision. (Hordon comments: "A good supervisor would be looking over Zalewski's shoulder, sensing what was going on, and would be a half-step ahead of the situation" [Hordon e-mail to Griffin 9 January 2007].) In any case, there is no sign, in this account, that Schipanni or anyone else at Boston Center had NEADS called. And there is still no sign of this several minutes later, when "the plane makes another dramatic turn—south toward New York City." Next, when controller Tom Roberts hands off the flight to New York controller John Hartling, telling him that Boston thinks it is hijacked, Hartling says that his reaction was: "I didn't believe him. Because I didn't think that that stuff would happen anymore, especially in this country"—as if there could be some other explanation for the plane's strange behavior and the foreign voice emanating from its cockpit. So he, instead of calling the military about AA 11, simply makes sure that UA 175 does not get very close to it, then hands AA 11 off to Dave Bottiglia, who has "no idea what is to come [his] way"—as if everyone who was going to be dealing with AA 11 would not have been keyed into the discussion long before. This story, to understate, does not have the ring of truth.

40 E-mail from Colin Scoggins, 1 January 2007.

41 E-mail from Hordon, 18 December 2006.

42 E-mail from Hordon, 18 December 2006.

43 E-mail from Hordon, 20 December 2006.

44 Paul Joseph Watson, "Boston Air Traffic Controller Says 9/11 An Inside Job," Prison Planet, 14 December 2006 (www.prisonplanet.com/articles/december2006/141206trafficcontroller.htm). This article is based on a telephone interview with Hordon by Rob Balsamo, the founder of Pilots for 9/11 Truth, 13 December 2006 (http://video.google.com/videoplay?docid=-9147890225218338952&hl=en).

45 Clarke 2.

46 O&D 188.

47 9/11CR 37.

48 O&D 186.

49 Tom Flocco, "Rookie in the 9-11 Hot Seat?" tomflocco.com, 17 June 2004 (http://tomflocco.com/fs/NMCCOpsDirector.htm).

50 O&D 235–36.

51 Flocco, "Rookie in the 9–11 Hot Seat?"

52 Tom Flocco, "9–11 Probe Continues to Bypass Executive Branch Testimony," tomflocco.com, 13 October 2003 (http://tomflocco.com/fs/911ProbeContinues.htm).

53 Flocco, "Rookie in the 9-11 Hot Seat?" citing *US News and World Report* 8 September 2003.

54 9/11CR 20. To anticipate: The first part is false because, as explained below in the text, Daniel Bueno of Boston Center contacted a military facility, Otis Air Force Base Tower, not only Cape TRACON, which is the FAA facility. The second part of the sentence is triply false: No one at Boston Center tried to contact the base at Atlantic City. Colin Scoggins, who suggested that NEADS try to get fighters from Atlantic City, did not suggest it at this time but later, during what was "probably [his] 4th or 5th call to them," when AA 11 was over New York City. And although Atlantic City was no longer an alert site, it, as explained in the text below, had fighters that perhaps could have been launched or, if already airborne for their daily training mission, diverted (e-mails from Scoggins, 11 and 12 January 2007). Besides getting all these things wrong, the 9/11 Commission even spelled Scoggins' first name "Collin" instead of "Colin" (9/11CR 458n101).

55 9/11CR 18–20.

56 E-mail from Hordon, 20 December 2006. Hordon's description corresponds with that given by Leslie Filson in 1999: "Crew chiefs and pilots also train together, always practicing for a scramble. . . . The alert pilots hone their skills in a number of ways: They fly with the 325th Fighter Wing as adversary pilots. . . and fly against one another. They also do practice scrambles with the Southeast Air Defense Sector" (Filson, *Sovereign Skies: Air National Guard Takes Command of 1st Air Force* [First Air Force, 1999] 96–97).

57 9/11CR 18. The quotation is from "FAA Order 7610.4J: Special Military Operations" (first effective on 3 November 1998, but with changes effective 3 July 2000, and 12 July 2001), ch. 7, "Escort of Hijacked Aircraft" (available at http://news.findlaw.com/cnn/docs/terrorism/chp7.html).

58 E-mail from Hordon, 20 December 2006.

59 9/11CR 17 and 458n101.

60 9/11CR 458n102.

61 9/11CR 18.

62 E-mail from Hordon, 20 December 2006.

63 Bronner 264. Hordon also finds this very suspicious, writing: "It is claimed that the first thing on the tapes is Dooley and Watson talking about love seats and couches. Now, most recordings are not 'open line' so that general conversation is overheard. Tapes are recording all the time, but the input is from 'keyed' mics or telephone receivers that have been 'picked up' to communicate with. *If* the 'couch' conversation were true, then why did it start right at that point? Didn't their shift start earlier?" (e-mail from Hordon, 2 January 2007).

64 Bronner 265.

65 Bronner 264; 9/11CR 20.

66 Hart Seely, "Amid Crisis Simulation, 'We Were Suddenly No-Kidding Under Attack,'" Newhouse News Service, 25 January 2002 (www.newhouse news.com/archive/story1a012802.html).

67 "Moments of Crisis: Part I: Terror Hits the Towers," ABC News, 3 October 2002 (http://web.archive.org/web/20021003210756/http://abcnews.go.com/onair/DailyNews/sept11_moments_1.html); "9/11: Interviews by Peter Jennings," ABC News, 11 September 2002.

68 This statement was made in the blog mentioned in note 102.

69 E-mail from Scoggins, 14 December 2006.

70 When I asked Scoggins about this apparent contradiction, he replied that it has been a problem for him, too. On the one hand, he knows that he "made all of these calls." On the other hand, he is quite certain that he did not get onto the floor until about 8:35. As a result, although he had tried to write up a chronology, he "couldn't get a timeline that made any sense" (Scoggins e-mail to Griffin, 8 January 2007).

71 E-mail from Scoggins, 31 December 2006.

72 E-mails from Scoggins, 8 and 11 January 2007.

73 9/11 Commission Hearing, 17 June 2004 (www.9-11commission.gov/archive/hearing12/9-11Commission_Hearing_2004-06-17.htm).

74 9/11 Commission Hearing, 17 June 2004.

75 E-mail from Scoggins, 30 December 2006.

76 9/11CR 19. According to the FAA's "Summary of Air Traffic Hijack Events, September 11, 2001" (www.gwu.edu/~nsarchiv/NSAEBB/NSAEBB165/faa7.pdf), Boston contacted both the ROC and the Herndon Command Center (see 8:25:00).

77 E-mail from Hordon, 12 January 2007.

78 Jim Dwyer, "Takeoffs Continued Until Second Jet Hit Trade Center, Transcripts Show," *New York Times* 30 December 2003 (www.mishalov.com/wtc_takeoffs.html).

79 E-mails from Scoggins, 8 January 2007 and 31 January 2007.

80 Leslie Filson, *Air War over America: Sept. 11 Alters Face of Air Defense Mission,* foreword by Larry K. Arnold (Public Affairs: Tyndall Air Force Base, 2003), 50.

81 Scoggins says that after calling the Otis Tower, Bueno told Cooper to call NEADS (e-mail from Scoggins, 12 January 2007).

82 Bronner 266.

83 Filson, *Air War over America,* 50.

84 Bronner 266.

85 E-mail from Hordon, 19 December 2006.

86 E-mails from Hordon, 19 December 2006 and 11 January 2007.

87 "PAVE PAWS, Watching North America's Skies, 24 Hours a Day" (http://web.archive.org/web/20010927062454/www.pavepaws.org/). The statement quoted in the text, which was on the site in 2003, has in the meantime been removed.

88 Bronner 266–67.

89 E-mail from Hordon, 31 December 2006.

90 E-mail from Scoggins, 1 January 2007.

91 E-mail from Scoggins, 14 December 2006.

92 Bronner 267.

93 E-mail from Hordon, 31 December 2006.

94 E-mail from Hordon, 31 December 2006.

95 E-mail from Hordon, 2 January 2007.

96 Bronner 266.

97 Bronner 267.

98 9/11CR 20.

99 This document, often referred to simply as CJCSI 3610.01A, is available at www.dtic.mil/doctrine/jel/cjcsd/cjcsi/3610_01a.pdf. Some students of 9/11 have thought that this document, with its statement about forwarding requests for DoD approval to the secretary of defense, changed the procedure. However, this same statement was already contained in the version of this document published in July 1997 (www.dtic.mil/doctrine/jel/cjcsd/cjcsi/3610_01.pdf).

100 The idea that no standard procedures should prevent "immediate responses" in emergency situations is also stated in other places in this memo of 1 June 2001. Section 4.4, after saying that the secretary of defense retains approval authority for various types of support, concludes by saying: "Nothing in this Directive prevents a commander from exercising his or her immediate emergency response authority as outlined in DoD Directive 3025.1." And Section 4.5 begins with these words: "With the exception of immediate responses under imminently serious conditions, as provided in paragraph 4.7.1., below. . . . " I have discussed this issue at greater length in the Afterword to the second edition of NPH.

101 O&D 165–66.

102 Scoggins made this remark in a response to a previous interrogator on a blog. In his first letter to me, 26 October 2006, in which he said he would be willing to answer questions, he said that he had "posted a little bit online on a few blogs." In response, I suggested that a good way to begin would be for him to send me those statements, which he did on 27 October 2006. The passage quoted here was in that material. FAA Order 7610.4J, which is the version that was in effect on 9/11, appears to be no longer publicly available, but Chapter 7, "Escort of Hijacked Aircraft," is available at http://news.findlaw.com/cnn/docs/terrorism/chp7.html.

103 Filson, Air War over America, 50.

104 9/11 Commission Hearing, 23 May 2003.

105 Filson 50.

106 E-mail from Scoggins, 12 December 2006.

107 E-mail from Scoggins 8 January 2007.

108 E-mail from Scoggins 8 January 2007.

109 Airman, December 1999 (www.af.mil/news/airman/1299/home2.htm).

110 Kevin Dennehy, "Local Reservists Await the Call," Cape Cod Times 15

September 2001 (www.capecodonline.com/special/terror/terrornews/local reservists15.htm).

111 NORAD, "Newspaper Article Contains Inaccuracies," news release, 1 November 2000 (http://web.archive.org/web/20020811103340/www.norad.mil/rel0016.htm).

112 That statement was cited in Nafeez Mosaddeq Ahmed, *The War on Freedom: How and Why America Was Attacked September 11, 2001* (Joshua Tree, CA: Tree of Life Publications, 2002) 151.

113 William B. Scott, "Exercise Jump-Starts Response to Attacks," *Aviation Week and Space Technology* 3 June 2002 (http://web.archive.org/web/20020917072642/www.aviationnow.com/content/publication/awst/20020603/avi_stor.htm).

114 Bronner 267.

115 Although it has widely been thought that the military would not shoot down passenger planes, especially over a city, a shot-down plane would cause far less death and destruction than a plane allowed to crash into a skyscraper. On this issue, see the later statement by Hordon.

116 Watson, "Boston Air Traffic Controller Says 9/11 An Inside Job."

117 E-mail from Hordon, 18 December 2006.

118 E-mail from Hordon, 8 January 2007.

119 This statement was in the blog mentioned in note 102.

120 E-mail from Scoggins, 8 January 2007.

121 E-mail from Hordon, 30 December 2006.

122 E-mail from Hordon, 2 January 2007.

123 9/11CR 21–23.

124 Bronner 268.

125 "NORAD's Response Times," 18 September 2001.

126 Miller, "Military Now Notified Immediately of Unusual Air Traffic Events." The same statement was made in "FAA Controllers Detail Sept. 11 Events" by Associated Press writer Steve LeBlanc (www.boston.com/news/daily/12/attacks_faa.htm).

127 Scott Simmie, "The Scene at NORAD on Sept. 11," *Toronto Star* 9 December 2001 (www.911readingroom.org/bib/whole_document.php?article_id=92).

128 "Moments of Crisis," ABC News, 3 October 2002.

129 Seely, "Amid Crisis Simulation, 'We Were Suddenly No-Kidding Under Attack.'"

130 Tom Brokaw, "America Remembers."

131 This discrepancy—whether the planes were 20 minutes away, as Brokaw, in conformity with NORAD's timeline of 11 September 2001, said, or just a couple of minutes away, as this controller said—is one of many indications that this story was also a falsehood. The point at hand, however, is that the story that the military is now telling on the basis of the NORAD tapes is very different from the story the military and the press had been telling prior to the summer of 2004.

132 Brokaw, "America Remembers."

133 This memo, dated 21 May 2003, is headed: "FAA Communications with NORAD on September 11, 2001: FAA Clarification Memo to 9/11 Independent Commission." It was widely understood to have been written by Laura Brown. But when it was discussed by the 9/11 Commission on May 23 (www.9-

11commission.gov/archive/hearing2/9-11Commission_Hearing_2003-05-23.htm),
it was presented by Commissioner Richard Ben-Veniste as written by "Mr. Asmus
and Ms. Schuessler." However, during a telephone conversation I had with Laura
Brown on Sunday, 15 August 2004, she confirmed that she had written the memo.
Nevertheless, the fact that it came to the Commission with Linda Schuessler's name
on it gives it added weight. She was the deputy director of system operations at the
Herndon Command Center and "was in charge" on 9/11, because Director Jack
Kies was out of town (FAA Employee Site, 2006 News Archives, 18 May 2006
[http://employees.faa.gov/news/employee_news/archive/news_update/index.cfm?ne
ws_archive=dsp_news_051806.cfm]). This memo is available at www.911truth.org/
article.php?story=2004081200421797.

134 9/11 Commission Hearing, 23 May 2003.

135 9/11CR 20.

136 9/11CR 24.

137 Bronner 267.

138 Bronner 268.

139 Bronner 268.

140 Bronner 09:07:20. This statement was not contained in the magazine
article but was available in the audio material that accompanied the online version.
This audio material was printed out, however, in a later online version
(www.vanityfair.com/politics/features/2006/08/norad200608).

141 The 9/11CR, besides saying that "the chain of command authorizing the
use of force [normally] runs from the president to the secretary of defense and
from the secretary to the combatant commander" (43), quotes military officials as
saying that they "would need 'executive' orders to shoot [a plane] down"
(458n98). Bronner, speaking of Nasypany, says: "he doesn't have the authority to
order a shootdown, nor does Marr or Arnold or Vice President Cheney, for that
matter. The order will need to come from President Bush."

142 See note 100.

143 E-mail from Hordon, 20 December 2006.

144 9/11CR 24.

145 9/11CR 459n120.

146 9/11 CR 459n120. The question of who was giving orders has added
importance in light of the reported statement of Captain Craig Borgstrom, one of
the Langley pilots, that they "were getting orders from a lot of different people"
(Filson, *Air War over America*, 66).

147 9/11CR 24.

148 Bronner 268

149 E-mails from Kyle Hence, 23 and 29 September 2004.

150 Filson, *Air War over America*, 50.

151 E-mail from Scoggins, 20 December 2006.

152 9/11CR 17.

153 Scott, "Exercise Jump-Starts Response to Attacks."

154 Walt Wasilewski, "174th Ready to Fly Again, If Called," *Post-Standard*
(Syracuse), 25 September 2001 (http://web.archive.org/web/20021104040712/
http://syracuse.com/news/content.ssf?/newsstories/20010925_cpnstor.html).

155 "Moments of Crisis," ABC News, 3 October 2002.

156 9/11CR 34.

157 9/11CR 34.

158 9/11CR 24.

159 9/11CR 34.

160 9/11CR 27.

161 *Village Voice* 13 September 2001; *Guardian* 17 October 2001.

162 Brokaw, "America Remembers." Pamela Freni likewise writes: "At 9:07AM a message was sent from the Air Traffic Control System Command Center in northern Virginia to every air traffic facility in the nation, announcing the first hijacking" (Pamela S. Freni, *Ground Stop: An Inside Look at the Federal Aviation Administration on September 11, 2001* [iUniverse, 2003] 59).

163 E-mail from Hordon, 22 December 2006.

164 9/11 Commission Hearing, 23 May 2003.

165 *Guardian,* 17 October 2001; *New York Times* 17 October 2001; *Boston Globe* 23 November 2001. The reported deviation in AA 77's flight course was shown in a map provided by *USA Today*; see "The Official Truth in Three Versions" (www.public-action.com/911/4flights.html).

166 *Arlington County: After-Action Report on the Response to the September 11 Attack on the Pentagon,* 2002 (www.arlingtonva.us/departments/Fire/edu/about/docs/after_report.pdf) C–45.

167 For Laura Brown's memo, see note 133.

168 Telephone conversation with Laura Brown, 15 August 2004.

169 Matthew Wald, "After the Attacks: Sky Rules; Pentagon Tracked Deadly Jet but Found No Way to Stop It," *New York Times* 15 September 2001 (www.attackonamerica.net/pentagontrackeddeadlyjet.html).

170 9/11 Commission Hearing, 23 May 2003. On Laura Brown as the author of this memo, see note 133.

171 9/11CR 36.

172 The other high official was Bill Peacock, the FAA director of air traffic services, who was in New Orleans. Having learned about the attack on the first tower and gotten to his hotel room, Pamela Freni reports, "He flipped through the channels and found CNN just in time to join the world in viewing the attack on the second tower. He determinedly dialed the phone, trying to connect with his staff. His call was routed to the phone in the conference room next door to his office at headquarters, into the never-ending teleconference. His deputy Jeff Griffith was serving as liaison to FAA Deputy Monte Belger, trying to gather a tactical notion of the attacks" (Freni, *Ground Stop,* 22).

173 9/11CR 28–29.

174 9/11CR 29–30.

175 9/11 Commission Hearing, 23 May 2003.

176 9/11CR 36.

177 Clarke 7.

178 9/11 Commission Hearing, 17 June 2004. There were, in fact, three officers in the "military cell" at Herndon that morning—Colonel John Czabaranek, Lt. Colonel Michael-Anne Cherry, and Major Kevin Bridges—and they reportedly become "immediately involved in coordinating FAA . . . Command Center actions with military elements." See (8:50AM) and (Before 9:03AM) in the "Complete 911 Timeline" at Cooperative Research (www.cooperativeresearch.org/ context.jsp? item=a903faamilitarylink#a903faamilitarylink).

179 9/11 Commission Hearing, 17 June 2004. The presence of the military liaison at FAA headquarters in Washington, DC, is mentioned by Pamela Freni, who speaks of "the onsite Department of Defense (DoD) liaison to the FAA" (Freni, *Ground Stop*, 21).

180 Clarke 7.

181 Cheney's statement was made on *Meet the Press*, NBC News, 16 September 2001. Riggs's statement is in "Spotlight on: Barbara Riggs," President's Council of Cornell Women, Spring 2006 (http://pccw.alumni.cornell.edu/ news/newsletters/spring06/riggs.html). My thanks to Matthew Everett for this and many of the other references in this chapter.

182 Jere Longman, *Among the Heroes: United 93 and the Passengers and Crew Who Fought Back* (HarperCollins, 2002) 107–10. Although, as I suggest later, the call was probably fabricated, rather than really being from her husband, Deema Burnett did receive the call and did contact the FBI.

183 Brokaw, "America Remembers."

184 Rowland Morgan, *Flight 93 Revealed: What Really Happened on the 9/11 'Let's Roll' Flight?* (New York: Carroll & Graf, 2006) 71.

185 "9/11: Interviews by Peter Jennings."

186 9/11CR 34.

187 Scott, "Exercise Jump-Starts Response to Attacks," *Cape Cod Times* 21 August 2002.

188 Richard Wallace, "What Did Happen to Flight 93?" Mirror.co.uk, 12 September 2002 (available at http://911research.wtc7.net/cache/planes/ evidence/mirror_whatdidhappen.html).

189 This exchange is quoted in Thierry Meyssan, *9/11: The Big Lie* (London: Carnot, 2002) 162.

190 O&D 150–51.

191 9/11CR 30.

192 9/11CR 41.

193 9/11CR 41. Bronner, repeating the claim with which the movie *United 93* ends, says that the shoot-down authorization was not given by President Bush until 10:18 (282). In saying this, he differs somewhat with the 9/11 Commission. It said that the authorization was probably first given sometime between 10:10 and 10:15. And whereas the Commission says that Cheney talked to the president at 10:18, it expresses skepticism about the claim, made by both Bush and Cheney, that Bush gave Cheney the authorization shortly after 10:00 (see 9/11CR 40–41 and O&D 245–46).

194 Associated Press, 13 September 2001.

195 General Myers Confirmation Hearing, Senate Armed Services Committee, Washington DC, 13 September 2001 (http://emperors-clothes.com/9-11backups/mycon.htm).

196 *Boston Herald* 15 September 2001. Wolfowitz's statement was also referred to in Matthew Wald's *New York Times* article of that day, "After the Attacks: Sky Rules."

197 Dave Foster, "UST Grad Guides Bombers in War," *Aquin*, 4 December 2002 (www.stthomas.edu/aquin/archive/041202/anaconda.html).

198 Matthew L. Wald with Kevin Sack, "'We Have Some Planes,' Hijacker Told Controller," *New York Times* 16 October 2001.

199 "9/11: Interviews by Peter Jennings."

200 9/11CR 37; Clarke 6–7; on the evacuation, see n. 14, above.

201 "Cheney Recalls Taking Charge from Bunker," CNN.com/Inside Politics, 11 September 2002 (http://archives.cnn.com/2002/ALLPOLITICS/09/11/ar911.king.cheney/index.html).

202 "9/11: Interviews by Peter Jennings," ABC News, 11 September 2002.

203 "9/11: Interviews by Peter Jennings."

204 Filson, *Air War over America,* 72.

205 Filson 68.

206 Filson 71.

207 This part of Arnold's testimony conflicts, of course, with his earlier statements, according to which the military knew about UA 93 a *long* time before it crashed.

208 Larry Arnold, "MG Larry Arnold on UAL Flight 93," NavySEALs.com, 8 June 2006 (www.navyseals.com/community/articles/article.cfm?id=9723).

209 Bronner 282.

210 Bronner 282.

211 Bronner 275. In 9/11CR the statement reads: "I just had a report that American 11 is still in the air, and it's on its way toward—heading toward Washington" (26).

212 9/11CR 34.

213 *Christian Science Monitor* 13 September 2001.

214 ABC News, September 6, 2002.

215 *New York Times* 13 September 2001; Seely, "Amid Crisis Simulation, 'We Were Suddenly No-Kidding Under Attack.'"

216 9/11CR 34.

217 "9/11: Interviews by Peter Jennings."

218 Bronner 267.

219 Seely, "Amid Crisis Simulation"; James Bamford, *A Pretext for War* (New York: Doubleday, 2004), 13–14.

220 Seely, "Amid Crisis Simulation."

221 Brokaw, "America Remembers."

222 9/11 Commission Hearing, 17 June 2004.

223 Bronner 275.

224 Bronner 275.

225 9/11CR 31.

226 Bronner 285, 264.

227 Bronner 282.

228 9/11CR 34.

229 See NPH, ch. 1–2.

230 Philip Shenon and Jim Dwyer, "Agency Says Military Did Not Lie to 9/11 Panel," *New York Times* 4 August 2006 (www.nytimes.com/2006/08/05/washington/05norad.html?ei=5090&en=336b951af522d8fe&ex=1312430400&adxnnl=1&partner=rssuserland&emc=rss&adxnnlx=1168974313–l/kVXgp+TGIqaZt5V53btg).

231 E-mail from Hordon, 18 December 2006.

232 E-mail from Hordon, 2 December 2007.

233 William M. Arkin, "When Seeing and Hearing Isn't Believing," *Washington Post* 1 February 1999 (www.washingtonpost.com/ac2/wp-dyn?pagename=article&node=&contentId=A45085-2000Feb28).

234 The accuracy that had been achieved by voice changers that were commercially available in 2004 is suggested by the following ad: "Is your spouse cheating on you? Call them and use a Telephone Voice Changer. Pretend to be their lover and tell him or her that your spouse knows about the affair" ("Telephone Voice Changers," Brickhouse Security [www.brickhousesecurity.com/telephone-voice-changers.html]). US intelligence agencies would probably have had such voice changers several years earlier.

235 Telephone interview with Laura Brown on 15 August 2004.

236 Mark Clayton, "Controllers' Tale of Flight 11," *Christian Science Monitor* 13 September 2001 (www.csmonitor.com/2001/0913/p1s2-usju.html).

237 A. K. Dewdney, "The Cellphone and Airfone Calls from Flight UA93," Physics 911, 9 June 2003 (http://physics911.net/cell phoneflight93.htm). The exact number of the alleged calls that were supposedly cell phone calls is debatable. Dewdney used the figure of 13. But I have, with Dewdney's permission, used the figure of 9, which is the number suggested by Rowland Morgan, *Flight 93 Revealed*, 49–51.

238 A.K. Dewdney, "Project Achilles Report: Parts One, Two and Three," Physics 911, 19 April 2003 (www.physics911.net/public/projectachilles.htm). In his essay, Dewdney applied this language to the likelihood that 13 calls would be completed. But in an e-mail of 21 November 2006, he agreed that it also applies to the likelihood that 9 calls would succeed.

239 Dewdney made these comments in the e-mail of November 21, mentioned in the previous note. The results of his twin-engine experiments are reported in Barrie Zwicker, *Towers of Deception: The Media Cover-Up of 9/11* (Gabriola Island, BC: New Society Publishers, 2006) 375.

240 A. K. Dewdney, "The Cellphone and Airfone Calls from Flight UA93."

241 9/11CR 11–12, 29.

242 Chris Dahler, "Cellphone Use in Aircraft May Not Be Dangerous," AVweb AVmail, October 1999 (www.avweb.com/other/avma9910.html).

243 *Aviation Week* 20 July 2004.

244 QUALCOMM Press Release, "American Airlines and QUALCOMM Complete Test Flight to Evaluate In-Cabin Mobile Phone Use," 15 July 2004 (www.qualcomm.com/press/releases/2004/040715_aa_testflight.html).

245 Longman, *Among the Heroes*, 129–33.

246 Dewdney, "The Cellphone and Airfone Calls." Although Dewdney in the second quotation wrote "cellphone calls," his suggestion could apply equally to the alleged Airfone calls.

247 A good test case is provided by the transcripts of the calls from "Tom Burnett" to Burnett's wife, Deena Burnett, because there were four of these calls, which contained considerable dialogue (available at www.tomburnett foundation.org/tomburnett_transcript.html). One noticeable fact is that, except for uttering Deena's name a few times, the caller never mentions a name. For example, when he, in his fourth call, asks about the children, he simply calls them "the kids." But the most suspicious fact is that when Deena then tells "Tom" that they are asking to talk to him, he says: "Tell them I'll talk to them later." This is

20 minutes after he had realized that the hijackers were on a suicide mission, planning to "crash this plane into the ground," and 10 minutes after he and others had decided they must, as soon as they are "over a rural area," try to gain control of the plane. The hijackers have already killed one person. So "Tom" knows that there is a good chance that he will die in the next few minutes, one way or the other. And yet, rather than taking this perhaps last opportunity to speak to his children, he tells his wife to tell them that he will "talk to them later"—a move that prevented him from having to demonstrate that he knew anything about them, even their names.

248 Greg Gordon, "Prosecutors Play Flight 93 Cockpit Recording," KnoxNews.com, 12 April 2006 (www.knoxsingles.com/shns/story.cfm?pk=MOUSSAOUI-04-12-06&cat=WW); quoted in Morgan, *Flight 93 Revealed*, 182, n. 87; emphasis added.

249 "United States v. Zacharias Moussaoui: Prosecution Trial Exhibits" (www.vaed.uscourts.gov/notablecases/moussaoui/exhibits/prosecution.html). My thanks to Elias Davidson for this information.

250 Editorial, "Our Porous Air Defenses on 9/11," *New York Times* 13 August 2006 (www.nytimes.com/2006/08/13/opinion/13sun2.html?_r=1&oref=slogin).

CHAPTER TWO: THE REAL 9/11 CONSPIRACY THEORY

1 WP 102; see also 254.

2 WP 102, 254, 255.

3 WP 86; see also 253.

4 WP 258.

5 WP 86, 253.

6 WP 259.

7 WP 268.

8 WP 86, 127.

9 WP 260.

10 WP 263.

11 9/11 Commission Hearing, 23 May 2003 (www.911commission.gov/archive/hearing2/9-11Commission_Hearing_2003-05-23.htm).

12 Clarke 7.

13 WP 264, quoting 9/11CR 34 (albeit imperfectly, leaving out "the" before "FAA").

14 WP 265. For the full discussion between Ben-Veniste and Arnold, see O&D 196–99.

15 WP 261.

16 WP 268.

17 WP 254.

18 E-mail from Robin Hordon, 16 January 2007. Without a transponder signal, Hordon emphasizes, positive radar contact could have been reestablished only with the help of the pilot, who must either report flying over some geographical point known to air traffic control or else execute two turns at the controller's instruction. Only upon seeing a radar target over this point or making these turns can the controller consider positive radar contact to have been established.

19 9/11 Commission Hearing, 23 May 2003.

20 9/11CR 225–26, 242, 520n56.

21 9/11CR 530n147.

22 WP 216.

23 WP 54.

24 9/11CR 39.

25 O&D 43.

26 The *San Francisco Chronicle* 11 September 2002, cited in Allan Wood and Paul Thompson, "An Interesting Day: President Bush's Movements and Actions on 9/11," Center for Cooperative Research (www.cooperativeresearch.org), under "When Did Bush First Learn of the Attacks." In another wording of the new story, Card said, "Not that many seconds later the president excused himself from the classroom" (MSNBC, 9 September 2002).

27 WP 253.

28 WP 116, 253, 256, 322.

29 WP 268.

30 WP 322.

31 WP 323.

32 WP 269–70.

33 WP 275.

34 WP 33.

35 WP 116.

36 Griffin, *Christian Faith and the Truth Behind 9/11: A Call to Reflection and Action* (Louisville: Westminster John Knox, 2006) 77.

37 WP 117.

38 WP 270.

39 9/11CR 47, 48.

40 Andrew J. Bacevich, *American Empire: The Realities and Consequences of US Diplomacy* (Cambridge: Harvard University Press, 2002) 44.

41 David Armstrong, "Dick Cheney's Song of America," *Harper's* October 2002.

42 On the various points in this paragraph, see ch. 6, "Imperial Motives for a New Pearl Harbor," in my *Christian Faith and the Truth Behind 9/11*.

43 Zbigniew Brzezinski, *The Grand Chessboard: American Primacy and Its Geostrategic Imperatives* (New York: Basic Books, 1997) 212, 24–25.

44 Project for the New American Century (PNAC), *Rebuilding America's Defenses: Strategy, Forces and Resources for a New Century*, September 2000 (www.newamericancentury.org) 51.

45 "Secretary Rumsfeld Interview with the New York Times," *New York Times* 12 October 2001 http://www.defenselink.mil/Transcripts/Transcript.aspx? TranscriptID=2097). For the statements by Bush and Rice, see O&D 116.

46 WP 278.

47 9/11CR xv, xvi. In WP, the former sentence is quoted as "facts and *causes* relating to . . ." (317; emphasis added).

48 WP 269–70.

49 WP 35, 28.

50 9/11CR xv.

51 WP 29.

52 Clarke is quoted as saying, with regard to the warning issued to the incoming Bush administration about the al-Qaeda threat: "It was very explicit.

Rice was briefed, and Hadley was briefed, and Zelikow sat in" (Philip Shenon, "Clinton Aides Plan to Tell Panel of Warning Bush Team on Qaeda," *New York Times* 20 March 2004).

53 WP 135.

54 Statement of the Family Steering Committee for the 9/11 Independent Commission, 20 March 2004 (www.911independentcommission.org/mar202004.html).

55 WP 320.

56 WP 38.

57 Quoted in Peter Lance, *Cover Up: What the Government Is Still Hiding about the War on Terror* (New York: Harper-Collins/ReganBooks, 2004) 139–40.

58 WP 273.

59 Ernest May, "When Government Writes History: A Memoir of the 9/11 Commission," *New Republic* 23 May 2005; cited in Bryan Sacks, "Making History: The Compromised 9-11 Commission," in Paul Zarembka, ed., *The Hidden History of 9-11-2001* (Amsterdam: Elsevier, 2006) 223–60, at 258 n. 10.

60 The fact that Zelikow was "involved in the drafting" of this document was revealed on PBS in *Frontline*'s "Interview with Barton Gellman" on 29 January 2003, shortly after Zelikow had become executive director of the 9/11 Commission. According to Gellman, a staff writer for the *Washington Post*, he had learned this from Zelikow during a telephone conversation the previous day. Perhaps Zelikow, realizing that it would not be politic for his role in drafting *NSS 2002* to be widely known, never mentioned it again. In any case, I am unaware of any reporter, aside from Gellman and James Mann (to be discussed later), who has mentioned Zelikow's role in *NSS 2002*.

61 "President Bush Delivers Graduation Speech at West Point," 1 June 2002 (www.whitehouse.gov/news/releases/2002/06/20020601-3.html).

62 *The National Security Strategy of the United States of America*, September 2002 (www.whitehouse.gov/nsc/nss.html); henceforth NSS 2002.

63 James Mann, *Rise of the Vulcans: The History of Bush's War Cabinet* (New York: Viking, 2004) 316.

64 NSS 2002 6, 15.

65 NSS 2002 15.

66 NSS 2002, cover letter.

67 Stefan Halper and Jonathan Clarke, *America Alone: The Neo-Conservatives and the Global Order* (Cambridge: Cambridge University Press, 2004) 142. Technically, the new doctrine is a doctrine of *preventive* war. But most writers, as Halper and Clarke illustrate, use the term "preemptive."

68 Stephen J. Sniegoski, "Neoconservatives, Israel, and 9/11: The Origins of the US War on Iraq," in D. L. O'Huallachain and J. Forrest Sharpe, eds., *Neoconned Again: Hypocrisy, Lawlessness, and the Rape of Iraq* (Vienna, VA: IHS Press, 2005) 81–109, at 81–82.

69 Halper and Clarke, *America Alone*, 4.

70 Max Boot, "Think Again: Neocons," *Foreign Policy* January/February 2004 (www.cfr.org/publication/7592/think_again.html) 18.

71 Ashton Carter, John Deutch, and Philip Zelikow, "Catastrophic Terrorism: Tackling the New Danger," *Foreign Affairs* November/December 1998: 80–94 (http://cryptome.quintessenz.at/mirror/ct-tnd.htm).

72 WP 28.

73 9/11CR 305.

74 Steven E. Jones, "Why Indeed Did the World Trade Center Buildings Collapse?" in ISO, 33–62, at 47.

75 FEMA, *World Trade Center Building Performance Study*, ch. 5, Sect. 6.2, "Probable Collapse Sequence," discussed in NPH 22.

76 Margie Burns, "Secrecy Surrounds a Bush Brother's Role in 9/11 Security," *American Reporter* 9/2021 (20 January 2003). Marvin Bush's role in the company is also mentioned in Craig Unger, *House of Bush, House of Saud: The Secret Relationship between the World's Two Most Powerful Dynasties* (New York & London: Scribner, 2004) 249.

77 WP 322.

78 Of the people listed on Alan Miller's "Patriots Question 9/11" website (http://patriotsquestion911.com), see especially Colonel Robert Bowman, Catherine Austin Fitts, Karen Kwiatkowski, Colonel Ronald Ray, Morgan Reynolds, Paul Craig Roberts, and Gregory Zeigler.

79 NPH 134–40.

80 WP 261.

81 9/11CR 40.

82 O&D 241–44.

83 WP 260, 264.

84 9/11CR 37; Clarke 6–7.

85 O&D 59.

86 O&D 125–26.

87 O&D 129–33.

88 O&D 28.

89 O&D 30.

90 O&D 36–37.

91 O&D 262–67.

92 O&D 30–31.

93 WP 228–231.

94 For Giuliani's complete statement, see "Who Told Giuliani the WTC Was Going to Collapse on 9/11?" (www.whatreallyhappened.com/wtc_giuliani.html). It is also in the film *911 Mysteries: Demolitions* (www.911Mysteries.com).

95 9/11CR 302.

96 Emergency Medical Services (EMS) Division Chief John Peruggia said that he was told that the "north tower was in danger of a near imminent collapse" (9/11 oral hist of John Peruggia, 17). Medical technician Richard Zarrillo, evidently a liaison between the OEM and EMS, said that he was told that "the buildings . . . are going to collapse" (9/11 oral hist of Richard Zarrillo, 5). Fire Marshal Stephen Mosiello and Deputy Assistant Chief of Safety Albert Turi also used the plural ("buildings") in reporting what they heard from Zarrillo in their oral histories. Turi reported that when Zarrillo was asked "where are we getting these reports?" his reply was: "you know, we're not sure, OEM is just reporting this." (For these oral histories, see "oral hist" under Abbreviations, above.)

97 In "A Brief History of New York City's Office of Emergency Management," we read: "1996: By executive order, the Mayor's Office of Emergency Management is created. The director reports directly to the Mayor, and serves as the local

director of Civil Defense." (Unfortunately, although in previous publications I had given the web page on which this "Brief History" was printed (www.nyc.gov/html/ oem/html/other/oem_history.html), it has now been removed as "outdated."

98 Oral hist of Chief Joseph Pfeifer, 23 October 2001.

99 Griffin, *Christian Faith and the Truth Behind 9/11*, 78.

100 WP 254.

101 WP 254.

102 9/11CR 499n130.

103 O&D 54.

104 9/11CR 36.

105 O&D 206–12. For Clarke's account, see *Against All Enemies* 3–5; for Mineta's account, see "Statement of Secretary of Transportation Norman Y. Mineta before the [9/11 Commission] May 23, 2003" (www.globalsecurity.org/ security/ library/congress/9-11_commission/030523-mineta.pdf).

106 9/11CR 462n189.

107 WP 135.

108 Anne Karpf, "Uncle Sam's Lucky Finds," *Guardian* 19 March 2002 (www.guardian.co.uk/september11/story/0,11209,669961,00.html).

109 Rowland Morgan and Ian Henshall, *9/11 Revealed: The Unanswered Questions* (New York: Carroll & Graf, 2005) 68.

110 Rowland Morgan, *Flight 93 Revealed: What Really Happened on the 9/11 'Let's Roll' Flight?* (New York: Carroll & Graf, 2006) 115. For Guy Smith's BBC documentary, see my discussion in the introduction, above.

111 Associated Press, 5 October 2001; *Boston Globe* 18 September 2001; *Independent* 29 September 2001.

112 9/11CR 1–2.

113 9/11CR ch. 1, note 1.

114 WP 245.

115 On this entire episode, see Morgan and Henshall, *9/11 Revealed*, 180– 83, or Morgan, *Flight 93 Revealed*, 81–96. As Morgan points out, Atta's bags, if being transferred from the Portland commuter plane to AA Flight 11, would have been held off that flight and opened only if Atta did not board that flight (89–90). Jay Kolar has pointed out, moreover, that the idea that Atta and al-Omari drove the Nissan Altima from Boston to Portland was an improvisation. The original story reported by the press was that the rented Nissan Altima was driven to Portland by Adnan Bukhari and Ameer Bukhari ("Two Brothers among Hijackers: CNN Report," 13 September 2001 [http://english.peopledaily.com.cn/200109/13/ eng20010913_80131.html]). After 9/11, however, the FBI learned that Adnan was still alive and that Ameer had died a year earlier. Their names on the list of hijackers for AA 11 were, therefore, replaced by two other brothers, Waleed and Wail al-Shehri and the Nissan was said to have been used by Atta and Omari. See Jay Kolar, "What We Now Know about the Alleged 9-11 Hijackers," in Zarembka, ed., *The Hidden History of 9-11-2001*, 3–45, at 13–18.

116 "Our Friends the Pakistanis," *Wall Street Journal* 10 October 2001 (www.opinionjournal.com/best/?id=95001298).

117 Michel Chossudovsky, *War and Globalisation: The Truth Behind September 11* (Canada: Global Outlook, 2002) 58; citing Agence France Presse, 10 October 2001.

118 Chossudovsky 51.

119 9/11CR 214.

120 Reuters, 15 September 2001, quoted in Chossudovsky, *War and Globalisation* 53.

121 O&D 110–12.

122 O&D 105–06.

123 9/11CR 331.

124 NPH 112.

125 9/11CR 172.

126 Josh Meyer, "2 Allies Aided Bin Laden, Say Panel Members," *Los Angeles Times* 20 June 2004 (www.truthout.org/cgi-bin/artman/exec/view.cgi/4/4932).

127 9/11CR 154.

128 Daniel Hopsicker, *Welcome to Terrorland: Mohamed Atta and the 9/11 Cover-up in Florida* (Eugene: MadCowPress, 2004); *Newsweek* 15 October 2001; *San Francisco Chronicle* 4 October 2001; "Terrorist Stag Parties," *Wall Street Journal* 10 October 2001 (www.opinionjournal.com/best/?id=95001298).

129 Rowland, *Flight 93 Revealed*, 93–95.

130 Rowland and Henshall, *9/11 Revealed*, 117–19.

131 Jay Kolar, "What We Now Know about the Alleged 9-11 Hijackers," 3–45, at 6–10.

132 WP 267.

133 WP 118.

134 David Bamford, "Hijack 'Suspect' Alive in Morocco," BBC News, 22 September 2001 (http://news.bbc.co.uk/1/hi/world/middle_east/1558669.stm).

135 David Harrison, "Revealed: The Men with Stolen Identities," *Telegraph* 23 September 2001 (www.portal.telegraph.co.uk/news/main.jhtml?xml=/news/2001/09/23/widen23.xml).

136 The Ahmed al-Nami contacted by Harrison was 33, whereas the man of that name who was allegedly on Flight 93, which evidently crashed in Pennsylvania, was only 21. See Christine Lamb, "The Six Sons of Asir," *Telegraph* 15 September 2002 (www.portal.telegraph.co.uk/news/main.jhtml?xml=/news/2002/09/15/wdoss215.xml).

137 9/11CR 5.

138 Kolar, 'What We Now Know about the Alleged 9-11 Hijackers," 22–27.

139 "Ziad Jarrah," Book Rags (www.bookrags.com/wiki/Ziad_Jarrah). My thanks to Jay Kolar for this reference.

140 Francis A. Boyle, "Bush, Jr., September 11th and the Rule of Law," available in *The Criminality of Nuclear Deterrence: Could The US War On Terrorism Go Nuclear?* (Atlanta: Clarity Press, 2002) or at www.ratical.org/ratville/CAH/CrimNukDetSI.html.

141 "White House Warns Taliban: 'We Will Defeat You'" (CNN.com, 21 September 2001). Four weeks after the attacks on Afghanistan began, a Taliban spokesman said: "We are not a province of the United States, to be issued orders to. We have asked for proof of Osama's involvement, but they have refused. Why?" See Kathy Gannon, AP, "Taliban Willing To Talk, But Wants US Respect" (www.brownsvilleherald.com/comments.php?id=P10017_0_1_0_C).

142 See "The Fake bin Laden Video" (www.whatreallyhappened.com/osamatape.html). Bruce Lawrence's statement is quoted in Kevin Barrett, "Top

U.S. Bin Laden Expert: Confession Video 'Bogus'" (www.911blogger.com/node/6317). Lawrence is the editor of *Messages to the World: The Statements of Osama Bin Laden* (London and New York: Verso, 2005).

143 Federal Bureau of Investigation, Most Wanted Terrorists (www.fbi.gov/wanted/terrorists/terbinladen.htm); Ed Haas, "FBI says, 'No Hard Evidence Connecting Bin Laden to 9/11'" Muckraker Report, 6 June 2006 (www.teamliberty.net/id267.html).

144 Mindy Kleinberg and Lorie Van Auken, "FSC Questions to the 9/11 Commission With Ratings of Its Performance in Providing Answers" (www.911pressfortruth.org/file_download/11), question 21.

145 See ch. 1, "9/11 and Prior False-Flag Operations," in Griffin, *Christian Faith and the Truth Behind 9/11.*

146 WP 118.

147 WP118–19.

148 WP 121–22.

149 WP 120–23.

150 WP 122, 119, 124.

151 WP 119.

152 9/11CR 145, 148, 149, 153, 154, 155.

153 See 9/11CR, ch. 5, notes 1, 10, 11, 16, 32, 40, and 41.

154 WP 124.

155 Ed Haas, "Government Spokesman Says, 'I Don't Understand the Public's Fascination with World Trade Center Building Seven,'" Muckraker Report, 21 March 2006 (www.teamliberty.net/id235.html).

156 Ed Haas, "Change in Venue or Date Will Not Alter Decision," Muckraker Report, 3 July 2006 (www.teamliberty.net/id273.html).

157 "*Popular Mechanics* Invited to the National 9/11 Debate," Muckraker Report, 24 August 2006; email of 1 March 2007.

158 WP 14–15. "Set Up to Fail" is the title of the first chapter.

159 WP 321.

160 Zogby International, "A Word about Our Poll of American Thinking toward the 9/11 Terrorist Attacks," Zogby International, 24 May 2006 (www.zogby.com/features/features.dbm?ID=231). For an interpretation, see "Zogby Poll Finds Over 70 Million Voting Age Americans Support New 9/11 Investigation," 911Truth.org, 21 May 2006 (www.911truth.org/article.php?story=20060522022041421).

161 WP 320–21, 319.

162 *9/11: Press for Truth* (http://video.google.com/videoplay?docid=5589099104255077250).

163 WP 268.

164 Thomas Hargrove and Guido H. Stempel, III, "Anti-Government Anger Spurs 9/11 Conspiracy Belief," NewsPolls.org, Scripps Survey Research Center at Ohio University, 2 August 2006 (http://newspolls.org/story.php?story_id=55).

165 The program, "9/11: Truth, Lies and Conspiracy," which wove snippets from various interviews together, was broadcast 10 September 2006 (www.cbc.ca/sunday/sep10-06.html). For the interview with Hamilton in its entirety, see "9/11: Truth, Lies and Conspiracy: Interview: Lee Hamilton," CBC News, 21 August 2006 (www.cbc.ca/sunday/911hamilton.html).

166 The interviewer, Evan Solomon, interviewed me for the same program, "9/11: Truth, Lies and Conspiracy: Interview: David Ray Griffin," CBC News, 25 August 2006 (www.cbc.ca/sunday/911griffin.html).

167 9/11CR 29.

168 9/11 Commission Hearing, 23 May 2003, panel 1.

169 Whereas Hamilton had long been a Washington insider, Kean had no prior experience with Washington or politics at the national level. The fact that Hamilton at least knew more than Kean is suggested by the fact that after the latter had helped produce the highly falsified ABC docudrama, *The Path to 9/11*, Hamilton lectured his good friend and former co-chair about his participation in this effort during a joint appearance at the National Press Club, saying that "to distort . . . an event of this consequence . . . in this kind of presentation . . . does not serve the country well." See Dana Milbank, "With 9/11 Film, Kean Finds Tough Critic in Hamilton," *Washington Post* 12 September 2006 (www.washingtonpost.com/wp-dyn/content/article/2006/09/11/AR2006091101084.html).

170 WP 216.

171 O&D 28; emphasis in original.

CHAPTER THREE: THE DISINTEGRATION OF THE WORLD TRADE CENTER

1 NIST (National Institute of Standards and Technology), draft, *Final Report of the National Construction Safety Team on the Collapses of the World Trade Center Towers*, June 2005 (http://911research.wtc7.net/wtc/official/nist/NISTNCSTAR1Draft_text.html).

2 Jim Hoffman, "Building a Better Mirage: NIST's 3-Year $20,000,000 Cover-Up of the Crime of the Century," 911 Research, Version 1.0, 8 December 2005 (http://911research.wtc7.net/essays/nist/index.html). Version 1.0 is the final version. Versions 0.9 and 0.98 had been posted on August 1 and August 21, respectively.

3 NISTFR. The response to criticisms, entitled "Events Following Collapse Initiation," constitutes Section 6.14.4.

4 "Fact Sheet: NIST's World Trade Center Investigation" (www.nist.gov/public_affairs/factsheet/nist_investigation_911.htm).

5 These points have been emphasized in Kevin Ryan, "What Is 9/11 Truth? The First Steps," *Journal of 9/11 Studies* 2 (August 2006): 1–6 (www.journalof911studies.com).

6 Donald Kennedy, "An Epidemic of Politics," *Science* 31 January 2003 (www.sciencemag.org/cgi/content/summary/299/5607/625).

7 "Politics and Science in the Bush Administration," Executive Summary 3 (www.democrats.reform.house.gov/features/politics_and_science/pdfs/pdf_politics_and_science_rep.pdf).

8 Union of Concerned Scientists, "Restoring Scientific Integrity in Policymaking" (www.ucsusa.org/scientific_integrity/interference/scientists-signon-statement.html).

9 AFAQs, Question 1.

10 "Boeing 707–767 Comparison" (www.whatreallyhappened.com/boeing_707_767.html). The second statement is quoted in Jim Hoffman, "The World Trade Center Demolition," section headed "The WTC Was Designed to Survive the Impact of a Boeing 767" (http://911research.wtc7.net/mirrors/guardian/WTC/wtc-demolition.htm).

11 NISTFR 2.3 (p. 20), 3.2 (p. 38) and 5.3.2 (p. 55).

12 AFAQs, Question 1.

13 For a video containing De Martini's statement, see *The 'Truss Theory': A Fantasy Concocted to Conceal a Demolition*, What Really Happened (www.whatreallyhappened.com/trusstheory.html). De Martini can also be seen making this statement in in *911 Mysteries: Demolitions* (www.911Mysteries.com).

14 John Skilling's statement is quoted in Eric Nalder, "Twin Towers Engineered to Withstand Jet Collision," *Seattle Times* 27 February 1993. It is partially quoted in James Glanz and Eric Tipton, *City in the Sky: The Rise and Fall of the World Trade Center* (New York: Times Books/Henry Holt, 2003) 138.

15 Robertson's statement is quoted in "The Fall of the World Trade Center," BBC 2, 7 March 2002 (www.bbc.co.uk/science/horizon/2001/ worldtrade centertrans.shtml).

16 I am using the term "explosives" very broadly to refer not only to explosives in the technical sense, such as RDX, but also to incendiary mixtures, such as thermite and thermate, and any other substances or devices that can be used to produce explosions.

17 AFAQs, Question 3.

18 "The Plane that Crashed into the Empire State Building," 20th Century History (http://history1900s.about.com/od/1940s/a/empirecrash.htm).

19 AFAQs, Question 1. As Jim Hoffman points out, this statement, with its contrast between the "large mass" of the plane and the "light steel" of the building, is very misleading. "In fact, the steel on a single floor of the tower was ten times the weight of a 767." See Jim Hoffman, "A Reply to the National Institute for Standards and Technology's *Answers to Frequently Asked Questions*" (http://911research.wtc7.net/reviews/nist/WTC_FAQ_reply.html).

20 AFAQs, Question 2.

21 NISTFR 22–23, 41.

22 Although technically there were only 236 perimeter columns, there were also 4 corner columns, which were inside. For the sake of brevity, I am referring to all 240 of these columns, which were around the perimeter as distinct from being in the core, as perimeter columns.

23 Thomas Eagar and Christopher Musso, "Why Did the World Trade Center Collapse? Science, Engineering, and Speculation," *JOM: Journal of the Minerals, Metals & Materials Society* 53.12 (2001), 8–11 (www.tms.org/pubs/journals/JOM/0112/Eagar/Eagar-0112.html).

24 See "Structures Can Be Beautiful: World's Tallest Buildings Pose Esthetic and Structural Challenge to John Skilling" and "How Columns Will Be Designed for 110-Story Buildings," *Engineering News-Record* 2 April 1964; these statements are quoted in Kevin Ryan, "What Is 9/11 Truth?"

25 Eric Douglas, "The NIST WTC Investigation—How Real Was The Simulation?" *Journal of 9/11 Studies* 6 (December 2006): 1–28.

26 Hoffman, "Building a Better Mirage," section entitled "Shrinking the Core Columns."

27 NIST tried to circumvent this problem, Hoffman points out, by modifying the trajectory of the flight, but this means that NIST's account of this trajectory disagrees with the video evidence.

28 Douglas, "The NIST WTC Investigation—How Real Was The

Simulation?" 10, citing NCSTAR 1–2B: 382. "NCSTAR" is an abbreviation for the report produced by the National Construction Safety Team Act, under which NIST carried out its investigations. What I am calling NIST's final report (NISTFR, in these notes) or simply the NIST report, is fairly brief, containing only 247 pages. But the entire report, which is some 10,000 pages long, includes 42 companion volumes containing the results of eight investigations. They are abbreviated NIST NCSTAR 1–1, NIST NCSTAR 1–2, on up to NIST NCSTAR 1–8. The entire set of documents, entitled *Final Reports of the Federal Building and Fire Investigation of the World Trade Center Disaster*, can be found at http://wtc.nist.gov/reports_october05.htm.

29 Douglas 9, quoting NIST NCSTAR 1–2B: 385.

30 Douglas 14.

31 Douglas 9–10, citing NIST NCSTAR 1–2B: 390.

32 Douglas 15, quoting NCSTAR 1–5: 181.

33 "Fact Sheet: NIST's World Trade Center Investigation" (www.nist.gov/public_affairs/factsheet/nist_investigation_911.htm), under question, "Why is NIST doing this investigation?"

34 Ryan, "What Is 9/11 Truth?" referring to NIST NCSTAR 1–6A, Appendix C, 263ff. (http://wtc.nist.gov/NISTNCSTAR1-6A.pdf). "In the end," Ryan adds, "they slid the results into a 12-page appendix to the final report."

35 Ryan, "What Is."

36 Therese McAllister, "Structural and Fire Protection Damage Due to Aircraft," Building and Fire Research Laboratory, NIST, 15 September 2005 (http://wtc.nist.gov/WTC_Conf_Sep13-15/session6/6McAllister.pdf).

37 Douglas, "The NIST WTC Investigation—How Real Was The Simulation?" 17.

38 AFAQs, Question 2.

39 AFAQs, Question 3.

40 AFAQs, Question 7.

41 Sheila Barter, "How the World Trade Center Fell," BBC News, 13 September 2001 (http://news.bbc.co.uk/1/hi/world/americas/1540044.stm).

42 Steven E. Jones, "Why Indeed Did the WTC Buildings Collapse?" in ISO, 33–62. For visual evidence of his points, Jones refers readers to the online version of his paper, which had been posted on his BYU website. But Jones was later forced to remove his paper from that site. The online version can now be read (under the title "Why Indeed Did the World Trade Center Buildings Completely Collapse?") in the *Journal of 9/11 Studies* 3 (September 2006): 1–48.

43 AFAQs, Question 7.

44 NISTFR 88.

45 AFAQs, Question 2.

46 Eagar and Musso, "Why Did the World Trade Center Collapse?"

47 Thomas Eagar, "The Collapse: An Engineer's Perspective," which is part of "Why the Towers Fell," *NOVA* 30 April 2002 (www.pbs.org/wgbh/nova/wtc/collapse.html).

48 AFAQs, Question 7.

49 Hoffman, "Building a Better Mirage."

50 AFAQs, Question 7.

51 Eagar, "The Collapse: An Engineer's Perspective," citing A. E. Cote, ed.,

Fire Protection Handbook, 17th ed. (Quincy, ME: National Fire Protection Association, 1992).

52 AFAQs, Questions 2, 3, 8, 13.

53 AFAQs, Question 7.

54 Sunder's statement is quoted in Andy Field, "A Look Inside a Radical New Theory of the WTC Collapse," Firehouse.com, 7 February 2004 (http://cms.firehouse.com/content/article/article.jsp?sectionId=46&id=25807).

55 NISTFR 179.

56 AFAQs, Question 9.

57 AFAQs, Question 9. To make clear that I did not leave out anything that would really support the view that the fires, in spite of giving off black smoke, were really quite hot, I will here quote the remainder of NIST's answer: "The visible part of fire smoke consists of small soot particles whose formation is favored by the incomplete combustion associated with oxygen-depleted burning. Once formed, the soot from the tower fires was rapidly pushed away from the fires into less hot regions of the building or directly to broken windows and breaks in the building exterior. At these lower temperatures, the soot could no longer burn away. Thus, people saw the thick dark smoke characteristic of burning under oxygen-depleted conditions."

58 James Fetzer, "Why NIST Hasn't Answered Its Own Questions," Scholars for 9/11 Truth (www.scholarsfor911truth.org/Why-NIST-hasn't-Answered-its-own-Questions.html).

59 Hoffman, "A Reply."

60 Eagar, "The Collapse: An Engineer's Perspective."

61 Eric Hufschmid, *Painful Questions: An Analysis of the September 11th Attack* (Goleta, CA: Endpoint Software, 2002) 40.

62 NISTFR 88.

63 NISTFR 88.

64 Hoffman, "Building a Better Mirage."

65 Eagar, "The Collapse: An Engineer's Perspective."

66 Mark H. Gaffney, "Dead on Arrival: The NIST 9/11 Report on the World Trade Center Collapse," Rense.com, 15 December 2006 (http://rense.com/general74/nist.htm).

67 AFAQs, Questions 2 and 8.

68 Quoted in "WTC 2: There Was No Inferno," What Really Happened (www.whatreallyhappened.com/wtc2_fire.html).

69 Quoted in "Tape Sheds Light on WTC Rescuers," CNN, 4 August 2002 (http://edition.cnn.com/2002/US/08/04/wtc.firefighters/index.html). The voices of the firefighters reportedly "showed no panic, no sense that events were racing beyond their control" (Jim Dwyer and Ford Fessenden, "Lost Voices of Firefighters, Some on 78th Floor," *New York Times* 4 August 2002 [www.mishalov.com/ wtc_lostvoicesfiredept.html]).

70 AFAQs, Question 7.

71 AFAQs, Question 7.

72 Kevin Ryan, "Propping Up the War on Terror: Lies about the WTC by NIST and Underwriters Laboratories," in ISO, 63–71, at 68.

73 Ryan 67–68.

74 AFAQs, Question 7.

75 Fetzer, "Why NIST Hasn't Answered Its Own Questions."

76 Samuel H. Marcus, *Basics of Structural Steel* (Reston, VA: Reston Publishing 1977) 20.

77 Ryan, "Propping Up the War on Terror," 68.

78 John Dobberstein, "Area Man Stirs Debate on WTC Collapse: South Bend Firm's Lab Director Fired After Questioning Federal Probe," *South Bend Tribune* 22 November 2004 (www.911truth.org/article.php?story=20041124095100856).

79 Ryan's letter to Frank Gayle is available in "UL Executive Speaks Out on WTC Study," 9/11Truth.org, 12 November 2004 (www.911truth.org/article.php?story=20041112144051451).

80 FEMA, "Interstate Bank Building Fire, Los Angeles, California," 1988 (www.lafire.com//famous_fires/880504_1stInterstateFire/FEMA-TecReport/FEMA-report.htm).

81 FEMA, "High-Rise Office Building Fire One Meridian Plaza Philadelphia, Pennsylvania" (www.interfire.org/res_file/pdf/Tr-049.pdf).

82 "Fire Practically Destroys Venezuela's Tallest Building" (www.whatreallyhappened.com/venezuela_fire.html).

83 FEMA, *World Trade Center Building Performance Study*, May 2002, Appendix A: "Overview of Fire Protection in Buildings," A–9 (www.fema.gov/pdf/library/fema403_apa.pdf).

84 Kevin Ryan, in his letter to Frank Gayle (see note 79), wrote in criticism of NIST's preliminary report: "This story just does not add up. If steel from those buildings did soften or melt, I'm sure we can all agree that this was certainly not due to jet fuel fires of any kind, let alone the briefly burning fires in those towers. . . . Please do what you can to quickly eliminate the confusion regarding the ability of jet fuel fires to soften or melt structural steel."

85 Ryan, "What Is 9/11 Truth?"

86 NISTFR 203 (PDF).

87 NISTFR xxxvii note, 82 note (PDF).

88 Hoffman, "Building a Better Mirage."

89 Ibid.

90 AFAQs, Question 2.

91 NISTFR 28, 143.

92 AFAQs, Question 2.

93 AFAQs, Question 6.

94 AFAQs, Question 6, quoting NISTFR 146 (Section 6.14.4).

95 AFAQs, Question 6.

96 Hoffman, "A Reply."

97 Gordon Ross, "Momentum Transfer Analysis of the Collapse of the Upper Storeys of WTC 1," *Journal of 9/11 Studies* 1 (June 2006): 32–39.

98 Sean Glazier, "Why the NIST 'Fact Sheet' Just Won't Do" (www.scholarsfor911truth.org/WhyNISTFactSheetWontDo.html).

99 Judy Wood, "A Refutation of the Official Collapse Theory" (http://janedoe0911.tripod.com/BilliardBalls.html). Wood, incidentally has a B.S. in civil engineering, an M.S. in engineering mechanics, and a Ph.D. in materials engineering science.

100 Steven Jones, "Why Indeed Did the WTC Buildings Collapse?" in ISO, 47–48, with reference to video evidence at www.911research.com/wtc/evidence/

videos/docs/south_tower_collapse.mpeg and photograph 16 of the online version of his paper (see note 42, above). This remarkable phenomenon is shown in *911 Mysteries: Demolitions* (www.911Mysteries.com).

101 C. Thurston, "Explosion or Collapse? The Semantics of Deception and the Significance of Categories," 4 November 2006 (www.truememes.com/semantics.html).

102 NISTFR 196.

103 Ryan, "Propping Up the War on Terror," 69.

104 NISTFR 142.

105 NISTFR 142.

106 Jones, "Why Indeed Did the WTC Buildings Collapse?" 53.

107 Ryan, "What Is 9/11 Truth?" For the claim that the "floor system deflection" reached "approximately 42 in," see NISTFR 98.

108 Gaffney, "Dead on Arrival."

109 Douglas, "The NIST WTC Investigation—How Real Was The Simulation?" 3, 8, 21.

110 Gaffney, "Dead on Arrival."

111 E-mail from Hoffman, November 2006.

112 AFAQs, Questions 2 and 12.

113 Fetzer, "Why NIST Hasn't Answered Its Own Questions."

114 AFAQs, Question 2.

115 Jones, "Why Indeed Did the WTC Buildings Collapse?" ISO 46.

116 Quoted in Liz Else, "Baltimore Blasters," *New Scientist* 183/2457 (July 24, 2004), 48 (http://archive.newscientist.com/secure/article/article.jsp?rp=1&id=mg18324575.700).

117 Hoffman, "A Reply."

118 Thurston, "Explosion or Collapse?"

119 AFAQs, Question 2.

120 "Explosive Testimony: Revelations about the Twin Towers in the 9/11 Oral Histories," ch. 2 of David Ray Griffin, *Christian Faith and the Truth Behind 9/11* (Louisville: Westminster John Knox, 2006). This essay was previously published at 911Truth.org (www.911truth.org/article.php?story=20060118104223192).

121 The *New York Times*, after finally succeeding with its suit to force the City of New York to release these 9/11 oral histories, made them publicly available (see "oral hist" in the Abbreviations, above).

122 Graeme MacQueen, "118 Witnesses: The Firefighters' Testimony to Explosions in the Twin Towers," *Journal of 9/11 Studies* 2 (August 2006): 49–123.

123 Quoted in Dennis Smith, *Report from Ground Zero: The Story of the Rescue Efforts at the World Trade Center* (New York: Penguin, 2002) 18.

124 Oral hist of Frank Cruthers, 4.

125 John Bussey, "Eye of the Storm: One Journey Through Desperation and Chaos," *Wall Street Journal* 12 September 2001 (http://online.wsj.com/public/resources/documents/040802pulitzer5.htm).

126 Dean E. Murphy, *September 11: An Oral History* (New York: Doubleday, 2002) 9–15.

127 Guzman's account, which was not included in my "Explosive Testimony," is contained in Mike Kelly, "Last Survivor Pulled from WTC Rebuilds

Life, Recalls Horror," *The Record* (Bergen County, New Jersey) 10 September 2003. It can be found at What Really Happened (www.whatreallyhappened.com/wtc_mcmillan.html). Incidentally, although Kelly refers to her as "Genelle Guzman McMillan," he reports that she did not marry Roger McMillan until two months after 9/11.

128 Greg Szymanski, "NY Fireman Lou Cacchioli Upset that 9/11 Commission 'Tried to Twist My Words,'" Arctic Beacon.com, 19 July 2005 (www.arcticbeacon.com/19-Jul-2005.html). Although the oral histories that were released on August 12 did not include one from Cacchioli, the fact that he was on duty is confirmed on page 4 of Thomas Turilli's oral history.

129 Oral hist of Karin Deshore, 15.

130 Oral hist of Kenneth Rogers, 3–4.

131 Oral hist of Timothy Burke, 8–9.

132 Oral hist of Edward Cachia, 5.

133 BBC, 11 September 2001.

134 Oral hist of Stephen Gregory, 14–16.

135 Greg Szymanski, "WTC Basement Blast and Injured Burn Victim Blows 'Official 9/11 Story' Sky High," Arctic Beacon.com, 24 June 2005 (www.arcticbeacon.com/24-Jun-2005.html).

136 Greg Szymanski, "Second WTC Janitor Comes Forward With Eyewitness Testimony Of 'Bomb-Like' Explosion in North Tower Basement," ArcticBeacon.com, 12 July 2005 (www.arcticbeacon.citymaker.com/articles/article/1518131/29079.htm).

137 "We Will Not Forget: A Day of Terror," *Chief Engineer* July 2002.

138 Quoted in Christopher Bollyn, "New Seismic Data Refutes Official Explanation," American Free Press, updated 12 April 2004 (www.americanfreepress.net/09_03_02/NEW_SEISMIC_/new_seismic_.html).

139 Oral hist of Lonnie Penn, 5.

140 Oral hist of Paul Curran, 11.

141 Oral hist of Bradley Mann, 5–7.

142 Greg Szymanski, "WTC Basement Blast and Injured Burn Victim Blows 'Official 9/11 Story' Sky High."

143 In the words of NISTFR: "The focus of the Investigation was on the sequence of events from the instant of aircraft impact to the initiation of collapse for each tower. For brevity in this report, this sequence is referred to as the 'probable collapse sequence,' although it includes little analysis of the structural behavior of the tower after the conditions for collapse initiation were reached. . . [Our simulation treats only] the structural deterioration of each tower from the time of aircraft impact to the time at which the building . . . was poised for collapse" (80n, 140).

144 AFAQs, Question 4.

145 Oral hist of James Curran, 10–11.

146 James Fetzer, "Why NIST Hasn't Answered Its Own Questions."

147 AFAQs, Question 5.

148 Christopher Bollyn, "New Seismic Data Refutes Official Explanation," American Free Press, updated 12 April 2004 (www.thetruthseeker.co.uk/article.asp?ID=2580); Craig T. Furlong and Gordon Ross, "Seismic Proof: 9/11 Was an Inside Job," Updated Version II, *Journal of 9/11 Studies* 3 (September

2006) (http://worldtradecentertruth.com).

149 See Jim Hoffman, "Seismic Records of the Twin Towers' Destruction: Clarifying the Relationship Between Seismic Evidence and Controlled Demolition Theories," Version 0.9, 31 October 2006 (http://911research.wtc7.net/essays/demolition/seismic.html).

150 AFAQs, Question 13.

151 "NIST Engineer, John Gross, Denies the Existance [sic] of Molten Steel" (http://video.google.com/videoplay?docid=-7180303712325092501&hl=en). Gross is one of the 13 members of the National Construction Safety Team listed at the beginning of NISTFR.

152 The quotations from Loizeaux and Tully are in Bollyn, "New Seismic Data Refutes Official Explanation." Bollyn said (e-mail of 27 October 2005) that these statements were made to him personally during telephone interviews with Tully and Loizeaux, probably in the summer of 2002. Bollyn added that although he is not positive about the date of the telephone interviews, he is always "very precise about quotes."

153 Quoted in James Williams, "WTC a Structural Success," *SEAU News: The Newsletter of the Structural Engineers Association of Utah*, October 2001 (www.seau.org/SEAUNews-2001-10.pdf).

154 William Langewiesche, *American Ground: Unbuilding the World Trade Center* (New York: North Point Press, 2002) 31. Ruvolo is quoted in the DVD *Collateral Damages* (www.collateraldamages.com). For just this segment plus discussion, see Steve Watson, "Firefighter Describes 'Molten Metal' at Ground Zero, Like a 'Foundry,'" Inforwars.net, 17 November 2006 (http://infowars.net/articles/november2006/171106molten.htm).

155 Glenn Stout, Charles Vitchers, and Robert Gray, *Nine Months at Ground Zero: The Story of the Brotherhood of Workers Who Took on a Job Like No Other* (New York: Scribner, 2006) 65, 66. (Thanks to Matthew Everett for the references in this and the previous note.)

156 Trudy Walsh, "Handheld APP Eased Recovery Tasks," *Government Computer News* 21, no. 27a, 11 September 2002 (www.gcn.com/21_27a/news/19930-1.html).

157 Professor Allison Geyh of Johns Hopkins, who was part of a team of public health investigators who visited the site shortly after 9/11, wrote: "In some pockets now being uncovered they are finding molten steel," *Magazine of Johns Hopkins Public Health,* late Fall 2001. Keith Eaton of the Institution of Structural Engineers (London), who somewhat later toured the site with an engineer, said that he was shown slides of "molten metal, which was still red hot weeks after the event" (*Structural Engineer* 3 September 2002) 6. Herb Trimpe, an Episcopalian deacon who served as a chaplain at Ground Zero, said, "The fires burned, up to 2,000 degrees, underground for quite a while. . . . I talked to many contractors and they said . . . beams had just totally been melted because of the heat." "The Chaplain's Tale," *Times-Herald Record* 8 September 2002 (http://archive.recordonline.com/adayinseptember/trimpe.htm).

158 Jones, "Why Indeed Did the WTC Buildings Collapse?" 35.

159 AFAQs, Question 13.

160 Jones, "Why Indeed Did the WTC Buildings Collapse?" 37.

161 AFAQs, Question 13.

162 Jones, "Why Indeed Did the WTC Buildings Collapse?" 38.

163 Fetzer, "Why NIST Hasn't Answered Its Own Questions."

164 AFAQs, Question 13.

165 Jones, "Why Indeed Did the WTC Buildings Collapse?" 39.

166 Each column, besides being at least 36 by 16 inches, had walls that were at least 4 inches thick at the base, then tapered off in the upper floors, which had less weight to support. Pictures of columns can be seen on page 23 of Eric Hufschmid's *Painful Questions*. The reason for the qualification "at least" in these statements is that Jim Hoffman has recently concluded that some of them were even bigger. With reference to his article "The Core Structures: The Structural System of the Twin Towers," 9-11 Research.wtc7.net, n.d. (http://911research.wtc7.net/wtc/arch/core.html), Hoffman has written (e-mail of 26 October 2005): "Previously I've been saying that the core columns had outside dimensions of 36 x 16, but I now think that at least 1/3 of them had dimensions of 54 x 22, based on early articles in the *Engineering News-Record* and photographs I took of close-up construction photos on display at the Skyscraper Museum in Manhattan. . . . Also, according to the illustration in the *Engineering News-Record*, the thickness of the steel at the bases was 5 inches, not 4 inches."

167 9/11CR 541n1.

168 AFAQs, Question 2.

169 Hoffman, "Your Eyes Don't Lie: Common Sense, Physics, and the World Trade Center Collapses," 9-11 Research.wtc7.net, 2004 (http://911research.wtc7.net/talks/radio/youreyesdontlie/index.html).

170 Quoted in Eric Hufschmid's video, *Painful Deceptions* (www.EricHufschmid.Net).

171 Quoted in Tom Held, "Hoan Bridge Blast Set Back to Friday," *Milwaukee Journal Sentinel* 19 December 2000 (www.jsonline.com/news/metro/dec00/hoan20121900a.asp).

172 E-mail from Hoffman, 27 September 2005. Hoffman also noted that "the lengths of the pieces bear little resemblance to the lengths of the steel parts known to have gone into the construction," which means that one could not reasonably infer that the pieces simply broke at their joints.

173 Liz Else, "Baltimore Blasters," 48.

174 Knight-Ridder, "Towers' Quick Collapse Surprises Engineers," 12 September 2001. (This story, even the cached version, has disappeared from the Internet.)

175 NISTFR 151.

176 Hoffman, "The Twin Towers Demolition," 9-11 Research.wtc7.net (http://911research.wtc7.net/talks/towers/slides.html).

177 Jim Hoffman, "The North Tower's Dust Cloud: Analysis of Energy Requirements for the Expansion of the Dust Cloud Following the Collapse of 1 World Trade Center," Version 3, 9-11 Research.wtc7.net, 16 October 2003 (http://911research.wtc7.net/papers/dustvolume/volumev3.html).

178 "The World Trade Center: Rise and Fall of an American Icon," History Channel, 8 September 2002.

179 Stout, Vitchers, and Gray, *Nine Months at Ground Zero*, 144.

180 This statement from Mount Sinai Medical Center's Philip Landrigan, a renowned authority on environmental health, is quoted in Ellen Barry, "Study

Links Health Risks, 9/11," *Los Angeles Times* 6 September 2006 (www.truthout.org/cgi-bin/artman/exec/view.cgi/64/22321).

181 Hoffman ("The Twin Towers Demolition") says that the clouds expanded to five times the diameter of the towers in the first ten seconds. The demolition of the Kingdome can be viewed at the website of Controlled Demolition, Inc. (www.controlled-demolition.com/default.asp?reqLocId= 7&reqItemId=20030317140323), that of the Reading Grain Facility at ImplosionWorld.com (http://implosionworld.com/reading.html).

182 Hoffman, "The North Tower's Dust Cloud."

183 Hoffman, "The Twin Towers Demolition."

184 Jeff King, "The WTC Collapse: What the Videos Show," Indymedia Webcast News, 12 November 2003 (http://ontario.indymedia.org/ display.php3?article_id=7342&group=webcast).

185 Sunder's statement is quoted in D9/11M 45.

186 AFAQs, Question 2.

187 Don Paul and Jim Hoffman, *Waking Up from Our Nightmare: The 9/11/01 Crimes in New York City* (San Francisco: Irresistible/Revolutionary, 2004) 7. For photos of horizontal ejections, see http://911research.wtc7.net/talks/ wtc/expulsion.html.

188 See "911 Eyewitness: Huge Steel Sections Ejected More than 600 Feet" (http://video.google.com/videoplay?docid=1807467434260776490).

189 Joan Killough-Miller, "The 'Deep Mystery' of Melted Steel," *WPI Transformations*, Spring 2002 (www.wpi.edu/News/Transformations/2002Spring/ steel.html).

190 Glanz, "Engineers Suspect Diesel Fuel in Collapse of 7 World Trade Center." I have here quoted Glanz's paraphrase of Barnett's statement.

191 Killough-Miller, "The 'Deep Mystery' of Melted Steel."

192 Jones, "Why Indeed," 35.

193 Killough-Miller, "The 'Deep Mystery' of Melted Steel."

194 See http://wpi.edu/News/Releases/20045/fpe.html.

195 *New York Times* 2 February 2002; quoted in Killough-Miller, "The 'Deep Mystery' of Melted Steel."

196 FEMA, *World Trade Center Building Performance Study*, Appendix C.

197 See the section headed "The ASCE's Disclosures of Steel Sulfidation" in Hoffman's "Building a Better Mirage."

198 FEMA, *World Trade Center Building Performance Study*, ch. 2. For visual evidence, see Jim Hoffman, "Video Evidence of the North Tower Collapse: North Tower Collapse Video Frames," 9-11 Research.wtc7.net, n.d. (http://911research. wtc7.net/wtc/evidence/videos/wtc1_close_frames.html).

199 James Glanz and Eric Lipton, "Towers Withstood Impact, but Fell to Fire, Report Says," *New York Times* 29 March 2002.

200 "Video Evidence of the North Tower's Destruction: North Tower Collapse Video Frames," 9-11 Research (http://911research.wtc7.net/ wtc/evidence/ videos/wtc1_close_frames.html).

201 Hoffman, "The Structural System of the Twin Towers: The Hat Trusses," 9-11 Research (http://911research.wtc7.net/wtc/arch/hattruss.html).

202 Hoffman quotes the section (6.14.2) of NISTFR in which this argument is made (144–45).

203 Hoffman, e-mail of 3 November 2006. Hoffman added: "I've seen the antenna drop explained as an optical illusion caused by the southward rotation of the top, but videos taken from the east clearly show that the southward rotation doesn't start until after the drop."

204 Don Paul and Jim Hoffman, *Waking Up from Our Nightmare* 34.

205 Steven Jones, "Why Indeed Did the WTC Buildings Collapse?" 48.

206 Quoted in Liz Else, "Baltimore Blasters."

207 Jim Hoffman, "Review of 'A New Standard for Deception: The NIST WTC Report': A Presentation by Kevin Ryan" (http://911research.wtc7.net/reviews/kevin_ryan/newstandard.html).

208 "Baosteel Will Recycle World Trade Center Debris," Eastday.com, 24 January 2002 (www.china.org.cn/english/2002/Jan/25776.htm).

209 The official investigators reportedly found that they had less authority than the clean-up crews, leading the House of Representatives' Committee on Science to report that "the lack of authority of investigators to impound pieces of steel for examination before they were recycled led to the loss of important pieces of evidence." See "Learning from 9/11: Understanding the Collapse of the World Trade Center," hearing, 6 March 2002, under "Background" (http://web.archive.org/web/20021128021952/http://commdocs.house.gov/committees/science/hsy77747.000/hsy77747_0.htm).

210 This removal was, moreover, carried out with the utmost care, because "the loads consisted of highly sensitive material." Each truck was equipped with a Vehicle Location Device, connected to GPS. "The software recorded every trip and location, sending out alerts if the vehicle traveled off course, arrived late at its destination, or deviated from expectations in any other way. . . . One driver . . . took an extended lunch break of an hour and a half. . . . [H]e was dismissed" (Jacqueline Emigh, "GPS on the Job in Massive World Trade Center Clean-Up," 1 July 2002 [http://securitysolutions.com/ar/security_gps_job_massive]).

211 *New York Times* 25 December 2001. This protest was echoed by Professor Abolhassan Astaneh-Asl, professor of civil engineering at the University of California at Berkeley, who said: "Where there is a car accident and two people are killed, you keep the car until the trial is over. If a plane crashes, not only do you keep the plane, but you assemble all the pieces, take it to a hangar, and put it together. That's only for 200, 300 people, when they die. In this case, you had 3,000 people dead. You had a major . . . manmade structure. My wish was that we had spent whatever it takes. . . . Get all this steel, carry it to a lot. Instead of recycling it. . . . After all, this is a crime scene and you have to figure out exactly what happened" (CBS News, 12 March 2002).

212 *Fire Engineering* January 2002. The first sentence is from Francis L. Brannigan, Glenn P. Corbett, and Vincent Dunn, "WTC 'Investigation'?: A Call to Action" (http://fe.pennnet.com/Articles/Article_Display.cfm? Section=Online Articles&SubSection=Display&PUBLICATION_ID=25&ARTICLE_ID=13002 6). The second sentence is from editor Bill Manning, "Selling Out the Investigation" (www.globalresearch.ca/articles/ MAN309A.html).

213 "Baosteel Will Recycle World Trade Center Debris."

214 See Margie Burns, "Secrecy Surrounds a Bush Brother's Role in 9/11 Security," *American Reporter* 9/2021 (20 January 2003), who reports that the company's present CEO, Barry McDaniel, said that the company had had an

ongoing contract to provide security at the World Trade Center "up to the day the buildings fell down." Marvin Bush's role in the company is mentioned in Craig Unger, *House of Bush, House of Saud: The Secret Relationship between the World's Two Most Powerful Dynasties* (New York: Scribner, 2004) 249.

215 AFAQs, Question 14.

216 James Glanz, "Engineers Suspect Diesel Fuel in Collapse of 7 World Trade Center," *New York Times* 29 November 2001 (http://killtown. 911review.org/wtc7/archive/nytimes_112901.html).

217 See FEMA, *World Trade Center Building Performance Study*, ch. 5, Sect. 6.2, "Probable Collapse Sequence," which I discussed in NPH 22.

218 See "Zogby Poll: Over 70 Million American Adults Support New 9/11 Investigation," 911Truth.org, 23 May 2006 (www.911truth.org/article.php?story= 20060522022041421). The poll itself can be read at www.zogby.com/features/ features.dbm?ID=231.

219 "Fact Sheet: NIST's World Trade Center Investigation" www.nist.gov/ public_affairs/factsheet/nist_investigation_911.htm).

. 220 Stacey Loizeaux, daughter of Mark Loizeaux, the president of Controlled Demolition, Inc., said during an interview in 1996: "The term 'implosion' was coined by my grandmother back in, I guess, the '60s. It's a more descriptive way to explain what we do than 'explosion.' There *are* a series of small explosions, but the building itself isn't erupting outward. It's actually being pulled in on top of itself. What we're really doing is removing specific support columns within the structure and then cajoling the building in one direction or another, or straight down" (PBS, "Interview with Stacey Loizeaux," *NOVA* Online, December 1996 [www.pbs.org/wgbh/nova/kaboom/loizeaux.html]).

221 FEMA, *World Trade Center Building Performance Study*, ch. 5.

222 "The Myth of Implosion" (www.implosionworld.com/dyk2.html).

223 Glanz, "Engineers Suspect Diesel Fuel in Collapse of 7 World Trade Center."

224 PBS, "Interview with Stacey Loizeaux," quoted in Ed Haas, "No Chance of *Truth* in WTC-7 Investigation," Muckraker Report, 19 April 2006 http://www.teamliberty.net/id243.html.

225 E-mail from Steven Jones, 10 October 2005.

226 Quoted in Glanz, "Engineers Suspect Diesel Fuel in Collapse of 7 World Trade Center."

227 Jones referred to "the three photos at the top of http://911research.wtc7.net/ talks/wtc/videos.html" and also to "a video close-up of the southwest corner of WTC 7 as this corner begins its steady drop to the ground: http://st12.startlogic.com/ ~xenonpup/Flashes/squibs_along_southwest_corner.htm."

228 Jones here referred to *Popular Mechanics, 9/11: Debunking the Myths*, March 2005 (the online title of which is "Debunking the 9/11 Myths" (www.popularmechanics.com/science/defense/1227842.html?page=1&c=y).

229 Jones here gives the equation ($y = .5gt^2$).

230 Jones, "Why Indeed Did the World Trade Center Buildings Collapse?" ISO 43. For the Implosion World website, see www.implosionworld.com/ cinema.htm. These squibs are also shown in *911 Mysteries: Demolitions* (www.911Mysteries.com).

231 Report from 1010 WINS NYC News Radio, contained in the documentary "911 Eyewitness" (http://video.google.com/videoplay?docid=

65460757734339444&q=911+eyewitness).

232 Quoted in Chris Bull and Sam Erman, eds., *At Ground Zero: Young Reporters Who Were There Tell Their Stories* (New York: Thunder's Mouth Press, 2002) 97.

233 UPN9 News; quoted in *Loose Change: Final Cut*.

234 Websites showing the collapse of WTC 7 include www.geocities.com/killtown/wtc7.html and www.whatreallyhappened.com/wtc7.html. DVDs showing it include *Painful Deceptions* (www.erichufschmid.net/ThePainfulDeceptions Video.html), *911 Mysteries: Demolitions* (www.911 Mysteries.com), *Loose Change* (www.loosechange911.com), *Improbable Collapse* (http://video.google.com/videoplay?docid=4026073566596731782), David Ray Griffin, "The Destruction of the World Trade Center" (http://www.peaceproject.com/books/dvd146.html). A number of YouTube videos are also listed in the story at www.911blogger.com/node/2807.

235 This interview can be seen at "Demo Expert Confirms WTC-7 Was 'Controlled Demolition'" (www.911blogger.com/node/2807).

236 Bachmann and Schneider are both quoted in Daniele Ganser, "Der erbitterte Streit um den 11. September," *Tages-Anzeiger* 9 September 2006 (http://tagesanzeiger.ch/dyn/news/ausland/663864.html). Heikki Kurttila's analysis is contained in "Collapse Examination of WTC 7," 18 November 2005 (www.saunalahti.fi/wtc2001/WTC7_collapse_examination.pdf).

237 Dean E. Murphy, *September 11*, 175–76.

238 Oral hist of Frank Fellini, 101, and of Vincent Massa, 17–18.

239 I have discussed the expectation of the collapse of WTC 7 in "The Destruction of the World Trade Center: Why the Official Story Cannot Be True," in my *Christian Faith and the Truth Behind 9/11*, 50–53. This essay is also in Paul Zarembka, ed., *The Hidden History of 9–11-2001* (Amsterdam: Elsevier, 2006) 79–122.

240 Kelly, "Last Survivor Pulled from WTC."

241 NIST made its progress report on WTC 7 available (http://wtc.nist.gov/progress_report_june04/appendixl.pdf).

242 NIST Awards: "WTC 7: Structural Analysis and Collapse Hypotheses" (http://wtc.nist.gov/solicitations/wtc_awardQ0186.htm).

243 Ed Haas, "No Chance of *Truth* in WTC-7 Investigation."

244 Oral hist of Decosta Wright, 11.

245 Oral hist of Thomas McCarthy, 10–11.

246 Oral hist of Chief Daniel Nigro, 10.

247 Quoted in Dennis Smith, *Report From Ground Zero: The Heroic Story of the Rescuers at the World Trade Center* (New York: Penguin Putnam, 2002) 160.

248 Oral hist of Tiernach Cassidy, 22.

249 For photographs and discussion, see Hufschmid, *Painful Questions* 62–65, and the section entitled "The 'Raging' Fires at WTC Tower Seven" in "The World Trade Center Fires (Not So Hot Eh?)" (http://belgrade.indymedia.org/news/2005/04/102_comment.php). Terry Schmidt's photograph can be seen on page 63 of Hufschmid's *Painful Questions*. Schmidt reports that he took this photograph between 3:09 and 3:16PM (personal correspondence, 8 January 2006).

250 Jacobson can be seen making this statement in Michael Berger's film, *Improbable Collapse: The Demolition of Our Republic*.

251 See FEMA, *World Trade Center Building Performance Study*, ch. 5: WTC 7, Sect. 6.2, "Probable Collapse Sequence" (available at http://911research. wtc7.net/mirrors/fema_wtc/fema403_ch5.pdf).

252 D9/11M 54. This damage can be seen in the *Improbable Collapse* video.

253 Hoffman, "Claims of Severe Damage to Building 7" (http://wtc7.net/damageclaims.html).

254 Michael Green, "'Science, Handmaiden of Inspired Truth,' Or Putting NIST in Perspective," 9-11 Research, 12 December 2006 (http://911research. wtc7.net/essays/green/hamburger.html). Green also reports that, after Hamburger had mentioned the core columns, an audience member asked how many core columns each tower had, to which Hamburger replied that he did not know— which Green calls "a remarkable admission from a key member of the NIST WTC team." Green also points to a *Wall Street Journal* story in which Hamburger is quoted as saying that, when he saw the South Tower collapse, it appeared to him "that charges had been placed in the building" (Joseph T. Hallinan, Thomas B. Burton, and Jonathan Eig, "Top Structural Engineers to Do Autopsy on Twin Towers to Assess Why They Fell," *Wall Street Journal* 19 September 2001).

CHAPTER FOUR: DEBUNKING 9/11 MYTHS

1 "9/11: Debunking the Myths," *Popular Mechanics*, March 2005. The title of the online version is "Debunking the 9/11 Myths" (www.popular mechanics.com/science/defense/1227842.html?page=1&c=y).

2 Jim Hoffman, "Popular Mechanics' Assault on 9/11 Truth," *Global Outlook* 10 (Spring–Summer 2005) 21–42, which is based on Hoffman, "*Popular Mechanics* Attacks Its '9/11 Lies' Straw Man," Version 1.2, 9 February 2005 (http://911research.wtc7.net/essays/pm/index.html); Jeremy Baker, "Contrary to *Popular (Mechanics')* Belief," *Global Outlook* 10 (Spring–Summer 2005) 14–19 (the quoted statement is on 14). See also Peter Meyer, "Reply to *Popular Mechanics* re 9/11" (www.serendipity.li/wot/pop_mech/reply_to_popular_mechanics.htm).

3 David Ray Griffin, "The Destruction of the World Trade Center: Why the Official Account Cannot Be True," in Griffin, *Christian Faith and the Truth Behind 9/11: A Call to Reflection and Action* (Louisville: Westminster John Knox Press, 2006) 34–56, at 208n58. This essay was previously published, in slightly different form, in *The Hidden History of 9-11-2001*, ed. Paul Zarembka (Amsterdam: Elsevier, 2006) 79–122, and originally at 911Review.com (http://911review.com/ articles/griffin/nyc1.html).

4 D9/11M.

5 Baker, "Contrary to *Popular (Mechanics')* Belief," 19.

6 Senator John McCain, "Foreword," D9/11M xi–xvi.

7 McCain xv.

8 McCain xiii.

9 McCain xi.

10 McCain xv.

11 McCain xii.

12 McCain xiv, xii.

13 Ed Haas, "FBI says, 'No Hard Evidence Connecting Bin Laden to 9/11'" Muckraker Report, 6 June 2006 (www.teamliberty.net/id267.html).

14 McCain xii–xiii.

15 McCain xiii.

16 Brief descriptions of these three incidents are provided in the first chapter of my *Christian Faith and the Truth Behind 9/11*.

17 George McT. Kahin, *Intervention: How America Became Involved in Vietnam* (Garden City: Anchor Press, 1987) 217–21.

18 McCain xv.

19 Christopher Bollyn, "The Hidden Hand of the C.I.A. and the 9/11 Propaganda of *Popular Mechanics*," American Free Press, 19 March 2005 (www.rense.com/general63/brutalpurgeofPMstaff.htm).

20 Bollyn, "9/11 and Chertoff: Cousin Wrote 9/11 Propaganda for PM," Rumor Mill News, 4 March 2005 (www.rumormillnews.com/cgi-bin/archive.cgi?read=66176).

21 James B. Meigs, "Afterword: The Conspiracy Industry," D9/11M 91–107, at 102–03.

22 D9/11M 103.

23 US Department of State, "The Top September 11 Conspiracy Theories," 25 October 2006 (http://usinfo.state.gov/media/Archive/2005/Jan/24-318760.html).

24 D9/11M xx.

25 D9/11M xix, xxi, xviii.

26 D9/11M 1.

27 D9/11M 2.

28 D9/11M 3.

29 D9/11M 4, 6.

30 9/11CR 530n147.

31 D9/11M 4.

32 9/11CR 226.

33 D9/11M 4–5.

34 9/11CR 242.

35 D9/11M 5.

36 D9/11M 5–6.

37 Amy Goldstein, Lena H. Sun, and George Lardner Jr., "Hanjour: A Study in Paradox," *Washington Post* 15 October 2001 (www.washingtonpost.com/ac2/wp-dyn?pagename=article&node=&contentId=A59451-2001Oct14&notFound=true).

38 "FAA Was Alerted To Sept. 11 Hijacker," CBS News, 10 May 2002 (www.cbsnews.com/stories/2002/05/10/attack/main508656.shtml).

39 Jim Yardley, "A Trainee Noted for Incompetence," *New York Times* 4 May 2002 (http://select.nytimes.com/gst/abstract.html?res=F20A11FD35550C778CDDAC0894DA404482).

40 D9/11M 6.

41 Goldstein, Sun, and Lardner.

42 Yardley.

43 D9/11M 6.

44 Stan Goff, "The So-Called Evidence is a Farce," Narco News 14, 10

October 2001 (http://narconews.com/Issue15/goff1.html).

45 Russ Wittenberg is quoted in Greg Szymanski, "Former Vietnam Combat and Commercial Pilot Firm Believer 9/11 Was Inside Government Job," *Lewis News* 8 January 2006 (www.lewisnews.com/article.asp?ID=106623).

46 Stan Goff, "The So-Called Evidence is a Farce."

47 Quoted in Szymanski, "Former Vietnam Combat and Commercial Pilot."

48 A simulation of this trajectory can be seen at "American 77 Final Maneuver" (www.youtube.com/watch?v=DzR-q0ijbV0) (the two 0's in this URL are zeros). The claim that the aircraft that flew this trajectory was "American 77" is, of course, simply a claim.

49 D9/11M xx.

50 Nafeez Mosaddeq Ahmed, *The War on Freedom: How and Why America Was Attacked September 11, 2001* (Joshua Tree, CA: Tree of Life Publications, 2002) 161–62, and NPH 40–41. Also, the difficulty of simply hitting the Pentagon, even without the downward spiral, had been raised by Thierry Meyssan by means of quoting President Hosni Mubarak of Egypt. Speaking as a former pilot, Mubarak said that hitting lower floors "is not an easy thing" and that the pilot would have needed to "have flown a lot in this area to know the obstacles which could meet him when he is flying very low with a big commercial plane to hit the Pentagon in a special place" (Thierry Meyssan, *9/11: The Big Lie* [London: Carnot, 2002] 26).

51 D9/11M 6.

52 E-mail from Ralph Omholt, 27 October 2006.

53 D9/11M xxi.

54 D9/11M 8–11.

55 Unless, of course, its defenders can explain why they had been defending a false claim and why the rest of their story is not rendered incredible by this fact.

56 D9/11M 14.

57 D9/11M 21.

58 *San Diego Union–Tribune* 12 September 2001.

59 Griffin, "Flights 11, 175, 77, and 93: The 9/11 Commission's Incredible Tales," 911Truth.org, 5 December 2005 (www.911truth.org/article.php?story=20051205150219651). This essay was later published as "Flights of Fancy: The 9/11 Commission's Incredible Tales about Flights 11, 175, 77, and 93," in *Global Outlook*, April 2006, and in Griffin, *Christian Faith and the Truth Behind 9/11*.

60 O&D 163–64.

61 D9/11M xv.

62 *USA Today* (17 September 2001) was told by Pentagon sources, it reported, that Andrews "had no fighters assigned to it." General Larry Arnold told MSNBC (23 September 2001), "We [didn't] have any aircraft on alert at Andrews."

63 "DCANG Mission," available at http://web.archive.org/web/20010408230859/www.dcandr.ang.af.mil/hq/index.htm. This statement was on the Andrews website when it was updated on 19 April 2001.

64 "DCANG Mission & Vision" (http://web.archive.org/web/20010914183708/www.dcandr.ang.af.mil/aboutDCANG/mission.htm). The date on this statement is 24 July 2001, but whether that is when the new statement was

posted, I do not know. Jared Israel, who was evidently the first one to call attention to this change, has written: "we cannot say *exactly* when the Mission Statement was removed. We can only say with certainty that it was between April 19 and September 13, 2001" (http://emperors-clothes.com/indict/ update630.htm).

65 Fox News, 11 September 2001. This interview is included in a film, *Pandora's Black Box*, produced by Pilots for 9/11 Truth (http://pilotsfor911 truth.org).

66 D9/11M 14–15.

67 O&D 272–73, quoting 9/11CR 31.

68 D9/11M 180–86. On the authorship of this memo by Laura Brown, see n. 136 of ch. 1.

69 D9/11M 192–93, 204–06. See Matthew Wald, "After the Attacks: Sky Rules; Pentagon Tracked Deadly Jet but Found No Way to Stop It," *New York Times* 15 September 2001 (www.attackonamerica.net/pentagontrackeddeadlyjet.html).

70 D9/11M 15.

71 E-mail from Hordon, 15 January 2007; e-mail from Scoggins, 16 January 2007.

72 D9/11M 15.

73 D9/11M 16, 17–18.

74 See O&D 157–58, discussing 9/11CR 20; the 9/11 Commission's statement about the New York Center's direct call is at 9/11CR 23.

75 D9/11M x.

76 D9/11M 155.

77 D9/11M xxi.

78 D9/11M 18.

79 D9/11M 18–19.

80 "Air Attack on Pentagon Indicates Weaknesses," *Newsday* 23 September 2001.

81 9/11CR 34.

82 9/11 Commission Hearing, 23 May 2003 (www.9-11commission.gov/ archive/hearing2/9-11Commission_Hearing_2003-05-23.htm), panel 1.

83 For Lee Hamilton's exchange with Mineta, see www.youtube.com/ watch?v=V7Vs7KNlpXU; for Roemer's exchange with Mineta, see www.youtube.com/watch?v=6Z2c8IKemYI. For a discussion, which includes the fact that this portion of Mineta's testimony has been removed from the official version of the video, see Gregor Holland, "The Mineta Testimony: 9/11 Commission Exposed," 911Truth.org, 1 November 2005 (www.911truth movement.org/archives/2005/11/post.php).

84 D9/11M 17.

85 D9/11M 17. The original claim is repeated, moreover, in Guy Smith's BBC documentary, *The Conspiracy Files: 9/11*. Davin Coburn, listed as one of the "researchers" for D9/11M, stated on camera that "there were like 4500 blips that looked identical across the United States."

86 Charles Lane, Don Phillips, and David Snyder, "A Sky Filled With Chaos, Uncertainty and True Heroism," *Washington Post* 17 September 2001 (www.washingtonpost.com/ac2/wp-dyn?pagename=article&node=nation/ specials/attacked&contentId=A41095-2001Sep16).

87 9/11CR 20.

88 O&D 167.

89 This interview was on the *Jack Blood Show*, 14 December 2006, hour 1 (www.realradioarchives.com/sounds/JB0829062.mp3).

90 D9/11M 21, quoting 9/11CR 18.

91 9/11CR 11.

92 D9/11M 20.

93 D9/11M 20.

94 Leslie Filson, *Air War over America: Sept. 11 Alters Face of Air Defense Mission,* foreword by Larry K. Arnold (Public Affairs: Tyndall Air Force Base, 2003) 72.

95 9/11 Commission Hearing, 23 May 2003.

96 9/11 Commission Hearing, 17 June 2004 (www.9-11commission.gov/archive/hearing12/9-11Commission_Hearing_2004-06-17.htm).

97 9/11 Commission Hearing, 17 June 2004.

98 9/11CR 16 352.

99 D9/11M 20, 22.

100 9/11CR 17.

101 9/11CR 344–45, quoted in O&D 264–65.

102 O&D 266–67.

103 Quoted in Joby Warrick and Joe Stephens, "Before Attack, US Expected Different Hit," *Washington Post* 2 October 2001 (www.washingtonpost.com/ac2/wp-dyn/A55607-2001Oct1?language=printer).

104 *New York Times* 3 November 2001; *Time* 4 April 1995.

105 Associated Press, 18 April 2002.

106 MDW News Service, 3 November 2000; *Mirror* 24 May 2002.

107 John J. Lumpkin, "Agency was to Crash Plane on 9-11," Associated Press, 22 August 2002; Pamela Hess, "US Agencies—Strange 9/11 Coincidence," UPI, 22 August 2002.

108 9/11 Commission Hearing, 13 April 2004, panel 1 (www.9-11commission.gov/archive/hearing10/9-11Commission_Hearing_2004-04-13.htm).

109 Steven Komarow and Tom Squitieri, "NORAD Had Drills of Jets as Weapons," *USA Today* 18 April 2004 (www.usatoday.com/news/ washington/2004-04-18-norad_x.htm). The exercise involving planes from Utah and Washington was named Amalgam Virgo 02. It was not held until 2002 but was planned in July 2001 (www.cooperativeresearch.org/context.jsp?item=a060101amalgamvirgo).

110 D9/11M 22.

111 Glen Johnson, "Facing Terror Attack's Aftermath: Otis Fighter Jets Scrambled Too Late to Halt the Attacks," *Boston Globe* 15 September 2001 (www.fromthewilderness.com/timeline/2001/bostonglobe091501.html).

112 D9/11M 24.

113 Linda Slobodian, "NORAD on Heightened Alert: Role of Air Defence Agency Rapidly Transformed in Wake of Sept. 11 Terrorist Attacks," *Calgary Herald* 13 October 2001 (http://911research.wtc7.net/cache/planes/analysis/norad/calgaryherald101301_scrables.html); Leslie Miller, "Military Now Notified Immediately of Unusual Air Traffic Events," Associated Press, 12 August 2002 (http://911research.wtc7.net/ cache/planes/analysis/norad/020812ap.html).

114 Griffin, "The Destruction of the World Trade Center: Why the Official Account Cannot Be True." This essay was first published in 2005 at 911Review.com (http://911review.com/articles/griffin/nyc1.html). It was next published in Paul Zarembka, ed., *The Hidden History of 9-11-2001* (Amsterdam: Elsevier, 2006) and then in my *Christian Faith and the Truth Behind 9/11*. The quoted statement is in note 35 of the first two versions and note 58 of the third one.

115 In the statement from Martin cited in Leslie Miller's AP story cited in note 113, the 67 scrambles occurred from "September 2000 to June 2001," which would be nine months. In the present statement, the months are reversed, making the period in question sixteen months. Having been unable to locate the *Colorado Springs Gazette* story, I do not know if *PM* introduced the error or if it simply did not notice the error in the *Gazette* story.

116 D9/11M 24–25.

117 Air Traffic Control Center, "ATCC Controller's Red Binder" (available at www.xavius.com/080198.htm), quoted in Ahmed, *The War on Freedom,* 148.

118 Slobodian, "NORAD on Heightened Alert."

119 General Accounting Office, "Continental Air Defense: A Dedicated Force Is No Longer Needed," 3 May 1994 (www.fas.org/man/gao/gao9476.htm).

120 Leslie Filson, *Sovereign Skies: Air National Guard Takes Command of 1st Air Force* (Tyndall, FL: First Air Force, 1999) 52.

121 D9/11M 23.

122 O&D 323n31.

123 "Fangs Bared: Florida's Eagles Stand Sentry Over Southern Skies," *Airman,* December 1999 (www.af.mil/news/airman/1299/home.htm).

124 "Retired Air Force Col: They Lied to Us About the War and About 9/11 Itself," 27 October 2005 (www.benfrank.net/blog/2005/10/27/oil_mafia_treason).

125 D9/11M 25.

126 Johnson, "Facing Terror Attack's Aftermath."

127 Filson, *Sovereign Skies,* 96–97.

128 *Airman,* December 1999 (www.af.mil/news/airman/1299/home2.htm).

129 D9/11M 28.

130 D9/11M 28.

131 D9/11M 28.

132 Professors Question 9/11 (http://patriotsquestion911.com/professors.html).

133 David Ray Griffin and Peter Dale Scott, ed., *9/11 and American Empire: Intellectuals Speak Out* (Northampton, MA: Olive Branch Press, 2006); Paul Zarembka, ed., *The Hidden History of 9-11-2001* (Amsterdam: Elsevier, 2006); Kevin Barrett, John B. Cobb, Jr., and Sandra Lubarsky, *9/11 and American Empire: Christians, Jews, and Muslims Speak Out* (Northampton: Olive Branch Press, 2007).

134 D9/11M 29.

135 D9/11M 29.

136 I so described it, in fact, in a note for my essay, "The Destruction of the World Trade Center."

137 D9/11M 30.

138 D9/11M 31, quoting Robertson's statement as provided in the *New Yorker,* 19 November 2001.

139 John Skilling's statement is quoted in Eric Nalder, "Twin Towers

Engineered to Withstand Jet Collision," *Seattle Times* 27 February 1993. It is partially quoted in James Glanz and Eric Tipton, *City in the Sky: The Rise and Fall of the World Trade Center* (New York: Times Books/Henry Holt, 2003) 138.

140 D9/11M 31.

141 Eagar and Musso, "Why Did the World Trade Center Collapse?"

142 For the video in which De Martini makes this statement, see "The 'Truss Theory': A Fantasy Concocted to Conceal a Demolition," What Really Happened (www.whatreallyhappened.com/trusstheory.html).

143 D9/11M 32–33.

144 D9/11M 35–36.

145 Greg Szymanski, "NY Fireman Lou Cacchioli Upset that 9/11 Commission 'Tried to Twist My Words,'" Arctic Beacon.com, 19 July 2005 (www.arcticbeacon.com/19-Jul-2005.html).

146 David Ray Griffin, "Explosive Testimony: Revelations about the Twin Towers in the 9/11 Oral Histories," 911Truth.org, 18 January 2006 (www.911truth.org/article.php?story=20060118104223192), quoting Szymanski, "NY Fireman Lou Cacchioli Upset." (This essay was later reprinted in my *Christian Faith and the Truth Behind 9/11*).

147 "Explosive Testimony," n. 43. It appears that my article did misrepresent Cacchioli with regard to his attempt to testify to staff members of the 9/11 Commission. Although my article does not directly say that he was frustrated because he was not permitted to give his testimony about explosives, it does, like Szymanski's article, imply it, whereas Cacchioli evidently told *PM* that he had wanted to talk about the ineffectiveness of the radios (D9/11M 36). But this is a secondary point. The primary issue is Cacchioli's description of occurrences that made him think at the time that explosives were going off.

148 Graeme MacQueen, "118 Witnesses: The Firefighters' Testimony to Explosions in the Twin Towers," *Journal of 9/11 Studies* 2 (August 2006): 49–106 (www.journalof911studies.com).

149 For the video of this conversation, see "Evidence of Demolition Charges in WTC 2," What Really Happened (www.whatreallyhappened.com/ wtc2_cutter.html).

150 Oral hist of Edward Cachia, 5.

151 Oral hist of Thomas Turilli, 4.

152 Randy Lavello, "Bombs in the Building" (www.prisonplanet.com/ analysis_lavello_050503_bombs.html).

153 Jim Hoffman, "*Popular Mechanics'* Attacks Its '9/11 Lies' Straw Man," Version 1.2, 9 February 2005 (http://911research.wtc7.net/essays/pm/index.html). Hoffman's critique was reprinted in slightly revised form as "Popular Mechanics' Assault on 9/11 Truth," *Global Outlook* 10 (Spring–Summer 2005) 21–42.

154 D9/11M 37, 38.

155 D9/11M 37.

156 Eagar and Musso, "Why Did the World Trade Center Collapse?"

157 D9/11M 158.

158 Hoffman, e-mail of 30 November 2006.

159 D9/11M 37, 38.

160 NISTFR 147.

161 D9/11M 39.

162 NISTFR 88.

163 NISTFR 88.

164 D9/11M 39.

165 D9/11M 38.

166 D9/11M 40.

167 Eagar and Musso, "Why Did the World Trade Center Collapse?"

168 See "Structures Can Be Beautiful: World's Tallest Buildings Pose Esthetic and Structural Challenge to John Skilling" and "How Columns Will Be Designed for 110-Story Buildings," *Engineering News-Record* 2 April 1964; cited in Kevin Ryan, "What Is 9/11 Truth?" The statements to which Ryan referred said that "live loads on these [perimeter] columns can be increased more than 2000% before failure occurs" and that "one could cut away all the first-story columns on one side of the building, and part way from the corners of the perpendicular sides, and the building could still withstand design live loads and a 100-mph wind force from any direction."

169 D9/11M 37.

170 D9/11M 41.

171 Jones, "Why Indeed Did the WTC Buildings Collapse?" 39.

172 D9/11M 41, quoting Alan Pense, professor emeritus of metallurgical engineering at Lehigh University.

173 Quoted in James Williams, "WTC a Structural Success," *SEAU News: The Newsletter of the Structural Engineers Association of Utah*, October 2001 (www.seau.org/SEAUNews-2001-10.pdf).

174 Christopher Bollyn, "New Seismic Data Refutes Official Explanation," American Free Press, updated 12 April 2004 (www.thetruthseeker.co.uk/article.asp?ID=2580).

175 William Langewiesche, *American Ground: Unbuilding the World Trade Center* (New York: North Point Press, 2002) 31.

176 D9/11M 44–45.

177 AFAQs, Question 2.

178 D9/11M 39.

179 Zdenek P. Bazant and Yong Zhou, "Why Did the World Trade Center Collapse? Simple Analysis," *Journal of Engineering Mechanics* 128/2 (January 2002). Strangely, *PM*, in citing this paper in the notes at the back of the book, does not mention Yong Zhou as co-author.

180 D9/11M 46.

181 Quoted in Christopher Bollyn, "New Seismic Data Refutes Official Explanation."

182 D9/11M 46–47.

183 "Epilogue: The Van Romero Episode" is printed at the end of the version of "The Collapse of the World Trade Center" contained in my *Christian Faith and the Truth Behind 9/11*. (In the previous versions of the paper, the material on Romero was contained in a long note.)

184 Olivier Uyttebrouck, "Explosives Planted In Towers, N.M. Tech Expert Says," *Albuquerque Journal* 11 September 2001 (www.public-action.com/911/jmcm/ABQjournal; scroll down).

185 John Fleck, "Fire, Not Extra Explosives, Doomed Buildings, Expert Says," *Albuquerque Journal* 21 September 2001 (www.public-action.com/911/jmcm/ABQjournal).

186 D9/11M 49.

187 Uyttebrouck, "Explosives Planted In Towers, N.M. Tech Expert Says."

188 Hoffman, *"Popular Mechanics'* Attacks Its '9/11 Lies' Straw Man."

189 D9/11M 52.

190 D9/11M 46. This is *PM's* paraphrase, not a direct quotation, of Loizeaux's statement.

191 D9/11M 53.

192 D9/11M 53–54.

193 D9/11M 53, 56.

194 D9/11M 56, 58.

195 See Sharon Seitz, "The Little Fireboat That Did," *Time Out New York* 313 (27 September–4 October 2001) (http://web.archive.org/web/20011031135350/www.timeoutny.com/aroundtown/313/313u.around.fireboat.box.html), and Huntley Gill, "Retired Fireboat Harvey Helps With World Trade Center Disaster," NYFD.com (www.firehouse.com/terrorist/17_Pharvey.html). The statement from NIST is in NIST NCSTAR 1-8, "The Emergency Response Operations" (http://wtc.nist.gov/NISTNCSTAR1-8.pdf) 110.

196 *America Rebuilds*, PBS documentary, 2002, now available as PBS Home Video, ISBN 0-7806-4006-3 (www.pbs.org/americarebuilds).

197 D9/11M 57–58.

198 *America Rebuilds*. Silverstein's statement can be viewed on a video (www.infowars.com/Video/911/wtc7_pbs.WMV) or heard on an audio file (http://VestigialConscience.com/PullIt.mp3).

199 D9/11M 57.

200 D9/11M 57–58.

201 This telephone call, preceded by Silverstein's statement and then the claim by PM's Davin Coburn that "the term 'pull it' is not a demolition term," can be heard at www.pumpitout.com/audio/pull_it_mix.mp3.

202 "9/11 Myths Busted!" *The O'Reilly Factor*, Fox News, 7 August 2006 (www.foxnews.com/story/0,2933,207406,00.html).

203 Russell Pickering, Pentagon Research (www.pentagonresearch.com).

204 D9/11M 59.

205 One problem is that no reference is given to support the claim about "hundreds of witnesses." The most extensive list of witnesses, provided by Eric Bart, contains 152 people, only some of whom claimed to have seen an airliner crash into the Pentagon. Others claimed to have seen something quite different (Eric Bart, "It Was a Plane Bomb," section entitled "Witness Accounts" (http://eric.bart.free.fr/iwpb/witness.html). Moreover, when another researcher, Jerry Russell, examined the 31 testimonies that provided "explicit, realistic and detailed claims" about an airliner striking the Pentagon, he found "substantial errors or contradictions in 21." For example, *USA Today* reporter Steve Anderson said that the plane "drug its wing along the ground before it hit the Pentagon." This, however, would have created a huge scar in the Pentagon lawn, which photographs showed not to exist. Russell also, looking at the list of explicit witnesses in light of the hypothesis that "'eyewitness' sources strongly linked to the US corporate and media elite might [have] provide[d] false testimony," found that "24 of 31 worked for either the Federal Government or the mainstream media" (Jerry Russell, "Eyewitnesses and the Plane-Bomb Theories" [www.911-

strike.com/PlaneBomb.htm]). To point out these problems is not to say that someone could not make a good case for the evidentiary value of the testimony of some of the reputed eyewitnesses; it is merely to say that *PM* did not do so.

206 D9/11M 65.

207 "Washington's Heroes: On the Ground at the Pentagon on Sept. 11," *Newsweek* 28 September 2003 (http://msnbc.msn.com/id/3069699).

208 Meigs, "Afterword: The Conspiracy Industry," D9/11M 96.

209 D9/11M 67.

210 See Probst's testimony in Eric Bart, "Witness Accounts," or in Vince Crawley, "Fortress Report," MilitaryCity.com, 11 September 2002 (www.military city.com/sept11/fortress1.html).

211 Dave McGowan, "September 11, 2001 Revisited: The Series: Act II," Center for an Informed America (www.davesweb.cnchost.com/nwsltr68.html).

212 D9/11M 67.

213 See, for example, Russell Pickering, Pentagon Research: Lamp Poles (www.pentagonresearch.com/lamps.html).

214 See, for example, Dave McGowan, "September 11, 2001 Revisited: The Series: Act II," and Richard Stanley and Jerry Russell, "The Five-Sided Fantasy Island: The Quantum Flight Path?" 911-Strike.com (www.911-strike.com/quantum-path.htm).

215 *The PentaCon: Eyewitnesses Speak, Conspiracy Revealed* (http://video.google.com/videoplay?docid=4196580169348087802), a 2007 film by the Citizen Investigation Team, headed by Aldo Marquis and Craig Ranke (www.thepentacon.com).

216 Stanley and Russell, "The Five-Sided Fantasy Island: The Quantum Flight Path?"

217 See *Pandora's Black Box*: Chapter 1, "Analysis of American 77 Flight Data," and Chapter 2, "Flight of American 77," at Pilots for 9/11 Truth (http://pilotsfor911truth.org). It is important to note that the titles, with their reference to "American 77," reflect the position of the NTSB, not Pilots for 9/11 Truth. As Rob Balsamo, the founder of that organization, says: "The NTSB claims the Flight Data Recorder is from AA77, but it could really be from any type of aircraft" (e-mail, 17 January 2007).

218 "Memorandum for the Secretary of Defense: Subject: Justification for US Military Intervention in Cuba," 13 March 1962 (PDF of original document available at www.gwu.edu/~nsarchiv/news/20010430/doc1.pdf) 10.

219 This statement, which was revealed in the new chapter of the updated version of Philippe Sands, *Lawless World: Making and Breaking Global Rules* (London: Penguin Books, 2006), was quoted in "Revealed: Bush and Blair Discussed Using American Spyplane in UN Colours to Lure Saddam into War," Channel 4 News (London) 2 February 2006 (available at www.afterdowningstreet.org/?q=node/7418).

220 D9/11M 63.

221 See the story at http://cf.newsday.com/911/victimsearch.cfm?id=200 and the list of occupants at www.cnn.com/SPECIALS/2001/trade.center/ victims/AA11.victims.html.

222 Natalie Patton, "Flight Attendant Made Call on Cell Phone to Mom in Las Vegas," *Las Vegas Review-Journal* 13 September 2001. See also "Profile:

Renee May," Center for Cooperative Research (www.cooperativeresearch.org/entity.jsp?entity=renee_may). She reportedly made the call at 9:12, when the plane would have still been too high for a cell phone call to have been successful. And the plane was said to be going at "a high rate of speed" (9/11CR 9), which by itself would probably have made the call impossible.

223 Quoted in Jim Hoagland, "The Limits of Lying," *Washington Post* 21 March 2002.

224 Quoted in Rowland Morgan, "Barbara Olson's Call from Flight 77 Never Happened," Global Echo, 2 December 2004 (http://globalecho.org/view_article.php?aid=2434).

225 See Hannity & Colmes, Fox News, 14 September 2001; *Larry King Live*, CNN, 14 September 2001 (http://edition.cnn.com/TRANSCRIPTS/0109/14/lkl.00.html); and Toby Harnden, "She Asked Me How to Stop the Plane," *Daily Telegraph* 5 March 2002. See "Barbara Olson Said to Call from Flight 77, but Account Is Full of Contradictions," Center for Cooperative Research (www.cooperativeresearch.org/entity.jsp?entity=barbara_olson).

226 Rowland Morgan and Ian Henshall, *9/11 Revealed: The Unanswered Questions* (New York: Carroll & Graf, 2005) 128–29.

227 Rowland Morgan, *Flight 93 Revealed: What Really Happened on the 9/11 'Let's Roll' Flight?* (New York: Carroll & Graf, 2006) 52.

228 The letter of inquiry, which was written at the instigation of Ian Henshall, was sent 6 December 2004. The response from Tim Wagner was sent the same day. The fact that AA had confirmed the absence of onboard phones on its Boeing 757s is mentioned in Rowland Morgan, *Flight 93 Revealed*, 52.

229 American Airlines, "Onboard Technology" (https://www.aa.com/content/travelInformation/duringFlight/onboardTechnology.jhtml). This statement is quoted in Rowland Morgan, "Barbara Olson's Call from Flight 77 Never Happened."

230 D9/11M 63.

231 Andrew M. Baker, M.D., "Human Identification in a Post-9/11 World: Attack on American Airlines Flight 77 and the Pentagon Identification and Pathology" (http://ndms.chepinc.org/data/files/3/266.pdf); Steve Vogel, "Remains Unidentified For 5 Pentagon Victims," *Washington Post* 21 November 2001 (www.washingtonpost.com/ac2/wp-dyn?pagename=article&node=&contentId=A61202-2001Nov20). Both of these reports are quoted on Pickering's website under "Evidence" (www.pentagonresearch.com/evidence.html).

232 This autopsy can be read on Pickering's site (www.pentagonresearch.com/093.html).

233 *After-Action Report on the Response to the September 11 Attack on the Pentagon: Arlington County*, 2002 (www.arlingtonva.us/departments/Fire/edu/about/docs/after_report.pdf), quoted in Pickering, Pentagon Research: Evidence ((www.pentagonresearch.com/evidence.html).

234 Col. H. Theodore Harcke, Major Joseph A. Bifano, and Capt. Kelly K. Koeller, "Forensic Radiology: Response to the Pentagon Attack on September 11, 2001," *Radiology* 223 (2002):7–8 (http://radiology.rsnajnls.org/cgi/content/full/223/1/7).

235 *After-Action Report on the Response to the September 11 Attack on the Pentagon*, C–45.

236 Jamie McIntyre interviewed by Judy Woodruff, "America Under Attack," CNN Breaking News, 11 September 2001 (http://transcripts.cnn.com/TRANSCRIPTS/0109/11/bn.35.html).

237 Meigs, "Afterword: The Conspiracy Industry," D9/11M 97.

238 Russell Pickering, quoting statements of McIntyre's posted on Pickering's website (www.pentagonresearch.com/video.html), made this point in an e-mail of 14 October 2006, to *Popular Mechanics*' editor-in-chief James Meigs.

239 Jamie McIntyre interviewed by Judy Woodruff. Some people have claimed that McIntyre later, in strongly supporting the view that the building was hit by a 757, contradicted his earlier statement that all the pieces he saw were "very small." The strongest evidence for this view seems to be this statement: "I was there on September 11, and I saw the wreckage of a plane, including large pieces" (see "Jamie McIntyre Contradiction #3" at www.youtube.com/watch?v=KV0XRVL2vrw). In his interview with Judy Woodruff on 9/11, however, he had said: "The biggest piece I saw was about three feet long, it was silver and had been painted green and red . . . . I also saw a large piece of shattered glass. It appeared to be a cockpit windshield or other window from the plane" (http://transcripts.cnn.com/TRANSCRIPTS/0109/11/bn.35.html). There is, therefore, no contradiction as long as it is understood that the "large pieces" he saw were "small enough that you can pick [them] up in your hand." Thus understood, his later affirmation of "large pieces" does not contradict his earlier report that there were "no large tail sections, wing sections, fuselage, nothing like that anywhere around."

240 Ralph Omholt, "9-11 and the Impossible: The Pentagon: Part One of an Online Journal of 9-11" (www.physics911.net/omholt.htm). Henceforth cited simply as "The Pentagon."

241 For Plaugher's statement, see "DoD News Briefing," Defense Link, Department of Defense, 12 September 2001. Although this briefing has been removed from the DoD, it has been preserved by Yale Law School's Avalon Project (www.yale.edu/lawweb/avalon/sept_11/dod_brief01.htm). To be sure, a month later, after there was time for Plaugher's memory to be "refreshed," he said that he did remember having seen "pieces of the fuselage, the wings, the landing gear, pieces of the engine" (quoted in NPH 34). For Evey's statement, see "Dod News Briefing on Pentagon Renovation," Defense Link, Department of Defense, 15 September 2001.

242 "Interview with April Gallop," George Washington's Blog, 13 July 2006 (http://georgewashington.blogspot.com/2006/07/interview-with-april-gallop.html).

243 Randy Dockendorf, "Tyndall Native Relives 9/11" (www.yankton.net/stories/091103/com_20030911017.shtml). Pickering, who has studied over 1,500 photographs from both inside and outside the Pentagon, says: "There are no photos that indicate aircraft passenger seats, luggage or cargo" (www.pentagonresearch.com/photographers.html).

244 McWethy's statement is quoted in *Covering Catastrophe: Broadcast Journalists Report September 11*, ed. Allison Gilbert et al. (New York: Bonus Books, 2002) 187. I am indebted to Matthew Everett for this reference.

245 *The NFPA Journal* 1 November 2001. This argument, Thierry Meyssan pointed out (*Pentagate* [London: Carnot, 2002], 14-17), was articulated by many defenders of the official account.

246 See, for example, Jim Hoffman's photographs and discussion at http://911research.wtc7.net/talks/noplane/enginerotor.html and the six following pages.

247 D9/11M photo section.

248 Dave McGowan, "September 11, 2001 Revisited: The Series: Act II."

249 D9/11M 63.

250 D9/11M 64.

251 General Stubblebine's statement, which is in the film *One Nation Under Siege*, can be seen at that film's website (www.undersiegemovie.com/moreinfo.html) or at YouTube (www.youtube.com/watch?v=Zsn4JA450iA).

252 D9/11M 66.

253 According to those who believe that the Pentagon was hit by a Boeing 757, or at least a large airplane of some type, the two best photographs are at www.geoffmetcalf.com/pentagon/images/5.jpg and www.geoffmetcalf.com/pentagon/images/6.jpg.

254 D9/11M 69, quoting Mete Sozen, who was one of the authors of the ASCE's *Pentagon Building Performance Report*.

255 D9/11M 67–68.

256 D9/11M 69.

257 Mete A. Sozen, Sami A. Kilic, and Christoph M. Hoffmann, "September 11 Pentagon Attack Simulations Using LS-Dyna," phase I, completed 11 September 2002 (www.cs.purdue.edu/homes/cmh/simulation/phase1).

258 Mete A. Sozen, Ayhan Irfanoglu, and Christoph M. Hoffmann, "September 11 Pentagon Attack Simulations Using LS-Dyna," phase III, as of 10 September 2006 (www.cs.purdue.edu/homes/cmh/simulation/phase3/index.html).

259 Pickering points out that Purdue's "liquefaction" theory is "without historical precedent or physical evidence"; see Pickering, Pentagon Research: Exit Hole (www.pentagonresearch.com/exit.html).

260 See Pentagon Research: The Pentagon, "Wedge Information" (www.pentagonresearch.com/pentagon.html), "Inner Rings" (www.pentagon research.com/innerrings.html), and "Exit Hole" (www.pentagonresearch.com/exit.html).

261 Pentagon news briefing, 15 September 2001.

262 See Pickering, Pentagon Research: Exit Hole.

263 NPH 31.

264 D9/11M 69–70.

265 D9/11M 70.

266 D9/11M 70.

267 Sami Yli-Karjanmaa, who to my knowledge has provided the best critique of this report, says: "The Report in no way comments on what caused a large hole to be created in the inner wall of the Pentagon's middle Ring. The Report only says this: 'There was a hole in the east wall of Ring C, emerging into AE Drive, between column lines 5 and 7 in Wedge 2. . . . The wall failure was approximately 310 ft from where the fuselage of the aircraft entered the west wall of the building'" ("The ASCE's Pentagon Building Performance Report: Arrogant Deception—Or an Attempt to Expose a Cover-up?" [www.kolumbus.fi/sy-k/pentagon/asce_en.htm]).

268 ASCE (American Society of Civil Engineers), *Pentagon Building*

Performance Report, January 2003 (http://fire.nist.gov/bfrlpubs/build03/PDF/b03017.pdf) 20, 40.

269 D9/11M 70.

270 "Washington's Heroes: On the Ground at the Pentagon on Sept. 11," *Newsweek* 28 September 2003 (http://msnbc.msn.com/id/3069699).

271 ASCE, *Pentagon Building Performance Report*, 40 (section 6.1).

272 Pentagon news briefing, 15 September 2001. Mitchell's statement agrees with the first known photograph of this hole, which shows no sign of any airplane parts (Pickering, Pentagon Research: Exit Hole Chronology [www.pentagonresearch.com/062.html]).

273 Pickering, Pentagon Research: Exit Hole.

274 Michael Meyer, "Pentagon C Ring Exit Hole Mystery," Scholars for 9/11 Truth," 10 June 2006 (www.scholarsfor911truth.org/ArticleMeyer_10June2006.html).

275 Michael Meyer, e-mail of 24 November 2006.

276 See "Exit Hole" and "Rapid Wall Breaching Kit" under "No Exit Hole Inspection" (www.pentagonresearch.com/091.html).

277 Pickering, asking this question, writes: "That area of 'C' ring had no windows on floor one and no doors in the unrenovated Wedge 2 where the exit hole is located. Maybe it was intended as a humane escape route for the people inside. If they wanted to do total destruction why would they have blast reinforced the front of the building in Wedge 1 (which was also the least occupied wedge)? People did make it out of the exit hole according to witnesses. . . . The aircraft nose was just a cover story because the RWBK [Rapid Wall Breaching Kit] makes a round hole and the nose of an aircraft is round and would appear logical to the uninformed."

278 See Judicial Watch, "CITGO Gas Station Cameras Near Pentagon Evidently Did Not Capture Attack," 15 September 2006 (www.judicialwatch.org/printer_5965.shtml). These videos can be seen on YouTube (www.youtube.com/watch?v=2LJvFjsl6zk).

279 In November 2006, long after the *PM* book had appeared, a video from the nearby Doubletree Hotel was released, but it also showed nothing identifiable. It is available on YouTube (www.youtube.com/watch?v=H285_DWX_bQ).

280 D9/11M 61.

281 D9/11M xv.

282 D9/11M 61.

283 For the documented evidence, see http://flight77.info/85tapes.gif, which shows a letter requesting 85 videos that had been mentioned by an FBI agent, and www.flight77.info/00new/n85reply.jpg, which shows a DoJ letter saying: "The material you requested is located in an investigative file which is exempt from disclosure."

284 *On the Story*, CNN, 20 May 2006 (http://transcripts.cnn.com/TRANSCRIPTS/0605/20/tt.01.html).

285 D9/11M 61.

286 See "Pentagon Photos Released," Associated Press, 8 March 2002 (www.pentagonresearch.com/Daily%20Herald%20War%20on%20Terrorism.htm).

287 D9/11M 65.

288 Omholt, "The Pentagon."

289 Omholt; scroll down about two fifths of the way. Omholt also points to

evidence of premeditation, saying: "Note in the right-hand picture the material conveniently available for that ground cover. That's asking a lot of 'coincidence'!"

290 See "Smoke and Fire," 9-11 Research (http://911research.wtc7.net/ pentagon/evidence/photos/smoke.html).

291 Pickering, Pentagon Research: Bob Pugh Video (www.pentagonresearch.com/ bob.html).

292 Omholt, "The Pentagon."

293 D9/11M 68.

294 Won-Young Kim and G. R. Baum, "Seismic Observations during September 11, 2001, Terrorist Attack," Spring 2002 (report to the Maryland Department of Natural Resources); available at www.cooperativeresearch.org.

295 For a defense of the 757 theory, see Jim Hoffman, "The Pentagon Attack: The No-Jetliner Claim" (http://911research.wtc7.net/talks/noplane/index.html).

296 Quoted in Szymanski, "Former Vietnam Combat and Commercial Pilot." (Later evidence has indicated that the trajectory involved 8,000 feet and a 330-degree turn.)

297 Ralph Omholt, e-mail of 27 October 2006; emphasis his.

298 Barara Honegger, "The Pentagon Attack Papers: Seven Hours in September: The Cloth that Broke the Lie," appendix to Jim Marrs, *The Terror Conspiracy: Deception, 9/11, and the Loss of Liberty* (New York: Disinformation, 2006), 439–65.

299 See, for example, Jim Hoffman's discussion under "Frequently Asked Questions: The Pentagon Attack" (http://911research.wtc7.net/faq/ pentagon.html#suicidepilot).

300 Information supporting these six points can be found on Pickering's Pentagon Research Website under "The Pentagon," "Attack Path," and "Impact Zone."

301 Pentagon Research: Attack Path (www.pentagonresearch.com/attack.html).

302 9/11CR 31.

303 "DOD Rehearsed Plane Hitting Pentagon," UPI, 22 April 2004 (http://web.archive.org/web/20050211062128/www.washtimes.com/upi-breaking/ 20040422-090447-8354r.htm).

304 Eric Schmitt, "Threats and Responses: War Games; Pentagon Rejected Pre-9/11 Hijacking Exercise," *New York Times* 14 April 2004 (http://select.nytimes.com/gst/abstract.html?res=F60E13F63D5F0C778DDDAD0 894DC404482); Bradley Graham, "Pentagon Crash Scenario Was Rejected for Military Exercise," *Washington Post* 14 April 2004 (www.washingtonpost.com/ ac2/wp-dyn?pagename=article&contentId=A9449-2004Apr13).

305 Matt Mientka, "Pentagon Medics Trained for Strike," *US Medicine*, October 2001 (www.usmedicine.com/article.cfm?articleID=272&issueID=31).

306 Gen. Lance Lord, "A Year Ago, A Lifetime Ago," *The Beam* 13 September 2002 (www.dcmilitary.com/dcmilitary_archives/stories/091302/19212-1.shtml).

307 D9/11M 65.

308 Federal Bureau of Investigation, "9/11 Investigation (PENTTBOM)" (www.fbi.gov/pressrel/penttbom/aa77/77.htm); discussed on Pickering's website under "Evidence" (www.pentagonresearch.com/evidence.html).

309 The NTSB has, in response to FOIA requests, issued various documents related to Flight 77 (www.ntsb.gov/info/foia_fri.htm). But these documents contain no report on the damage to the Pentagon.

310 Ed Haas, "FBI Says, 'No Hard Evidence Connecting Bin Laden to 9/11'" Muckraker Report, 6 June 2006 (www.teamliberty.net/id267.html).

311 Colonel George Nelson, USAF (ret.), "Impossible to Prove a Falsehood True: Aircraft Parts as a Clue to Their Identity," Physics 911, 23 April 2005 (www.physics911.net/georgenelson.htm).

312 D9/11M 77.

313 D9/11M 80.

314 D9/11M 19.

315 "9/11: Interviews by Peter Jennings," ABC News, 11 September 2002 (http://911research.wtc7.net/cache/pentagon/attack/abcnews091102_jenningsint erviews.html).

316 Quoted in Filson, *Air War over America*, 71.

317 Filson 68.

318 Dave Foster, "UST Grad Guides Bombers in War," *Aquin*, 4 December 2002 (www.stthomas.edu/aquin/archive/041202/anaconda.html). Kuczynski's own plane, an E-3 Sentry, was unarmed, so although he said, "I was given direct orders to shoot down an airliner," he had to mean that his trio of planes was given the order.

319 9/11CR 37; Clarke, *Against All Enemies*, 6–7.

320 9/11CR 40–41.

321 O&D 245–46, citing *Newsweek* 20 June 2004.

322 D9/11M 81. Nine such witnesses are quoted in Paul Thompson's timeline; see "(Before and After 10:06AM) September 11, 2001: Witnesses See Low-Flying, Small White Jet at Flight 93 Crash" (www.cooperativeresearch.org/timeline.jsp?timeline=complete_911_timeline&day_of_9/11=ua93#a1006treetop).

323 *Pittsburgh Post-Gazette* 16 September 2001.

324 Jeff Pillets, "In Rural Hamlet, the Mystery Mounts; 5 Report Second Plane at Pa. Crash Site," *Bergen Record* 14 September 2001 (www.flight93 crash.com/second-plane-at-flight93-crash-site.htm).

325 Richard Wallace, "What Did Happen to Flight 93?" *Daily Mirror* 12 September 2002 (available at http://911research.wtc7.net/cache/planes/evidence/mirror_whatdidhappen.html).

326 "Unanswered Questions: The Mystery of Flight 93," *Independent* 13 August 2002 (available at http://911research.wtc7.net/cache/planes/attack/independent_f93.html).

327 Alan Levin, Marilyn Adams, and Blake Morrison, "Part I: Terror Attacks Brought Drastic Decision: Clear the Skies," *USA Today* 12 August 2002 (www.usatoday.com/news/sept11/2002-08-12-clearskies_x.htm). As that article pointed out, the FAA had at 9:25 ordered a national groundstop, which meant no more civilian aircraft were to take off.

328 Susan Mcelwain, reporting that the FBI at first tried to tell her that there was no white plane, said: "But I saw it and it was there before the crash and it was 40 feet above my head." Tom Spinelli said: "I saw the white plane. . . . It was flying around all over the place like it was looking for something. I saw it before and after the crash." Both statements are quoted in Wallace, "What Did Happen to Flight 93?"

329 John Doe II, "And Kiss the Official UA Theory Good-bye," Democratic Underground, January 2005 (www.democraticunderground.com/discuss/

duboard.php?az=view_all&address=125x28985).

330 D9/11M 83; quoting (but without giving the article's name) Michel Chossudovsky, "More Holes in the Official Story: The 9/11 Cell Phone Calls," Centre for Research on Globalisation, 10 August 2004 (http://globalresearch.ca/articles/CHO408B.html).

331 D9/11M 83; quoting A. K. Dewdney, "The Cellphone and Airfone Calls from Flight UA93," Physics 911, 9 June 2003 (http://physics911.net/cell phoneflight93.htm).

332 D9/11M 84.

333 CTIA—The Wireless Association, "Overview" (www.ctia.org/aboutCTIA/index.cfm) and "Industry Topics: Homeland Security" (www.ctia.org/industry_topics/topic.cfm/TID/33).

334 D9/11M 83–84.

335 Betsy Harter, "Final Contact," *Telephony's Wireless Review* 1 November 2001 (http://wirelessreview.com/ar/wireless_final_contact).

336 "Will They Allow Cell Phones on Planes?" *The Travel Technologist* 19 September 2001 (www.elliott.org/technology/2001/cellpermit.htm).

337 Harter, "Final Contact."

338 Both quoted statements are found at the end of A.K. Dewdney, "Project Achilles Report: Parts One, Two and Three," Physics 911, 19 April 2003 (www.physics911.net/projectachilles).

339 E-mail of 21 November 2006.

340 See Morgan, *Flight 93 Revealed*, 49–51. The nine calls would be those from Jeremy Glick, Marion Britton, CeeCee Lyles, Sandy Bradshaw, Elizabeth Wainio, the first and third calls from Tom Burnett, and the 9:58 call usually attributed to Edward Felt.

341 See the accounts in Jere Longman, *Among the Heroes: United Flight 93 and the Passengers and Crew Who Fought Back* (New York: HarperCollins, 2002) chaps. 9–16.

342 D9/11M 85.

343 D9/11M

344 For the calls from both "Wainio" and "Burnett," see the valuable analysis in John Doe II, "UA 93: Cell Phones and Airphones," Democratic Underground, 18 July 2005 (www.democraticunderground.com/discuss/duboard.php?az=show_mesg&forum=125&topic_id=48029&mesg_id=48029).

345 D9/11M 85.

346 9/11CR 11, 29.

347 D9/11M 86.

348 "Telephone Voice Changers," Brickhouse Security (www.brickhouse security.com/ telephone-voice-changers.html).

349 Newseum, *Running Toward Danger* (Lanham: Rowman & Littlefield, 2002) 148.

350 Newseum, 149.

351 David McCall, *From Tragedy to Triumph* (Johnstown, Penn.: Noah's Ark, 2002) 25.

352 McCall 29–30.

353 Glenn J. Kashurba, *Quiet Courage: The Definitive Account of Flight 93 and Its Aftermath* (Somerset, Penn.: SAJ Publishing, 2006) 38.

354 Peter Perl, "Hallowed Ground," *Washington Post*, 12 May 2002

(www.washingtonpost.com/ac2/wp-dyn/A56110-2002May8).

355 D9/11M 87–88.

356 I am indebted for this observation to John Doe II, "And Kiss the Official UA Theory Good-bye."

357 "Officials Find Data Recorder at Site of Pa. Crash," *New York Times* 14 September 2001; Mike Billington, "Rural Pa. Residents Reach Out to Investigators," *News Journal* (Wilmington, DE) 16 September 2001.

358 Ken Zapinski, "A Blur in the Sky, Then a Firestorm," *St. Petersburg Times* 12 September 2001 (www.sptimes.com/News/091201/Worldandnation/A_blur_in_the_sky__th.shtml).

359 WPXI TV 11 Pittsburgh, 13 September 2001.

360 "NORAD's Response Times," 18 September 2001 (available at www.standdown.net/noradseptember182001pressrelease.htm).

361 Jonathan D. Silver, "What Was the Danger to City? Doomed United Flight 93 Passed Just South of Pittsburgh," *Pittsburgh Post-Gazette* 13 September 2001 (http://911research.wtc7.net/cache/planes/analysis/flight93/postgazette_20010913flightpath.html). The other story was Tom Gibb, James O'Toole, and Cindi Lash, "Investigators Locate 'Black Box' from Flight 93; Widen Search Area in Somerset Crash," *Pittsburgh Post-Gazette* 13 September 2001 (http://post-gazette.com/headlines/20010913somersetp3.asp).

362 William Bunch, "We Know It Crashed, But Not Why," *Philadelphia Daily News* 15 November 2001 (www.whatreallyhappened.com/flight_93_crash.html); Jonathan Silver, "Day of Terror: Outside Tiny Shanksville, a Fourth Deadly Stroke," *Pittsburgh Post-Gazette* 12 September 2001 (www.post-gazette.com/headlines/20010912crashnat2p2.asp); Alan Levin, Marilyn Adams, and Blake Morrison, "Terror Attacks Brought Drastic Decision: Clear the Skies," *USA Today* 12 August 2002 (www.usatoday.com/news/sept11/2002-08-12-clearskies_x.htm).

363 Dennis Roddy, "Flight 93: Forty Lives, One Destiny," *Pittsburgh Post-Gazette* 28 October 2001 (www.post-gazette.com/headlines/ 20011028flt93 mainstoryp7.asp).

364 Kim and Baum, "Seismic Observations During September 11, 2001, Terrorist Attack," cited in 9/11CR 461n168.

365 9/11CR 30.

366 *New York Observer* 11 February 2004, quoted in Paul Thompson and the Center for Cooperative Research, *The Terror Timeline: Year by Year, Day by Day, Minute by Minute* (New York: HarperCollins, 2004) 446. This lack of any independent investigation by the NTSB is supported by William Bunch, who wrote: "The NTSB referred all questions to the FBI" (William Bunch, "Three-Minute Discrepancy in Tape: Cockpit Voice Recording Ends Before Flight 93's Official Time of Impact," *Philadelphia Daily News* 16 September 2002 [available   at www.propagandamatrix.com/three_minute_discrepency_in_tape.htm]).

367 9/11CR 462n168.

368 Jim Hoffman, "Notable Retractions: Won Young Kim" (http://911research.wtc7.net/planes/analysis/flight93/kim.html).

369 Kim and Baum, "Seismic Observations during September 11, 2001, Terrorist Attack." ("UTC" refers to Universal Coordinated Time, which has largely superseded GMT [Greenwich Mean Time].)

370 9/11CR 462n168, citing an e-mail from Won-Young Kim, "Re: UA Flight 93," 7 July 2004.

371 Hoffman, "Notable Retractions: Won Young Kim."

372 Kim's website is at www.ldeo.columbia.edu/~wykim.

373 "Wallace Named Strategic Research Directorate Leader," Los Alamos National Laboratory, 4 March 2004 (www.lanl.gov/news/index.phh/ fuseaction/ home.story/story_id/2334).

374 Quoted in Bunch, "Three-Minute Discrepancy in Tape"; also in Morgan, *Flight 93 Revealed*, 148, 149.

375 Bunch, "Three-Minute Discrepancy in Tape."

376 Jere Longman, *Among the Heroes*, 269–73. This event occurred 18 April 2002.

377 "Families Say Flight 93 Tapes Prove Heroism," CNN, 29 April 2002 (www.cnn.com/2002/US/04/19/rec.flight.93.families).

378 Longman, *Among the Heroes*, 271.

379 9/11CR 14.

380 Morgan, *Flight 93 Revealed*, 54.

381 John Doe II, "Flight 93: Too Many Contradictions," Democratic Underground, 20 October 2004 (www.democraticunderground.com/discuss/ duboard.php?az=view_all&address=125x23179).

382 D9/11M 86–87.

383 D9/11M 88–89.

384 "Unanswered Questions: The Mystery of Flight 93," *Independent*, 13 August 2002; Wallace, "What Did Happen to Flight 93?"

385 Christopher Bollyn, "9–11 Mysteries Remain," AmericanFreePress.net, updated 17 September 2004 (www.americanfreepress.net/html/9-11_mysteries.html).

386 Richard Gazarik and Robin Acton, "Black Box Recovered at Shanksville Site," *Pittsburgh Tribune-Review* 14 September 2001 (www.pittsburghlive.com/ x/pittsburghtrib/s_1290.html).

387 D9/11M 89, quoting Tom Gibb, James O'Toole, and Cindi Lash, "Investigators Locate 'Black Box' from Flight 93; Widen Search Area in Somerset Crash," *Pittsburgh Post-Gazette* 13 September 2001 (http://post-gazette.com/ headlines/20010913somersetp3.asp).

388 D9/11M 89–90.

389 Kashurba, *Quiet Courage*, 35.

390 Jonathan Silver, "Day of Terror: Outside Tiny Shanksville, a Fourth Deadly Stroke," *Pittsburgh Post-Gazette* 12 September 2001 (www.post-gazette.com/headlines/20010912crashnat2p2.asp).

391 Debra Erdley, "Crash Debris Found 8 Miles Away," *Pittsburgh Tribune-Review* 14 September 2001 (www.pittsburghlive.com/x/pittsburghtrib/s_12967.html). Bill Heltzel and Tom Gibb, "2 Planes Had No Part in Crash of Flight 93," *Pittsburgh Post-Gazette* 16 September 2001 (www.post-gazette.com/ headlines/20010916otherjetnat5p5.asp); Richard Wallace, "What Did Happen to Flight 93?" *Daily Mirror* 12 September 2002.

392 "America Under Attack: FBI and State Police Cordon Off Debris Area Six to Eight Miles from Crater Where Plane Went Down," CNN, 13 September 2001 (http://transcripts.cnn.com/TRANSCRIPTS/0109/13/bn.01.html).

393 Erdley, "Crash Debris Found 8 Miles Away."

394 Kashurba, *Quiet Courage*, 35.

395 Erdley.

396 Erdley.

397 "FBI Does Not Rule Out Shootdown of Penn. Airplane," Reuters, 13 September 2001 (http://web.archive.org/web/20011218031530/ http://investor. cnet.com/investor/news/newsitem/ 0-9900-1028-7147291-0.html).

398 Gazarik and Acton, "Black Box Recovered at Shanksville Site."

399 Robin Acton and Richard Gazarik, "Human Remains Recovered in Somerset," *Pittsburgh Tribune-Review* 13 September 2001 (www.pittsburghlive.com/ x/pittsburghtrib/s_47536.html).

400 Ken Zapinski, "A Blur in the Sky, Then a Firestorm."

401 Bunch, "We Know It Crashed, But Not Why."

402 "Hijack Ends in Pennsylvania Crash," ABCNews.com, 11 September 2001 (available at http://911research.wtc7.net/cache/planes/evidence/ abcnews_ airplanecrash010911.html).

403 "No Survivors Reported in Pennsylvania Plane Crash," News Channel 5, 11 September 2001 (http://911research.wtc7.net/cache/planes/evidence/ newsnet5_nosurvivors.html).

404 Kashurba, *Quiet Courage*, 13, 66.

405 Bunch, "We Know It Crashed, But Not Why." Incidentally, although Bunch spelled the mayor's name "Stuhl," it is spelled "Stull," Devvy Kidd has pointed out ("Asking Questions at the Flight 93 Crash Site," 11 September 2005 [www.devvy.com/flight_93_part_1.html]).

406 Bunch, "We Know It Crashed, But Not Why."

407 Wallace, "What Did Happen to Flight 93?"

408 William B. Scott, "Exercise Jump-Starts Response to Attacks," *Aviation Week and Space Technology* 3 June 2002; *Cape Cod Times* 21 August 2002.

409 "Surprise Trip for Donald Rumsfeld," CNN, 24 December 2004 (http://edition.cnn.com/TRANSCRIPTS/0412/24/nfcnn.01.html).

410 Colin Perkel and Beth Gorham, "Missile Rejection Perplexes US," *Canadian Press* 23 February 2005 (www.curevents.com/vb/showpost.php? p=51773&postcount=1; scroll down).

411 For a discussion of these facts and the difficulties of trying to construct a coherent account of what happened from them, see John Doe II, "Proof That Official UA 93 Story Is a Hoax" (www.democraticunderground.com/discuss/ duboard.php?az=view_all&address=125x37066).

CONCLUSION

1 Terry Allen, "The 9/11 Faith Movement," *In These Times* 11 July 2006 (www.inthesetimes.com/site/main/article/2702).

2 See NPH, ch. 1, and *Christian Faith and the Truth Behind 9/11*, ch. 3.

3 See Sharon Seitz, "The Little Fireboat That Did," and Huntley Gill, "Retired Fireboat Harvey Helps With World Trade Center Disaster," NYFD.com (www.firehouse.com/terrorist/17_Pharvey.html).

4 NIST NCSTAR 1–8 (http://wtc.nist.gov/NISTNCSTAR1-8.pdf) 110.

5 David Ray Griffin, "The Destruction of the World Trade Center: Why the Official Account Cannot Be True," has been published at 911Review.com (http://911review.com/articles/griffin/nyc1.html); in Paul Zarembka, ed., *The*

Hidden History of 9-11-2001 (Amsterdam: Elsevier, 2006); and in Griffin, *Christian Faith and the Truth Behind 9/11*.

6 As I wrote in the essay mentioned in the previous note: "Firefighters who had been fighting the fires in the building said they were ordered to leave the building, after which a collapse zone was established. As medical worker Decosta Wright put it: 'they measured out how far the building was going to come, so we knew exactly where we could stand,' which was '5 blocks away.'"

7 "The 9/11 Conspiracy Nuts: How They Let the Guilty Parties of 9/11 Slip Off the Hook," *Counterpunch* 9/10 September 2006 (www.counterpunch.org/cockburn09092006.html).

8 Although articles on 9/11 by regular contributors to *Counterpunch* who have come to doubt the official conspiracy theory, such as Bill Christison and Paul Craig Roberts, have appeared elsewhere, such articles have, at this writing, never appeared in *Counterpunch*. Cockburn has, however, opened *Counterpunch*'s pages to a US weapons scientist, Manuel Garcia, Jr., to defend the official version of the collapses of the Twin Towers and WTC 7. Garcia, who works at the Lawrence Livermore National Laboratory in California, wrote three essays—"The Physics of 9/11," "The Thermodynamics of 9/11," and "Dark Fire: The Fall of WTC 7"—which have been included in a "Counterpunch Special Report: Debunking the Myths of 9/11" (www.counterpunch.org/ninelevenconsp11252006.html). At least with Garcia on board, Cockburn can point out that if his acceptance of the official story involves a magical view of the collapses, this view is shared by a physicist with a Ph.D. For a critique of Garcia's essays, the first two of which are headed "We See Conspiracies That Don't Exist," consult Kevin Ryan, "Manuel Garcia Sees Physics That Don't Exist," 911Blogger.com, 27 December 2006 (www.911blogger.com/ node/5272).

9 Dean E. Murphy, *September 11: An Oral History* (New York: Doubleday, 2002) 9–15.

10 Quoted in Susan Hagen and Mary Carouba, *Women at Ground Zero: Stories of Courage and Compassion* (Indianapolis: Alpha Books, 2002) 65–66, 68.

11 Gerald M. Carbone, "The Miracle of Ladder 6 and Josephine," *Providence Journal* 11 September 2002 (www.projo.com/words/st20021016.htm).

12 Christopher Hayes, "9/11: The Roots of Paranoia," *Nation* 8 December 2006 (www.thenation.com/doc/20061225/hayes).

13 Jim Dwyer, "2 US Reports Seek to Counter Conspiracy Theories About 9/11," *New York Times* 2 September 2006 (www.911review.com/reviews/nyt/markup/02conspiracy.html).

14 Although Dwyer's quotation had "molten steel," Jones is always careful to say "molten metal," because when steel is melted by thermite, which he suspects was used, molten iron is produced.

15 Trudy Walsh, "Handheld APP Eased Recovery Tasks," *Government Computer News* 21.27a (11 September 2002) (www.gcn.com/21_27a/news/19930-1.html).

16 Matthew Rothschild, "Enough of the 9/11 Conspiracy Theories, Already," *Progressive* 18 September 2006 (www.alternet.org/story/41601/).

17 NPH 18–19.

18 NPH 19.

19 This retort is a variation on a New England minister's reply, as quoted by

Sidney E. Mead: "I cannot permit your ignorance, however vast, to take precedence over my knowledge, however limited" ("Church History Explained," *Church History* 32/1 [March 1963] 17–31 [available at http://links.jstor.org/sici?sici=0009-6407(196303)32%3A1%3C17%3ACHE% 3E2.0.CO%3B2-C]).

20 Bill Christison on the *Alex Jones Show*, quoted in Paul Joseph Watson, "28-Year Career CIA Official Says 9/11 An Inside Job," Prison Planet.com, 7 September 2006 (http://propagandamatrix.com/articles/september2006/070906insidejob.htm).

21 Bill Christison, "Stop Belittling the Theories About September 11," www.dissidentvoice.org, 14 August 2006 (www.dissidentvoice.org/Aug06/Christison14.htm).

22 Christison, quoting Webster Tarpley's address at the American Scholars Symposium, "9/11 and the Neo-Con Agenda," at the Los Angeles Sheraton, 24–25 June (available at http://video.google.com/videoplay?docid=-4258946892514662399).

23 "9/11: The Myth and the Reality," 911Truth.org, 5 April 2006 (www.911truth.org/article.php?story=20060405112622982); forthcoming in James H. Fetzer, ed., *The 9/11 Conspiracy: Experts and Scholars Speak Up for Truth* (Peru, IL: Open Court, 2006); also available on a DVD (http://911TV.org).

24 Alexander Cockburn, "The Decline of the Left," Free Press, 30 September 2006 (www.freepress.org/columns/display/2/2006/1440). Since then, this claim has been made, even more strongly, by George Monbiot, who has written: "Why do I bother with these morons [meaning representatives of the 9/11 truth movement]? Because they are destroying the movements some of us have spent a long time trying to build. Those of us who believe that the crucial global issues— climate change, the Iraq war, nuclear proliferation, inequality—are insufficiently debated in parliament or congress, that corporate power stands too heavily on democracy, that war criminals, cheats and liars are not being held to account, have invested our efforts in movements outside the mainstream political process. These, we are now discovering, are peculiarly susceptible to this epidemic of gibberish. . . . The 9/11 conspiracy theories are a displacement activity. . . , something you do because you feel incapable of doing what you ought to do. . . . Faced with the mountainous challenge of the real issues we must confront, the chickens in the 'truth' movement focus instead on a fairytale, knowing that nothing they do or say will count, knowing that because the perpetrators don't exist, they can't fight back. They demonstrate their courage by repeatedly bayoneting a scarecrow" ("9/11 Fantasists Pose a Mortal Danger to Popular Oppositional Campaigns," *Guardian* 20 February 2007 [www.guardian.co.uk/commentisfree/story/0,,2017006,00.html]). Although Monbiot questions our sincerity, I do not question his but only his awareness of the facts about 9/11. He says, for example, that "the magazine *Popular Mechanics* . . . has ripped the demolition theories apart." In response, I have written "Morons and Magic: A Reply to George Monbiot," Information Clearing House, 7 March 2007.

25 David Ray Griffin, "The Truly Distracting 9/11 Conspiracy Theory: A Reply to Alexander Cockburn," *Le Monde Diplomatique*, Nordic Edition, March 2007 (http://www.lmd.no/index.php?article=1408#fotnoter).

26 Griffin, *Christian Faith and the Truth Behind 9/11*, 183. This statement can serve as my reply, in advance, to Monbiot's charge that the 9/11 truth movement's story draws campaigners away.

27 "You Can Do Anything with a Bayonet Except Sit On It," TomDispatch.com

interview with Mark Danner, 26 February 2006 (http://markdanner.com/ nyt/022606_tomdispatch.htm). Giorgio Gamben, after employing the concept of the "state of exception" in his *Homo Sacer: Sovereign Power and Bare Life*, trans. Daniel Heller-Roazen (Stanford: Stanford University Press, 1998), developed it much more fully in *State of Exception*, trans. Kevin Attell (Chicago: University of Chicago Press, 2006).

28 See, for example, Peter Phillips with Bridget Thornton and Celeste Vogler, "Parameters of Power in the Global Dominance Group: 9/11 & Election Irregularities in Context," in ISO, 169–97.

Index

A

AA (American Airlines) 11 (Flight 11), 35–55, 94, 127, 225, 232, 331n6. *See also* phantom Flight 11
AA 77 (Flight 77), 28, 63–66, 74, 97, 99, 120, 225, 227, 229–30, 262–88, 365n48
Against All Enemies, 68, 116, 120
Agamben, Giorgio, 320, 384–85n27
Ahmad, General Mahmoud, 123–25
Ahmed, Nafeez, 2, 220, 337n112
Airfone calls, 89–91, 126–27, 266
Airwar over America, 45, 50, 73, 76
Alert fighters, 62–63, 223–24, 241
Allen, Terry, 10, 12, 21, 310–12, 36, 318, 325–26n32
Andrews Air Force Base, 62, 224–26, 365n62
Arendt, Hannah, 209
Arias, Donald, 62, 77, 225
Arkin, William, 84–85, 342n233
Armitage, Richard, 125
Arnold, General Larry, 28–30, 49–50, 52, 58, 67–68, 73–74, 76, 78–79, 80–82, 83, 85, 93, 97–98, 234, 290, 338n141, 341n207, 343n14, 365n62
Athearn, Daniel, viii

B

Bacevich, Andrew, 344n40
Bachmann, Hugo, 200, 243
Baer, Robert, 12–13, 18, 20, 320
Bailey, Roger, 304, 305
Baker, Dr. Andrew, 267–68, 373n231
Baker, Jeremy, 207, 246, 363n2
Baker, Paul, 161–62
Balsamo, Rob, 334n44, 372n217
Bamford, David, 127
Bamford, James, 341n219
Barnett, Jonathan, 190, 198–99
Barrett, Kevin, 329n82, 368n133
Bart, Eric, 371n205
Baum, Gerald, 281, 299–301, 377n294
Bazant, Zdenek, 254, 370n179
Becker, Gary, 2
Belger, Monte, 44, 69, 339n172
Ben–Veniste, Richard, 58, 66, 68, 78, 97, 98, 116, 338n133, 343n14
Berg, Philip J., 14
Berger, Michael, 363n250
Berlet, Chip, 22
Biederman, Ronald, 190
Biggio, Terry, 41, 44
Binalshibh, Ramzi, 130–31
Bingham, Mark, 89
Bin Laden, Osama (Usama), 8, 12, 21, 101, 104, 105, 117, 128–29, 208, 209, 287
Birnback, Marc, 221
Boeing 707 and 767 (comparison), 145–46
Bohrer, David, 72–74
Bollyn, Christopher, 212–13, 216, 356n138, 357n152, 364nn19,20
Bolton, Josh, 72, 74

Bomboy, Paul, 297
Boot, Max, 110
Borgstrom, Capt. Craig, 338n146
Boston Center (FAA), 35, 53, 83, 332n3, 334n54, 335n76
Bottiglia, Dave, 57, 333n39
Bowman, Col. Robert, 14, 241, 346n78
Boyle, Francis A., 348n140
Bradshaw, Sandy, 379n340
Bridges, Major Kevin, 339n178
Britton, Marion, 379n340
Brokaw, Tom, 56–57, 64, 70, 77, 332n33, 333n39
Bronner, Michael, 4–5, 6, 26, 27–94, 95, 97, 340n193
Brooks, Chadwick, 264
Brown, Hyman, 153
Brown, Laura, 38, 57–58, 65–66, 68, 86, 97, 99, 116, 120, 226–27, 337–38n133, 333nn167,168, 366n68
Brzezinsky, Zbigniew, 105, 344n43
Bueno, Daniel, 45, 51, 334n54, 335n81
Building 7. *See* WTC 7
Bukhari, Adnan and Ameer, 347n115
Bülow, Andreas von, 14
Bunch, William, 301, 380n362, 380n366
Burke, Timothy, 177
Burnett, Deena, 70, 340n182, 342n247
Burnett, Tom, 70, 296, 342–43n247, 379n340
Burns, Joseph, 186
Bush, President George H.W., 31
Bush, President George W., 1, 2, 15–17, 25, 100–01, 104–11, 112, 144, 265–66, 290–91, 340n193
Bush, Marvin, 114, 117, 193, 346n76
Bussey, John, 176
Butler, Bill, 313
Butler, Lt. Col. Steve, 14, 327n42
Butler, Terry, 298

C

Cabell, Brian, 305
Cacchioli, Louie, 177, 246–48, 356n128, 369n147
Cachia, Edward, 177, 248
Callahan, Greg, 70
Canavan, Gen. Mike, 64
Card, Andrew, 72, 74, 101, 344n26
Carouba, Mary, 383n10
Cassidy, Tiernach, 203, 204
Cell phone calls, 26, 87–91, 99, 126–27, 136–37, 215, 266, 292–97, 317
Cellucci, Paul, 307
Chaney, Rick, 292
Chapin, Tom, 161
Cheney, Vice President Dick, 69, 104–05, 111; and PEOC, 31–33, 71, 72, 116, 138–39, 331–32n18; shootdown authorization by, 28, 71–74, 93, 138–39, 290–91, 338n141, 340n193
Cherry, Lt. Col. Michael–Anne, 339n178
Chertoff, Benjamin, 6, 212–13, 216, 238
Chertoff, Michael, 6, 212–13, 216

Chevrette, Peggy, 217–18
Chiesa, Giulietto, 14
Chossudovsky, Michel, 14, 124, 292, 347n117, 379n330
Christison, Bill, 3, 14, 318–19, 383n8
Clarke, Jonathan, 109, 110, 345n67
Clarke, Richard, 32, 37, 68, 69, 72, 84, 97, 107, 116, 120, 136–37, 236, 289, 290, 331n14, 344–45n52
Coburn, Davin, 228, 232, 259, 366n85, 371n201
Cockburn, Alexander, 13–15, 18–20, 21, 312–13, 318, 319, 383n8
Coffin, William Sloane, 14
Collapse:
    at virtually free–fall speed, 165–69, 180;
    global, 164–65;
    pancake, 113, 165–66, 185, 253–54;
    progressive, 163–64, 166;
    symmetrical, 186–87
Conspiracy theories:
    generic, 8–9, 101;
    official and alternative, 8–15, 21–26, 103, 129, 207–11;
    one–sided use of term, 7, 8–15, 101–02, 207–08, 325n25;
    rational and irrational, 8–9, 26, 95, 98, 102–36, 205–06;
    scientific & unscientific, 24, 26, 112, 205–06
Controlled demolition, 173, 194, 242
Controlled Demolition, Inc., 174, 178, 185–86, 200–02, 206, 359n181
Cooper, Joe, 43, 44, 45, 51, 335n81
Corley, Gene, 316
Cox, Harvey, 14

D
D'Agostino, Sal, 313
Danner, Mark, 320, 328n63, 384n27
David, Felipe, 178
Debunking, 4–15, 95, 119, 213
Debunking 9/11 Myths, 5, 6, 7, 134, 207–307
Decker, Dennis, 291–92
Delasko, Carol, 305
DeMartini, Frank, 146–47, 246, 351n13
Deskins, Col. Dawne, 42, 43, 76–77
Deutch, John, 111
Dewdney, A. K., 14, 87–88, 292, 294–95, 342nn237–40, 246, 379n338
Dixon, Brian, 247
Doe, John, II, 378n329, 379n344, 380n356, 382n411
Dooley, Sgt. Maureen, 56, 78, 335n63
Douglas, Eric, viii, 149, 150, 170, 171, 351n25
Duffy, Lt. Col. Timothy, 45, 46, 52, 58
Dunbar, David, 5, 134, 215
Dwyer, Jim, 5, 9, 314–15, 324n18, 383n14

E
Eagar, Thomas, 149, 153–55, 156, 157, 165, 185, 189, 246, 249, 250, 251, 351n23, 352n47

Ecological crisis, 317–21
Eisenhower, President Dwight, 96
Ellsberg, Daniel, 17
Else, Liz, 355n116
Empire State Building, 148, 244–46
Empiricism, 15–23
Erdley, Debra, 382n391
Evans, Stephen, 177
Everett, Matthew, 340n181
Evey, Lee, 270, 275
Explosions, 175–79, 199, 246–48, 312–13
Explosives, 203, 167, 202–03, 246–47, 351n16

F
FAA (Federal Aviation Administration):
    blamed for 9/11 attacks, 4, 52, 60, 63, 80, 93, 105;
    Boston Center of, 35, 53, 83, 332n3, 334n54, 335n76;
    Cape Cod facility of, 39, 45;
    headquarters, 35, 40, 64, 67, 69, 83;
    Herndon Command Center of, 35–55, 64, 67, 68, 338n133;
    notification of military by, 28–29, 93;
    protocols of, 39–45, 60–61, 120–21;
    standard procedures of, 34–36;
    tapes, 28, 53, 86
Falk, Richard, 1, 14
False–flag operations, 129–30, 210, 265
Family Steering Committee (FSC), 107, 111
Faram, Mark, 271
Farmer, John, 30, 80
FBI, 86, 120, 123, 127, 128, 132, 209, 268–69, 280–81, 287–88
Flight 93 Revealed, 266, 347nn110, 115
Flocco, Tom, 37–38
Frini, Pamela S., 339nn162,172, 340n179
Fritz, Tom, 306
Fuchek, Greg, 182, 315

G
Gabrielle, Monica, 135
Gaffney, Mark, 158, 171–72, 353n66
Gallop, April, 270
Garcia, Andrew, 296
Garcia, Manuel, Jr., 383n8
Garvey, Jane, 68, 87, 116, 120, 289
Gates, Robert, 242
Gayle, Frank, 157, 161
Gazarik, Richard, 381n386
Gellman, Barton, 345n60
Geyh, Allison, 357n157
al–Ghamdi, Saeed, 122
Gibney, Major Rick, 288
Gibson, Charlie, 32
Gill, Huntley, 371n195
Ginzburg, Susan, 122
Giuliani, Rudy, 117–19, 201–02, 346n94
Glanz, James, 191, 195, 359n190, 361n216
Glazier, Sean, 168
Glick, Jeremy, 379n340

Global warming, 318–20, 321
Goff, Stan, 219–20, 315n44
Gorton, Slade, 106, 111
Gorelick, Jamie, 234–35
Graf, Alexa, 293–94
Grand-Pre, Donn de, 288
Gray, Bobby, 182, 188
Green, Michael, 206, 363n254
Gregory, Stephen, 279–80
Griffin, David Ray (discussed), 10, 11–16, 18, 20, 22, 26, 311, 316, 317, 325–26n32
Griffith, Jeff, 339n172
Gross, John L., 181, 357n151
Grossman, Lev, 10–11
GTE Airfones, 89–91, 126–27, 266
Gutierrez, Carlos, 143
Guzman, Genelle, 176–77, 202, 355–56n127

H

Haack, Susan, 329n76
Haas, Edward, viii, 128–29, 133–34, 202, 330n87, 349nn143,155–57, 364n13
Haass, Richard, 109
Hagan, Susan, 383n10
Halper, Stefan, 109, 110, 345n67
Hamburger, Ronald, 206, 363n254
Hamilton, Lee H., 5, 27, 31–32, 95–142 (esp. 136–42), 331n14, 349n165, 350n169
Hanjour, Hani, 99–100, 116, 126, 216–20, 262, 282–85, 287
Harcke, Col. H. Theodore, 373n234
Hargrove, Thomas, 324n12
Harrison, David, 127, 348nn135,136
Harter, Betsy, 379n335
Hartling, John, 333n39
Harvey, Thomas E., 212
Haugen, Gen. Mike J., 71
Hayes, Christopher, 313–14, 318
Hence, Kyle, 62, 225
Henshall, Ian, viii, 126, 266–67, 373n228
Herbert, Dr. Robert, 17
Herndon Command Center, 35–55, 64, 67, 68, 338n133
Herring, Capt. Tom, 51, 241
Hess, Michael, 199
Heyward, Carter, 14
Hijackers (alleged), 100, 101, 121–32, 216–20
Hodgkins, Mark, 75
Hoffman, Jim, viii, 143, 150, 153, 154, 156, 158, 164, 167, 168, 172–73, 174–75, 185, 186, 187, 188, 189, 191, 192, 205, 207, 249, 256, 300, 301, 350n2, 351nn19,27, 358n166, 358n172, 359n181, 360n203
Hoglan, Alice, 89
Holland, Gregor, 366n83
Honegger, Barbara, 377n298
Hopsicker, Daniel, 33, 348n128
Hordon, Robin, viii, 19, 36–54 passim, 60–61, 63, 64, 83–84, 99, 333n39, 337n115, 343n18
Horsley, Richard, 14
Hough, Joseph H., 14

Hufschmid, Eric, 353n61, 358n170
Hussein, Saddam, 12, 16
Hyver, Laeti, 266

I

Implosion, 197–98, 205, 359n181, 361n220
Inference to the best explanation, 23–24
Iraq war, 2, 16, 172, 265–66, 318–19
Isaac, Paul, 248
ISI (Inter-Services Intelligence), 123–25, 137
Israel, Jared, 366n64
Ivashov, Gen. Leonid, 14, 327n46

J

Jacobsen, Mark, 204
Jaqua, Ann, vii
Jarrah, Ziad, 122, 128, 217, 268, 302, 348n139
Jellinek, Capt. Michael, 56, 97, 226
Jenkins, Dr. Cate, 17
Jennings, Peter, 32, 42, 70, 72, 76
Johnson, Glen, 237, 241, 367n111
Johnson, Lyndon, 17
Jones, Steven, 2, 113, 153, 169–70, 171, 174, 181, 182–83, 184, 190, 192, 199, 243, 251–52, 253, 314–15, 324n6, 352n42, 361nn227–230, 383n14
Jowenko, Danny, 200, 243

K

Kashurba, Glenn J., 379n353
Kean, Thomas H., 4, 5, 27, 95–136, 139, 350n169
Keane, Sue, 313
Keefer, Michael, 22
Keller, Catherine, 14
Kemper, Rick, 293, 294, 295–96
Kennedy, A. L., 14
Kerrey, Bob, 69, 125
Kidd, Devvy, 382n405
Kies, Jack, 339n133
Killough-Miller, Joan, 359n189
Kilsheimer, Allyn E., 263, 277
Kim, Won-Young, 281, 299–301, 377n294
King, Jeff, 189, 316
King, John, 331n14
Kleinberg, Mindy, 349n144
Knoblauch, Loring, 161
Kolar, Jay, 126, 347n115, 348n139
KSM. See Mohammed, Khahil Sheikh
Kuczynski, Lt. Anthony, 71, 290, 378n318
Kuhn, Thomas, 328n57
Kurtilla, Heikki, 201, 243
Kwiatkowski, Karen, 346n78

L

LaGasse, William, 264
Lance, Peter, 331n13, 345n57
Landrigan, Philip, 358n180
Lang, Col. Patrick, 388n64
Langewiesche, William, 182, 253, 357n154
Langley fighters, 28, 74–79, 81, 84, 94, 97, 224
Lavello, Randy, 369n152

Lawrence, Bruce, 128
Leidig, Capt. Charles, 37–38
Levin, Carl, 70
Lichty, Barry, 307
Lipton, Eric, 191
Loizeaux, Mark, 174, 178, 181, 186, 192, 198,
    202, 253, 254, 257, 260, 357n152
Loizeaux, Stacey, 198, 361n220
Longman, Jere, 70, 340n182
Lord, Gen. Lance, 286
Lubarsky, Sandra, 329n82, 368n133
Lyles, CeeCee, 296, 379n340
Lyles, Lorne, 296

M

MacQueen, Graham, 175, 247, 355n122
Madigan, Pat, 297
Madsen, Wayne, 14
Magnusson, Jon, 245–46, 251, 252
Mann, Bradley, 178–79
Mann, James, 109, 345n63
Manning, David, 328n63
Markham, Ian, 16
Marquis, Aldo, 372n215
Marr, Col. Robert, 49–51, 52, 59, 61–63, 73–74,
    78–79, 82, 84, 97, 234, 289, 290, 338n141
Martin, Major Douglas, 227, 234, 238
Martin, Lino, 333
Mason, Don, 263–64, 265
Masood, Ahmad Shah, 123–24
May, Capt. Eric H., 14
May, Ernest, 108, 345n59
May, Renee, 266
McCain, John, 6, 207–11, 225, 270, 279
McCarthy, Thomas, 203, 204
Mcelwain, Susan, 70, 292, 306–07, 378n328
McEntee, Sgt. Sean, 225
McGovern, Ray, 14, 328nn63,64
McGowan, Dave, 263, 271
McIlvaine, Bob, 135
McIntyre, Jamie, 269–70, 273, 279, 374n239
McKinley, Gen. Craig, 58
McMurtry, John, 14
McWethy, John, 270
Meacher, Michael, 14
Mead, Sydney, 383–84n19
Meigs, James B., 134, 212, 215–16, 232, 261,
    263, 364n21, 374n238
Meyer, Harry, 203
Meyer, Jon, 294
Meyer, Michael, 278
Meyssan, Thierry, 271, 275, 340n189, 364n50,
    374n245
al-Mihdhar, Khalid, 126
Military:
    as giving false testimony, lying, 4, 5, 6, 27,
        29–30, 80–82, 91–92, 93–94, 98;
    exercises, 236–37, 367n109, 377n304;
    interceptions, 237–41;
    radar, 46–48
Miller, Alan, 326n39, 346n78
Miller, Leslie, 55–56, 332n30

Miller, Mark Crispin, 14
Mineta, Norman, 31–32, 71, 72, 120, 138,
    229–30, 331n14, 366n83
Mitchell, Terry, 277
Mlakar, Paul, 271, 272, 276
Mohammed, Khalid Sheikh (KSM), 101, 130–32
Molten metal, 113, 198, 248–53, 383n14
Monbiot, George, 326n37, 384n24
Moore, Michael, 8
Morgan, Rowland, viii, 70, 126, 266–67, 302,
    340n184, 342n237, 373n224
Mosiello, Stephen, 346n96
Mount Sinai Medical Center, 17, 188, 358n180
Moussaoui, Zacarias, 90
Murad, Abdul Hakim, 235
Murphy, Dean E., 355n126
Musso, Christopher, 351n23
Muwakkil, Salim, 11–12, 22–23
Myers, Gen. Richard, 52, 68, 70, 71, 74, 97, 116,
    117, 120, 234–35, 289

N

al-Nami, Ahmed, 348n136
Nash, Major Daniel, 46, 60, 70, 307
Nasypany, Major Kevin, 46, 47, 48, 49, 59, 60,
    61, 75, 78–79, 82, 84, 338n141
Nation, 12–13, 313
National Institute of Standards and Technology.
    See NIST
National Military Command Center. See NMCC
National 9/11 Debate, 133–34, 136
National Transportation Safety Board. See NTSB
Naudet brothers, 248
NCSTAR, 352n28
NEADS (Northeast Air Defense Sector), 28–29,
    35–55, 227;
    technicians, 41–42, 56
Nelson, George, viii, 14, 287
Neoconservatives (neocons), 104–05, 110
Newman, Michael, 6, 133
New Pearl Harbor, 2, 4, 115
New York Times, 5, 30, 355n121
Nigro, Daniel, 203
9/11 Commission Report, 2–142
    as cover-up, 2;
    as deceitful, 30–34, 59;
    omissions and distortions in, 31–34, 54,
        56, 59, 60, 65, 66, 69
    passim, 216–20, 222, 228, 230, 235–36,
        289, 296, 298;
*9/11 Commission Report: Omissions and
    Distortions*, 2, 99–100, 117–20, 222, 224, 289
9/11 Mysteries: Demolitions, 174, 178, 346n94
9/11 Revealed, 266, 347nn109, 115
9/11 truth movement, 2, 12, 13–15, 114
NIST (National Institute of Standards and
    Technology), 5, 114, 140, 143–206;
    as agency of Bush administration, 6, 25–26,
        143, 193, 195, 310, 315;
    "Answers to Frequently Asked Questions,"
        5, 143, 315;
    refusal to debate, 133

NIST NCSTAR, 352n28
NIST report, 5, 6–7, 143, 242–61;
    as unscientific, 23–24, 25, 149–52, 157–58,
        164, 167, 171–73, 184, 206
NMCC (National Military Command Center),
    29, 56, 58, 63, 70, 73, 83, 227;
    and hijacking protocol, 40, 44, 50, 53;
    teleconference run by, 37–38, 43, 58, 290
NORAD (North American Aerospace
    Defense Command), 28–29, 227, 233–35;
    alert fighters available to, 62–63, 223–24,
        241;
    interceptions by, 237–41;
    military exercises (war games) by, 236–37,
        367n109, 377n304;
    timeline of September 11 (2001), 29, 55,
        92, 95, 96
NORAD tapes, 4–5, 27–94;
    as authentic military history of 9/11, 30,
        42, 52–53, 61, 66, 73, 79, 83;
    cherry-picking, 53–54, 83;
    doctoring of, 83–86
NSS 2002, 108–09, 111, 345n62
NTSB (National Transportation
    Safety Board), 264, 277, 287, 298, 299, 303,
    304, 377n309, 380n366
Nunn, Senator Sam, 236

O

O'Dowd, John, 187–88
Office of Emergency Management (OEM), 118,
    346–47n97
O'Huallachain, D.L., 328n64
Oldham, Joe, 212
Olmstead, Dr. Thomas, 268
Olson, Barbara, 266, 267, 373nn224, 225
Olson, Ted, 266–67
al-Omari, Abdullah, 122–23
Omholt, Ralph, viii, 216, 220, 270, 280, 281,
    282, 374n240, 376–77n289
Operation Northwoods, 210, 265
Oral histories of 9/11, 355n121
O'Reilly, Bill, 261
Otis fighter jets, 45, 49, 52, 58–63, 94
Otis military facilities, 45, 46, 49, 50, 51, 52,
    56, 223–24

P

Paik, Edward, 264
Palast, Greg, 328n63
Paradigmatic thinking, 7, 15–17
Paul, Don, 189, 193, 359n187
Pax Americana, 104–05, 208
Peacock, Bill, 339n172
Pecoraro, Mike, 178
Penn, Lonnie, 178
Pentagon:
    attack on, 99, 112, 120;
    black boxes found in, 263;
    C-ring "exit hole," 264, 275–78;
    Citgo station by, 264, 269;

clipped light poles, 264–65;
    DNA identification of victims, 267–69;
    eyewitness evidence, 262–63, 271;
    missile hypothesis about, 271, 275, 283;
    removal of evidence from, 280, 286;
    videos of, 117, 279–80, 376n279
Pentagon Building Performance Report, 26,
    271, 272, 276, 277, 375n254, 267, 268
PEOC (Presidential Emergency Operations
    Center), 31–32, 71–72
Perle, Richard, 104
Phantom Flight 11, 28, 74–79, 81, 84, 93, 97,
    223, 229
Phillips, Jeff, 297
Phillips, Peter, 385n28
Pickering, Russell, viii, 262, 276, 277–78, 280–
    81, 284–86, 374n238, 374n243, 375n259,
    376n277
Pilots for 9/11 truth, 15, 232, 264, 366n65,
    372n217
Plaugher, Ed, 270, 374n241
PNAC. See Project for the New American Century
Polls about 9/11, 3, 7, 135, 136
Popular Mechanics, 5–6, 26, 134, 141, 207–
    307, 313–14, 361n228
Powell, Colin, 88, 128
Powell, Jeremy, 42, 43
Press treatment of 9/11, 3, 7–26, 309–21
Probst, Frank, 263, 273
Professors Question 9/11, 15, 242
Project for the New American Century (PNAC),
    104–05, 110, 111, 208
Protocol: emergency and hijack, 39–45, 60–61,
    227–28
Pugh, Bob, 280–81

Q

al-Qaeda, 8, 101, 104, 105, 107, 114, 119–20,
    121–32, 142, 197, 208–11, 344–45n52
QUALCOMM, 293, 342n244

R

Raney, Brenda, 294
Ranke, Craig, 372n215
Raskin, Marcus, 14
Rather, Dan, 200
Ray, Col. Robert D., 14, 327n49, 346n78
Reagan, Brad, 5, 134, 215
Reynolds, Morgan, 14, 242, 346n78
Rice, Condoleezza, 6, 31, 32, 72, 107, 111, 116,
    124, 331n14
Riggs, Barbara, 69
Roberts, Paul Craig, 10–11, 14, 346n78, 383n8
Roberts, Tom, 333n39
Robertson, Leslie, 147, 181–82
Rodriguez, William, 178, 179
Roemer, Tim, 32, 138, 331n14
Rogers, Kenneth, 177
Romero, Van, 255
Rose, David, 330n85
Ross, Gordon, 168

Rothschadl, Judy, 270
Rothschild, Matthew, 9–10, 18, 20, 21, 24–26, 315–18
Rountree, Stacia, 56, 78
Rove, Karl, 72, 111
Rowe, Korey, 10
Rudman, Senator Warren, 241
Ruether, Rosemary, 14
Rumsfeld, Donald, 52, 68, 99, 104, 116, 117, 120, 275, 276, 285, 289, 307
Russell, Jerry, 371n205, 361n214
Ruvolo, Phillip, 183, 357n154
Ryan, Kevin, 151, 157, 158, 161–62, 163, 170, 171, 350n5, 351n24, 352n34, 354nn79, 84, 370n168, 383n8

S

Saari, Steve, 241
Sacks, Bryan, 16, 345n59
Sanchez, José, 178
Sands, Philippe, 372n219
Schiavo, Mary, 299
Schipanni, John, 35, 44, 333n39
Schmidt, Terry, 203–04
Schneider, Jörg, 200, 243
Scientific explanation, 7, 23–26
Scientists-for-hire, 8, 23, 24, 144
Scoggins, Colin, 36, 38, 43, 44, 45, 46, 48, 50, 51, 53–54, 62, 75–77, 78, 224, 334n54, 335n70, 336n102
Scott, Col. Alan, 28–30, 58, 74, 79, 80–82, 85, 99, 234
Scott, Peter Dale, 14, 368n133
Scott, William B., 33n113
Secret Service, 38, 69, 100–01, 331n18, 332n20
Seely, Hart, 56, 335n66
Seitz, Sharon, 361n195
Sheen, Charlie, 216
al-Shehri, Wail, 347n115
al-Shehri, Waleed, 33–34, 127, 347n115
Sisson, Hal, 325
Sisson, Richard, 190
Shapley, Linda, 306
Sharpe, J. Forrest, 328n64
Silverstein, Larry, 117, 260, 311, 371n201
Skilling, John, 147, 245, 246, 351n14
Sliney, Ben, 43–44, 68
Slobodian, Linda, 332n30, 367n113
Smith, Dennis, 362n247
Smith, Guy, 5–6, 11, 122, 150, 185, 207, 212, 232, 259, 305, 325n31, 347n10, 366n85
Sniegoski, Stephen, 110, 345n68
Snyder, Mike, 237–38
Solomon, Evan, 136–41, 350n166
Sozen, Mete, 26, 273–75, 375nn254, 257, 258
Spangler, Scott, 297
Spence, Gerry, 14
Spinelli, Tom, 378n328
Squibs, 180–81, 199, 253–54, 316
Stand-down order, 29, 52, 63, 94, 95–98, 112, 115, 116, 222–37
Stanley, Richard, 264, 372n214

Steiner, Gen. Carl, 85
Stempel, Guido H., 324n12
Stewart, Payne, 237, 238, 240
Stop, Jim, 306
Stout, Glenn, 357n155
Stubblebine, Albert, 272
Stull, Ernie, 306, 382n405
Sturm, Douglas, 14
al-Sugami, Satam, 121
Sunder, Shyam, 155, 189, 205, 253–54, 258
Svonavec, Jim, 303
Szupinka, Lyle, 303–04
Szymanski, Greg, 246–47, 356nn128, 135, 136, 365n45, 369n145

T

Taliban, 117, 124, 128, 348n141
Tardio, Dennis, 176
Tarpley, Webster, 319, 384n22
Temyer, Laura, 306
Tenet, George, 123–24, 130
Thompson, Paul, 2, 344n26, 378n322, 380n366
Thornsberg, Tim, 298
Thornton, Bridget, 385n28
Thurston, Chuck, 170, 175, 355n101
Tinsley, Nikki, 17
Tomb, Rex, 128–29, 287
Transponders, 48, 231–33
Treacy, Lt. Col. Jon, 45, 52
Trimpe, Herb, 357n157
Tully, Peter, 181, 357n152
Turcios, Robert, 264
Turi, Albert, 346n96
Turilli, Thomas, 248, 356n128
Twin Towers, 2, 24–25, 112;
    columns in, 149–50, 165, 186–87, 351n22, 358n166, 363n254;
    deepest mystery of, 190–91;
    disintegration of, 145, 169–70, 175, 194, 316;
    explosions in, 175–79;
    features of destruction of, 100, 113–14, 140–42;
    fires in, 152–63;
    molten metal under, 113, 181–84;
    pancake theory, 113, 165–66, 185, 253–54;
    pulverization, 113, 169–70;
    removal of steel, 117, 157, 192–93, 202;
    squibs, 180–81;
    sturdiness of, 244–46, 251;
    total (global) collapse, 184–86;
        antenna drop (North Tower), 191;
        North and South Tower comparison, 59–51, 159;
        tipping and disintegration (South Tower), 192

U

UA (United Airlines) 93 (Flight 93), 4–5, 26, 66–74, 78, 93, 97, 223, 288–307;
    as shot down, 4–5, 26, 28, 29, 70–74, 93, 116, 291;

passports and bandana from, 121–22;
telephone calls from, 86–91, 136–37
UA 175 (Flight 175), 28, 55–63, 96–97;
no-windows-claim about, 221
pod-claim about, 221, 223;
Underwriters Laboratories (UL), 51, 157, 160, 171
Unger, Craig, 346n76
United 93 (the movie), 4, 26, 44, 66, 73–74, 89, 90, 91
Unocal, 124
Uyttebrouck, Olivier, 370n184

V

Van Auken, Lorie, 349n144
Varcapode, Bob, 57
Veliz, Teresa, 176, 313
Veterans for 9/11 Truth, 15
Vickers, Charlie, 182
Vogel, Steve, 373n231
Vogler, Celeste, 385n28
Voice Morphing, 84–92

W

Wagner, Tim, 267, 373n228
Wainio, Elizabeth, 296, 379n340
Wald, Matthew, 340n198, 366n69
Walker, Wirt, 114, 117, 193
Wallace, Richard, 340n188, 378n325
Wallace, Terry, 301
Walter, Mike, 271
War games, 236–37, 367n109, 377n304
Watson, Paul Joseph, 333n44
Watson, Shelley, 56, 335n63
Weinberger, Casper, 225–26
Weston, Burns, 14
Winfield, Brig. Gen. Montague, 37, 56, 63, 70, 72, 74, 97, 289, 290
Wise, Chris, 153
Wishful-and-fearful thinking, 7, 18–23, 209
Without Precedent, 5, 6, 27, 92, 95.
    See also Kean, Thomas H., and Hamilton, Lee H.
Wittenberg, Russ, 14–15, 216, 219, 220
Wolfowitz, Paul, 71, 104–05, 115, 289
Wood, Allan, 344n26
Wood, Judy, 169, 181, 354n99
Worby, David, 17, 329n71
Worcester Polytechnic Institute, 190
World Trade Center, 110, 242–61.
    See also Twin Towers; WTC 7
Wright, Decosta, 203, 383n6
WTC 7 (Building 7), 2, 24–25, 100, 112, 114, 117, 140–42, 194–206, 257–61, 314, 316–17;
explosions in, 199–200;
FEMA report on, 195–96, 197, 204;
fires in, 202–04;
foreknowledge of collapse of, 201–02;
9/11 Commission on, 196;
Silverstein's suggestion to "pull it," 260, 311;
special difficulties for official theory, 195–202

Y

Yardley, Jim, 364n39
Yates, Chris, 224, 235
Yousef, Ramzi, 235

Z

Zalewski, Pete, 35, 43, 44, 333n39
Zapinski, Ken, 380n358
Zarembka, Paul, 345n59, 368n133
al-Zawahiri, Ayman, 104
Zeigler, Capt. Gregory, 15, 346n78
Zelikow, Philip, 10, 31–34, 94, 103, 106–11, 139, 229, 300, 345n60
Zhou, Young, 370n179
Zinn, Howard, 14
Zwicker, Barrie, 14, 325, 330n89, 342n239